# Caravan
## Out & About Live
www.outandaboutlive.co.uk

Published by
Warners Group Publications

Printed in the UK by
Warners Midlands
West St, Bourne
Lincolnshire PE10 9PH
Tel: 01778 391000

**Editorial**
**Editor** Peter Rosenthal
**Deputy Editor** Claire Tupholme
**Database Manager**
Wendy Pennycook

**Advertising**
**Head of Advertising** Fleur Chivers
**Sales Executive**
Ashleigh Westbrook
Tel: 01778 392050
Email: ashleighw@warnersgroup.co.uk
**Sales Executive**
Laura Waltham
Tel: 01778 391027
Email: lauraw@warnersgroup.co.uk

**Publisher** John Greenwood

**Production**
Katie Phillips
Jean Waterfall

**Design**
Jayne Thorpe
Sarah Machin
Amie Carter

**Front Cover** Newberry Valley, Devon
**Inset** Woodland Waters, Lincolnshire
**This page** Trevella Caravan & Camping Park, Cornwall

# CARAVAN HOLIDAY

GW01495744

## TAKE THIS GLOVEBOX GUIDE ON A TRIP...
This guidebook has been fully updated for 2012 and details a wide range of parks from across the UK that cater for holiday homes and lodges, as well as touring pitches. The parks are sorted by region, then by county and town. For the index of regions and counties, flip to page 13.

## ... AND PLAN AHEAD WITH CAMPSITE FINDER
To find more information, reviews, prices and photos of all the campsites featured in this guide, simply visit www.outandaboutlive.co.uk and click on the Campsite Finder links. Many have been reviewed by our team following a site visit so you can be sure of accurate information written by the team behind Caravan and MMM.

## THE CARAVAN CLUB
This guidebook has been sponsored by the Caravan Club who are widely regarded as one of the standard-bearers when it comes to high quality campsites - see the list on p15. They offer 200 plus parks, many of which are star graded. To find out more information visit www.caravanclub.co.uk or call 0800 521761.

## KEY TO SYMBOLS AND ABBREVIATIONS

**Top 101** Sites have previously been recommended by readers of Caravan magazine.

**Premier Parks** are a group of parks linked by their high quality. Each one has to be rated by our team.

- **(5m)** Distance from nearest town/village
- **BH&HPA** Brit Hol & Home Parks Assoc.
- **NCC** Member of National Caravan Council
- Accepts motorhomes
- Accepts caravans
- Accepts tents
- Has holiday homes
- Has lodges
- Cars can be parked alongside pitches
- Electric hook-ups available
- Shower on site
- Waste water disposal point on site
- Bottled gas available
- Chop on site
- Bar on site
- Restaurant / seated hot food outlet on site
- Washing machine facilities on site
- Drying available on site
- Indoor games room
- Indoor swimming pool
- Outdoor swimming pool
- Dogs accepted
- Entertainment provided
- Wheelchair-friendly facilities provided
- Motorhome waste empty point
- Tourist board star rating
- Toilet facilities available
- Train station nearby
- Bus service nearby
- Chemical disposal point available
- Park open all year
- Takeaway on site
- Farm produce available
- Fishing
- Storage facilities available
- Wi-Fi available

Visit www.caravanclub.co.uk

# Get away from it all with The Caravan Club

**Around 2,500 peaceful havens with exclusive access to a maximum of five Club members at any one time**

Monaughty Poeth, Shropshire, Certificated Location

We all like a little peace and quiet at times and staying at one of The Caravan Club's Certificated Locations gives you that chance. Chill out at a CL and you'll discover havens of peace, accompanied perhaps just by the lowing of cows or the trill of a songbird.

With 2,500 or so to choose from, there's bound to be one close to anywhere you might choose, whether coastal, in perfect countryside or close to a chosen attraction.

They're for Caravan Club members only, so, to discover the delights of CLs, why not join today.

### What is a Certificated Location?

- Mostly rural sites with no more than 5 pitches
- Very exclusive: access restricted to Caravan Club members only
- Checked by The Caravan Club every year
- Most have electric hook-up, some even showers, toilets or hardstandings
- Certificated Locations are one of the main reasons people join The Caravan Club

Shawgate Farm, Staffordshire, Certificated Location

Seaforth Highland Country Estate, Brahan, Certificated Location

## Join online today
**www.caravanclub.co.uk/parks**
or call on 0800 328 6635
Calls may be recorded

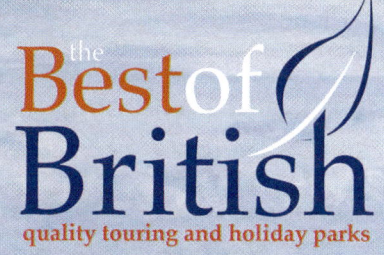

# the Best of British
## quality touring and holiday parks

... group of five star privately owned
... restigious Touring and Holiday Parks
... suit all tastes, with a warm and
... iendly welcome wherever you go

www.bob.org.uk

**What are you looking for?** We all have different requirements for our holidays and this guide concentrates on presenting a flavour of our member parks to enable you to choose which appeal to you.

In order to tailor your holiday to just what you want, contact the park you are interested in for details of their facilities and their prices – then you can tailor-make your holiday to suit you and your family!

*Enjoy your holiday* **Choose a Best of British Park!**

# SOUTH WEST ENGLAND

### SOMERSET

A uniquely peaceful park based on a garden theme, with pitches set amongst lawns. It is within 800 metres of a championship fly fishing lake & the surrounding country park is a haven for bird watchers and walkers.

### BATH CHEW VALLEY
Ham Lane
Bishop Sutton, Nr Bath
North East Somerset BS39 5TZ
**Tel: 01275 332127**
Email: enquiries@bathchewvalley.co.uk
www.bathchewvalley.co.uk

### TOURING, CARAVAN AND CAMPING PARK

### DEVON

Superb family run holiday park with wonderful sea views, offering excellent facilities for touring, camping, luxury lodges and holiday caravans. Bar meals, nightly entertainment and heated pools.

### BEVERLEY PARK
Goodrington Road, Paignton
South Devon TQ4 7JE
**Tel: 01803 661976**
Fax: 01803 845427
Email: info@beverley-holidays.co.uk
www.beverley-holidays.co.uk

### HOLIDAY PARK

### CORNWALL

Award winning site open all year. Situated in beautiful Cornish countryside. Licenced shop, takeaway food, childrens adventure play area, heated amenity block, hardstanding pitches. Adult special offers available.

### DOLBEARE PARK
Landrake, Saltash
Cornwall PL12 5AF
**Tel: 01752 851332**
Fax: 01752 547871
Email: reception@dolbeare.co.uk
www.dolbeare.co.uk

### TOURING PARK

### DEVON

This 15th century farmstead, once besieged by irate roundheads, nestles in a picturesque valley set in thirty acres of glorious Devon. Shop, games room, T.V., tennis-court, children's adventure & dog exercise areas, generous pitches.

### DORNAFIELD
Two Mile Oak, Newton Abbot
Devon TQ12 6DD
**Tel: 01803 812732**
Fax: 01803 812032
Email: enquiries@dornafield.com
www.dornafield.com

### CARAVAN AND CAMPING PARK

### CORNWALL

One of Cornwall's premier parks and winner of Cornwall's Holiday Park of the Year Award. Set in fabulous countryside minutes from Newquay. Facilities include the Oasis indoor and outdoor Fun Pools complex.

### HENDRA PARK
Newquay
Cornwall TR8 4NY
**Tel: 01637 875778**
Fax: 01637 879017
Email: enquiries@hendra-holidays.com
www.hendra-holidays.com

### HOLIDAY PARK

### DEVON

This 5 star touring & camping park is ideally situated amidst the North Devon countryside, only a few miles from the coast's golden beaches and Exmoor National Park. With 120 sheltered, level pitches for touring units.

### HIDDEN VALLEY
West Down, Nr Braunton
Near Ilfracombe
Devon EX34 8NU
**Tel: 01271 813837**
Email: info@hiddenvalleypark.com
www.hiddenvalleypark.com

### HOLIDAY PARK

### DORSET

Just 500 metres from a lovely unspoilt beach, the park is at clifftop height overlooking the sweeping Lyme Bay. The leisure facilities offer a wide range of activities to make you feel healthier and relaxed. Wide choice of bar food.

### HIGHLANDS END
Eype, Bridport
Dorset DT6 6AR
**Tel: 01308 422139**
Fax: 01308 425672
Email: holidays@wdlh.co.uk
www.wdlh.co.uk

### HOLIDAY PARK

### DORSET

Award winning 5 star holiday park, deep in the Dorset countryside but only 8 miles from sandy beaches. Offering tenting & touring pitches, grass, hardstanding or 'executive'. Luxury lodges also for hire.

### MERLEY COURT
Merley, Wimborne
Dorset BH21 3AA
**Tel: 01590 648331**
Fax: 01590 645610
Email: holidays@shorefield.co.uk
www.shorefield.co.uk

### HOLIDAY PARK

# SOUTH WEST ENGLAND

### DEVON

Sidmouth's multi award winning Park. Oakdown is landscaped into groves for privacy, with floral displays to delight you. Oak Mead Golf offers an excellent pitch and putt and refreshments in a welcoming reception/café.

### OAKDOWN

Gatedown Lane, Weston
Sidmouth, Devon EX10 0PT
**Tel: 01297 680387**
Fax: 01297 680541
Email: enquiries@oakdown.co.uk
www.oakdown.co.uk

### HOLIDAY PARK

### SOMERSET

*Exclusively for Adults*

Exceptional family run adults only touring park with 5 star amenities. Set in Somerset countryside with views of the Mendip hills. Perfect for walking, cycling, fishing and touring. Shop and off-licence, heated amenities block.

### THE OLD OAKS

Wick Farm, Wick
Glastonbury
Somerset BA6 8JS
**Tel: 01458 831437**
Email: info@theoldoaks.co.uk
www.theoldoaks.co.uk

### CARAVAN AND CAMPING PARK

### CORNWALL

Polmanter is the ideal location for those visiting and touring in West Cornwall. Excellent amenities and within walking distance of some of the most beautiful beaches in West Cornwall. No single sex groups.

### POLMANTER

St Ives
Cornwall
TR26 3LX
**Tel: 01736 795640**
Email: reception@polmanter.co.uk
www.polmanter.co.uk

### TOURING PARK

### DEVON

Facilities include a centrally-heated amenities block with disabled facilities, a bar and restaurant, dog exercising areas, tropical conservatory, outdoor and undercover play areas and much more.

### ROSS PARK

Park Hill Farm, Moor Road, Ipplepen
Newton Abbot, Devon TQ12 5TT
**Tel: 01803 812983**
Fax: 01803 812983
Email: enquiries@rossparkcaravanpark.co.uk
www.rossparkcaravanpark.co.uk

### TOURING PARK

### HAMPSHIRE

Award winning centre nestled in the New Forest National Park. Woodland walks, cycle hire centre, gym, two family swimming pools, horse riding, trout fishing or indulge in a treatment in the beauty therapy suite.

### SANDY BALLS

Godshill, Fordingbridge, New Forest
Hampshire SP6 2JZ
**Tel: 0845 2702248**
Fax: 01425 653067
Email: post@sandyballs.co.uk
www.sandyballs.co.uk

### HOLIDAY CENTRE

### CORNWALL

Beautiful 5 star family run holiday, touring and camping park in south Cornwall. Outdoor heated pool, barbecue areas, tennis, volleyball, pitch 'n' put, badminton, giant chess and draughts, café and well stocked shop.

### SEAVIEW INTERNATIONAL

Boswinger, St Austell
PL26 6LL
**Tel: 01726 843425**
Fax: 01726 843358
Email: holidays@seaviewinternational.com
www.seaviewinternational.com

### TOURING AND HOLIDAY HOME PARK

### CORNWALL

Family-run holiday park set in 20 acres of beautiful grounds in a quiet picturesque wooded valley one mile from the sea. Stay in one of our modern caravans, apartments or your own caravan, tent or motorhome.

### SUN VALLEY

Pentewan Road, St Austell
Cornwall PL26 6DJ
**Tel/Fax: 01726 843266**
Email: reception@sunvalleyholidays.co.uk
www.sunvalleyholidays.co.uk

### HOLIDAY PARK

### DORSET

Set in 20 acres of stunning parkland, situated in the grounds of the former South Lytchett Manor. A dog friendly site with acres of dog walking including an area where you can exercise your dog off lead.

### SOUTH LYTCHETT

Dorchester Road
Poole
BH16 6JB
**Tel: 01202 622577**
Email: info@southlytchettmanor.co.uk
www.southlytchettmanor.co.uk

### HOLIDAY PARK

### CORNWALL

A haven of tranquillity far from the stresses of modern day living. Nestling in a valley surrounded by farmland, we are the perfect rural retreat. Just a mile from the sea, within easy reach of many places of interest.

### TRETHEM MILL

St Just In Roseland, Nr St Mawes
Truro, Cornwall TR2 5JF
**Tel: 01872 580504**
Fax: 01872 580968
Email: reception@trethem.com
www.trethem.com

### TOURING PARK

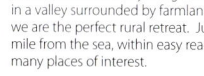

# SOUTH WEST ENGLAND

### DORSET
A warm, friendly welcome awaits you at our 40 acre woodland park. Enjoy the tranquility on the park, or the walks in the surrounding Wareham Forest and heath-land. Park is ideal for couples and younger families.

### WAREHAM FOREST
North Trigon, Wareham
Dorset BH20 7NZ
**Tel: 01929 551393**
Fax: 01929 558321
Email: holiday@warehamforest.co.uk
www.warehamforest.co.uk

**TOURING PARK**

### SOMERSET
*Exclusively for Adults*
Attractively landscaped park for adults only, situated in a beautiful area close to the Somerset/Devon border. Spacious all weather hardstandings, all with views and surrounded by extensive shrubs.

### WATERROW
Waterrow, Wiveliscombe
Taunton, Somerset TA4 2AZ
**Tel: 01984 623464**
Email: waterrowpark@yahoo.co.uk
www.waterrowpark.co.uk

**TOURING, CARAVAN AND CAMPING PARK**

### DEVON
A family run park with breathtaking countryside views of Dartmoor and the River Exe. Close to the renowned beauty spot of Woodbury Common – some three thousand acres of unspoilt open heathland.

### WEBBERS PARK
Castle Lane, Woodbury
Exeter EX5 1EA
**Tel: 01395 232276**
Fax: 01395 233389
Email: reception@webberspark.co.uk
www.webberspark.co.uk

**TOURING AND HOLIDAY HOME PARK**

### DORSET
The park lies on the Dorset / Devon border. Walkers are spoilt for choice with coastal views or rolling inland vistas. Enjoy our superb indoor swimming pool, tennis court, coarse fishing lake, indoor/outdoor play areas.

### WOOD FARM
Axminster Road, Charmouth
Dorset DT6 6BT
**Tel: 01297 560697**
Fax: 01297 561243
Email: holidays@woodfarm.co.uk
www.woodfarm.co.uk

**TOURING AND HOLIDAY HOME PARK**

### CORNWALL
Overlooks Bude Bay and countryside; many safe sandy beaches lie within 1½ miles. We have excellent facilities for touring and camping, with luxury holiday homes for hire. Visitors can also enjoy use of our Lodge takeaway.

### WOODA FARM
Poughill, Bude
Cornwall EX23 9HJ
**Tel: 01288 352069**
Fax: 01288 355258
Email: enquires@wooda.co.uk
www.wooda.co.uk

**HOLIDAY PARK**

### DEVON
Just a few minutes from the waterside town of Dartmouth and South west Coast Path. Indoor play area, outdoor rides and falconry centre. Immaculate facilities with Adult special offers available in low season.

### WOODLANDS GROVE
Blackawton
Totnes, Devon TQ9 7DQ
**Tel: 01803 712598**
Fax: 01803 712680
Email: holiday@woodlandsgrove.com
www.woodlandsgrove.com

**CARAVAN AND CAMPING PARK**

### DEVON
Devon Tourism Awards - Holiday Park of the Year. Set in an Area of Outstanding Natural Beauty. Get active with hiking, biking, tree-surfing, canoeing and horse riding plus stunning beaches all within easy reach.

### WOODOVIS PARK
Gulworthy
Tavistock, Devon PL19 8NY
**Tel: 01822 832968**
Fax: 01822 832948
Email: info@woodovis.com
www.woodovis.com

**HOLIDAY PARK**

# SOUTH EAST ENGLAND

### KENT
This beautiful park offers the perfect holiday location. Facilities include large children's playground, sports field, games room, television lounge, centrally heated showers, full facilities for disabled people and large 'Adults Only' section.

### BROADHEMBURY
Steeds Lane, Kingsnorth
Ashford, Kent TN26 1NQ
**Tel: 01233 620859**
Fax: 01233 620859
Email: holidaypark@broadhembury.co.uk
www.broadhembury.co.uk

**TOURING AND HOLIDAY HOME PARK**

# SOUTH EAST ENGLAND

### ISLE OF WIGHT

Well managed park in peaceful village location. 170 pitches in 11 acres of paddocks. Excellent touring facilities. A new facilities block with the highest specification, containing excellent amenities, is now open.

### THE ORCHARDS
Main Road, Newbridge
Yarmouth, Isle of Wight PO41 0TS
**Tel: 01983 531331/531350**
Fax: 01983 531666
Email: admin@orchards-holiday-park.co.uk
www.orchards-holiday-park.co.uk

**HOLIDAY PARK**

### KENT

Quex is a picturesque, level and partly-wooded park with a peaceful, quiet atmosphere. The lovely sandy beach at Minnis Bay is only two miles away. There is a children's play area. Grocery shop and laundry.

### QUEX PARK
Park Road, Birchington
Kent CT7 0BL
**Tel: 01843 841273**
Fax: 01843 841273
Email: Info@keatfarm.co.uk
www.keatfarm.co.uk

**TOURING AND HOLIDAY HOME PARK**

### KENT

5 star, quality park set in idyllic rural surroundings. In the centre of the Mannington's 150 acre farm, the 15 acre touring park offers quality facilities all year round. Truly a park for all seasons.

### TANNER FARM
Goudhurst Road, Marden, Tonbridge
Kent TN12 9ND
**Tel: 01622 832399**
Fax: 01622 832472
Email: enquiries@tannerfarmpark.co.uk
www.tannerfarmpark.co.uk

**TOURING, CARAVAN AND CAMPING PARK**

# WALES

### CEREDIGION

Well landscaped, award-winning park on the edge of the village of Cenarth with its famous salmon-leap waterfalls. Luxurious health and leisure complex with fitness suite, pool, spa, sauna/steam rooms, bar etc.

### CENARTH FALLS
Cenarth, Newcastle Emlyn
Ceredigion SA38 9JS
**Tel: 01239 710345**
Fax: 01239 710344
Email: enquiries@cenarth-holipark.co.uk
www.cenarth-holipark.co.uk

**TOURING AND HOLIDAY HOME PARK**

### CARMARTHENSHIRE

Award winning family run park. Heated amenity block, family rooms, laundry, super pitches and motor caravan service point. At the foot hills of the Brecon Beacons, ideal for touring, walking and cycling.

### ERWLON
Brecon Road, Llandovery
Carmarthenshire SA20 0RD
**Tel: 01550 721021/720332**
or 01550 720332
Email: enquiries@erwlon.co.uk
www.erwlon.co.uk

**TOURING, CARAVAN AND CAMPING PARK**

### ISLE OF ANGLESEY

Award-winning park in a rural setting, tranquil and relaxing atmosphere. Ideal for couples and families seeking a peaceful holiday. Near to several sandy beaches with delightful coastal walks. Immaculate facilities.

### HOME FARM
Marianglas
Isle of Anglesey LL73 8PH
**Tel: 01248 410614**
Fax: 01248 410900
Email: enq@homefarm-anglesey.co.uk
www.homefarm-anglesey.co.uk

**TOURING AND HOLIDAY HOME PARK**

### NORTH WALES

Enjoy handmade crafts, or dine in the Shippon Restaurant in the beautiful Edwardian buildings; sample our own Real Ale; or have homemade cream teas in the gardens with views over the Dee Valley.

### THE PLASSEY
Eyton, Wrexham
North Wales LL13 0SP
**Tel: 01978 780277**
Fax: 01978 780019
Email: enquiries@theplassey.co.uk
www.plassey.com

**LEISURE PARK**

### GWYNEDD

A 5 STAR, family run, dog friendly Park. Overlooking Cardigan Bay and miles of sandy beach. Facilities include: Launderette, Showers, Washroom, Shop, Dog Walking Field and Children's Play area.

### TRAWSDIR
Llanaber, Barmouth
Gwynedd LL42 1RR
**Tel: 01341 280999**
Fax: 01341 280740
Email: enquiries@barmouthholidays.co.uk
www.barmouthholidays.co.uk

**CARAVAN AND CAMPING PARK**

# CENTRAL ENGLAND

### SHROPSHIRE
### BEACONSFIELD
**TOURING AND HOLIDAY HOME PARK**

Tranquil, picturesque, family-run park created for the discerning and exclusively for adults (over 21 yrs). We have an á la carte restaurant for special occasions, indoor swimming pool/steam room, fly and coarse fishing.

Upper Battlefield, Shrewsbury
Shropshire SY4 4AA
**Tel: 01939 210370**
Fax: 01939 210349
Email: mail@beaconsfield-farm.co.uk
www.beaconsfield-farm.co.uk

### OXFORDSHIRE
### LINCOLN FARM
**CARAVAN AND CAMPING PARK**

Award winning park situated in the heart of Standlake with two pubs a short walk away. Five star facilities including a laundrette. We have two indoor swimming pools, saunas, jacuzzis and a steam room.

High Street, Standlake
Nr Witney, Oxfordshire OX29 7RH
**Tel: 01865 300239**
Fax: 01865 300127
Email: info@lincolnfarmpark.co.uk
www.lincolnfarmpark.co.uk

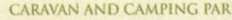

### SHROPSHIRE
### OXON HALL
**TOURING AND HOLIDAY HOME PARK**

Set in attractive tree-fringed land close to Shrewsbury and well situated for visiting Ironbridge and the Welsh Marches. Our facilities are maintained to the highest standards. Well stocked accessory and food shop.

Welshpool Road, Shrewsbury
Shropshire SY3 5FB
**Tel: 01743 340868**
Fax: 01743 340869
Email: oxon@morris-leisure.co.uk
www.morris-leisure.co.uk

### HEREFORD
### POSTON MILL PARK
**TOURING AND HOLIDAY HOME PARK**

A haven for relaxing, set in Herefordshire's Golden Valley, with a restaurant and farm shop on site. For fun try your hand at our 9 hole 'pitch and putt' golf course or try your hand at fishing in the river Dore.

Peterchurch, Golden Valley
Hereford HR2 0SF
**Tel: 01981 550225**
Fax: 01981 550000
Email: info@poston-mill.co.uk
www.bestparks.co.uk

### WARWICKSHIRE
### SOMERS WOOD
**TOURING PARK**

Located in the heart of England offering peace and tranquility exclusively for adults. A 27 hole golf course, floodlit driving range and restaurant/bar facilities are available to use at the adjacent Golf Centre.

Somers Road, Meriden
North Warwickshire CV7 7PL
**Tel: 01676 522978**
Fax: 01676 522978
Email: enquiries@somerswood.co.uk
www.somerswood.co.uk

### HEREFORDSHIRE
### TOWNSEND
**CARAVAN AND CAMPING PARK**

On the edge of Pembridge, one of Herefordshires' most beautiful 'Black & White' villages. Spacious 12 acre, touring and camping park with luxurious heated facilities. Onsite award-winning Farm Shop.

Townsend Farm
Pembridge, Leominster
Herefordshire HR6 9HB
**Tel: 01544 388527**
Fax:
Email: info@townsendfarm.co.uk
www.townsendfarm.co.uk

# EASTERN ENGLAND

### LINCOLNSHIRE
### BAINLAND
**COUNTRY PARK**

The park evokes a real sense of peace and seclusion with excellent leisure facilities. Set in 42 acres surrounded by woodland, our park's first-rate recreational opportunities complement those of the Lincolnshire Wolds.

Horncastle Road, Woodhall Spa
Lincolnshire LN10 6UX
**Tel: 01526 352903**
Fax: 01526 353730
Email: bookings@bainland.co.uk
www.bainland.co.uk

### LINCOLNSHIRE
### BROOKSIDE
**CARAVAN AND CAMPING PARK**

Superb, modern facilities which along with the usual amenities boasts individual washrooms in the ladies and gents. Indoor food preparation facilities. Peaceful and relaxing views over trees and woodland.

Stather Road, Burton-upon-Stather
Scunthorpe,
North Lincs DN15 9DB
**Tel: 01724 721369**
Email: brooksidecp@aol.com
www.brooksidecaravanpark.co.uk

# EASTERN ENGLAND

### LINCOLNSHIRE
Join us for peace and tranquility at our 5 star site, 1.5 miles from Sutton-On-Sea. Wonderful beaches and a long promenade for bicycles/wheelchairs. Fully stocked tourist information cabin including library.

### CHERRY TREE
Cherry Tree Cottage
Huttoft Road, Sutton-On-Sea
Lincolnshire LN12 2RU
Tel: 01507 441226
Email: info@cherrytreesite.co.uk
www.cherrytreesite.co.uk

**TOURING PARK**

### CAMBRIDGE
Pleasant touring park, which is located some five miles west of Cambridge. The park has excellent toilet and shower amenities and careful siting of pitches around the perimeter gives a wonderful feeling of spaciousness.

### HIGHFIELD FARM
Long Road, Comberton
Cambridge CB23 7DG
Tel/Fax: 01223 262308
Email: enquiries
@highfieldfarmtouringpark.co.uk
www.highfieldfarmtouringpark.co.uk

**TOURING PARK**

### CAMBRIDGESHIRE
Quiet, attractive, rural site provides a central Cambridgeshire location. At the heart of the site is a green oak timber-framed building which houses reception, a shop, café, bar and award winning restaurant.

### STROUD HILL
Fen Road, Pidley
Cambridgeshire PE28 3DE
Tel: 01487 741333
Fax: 01487 741 365
Email: stroudhillpark@btconnect.com
www.stroudhillpark.co.uk

**TOURING PARK**

### NORFOLK
A quiet, friendly, 5 star quality family park positioned in tranquil countryside. 60 hard standing all-weather pitches. Five exclusive CL premier pitches. Guest house and SC cottages also available. Arrivals after 1.30pm please.

### THE OLD BRICK KILNS
Little Barney Lane, Barney
Fakenham, Norfolk NR21 0NL
Tel: 01328 878305
Fax: 01328 878948
Email: enquiries@old-brick-kilns.co.uk
www.old-brick-kilns.co.uk

**CARAVAN AND CAMPING PARK**

### NORFOLK
Exclusively for adults only, our five-star country park offers the perfect retreat in which to relax. The main facilities are fully heated and a guest TV lounge provides a small library. Centrally situated in picturesque North Norfolk.

### TWO MILLS
Yarmouth Road, North Walsham
Norfolk NR28 9NA
Tel: 01692 405829
Fax: 01692 405829
Email: enquiries@twomills.co.uk
www.twomills.co.uk

**TOURING PARK**

# NORTHERN ENGLAND

### CO. DURHAM
Delightful, peaceful and secluded retreat, situated between the pretty villages of Neasham and Hurworth-on-Tees, with private fishing and riverside walks. Ideally situated for exploring the Yorkshire Dales and Teesdale Moors.

### NEWBUS GRANGE
Newbus Grange Country Park
Hurworth Road, Neasham, Nr Darlington
Co. Durham DL2 1PE
Tel: 01325 720973
Email: newbusgrangecp@btconnect.com
www.maguirescountryparks.co.uk

**STATIC HOLIDAY HOME PARK**

### NORTHUMBERLAND
Situated in North Northumberland's 'Secret Kingdom', two miles from the Scottish Border and 1.5 miles from the historic town of Berwick-upon-Tweed, the park is open all year round and has 5 star facilities.

### ORD HOUSE
East Ord, Berwick-upon-Tweed
Northumberland TD15 2NS
Tel: 01289 305288
Fax: 01289 330832
Email: enquiries@ordhouse.co.uk
www.maguirescountryparks.co.uk

**COUNTRY PARK**

### CUMBRIA
Set in picturesque, unspoilt countryside in the heart of the Lake District, tranquil yet accessible. Specially designed adventure play areas and many natural features. Comfort and fresh air aplenty.

### PARK CLIFFE
Birks Road, Windermere
Cumbria LA23 3PG
Tel: 01539 531344
Fax: 01539 531971
Email: info@parkcliffe.co.uk
www.parkcliffe.co.uk

**TOURING, CAMPING AND HOLIDAY HOME PARK**

# NORTHERN ENGLAND

### LANCASHIRE
### RIVERSIDE

A secluded level park on the banks of the River Wenning, situated in beautiful countryside, within walking distance of High Bentham. Great adventure play area, new fishing lake and nearby 18 hole golf course.

High Bentham
Lancaster LA2 7FJ
**Tel: 01524 261272**
Fax: 01524 262835
Email: info@riversidecaravanpark.co.uk
www.riversidecaravanpark.co.uk

**TOURING AND HOLIDAY HOME PARK**

### CUMBRIA
### WILD ROSE

Set in the stunning Eden Valley. Facilities include a well stocked shop (seasonal), a licensed restaurant with take away, laundrette and children's play areas. We also hire out five Wigwams which offer the chance to camp in style.

Ormside, Appleby-in-Westmorland
Cumbria CA16 6EJ
**Tel: 017683 51077**
Fax: 017683 52551
Email: reception@wildrose.co.uk
www.wildrose.co.uk

**TOURING AND HOLIDAY HOME PARK**

# SCOTLAND

### MORAY
### ABERLOUR GARDENS

Set in 5 acre Victorian walled garden of Aberlour House. 500m from the River Spey and in the heart of the Speyside Malt Whisky Trail. Within easy reach of the Moray Coast and Cairngorm National Park.

Aberlour on Spey
Moray AB38 9LD
**Tel: 01340 871586**
Fax: 01340 871586
Email: info@aberlourgardens.co.uk
www.aberlourgardens.co.uk

**TOURING AND HOLIDAY HOME PARK**

### DUMFRIES/GALLOWAY
### BRIGHOUSE BAY

1200 exclusive acres. This wildlife haven with woods adjacent has extensive nature trails & its own sandy beach. Exceptional amenities include 18-hole and 9 hole golf courses, bar and bistro, indoor pool, jacuzzi, steam room.

Borgue, Kirkcudbright
Dumfries and Galloway DG6 4TS
**Tel: 01557 870267**
Fax: 01557 870319
Email: info@brighouse-bay.co.uk
www.gillespie-leisure.co.uk

**HOLIDAY PARK**

### DUMFRIES/GALLOWAY
### KIPPFORD

Over 25 acres with many wonderful views and partly set around granite outcrops. Touring and camping pitches are located on the level. Red squirrels abound, coastal and forest walks, cycle trails and a 9 hole golf course.

Kippford, Dalbeattie
Kirkcudbrightshire DG5 4LF
**Tel: 01556 620636**
Fax: 01556 620607
Email: info@kippfordholidaypark.co.uk
www.kippfordholidaypark.co.uk

**TOURING AND HOLIDAY HOME PARK**

### ANGUS
### RIVERVIEW

Riverview is a friendly park which is maintained to an exceptionally high standard and enjoys magnificent views across the River Tay. Our facilities include games room, play-park, heated toilets & showers, laundry and leisure suite.

Marine Drive
Monifieth
Angus DD5 4NH
**Tel: 01382 535471**
Fax:
Email: info@riverview.co.uk
www.riverview.co.uk

**TOURING AND HOLIDAY HOME PARK**

### STIRLING
### TROSSACHS

The 40 acre park has 45 exclusive touring pitches (mostly fully-serviced – with water, drainage, electricity and TV hook-up) on south-facing landscaped terraces and bordered to the north by a glorious oak and bluebell wood.

By Aberfoyle
Stirling FK8 3SA
**Tel: 01877 382614**
Fax: 01877 382732
Email: info@trossachsholidays.co.uk
www.trossachsholidays.co.uk

**HOLIDAY PARK**

---

**A warm welcome wherever you go**
Whichever Best of British Park you choose, you can be sure that you will receive the warmest of welcomes and a very high high level of customer service.

*Enjoy your holiday* **Choose a Best of British Park!**

**ARE YOU A BEST OF BRITISH LOYALTY CARDHOLDER?**
Register for a *loyalty card*, get information on special offers, sign up for the newsletter or post a review of the park(s) you've visited

Visit **www.bob.org.uk**
and register online or write to
PO Box 20249 Edinburgh EH9 2YZ

**FACILITIES KEY** For further information on other facilities please contact the park direct

✓ Available
✗ Not Available

The best of British Touring and Holiday Parks is the trading name of Lucaspark (1994) Limited, PO Box 20249, Edinburgh EH9 2YZ • Company Number: 2865560 • VAT Registration Number: 733 1434 77 • Contact Best of British at office@bobpr.co.uk • © Copyright Lucaspark (1994) Limited

The information about individual parks in this brochure has been supplied by the parks themselves. Whilst these parks were initially inspected by Best of British to ensure that they attained the required standard, no guarantee can be given by Best of British that the parks maintain this standard, nor is it possible for Best of British to check each and every detail regarding facilities in relation to the parks. Whilst every effort is made to ensure that the information regarding the parks is correct, Best of British do not guarantee and neither it nor any of its officers or agents accept any responsibility should this information be incorrect. In making any booking, whether or not through this brochure, you are deemed to be dealing with the parks direct and any matter of complaint or difficulty is the sole responsibility of the parks themselves. Best of British acts at all times as agent for and on behalf of the parks included within this brochure and the individual Parks reserve the right to alter or rescind any of the published facilities or specifications. Park owners reserve the right to alter prices in the light of any VAT amendments made.

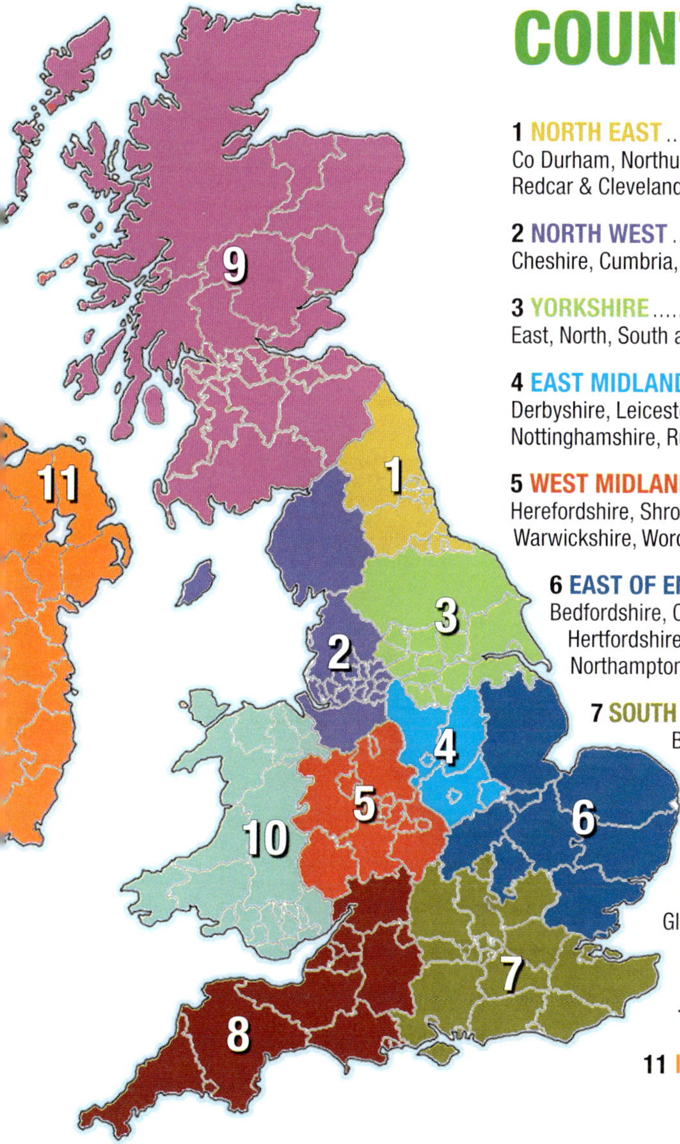

# REGIONS & COUNTIES INDEX

**1 NORTH EAST** ..................................... PAGE 16
Co Durham, Northumberland,
Redcar & Cleveland, Tyne & Wear

**2 NORTH WEST** ..................................... PAGE 20
Cheshire, Cumbria, Lancashire, Merseyside

**3 YORKSHIRE** ........................................ PAGE 34
East, North, South and West Yorkshire

**4 EAST MIDLANDS** ............................... PAGE 46
Derbyshire, Leicestershire,
Nottinghamshire, Rutland

**5 WEST MIDLANDS** .............................. PAGE 51
Herefordshire, Shropshire, Staffordshire,
Warwickshire, Worcestershire

**6 EAST OF ENGLAND** ..................... PAGE 59
Bedfordshire, Cambridgeshire, Essex,
Hertfordshire, Lincolnshire, Norfolk,
Northamptonshire, Suffolk

**7 SOUTH EAST** .......................... PAGE 79
Berkshire, Buckinghamshire, East
Sussex, Hampshire, Isle of Wight,
Kent, London, Oxfordshire,
Surrey, West Sussex

**8 SOUTH WEST** ...... PAGE 98
Cornwall, Devon, Dorset,
Gloucestershire, Somerset, Wiltshire

**9 SCOTLAND** .......... PAGE 149

**10 WALES** ............... PAGE 174

**11 IRELAND** ................. PAGE 201

**Find over 3,300 campsites!**
To find even more great campsites for **caravans, motorhomes, tents** and **trailer tents**, as well as **holiday homes** and **lodges**, simply visit our website.

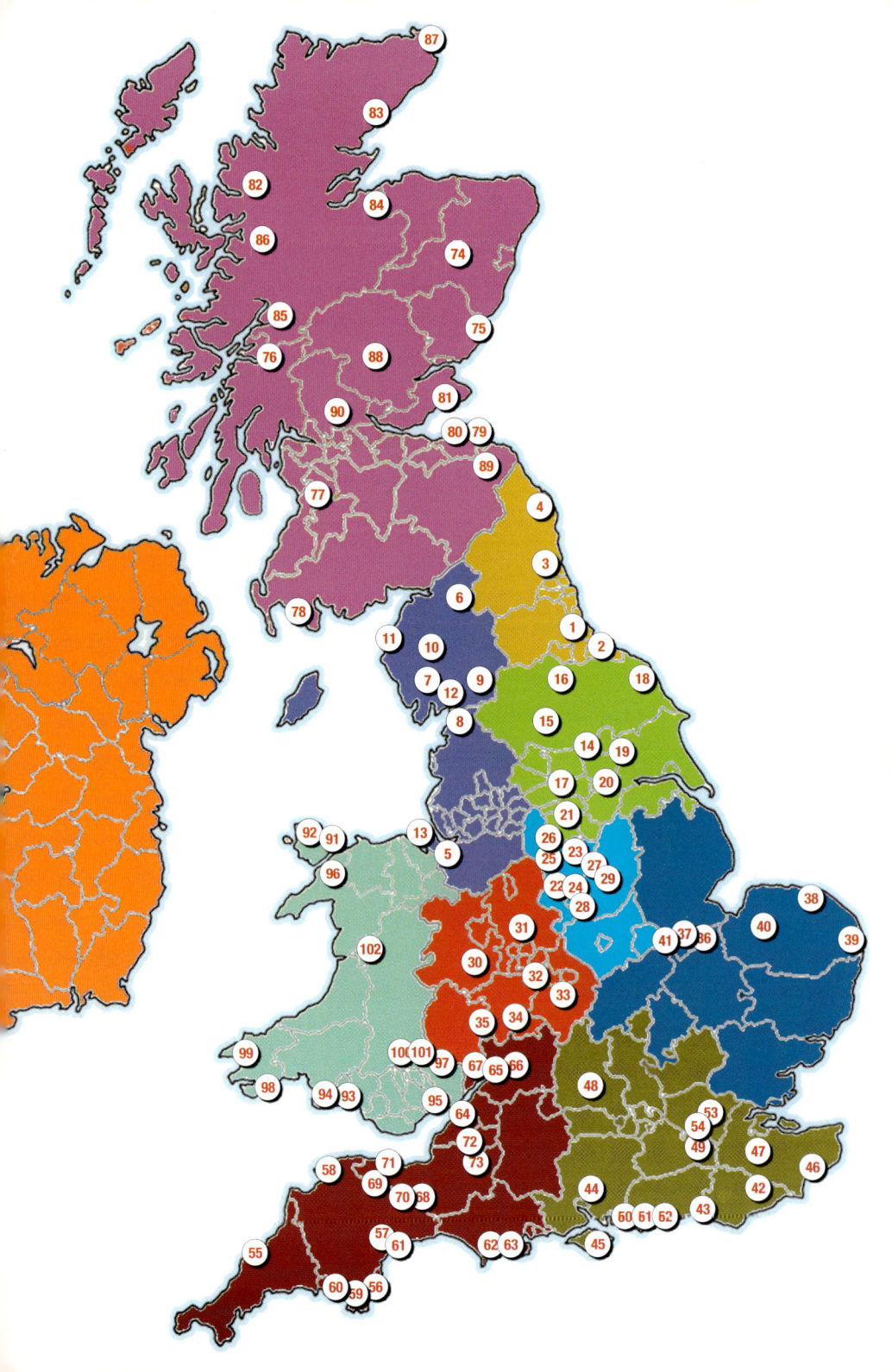

# TOP-RATED CLUB SITES

All the Caravan Club sites listed in this index have been officially star-rated by the British Graded Holiday Parks scheme

| SITE NAME | PAGE |
|---|---|
| **NORTH EAST** | |
| 1 Grange | 16 |
| 2 White Water Park | 17 |
| 3 River Breamish | 17 |
| 4 Seaview | 18 |
| **NORTH WEST** | |
| 5 Chester Fairoaks | 20 |
| 6 Englethwaite Hall | 22 |
| 7 Park Coppice | 23 |
| 8 Meathop Fell | 23 |
| 9 Low Park Wood | 23 |
| 10 Low Manesty | 25 |
| 11 Dockray Meadow | 25 |
| 12 Braithwaite Fold | 28 |
| 13 Wirral Country Park | 34 |
| **YORKSHIRE** | |
| 14 Knaresborough | 37 |
| 15 Lower Wensleydale | 37 |
| 16 Hargill House | 39 |
| 17 Strid Wood | 41 |
| 18 Low Moor | 43 |
| 19 Beechwood Grange | 43 |
| 20 Rowntree Park | 44 |
| 21 Lower Clough Foot | 45 |
| **EAST MIDLANDS** | |
| 22 Blackwall Plantation | 46 |
| 23 Chatsworth Park | 47 |
| 24 The Firs | 47 |
| 25 Grin Low | 47 |
| 26 Losehill | 48 |
| 27 Poolsbrook | 48 |
| 28 Elvaston Castle | 48 |
| 29 Clumber Park | 51 |
| **WEST MIDLANDS** | |
| 30 Presthope | 53 |
| 31 Uttoxeter Racecourse | 55 |
| 32 Chapel Lane | 55 |
| 33 Warwick Racecourse | 57 |
| 34 Broadway | 57 |
| 35 Bromyard Downs | 58 |
| **EAST OF ENGLAND** | |
| 36 Houghton Mill | 59 |
| 37 Ferry Meadows | 60 |
| 38 Seacroft | 69 |
| 39 Great Yarmouth | 71 |
| 40 The Covert | 74 |
| 41 Top Lodge | 75 |
| **SOUTH EAST / LONDON** | |
| 42 Normanhurst | 80 |
| 43 Sheepcote Valley | 81 |
| 44 Morn Hill | 86 |
| 45 Southland | 88 |
| 46 Black Horse Farm | 90 |
| 47 Bearsted | 91 |
| 48 Burford | 94 |
| 49 Alderstead Heath | 96 |
| 50 Rowan Park | 96 |
| 51 Littlehampton | 98 |
| 52 Northbrook Farm | 98 |
| 53 Abbey Wood | 93 |
| 54 Crystal Palace | 93 |
| **SOUTH WEST** | |
| 55 Trewethett Farm | 114 |
| 56 Hillhead | 119 |
| 57 Exeter Racecourse | 122 |
| 58 Brook Lea | 123 |
| 59 Broad Park | 124 |
| 60 Plymouth Sound | 127 |
| 61 Putts Corner | 128 |
| 62 Crossways | 134 |
| 63 Haycraft | 136 |
| 64 Baltic Wharf | 139 |
| 65 Cheltenham Racecourse | 140 |
| 66 Moreton-in-Marsh | 141 |
| 67 Tewkesbury Abbey | 141 |
| 68 Five Acres | 144 |
| 69 Exmoor House | 145 |
| 70 Lakeside | 145 |
| 71 Minehead | 146 |
| 72 Wincanton Racecourse | 148 |
| 73 Longleat | 149 |
| **SCOTLAND** | |
| 74 The Invercauld | 150 |
| 75 Lochside | 152 |
| 76 North Ledaig | 154 |
| 77 Craigie Gardens | 155 |
| 78 New England Bay | 160 |
| 79 Yellowcraig | 160 |
| 80 Edinburgh | 161 |
| 81 Balbirnie | 161 |
| 82 Kinlochewe | 162 |
| 83 Dalchalm | 163 |
| 84 Culloden Moor | 165 |
| 85 Bunree | 166 |
| 86 Morvich | 166 |
| 87 Dunnet Bay | 167 |
| 88 Maragowan | 170 |
| 89 Gibson Park | 172 |
| 90 Blair Drummond | 173 |
| **WALES** | |
| 91 Penrhos | 174 |
| 92 Cae Mawr | 175 |
| 93 Gowerton | 177 |
| 94 Pembrey Country Park | 178 |
| 95 Tredegar House | 185 |
| 96 Coed Helen | 188 |
| 97 Pandy | 185 |
| 98 Freshwater East | 195 |
| 99 Lleithyr Meadow | 196 |
| 100 Aberbran | 197 |
| 101 Brynich | 198 |
| 102 Gwern-y-Bwlch | 199 |

# NORTH EAST

## CO DURHAM

### Barnard Castle

**(2m). Barnard Castle Camping & Caravanning Club Site, Dockenflatts Lane, Barnard Castle, Co Durham DL12 9DG.** 01833 630228 . www.campingandcaravanningclub.co.uk. Well placed for exploring the Pennines and the city of Durham. Within easy walking distance of Barnard Castle. 90 pitches set in 10 acres. Non-members welcome. Caravans, motorcaravans and tents accepted. Visit Britain Tourism in Excellence Award - Caravan Holiday Park of the Year. NE England runner up. Loo Of The Year (5 stars). Fishing, golf, horse riding, swimming pool and tennis all nearby. Special deals available for families and backpackers. From Barnard Castle take B6277 towards Middleton-in-Teeside, after 1m at Club sign turn L, site 500yd on L. Open: 1 April - 31 October. ★ ★ ★ ★ ★ NCC

**(8m). Cote House Farm, Cote House Road, Middleton-in-Teesdale, Barnard Castle, Co Durham DL12 0PN.** 01833 640515. Fishing, sailing, shops etc within 2m. Golf 8m. Walking area - Pennine Way 1.5m up road. By Grassholme Reservoir, 1m out of Mickleton village up Kelton road, by river Lune, inc Cote House Wood. Open: 1 March - 31 October.

**(5m). Doe Park Farm Caravan Site, Cotherstone, Barnard Castle, Co Durham DL12 9UQ.** 01833 650302. www.doepark.co.uk. The park is attractively situated in Dales countryside on the edge of the pretty village of Cotherstone. River fishing available near site. Golf course 4m, garage 2m, nearest shop (inc PO and papers) 0.5m. Doctors 4m. Bar meals, restaurants etc 0.5-2m. Nature reserve on farm. Join B6277 at Barnard Castle, travelling towards Middleton in Teesdale. Site on L 0.5m past Cotherstone. Open: 1 March - 31 October. ★ ★ ★ ★ BH&HPA

**(3m). Hetherick Caravan Park, Kinninvie, Barnard Castle, Co Durham DL12 8QX.** 01833 631173. www.hetherickcaravanpark.co.uk. Pleasant park located in the heart of beautiful Teesdale. Pretty market town of Barnard Castle 3m. Ideally situated for all local attractions. Golf course and sports centre (including swimming pool) within 2m. Owner supplied copy. Located near Kinninvie, just off B6279 from Staindrop or B6278 from Barnard Castle. Open: 1 March - 31 October. BH&HPA

**(8m). Mickleton Mill Caravan Park, Mickleton, Barnard Castle, Co Durham DL12 0LS.** 01833 640317. On site fishing on the river Lune is available to caravanners. On B6277 towards Barnard Castle. Follow road to Mickleton. Turn R just past Blacksmiths Arms, at bottom of road bear to the L. Open: 15 March - 31 October. BH&HPA

**(1.5m). Pecknell Farm, Lartington, Barnard Castle, Co Durham DL12 9DF.** 01833 638357. Hardstands for 5 motor caravans. Nearest shops, golf, swimming, PO, doctors are in Barnard Castle. Many lovely walks nearby. 1hr away from lakes. AA 3 pennants. On B6277 on right hand side 0.5m from Barnard Castle. Open: 1 April - 31 October.

**(2m). Teesdale Barnard Castle Caravan Club Site, Lartington Lane, Barnard Castle, Co Durham DL12 9BD.** 01833 637999. www.caravanclub.co.uk. Slightly sloping site with views overlooking the sea. Beach 1m. Hardstandings. Toilet blocks. Privacy cubicles. Laundry facilities. Veg prep. Gas & Gaz. MV service point. Late night arrivals area. Ideal for families. Members only. No tents. See website for standard directions to site. Open: 23 March - 31 October. NCC

### Bishop Auckland

**(4m). Witton Castle, Witton-le-Wear, Bishop Auckland, Co Durham DL14 0DE.** 01388 488230. www.wittoncastle.co.uk. Caravan storage. Bars. Fly fishing. Swimming pool. Paddling pool, children's playground. Bar meals. Special facilities for rallies. Periodic special events. Shopping 2m. Golf 4m. Cinema 10m. Owner supplied copy. Off A68 and between Toft Hill and Witton-le-Wear. Open: 1 March - 31 October. BH&HPA

### Consett

**(3m). Allensford Caravan & Country Park, Castleside, Consett, Co Durham DH8 9BA.** 01207 505572. Large children's adventure park, picnic areas and open recreation areas. Fishing and woodland walks from park. Horse riding (2m), Golf (4m). Owner supplied copy. The park is easily found from the A1 motorway by taking the A68 heading towards Castleside. Keep on the A68 for Allensford and the park can be found alongside the river Derwent. Open: 1 March - 31 October. BH&HPA

### Darlington

**(4m). Newbus Grange Country Park, Hurworth Road, Neasham, Darlington, Co Durham DL2 1PE.** 01325 720973. www.newbusgrangecountrypark.co.uk. Newbus Grange offers owner occupied holiday homes in delightful peaceful surroundings, situated between the pretty villages of Neasham and Hurworth. Private fishing, good local food, riverside walks, bus to Darlington. David Bellamy Silver Conservation Award. Take A66 Darlington bypass, at football stadium roundabout SP Neasham, 2m to T junction turn R, 500 yds on L. Open: 18 January - 3 January. ★ ★ ★ ★ BH&HPA

**(10m). Winston Caravan Park, The Old Forge, Winston, Darlington, Co Durham DL2 3RH.** 01325 730228. www.touristnetuk.com/ne/winston. Disabled person's holiday home for hire. Sports centre, play park, tennis court, football, netball pitch 300yds, golf course, fishing. PO, shops and doctors 2m. Pub 400yds. On A67, 10m W of Darlington, turn L into Winston Village follow road for 400yds then turn R into site. 5.5m from Barnard Castle. Open: 1 March - 31 October. ★ ★ ★

### Durham

**(4.5m). Finchale Abbey Farm, Finchale, Durham, Co Durham DH1 5SH.** 01913 866528. www.finchaleabbey.co.uk. ADULT ONLY PARK. Cafe on site, bar at golf range. 24h security. River walks. Hardstandings. Credit cards accepted. Shops 1.5m walk, fishing, golf course within 15mins walk. Beautiful countryside park. David Bellamy Silver Conservation Award. Off A1(M) at Chester-Le-Street, on A167 (S) follow signs for Arnison Centre. Then signs for Finchale Priory. Open: All year. ★ ★ ★ ★ BH&HPA NCC

**(2.5m). Grange Caravan Club Site, Meadow Lane, Durham, Co Durham DH1 1TL.** 01913 844778. www.caravanclub.co.uk. An open and level site within easy reach of the historic city of Durham. Advance bookings essential. Non-members and tent campers welcome. Hardstandings. Dog walk. Toilet blocks with privacy cubicles and laundry facilities. Fishing and golf nearby. Ideal for families. See website for standard directions to site. Open: All year. ★ ★ ★ ★ ★ NCC

### Hartlepool

**(7m). Crimdon Dene Holiday Park, Coast Road, Blackhall Colliery, Hartlepool, Co Durham TS27 4BN.** 01429 267801. www.park-resortstouring.com. New all

# NORTH EAST

weather sports court in 2008. Amusements, FREE kids club. Family bar. Nearby shops, PO, doctors, garages. Outdoor play area, indoor swimming pool. David Bellamy Gold Conservation Award. From A19, take B1281 turning SP to Blackhall and drive through Castle Eden, turn L after about 0.5m SP Blackhall. After 3m, turn R at T junction on to A1086, towards Crimdon. After 1m the park is SP. Open: 21 March - 31 October. BH&HPA NCC 2⛳

### Stanley

(1m). **Bobby Shafto Caravan Park, Money Hills, Beamish, Stanley, Co Durham DH9 0RY.** *01913 701776.* www.bobbyshaftocaravanpark.co.uk. Licensed club. Children's play area. Take A693 for 5m from Chester-le-Street to Beamish. Open: 1 March - 31 October. ★★★ BH&HPA 75 56

### Stockton-on-Tees

(1.25m). **White Water Park Caravan Club Site, Tees Barrage, Stockton-on-Tees, Co Durham TS18 2QW.** *01642 634880.* www.caravanclub.co.uk. This pleasantly landscaped site is adjacent to the largest white water canoeing and rafting course built to international standard in Britain. Baby and toddler washroom. MV service point. TV, information rooms and play equipment. Golf and NCN route nearby. Good area for walking. Facilities for disabled. Ideal for families. Non-members and tent campers welcome. See website for standard directions to site. Open: All year. ★★★★★ NCC 115 115

### Weardale

**Heather View Caravan Park, Stanhope, Weardale, Co Durham DL13 2PS.** *01388 528728.* www.heatherview.co.uk. Shop, set by the river Wear 5mins walk from picturesque Stanhope, great fishing and stunning views. Owner supplied copy. Near A689 & Stanhope. Open: 1 March - 31 October. BH&HPA 360

## NORTHUMBERLAND

### Alnwick

(0.5m). **Alnwick Rugby Club Campsite, St James Estate, Alnwick, Northumberland NE66 1BG.** *01665 602342.* www.alnwickrugby.com. Tourers only use of club rooms when open. For bookings write to Mr D R Bell, 4 Bondgate Without, Alnwick NE66 1PP. Golf course, shops, PO all within 1km. On outskirts of Alnwick (S) within sight of the A1, from A1 S Alnwick signpost take slip road, L at bottom then second L. Open: 1 May - 31 August. ★

(1m). **Dunstan Hill Camping & Caravanning Club Site, Dunstan, Alnwick, Northumberland NE66 3TQ.** *01665 576310* . www.campingandcaravanningclub.co.uk. The site is set in 14 acres in the shadow of Dunstan Borough Castle and 1m from coast with a footpath to beach from site. Non-members welcome and may join at the site. All units accepted. One of the park's major attractions is Kielder Water, Europe's largest man-made lake is nearby. Close to Alnwick Castle, a location used in the recent Harry Potter films. Special deals available for families and backpackers. Loo Of The Year (4 stars). From A1 take B1340 signed Seahouses. R at T junction at Christon Bank. Take 2nd R SP Embleton, 3rd L on to B1339 coastal route, site 2m on L. Open: 1 April - 31 October. ★★★★ 150 150

(9m). **Newton Hall, Newton Hall, Newton-by-the-Sea, Alnwick, Northumberland NE66 3DZ.** *01665 576239.* www.newtonholidays.co.uk. 1m from local shops, 9m from Alnwick Castle and Bamburgh Castle. Park is close to Sandy Bay (0.75m approx). Open: 25 March - 30 October. ★★★★ BH&HPA 16 16

**River Breamish Caravan Club Site, Powburn, Alnwick, Northumberland NE66 4HY.** *01665 578320.* www.caravanclub.co.uk. Set amid the Cheviot Hills, with excellent walking and cycling in the immediate area. Toilet blocks with privacy cubicles and laundry facilities. Baby and dog walk on site. Non members and tent campers welcome. Facilities for the disabled. See website for standard directions to site. Open: 23 March - 5 November. ★★★★★ NCC 76 76

### Ashington

(6m). **Sandy Bay Holiday Park, North Seaton, Ashington, Northumberland NE63 9YD.** *01670 815055.* www.parkresortstouring.com. Indoor pool, water resorts programme, adventure playground, sports court, shop, laundrette, amusements, takeaway, FREE kids clubs, FREE family evening entertainment. Restaurant, Koi carp lake. Dartc. Pool table. Alnwick Castle. David Bellamy Silver Conservation Award. From A1 at Seaton Burn, go on A19, at roundabout go on to A189 to Ashington, head N. At first roundabout on A189 turn R on to B1334 towards Newbiggin by Sea. Park is on right-hand side. Open: 10 April - 31 October. ★★★ BH&HPA NCC 520

(2m). **Wansbeck Riverside Caravan & Camping Site, Green Lane, Ashington, Northumberland NE63 8TX.** *01670 812323.* www.northumberland.gov.uk. Touring site set in picturesque Wansbeck Riverside Park. On the banks of the river Wansbeck, and an ideal touring base. A warden lives on the site and runs a well-stocked shop. Children's play area & paddling pool. Owner supplied copy. SP off the A1068, guide post to Ashington Road (brown sign). Open: All year. ★★ 44

### Bamburgh

(1m). **Glororum Caravan Park, Glororum, Bamburgh, Northumberland NE69 7AW.** *01668 214457.* www.northumbrianleisure.co.uk. Peaceful surroundings within easy reach of Holy Island, the Farne Islands, Cheviots and many historic castles. Nearby facilities for horse-riding, swimming, golf, tennis and boat trips. 1m from Bamburgh on the Adderstone (B1341) or from A1 take B1341 at Adderstone garage and continue for 4m. Open: 9 March - 31 October. ★★★ NCC 15 80 150

(3m). **Waren Caravan And Camping Park, Waren Mill, Bamburgh, Northumberland NE70 7EE.** *01668 214366.* www.meadowhead.co.uk. 250 pitches in a flat 4 acre park. Large heated toilet block with 6 privacy cubicles, including disabled facilities. Wonderfully scenic. Follow B1342 from A1 to Waren Mill towards Bamburgh. By Budle Bay turn R and follow signs to park. Open: 12 March - 31 October. ★★★★ BH&HPA 82 82 27

### Belford

**The Kaims Holiday Park (was Bradford Kaims), Bradford House, Belford, Northumberland NE70 7JT.** *01668 213432.* ★★★

### Berwick-upon-Tweed

**Berwick Holiday Park (Haven), Magdalene Fields, Berwick-upon-Tweed, Northumberland TD15 1NE.** *0871 1680406.* www.haven.com. Located indoor and outdoor pools, outdoor bowling, amusements, kid's clubs. Mash and Barrel lounge-bar-cafe. Live entertainment daily. Supermarket complex. Outdoor multisports court/indoor soft play area. 2 sandy beaches with access. Rose Award. Welcome

# NORTH EAST

Host Award Investor in People. Golf course next door, outdoor Funzone includes play area, bouncy castle and trampolines. David Bellamy Gold Conservation Award. Park SP on A1 from both north and south and you will find signs directing you to Berwick Holiday Park in the town. Open: 18 March - 31 October. ★ ★ ★ ★ ★ BH&HPA NCC ⚑ ♿ ♪ ♿ ⚑ ⚑ ✕ ♿ ⚑ ♿ ♿ ♿ 270⚑

**(7m). Haggerston Castle Holiday Park (Haven), Beal, Berwick-upon-Tweed, Northumberland TD15 2PA.** *0871 2310865* . www.caravancamping.co.uk. Heated indoor and outdoor swimming pools. New luxury spa treatment rooms. Club. Bars. Entertainment. Horse riding. Boating lake. Chinese restaurant. Burger King. Tennis courts. 9-hole golf course. Mini market. Bike hire. Crazy golf. Rose award. Welcome Host Award, Investor in People. Golf courses nearby. Beach 5m. David Bellamy Gold Conservation Award. Park SP from A1. Open: 18 March - 31 October. ★ ★ ★ ★ ★ BH&HPA NCC ⚑ ⚑ ♿ ♪ ♿ ⚑ ✕ ⚑ ♿ ♿ ♿ 153⚑ 153⚑ 1750⚑

**(1.5m). Ord House Country Park, East Ord, Berwick-upon-Tweed, Northumberland TD15 2NS.** *01289 305288* . www.ordhouse.co.uk. Licensed club. Silver Award Green Tourism Business Scheme. AA 5 pennants. Award winner. Toilet & Amenity Building & Disabled Suite. Members of the Best of British. Licensed club within the 18th century manor house. Mini golf & children's play area. Camping & caravanning accessory shop. Golf & sports centre within 1.5m. Shops & PO outside park entrance. GS. David Bellamy Gold Conservation Award. Off Berwick bypass (A1) at East Ord. Open: All year. ★ ★ ★ ★ ★ BH&HPA ⚑ ⚑ ♿ ⚑ ♿ ♿ ♿ ✕ ⚑ ⚑ ⚑ 25⚑ 75⚑ ▲ 418⚑

**(0.5m). Seaview Caravan Club Site (Berwick), Bilendean Road, Spittal, Berwick-upon-Tweed, Northumberland TD15 1QU.** *01289 305198* . www.caravanclub.co.uk. Excellent views of the Tweed and old town. Good site for children with safe bathing and play facilities at Spittal beach. Tent campers and non-members welcome. Hardstandings available. Advance booking advised BH and July and August. Privacy cubicles. Baby/toddler washroom. Veg prep. MV service point. Golf, cycling and water sports nearby. See website for standard directions to site. Open: 23 March - 7 January. ★ ★ ★ ★ ⚑ ♿ ⚑ ♿ ♿ ♿ ♿ 98⚑ 98⚑

## Chathill

**Beadnell Bay Camping & Caravanning Club Site, Beadnell, Chathill, Northumberland NE67 5BX.** *01665 720586* . www.campingandcaravanningclub.co.uk. 6-acre site with 150 pitches with full facilities next to the beach. Ideal for exploring Northumberland coastline and within easy reach of A1. NO TOWED CARAVANS PERMITTED. Non-members accepted. Motorhomes & tents welcome. A superb site for walkers and cyclists. Special deals available for families and backpackers. Site is on L after Beadnell Village, just beyond left hand bend. 10m from Alnwick. Follow 'Seahouses' SP. 20m from Berwick-upon-Tweed. Open: 14 April - 26 September. ★ ★ ★ NCC ⚑ ♿ ♿ ⚑ ⚑ ♿ ♿ 150⚑ ⚑

## Haltwhistle

**(3m). Hadrians Wall Camping and Caravan Site, Melkridge Tilery, Melkridge, Haltwhistle, Northumberland NE49 9PG.** *01434 320495* . www.hadrianswallcampsite.co.uk. 0.5m from Hadrian's Wall world heritage site. 300yd S of B6318, 1m W of Once Brewed. 2m due N of Melkridge (A69). Open: All year. ★ ★ ★ ⚑ ⚑ ♿ ⚑ ♿ ⚑ ⚑ ⚑ ⚑ 3⚑ 20⚑ 35▲

**(1.5m). Haltwhistle Camping & Caravanning Club Site, Burnfoot Park Village, Haltwhistle, Northumberland NE49 0JP.** *01434 320106* . www.campingandcaravanningclub.co.uk. Site is in the National Trust Bellister Castle Estate on south bank of South Tyne river and 4m from Hadrian's Wall. Close to the Pennine Way on the banks of river South Tyne. All units accepted. Non-members welcome. Fishing available on site. Special deals available for families and backpackers. From A69, take Alston road S (A689). Coanwood and Halton Lea Gate. Follow site signs. Open: 1 April - 31 October. ★ ★ ★ ★ NCC ⚑ ⚑ ♿ ⚑ ♿ ♿ ♿ ⚑ ⚑ ⚑ 50⚑ 50⚑

**(1m). Seldom Seen Caravan Park, Haltwhistle, Northumberland NE49 0NE.** *01434 320571* . Quiet, riverside park. Bird watching, peaceful walks. 2m Hadrian's Wall World Heritage site. Nr Northumberland National Park, Historical Borders, High Pennines AONB. Golf 5m. David Bellamy Gold Conservation Award. Off A69. SP Haltwhistle. Open: 1 March - 31 October. BH&HPA ⚑ ⚑ ♿ ⚑ ♿ ♿ ⚑ ⚑ ♿ 20⚑ ▲ 50⚑

**(5m). Yont The Cleugh, Coanwood, Haltwhistle, Northumberland NE49 0QN.** *01434 320274* . www.yontthecleugh.co.uk. A quiet park in outstanding unspoilt location. Near main Roman wall sites Bar. Children's play area. SP 4.5m off A69 and 3.5m off A689. Open: 1 March - 7 November. BH&HPA ⚑ ⚑ ♿ ⚑ ⚑ ⚑ 12⚑ 20⚑ ▲

## Hexham

**(10m). Barrasford Park Caravan Park, Front Drive, Barrasford Park, Hexham, Northumberland NE48 4BE.** *01434 681210*. 60 acres of woodland. Laundry. Licensed clubhouse. Salmon fishing within 2m. 8m N of Corbridge off A68. Open: 1 April - 31 October. ★ ★ ⚑ ⚑ ♿ ⚑ ♿ ⚑ ⚑ ⚑ ⚑ ♿ 21⚑ ▲ 120⚑

**(0.5m). Bellingham Camping & Caravanning Club Site, Brown Rigg, Bellingham, Hexham, Northumberland NE48 2JY.** *01434 220175*. www.campingandcaravanningclub.co.uk. 4 camping pods also available for hire. Fishing, golf, canoe launch, swimming 0.5m from site. Pennine way adjacent to site. Village 0.5m, shops, pubs and restaurant. Dog walk on site. 8m Kielder Water. 10m Hadrian's Wall. Walks straight from site. From A68 take the B6320 to Bellingham. Open: 11 March - 30 October. ★ ★ ★ ★ ⚑ ⚑ ♿ ⚑ ♿ ♿ 65⚑ 65⚑ 15▲

**(1.5m). Causey Hill Caravan Park, Causey Hill, Hexham, Northumberland NE46 2JN.** *01434 602834*. Quiet Country Park, woodland walks, wildlife pond. Fishing, golf courses nearby. Many hardstandings, all electric. Stunning views. Unique park, static caravans for sale. 1.5m SW Hexham. Follow B6306 or signs for Hexham racecourse and then Causey Hill. Open: 1 March - 31 October. ★ ★ ★ BH&HPA NCC ⚑ ⚑ ♿ ⚑ ♿ ♿ ⚑ ⚑ ⚑ ♿ 10⚑ 40⚑

**(2m). Fallowfield Dene Caravan Park, Acomb, Hexham, Northumberland NE46 4RP.** *01434 603553*. www.fallowfielddene.co.uk. Roman wall nearby. Managers: Joe & Alison Richardson. 2m N of Hexham via A69 bypass (N of river Tyne) for 0.5m W. Turn N on to A6079. Site is 1m beyond village of Acomb. Open: 14 March - 2 November. ★ ★ ★ ★ BH&HPA ⚑ ⚑ ♿ ⚑ ♿ ♿ ⚑ ⚑ ⚑ ♿ 150⚑ ⚑

**(2m). Hexham Racecourse, Yarridge Road, Hexham, Northumberland NE46 2JP.** *01434 606847*. www.hexham-racecourse.co.uk. Situated on the second highest racecourse in Britain with dramatic views across large area of Northumberland. Dog walk. Advance booking not essential. Shops, doctor, dentist, golf course all within 2m. Off A69 on B6306, turn L after 3m. 1.5m to site. Open: 22 April - 9 October. ★ ★ ★ ⚑ ⚑ ♿ ⚑ ♿ ♿ ⚑ ⚑ ♿ 19⚑ 40⚑ 10▲

**Kielder Water Caravan Club AS, Leaplich Waterside Park, Falstone, Hexham, Northumberland NE48 1AX.** *01434 251000*. www.nwl.co.uk/kielder. A fabulous site for an active holiday, with some pitches overlooking Kielder Water,

# NORTH EAST

the largest man-made lake in Western Europe. Ideal family site with water sports, pony trekking, horse riding, orienteering, bird watching, cycling and crazy golf. All pitches on hardstandings but awnings possible. Dog walk. Non-members and tent campers welcome. Toilet blocks and laundry facilities. Motorhome service point. See website for standard directions to site. 4m from Kielder. Open: 1 April - 31 October. ★★★★ ♿ ⚲ ⚘ ⚹ ⚭ ⛺ ♨ ♿ 83🚐 83🚙

(6m). **Poplars Riverside Caravan Park, Haydon Bridge, Hexham, Northumberland NE47 6BY.** *01434 684427.* A secluded small riverside site at Haydon Bridge. Fishing on site. Near village and convenient for Hadrian's Wall. Railway station in village. Ideal for walking and cycling. Near the A69 Newcastle-upon-Tyne to Carlisle road. Come into Haydon Bridge, look for caravan sign near bridge. Open: 1 March - 31 October. ★★★★ BH&HPA ♿ ⚹ ⚭ ⚲ ⚘ ⛺ 🚗 ♨ ♿ 11🚐 △ 31🚙

## Morpeth

(0.25m). **Clennell Hall Riverside Holiday Park, Clennell, Morpeth, Northumberland NE65 7BG.** *01669 650341.* www.clennellhall.co.uk. Quiet family-run site at the foot of the Cheviot Hills. Located amidst spectacular countryside in upper Coquetdale, Alwinton, Rothbury in Northumberland and next to the Northumberland National Park. No busy roads or traffic nearby, just the gentle bleating of sheep in the surrounding fields, penetrates the tranquillity of this ideal retreat. Children's play area. AA 3 Pennants. Via Rothbury, B6341 after 4m turn R signed Alwinton. Over 2nd bridge turn R signed Clennell Hall. Open: 1 March - 31 October. BH&HPA NCC ♿ ⚲ ⚭ ⚹ ⚘ ⛺ 🍴 ♨ ♿ 50🚐 △ 14🚙

**Nunnykirk Caravan Club Site, Morpeth, Northumberland NE61 4PZ.** *01669 620762.* www.caravanclub.co.uk. 5.5m from Rothbury. Peace and tranquillity reign at this attractive site, making it a haven for wildlife, and a bird watcher's paradise. Own sanitation required. Good area for walking, dog walk nearby. Fishing within 5m. Non-members welcome. No tents. Use website for standard directions to site. Open: 5 April - 1 October. NCC ♿ ⚹ ⚲ ⚘ 🚗 ♨ 84🚐 84🚙

## Newbiggin-by-the-Sea

**Church Point Caravan Park, High Street, Newbiggin-by-the-Sea, Northumberland NE64 6DP.** *0844 0502556.* www.park-resorts.com. Guests have full use of all facilities at nearby Sandy Bay Holiday Park, including swimming pool, restaurant, laundrette, family entertainment, shop, take away. No under 18 years groups. David Bellamy Silver Conservation Award. Owner supplied copy. 4m from Ashington. Open: 19 March - 30 October. BH&HPA NCC ♿ ⚭ 🚐 115🚙

## Newcastle upon Tyne

(8m). **Border Forest Caravan Park, Cottonshopeburnfoot, Otterburn, Newcastle upon Tyne, Northumberland NE19 1TF.** *01830 520259.* www.borderforest.com. Family run park situated in beautiful Northumberland Border country. Directly onto Pennine Way and Kielder Forest. Free hot showers. Timber lodge hire. Bed and breakfast. Restaurant nearby. David Bellamy Gold Conservation Award. Adjacent A68. 6m S of Scottish border (Carter bar). 8m N of Otterburn. Open: All year. ★★★★ BH&HPA ♿ ⚹ ⚭ ⚲ ⚘ ⛺ 🚗 ♨ ♿ 36🚐 36🚙 △

## Prudhoe

(1.4m). **The High Hermitage Caravan Park, Ovingham, Prudhoe, Northumberland NE42 6HH.** *01661 832250.* www.highhermitagecaravanpark.co.uk. Communal BBQ, giant draught/chess board. Distance to shops, PO, doctor 1m. Distance to chemists, garage, playgrounds, rail station, restaurants, Pubs 1.5m. Fishing rights on boundary riverbank. Cinema, theatre, museum, towns of Newcastle and Hexham 12m. Metro shopping centre 10m. Golf course 4m. No dogs or cats. Off A69. SP 'Wylam' and follow main road to apparent T-junction SP R to Ovingham, continue on main road 1.5 m towards Ovingham along riverside. Just after paved and railed-in water extraction point, turn R into drive entrance (concealed). Open: 1 March - 7 January. ★★★ BH&HPA ♿ ⚹ ⚭ ⚲ ⚘ ⛺ ♨ ♿ 5🚐 5🚙 △ 28🏕

## Seahouses

**Seafield Caravan Park (Seahouses), Seahouses, Northumberland NE68 7SP.** *01665 720628.* www.seafieldpark.co.uk. Situated central for Seahouses giving access to shops and all local amenities. Superior well-equipped holiday homes, fully serviced touring pitches. Play park, coffee shop, swimming pool and gym. David Bellamy Gold Conservation Award. Travelling S leave A1 at Alnwick and follow B1340 direct to Seahouses. If travelling from N leave A1 at Belford and follow B1342 through Bamburgh to Seahouses. Open: 9 February - 9 January. ★★★★★ BH&HPA ♿ ⚹ ⚭ ⚲ ⚘ ⛺ 🍴 🚗 ♨ ♿ 18🚐 388🚙

## Stocksfield

(4m). **Wellhouse Caravan & Camping Park, Wellhouse Farm, Newton, Stocksfield, Northumberland NE43 7UY.** *01661 842193.* www.wellhousefarm.co.uk. Quiet family site. Ideal for visiting Northumberland and surrounding areas. 1m from A69 on B6309 to Matfen & Stamfordham. 9m from Hexham. 1m from B6318, Hadrians Wall. 2m from Corbridge fishing and golf. Open: 1 April - 31 October. ★★★ ♿ ⚹ ⚲ ⚘ ⛺ ♨ ♿ 10🚐 40🚙 △

## Wooler

(0.25m). **Highburn House Country Holiday Park, Wooler, Northumberland NE71 6EE.** *01668 281344.* www.highburn-house.co.uk. Farm park with good views over the Cheviot Hills. Shops, pubs, doctors, dentist etc. 0.25m from park. Takeaway meals, cafe/restaurant, diary produce available nearby. Castles, light railway, wild cattle. Scottish border all within 7m of park. Golf course 2m. From A1 take A697 to Wooler, turn L to High Street at the top turn L into Burnhouse road, park is on L. Open: 1 March - 31 October. ★★★★ BH&HPA ♿ ⚹ ⚭ ⚲ ⚘ ⛺ 🚗 ♨ ♿ 35🚐 35🚙 △ 43🏕

(2m). **Riverside Country Park (North Dales), South Road, Wooler, Northumberland NE71 6NJ.** *01668 281447.* www.northdales.co.uk. Situated on edge of Northumbria National Park. Indoor pool. Family lounge bar and clubroom. From South take A697 off A1, SP Coldstream to Wooler about 35m. Park on left hand side on outskirts of village. Open: 9 March - 31 October. BH&HPA ♿ ⚹ ⚭ ⚲ ⚘ ⛺ 🍴 🚗 ♨ ♿ 55🚐 △ 395🚙

## REDCAR & CLEVELAND
### Saltburn-by-the-Sea

**Margrove Park Holidays, Boosbeck, Saltburn-by-the-Sea, Redcar & Cleveland TS12 3BZ.** *01287 653616.* Free showers. Manager: K & M Crossman. 2m to shops. PO 1m. Fishing, golf course nearby. Plenty of walking 0.5m to Cleveland Way. From Guisbrough follow A171 (SP Whitby) for about 2m. When you should turn L on to the minor road sp Margrove Park and Lingdale in about 0.25m, the dip in road, turn R into the site. Open: 1 April - 31 October. ♿ ⚭ ⚲ ⚘ ♨ 🚐 🚙

## TYNE & WEAR
### Rowlands Gill

**Derwent Park Caravan & Camping Park, The Bungalow, Derwent Park, Rowlands Gill, Tyne & Wear NE39 1LG.**

# NORTH EAST / NORTH WEST

01207 543383. Flat, sheltered site by river. Hot showers, laundry, playground, tennis, bowls, crazy golf and trout fishing. Near Beamish and Gateshead Metro Centre. 2m from shops, clubs, restaurants. At junction of A694 and B6314 in Rowlands Gill, 7m SW of Newcastle-upon-Tyne. Open: 1 March - 31 October. ★★★★ 35 A 24

## South Shields

Lizard Lane Camping & Caravan Park, Marsden, South Shields, Tyne & Wear NE34 7AB. 01914 544982. 9 hole putt on site. Children's play area up to 8 years. Close to museums, leisure centre and Roman remains. Fees on request (advance bookings only for weekly stays). Sea 100yd. Owner supplied copy. 2m SE of South Shields town centre via A183. Open: Contact site direct. ★★★

## Whitley Bay

(2m). Old Hartley Caravan Club Site, Whitley Bay, Tyne & Wear NE26 4RL. 01912 370256. www.caravanclub.co.uk. Slightly sloping site with views overlooking the sea. Beach 1m. Hardstandings. Toilet blocks. Privacy cubicles. Laundry facilities. Veg Prep. Gas & Gaz. MV Service point. Late night arrivals area. Ideal for families. Members only. No tents. See website for standard directions to site. Open: 23 March - 5 November. NCC 64 64

## CHESHIRE

### Chester

(3m). Birch Bank Farm Campsite, Stamford Lane, Christleton, Chester, Cheshire CH3 7QD. 01244 335233. www.birchbankfarm.co.uk. A small site on a working farm in the green Cheshire countryside and free of traffic noise. Turn R off A51 Chester to Nantwich road, opposite Vicars Cross golf club, Christleton-Waverton road. Open: 1 May - 31 October. 10 10

(4m). Chester Fairoaks Caravan Club Site, Rake Lake, Little Stanney, Chester, Cheshire CH2 4HS. 01513 551500. www.caravanclub.co.uk. A very pleasant, open and level site with oak trees on the boundary, conveniently located just off the M53. Some hardstandings, toilet block, laundry point, play equipment and dog walk on site. Golf, fishing and NCN route within 5m. Non-members and tent campers admitted. See website for standard directions to site. Open: All year. ★★★★★ NCC 100 100

(3m). Chester Southerly Touring Park, Rough Hill, Marlston-cum-Lache, Chester, Cheshire CH4 9LB. 01244 671308. www.chestersoutherly.co.uk. All pitches are level and attractively situated. Sports and shopping facilities etc. in Chester. Play area, public telephone. Calor Gas. Ideal touring base. Rallies by arrangement. Off A55 and A483. Open: All year. 70

(2.5m). Netherwood Touring Park (Adults only), Whitchurch Road, Chester, Chester, Cheshire CH3 6AF. 01244 335583. www.netherwoodtouringsite.co.uk. Hot and cold showers, razor points, hand and hairdryers. Chemical toilet disposal point. No children. Borders Shropshire Union Canal. 2.5m from the centre of Chester. OS map ref: 117447648. On A41. GPS coordinates: Lat: 53 10 39N, long: 2 49 46W. A41 Chester-Whitchurch road. Open: 1 March - 31 October. 15 15

(7m). Northwood Caravan Park, Dog Lane, Kelsall, Chester, Cheshire CW6 ORP. 01829 752569. www.northwood-hall.co.uk. An idyllic setting, this attractive family run park is set amongst oak and chestnut trees. Near to Delamere Forest. Seasonal pitches available. Fishing, tennis 1m. Golf courses 3-5m. Cinema/shopping 7m. M6, J18 follow signs for Chester on A54. Take second left hand exit for Kelsall. Turn L down Dog Lane adjacent the Royal Oak Pub, park is 1m down on R. Open: All year. 30 30 A 2

### Frodsham

(2.5m). The Ridgeway Country Holiday Park, The Ridgeway, Alvanley, Frodsham, Cheshire WA6 6XQ. 01928 734981. www.ridgewaypark.com. Non residential park - holiday caravans for hire and sale and wood-clad lodges for hire. Shopping & cinema 15mins, swimming pool 25mins into Chester. Golf, sailing, horse riding, fishing nearby. J12, M56, follow A56 towards Frodsham. Shortly after passing through the market town, turn L on to B5393. Keep on road until you pass Foxhill centre, then immediately turn L on to 'The Ridgeway'. Open: 1 March - 17 December. ★★★★ BH&HPA 48

### Knutsford

(5m). Woodlands Park Caravan Site, Woodlands Park, Wash Lane, Allostock, Knutsford, Cheshire WA16 9LG. 01565 722194 . Dogs allowed with permission. Fishing on site, golf course nearby. 3m to shops. GS. Open March 1-January 6 for holiday caravans. J19, M6, go to Knutsford, park S of Knutsford on A50. Open: 1 March - 31 October. BH&HPA 30

### Macclesfield

(4m). Stoneyfold Caravan Park, off Leek Road, Bosley, Macclesfield, Cheshire SK11 0PR. 01625 422832. www.stoneyfoldcaravanpark.co.uk. Very quiet, woodland site with magnificent views and wildlife. Owner supplied copy. About 4m from Macclesfield on Leek road, nearside, 0.5m short of A523/A54 crossroads, up lane near Tilcon sign. Open: 1 March - 15 January. BH&HPA 30

(6m). Strawberry Wood Caravan Park, Farm Lane, Lower Withington, Macclesfield, Cheshire SK11 9DU. 01477 571407. www.strawberrywoodcaravanpark.co.uk. Small, quiet site set in mature woodland. Hardstanding. Close to Jodrell Bank radio telescope. Fishing available on site. From J18, M6 take A535 to Macclesfield after 4m take B5392, site entrance 700yd on right hand side. Open: 1 March - 31 October. 25 25

### Malpas

(1m). The Glen CL, Mill Lane, Bulkeley, Malpas, Cheshire SY14 8BL. 01829 720514. Peace and seclusion guaranteed in beautiful area of Shropshire. Due to the tranquility, the Glen is not suitable for children. On A4117 E off A456 Birmingham, Kidderminster, W off A49 Shrewsbury, Ludlow A4117. Open: All year. BH&HPA

### Northwich

(5m). Daleford Manor Caravan Park (Caravan Club AS), Daleford Manor, Daleford Lane, Sandiway, Northwich, Cheshire CW8 2BT. 01606 889545 . www.dalefordmanorcaravanpark.co.uk. Blakemere craft centre, excellent fishing 1m away. Butcher's and amenity shops in local village. Off A556, Daleford Lane then take 1st R turn onto farm lane where park is located. Sandiway golf course 2m away. Open: 1 March - 1 January. BH&HPA 10 10

Delamere Forest Camping & Caravanning Club Site, Station Road, Delamere, Northwich, Cheshire CW8 2HZ. 01606 889231 . www.campingandcaravanningclub.co.uk. The wonderful new club site at Delamere Forest has many environmentally friendly features to complement the beauty of the forest and is a stone's throw from the Go Ape theme park. Located on the B5152 is accessible from the A556, the B5152 and close to the M6. Open: 1 January - 31 December. ★★★★★ NCC 80 80

# NORTH WEST

(4m). **Lamb Cottage Caravan Park** (Tranquil adults-only), Dalefords Lane, Whitegate, Northwich, Cheshire CW8 2BN. *01606 882302*. www.lambcottage.co.uk. Peaceful retreat on award winning adults only park. Booking essential. Open March-end December for statics. A556 to Sandiway PO/off licence, take road to Winsford, 1.5m on R, white cottage, sign on front. Open: 1 March - 31 October. ★★★★★ BH&HPA

(4.5m). **Woodbine Cottage Caravan Park**, Warrington Road, Acton Bridge, Northwich, Cheshire CW8 3QB. *01606 852319*. A beautiful country site on the banks of the river Weaver at the heart of Cheshire. Convenient for many places of interest around Cheshire (Anderton Boat Lift, Delamere Forest Craft Centres, Gullivers World). Shopping precinct, doctor 1m; 5 golf courses within 4m; fishing ponds 2m. From M56 J10, take A49 towards Whitchurch, carry on past Riverside on L then park entrance on L. Open: 1 March - 31 October.

## Stockport

(7.5m). **Elm Beds Caravan & Camping Site**, Elm Beds Road, Poynton, Stockport, Cheshire SK12 1TG. *01625 872370*. www.peaksandplains.co.uk. Hot & cold showers and basins. Shaver points. Gas supplies. Accessed from A6 or A523. At Poynton 2m east off A523. At Poynton 2m east off A523. Hot & cold showers and basins. Shaver points. Gas supplies. Open: 1 March - 31 October. BH&HPA

## Warrington

(5m). **Holly Bank Caravan Park**, Warburton Bridge Road, Rixton, Warrington, Cheshire WA3 6HU. *01925 752842*. Chemical toilet disposal point. Shaver points. Gas. Laundry facilities. Games room. Free showers. Public telephone. AA 3 pennants. 440yd to 3 pubs, shop (village). 2m E of M6 J21. On A57 (Irlam). Turn R at lights into Warburton Bridge Road. Entry on L. Open: All year.

## Winsford

(3m). **Elm Cottage Touring Park**, Elm Cottage, Chester Lane, Little Budworth, Winsford, Cheshire CW7 2QJ. *01829 760544*. www.elmcottagecp.co.uk. Supermarkets, doctors, dentists and vets within a 5m radius. Good fishing and golf courses nearby. Free tyre inflation facility on site. David Bellamy Gold Conservation Award. W of Winsford on A54. The Shrewsbury Arms is only 400yd away. Open: 10 February - 25 January. ★★★★ BH&HPA

(1m). **Lakeside Caravan Park (Winsford)**, Stockshill, Winsford, Cheshire CW7 4EF. *01606 861043*. www.thornleyleisure.co.uk. Boating and fishing lake. Doctors, town centre, amenities, leisure centres, golf course all available nearby. Off A54 near Winsford. Open: 1 March - 16 January. ★★★★ BH&HPA

■**New Farm (Cheshire)**, New Farm, Long Lane, Wettenhall, Winsford, Cheshire CW7 4DW. *01270 528213*. www.newfarmcheshire.co.uk. Adult only caravan park set in a picturesque part of Cheshire, 17 miles from the walled city of Chester. New Farm welcomes tourers and motorhomes to their relaxed and tranquil park. There is easy access to a level site with gravel road and 17 hardstandings. There is a well-maintained shower and toilet block. On site there are three coarse fishing lakes. Wettenhall is conveniently placed for Nantwich and is only a few minutes drive from several country pubs, a Coop and post office. There's a pub within walking distance Open: All year.

## CUMBRIA
### Ambleside

(5m). **Hawkshead Hall**, Hawkshead Hall Farm, Hawkshead, Ambleside, Cumbria LA22 0NN. *01539 436221*. www.hawksheadhall-campsite.com. 10mins walk to village, various shops, inns and cafes. Owner supplied copy. S of Ambleside on B5286, 0.25m before Hawkshead Village. Open: 15 March - 8 November.

**PREMIER PARKS 2011** ■(1.5m). **Skelwith Fold Caravan Park**, Ambleside, Cumbria LA22 0HX. *01539 432277*. www.skelwith.com. Warm welcome to all those who have not yet discovered the serenity and beauty of Skelwith Fold Caravan Park. A haven of peace and tranquillity set in 130 acres of natural woodland, home to the red squirrel, red and roe deer, badgers, rabbits and pole cats. An ideal relaxing base for those who wish to walk the fells or explore the many attractions offered by the Lake District. We are proud of our many awards. David Bellamy Gold Conservation Award. Leave M6 at J36 and take A591 to Ambleside. Follow A593 for Coniston at Clappersgate turn L on to B5286. Park is 1.5m from Ambleside and 3m from Hawkshead. Open: 1 March - 15 November. ★★★★★ BH&HPA 100 100

(5m). **The Croft Caravan & Camp Site**, North Lonsdale Road, Hawkshead, Ambleside, Cumbria LA22 0NX. *01539 436374*. www.hawkshead-croft.com. Showers, shaving and hairdryer points. TV room. Laundry. Shops in village also Beatrix Potter gallery and Wordsworth's grammar school. On B5286 at Hawkshead village. Open: 11 March - 6 November. ★★★★ BH&HPA

### Appleby-in-Westmorland

(3.5m). Wild Rose Park, Ormside,

*A jewel set in the heart of English Lakeland*
The perfect haven for your motorhome or touring caravan. Skelwith Fold's 130 acres offers a tranquil setting even in Lakelands peak season. Open from 1st March to 15th November.
**Skelwith Fold Caravan Park**
Ambleside, Cumbria, LA22 0HX
**015394 32277**
www.skelwith.com

# NORTH WEST

**Appleby-in-Westmorland, Cumbria CA16 6EJ.** 01768 351077. www.wildrose.co.uk. Recreation room. Heated outdoor swimming and paddling pools. TV. Play areas with safety surfaces. Laundrette. Off-licence. Restaurant. Takeaway. Indoor nursery room. Licensed mini-market. Pitch & putt. Reduced facilities in winter. Superb mountain views. Golf course 5m. GS. David Bellamy Gold Conservation Award. From Appleby on B6260 to Orton. In 1.5m turn E on Ormside and Soulby road. At first crossroad turn L to Ormside. After 600yd turn R into lane, then a further 600yd into drive to site. Open: All year. ★★★★★ BH&HPA 50 162 10

### Barrow-in-Furness

**(5m). South End Caravan Park, Walney Island, Barrow-in-Furness, Cumbria LA14 3YQ.** 01229 472823. www.walneyislandcaravanpark.co.uk. Gas supplies. Family run park with indoor swimming pool and club house. Close to beach. Tennis court, bowling green, children's playground. Owner supplied copy. Take exit 36 from M6, A590 to Barrow. From Ramsden Sq. follow Walney signs, 3m S of Bridge. Open: 1 March - 30 October. BH&HPA NCC 20 200

### Beckermet

**(4.5m). Tarnside Caravan Park, Braystones, Beckermet, Cumbria CA21 2YL.** 01946 822777. www.seacote.com. Fishing - sea and freshwater. Beside lovely beach, caravan club & restaurant. Convenient for western lakes and falls. A595 S of Egremont. 2m S of Egremont follow tourist signs on B5345. Open: 1 March - 15 January. BH&HPA 20 53

### Brampton

**(7m). Cairndale Caravan Site, Cumwhitton, Heads Nook, Brampton, Cumbria CA8 9BZ.** 01768 896280. Calor Gas. Golf, fishing, shopping centre, PO, pubs, restaurant, doctors within 6-9m. Owner supplied copy. Country park off A69 at Warwick Bridge, follow road to Corby-Cumwhitton, turn L at Cumwhitton village. Open: 1 March - 31 October. BH&HPA 5 17

**Irthing Vale Caravan Park, Old Church Lane, Brampton, Cumbria CA8 2AA.** 01697 73600. Flat, well-drained site. Near Hadrian's Wall and 9m NE from cathedral City of Carlisle. Lake District, Solway coast and Scotland within easy reach. Owner supplied copy. 0.5m N of Brampton off A6071. Open: 1 March - 31 January. 20

### Carlisle

**(3m). Dalston Hall Holiday Park, Dalston Hall, Dalston, Carlisle, Cumbria CA5 7JX.** 01228 710165. www.dalstonhallholidaypark.co.uk. Small, well maintained, family run park set in 94 acres of wooded park and within easy reach of the Lake District, Solway Firth and Border Counties. 9 hole golf course. Clubhouse. Laundry. Playground. Hot showers. Fishing. Hardstandings with electric and water to each pitch. Off M6 exit 42 to Dalston Village on B5299, direction Carlisle 1m N of Dalston. Open: 1 March - 31 January. ★★★ BH&HPA 50 52

**(4m). Dandy Dinmont Caravan & Camping Site, Blackford, Carlisle, Cumbria CA6 4EA.** 01228 674611. www.caravan-camping-carlisle.itgo.com. MAINLY ADULT SITE. 27 pitches for tourers and motor caravans. Good base for visiting Carlisle, Roman wall and Border country. Only 45mins from Lake District. An ideal overnight halt. Superstore, PO, horse riding within 2m - golf, hospital within 4m. Leave M6 J44. Take A7 Galashiels road, park is about 1.5m N on the R after Blackford village sign. Open: 1 March - 31 October. ★★★★ BH&HPA 27

**(6.5m). Englethwaite Hall Caravan Club Site, Armathwaite, Carlisle, Cumbria CA4 9SY.** 01228 560202. www.caravanclub.co.uk. A tranquil site, located in the Eden Valley. No sanitation. Dog walk and exercise field on site. Non-members welcome. No tents. Motorhome service point. Great for walkers. All hardstanding, part sloping, gas, gaz, information room, storage, quiet and peaceful off peak. See website for standard directions to site. Open: 30 March - 5 November. ★★★★ NCC 63 63

**(8m). Oakbank Lakes Country Park, Longtown, Carlisle, Cumbria CA6 5NA.** 01228 791108. Sixty acre site with four lakes with carp and trout. Salmon and sea fishing available. Bird sanctuary. Game bird breeding unit. Owner supplied copy. 1m N of Longtown on the A7. Open: All year. BH&HPA 12 12

**(4m). Orton Grange Caravan Park R, Wigton Road, Carlisle, Cumbria CA5 6LA.** 01228 710252. www.barton-park-homes.co.uk. Based in the beautiful Cumbrian countryside, Orton Grange is a private haven for the retired/semi-retired. Located 4m from Carlisle. Off A595 from Carlisle. Open: All year. ★★★★ 4

**(7m). Skiddaw View Holiday Park, Bothel, Bassenthwaite, Carlisle, Cumbria CA7 2JN.** 01697 320919. www.skiddawview.co.uk. Laundry, tourist info, public phone, play area. Shops etc 7m. Owner supplied copy. Off A591, near junction with A595. SP 'Sunderland Village'. 7m to Cockermouth. Open: All year. ★★★★ BH&HPA 110

### Cockermouth

**(1m). Graysonside Farm, Lorton Road, Cockermouth, Cumbria CA13 9TQ.** 01900 822351. www.graysonside.co.uk. Off B5292, 2 miles from A66.. Ideal base to tour the lakes and Western coast. Lovely views of the Lorton/Buttermere fells. Dogs allowed by request only. Owner supplied copy. Off B5292, 2 miles from A66.. Ideal base to tour the lakes and Western coast. Lovely views of the Lorton/Buttermere fells. Dogs allowed by request only. Open: 1 April - 1 November. 5 5

**(1m). Violet Bank Holiday Home Park Ltd, Simonscales Lane, Cockermouth, Cumbria CA13 9TG.** 01900 822169. www.violetbank.co.uk. Children's play area. 1m shopping, 3m golf course. David Bellamy Gold Conservation Award. Owner supplied copy. Leave Cockermouth on the A5292 Lorton Road. After 0.25m turn R up Vicarage Lane which leads to Simonscales Lane and Holiday Home Park. Open: 12 February - 12 January. ★★★★ BH&HPA NCC 93

**(4m). Wheatsheaf Inn, Low Lorton, Cockermouth, Cumbria CA13 9UW.** 01900 85199. www.wheatsheafinnlorton.co.uk. Fishing available for coarse fish and trout, salmon and sea trout. Cocker and Derwent rivers. Shops, doctors, PO within 4m. Greta 8m. Situated on B5289 towards Buttermere and Loweswater. Open: 1 March - 15 November. 20 22

**(4.5m). Whinfell Caravan Park & Campsite, Lorton Vale, Cockermouth, Cumbria CA13 0RQ.** 01900 85260. A small, secluded park, well-placed for the western lakes and fells and set in the tranquillity of the Vale of Lorton. 3m to nearest lake. 4m to Cockermouth town centre. Dogs must be on leads. Owner supplied copy. Off B5289 through Low Lorton, SP. Open: All year. 5 5 19

# NORTH WEST

**(0.25m). Wyndham Hall Caravan Park, Old Keswick Road, Cockermouth, Cumbria CA13 9SF.** 01900 822571. www.wyndhamholidaypark.co.uk. Seasonal holiday caravans for sale. Walking distance to Cockermouth, pubs, cafes, takeaways, petrol stations, 3 supermarkets, library and 'Wordsworth House'. No single sex groups. Owner supplied copy. On old A66 Keswick to Cockermouth, turn R at Castle Inn sign (end of Bassenthwaite Lake) then bear L to Embleton-Cockermouth, entrance on L on outskirts of Cockermouth. Open: 1 March - 31 October. 4🚐 8🚐 A 78

## Coniston

**(1m). Coniston Hall Campsite, Haws Bank, Coniston, Cumbria LA21 8AS.** 01539 441223. Size of site: 20 acres. Owner supplied copy. S of Coniston village centre. Turn off the A593 at Hawes Bank towards the lake. Open: 1 March - 31 October. 50🚐 🚐 A

**(3m). Hoathwaite Farm Caravan & Campsite CS, Torver, Coniston, Cumbria LA21 8AX.** 01539 441349. This is an extremely basic campsite and campers are expected to bring their own toilet facilities and there is a facility for emptying these on site. We can accommodate tents, campervans and caravans. Organised groups such as scouts can be accommodated in a separate field. A590-3m S of Coniston on Torver road turn L at green railings. Turn L again over first cattle grid. Open: All year. 🚐 🚐 A

**(1.25m). Park Coppice Caravan Club Site, Coniston, Cumbria LA21 8LA.** 01539 441555. www.caravanclub.co.uk. Set in 63 acres of National Trust woodland with many facilities for younger families including junior orienteering, nature trail and toddler's play area. Nearby lake offers sailing and water sports. Advance booking essential. Non members and tent campers welcome. Toilet block and laundry facilities. Motorhome service point. Fishing. Ideal for walking. See website for standard directions to site. Open: 23 March - 5 November. ★★★★ NCC 280🚐 280🚐 A

## Dent

**(4m). Ewegales Farm Camping Site, Dentdale, Dent, Cumbria LA10 5RH.** 01539 625440. Shower. Good for fishing - good flat field by river. Leave M6 at J37 on to A684 to Sedbergh. Site 3m E of Dent. Open: 1 March - 31 October. 6🚐 5🚐 A

## Flookburgh

**(3.5m). Lakeland Leisure Park (Haven), Moor Lane, Flookburgh, Cumbria LA11 7LT.** 0871 2310583. www.caravancamping.co.uk. Convenience store. Entertainment complex, arcade, restaurant. Indoor and outdoor heated pools. Tennis courts. Pony-trekking, stables on park. Welcome Host Award, Investor in People. David Bellamy Gold Conservation Award. M6, J36 on to A590. Turn L on to A6/A590 for Barrow-In-Furness. B5277 through Grange-over-Sands, then Allithwaite and into Flookburgh. Turn L at the village square and travel 1m down this road to the park. Open: 18 March - 31 October. ★★★★ BH&HPA NCC 100🚐 100🚐 A 1170

## Grange-over-Sands

**(4m). Greaves Farm Caravan Park, Field Broughton, Grange-over-Sands, Cumbria LA11 6HU.** 01539 536329. www.greavesfarmcaravanpark.co.uk. Small, quiet, family run, grassy site with 6-berth luxury fully-serviced caravans. Ideal for exploring the lakes. Personal supervision. Booking essential. Calor Gas. M6, J36 follow A590 SP Barrow. About 1m before Newby Bridge, L at cross roads Cartmel/Staveley. Site 1m on L before church. Open: 1 March - 31 October. ★★★★ BH&HPA 3🚐 10🚐 A 20🚐

**(2.5m). Meathop Fell Caravan Club Site, Grange-over-Sands, Cumbria LA11 6RB.** 01539 532912. www.caravanclub.co.uk. An ideal base from which to explore N Lancashire and southern Lake District. Gas. Advance booking essential Bank Holidays, Xmas and New Year. MV service point, playground. Non-members welcome. No tents. Toilet blocks with privacy cubicles, laundry facilities and baby/toddler washroom. Golf nearby. Ideal for families. See website for standard directions to site. Open: All year. ★★★★★ NCC 131🚐 131🚐

**(4.5m). Oak Head Caravan Park, Ayside, Grange-over-Sands, Cumbria LA11 6JA.** 01539 531475. www.oakheadcaravanpark.co.uk. AA 3 stars 74%. Garage, shops, PO, cafe/restaurant, dairy produce, fishing, golf all within 4m . M6, 36,14m on A590 to Newby Bridge. 2m to Lake Windermere. 4.5m to Grange-over-Sands railway station. Follow signs for Ayside along new A590 bypass. Open: All year. 30🚐 A 71

## Holmrook

**(9m). Eskdale Camping & Caravanning Club Site, Boot, Holmrook, Cumbria CA19 1TH.** 01946 723253 . www.campingandcaravanningclub.co.uk. Described by Wainwright as 'one of the loveliest Lakeland valleys', walkers can reach England's highest peak and deepest lake from the site. 10 camping pods, camping barn and licensed shop available. When approaching from A6, J38 allow plenty of time, follow the road numbers A590-A5092-A595. Open: 1 March - 14 January. ★★★★★ NCC 80🚐 A

**(0.5m). Seven Acres Caravan Park, Holmrook, Cumbria CA19 1YD.** 01946 822777. www.seacote.com. Flat, grassy, sheltered park. Payphones. Golf, fell walking, mountain climbing, fishing, boating, rambling, horse riding all available nearby. PO, shops, pubs, restaurants and cafes in Gosforth. Close to Wasdale/Eskdale. S of Gosforth on A595 west Cumbria coast road. Open: 1 March - 15 January. BH&HPA 39🚐 39🚐 A 78

## Kendal

**(2m). Kendal Camping & Caravanning Club Site, Millcrest, Shap Road, Kendal, Cumbria LA9 6NY.** 01539 741363 . www.campingandcaravanningclub.co.uk. A good base for touring the Lake District, just a few miles outside Kendal. The forest of Bowland is nearby. Bird watchers will enjoy a visit to Leighton Moss Bird Reserve. All units accepted. Non-members welcome. Site shop stocked with essentials. Special deals available for families and backpackers. 1.5m N of Kendal; on the R hand side of A6. N of nameplate 'Skelsmergh'. Open: 1 April - 31 October. ★★★★ NCC 50🚐 50🚐

**(3m). Low Park Wood Caravan Club Site, Sedgwick, Kendal, Cumbria LA8 0JZ.** 01539 560186. www.caravanclub.co.uk. Peaceful location on National Trust land, with several walks from site. River fishing (permits available). Gas. Advance booking essential weekends, Bank Holidays, July and August. Dog walk. Non-members welcome. No tents. Toilet blocks with laundry facilities. MV service point. Ideal for families. Varied bird life. See website for standard directions to site. Open: 23 March - 5 November. ★★★★ NCC 141🚐 141🚐

# NORTH WEST

**(3m). Pound Farm (North Dales), Crook, Kendal, Cumbria LA8 8JZ.** 01539 821220. www.northdales.co.uk. Sheltered park 5m from Lake Windermere. Newly developed pitches available for lodges. Golf, cinema & town for shopping 3m. M6, J36 follow A591 to roundabout. Exit roundabout on to B5284, Pound Farm 1.8m on L. Open: 1 March - 15 November. BH&HPA ★★★★ 10🚐 10⛺ ⚡

**(3m). Ratherheath Lane Caravan Park, Chain House, Kendal, Cumbria LA8 8JU.** 01539 821154. www.lakedistrict-caravans.co.uk. Close to all Lake District attractions. Small, suits couples. Exit M6, J36 follow A591 for Windermere. Take B5284 to Crook. Park is 1.5m on the R. Open: 1 March - 15 November. ★★★★ BH&HPA 8🚐 12⛺

**(3m). The Ashes Caravan Park (Adults only), New Hutton, Kendal, Cumbria LA8 0AS.** 01539 731833. www.ashes-caravanpark.co.uk. Small, friendly touring park in peaceful countryside with delightful Cumbrian views. Ideal for holidays exploring the lakes and Yorkshire Dales or an overnight halt. Adults only 18 years and over. Wi-Fi available. From M6 J37, take A684 to Kendal for 2m. Turn L at cross-roads to New Hutton village. Site on R in 0.75m. Only approach/depart via A684. Open: 1 March - 5 November. ★★★★ BH&HPA 25🚐 25⛺

**(2.5m). Windermere Camping & Caravanning Club Site, Ashes Lane, Staveley, Kendal, Cumbria LA8 9JS.** 01539 821119 . www.campingandcaravanningclub.co.uk. The site is situated in an unrivalled rural location of the Lake District. Overlooking the fells of South Lakes. Set in 22 acres and located 5m south of Windermere, close to the village of Staveley. Non-members welcome. All unit accepted. Special deals available for families and backpackers. On-site facilities include a licensed bar, takeaway, dedicated backpackers facilities, laundry, toilet and showers, play area and dog walk. Fishing, golf, horse riding and water sports available locally (3-5m). Loo Of The Year (5 stars). David Bellamy Gold Conservation Award. Signed off A591. 0.75m from roundabout with B5284 towards Windermere. Open: 11 March - 14 January. ★★★★★ NCC 250🚐 250⛺

## Keswick

**(3m). Burns Farm Caravan and Campsite, Burns Farm, St Johns In The Vale, Keswick, Cumbria CA12 4RR.** 01768 79112. www.burns-farm.co.uk. Quiet family run site. Beautiful views. Perfect walking country. Facilities block. 3 cottages for hire. AA 3 pennants. 15m from M6 j40, take A66 Keswick, second L past Threlkeld village, SP Castlerigg-Stone Circle and Burns Farm caravan site. Open: 7 March - 14 November. BH&HPA NCC 32⛺

**(1.5m). Castlerigg Hall, Castlerigg Hall, Keswick, Cumbria CA12 4TE.** 01768 774499. www.castlerigg.co.uk. Spectacular views of lakes and mountains. Tea room. Fully serviced pitches available. Fees on application. Turn R off A591 Keswick to Ambleside. Open: 7 March - 5 November. ★★★★ BH&HPA 53🚐 7⛺

**◼ Dalebottom Farm Caravan & Camping Site, Naddle, Keswick, Cumbria CA12 4TF.** 01768 74713. www.dalebottomfarm.co.uk. A family run site in the heart of the picturesque Naddle Valley in the Lake District. Perfectly located to explore the beauty of Lakeland and participate in walking, sailing, pony trekking, climbing, fishing and golfing. Approx 2 miles away is the Ancient Castlerigg Stone Circle which is accessible by footpath from the site. Keswick town nearby. Pitches have 5 amp electric hook-ups and good views across the fells. 2.5m South of Keswick on the A591 Ambleside/Windermere Road. Open: March - October.

**(0.5m). Derwentwater (The Oval) Camping & Caravanning Club Site, Crow Park Road, Keswick, Cumbria CA12 5EN.** 01768 772579 . www.campingandcaravanningclub.co.uk. Within the heart of the Lake District National Park, beside the peace of Lake Derwentwater. Non-members welcome. Caravans and motorcaravans only (no tents). All service pitches available. No awnings permitted. Golf, pony trekking, rock climbing, paragliding and swimming are all available in the area. Special deals available for families and backpackers. David Bellamy Silver Conservation Award. From M6 J40 follow A66 for 13m, SP Keswick/Workington. At roundabout SP Keswick turn L. At T junction turn L to Keswick town centre. At mini roundabout turn R. Take road to R of church. Site on L. Open: 1 March - 5 January. ★★★★ NCC 17🚐 17⛺

**(0.5m). Derwentwater (Walker Park) Camping & Caravanning Club Site, Crow Park Road, Keswick, Cumbria CA12 5EN.** 01768 772579 . www.campingandcaravanningclub.co.uk. Within the heart of the Lake District National Park, beside the peace of Lake Derwentwater. Non-members welcome. Caravans and motorcaravans only (no tents). All service pitches available. No awnings permitted. Golf, pony trekking, rock climbing, paragliding and swimming are all available in the area. Special deals available for families and backpackers. David Bellamy Silver Conservation Award. From M6 J40 follow A66 for 13m, SP Keswick/Workington. At roundabout SP Keswick turn L. At T junction turn L to Keswick town centre. At mini roundabout turn R. Take road to R of church. Site on L. Open: 2 May - 26 September. ★★★★ NCC 26🚐 26⛺

**(5m). Herdwick Croft, Ouse Bridge, Bassenthwaite Lake, Keswick, Cumbria CA12 4RD.** 01768 776241. www.herdwick-croft.co.uk. All pitches serviced. New shower & toilet block. Beautiful location, peace and quiet. Golf, riding. Animal farm. Owner supplied copy. Off A591 north end of Bassenthwaite lake. Open: 22 April - 31 October. 10🚐 42⛺

**(0.5m). Keswick Camping & Caravanning Club Site, Crow Park Road, Keswick, Cumbria CA12 5EP.** 01768 772392 . www.campingandcaravanningclub.co.uk. Beautiful woodland park with lake frontage and jetty. Some hardstanding. Non-members welcome. All units accepted. Special deals available for families and backpackers. David Bellamy Silver Conservation Award. Off A66, follow signs for Keswick. Turn L at roundabout, turn left at T-junction. At mini-roundabout turn R, take road to R of church. Turn R up narrow lane, after rugby club. Open: 3 February - 28 November. ★★★★ NCC 250🚐 250⛺

---

### DALEBOTTOM FARM CARAVAN & CAMPING PARK
NADDLE KESWICK, CUMBRIA CA12 4TF  **Tel: 017687 72176**
**"HEART OF LAKELAND"**
Peacefully situated in the picturesque Naddle Valley two miles south of Keswick on A591 Windermere road. Touring & Tenting pitches. Electric hook ups. Toilet & Shower Facilities. Static Caravans & Country Cottages to let. Colour TV Toilet & Shower Facilities in all units. Static Caravans Tourers Tents March 1st to November 1st. Country Cottages available all year. S.A.E. for brochure to: Proprietors: Messrs Kitching

# NORTH WEST

**(1m). Low Briery Riverside Village,** Penrith Road, Keswick, Cumbria CA12 4RN. 01768 772044. www.keswick.uk.com. Nestled in wooded valley with river alongside. Range of accommodation - static caravans, lodges, cottages. Short walk from Keswick. Just upriver from Keswick on eastern side. Access off interchange A66 and Keswick access road. Open: 3 January - 29 October.
★★★★ 🚾🐕🚽🚐 75🔌🚐

**(4m). Low Manesty Caravan Club Site,** Manesty, Keswick, Cumbria CA12 5UG. 01768 777275. www.caravanclub.co.uk. Set in National Trust woodland, close to Derwentwater with views over fells. Ideal location for lakes and walking. Own sanitation required. Advance booking advised and essential Bank Holidays, June to end September and late October. Non-members admitted. No tents. MV service point. Fishing and water sports. Some hardstanding, steel awning pegs required. Gas and Gaz, dog walk nearby, quiet and peaceful off peak. NCN cycle route within 5m. Recycling facilities. See website for standard directions to site. 2m from Borrowdale. Open: 30 March - 5 November. ★★★★ NCC 🚾🐕🚽 🚽🚾🚐 60🔌 60🔌

**(8.5m). North Lakes Caravan and Camping Park,** Bewaldeth, Bassenthwaite Lake, Keswick, Cumbria CA13 9SY. 01768 776510. www.northlakesholidays.co.uk. 85 mixed pitches in total. 30-acre park for people who enjoy peace and quiet in the less commercialised northern end of the Lake District. Bar. Laundry. Facilities block. TV area. Coarse fishing lake. On A591. N of Keswick. Open: 1 March - 31 October. 🐕♫🚽🚾 🍴🚾🐕🚐 85🔌 🛁

**(2.5m). Scotgate Holiday Park,** Braithwaite, Keswick, Cumbria CA12 5TF. 01768 778343. www.scotgateholidaypark.co.uk. Licensed shop and restaurant. 7 chalets for hire also available. Mobile PO on site Friday 12-1. Lodges for sale. W of Keswick, just off A66 on B592 entrance to Braithwaite village. Open: All year. ★★★★ BH&HPA 🚾🐕♫🚽🚾🛁🚐 7🔌 28🔌 150▲ 29🔌 2🛁

**(6m). Trafford Caravan Site, Low Wood,** Bassenthwaite, Keswick, Cumbria CA12 4QH. 01768 776298. www.tralee.com. Situated at the foot of Skiddaw with beautiful views all round. Level site suitable for disabled people and wheelchairs. Owner supplied copy. On A591. Quiet, Lakeland park on Carlisle road. 6m from roundabout outside Keswick. Open: 1 April - 31 October. 🚾🐕🚽🚾🚐 12🔌▲ 53🔌

## Kirkby Lonsdale

**(0.5m). Woodclose Park, Casterton,** Kirkby Lonsdale, Cumbria LA6 2SE. 01524 271597. www.woodclosepark.com. Set within the beautiful valley of the River Lune between the Yorkshire Dales and the Lake District National Park, Woodclose Park is a quiet and serene place set within 9 acres providing a unique holiday base in an Area of Outstanding Natural Beauty, within walking distance of Kirby Lonsdale. We welcome touring caravans, motorhomes, tents and on-site wigwams. Golf, horse riding, leisure club nearby with cycle hire available on site. David Bellamy Gold Conservation Award. Enjoy England Gold Award winner. M6, J36 then A65, 0.5m SE of Kirkby Lonsdale. Open: 1 March - 31 October. ★★★★★ BH&HPA NCC 🚾🐕🚽♫🚾🐕🚐 🛁🚾🚐 12🔌 17🔌 4▲ 6🛁

## Kirkby Stephen

**(4m). Bowber Head, Bowber Head, Ravenstonedale, Kirkby Stephen,** Cumbria CA17 4NL. 01539 623254. www.cumbriaclassiccoaches.co.uk. Excellent centre for both the Lakes and the Dales. Beautiful views of Wildboar and the Howgill Fells. TV hook-ups. Bottled gas available. Payphone. Dogs allowed under control. Camping and Caravanning Club listed. Classic coach service operated from site. 4.5m S of Kirkby Stephen, SP off the A683. Open: 1 March to 31 October. 🚾🐕🚽🚾🚐 🍴🚾🐕🚐 2🔌 5🔌▲ 🛁

**(1m). Pennine View Caravan and Camping Park, Station Road, Kirkby Stephen,** Cumbria CA17 4SZ. 01768 371717. Set near the market town of Kirkby Stephen, offers 58 touring pitches (some on hardstandings). Ideal base for exploring the Dales and Lake District. River Eden borders site. Outdoor play area. Pub nearby. M6, J38 follow A685 for 11m, site on R. A66 at Brough follow A685 for 5m site on L. Open: 10 March - 31 October. ★★★★ BH&HPA 🚾🐕🚽♫🛁 🍴🚾🐕🚐 43🔌▲

## Lamplugh

**Dockray Meadow Caravan Club Site, Lamplugh, Cumbria CA14 4SH.** 01946 861357. www.caravanclub.co.uk. Conveniently set on N edge of Lake District with mountain walks off site. All hardstanding. Gas. Advance booking essential Bank Holidays. No sanitation. MV service point. Non-members welcome. No tents. Fishing nearby. Good for walking. Part sloping, steel awning pegs required, gas and Gaz. Information room, dog walk nearby, quiet and peaceful off peak, NCN cycle route within 5m. See website for standard directions to site. 4m from Ennerdale Bridge. Open: 30 March - 5 November. ★★★★ NCC 🚾🐕🚽♫🚾🐕 🍴🚾🐕🚐 53🔌 53🔌

## Maryport

**(6m). Manor House Caravan Park (Maryport), Edderside Road, Allonby, Maryport, Cumbria CA15 6RA.** 01900 881236. www.manorhousepark.co.uk. Licensed club. Sauna and fitness room. From Maryport, take A596, pick up the B5300 to Allonby. 1m after Allonby take a R turn to Edderside. Open: 1 March - 15 November. ★★★ BH&HPA 🐕🚾🚐 ♫🚽🚾🐕🚾🚐🛁 3🔌 20🔌 ▲ 152🔌

**(5m). Spring Lea Caravan And Leisure Centre, Allonby, Maryport, Cumbria CA15 6QF.** 01900 881331. www.springlea.co.uk. 40 touring pitches. 2 minutes away from a sandy beach. Indoor pool complex, outdoor playground, amusement arcade & bar. Situated midway between Maryport and Silloth on B5300. Open: 1 March - 31 October. ★★★★ BH&HPA 🐕🚾♫🚽🚾🐕🛁🍴🚐 🚾🐕🛁🚾🚐 35🔌▲ 95🔌

## Millom

**(1m). Butterflowers Holiday Homes, Port Haverigg, Millom, Cumbria LA18 4HB.** 01229 772880. www.butterflowers.net. Indoor swimming pool. Follow signs from Harbour Hotel past the Beach Cafe, the entrance is on the R before the Inshore Rescue. Open: All year. BH&HPA 🐕♫ 🚾🐕🚽🚾🚐 80🔌 🛁

## Milnthorpe

**(4m). Fell End Caravan Park, Slackhead Road, Hale, Milnthorpe, Cumbria LA7 7BS.** 01524 781453. www.fellendcaravanpark.co.uk. Close to Silverdale/Arnside area of outstanding natural beauty. Beautifully developed and landscaped park incorporating natural features including woodlands and limestone pavements. Shop, bar, restaurant. Shops 2m, golf course 3m. Cinema 15m. David Bellamy Gold Conservation Award. Off M6 junction 35, off A6 at sign marked 'Sites'. Next to wildlife oasis just past Cumbria border sign. Follow brown signs. Open: All year. ★★★★★ BH&HPA 🚾🐕🚽♫🚾🐕🚽🛁 🍴🚾🐕🚐 80🔌 80🔌 4🛁

**(2.5m). Hall More Caravan Park, Hale, Milnthorpe, Cumbria LA7 7BP.** 01524 781453. www.hallmorecaravanpark.co.uk. Three-acre trout lake on premises. Close to Silverdale/Arnside area of outstanding natural beauty. Good base for walking and exploring. Shops 2m, golf course 3m, cycle hire 5m, cinema 15m. David Bellamy Silver Conservation Award. Open March-December for statics. M6, J35. Follow A6 towards Milnthorpe for 4m. Take the first L marked Arnside with tourism signs for

# NORTH WEST

sites. Follow the unclassified road and the park is less than 1m. Open: 1 March - 4 January. BH&HPA 34 34

**Hazelslack Caravan Site, Carr Bank House, Carr Bank, Milnthorpe, Cumbria LA7 7LG.** *01524 701482.* Site 200yd on R. Edge of Lake District and near coast. Owner supplied copy. 3m SW of Milnthorpe. From Milnthorpe follow Arnside road. Go almost to Arnside then SP for Carr Bank and bear R along this road, turning L after 0.5m along narrow lane. Open: 1 March - 31 October.

**(6m). Waters Edge Caravan Park, Crooklands, Milnthorpe, Cumbria LA7 7NN.** *01539 567708.* www.watersedgecaravanpark.co.uk. Family run park with modern facilities. Easy access to Lakes, Yorkshire and Morecambe Bay. Lounge and licensed bar. Restaurant within 300yds. Takeaway 3m. Open countryside. Nearby fishing, tennis, golf, riding, etc. One mile from M6, Jct 36. Take A65 towards Kirkby Lonsdale then left at roundabout to A65 Crooklands. Site is on right-hand side before Crooklands hotel. Open: 1 March - 14 November. ★★★★ BH&HPA 26

## Penrith

**(7m). Beckses Caravan Park, Penruddock, Penrith, Cumbria CA11 0RX.** *01768 483224.* Small, pleasant site on the edge of Lake District National Park. AA 3-pennants. English Lakes member. M6, J40 take A66 (SP Keswick). Continue for about 6m, then turn R on to B5288 (SP Greystoke). Beckses Park is 150yd on the R. Open: 22 March - 31 October. 23 15

**(7m). Cove Caravan & Camping Park, Lake Ullswater, Watermillock, Penrith, Cumbria CA11 0LS.** *01768 486549.* www.cove-park.co.uk. RAC appointed. Very clean & superb location. 17 mixed pitches in total. Peaceful park sheltered by nearby fells and overlooking Lake Ullswater. Excellent facilities, well maintained. Shop next door, lake 1.5m. AA 3 pennants. From M6 J40, A66 Keswick, roundabout A592 to Ullswater. T Junction, right, Brackenrigg Inn - right. Cove Park is 1.5m on L. Open: 15 March - 31 October. BH&HPA 17 17

**(9m). Gill Head Caravan & Camping Park, Gill Head Farm, Troutbeck, Penrith, Cumbria CA11 0ST.** *01768 779652.* www.gillheadfarm.co.uk. AA 4 pennants. A beautiful maintained site with panoramic views of Northern Fells with modern facilities in ideal location for lakes. Owner supplied copy. Midway between Penrith and Keswick on A66, take A5091 (Ullswater Road). First R

200yd from junction we are first on R. Open: 22 April - 1 November. 10 25 17

**(14m). Gillside Caravan & Camping Site, Gillside, Glenridding, Penrith, Cumbria CA11 0QQ.** *01768 482346.* www.gillsidecaravanandcampingsite.co.uk. Bunkhouse accommodation. Owner supplied copy. Take the A592 to Glenridding, SP for Gillside Camping first L after Travellers Rest. Situated at the foot of Hellvellyn and 5mins walk from Lake Ullswater. Open: 1 March - 15 November. 5 5 30

**(8m). Hopkinsons Whitbarrow Hall Caravan Park, Whitbarrow Hall Caravan Park, Berrier, Penrith, Cumbria CA11 0XB.** *01768 483456.* www.hopkinsons-caravanpark.co.uk. Bar. Laundrette. Showers. Kitchen for campers' use. Calor Gas stockist. AA 3-Pennant award. Dogs must be on leads. Strict 5mph speed limit. Owner supplied copy. J40, M6 take A66 towards Keswick, after 8m turn R at Sportsman's Inn, SP Hutton Roof. Site 0.5m from A66. Open: 1 March - 31 October. 80 167

**(2m). Lowther Holiday Park, Eamount Bridge, Penrith, Cumbria CA10 2JB.** *01768 863631.* www.lowther-holidaypark.co.uk. AA 4 pennants. Fishing on site, golf 3m, PO and doctors/hospital 2m. David Bellamy Gold Conservation Award. J 40, take A66 E then A6 S. Open: 1 March - 14 November. ★★★★ BH&HPA 196 390

**(6m). Park Foot Caravan & Camping Park, Howtown Road, Pooley Bridge, Penrith, Cumbria CA10 2NA.** *01768 486309.* www.parkfootullswater.co.uk. Views of Lake Ullswater with access. Licensed bar, restaurant and takeaway. Laundry, car wash, public telephone, children's club during summer school holidays. Sailing, windsurfing, canoeing, fishing, walking, pony trekking, tennis, bike hire, shop and two play areas. Calor Gas. AA 3 pennants. 6m golf, cinema, shopping centre. Dogs must be kept on lead. No single sex groups. M6 J40 - A66 Keswick/Ullswater, take A592 Ullswater, L at junction. In Pooley Bridge take Howtown road R at church. R at crossroads, 1m on L. Open: 1 March - 15 November. ★★★ BH&HPA 30 32 130

**(0.5m). Thacka Lea Caravan Park, Thacka Lane, Penrith, Cumbria CA11 9HX.** *01768 863319.* Off A6. Open: 1 March - 31 October. 15 25

**(9m). The Cross Fell Caravan and Camping Park, The Fox Inn, Ousby, Penrith, Cumbria

CA10 1QA.** *07900 585342.* www.crossfellcaravanpark.co.uk. Flat, well-drained site. Behind village Inn. Beautiful countryside. 9m NE of Penrith. Leave M6, J40 on to A686 Alston Road. Take second R, 1.5m after Langwathby. Site is 2m at Ousby. Open: All year. 2 7 29

**(6m). The Quiet Site, Ullswater, Penrith, Cumbria CA11 0LS.** *01768 727016.* www.thequietsite.co.uk. Family run site in idyllic location. Large adventure playground. Caravan and motorcaravan storage available. Fishing nearby. David Bellamy Gold Conservation Award. M6, J40. A66 to Keswick. A592 to Ullswater. Turn R at lake, turn R at Brackenrigg Inn. Site on R after 1.5m. Open: All year. ★★★★★ BH&HPA NCC 20 20 40

**(9m). Troutbeck Camping & Caravanning Club Site, Hutton Moor End, Troutbeck, Penrith, Cumbria CA11 0SX.** *01768 779249.* www.campingandcaravanningclub.co.uk. Quiet site for families and walkers. Licensed shop. Golf course just down the road. Rookin House activity centre 2m. Open March-November plus Xmas and New Year. On A66 9.5m W of M6 J40, turn L for Wallthwaite, site SP. 8m from Keswick. Open: 4 Mar - 30 Nov & 26 Dec - 2 Jan. ★★★★ BH&HPA 24 24 19

**(9m). Troutbeck Head Caravan Club Site, Troutbeck, Penrith, Cumbria CA11 0SS.** *01768 483521.* www.caravanclub.co.uk. Fabulous for nature lovers and walkers. The site sits in a valley alongside a babbling brook, below Great Mell Fell. Baby and toddler washroom. MV service point. Games room and play area. Dog walk on site. Fishing, golf, water sports and NCN route nearby. Good area for walking. Facilities for disabled. Ideal for families. Non-members welcome. See website for standard directions to site. Open: 23 March - 5 November. ★★★★★ NCC 151 151

**(7m). Ullswater Caravan, Camping & Marine Park, Watermillock, Penrith, Cumbria CA11 0LR.** *01768 486666.* www.uccmp.co.uk. At telephone box. Playground. Bar/games and TV room open during main season. Shop. Lake access 1m. Fishing, boating. Ideal for touring the lakes. M6, J40, on A592 turn R SP Longthwaite & Watermillock Church. Open: 1 March - 14 November. BH&HPA 120 58 62

**(5m). Waterfoot Park, Soulby, Penrith, Cumbria CA11 0JF.** *01768 486302.* www.waterfootpark.co.uk. Parkland site in grounds

# NORTH WEST

of a Georgian mansion. Site is well laid out with serviced static caravan pitches and an excellent touring area with a mix of hardstanding for ease of siting and lawn areas for awnings or recreation. Children's play area on site. Walking distance of Ullswater 'Steamers' Pier for cruises on Lake Ullswater. Water sports, pony trekking. Fishing, golf, cinema, shopping, lake cruises nearby. David Bellamy Gold Conservation Award. Take J40, M6, join A66 for about 1m then take A592, park is on RH side. Sat Nav not compatible. Open: 1 March - 14 November. ★★★★★ BH&HPA NCC

**(18m). Westmorland Caravan Park, Orton, Penrith, Cumbria CA10 3SB.** 01539 711322. www.westmorlandltd.com. Hardstanding - dog walk - Shops and cafe on service area 500yd + discount vouchers for meals in the cafe, hotel restaurant and farm shop produce. Perfect base for exploring the Lake District, or a convenient stopover whether you are travelling North or South. David Bellamy Gold Conservation Award. The site is next to Westmorland's award winning northbound Tebay Services on M6, between junctions 38 & 39, easily reached from southbound carriageway using the link road between the two service areas. Open: 18 March - 13 November. ★★★★★ BH&HPA

## Pooley Bridge

**(0.5m). Hillcroft Caravan Park (North Dales), Roehead Lane, Pooley Bridge, Cumbria CA10 2LT.** 01768 486363. www.northdales.co.uk. Elevated location with magnificent views. Ideal for fell walking, sailing, windsurfing and canoeing. Boat hire nearby. Dogs allowed if kept on a lead. Pooley Bridge 250yd, shops, PO etc. 4 pods new in 2009. Off M6 follow Northlakes, then Pooley Bridge, through village to crossroad, straight on. Open: 1 March - 15 November. BH&HPA

**(0.25m). Ravenglass Camping & Caravanning Club Site, Ravenglass, Cumbria CA18 1SR.** 01229 717250. www.campingandcaravanningclub.co.uk. The site is set in 5 acres of mature woodland which was once part of the Muncaster Castle Estate. This is walkers' paradise on Cumbria's western coast, where the Lake District National Park meets the sea. On site facilities include toilet, showers, laundry, CDP, washing up sinks and a play area. All unit types accepted. Non-members welcome. Special deals for families and backpackers. Turn L at 30mph sign into private road. Site entrance is 25yd on L. Open: 1 Feb - 30 Nov & 19 Dec - 2 Jan. ★★★★ NCC

## Seascale

**(6m). Church Stile Camp Site, Wasdale, Seascale, Cumbria CA20 1ET.** 01946 726252. www.churchstile.com. Excellent climbing. Beautiful views, pretty little village. Good for families and couples. Fell walking near lake, sheltered, well run family site. Two inns serving bar meals. Sorry no touring caravans. Shower block newly refurbished. Owner supplied copy. Off A595. 4m E of Gosforth to Nether Wasdale site by church. Open: 1 April - 1 November. BH&HPA

## Sedbergh

**(5m). Conder Farm, Dent, Sedbergh, Cumbria LA10 5QT.** 01539 625277. Small, family site of 1.5 acres. Quiet with beautiful views. Shop 500yd. Owner supplied copy. Turn in Sedbergh (J37, M6) Dent 5.5m. From Sedbergh turn R at George and Dragon (Dent), from Hawes turn L at George and Dragon. Open: 1 March - 31 October.

**(2.5m). Cross Hall Farm Caravan Park, Cautley, Sedbergh, Cumbria LA10 5LY.** 01539 620668. www.cautleycaravans.co.uk. Quiet, family park nestling at the foot of the Howgill fells. Abundance of walking, flora and fauna. Shopping 2.5m,

golf course 4m. Fell walking from site. Lake District nearby. Owner supplied copy. Off A683 to Kirkby Stephen and Brough overlooking the Howgill Fells and 1.5m to Cautley Spout. Open: 1 April - 31 October.

## Silloth

**Hylton Caravan Park, Eden Street, Silloth, Cumbria CA7 4AY.** 01697 332666. www.stanwix.com. 93 mixed pitches in total. Ideal base to tour lakes and border counties. Sister park to Stanwix 0.5m away. Full facilities available to Hylton Park holidaymakers. Telephone for brochure. AA 4 star rating, 70%. 18 hole golf course 1m. On A596 at Wigton take B5302 to Silloth. Entering Silloth follow signs to Hylton Park, 0.5m. Open: 1 March - 15 November.

**(3m). Rowanbank Caravan Park, Beckfoot, Silloth, Cumbria CA7 4LA.** 01697 331653. www.rowanbankcaravanpark.co.uk. On site wardens. Set in beautiful quiet countryside right next to unspoilt Solway beaches. Owner supplied copy. M6, J41 take B5305 to Wigton, then B5302 to Silloth. At Silloth take A5300 coast road to Maryport, park is about 3m on left hand side. Open: 1 February - 31 December. BH&HPA

**(1m). Stanwix Park Holiday Centre, Greenrow, Silloth, Cumbria CA7 4HH.** 01697 332666. www.stanwix.com. 121 mixed pitches in total. Large holiday centre - caravans for hire, tents and touring caravans welcome. Indoor leisure centre, pools, gym etc. Ten pin bowling, family entertainment, bars, disco and cabaret. Golf, fishing, bowling, tennis and shops. Ideal base to explore Lakes and historic Carlisle. Open all year except Xmas Day. On A596 at Wigton take B5302 To Silloth. Entering Silloth follow signs to Stanwix Park, about 1m. Open: All year. ★★★★★ BH&HPA NCC

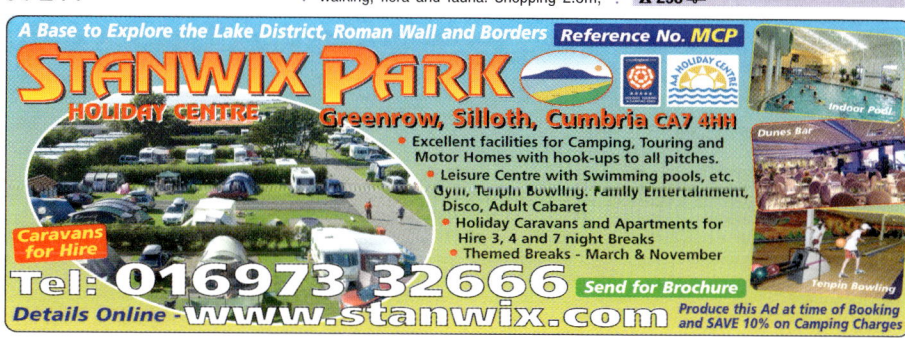

CARAVAN & HOLIDAY PARKS 2012 27

# NORTH WEST

**(1m). Tanglewood Caravan Park, Causeway Head, Silloth, Cumbria CA7 4PE.** 01697 331253. www.tanglewoodcaravanpark.co.uk. Play area. Off-licence. Bottled gas. Pets allowed (free of charge). Club house. Pub on site. Modern, fully-serviced caravans with colour TV. Brochure with tariff available. Golf course, shops, PO, doctor available within 2m. On B5302. 4m on from Abbeytown, on L before Silloth. Open: 1 January - 31 January. ★★★ BH&HPA

### St Bees

**(0.5m). Seacote Park, The Beach, St Bees, Cumbria CA27 0ET.** 01946 822777. www.seacote.com. Adjoining lovely beach in historic village. Pitches for motorhomes, tourers, tents and static caravans for hire. Restaurant and bar. Cliffop walks, golf course close by. Children welcome. Fishing. PO and shops in St Bees village. Fringe of Lake District. From M6 J40. A66 W then A595 to Whitehaven (4m) then B5345 to St Bees. Open: 1 March - 15 January. ★★★★ BH&HPA

### Ulverston

**(0.25m). Bardsea Leisure Park, Priory Road, Ulverston, Cumbria LA12 9QE.** 01229 584712. www.bardsealeisure.co.uk. Sheltered, select site in disused quarry. Extensively landscaped. Free hot showers. Dog exercise area. Fishing on site. Golf course, beach 1m. M6, J36, take A591 Kendal, A590 Barrow and A5087 coast road. Open: All year. ★★★★ BH&HPA

**(7m). Birchbank Farm, Blawith, Ulverston, Cumbria LA12 8EW.** 01229 885077. www.birchbank.co.uk. Small farm site alongside stream and next to open fell. Ideal for walking or touring south lakes. Ulverston for shops etc 7m, Coniston water 5m. Owner supplied copy. 3m SW of Coniston Water. On A5092, 0.5m W of Gawthwaite turn for Woodland, site 1.7m on N. Open: 1 May - 31 October.

**(3m). Black Beck Caravan Park, Bouth, Nr Newby Bridge, Ulverston, Cumbria LA12 8JN.** 01229 861274. www.blackbeck.com. Sauna/hot tub/gym area on site. Small hire fleet now available. Zoo, activity centre, swimming, baths, cinema. All amenities available within 5m radius. No pets in hire vans. No single sex groups. Rose Award. Owner supplied copy. M6, J36,A590 for Barrow and South Lakes. After Newby Bridge Bouth crossroads turn R, then L, first R. Open: 4 March - 10 November. ★★★★★

**(9m). Crake Valley Holiday Park, Water Yeat, Blawith, Ulverston, Cumbria LA12 8DL.** 01229 885203. www.crakevalley.co.uk. Adjacent to southern end of Coniston water in a quiet, rural situation, consisting of 10 static caravans and 5 timber lodges. Tents available from May till September. David Bellamy Gold Conservation Award. Owner supplied copy. On A5084 between Greenodd and Torver, 5m from Coniston village. Open: 3 March - 3 November. ★★★★★ BH&HPA

**(5m). Seacroft Park, Newbiggin, Ulverston, Cumbria LA12 0RJ.** 01539 823659. www.seacroftpark.co.uk. Quiet park, only a few metres from the sea. Owner supplied copy. Follow Bardsea road from Ulverston to Newbiggin. Park in LHS of road. Open: 1 March - 15 January.

### Whicham

**Silecroft Camping & Caravan Park, Silecroft, Whicham, Cumbria LA18 4NX.** 01229 772659. silecroftcountrypark.com. Golf course 100yds from beach. 1m from mountains. Indoor swimming pool. A591 to Greenodd, take A5092 to coast road, follow signs. 3m from Millom. Open: 1 March - 31 October. ★★★ BH&HPA

### Wigton

**(3.5m). Blaithwaite Christian Centre, Blaithwaite House, Wigton, Cumbria CA7 0AZ.** 01697 342319. www.blaithwaite.co.uk. Showers. Games room and field. Owner supplied copy. Off A595. Open: 22 April - 31 October.

**(0.5m). Solway Holiday Village, Silloth, Wigton, Cumbria CA7 4QQ.** 01697 331236. www.hagansleisure.co.uk. Open space, fresh air and spectacular views of some of England's most breathtaking scenery - all this can be yours with a visit to Solway Holiday Village. Located in the unspoiled seaside Victorian town of Silloth-on-Solway, this 120 acre family park has something for everyone. Facilities include indoor heated pool, kids' club, licensed bars with live entertainment, indoor & outdoor play areas, tennis, golf and much more. Carlisle M6, J44 to Wigton on A595/596, follow Silloth sign, take B5302 end of Wigton bypass - park is 10yd on R. Open: 1 March - 12 November. ★★★ BH&HPA NCC

**The Larches Caravan Park (Adults only), Mealsgate, Wigton, Cumbria CA7 1LQ.** 01697 371379.

### Windermere

**(0.5m). Braithwaite Fold Caravan Club Site, Glebe Road, Bowness-on-Windermere, Windermere, Cumbria LA23 3GZ.** 01539 442177. www.caravanclub.co.uk. This is an attractively laid out site, close to the shores of Lake Windermere and within easy walking distance of the town. Windermere has an excellent sailing centre from which to enjoy sailing, windsurfing and canoeing and you can hire equipment and take instruction. All hardstanding pitches, toilet block, laundry facilities, MV waste point, vegetable preparation area and dog walk. Non members welcome. No tents. See website for standard directions to site. Open: 23 March - 5 November. ★★★★ NCC

**(0.25m). Fallbarrow Caravan Park, Rayrigg Road, Windermere, Cumbria LA23 3DL.** 01539 569835. www.slholidays.co.uk. Beautiful lakeside park with 'state of the art' multi hook-up pitches. High standards of park facilities include boat launching and friendly 'Boathouse' pub with beer garden, bar meals, family room, children's play area. Also cafe deli and shop 'The Barn' available for coffees, snacks, groceries and locally produced foods. Shops 400yd. Cinema and boating 800yd. Cycle hire 1m. Gym, swimming (at sister park White Cross Bay - charges apply) 3m. Golf 4m. David Bellamy Gold Conservation Award. M6, J36 follow A591 to Windermere until you reach the town centre. Turn L following sign for Bowness 1.5m. At Bowness turn R at mini-roundabout SP Keswick, Steamboat Museum. Park is 300yd on the L. Open: 1 March - 14 January. ★★★★ BH&HPA

**Hill of Oaks, Tower Road, Windermere, Cumbria LA12 8NR.** 01539 531578. www.hillofoaks.co.uk. Nestling on the slopes of ancient woodland, Hill of Oaks offers exclusive lake frontage for more than a kilometre along the shore of Lake Windermere for that holiday base with a difference. The Park welcomes touring caravans, motor homes and holiday home pitches for sale on site. Facilities include children's play area, boat launching, on site shop, fishing, golf nearby and a range of water sports. David Bellamy Gold Conservation Award. M6, J36, travel towards Newby Bridge A590, turn R at roundabout A591 towards Bowness for 3m. Open: 1 March - 14

# NORTH WEST

November. ★★★★★ BH&HPA NCC 43⇆ 215⌂

**(2.5m). Limefitt Park (South Lakeland Parks), Patterdale Road, Windermere, Cumbria LA23 1PA.** *01539 569335.* www.slholidays.co.uk. Spectacular Lakeland valley location. 10mins drive Lake Windermere. Friendly Lakeland pub with bar meals, Shops, cinema 3m. Sailing, fishing, swimming, boat launch nearby. M6, J36 follow signs 'South Lakes', then 'Windermere'. 0.5m beyond Windermere turn R at mini roundabout taking A592. Patterdale Road, SP 'Ullswater' Limefitt is 2m on R. Open: 1 March - 14 January. ★★★★★ BH&HPA 49⌂

**(5m). Park Cliffe Camping & Caravan Estate, Birks Road, Windermere, Cumbria LA23 3PG.** *01539 531344.* www.parkcliffe.co.uk. Cumbria Tourism Holiday Park of the Year Award Winner 2011. Set in 25 acres of picturesque scenery above the eastern shores of Lake Windermere, Park Cliffe offers pitches for tourers, motorhomes and tents, as well as offering holiday homes and camping pods for hire. Facilities include; restaurant, bar, takeaway, shop, games room & adventure playground. Private bathrooms for hire. Bowness on Windermere, cinema, golf course, tennis, sailing and boat launching (4m), Kendal (15m). David Bellamy Gold Conservation Award. M6, J36. A590 to Barrow. At Newby Bridge, turn R on to A592. 3.5m turn R into Birks Road. Park is 0.3m on R. Open: 1 March - 11 November. ★★★★★ BH&HPA 60⇆ 60⌂ 100▲ 3⌂

**(2m). White Cross Bay Leisure Park And Marina, Ambleside Road, Windermere, Cumbria LA23 1LF.** *01539 569835.* www.slholidays.co.uk. Located on the shores of Lake Windermere, White Cross Bay offers lots to do for the whole family. Restaurant, bar, fast food, tennis court, marina, indoor pool, play area and games room. Shopping, cinema, boating 2m. Golf course 7m. David Bellamy Gold Conservation Award. From J36 on M6 follow signs to Windermere then A591 to Ambleside, park 2m from Windermere. Open: 1 March - 14 January. ★★★★★ BH&HPA NCC 63⌂

### Workington

**Inglenook Caravan Park, Fitz Bridge, Lamplugh, Workington, Cumbria CA14 4SH.** *01946 861240.* Flat site with tarmac and gravel roads in beautiful surroundings. Fishing and horse riding nearby. Beach 10m. Play area. Rose Award. Leave A66 at Cockermouth on to A5086 to Lamplugh. L past 'Lamplugh Tip' pub. Site 0.5m on R. 7m from Cockermouth/ Workington. Open: All year. ★★★★ BH&HPA 5⇆ 12⌂ ▲ 40⌂

## LANCASHIRE
### Blackpool

**(3m). Blackpool South Caravan Club Site, Cropper Road, Marton, Blackpool, Lancashire FY4 5LB.** *01253 762051.* www.caravanclub.co.uk. Probably the nearest site to Blackpool. Ideal location for the family holiday. Toilet blocks. Laundry facilities. Baby/toddler washroom. Veg prep. MV service point. Information room. Golf, fishing & water sports nearby. Good area for walking. Members only. No tents. See website for standard directions to site. Open: 23 March - 3 January. NCC 96⇆ 96⌂

**(3m). Clifton Fields Caravan Park, Peel Road, Peel, Blackpool, Lancashire FY4 5JU.** *01253 761676.* www.clifton-fields.co.uk. Laundrette and ironing room. Telephone. TV and games room. Action time play centre. Hardstandings for tourers. Chemical disposal. Calor Gas exchange. Golf course, cinema, shopping centre available within 3m. Owner supplied copy. Travelling on M55 take exit 4 turn L on to A583 to Kirkham. At roundabout go straight across to traffic lights. At lights turn R and immediately L on to Peel Road, 2nd caravan park on R. Open: 1 March - 31 October. BH&HPA 6⇆ 52⌂ 94⌂

**Hill View Caravan Park, Cartford Lane, Little Eccleston, Blackpool, Lancashire PR3 0PT.** *01253 890003.* Newly developed park. Hardstandings. Rural setting within easy reach of coast and lakes. Local shops, PO and weekly market 10mins walk. Payphone. Owner supplied copy. ▲ 20⌂

**(3m). Marton Mere Holiday Village (Haven), Mythop Road, Blackpool, Lancashire FY4 4XN.** *0871 2310881.* www.caravancamping.co.uk. Investor in People. Bowling green, Indoor heated pool with water chute. Bowlingo bowling. Outdoor Splashzone, multi sports court. Fencing, table tennis, family entertainment. Adventure golf. Cafe. Showbar. Bike hire, trampolines, kids mini go-karts. Marton Mere nature reserve. David Bellamy Gold Conservation Award. M55, J4. Turn R at the roundabout and take the A583 towards Blackpool. Pass the Windmill and turn R at the Clifton Arms traffic lights, on to Mythop Road. The park is 150yd on the L. Open: 18 March - 31 October. ★★★★ BH&HPA NCC 197⇆ 197⌂ 1118⌂

**(3m). Newton Hall Holiday Centre, Staining Road, Staining, Blackpool, Lancashire FY3 0AX.** *01253 882512.* www.newtonhall.net. Flat green bowling complex. Heated indoor pool. Amusement arcade. Cafe. Laundrette. Children's play area. Fishing pond. Golf course, shopping, pleasure beach, Blackpool attractions. Owner supplied copy. M55, J4 SP Blackpool head for Staining. On B5266. Open: 4 March - 10 November. ★★★★ 750⌂

**(3m). Pipers Height Caravan & Camping Park, Peel Road, Blackpool, Lancashire FY4 5JT.** *01253 763767.* www.pipersheight.co.uk. Families only. Fees by arrangement. Licensed club house with entertainment high season - restaurant. S of Blackpool from M55, J4. 40yd to Peel Corner turn into Peel Road, site is 50yd on R. Open: 1 March - 31 October. BH&HPA 40⇆ 100⌂

**(10m). Sandy Bay Caravan Park, Pilling Lane, Preesall, Blackpool, Lancashire FY6 0HG.** *01253 810883.* www.sandybaycaravansite.co.uk. Adjacent to beach. 10mins from all amenities. Owner supplied copy. Off M55, J3 & A585 for Fleetwood. 3rd traffic lights right on to A588. Follow Knott End (B5377) to T junction, L then 1st R into Pilling Lane. Open: 1 March - 4 January. 54⌂

**(5m). Stanah House Caravan Park, River Road, Thornton, Blackpool, Lancashire FY5 5LR.** *01253 824000.* A small, select, touring caravan site overlooking the river Wyre with good views of the Fells and Lake District mountains. Modern, fully-tiled toilet block with shower rooms and all amenities including laundry room. Adventure play area for children. Exit 3 M55, A585 Fleetwood R at roundabout, sign to river turn R. Open: 1 March - 31 October. ★★★★ 50⌂ ▲

**(6m). Windy Harbour Holiday Park, Little Singleton, Blackpool, Lancashire FY6 8NB.** *01253 883064.* www.windyharbour.net. Fully serviced pitches. Hardstanding for vehicles. Toilet and amenity facilities with free hot water and showers, washing up facilities. Rally rates for group bookings on request. Indoor heated swimming pool, junior and teen club, children's play area. Coarse fishing ponds, amusement arcade. Fish and chip shop, snack bar cafe. J3, M55. Take third exit off roundabout, SP A585 Fleetwood, and follow road for about

Visit www.caravanclub.co.uk                    CARAVAN & HOLIDAY PARKS 2012  **29**

# NORTH WEST

3m until set of traffic lights. Go straight on, park entrance is about 300m straight ahead. Open: 1 April - 31 October. ★★★ 25 200 200

## Burnley

(6m). **Bridge Heywood Caravan Park**, Read, Burnley, Lancashire BB12 7RR. 01254 886103. Quiet and select family run holiday park situated on the river Calder in the beautiful Ribble Valley yet just 1m from the village of Read. Owner-occupied caravans. Owner supplied copy. Off A671 Whalley to Read road. Open: 1 March - 6 January. BH&BPA 18 18 86 3

## Bury

(1.25m). **Burrs Country Park Caravan Club Site**, Woodhill Road, Bury, Lancashire BL8 1DA. 01617 610289. www.caravanclub.co.uk. Burrs has much to offer: relaxing river and countryside walks. Handy for trips into Manchester. Ideal for families. Double barrier system - arrivals before 8pm. Non-members welcome. No tents. See website for standard directions to site. Using sat nav include 'Woodhill Road'. Open: 9 February - 7 January. ★★★★ NCC 85 85

## Carnforth

(2m). **Bay View (Bolton Holmes)**, A6 Main Road, Bolton Le Sands, Carnforth, Lancashire LA5 8ES. 01524 732854. www.holgates.co.uk/bay-view/home. On shore front. Recently upgraded with brand new bar and restaurant. Spectacular sea views over Morecambe Bay. On site shop and reception area. 20m to the central lakes. David Bellamy Gold Conservation Award. J35 M6, A6 3m S of Carnforth. 7m N of Lancaster. Down Mill Lane. Open: 1 March - 31 October. ★★★★ BH&HPA 20 200 2

(5m). **Gibraltar Farm**, Silverdale, Carnforth, Lancashire LA5 0UA. 01524 701736. www.gibraltarfarm.co.uk. Peaceful situation near beach and woodland. Owner supplied copy. SP Silverdale N out of Carnforth. At Silverdale turn W on road SP to hospital and Gibraltar, to T-junction in Lindeth Road; farm entrance approximately 1m along road. Open: 1 March - 30 November. 15

(6m). **Hollins Farm**, Far Arnside, Silverdale, Carnforth, Lancashire LA5 0SL. 01524 701508. www.holgates.co.uk. Beautiful farm site overlooking Morecambe Bay, lots of farm animals to see and collect our own eggs. Short walk to Silverdale park with free use of all leisure facilities including swimming pool. Owner supplied copy. J35, M6, follow signs for Holgates. Open: 14 March - 31 October. ★★★★ BH&HPA 5 25

(3m). **Old Hall Caravan Park**, Capernwray, Carnforth, Lancashire LA6 1AD. 01524 733276. www.oldhallcaravanpark.co.uk. Over 80-acres of private woodland adjoining park. Public phone. David Bellamy Gold Conservation Award. Off A6 and M6 at J35 to Over Kellet, turn L to Capernwray. Park is 1.5m on R. Open: 1 March - 10 January. ★★★★★ 38 38

(3m). **Red Bank Farm**, Bolton-le-Sands, Carnforth, Lancashire LA5 8JR. 01524 823196. www.redbankfarm.co.uk. Cafe on site. Working farm. Pets corner. On the shore. Pubs, restaurants, shop, PO 1m. Golf 3m. From A6 at Bolton-le-Sands take A5015 to Morecambe, after 500yd turn sharp R, signed shore, R again over railway bridge, turn L along the shore. Open: 6 April - 31 October. 30 40

(2m). **Sandside Caravan & Camping Park**, The Shore, Bolton-le-Sands, Carnforth, Lancashire LA5 8JS. 01524 822311. Small, quiet site close to beach. Modern facilities block. Owner supplied copy. From J35, M6 follow signs for Morecambe about 3m, turn R after Far Pavillion Indian restaurant. Open: 1 March - 31 October. BH&HPA 10 60 35

(1m). **Scout Crag Holiday Park**, Silverdale Road, Warton, Carnforth, Lancashire LA5 9RY. 01524 734579. www.dalyparks.co.uk. Bottled gas. Shops, doctor, dentist, garages, golf, fishing, pubs all within 2m. Owner supplied copy. Exit 35 off M6, follow signs for Lancaster, in Carnforth turn right at lights, follow Warton sign, turn left for Silverdale approximately 1m along road. Open: 18 March - 4 January. BH&HPA 103

**Silverdale Holiday Park (Holgates)**, Cove Road, Silverdale, Carnforth, Lancashire LA5 0SH. 01524 701508. www.holgates.co.uk/silverdale/home. In an Area of Outstanding Natural Beauty. AA campsite of the year 2011. Overlooks Morecambe Bay. On-site pool, sauna, shop, restaurant & bar. 2 adventure playgrounds. Coast 10 mins walk. From M6 Jct 35. Take A601 for Carnforth. In town centre follow signs for 'Silverdale'. After level crossing, at 'T' Jct follow signs for 'Holgates'. Open: 15 December - 1 November.

## Clitheroe

(1.5m). **Clitheroe Camping & Caravanning Club Site**, Edisford Road, Clitheroe, Lancashire BB7 3LA. 01200 425294. www.campingandcaravanningclub.co.uk. 6 acre site accepting all units types. On the banks of the river Ribble in the Ribble Valley, in sheltered wooded setting. Adjacent to site are a pitch and putt, and miniature steam railway. The Yorkshire Dales are a popular destination with site visitors. Two ancient hunting forests encompass Clitheroe, those of Pendle and Bowland. The charming ancient market town of Clitheroe is 20mins walk from the site. Non members welcome. Special deals available for families and backpackers. A671 to Clitheroe. L at sports centre. Turn into Greenacre Road L at Edisford Road T Jct. Sports Centre on R, site 50yd on L. Open: 1 April - 31 October. ★★★★ NCC 80 80

(6m). **Rimington Caravan Park (Adults only)**, Hardacre Lane, Gisburn, Clitheroe, Lancashire BB7 4EE. 01200 445355. www.rimingtoncaravanpark.co.uk. Licensed bar. Luxury bathroom. Laundry. Public phone. Hairdryers. Wi-Fi, games room. Quiet countryside park. Shopping in village 1m. Town 5m. Golf courses 5 and 8m. Off A682. 1m E of Gisburn Village, SP for Nelson etc. 1st R again. Open: 1 March - 15 November. ★★★★★ BH&HPA 4 140

(1m). **Shireburn Caravan Park** R, Waddington Road, Edisford Bridge, Clitheroe, Lancashire BB7 3JG. 01200 423422. www.shireburnepark.co.uk. Woodland park in Forest of Bowland adja-

Located in its own peaceful wooded valley close to the Lake District, Morecambe Bay and the Yorkshire Dales.
Visit Britain 5 star, AA 3 pennant and David Bellamy Gold Conservation Award.
**Old Hall Caravan Park is your perfect getaway.**
Old Hall Caravan Park, Capernwray, Carnforth, Lancashire, LA6 1AD
01524 733276 // info@oldhallcaravanpark.co.uk
www.oldhallcaravanpark.co.uk

# NORTH WEST

cent to the river Ribble. Licensed clubhouse on site. Laundrette. Fishing nearby. Luxury caravans for hire. Victorian country house with self catering apartments - open all year. Brochure with pleasure. Open March 1-October 31, all year for luxury apartments. Owner supplied copy. Off B6246. Open: 1 March - 31 October. **BH&HPA** 143

**Stubbins Vale Caravan Site, Stubbins Lane, Sabden, Clitheroe, Lancashire BB7 9EP.** *01282 778007*. In the heart of Sabden village close to Pendle Hill and The Ribble Valley. Owner supplied copy. Off A59 & A671. Open: All year. **BH&HPA** 38

**(2m). Three Rivers Woodland Park, Eaves Hall Lane, West Bradford, Clitheroe, Lancashire BB7 3JG.** *01200 423523*. www.threeriverspark.co.uk. Indoor heated swimming pool. Club open all year. Weekend entertainment. Woodland nature trails. New luxury amenities block open. Laundrette. Play area. No children in residential homes. GS. Relaxed site, no security barriers and few rules on where to pitch, control of dogs and children. Stunning location. David Bellamy Gold Conservation Award. Turn off A59 at 'Clitheroe North' sign. Continue into West Bradford village. Turn L at T-junction. Take next R, Eaves Hall Lane. Open: All year. ★ ★ ★ ★ **BH&HPA** 10 80 A 8

**Todber Holiday Park, Burnley Road, Gisburn, Clitheroe, Lancashire BB7 4JJ.** *01539 569835*. www.slholidays.co.uk/Todber. A quiet park nestled in the heart of ribble Valley with stunning views. Static caravans only. Bar, shop, laundry, children's play area, entertainment, licensed club house. Volleyball, football. Fishing 1m, shops 2m, golf 5m, cinema 10m. Off A59 on A682 towards Burnley, also J13 from M65, 6m towards Gisburn and Kendal. Open: 1 March - 6 January. **BH&HPA** 305

### Fleetwood

**(1m). Broadwater Holiday Centre, Fleetwood Road, Fleetwood, Lancashire FY7 8JX.** *01253 872796*. www.broadwater.co.uk. New outdoor crown bowling green. Shop, PO 5 mins walk, Supermarkets (ASDA, Morrisons) 5mins drive. Sauna and Jacuzzi for over 16 years of age. Owner supplied copy. J3, M55. On A585 Thornton to Fleetwood. Follow signs to Fleetwood Eros Roundabout, turn R; we are 1st on L. Open: 4 March - 15 November. ★ ★ 360

**(1.5m). Cala Gran Holiday Park (Haven), Fleetwood Road, Fleetwood, Lancashire FY7 8JY.** *0871 4680496*. www.haven.com. Indoor pool, outdoor splash zones sports and leisure facilities. Kids' Club. Licensed club with family entertainment. Mini market. Sauna, owners lounge. Cabaret room, sports bar, amusements, bouncy castle, play area. Blackpool's Golden Mile and Pleasure beach. David Bellamy Silver Conservation Award. M6 then M55. J3 take A585 to Fleetwood, SP to Fleetwood/Thornton. At the 4th roundabout with the Nautical College on the L, take 3rd exit and the park is along this road on the L. Open: 18 March - 31 October. ★ ★ ★ ★ **BH&HPA NCC** 400

### Kirkham

**(1.5m). Mowbreck Park R, Mowbreck Lane, Wesham, Kirkham, Lancashire PR4 3HA.** *01772 682494*. www.mowbreckpark.co.uk. Good local transport. Fishing nearby. Peaceful park set in picturesque countryside, yet close to local amenities. From M55, J3. Turn L to Kirkham, L at roundabout to Wesham. L by St Joseph Church on to Mowbreck Lane. Open: 1 March - 16 January. ★ ★ ★ ★ ★ **BH&HPA NCC** 171

### Lancaster

**(6m). Moss Wood Caravan Park, Crimbles Lane, Cockerham, Lancaster, Lancashire LA2 0ES.** *01524 791041*. www.mosswood.co.uk. Fishing 400yd. Parachuting, microlights 2m. Golf, horse riding 3m. David Bellamy Gold Conservation Award. M6, J33 turn L on to A6, after about 1m turn R at front of white house onto Cockerham Road, continue to T junction. Turn R. At next T junction (Manor Pub) turn L. After 1m down on R. BEWARE OF HORSES ON CRIMBLES LANE. Open: 1 March - 31 October. ★ ★ ★ ★ ★ **BH&HPA NCC** 20 20 130

**(11m). Riverside Caravan Park (Lancaster), High Bentham, Lancaster,** Lancashire LA2 7FJ. *01524 261272*. www.riversidecaravanpark.co.uk. Laundry room, indoor games room, outdoor adventure playground, fishing on private stretch of river. 2 holiday cottages available for rent. Market town of Bentham with shops, pubs and takeaways 5 mins walk from park and golf course. David Bellamy Gold Conservation Award. M6 J34, turn on to A683 towards Kirkby Lonsdale. Turn R before Hornby on to B6480, SP to High Bentham. R turn by Black Bull Hotel. Park is 0.5m on R. Open: 1 Mar - 14 Dec & 29 Dec - 2 Jan. ★ ★ ★ ★ ★ **BH&HPA** 60 60 205

**(3m). Slyne Caravan Park, Bottomdale Road, Slyne, Lancaster, Lancashire LA2 6BG.** *01524 823322*. www.slyne-caravanpark.co.uk. Shops, PO, doctor and golf course all available nearby. Manager on the park. Owned holiday homes only, no rentals. Owner supplied copy. Off A6. First R after Cross Keys Pub when approaching from Lancaster direction. Open: 1 March - 16 January. **BH&HPA** 82

**(5m). Wyreside Lakes Fishery Camping Site, Sunnyside Farmhouse, Bay Horse, Lancaster, Lancashire LA2 9DG.** *01524 792093*. www.wyresidelakes.co.uk. Small site. 1m from PO, Fisherman's Rest licensed bar restaurant. Toilets (inc disabled), shower block, washroom. Outside washing up/water area. Carp, pike, mixed coarse fishing 8 lake complex. Entertainment every weekend from April to December. Tourist information on site. M6, J33, turn L and follow the brown signs. Open: 14 February - 3 January. ★ ★ ★ **NCC** 8 8 70 A 1

### Morecambe

**Glen Caravan Site, Westgate, Morecambe, Lancashire LA3 3EL.** *01524 423896*. glencaravans.mwanet.com. Golf, cinema, shopping centre all within 2m. Owner supplied copy. Site located within Morecambe on Westgate Road. 10-15mins walk to the promenade west end. Open: 1 March - 31 October. 5 20 36

**(3m). Melbreak Caravan Site, Carr Lane, Middleton, Morecambe, Lancashire LA3 3LH.** *01524 852430*. Golf, fishing, shops, PO and doctors all within 2m. Sandy

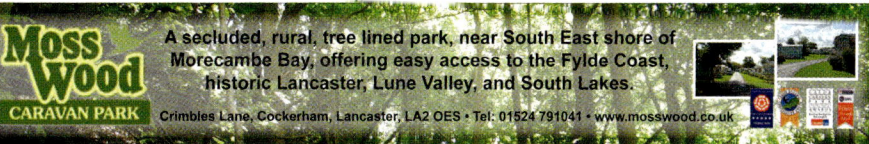

# NORTH WEST

beach 1m. A589 out of Morecambe SP to Middleton. Open: 1 March - 31 October. ★★★ BH&HPA 10🛏 10🚐 ⛺ 32

**Ocean Edge Leisure Park**, Moneyclose Lane, Heysham, Morecambe, Lancashire LA3 2XA. 01539 569235. www.slholidays.co.uk. GS. Indoor heated pool and sauna, boat launch, bowling green. Indoor children's play area, cabaret lounge, 10 mins drive from Morecambe. Golf 2m, shops 3m, cinema 5m. Follow M6, A589, B5273 to Lancaster, Morecambe and Port of Heysham at traffic lights at Moneyclose Inn, turn L access road to the park. Open: 18 February - 3 January. ★★★ BH&HPA 791

(0.5m). **Regent Leisure Park**, Westgate, Morecambe, Lancashire LA3 3DF. 01539 569235. www.slholidays.co.uk. Fantastic for families wanting a fun packed holiday. Play area. Laundrette. 2 heated outdoor pools. Nightclub complex. Children's indoor play centre. Fast food bar. Entertainment. Cinema, shops 1m, golf 3m. M6, J34 and follow A589 to Morecambe for 2.5m. First L @ 3rd roundabout on L 1.5m. Open: 1 March - 15 January. ★★★★ BH&HPA 445

(3m). **Riverside Caravan Park (Morecambe)**, Snatchems, Morecambe, Lancashire LA3 3ER. 01524 844193. www.riverside-morecambe.co.uk. Supermarket and leisure centre with swimming pool only 1m, golf courses nearby. Country pub next to site. No single sex groups. Owner supplied copy. Exit 34 off M6 follow signs for Morecambe. Cross river and L at roundabout on Morecambe road. Straight on at roundabout for 0.5m, next door to Golden Ball Hotel. Open: 5 March - 31 October. BH&HPA 53

(0.75m). **Venture Caravan Park**, Langridge Way, Westgate, Morecambe, Lancashire LA4 4TQ. 01524 412986. www.venturecaravanpark.co.uk. Play area. Public phone. Off-licence. Specially adapted holiday caravans for the disabled. Indoor heated swimming pool. Bar with entertainment and bar meals eat in or take away. Award winning en-suite toilet facilities. GS. Cinema, shopping centre 1.25m; golf course, leisure centre 1.5m. 1m from seafront, off A589, 6m from J34, M6. Open: All year. ★★★★ NCC 56🛏 56🚐 56⛺ 15

(0.25m). **Westgate Caravan Park R**, Westgate, Morecambe, Lancashire LA3 3DE. 01524 411448. Private holiday homes, tourers & rentals. 15 minute walk from Morecambe promenade. Morecambe offers plenty to see and do & sandy beaches. Off A589. Open: 1 March - 31 October. ★★★★ BH&HPA 16🛏 16🚐 186

## Ormskirk

(1.5m). **Abbey Farm Caravan Park**, Dark Lane Farm, Ormskirk, Lancashire L40 5TX. 01695 572686. www.abbeyfarmcaravanpark.co.uk. Quiet, peaceful park 1.5m on R, entrance alongside white cottage. First class facilities. Playground. Library. Off licence, shop. David Bellamy Silver Conservation Award. M6, J27-A2509 SP Parbold Island, L B5240 immediate R. Open: 1 March - 31 October. ★★★★ BH&HPA 10🚐 50 44

(6m). **Hurlston Hall Golf & Country Club**, Southport Road (A570), Ormskirk, Lancashire L40 8HB. 01704 841064. www.hurlstonhallcaravanpark.co.uk. Part of Hurlston Hall golf and country club, discount for visitors for golf, leisure, fishing, restaurant facilities on site. GS. Close to Ormskirk & Southport. Easily accessible from M58 & A59. Open: 1 March - 31 October. ★★★★ BH&HPA 60🚐 51

(5m). **Shaw Hall Caravan Park**, Smithy Lane, Scarisbrick, Ormskirk, Lancashire L40 8HJ. 01704 840298. www.shawhall.co.uk. Clubhouse with entertainment. Owner supplied copy. 4m E of Southport off A570. Situated on Leeds/Liverpool canal 6m from Southport. Open: 15 February - 31 January. BH&HPA NCC 37🚐 300

## Poulton-le-Fylde

(7m). **Maaruig Caravan Park**, 71 Pilling Lane, Preesall, Poulton-le-Fylde, Lancashire FY6 0HB. 01253 810364. Off B3314 to New Polzeath. Open: 1 April - 31 October. 31

## Preston

(15m). **Beacon Fell View Caravan Park**, 110 Higher Road, Longridge, Preston, Lancashire PR3 2TF. 01772 783233. www.haganslesiure.co.uk. Commanding breathtaking views over the Ribble Valley, Beacon Fell View Holiday Park is set in 30 acres of beautiful landscaped parkland, and is sure to offer you and your family a holiday to remember. Facilities include an indoor heated pool, a family clubhouse with live entertainment, indoor & outdoor play areas and kid's club. Gym and sauna, adults only bar. Leave M6 J32 to Garstang A6. Follow sign to Longridge (not Beacon Fell). At Longridge, straight across roundabout then L at White Bull. Park 1m on R. Open: 1 March - 12 November. ★★★ BH&HPA NCC 70🚐 ⛺ 38

(9m). **Bridgehouse Marina and Caravan Park**, Nateby Crossing Lane, Nateby, Preston, Lancashire PR3 0JJ. 01995 601612. www.bridgehousemarina.co.uk. A lovely, landscaped site on a flat field. The site adjoins a canal and boat-filled marina. Well placed for touring central Lancashire. Off A6. Open: 1 March - 4 January. ★★★ BH&HPA 50🚐 20

(10m). **Claylands Caravan Park**, Cabus, Garstang, Preston, Lancashire PR3 1AJ. 01524 791242. www.claylands.com. 14 acres of woodland alongside the river Wyre with excellent coarse fishing available on site also bar and restaurant. Ring for free brochure. David Bellamy Gold Conservation Award. Off J33 S 4m on the A6, 0.5m passed Cabus caravan mart and garage. Open: 1 March - 31 January. ★★★★ BH&HPA 40 A

(11m). **Leisure Lakes Caravan & Camping Park**, Mere Brow, Tarleton, Preston, Lancashire PR4 6JX. 01772 813446. www.leisurelakes.co.uk. Set in 90 acres with pleasant walks and open spaces for children. Full Tourist Board facilities. AA 2-pennant and RAC approved. Coarse fishing. Golf range, 9 hole golf course. Jet skis and windsurfing. PH on site. Village shop. New children's playground, and abundance of activities on site. Off A565 Southport to Preston road. 6m Southport. Open: All year. ★★ BH&HPA 110 A

(3m). **Primrose Bank Caravan Park**, Singleton Road, Weeton, Preston, Lancashire PR4 3JJ. 01253 836273. www.primrosecaravanpark.co.uk. All touring pitches are fully serviced & include hardstanding for caravan, car, awning. Fishing 1m, golf 2m. David Bellamy Gold Conservation Award. Open March-January, all year for lodges. 1.5m S of Singleton on B5260 and 5m E of Blackpool. Leave M55 towards Fleetwood on A585 then B5260 is third on L. At T junction the park is 1m on L. Open: 1 March - 15 January. BH&HPA 30🚐 35 A

**Queensgate Caravan Park**, Little Eccleston, Garstang, Preston, Lancashire PR3 0ZQ. 01995 670223. The trough of Bowland, Lake District and the historical city of Lancaster are all within an hour's drive. We are 0.5m from Gt Eccleston Village, with its shops, PO,

# NORTH WEST

pubs, restaurants and weekly market. Owner supplied copy. M6 motorway M55, 3rd junction, follow Fleetwood sign to first set of traffic lights, turn R on A586 for 1m, park is on L. Blackpool 6.5m. Open: 1 March - 4 January. BH&HPA 53

**(7m). Royal Umpire Caravan Park, Southport Road, Croston, Preston, Lancashire PR26 9JB.** 01772 600257. www.royalumpire.co.uk. Relax amid the best of the north west, Britain's favourite tourist attractions within an hour's drive of this renowned touring park. 10m E of Southport, 5m W of Chorley, 1m E of Croston village. David Bellamy Silver Conservation Award. On A581 midway between A59 and A49. Open: All year. ★★★ BH&HPA 200 200

**(10m). Smithy Caravan Park (Preston), Cabus Nook Lane, Winmarleigh, Garstang, Preston, Lancashire PR3 1AA.** 01995 606200. Excellent service block, free showers. On the Preston-Lancaster Canal. Peaceful and relaxing park. Ideal for the lakes, Morecambe and Blackpool. Owner supplied copy. M6, J32 join A6 north after 8m turn R at traffic lights on to B5272 Cockerham Road. After 1.5m turn R at Smith Garage, park on R over canal bridge. Open: 1 March - 5 January. BH&HPA 87

**(8m). Wyreside Farm Park, Allotment Lane, St Michaels-on-Wyre, Garstang, Preston, Lancashire PR3 0TZ.** 01995 679797. riverparks.co.uk. 10 mixed pitches in total. Fishing river (adjacent to park), ponds - 500yd. Pub, garage, bowls, tennis all within village. Golf, microlighting, clay pigeon shooting, large car boot all within 2m. Market town of Garstang 4m (5mins drive max) David Bellamy Gold Conservation Award. From South, M6, J32, A6 North Garstang. 3.5m Bilsborrow, L into St Michael's Road. 3.5m St Michael roundabout, turn R past church, past pub and garage. Allotment Lane on right hand side. Open: 1 March - 31 October. ★★★ BH&HPA 10 16

### Rochdale

**Gelderwood Country Park (Tranquil adults-only), Ashworth Road, Rochdale, Lancashire OL11 5UP.** 01706 364858. www.gelderwoodcaravanpark.co.uk. Adults only site of 34 pitches in 15 acres of woodland. Several restaurants within walking distance. 0.25 miles from Ashworth. J18, M62 to M66 (SP Bury) at second exit L, J2 leave M66 turn R on to A58 (SP Heywood) at Morrison's supermarket turn L into Bamford Road B6222 to T-junction. Turn L after 100yd turn R into Ashworth Road, park on R. Open: All year. ★★★★★ BH&HPA 10 35

**(4m). Hollingworth Lake Caravan Park R, Rakewood, Littleborough, Rochdale, Lancashire OL15 0AT.** 01706 378661. Rural area. Overlooking lake, restaurant and bar 1m. Showers. Laundry. Dryer. Golf, shops, PO, doctors within 1.5m. Pony trekking. Large fishing and boating lake nearby. Owner supplied copy. J21, M62. Follow Hollingworth Lake Country Park sign to Fisherman's Inn/Wine Press. Take Rakewood road then second R. Open: All year. ★★★ BH&HPA 15 40

### Thornton Cleveleys

**(7m). Kneps Farm Holiday Park, River Road, Thornton Cleveleys, Lancashire FY5 5LR.** 01253 823632. www.knepsfarm.co.uk. Quiet, family run park with luxurious amenities, family bathrooms and facilities for the disabled. A rural retreat close to Blackpool and Wyre countryside. From A585 Kirkham to Fleetwood take B5412 at roundabout signed Little Thornton. Turn R at mini roundabout after school on to Stanah Road, straight over second mini roundabout leading to River Road. Open: 1 March - 15 November. BH&HPA 5 40 4

## MERSEYSIDE
### Formby

**(1.5m). Formby Point Caravan Park, Lifeboat Road, Formby, Merseyside L37 2EB.** 01704 874367. www.formbypointcaravanpark.co.uk. Grassy and well-drained park. Near sea, beach and pinewoods. In conservation area. Convenient for Liverpool and Southport. Open March - October for statics. Owner supplied copy. 2m W of A565. Open: 1 April - 31 October. BH&HPA 20 280

### Southport

**(4m). Riverside Holiday Park (Southport), Southport New Road, Banks, Southport, Merseyside PR9 8DF.** 01704 228886. www.riversideleisurecentre.co.uk. Set in acres of pleasant meadow. Fishing on site. Play area, disco, laundrette, showers. Calor Gas and Camping Gaz stockist. Excellent entertainment for adults and children. Cafe. Country & western and cabaret acts. AA holiday centre. David Bellamy Bronze Conservation Award. Owner supplied copy. 2.5m W of Tarleton Cross Roads on S of A565, E Southport. Open: All year. ★★★ BH&HPA NCC 230 230 375 20

**Southport Caravan Club Site, The Esplanade, Southport, Merseyside PR8 1RX.** 01704 565214. www.caravanclub.co.uk. Situated on the Esplanade of traditional seaside resort, close to famous sands. Dog walk off site. Privacy cubicles. Baby washroom. Veg prep. MV service point. Information room. Play area. Golf and water sports nearby. Ideal for families. Members only. No tents. See website for standard directions to site. Open: 23 March - 31 October. NCC 100 100

**(6m). Willowbank Holiday Home & Touring Park, Coastal Road, Ainsdale, Southport, Merseyside PR8 3ST.** 01704 571566. www.willowbankcp.co.uk. Quiet relaxed atmosphere on park. 4 golf courses nearby. Children's play area. Dog walk. Cinema, swimming pool 6m. Southport resort attractions. Good public transport system. Cycle paths. AA 3 pennants. David Bellamy Gold Conservation Award. From Liverpool take A565 Southport past Formby. RAF Woodvale on L, turn L into coastal road SP Ainsdale Beach, park 150yd on the L. Open: 1 March - 31 January. ★★★★★ BH&HPA 87 87

### Wirral

**Parkfield Farm CL, Park Lane, Wirral, Merseyside CH47 8XT.** 0151 6323519. www.caravanclub.co.uk. A sheltered site for members only, found down a narrow country lane facing a large fishing pool. A nice flat field in pleasant surroundings. Off A553. Open: All year.

## WILLOWBANK HOLIDAY HOME & TOURING PARK
- 87 Mixed pitches with electricity hook up • Luxury heated shower and toilet facilities • Laundry
- Dish washing facilities • Separate shower and toilet room with wheelchair access • Childrens' play area
- Dog exercise area • Breathable ground sheets only (No carpet or plastic sheets) • Strictly no vans or commercial vehicles admitted to the park • Early booking is essential for busy periods and special events.

Coastal Road, Ainsdale, Southport, PR8 3ST • info@willowbankcp.co.uk • 01704 571566

# NORTH WEST / YORKSHIRE

**Wirral Country Park Caravan Club Site**, Station Road, Thurstaston, Wirral, Merseyside CH61 OHN. *01516 485228. www.caravanclub.co.uk.* The site has several flat grassy pitching areas separated by trees and shrubs, some overlooking the Dee estuary which is easily accessible. MV service point. Play equipment. Golf, NCN route nearby. Good area for walking. Ideal for families. Quiet and peaceful off-peak. Non-members welcome. No tents. See website for standard directions to site. Open: 23 March - 5 November. ★★★★ NCC ♿ 93🚐 93🏕

## EAST YORKSHIRE
### Brandesburton

(1m). **Fosse Hill Caravan Park & Jet Ski Centre**, Catwick Lane, Brandesburton, East Yorkshire YO25 8SB. *01964 542608. www.fossehill.co.uk.* Friendly caravan park with 75 pitches for caravans, tents and motorcaravans. Children's play area, some pitches have lakeside views. 4m inland from Hornsea. Fishing, golf nearby. 1m to restaurants, PO, butchers etc. From M62, exit 38. Take B1230 E to Beverley and A165 towards Bridlington at signpost. Open: 1 March - 31 October. ★★★ BH&HPA ♿ 75🚐 75🏕

### Bridlington

(6m). **Barmston Beach Holiday Park**, Sands Lane, Barmston, Bridlington, East Yorkshire YO25 8PJ. *0843 3092591. www.park-resorts.com.* Situated on to the beautiful Yorkshire coast. Licensed club. Free kids club. Shop, laundrette, takeaway and restaurant. Amusements. Outdoor play area, heated outdoor pool with splash area. Visiting entertainment cabaret. 4 golf courses within 10m. Yorkshire Moors steam railway. Historic cities of Beverley and York. David Bellamy Silver Conservation Award. Southbound take main A165 from Bridlington to Kingston-upon-Hull. Northbound, take main A165 from Hull. Barnston Beach is SP about 6m S of Bridlington. Open: 1 March - 1 January. ★★★★ BH&HPA NCC 360🚐

(0.5m). **North Bay Leisure Park**, Lime Kiln Lane, Bridlington, East Yorkshire YO16 6TG. *01262 673733. www.northbayleisurepark.com.* Caravans and lodges for sale on large plots complete with private parking bay. David Bellamy Bronze Conservation Award. Owner supplied copy. Off B1255, follow signs for North Beach parking. Superbly located within Bridlington and only 300 metres from the North Beach and promenade. Open: All year. ★★★★ BH&HPA 324🚐

(1m). **South Cliff Caravan Park**, South Cliff, Wilsthorpe, Bridlington, East Yorkshire YO15 3QN. *01262 671051. www.southcliff.co.uk.* All touring pitches hardstanding. Multi purpose play area. Club, shop. Golf course and boat launch nearby. On A165 Hull to Bridlington. Open: 1 March - 30 November. ★★★★ BH&HPA 184🚐 A 766🏕

(2m). **The Poplars Touring Park and Motel**, 45 Jewison Lane, Sewerby, Bridlington, East Yorkshire YO15 1DX. *01262 677251. www.the-poplars.co.uk.* Quiet, small touring park with modern toilet and shower facilities. Adjacent to family pub and restaurant. Golf course and coastal path within 1m. Owner supplied copy. From N side of Bridlington take B1255 to Flamborough, take 2nd L off Z-bend. Open: 4 March - 31 October. ★★★★ BH&HPA 6🚐 30🏕

### Driffield

(10m). **Dacre Lakeside Park**, New Road, Brandsburton, Driffield, East Yorkshire YO25 8RT. *01964 543704. www.dacrepark.co.uk.* Lake used for fishing, windsurfing, sailing, canoeing. Tennis court, clubhouse. (Golf, clay pigeon shooting and jet skiing nearby). Hot tubs on lodge verandas. Village pubs and Chinese and fish and chips within walking distance. Beverley shopping 6m. Open all year. Take first exit L at Brandesburton roundabout on the A165 Beverley-Bridlington. Follow road for 700yd and turn L on to park entrance. Open: 1 March - 2 January. ★★★★ BH&HPA 120🚐

(9m). **Skipsea Sands Holiday Park**, Mill Lane, Skipsea, Driffield, East Yorkshire YO25 8TZ. *01262 468210. www.park-resortstouring.com.* Close to beach with bars, amusements, laundrette and play area. Indoor swimming pool, ten pin bowling, fitness suite, sports facilities. Follow B1249 from Driffield or A165 from Bridlington. Turn on to B1249 at Beeford. Follow brown tourist signs from Skipsea village. 10m from Bridlington. Open: 1 March - 31 October. ★★★★ NCC 90🚐 A 710🏕

(3m). **Skirlington Leisure Park**, Skipsea, Driffield, East Yorkshire YO25 8SY. *01262 468213. www.skirlington.com.* 9-hole putting course. Fishing pond. Indoor swimming pool. Restaurant and bars with full entertainment in season. Situated between the villages of Skipsea and Atwick on B1242. 1.5m from Hornsea. Open: 26 February - 31 October. ★★★★★ BH&HPA 225🚐 A 566🏕

(9m). **Thorpe Hall Caravan Park**, Rudston, Driffield, East Yorkshire YO25 4JE. *01262 420393. www.thorpehall.co.uk.* 4.5 acres situated in former walled garden at Thorpe Hall. Own coarse fishery. Shops, golf course, sea fishing, PO, hospital minor injuries within 4m. David Bellamy Gold Conservation Award. 4m W from Bridlington on the B1253. Open: 1 March - 31 October. ★★★★ BH&HPA 78🚐 78🏕

### Hull

(8m). **Burton Constable Holiday Park & Arboretum**, The Old Lodges, Sproatley, Hull, East Yorkshire HU11 4LN. *01964 562508. www.burtonconstable.co.uk.* Modern facilities. Shaver points. Licensed club. Telephone. Snooker room. Fishing nearby. PO 1m, golf 3m, doctor 5m. David Bellamy Gold Conservation Award. On B1238 Hull to Aldborough. Modern facilities. Shaver points. Licensed club. Telephone. Snooker room. Fishing nearby. PO 1m, golf 3m, doctor 5m. David Bellamy Gold Conservation Award. Open: 1 March - 31 October. ★★★★ BH&HPA 5🚐 125🏕 20A

(17m). **Patrington Haven Leisure Park**, Haven Road, Patrington Haven, Hull, East Yorkshire HU12 0BR. *01964 630071. www.phlp.co.uk.* Swimming pool. Sauna. Steam room. Fitness centre. Sun bed with small charge. Flat green bowls. Pitch and putt golf. Fishing lake. Equestrian centre. Supermarket on park. PO, chemist and 4 pubs 1m away in the village of Patrington. Amusements, shops

34 CARAVAN & HOLIDAY PARKS 2012

# YORKSHIRE

pubs, beach 5m (Withernsea). Hull 17m W of Patrington. Owner supplied copy. M62 E towards Hull continue on A63 carriageway. Through Hull on dual carriageway, follow signs A1033 Withernsea. When reading Patrington village, take first R opposite 'The Railway' PH. Follow signs to the park. Open: 7 March - 7 January. ★★★★★ BH&HPA 🏠🐕🚐♿🔥⛽ ♿🚻 490⚡

**(3m). Sand le Mere Holiday Village, Southfield Lane, Tunstall, Hull, East Yorkshire HU12 0JF.** 01964 670403. www.sand-le-mere.co.uk. Amenities include pub, club, shop, cafe, restaurant, heated swimming pool, fitness room, play area, bowling and fishing. Children allowed. Disabled toilets. Golf, Tesco's 3m. Cinema, shopping centre 20m. M62 on to A63 Hull-Hedon. R on to A1033, R on to B1362, L on to local roads, Roos. R on to B1242. Open: All year. ★★★★ ⛽🏠🐕🚐♿🔥⛺✂️🛒🚻 ♿ 10⚡ 17⚡ ▲ 46⚡ 6♨️

## Skipsea

**Mill Farm Country Park (Skipsea), Mill Lane, Skipsea, East Yorkshire YO25 8SS.** 01262 468211. Booking office is at Mill Farm on the R. Bridlington 8m. Level site surrounded by mature hedges. Shaver points, showers, pot washing with free hot water. Sea 0.5m. Pub in the village. Shop/PO, cafe/restaurant, bottle gas supply, swimming pool, fishing and golf available nearby. Owner supplied copy. A165 Hull to Bridlington. At Beeford take the B1249 to Skipsea. At the cross roads turn R, then first L up Cross Street, which leads on to Mill Lane. Open: 1 April - 30 September. 🏠🐕🚐♿🔥♿ 35⚡ 35⚡ ▲

## Withernsea

**(1m). Willows Holiday Park, Hollym Road, Withernsea, East Yorkshire HU19 2PN.** 01964 612233. www.willowsholidaypark.co.uk. Showers, club, play area, coarse fishing lake, mini-golf. Laundry. Electric hook-ups bookable in advance. Located within easy reach of sea and town centre. Luxury caravans to hire. 0.25m to golf course, Tesco supermarket. 0.75m to town centre. No pets in hire vans. No single sex groups. Open March 4-January 3 (October 31 for tourers). Owner supplied copy. On A1033. First on the L on entering Withernsea. Open: 4 March - 31 October. ★★★★ BH&HPA 🏠🐕🚐 ♿🔥⛽♿ 5⚡ 40⚡ 168⚡

**(0.5m). Withernsea Sands Holiday Park, Waxholme Road, Withernsea, East Yorkshire HU19 2BS.** 01964 612189. www.park-resortstouring.com. Adventure playground, new children's play area, amusements, on-site shop. Bar, indoor swimming pool. Sandy beach 200yds. Newly refurbished touring toilet/shower facilities. David Bellamy Bronze Conservation Award. From J88 on the M62 take the A63 through Hull. At the end of the dual carriageway, turn R on to the A1033, and follow signs for Withernsea. Follow A1033 through the village and turn on to B1242. The park is 0.5m on R. Open: 20 March - 31 October. ★★★ BH&HPA NCC ⛽🏠🐕🚐♿🔥⛺🛒🚻 ✂️⛽♿🚐 115⚡ 40⚡

# NORTH YORKSHIRE
## Acaster Malbis

**Poplar Farm Caravan Park (Acaster), Acaster Malbis, North Yorkshire YO23 2UH.** 01904 706548. Family run park on the banks of river Ouse, river-bus service to York every day. Bar and restaurant. 4m S of York, turn off A64 at Copmanthorpe junction (A1237) follow signs. Open: 1 March - 31 October. BH&HPA 🏠🐕🚐 ♿⛺🔥🛒🚻 ⚡ 80⚡ ▲ 54⚡

## Boroughbridge

**(0.75m). Boroughbridge Camping & Caravanning Club Site, Bar Lane, Roecliffe, Boroughbridge, North Yorkshire YO51 9LS.** 01423 322683 . www.campingandcaravanningclub.co.uk. Near to Moors and Dales on the banks of river Ure with fishing and boating. All units accepted. Non-members welcome. A popular site for campers and caravanners who enjoy boating and fishing. The site also boasts a recreation hall with pool table and TV. Special deals available for families and backpackers. Loo Of The Year (5 stars). From A1(M) J48 follow sign for Bar Lane Industrial Estate and Roecliffe. Site 0.25m from roundabout. Open: 1 January - 31 December. ★★★★★ NCC 🏠🐕🚐♿🔥⛽ 🚻✂️🚐🛒♿ 85⚡ 85⚡ ▲

## Cawood

**(9m). Cawood Holiday Park, Ryther Road, Cawood, North Yorkshire YO8 3TT.** 01757 268450. www.cawoodpark.com. 57 pitches in 12 acres of parkland with its own lake. Equidistant to Leeds and York. On-site shop, bar (weekend entertainment), fishing. Off the B1223 from Cawood. Open: All year. ★★★★ BH&HPA ⛽🏠🐕🚐♿🔥⛺♿🚐 ⚡🛒♿ 10⚡ 50⚡ 10⚡ 8♨️

## Coneysthorpe

**(17m). Castle Howard Caravan & Camping Site, Coneysthorpe, North Yorkshire YO60 7DD.** 01653 648316. www.castlehoward.co.uk. Good touring centre, adjoining 70-acre lake. Well-drained site, good position for woodland and country walks. Dogs allowed under strict control. Fees on application. 6m SW of Malton. follow Castle Howard signs. Open: 1 March - 31 October. ★★★★ BH&HPA 🏠🐕🚐♿🔥⛽♿ 40⚡ ▲ 160⚡

## Filey

**(6m). Blue Dolphin Holiday Park (Haven), Gristhorpe Bay, Filey, North Yorkshire YO14 9PU.** 0871 2310893. www.caravancamping.co.uk. Amusement arcade. Indoor and outdoor swimming pools. Supermarket. Bars. Indoor Funzone. Adventure playgrounds. Mini ten-pin bowling. All-weather sports court. Kid's clubs. Family entertainment. Crazy golf. Cinema, Scarborough 5m. York 35m. David Bellamy Gold Conservation Award. Park lies directly on A165 between Bridlington and Scarborough and is situated about 2m N of Filey. Open: 18 March - 31 October. ★★★★ BH&HPA NCC ⛽🏠🐕🚐 🔥⛺🛒♿🚻✂️⛽♿🚐 ♿ 260⚡ 260⚡ ▲ 210⚡

**(2m). Crows Nest Caravan Park, Gristhorpe, Filey, North Yorkshire YO14 9PS.** 01723 582206. www.crowsnestcaravanpark.com. Privately owned park with full facilities. An ideal place for that quiet, relaxing family holiday or weekend break. Friendly atmosphere and helpful staff. Shop, bar, indoor heated swimming pool, games room, play area, fish & chip shop. No single sex groups. Rose Award. 2m N of Filey, 5m S of Scarborough off A165. Open: 1 March - 31 October. ★★★★ ⛽🏠🐕🚐♿🔥⛽🛒🚻♿ 18⚡ 50⚡ ▲ 237⚡

**(0.5m). Filey Brigg Camping & Caravan Park, North Cliff, Filey, North Yorkshire YO14 9ET.** 01723 513852. Well-equipped holiday site. Maximum stay 21 days. Path to beach. Laundry. AA 3 pennant site. Owner supplied copy. On the A165 road to Scarborough. On cliffs immediately north of Filey. Open: 22 April - 31 October. ★★★ BH&HPA 🏠🐕🚐♿✂️🛒♿ 🚐 140⚡ ▲

**(2m). Muston Grange Caravan Park, Muston Road, Filey, North Yorkshire YO14 0HU.** 01723 512167. www.mustongrange.com. Hardstanding pitches, fully serviced, new shower/laundrette block and small shop/reception. Childrens' play park. Pets welcome on leads. Outskirts to Filey Town. Quiet family fun park. 10mins walk to 5m of golden beach. Open: 6 March - 6 November. 🏠🐕🚐 ♿🔥⛽ ⛽🔥♿🚐 250⚡ 250⚡

# YORKSHIRE

(3m). Orchard Farm Holiday Village (Filey), Stonegate, Hunmanby, Filey, North Yorkshire YO14 0PU. *01723 891582*. www.orchardfarmholidayvillage.co.uk. 14 acres. Level, secluded site with full amenities. Indoor pool, bar, entertainment, play area, private fishing. Award winning beaches. Historical village. Turn W off A165 road at Royal Oak railway crossing, proceed to SP Hunmanby Park 0.5m on R, follow caravan/camping signs. Open: 1 March - 31 October. ★★★★★ BH&HPA 90 46

(3m). Primrose Valley Holiday Park (Haven), Primrose Valley, Filey, North Yorkshire YO14 9RF. *0871 2310892*. www.caravancamping.co.uk. Blue Flag Award, Welcome Host Award, Investor in People. Large multi-level heated pool complex. Multi-sports court. Adventure playground, climbing wall, boating lake, funfair, abseiling, go-karts, convenience store, 2 cabaret bars, sports bar, restaurants, family entertainment. David Bellamy Gold Conservation Award. Park is situated directly on A165 between Scarborough and Bridlington and is about 3m S of Filey. Open: 18 March -31 October. ★★★★★ BH&HPA NCC 49 49 1927

(5m). Reighton Sands Holiday Park (Haven), Reighton Gap, Filey, North Yorkshire YO14 9SH. *0871 2310894*. www.caravancamping.co.uk. Heated indoor swimming pool. Free kid's club. Family entertainment. Ten-pin bowling. Adventure playground. Convenience store. Outdoor sports. Soft play area. Golf course 3m. David Bellamy Gold Conservation Award. Park is situated on A165 between Bridlington and Filey. Open: 18 March - 31 October. ★★★ BH&HPA NCC 122 122 1135

## Guisborough

(1m). Tocketts Mill Caravan Park, Skelton Road, Guisborough, North Yorkshire TS14 6QA. *01287 610182*. www.tockettsmill.co.uk. Close to North Yorkshire Moors National Park, Whitby and coast. Fishing, golf, swimming, etc nearby. David Bellamy Gold Conservation Award. Owner supplied copy. Off A173 about 1m from Guisborough on road to Skelton. Open: 7 March - 31 October. ★★★★ BH&HPA NCC 89

## Harrogate

(2m). Bilton Park, Bilton Lane, Village Farm, Harrogate, North Yorkshire HG1 4DH. *01423 863121*. www.biltonpark.co.uk. 25 grass pitches on a well-drained touring field. Outdoor play area. Reception sells basics. Between Knaresborough & Harrogate. Own fishing. From A59 in Harrogate (between A661 & A61). Turn into Bilton Lane at Skipton Inn. Park 1.5m down Bilton Lane. Open: 1 April - 31 October. BH&HPA 25 

(4m). High Moor Farm Caravan Park, Skipton Road, Harrogate, North Yorkshire HG3 2LT. *01423 563637*. www.highmoorfarmpark.co.uk. Holiday site surrounded by trees, on the edge of Yorkshire Dales. Ideal touring base. Club. Golf on site. Bowling green. On A59 Harrogate to Skipton. Open: 1 April - 31 October. ★★★★★ BH&HPA 6 160 158

(12m). Low Wood Caravan Park, Pateley Bridge, Harrogate, North Yorkshire HG3 5PZ. *01423 711433*. Follow Low Wath road out of Pateley Bridge turn L after Water Mill Inn to Heathfield, 300yd L and follow signs to park. 2nd park on L. Open: 22 April - 31 October. BH&HPA 48

(3m). Ripley Caravan Park, Ripley, Harrogate, North Yorkshire HG3 3AU. *01423 770050*. www.ripleycaravanpark.com. A level country park with indoor heated pool, laundrette, playground, games and nursery play room, sauna and football pitch. Golf course nearby - PO in village. Maximum 2 dogs (depending on breed). David Bellamy Gold Conservation Award. Take A61 N Harrogate to Ripon, at Ripley roundabout take B6165 to Knaresborough, site 300yd on L. Open: 1 April - 31 October. ★★★★★ BH&HPA 100 100 80

(14m). Riverside Caravan Park (Harrogate), Low Wath Road, Pateley Bridge, Harrogate, North Yorkshire HG3 5HL. *01423 711383*. www.nidderdale.co.uk/riversidecaravanpark. Situated by the River Nidd, 5 mins walk from the market town of Pateley Bridge. Children's playground, fishing & boating available. B6265 or B6165 into Pateley Bridge, situated about 0.25m along Low Wath Road on the R. Open: 22 April - 31 October. BH&HPA 5 47 110

(2m). Rudding Park, Follifoot, Harrogate, North Yorkshire HG3 1JH. *01423 871350*. www.ruddingpark.com. Set in beautiful parkland. Ideal touring centre. Facilities include heated outdoor swimming pool, playground, 18 hole golf course, 6 hole short course and driving range, shop, Deer House family pub. Cinema, Clocktower restaurant nearby. GS. David Bellamy Gold Conservation Award. S of Harrogate, just off the A658 linking the A61 from Leeds to the A59 York Road. Open: 4 March - 31 January. ★★★★★ BH&HPA NCC 7 77 77 20 20

(1m). Shaw's Trailer Park, Knaresborough Road, Harrogate, North Yorkshire HG2 7NE. *01423 884432*. Street lighting, doctor and health centre next door. Bus stop at entrance to Harrogate. Pub 300yds. PO, shops, garages and hospital nearby. Fishing/boating at Knaresborough 2m, golf course 1m. SAE for brochure. AA 3 pennants. On A59 between Harrogate and Knaresborough (2.5m). Entrance next to Johnson's cleaners. Open: All year. 10 45

(20m). Studfold Farm, Lofthouse, Harrogate, North Yorkshire HG3 5SG. *01423 755210*. www.studfoldfarm.co.uk. 41 mixed pitches in total. Ideal for touring other Yorkshire Dales. Level site on working farm. Wonderful views in AONB. Excellent centre for walking, bird watching. Recently opened award winning 'Explore, Discover and Learn' trail, suitable for families. Discounts for campers. Village, PO 0.5m. Shopping, golf, fishing 7-10m. Owner supplied copy. 7m from Pately Bridge at head of Nidderdale. Open: 1 April - 31 October. ★★★★ BH&HPA 41 60

(15m). Westfield Farm, Heathfield, Pateley Bridge, Harrogate, North Yorkshire HG3 5BX. *01423 711880*. Shops, PO, cafe and takeaways 2m, nearest pub 0.5m. Owner supplied copy. Off B6265 Pateley Bridge to Ripon. At Pately Bridge take Ramsgill Road after 1m turn L towards Heathfield, L again in 100yd, site is the third on the L. Open: 1 April - 31 October. BH&HPA 6 60

## Hawes

(0.5m). Bainbridge Ings Caravan and Campsite, Hawes, Hawes, North Yorkshire DL8 3NU. *01969 667354*. www.bainbridge-ings.co.uk. Fishing nearby. Good centre for walking and touring the Yorkshire Dales. Shops, bus service within 0.5m. Train station, 7m. Lovely views from site of surrounding hills. Washing machine and tumble dryer on site. Approaching Hawes from Bainbridge on the A684 turn L at SP marked Gayle 300yd. Open: 1 April - 31

# YORKSHIRE

October. ★★★ 🏠🐕🛁🚿♿🍴🅿️🅿️🎮
🚐🚗♿🚿 10🚐 30🚐 🅰️ 2⛺

**(0.25m). Brown Moor Caravan Club Site, Brunt Acres Road, Hawes, North Yorkshire DL8 3PS.** *01969 667338.* www.caravanclub.co.uk. The site is in beautiful Wensleydale between the river Ure and the market town of Hawes. Toilet blocks, laundry facilities, baby and toddler washroom and MV service point. Dog walk and games room on site. Good area for walking. Fishing nearby. Ideal for families, facilities for disabled. Quiet and peaceful off-peak. Members only. No tents. See website for standard directions to site. Open: 23 March - 7 January. NCC 🏠🐕♿🛁🚿🍴🎮🅿️
🚐🚗♿ 110🚐 110🚐

**(0.25m). Honeycott Caravan Park, Ingleton Road, Hawes, North Yorkshire DL8 3LH.** *01969 667310.* www.honeycott.co.uk. Owner occupied static holiday caravans only. W of Hawes on the B6255 to Ingleton. 17m W of Leyburn. 20m from M6. Open: 1 March - 31 October. ★★★★ BH&HPA 🏠🐕🛁🚿♿🎮🅿️
🐾♿ 5🚐 5🚐 5🅰️

**(2m). Shaw Ghyll Farm Caravan and Camping Site, Simonstone, Hawes, North Yorkshire DL8 3LY.** *01969 667359.* A beautiful, secluded site by a small trout stream with a magnificent backdrop of hills. New facilities block. Hot showers. Hair & hand dryers. River fishing, fell walking. Follow signs from Hawes to Muker, for 2m. the site is 400yd past Simonstone Hotel on the L. Open: 1 March - 31 October. 🐕🐾♿🚗🎮
🚐 10🚐 🅰️ 6⛺

## Helmsley

**(4m). Foxholme Touring Caravan And Camping Park (Adults-Only), Harome, Helmsley, North Yorkshire YO62 5JG.** *01439 771904.* ADULTS ONLY. 60 mixed pitches in total. Well sheltered by trees. Washbasins in private cubicles. Send stamp for brochure. Leave Helmsley on A170 in direction of Scarborough, take 1st turn R SP Harome, in village turn L at church and then follow signs. Open: 15 March - 31 October. ★★★★ BH&HPA 🏠🐕🛁♿🚿🎮🅿️
♿ 🚐 60🚐 🅰️

**(2m). Golden Square Caravan & Camping Park, Oswaldkirk, Helmsley, North Yorkshire YO62 5YQ.** *01439 788269.* www.goldensquarecaravanpark.com. Secluded site surrounded by open countryside and woodland. Magnificent views. Luxury 'Award Winning' facilities block - refurbished in 2006 with underfloor heating. Disabled/family bathroom. Laundrette. Shop. Outdoor/indoor play areas. Sports centre, fishing and golf nearby. Deluxe all service pitches, seasonal pitches and storage compound. S of Helmsley. Off B1257 Malton Road to Ampleforth. Ampleforth 1m on caravan route. Open: 1 March - 31 October. ★★★★★ BH&HPA 🏠🐕🛁🚿♿
🎮🍴🅿️🚐🚗♿🚿🎮🅿️♿ 110🚐
110🚐 🅰️🎮

## Ingleton

**(1.5m). Trees Holiday Home Park, Westhouse, Ingleton, North Yorkshire LA6 3DP.** *01524 241511.* www.greenwoodleghe.co.uk. Set in beautiful scenery. Ideal for walking and touring. Excellent centre for Yorkshire Dales and Lake District. 1.5m to Ingleton. Famous area for mountains, waterfalls and caves. Owner supplied copy. Along A65 N of Ingleton, to hamlet called Westhouse. Open: All year. BH&HPA
🏠🐕🐾❄️🎮🅿️ 🚐 9🚐 20⛺

## Kirkbymoorside

**(4m). Wombleton Caravan & Camping Park, Wombleton, Moorfield Lane, Kirkbymoorside, North Yorkshire YO62 7RY.** *01751 431684.* www.wombletoncaravanpark.co.uk. Quiet and level with excellent modern facilities. Seasonal/storage pitches available. 4m E of Helmsley, stay on A170 until you see sign for Wombleton. Go straight through village, turn L for park. Open: 1 March - 31 October. ★★★★★ BH&HPA 🏠🐕
🐾♿🎮🅿️🚐🚗♿🚿🎮🅿️ 78🚐 🅰️

## Knaresborough

**(3m). Allerton Park Caravan Park, Allerton Mauleverer, Knaresborough, North Yorkshire HG5 0SE.** *01423 330569.* www.yorkshireholidayparks.co.uk. Peaceful woodland park setting E of A1. Touring base for York area and Moors. Timber lodges, holiday homes for sale and hire. No single sex groups or groups under 25 years old. David Bellamy Silver Conservation Award. Rose Award. From A1 take A59 1m towards York. Open: 1 February - 3 January. ★★★★ BH&HPA 🏠🐕🛁♿🚿🎮🅿️ 10🚐 40🚐
🅰️ 100⛺

**(2m). Kingfisher Caravan Park (Farnham), Low Moor Lane, Farnham, Knaresborough, North Yorkshire HG5 9JB.** *01423 869411.* Sheltered area for touring caravans and level hardstandings for motor caravans. Facilities with free hot water, washing up area, showers, laundry, large playground. Most sporting facilities nearby. Fishing available. From Knaresborough take A6055 signed Boroughbridge, turn L for Farnham. Turn L. Site 1m from church on the L. Open: 1 March - 1 November. ★★★★ BH&HPA 🏠🐕🐾♿🎮🅿️🍴🚗♿
5🚐 30🚐 🅰️ 88⛺ 🎮

**(2m). Knaresborough Caravan Club Site, New Road, Scotton, Knaresborough, North Yorkshire HG5 9HH.** *01423 860196.* www.caravanclub.co.uk. The site offers a gateway to the Yorkshire Dales and the many attractions of the North of England. Toilet blocks with privacy cubicles, laundry facilities and baby/toddler washroom. MV service point and vegetable preparation area. Fishing, golf and NCN within 5m. Dog walk nearby, good area for walking. Ideal for families. Non-members and tent campers welcome. See website for standard directions to site. Open: 23 March - 7 January. ★★★★★ NCC
🏠🐕🛁♿🚿🎮🍴🅿️🚐🚗♿
74🚐 74🚐 🅰️

## Leyburn

**(4m). Akebar Park, Wensleydale, Leyburn, North Yorkshire DL8 5LY.** *01677 450201.* www.akebarpark.com. 10 bay golf driving range, a challenging 18 hole golf course. Activities such as fishing, walking, golf, petanque, croquet and boules are all available, as well as our traditional pub situated at the entrance to the park. 7m W of A1, at Leeming Bar on the A684 signed from A1. Open: 1 March - 1 January. BH&HPA 🏠🐕🛁♿🚿🎮🅿️
🍴🚐🚗🍴♿🎮🅿️🚐🚗♿ 210🚐
🅰️ 207🎮

**(3m). Constable Burton Hall Caravan Park, Constable Burton, Leyburn, North Yorkshire DL8 5LJ.** *01677 450428.* NO TENTS OR TRAILER TENTS. Milk, newspapers and gas sales only. Restaurant & pub opposite site entrance. Wardens: Tony & Barbara Knowles. Golf course nearby. Constable Burton Hall Gardens open to the public. Leave A1 at A684 between Bedale and Leyburn. Open: 19 February - 31 October. ★★★★ BH&HPA 🏠🐕🛁
🐾♿🎮🅿️🚐🚗♿ 5🚐 110🚐

**(1m). Lower Wensleydale Caravan Club Site, Harmby, Leyburn, North Yorkshire DL8 5NU.** *01969 623366.* www.caravanclub.co.uk. Set within the hollow of a disused quarry, now overrun with wildflowers and mosses. Non-members welcome. Tent campers welcome in a separate area. No late arrivals area. Toilet blocks. Privacy cubicles. Laundry facilities. Veg prep. Waste disposal for motorhomes. Information room. Good area for walking. See website for standard directions to site. Open: 30 March - 5 November. ★★★ NCC 🏠🐕🛁♿🚿🎮🅿️
🚐🚗♿ 92🚐 92🚐 🅰️

# YORKSHIRE

(9m). Street Head Caravan Park, Newbiggin, Bishopdale, Leyburn, North Yorkshire DL8 3TE. *01969 663472*. www.streetheadcaravanpark.co.uk. Small, quiet caravan & camping park in middle of Yorkshire Dales National Park. Owner supplied copy. Off A684 Leyburn to Hawes. About 2m from Aysgarth. On B6160 and adjacent to Street Head Inn. Open: 1 March - 31 October. BH&HPA

## Malton

(8m). Flamingo Land Resort, Kirby Misperton, Malton, North Yorkshire YO17 6UX. *0871 9118000*. www.flamingoland.co.uk. Leisure complex, golf course, evening venues situated within family fun park with over 100 free attractions, including rollercoaster, family rides, 6 shows and an extensive zoo. Off A169 Malton to Pickering road. Open: 1 April - 1 November. BH&HPA

(10m). The Snooty Fox, East Heslerton, Malton, North Yorkshire YO17 8EN. *01944 710554*. Ganton golf 10 mins away. Wold Way, close to coast and Dales. Dogs on lead welcome (extra charge). Off A64. Open: All year.

(4m). Wolds Way, West Farm, West Knapton, Malton, North Yorkshire YO17 8JE. *01944 728463*. www.ryedalesbest.co.uk. An open level site next to a working farm with views over the Vale of Pickering. Heated toilet block, shop selling camping basics. See website. Open: 5 March - 31 October.

## Northallerton

(6m). Cote Ghyll Caravan & Camping Park, Osmotherley, Northallerton, North Yorkshire DL6 3AH. *01609 883425*. www.coteghyll.com. Beautiful family site in peaceful valley of North York Moors National Park with Stream. Luxury heated shower blocks with bathroom. 77 pitches in total. Super pitches, seasonals, caravan storage and ROSE AWARD HOLIDAY CARAVANS FOR HIRE AND SALE. Play area and stream. Village pubs/shops within 10mins walk. Adjacent to Cleveland Way, coast to coast, Lyke Wake Walk and National Cycleway. Golf, fishing, horse riding, sports centre and market towns all within 6m. Exit A19 at A684 Northallerton junction, travel into Osmotherley village. Turn L in village centre and follow road for 0.25m to the park. Open: 1 March - 31 October.

(4m). Otterington Park, Station Farm, South Otterington, Northallerton, North Yorkshire DL7 9JB. *01609 780656*. www.otteringtonpark.com. Shops, PO, doctors, golf course available in Northallerton. Fishing on site. Pub food 1m. David Bellamy Gold Conservation Award. Located on the A167 near South Otterington, N off the A61. Open: 1 March - 31 October. BH&HPA

(6m). Pembroke Caravan Park, Leeming Bar, Northallerton, North Yorkshire DL7 9BW. *01677 422652*. Good A1 stopover. Ideally situated for touring the Yorkshire Dales, Yorkshire Moors and the historic city of York. PO and pub with bar food in small village. Golf course 3m. Fishing 2m. 0.5m from A684, 1m from A1. 3m from Bedale. Open: 1 March - 31 October.

## Pickering

(1.5m). Black Bull Caravan Park, Malton Road, Pickering, North Yorkshire YO18 8EA. *01751 472528*. www.blackbullcaravanpark.co.uk. Quiet family site. On site ladies and gents toilet and shower block. Children's playground, playfield, games room, take away and bar meals. Static holiday caravans for hire on separate field. Nearby swimming, fishing, tennis, golf, steam railway, theme park and zoo, shops, bars and restaurants. S of Pickering on A169. Situated behind Black Bull PH. Open: 1 March - 31 October.

(2m). Overbrook Caravan Park (Tranquil adults-only), Maltongate, Thornton-le-Dale, Pickering, North Yorkshire YO18 7SE. *01751 474417*. www.overbrookcaravanpark.co.uk. Exclusively for adults, level well drained site, resident owners. 0.5m level walk to shops, PO, PHs, tea rooms and bus route. Centrally located for sight-seeing. David Bellamy Gold Conservation Award. Off A170. Turn down Maltongate, following stream or turn off A169 towards Thornton-le-Dale site of old railway station on R. Open: 1 March - 7 January. BH&HPA

(10m). Rosedale Caravan Park, Rosedale Abbey, Pickering, North Yorkshire YO18 8SA. *01751 417272*. www.flowerofmay.com. AA 4 pennants - nestling in beautiful valley, walking and touring country. Luxurious new toilet blocks. Dogs by arrangement. Off A170 (near Pickering) to Rosedale. Open: 9 April - 17 October. BH&HPA

(7m). Spiers House (Forest Holidays) Caravan & Camping Site, Cropton, Pickering, North Yorkshire YO18 8ES. *01751 417591*. www.forestholidays.co.uk. Refurbished in 2008. Perfect base for exploring the North York Moors National Park. Easy driving distance of York, Scarborough and Whitby. Bookings and brochure requests on 0845 1308224. A170 W from Pickering. 1m N of Cropton on the Rosedale road turn R to site. Open: All year.

(8.75m). The Howard (Rosedale Abbey) Caravan Club Site, Rosedale Abbey, Pickering, North Yorkshire YO18 8SA. *01751 417842*. www.caravanclub.co.uk. Attractive riverside site in the heart of the North Yorkshire Moors National Park. The coast is within easy driving distance and shopping available in Pickering. Own sanitation required. Members only. No tents. See website for standard directions to site. Open: 30 March - 5 November. NCC

(1.5m). Upper Carr Caravan Park, Upper Carr Lane, Malton Road, Pickering, North Yorkshire YO18 7JP. *01751 473115*. www.uppercarrchaletandtouringpark.co.uk. Level, family park with licensed shop, laundry, pets corner, play area, cycle hire, payphone. Golf, pub, swimming, walking and fishing nearby. 30 mins to York, Scarborough, Whitby and North Moors National Park. Brochure available. Off A169, S of Pickering. Open: 1 March - 31 October. BH&HPA

(6m). Vale Of Pickering Caravan Park, Carr House Farm, Allerston, Pickering, North Yorkshire YO18 7PQ. *01723 859280*. www.valeofpickering.co.uk. Super modernised facilities. Ladies & gents bath. Hairdryer. Gas supplies. Fishing 1m. Forestry walks 2m. Large play area. Microwave oven. Fully lit. Spirit licence. Play and games area. David Bellamy Gold Conservation Award. E of Pickering off A170 (Scarborough) & B1415 (Malton). Open: 4 March - 3 January. BH&HPA

(2.5m). Wayside Caravan Park, Wrelton, Pickering, North Yorkshire YO18 8PG. *01751 472608*. www.waysideparks.co.uk. Touring centre for moors. South facing park with country views and modern facilities. Historic steam railway. Fishing, golf course, service station and shop, PO all nearby. Pub/restaurant 200yd. Off A170 from Pickering 2.5m W at Wrelton - SP. Open: 1 April - 30 September.

# YORKSHIRE

★★★★★ BH&HPA 🏠 15

## Richmond

**(2m). Brompton Caravan Park, Brompton on Swale, Richmond, North Yorkshire DL10 7EZ.** 01748 824629. www.bromptoncaravanpark.co.uk. Friendly site set on banks of river Swale. Fully serviced pitches. Free heated showers/washing up water. Baby change facilities. Suitable for families and semi-retired/retired. Licenced shop. Play area. Dawn to dusk lighting. Some special offers, phone for details. On site take away for pizza, burgers and chips. David Bellamy Gold Conservation Award. Leave A1 at Catterick A6136 exit, take B6271 to Brompton-on-Swale. Park 1m on L after Brompton-on-Swale on Richmond road. Open: 20 March - 31 October. ★★★★★ BH&HPA 177 A 3

**(3.5m). Hargill House Caravan Club Site, Gilling West, Richmond, North Yorkshire DL10 5LJ.** 01748 822734. www.caravanclub.co.uk. Part sloping site with views over the Yorkshire Dales National Park. Non-members welcome. No tents. Hardstandings. Toilet blocks. Privacy cubicles. Laundry facilities. Veg prep. MV service point. Information room. Golf, fishing nearby. Good area for walking. Dog walk. See website for standard directions to site. Open: 23 March - 5 November. ★★★★ NCC 66 66

**Orchard Caravan Park (Richmond), Mill Holme, Reeth, Richmond, North Yorkshire DL11 6TT.** 01748 884475. Yorkshire Dales all grassed park in quiet secluded orchard beside the river Swale, 5mins walk from all the facilities offered by Reeth Village. Ideal base for walkers. Owner supplied copy. Leave Richmond on the A6108 to Leyburn after 5m to R on the B6270 to Reeth - bear L opposite village store. Open: 1 March - 31 October. BH&HPA 3 12 A 25

**Park Lodge Camping site, Keld, Richmond, North Yorkshire DL11 6LJ.** 01748 886274. www.rukins-keld.co.uk. Good base for touring the Dales. An hour's drive to Lakes. Fees on application. In Keld village on B6270, 3m NW of Muker, 9m from Hawes, 23m from Richmond and 11m from Kirkby Stephen. Open: All year.

**(3m). Scotch Corner Caravan Park, Scotch Corner, Richmond Road, Richmond, North Yorkshire DL10 6NS.** 01748 822530. www.scotchcornercaravanpark.co.uk. Fishing, golf available at Richmond (3m), very convenient night halt only 0.25m from A1. Access to nearby leisure centre. From Scotch Corner take A6108 Richmond road for 250yd then across to other carriageway and return 200yd to site entrance. Bar & restaurant adjacent. Open: 1 April - 31 October. BH&HPA 96

**(24m). Usha Gap Camping & Caravan Park, Usha Gap, Muker-In-Swaledale, Richmond, North Yorkshire DL11 6DW.** 01748 886214. www.ushagap.btinternet.co.uk. Small family run site on farm. Washing up facilities. Dryer. 0.25m from village shop and pub. Shop, PO, pub serving meals, fishing all within 0.25m. B6270. 20m from Richmond, W of Richmond along Swale Dale or over Butter Tubs Pass from Hawes. Open: All year. 12 12 A

## Ripon

**(1.5m). Black Swan Holiday Park, Black Swan Hotel, Fearby, Masham, Ripon, North Yorkshire HG4 4NF.** 01765 689477. www.blackswanholiday.co.uk. 45m view over the Vale of York. Off A6108, 0.25m NW of Masham, site 2m L at rear of Black Swan. Open: 1 March - 31 October. ★★★★ BH&HPA 5 50

**(9m). Old Station Holiday Park, Low Burton, Ripon, North Yorkshire HG4 4DF.** 01765 689569. www.oldstationmasham.co.uk. Quiet secluded park, footpaths to town 0.5m. Garage nearby sells gas, shops, PO and doctor. Many nice walks by river or further. Child's play park nearby. Brewery tours. Many local events. AA 3 pennants. From A1. Sinderby J on to B6267 to Masham W. From Harrogate A61 to A6108 N. Ripon-Masham. From Leyburn A6108 S. Open: 1 March - 30 November. BH&HPA 50 A

**(1m). River Laver Holiday Park, Studley Road, Ripon, North Yorkshire HG4 2QR.** 01765 690508. www.riverlaver.co.uk. Level, secluded, family-run park with excellent facilities. Hardstandings available with drain and water point. Ideal base for touring the Yorkshire Dales and North Yorkshire moors. Shop and gas sales on site. Golf 2m, shopping 1m, cinema 10m. Holiday homes for sale on exclusive new development. 0.75m from Ripon centre - off B6265 towards Fountains Abbey. Open: 1 March - 25 November. BH&HPA 18 100

**(0.5m). Riverside Meadows (Ripon), Ure Bank Top, Ripon, North Yorkshire HG4 1JD.** 01765 602964. www.flowerofmay.com. Tent and touring caravan park for families only. AA 3 pennants - tranquil setting amidst trees above river. Ideal for touring Dales or Yorkshire Moors. Off A61 at Ripon. Open: 25 March - 14 October. BH&HPA 10 100 200 A

**(5.5m). Sleningford Watermill, North Stainley, Ripon, North Yorkshire HG4 3HQ.** 01765 635201. www.sleningfordwatermill.co.uk. Beautiful, quiet riverside site. A holiday flatlet also available for hire. On-site fly fishing and white water canoeing on River Ure. Ideal for walking, bird and wild flower spotting. Central for Herriot country and the N Yorks Dales. PO & garage 1-2m away. Doctor's surgery 4m. Golf courses, shops 5m. Campsite has its own small store and canoe shop. David Bellamy Gold Conservation Award. Follow signs for Lightwater Valley, taking A6108 out of Ripon, site is clearly SP. Alternatively leave A1 at the B6267 Masham to Thirsk road and follow Lightwater Valley signs. Open: 1 April - 31 October. ★★★★ BH&HPA 48 50 A

**(5m). Woodhouse Farm Country Park, Woodhouse Farm, Winksley, Ripon, North Yorkshire HG4 3PG.** 01765 658309. www.woodhousewinksley.com. TV and games room. Play equipment. Ideal touring base for Yorkshire Dales. Licensed restaurant serving home cooked food and real ale. David Bellamy Silver Conservation Award. After 3.5m off B6265 Ripon to Pateley Bridge at Winksley and Grantley right hand turn-off. Open: 15 March - 31 October. ★★★★ BH&HPA 5 100 A

## Scarborough

**(4m). Arosa Caravan Park, Ratten Row, Seamer, Scarborough, North Yorkshire YO12 4QB.** 01723 862166. www.arosacamping.co.uk. Quiet, family site in picturesque countryside. Ideal for touring. Full modern facilities. TV & games room. Play area. Laundrette. Public phone. Club house. Entertainment in high season. 4m S of Scarborough on A64 York road. From York, 1st L in Seamer. Open: 1 March - 4 January. ★★★★ BH&HPA 104 104 A

**(4m). Brown's Caravan Park, Mill Lane, Cayton Bay, Scarborough, North Yorkshire YO11 3NN.** 01723 582303. www.brownscaravanpark.com. Licensed bar serving food with children's room and play area. Village 1m with shops, PO. 3m S of Scarborough, just off A165. Turn R at Cayton Bay traffic lights. Open: 1 March

CARAVAN & HOLIDAY PARKS 2012 39

# YORKSHIRE

- 31 October. ★★★★ BH&HPA 35♲

(3m). **Cayton Village Caravan Park, Mill Lane, Cayton Bay, Scarborough, North Yorkshire YO11 3NN.** 01723 583171. www.caytontouring.co.uk. The very best of coast and country. Luxurious facilities, playground, recreation area, site shop and dog walk. Seasonal pitches, winter storage and caravan sales. Super sites, hardstanding and grass pitches. Bus service from park entrance. Low season supersaver and OAP discounts. Location: Beach 0.5m, Scarborough 3m, Filey 4m, adjoining village with pubs, chip shop and PO. Fishing nearby. David Bellamy Gold Conservation Award. Wi-Fi catering for The Laurels super sites. From A165 S of Scarborough, turn inland at Cayton Bay, park 0.5m on right hand side. From A64 take B1261 SP Filey. In Cayton, take second L after Blacksmiths Arms, park is 200yd on L. Open: 1 March - 31 October. ★★★★ BH&HPA 269 41

**Coachman Caravan Park (Adults only), Pickering Road West, Snainton, Scarborough, North Yorkshire YO13 9PL.** 01723 864596. www.coachmancaravanpark.co.uk. Fishing nearby. Shop/PO in adjacent village. Golf driving range nearby. Brochure available. 8m from Pickering. Adults only. Ideal walking/cycling. Between Pickering and coast. Open: 1 March - 31 October. 12

(5m). **Flower Of May, Lebberston Cliff, Scarborough, North Yorkshire YO11 3NU.** 01723 584311. www.flowerofmay.com. Games room. Family room. Bar. Laundry. Supermarket. Free play area. Indoor heated pool. Dogs allowed by arrangement (one per pitch). Golf, basketball, bowling. On A165 Filey to Scarborough. Open: 1 April - 28 October. ★★★★ BH&HPA

20 250 A 20

(2m). **Jacobs Mount Caravan And Camping Site, Stepney Road, Scarborough, North Yorkshire YO12 5NL.** 01723 361178. www.jacobsmount.com. Level, all weather pitches. Tap, drain, electric etc. Licensed club. Bar meals. 2 Play areas. Family room. New centrally heated showers. Laundry facilities. Street lights. Rose Award. AA-5 flags. 2m W of town centre on A170 Thirsk Road. Open: 3 March - 4 November. ★★★★ BH&HPA 16 140 A 60

(8m). **Jasmine Park, Cross Lane, Snainton, Scarborough, North Yorkshire YO13 9BE.** 01723 859240. www.jasminepark.co.uk. Quiet picturesque park in the ideal location for exploring coast and countryside, with level pitches. Multi award winning park. Please see our website or call for a brochure pack. David Bellamy Gold Conservation Award. Turn S off A170 in Snainton (midway between Pickering and Scarborough), SP. Open: 1 March - 31 October. ★★★★★ 17 60 80 A 4

(5m). **Lebberston Touring Park, Filey Road, Lebberston, Scarborough, North Yorkshire YO11 3PE.** 01723 585723. www.lebberstontouring.co.uk. Quiet country location with well spaced pitches, enjoying extensive south facing views. Ideal for those seeking a peaceful, relaxing break. Fully modernised amenity blocks. Dog area. Perfect base for exploring this beautiful diverse area. David Bellamy Gold Conservation Award. From A64 or A165 take B1261 to Lebberston. 3m from Filey. Open: 1 March - 31 October. ★★★★★ BH&HPA 50 125

(2m). **Scalby Close Park, Burniston Road, Scarborough, North Yorkshire YO13 0DA.** 01723 365908. www.scalbyclosepark.co.uk. Family owned and run with level, sheltered pitches. Fully insulated and heated holiday homes for hire. Ideal for touring N Yorkshire Moors and coast. Just 2m from Scarborough's North Bay attractions, pools, boating, etc. David Bellamy Gold Conservation Award. Park signed 400yds on A165 N of Scarborough. Open: 2 March - 4 November. ★★★★ BH&HPA 5 42 5

(1m). **Scarborough Camping & Caravanning Club Site, Field Lane, Burniston Road, Scarborough, North Yorkshire YO13 0DA.** 01723 366212. www.campingandcaravanningclub.co.uk. The site is set in 20 acres with stunning views over the Yorkshire countryside. Situated high on the hills outside the village of Scalby and just N of the Victorian seaside resort of Scarborough. All units welcome. Some all weather pitches available. Laundry facilities, children's play area. Swimming, fishing and tennis all available nearby. Non-members welcome. Special deals available for families and backpackers. Visit Britain Caravan Holiday Park of the Year. Yorkshire finalist. Loo Of The Year (4 stars). On W side of A165, 1m N of Scarborough. Open: 1 April - 31 October. ★★★★ NCC 300 300 A

(4m). **Spring Willows, Main Road, Staxton, Scarborough, North Yorkshire YO12 4SB.** 01723 891505. www.springwillows.co.uk. Bar. Free hot showers. Swimming pool. Sauna. Bistro. Playground. Children's club. Free entertainment. AA 4 pennants. A64 Filey to Bridlington road to Staxton roundabout. Open: 3 February - 7 January. ★★★★ BH&HPA 64 64 20 A 3 1

(6m). **St Helens In The Park, Wykeham Estate, Wykeham, Scarborough, North Yorkshire YO13 9QD.** 01723 862771. www.sthelenscaravanpark.co.uk.

Want to find your nearest Premier Park? Then visit www.mmm-premier-parks.co.uk

MMM PREMIER PARK 2012

# YORKSHIRE

Hardstandings on adult only area. In North Yorkshire Moors National Park. New 'zip slide' on playground and bike hire on site. Unusual animals (alpacas) on site. Pets welcome. Fishing 1m. David Bellamy Gold Conservation Award. Situated on the A170 Scarborough to Pickering road. Open: 15 February - 3 January. ★★★★ BH&HPA 🐕🎣🚴🏊🎾🏰🎯🍴⛽🚿🚻 ♿🐾🚐200🚙🅿

(5m). **West Ayton Caravan Club Site**, Cockrah Road, West Ayton, Scarborough, North Yorkshire YO13 9JD. *01723 862989*. www.caravanclub.co.uk. 4m from Scarborough's safe beaches. Ideal family holiday site. Privacy cubicles. Baby/toddler washroom. Veg prep. MV service point. Playfield and play equipment. Golf, fishing nearby. Members only. No tents. See website for standard directions to site. Open: 23 March - 5 November. NCC 🏕️🐕🎣🚴🏊🎾🏰🍴⛽🚿🚻♿ 🐾164🚐164🚙

## Selby

(4m). **The Ranch Caravan Park**, Cliffe Common, Selby, North Yorkshire YO8 6EF. *01757 638174*. www.theranchcaravanpark.co.uk. Set in 6 acres of woodland, family run site ideally situated in the heart of Yorkshire. Various leisure activities nearby. Village shop and pub. Credit cards accepted. Wi-Fi. M62, J37 (Goole), take A63 towards Selby. At Cliffe turn R and travel for 1m, then turn L at crossroads. Entrance to park 80yd on the R. Open: 5 February - 5 January. ★★★★ BH&HPA 🛜🏕🐕🎣🚴🏊🎾🏰🎯🍴⛽🚿🚻 ♿ 🌀 50🚐 50🚙 🅿

## Settle

(2.5m). **Knight Stainforth Hall Camping & Caravan Park**, Little Stainforth, Settle, North Yorkshire BD24 0DP. *01729 822200*. www.knightstainforth.co.uk. Beside river in Dales National Park. Booking advised. Fees on application. Turn off A65 into Settle, then turn opposite Settle community college on to Stack House lane, site is then 2m. Open: 1 March - 31 October. ★★★★ BH&HPA NCC 🏕🐕🎣🚴🏊🎾🏰⛽🚿🚻♿ 🐾 50🚐 50🚙 🅿 60⛺

(1m). **Langcliffe Caravan Park**, Settle, North Yorkshire BD24 9LX. *01729 822387*. www.langcliffe.com. Children's playground. Golf course, fishing, swimming pool, restaurants and pubs all within 1m. Set in beautiful surroundings 1m from Settle with all amenities. David Bellamy Gold Conservation Award. Off A65 on to B6480 continue on B6479 to Horton in Ribblesdale. Go past Watersbed Mill and take next turning L. Park is at end of lane.

Open: 1 March - 15 January. ★★★★ BH&HPA 🏕🐕🎣🚴🏊🎾🏰⛽🚿🚻♿ 10🚐 50🚙 🅿 55⛺

## Sheriff Hutton

(1.5m). **Sheriff Hutton Camping & Caravanning Club Site**, Bracken Hill, Sheriff Hutton, North Yorkshire YO60 6QG. *01347 878660*. www.campingandcaravanningclub.co.uk. A 10 acre site with 90 pitches. Convenient for visiting York, North Yorkshire Moors National Park and east coast. All units accepted. Non-members welcome. Seaside resorts Bridlington, Scarborough and Filey are within easy reach. Special deals available for families and backpackers. From York follow Earswick/Strensall signs. Keep L at filling station and Ship Inn. Site 2nd on R. Open: 1 April - 31 October. ★★★★ NCC 🏕🐕🎣🚴🏊🎾🏰⛽🚿🚻♿ 90🚐 90🚙 🅿

## Skipton

(4.5m). **Eshton Road Caravan Park**, Eshton Road, Gargrave, Skipton, North Yorkshire BD23 3PN. *01756 749229*. Fishing on site. Golf course 4m. Shops, PO, doctor 5mins walk. Off A65. Open: All year. BH&HPA 🏕🐕🎣🚴🏊🎾🏰❄🍴⛽ 🚿🚻♿ 10🚐 20🚙 🅿

(14m). **Fold Farm Campsite**, Fold Farm, Kettlewell, Skipton, North Yorkshire BD23 5RH. *01756 760886*. Quiet, scenic, amid moors. Fees on application. N of Skipton via B6160, close to village. From King's Head Inn in village centre, upstream for 100yd, farm, upstream for further 300yd, camp site. Open: 20 March - 31 October. 🏕🐕🏊⛽🚻 🚐🚙 🅿

(15m). **Hawkswick Cote Park (North Dales)**, Arncliffe, Skipton, North Yorkshire BD23 5PX. *01756 770226*. www.northdales.co.uk. Set in unspoilt countryside, offers both touring pitches & holiday homes. Well-stocked licensed shop. Near Lightwater Valley. From Skipton take B6265, at Threshfield take B6160. 1/4m past Kilnsey bear L towards Arncliffe. Hawkswick Cote is 1.5m on L. Open: 3 March - 10 November. ★★★★ BH&HPA NCC 🏕🐕🎣🚴🏊🎾🏰 ⛽🚿🚻♿ 10🚐 30🚙 🅿 97⛺

(8m). **Howgill Lodge Camping & Caravanning Park**, Barden, Skipton, North Yorkshire BD23 6DJ. *01756 720655*. www.howgill-lodge.co.uk. Family run park, B&B also available. Quiet with beautiful views over Wharfedale. Ideal walking area. Dogs allowed with tourers only. Nearest pub 1m. Nearest town Skipton 7m. David Bellamy Gold Conservation Award. Turn off B6160 at Barden Tower, park 1m on R, along lane by phone box. Open: 1 April - 1 November. ★★★★★ BH&HPA 🏕🐕🎣🚴 🏊🎾🏰⛽🚿🚻♿ 15🚐 15🚙 🅿 6⛺

**Strid Wood Caravan Club Site**, Bolton Abbey, Skipton, North Yorkshire BD23 6AN. *01756 710433*. www.caravanclub.co.uk. Set in open glade surrounded by woodland and the Yorkshire Dales. Non-members welcome - No tents, advance booking essential. All hardstanding, steel awning pegs required, dog walk on site. Privacy cubicles. Baby changing facilities. Veg prep. Motorhome service point. Information room. Good area for walking. Water sports nearby, quiet and peaceful off peak. See website for standard directions to site. Open: 23 March - 7 January. ★★★★★ NCC 🏕🐕 🐾🎣🚴🏊🎾🏰⛽🚿🚻♿ 57🚐 57🚙

(1.2m). **Tarn House Caravan Park**, Stirton, Skipton, North Yorkshire BD23 3LQ. *01756 795309*. www.tarnhouse.net. Only one dog allowed per van but no Alsatians, Rottweilers or Pit Bulls etc. Owner supplied copy. Off B6265. Take the Skipton bypass, on the N roundabout go SW on road signed 'Local traffic only'. After 200yd turn R, SP. Open: 1 March - 31 October. ★★★★ NCC 🏕 32🚐 224⛺ 🅿

(6m). **Threaplands House Farm**, Cracoe, Skipton, North Yorkshire BD23 6LD. *01756 730248*. Calor and Camping Gaz on site. Bakery on site selling bread, cakes etc and milk, eggs. Shops, doctor, PO, shopping within 3m. Golf course, fishing, cinema 6m. Access via Skipton to Grassington B6265. Open: 1 March - 31 October. BH&HPA 🏕🐕🎣⛽🚻♿ 🐾 30🚙 🅿

**Wharfedale Caravan Club Site**, Long Ashes, Threshfield, Skipton, North Yorkshire BD23 5PN. *01756 753340*. www.caravanclub.co.uk. Set in the heart of the Yorkshire Dales, the site is screened with mature trees and is in two fields divided by one of the dry stone walls characteristic of the area. Baby and toddler washroom. MV service point. Play equipment and dog walk on site. Good area for walking and fishing nearby. Ideal for families. Members only. No tents. See website for standard directions to site. Open: 23 March - 7 January. NCC 🏕🐕🎣🚴🏊🎾🏰⛽ 🚿🚻♿ 118🚐 118🚙

(9m). **Wood Nook Caravan Park**, Skirethorns, Threshfield, Skipton, North Yorkshire BD23 5NU. *01756 752412*. www.woodnook.net. Licensed shop. Children's play area. Golf, cinema, supermarkets 9m. Fishing 2m. David Bellamy Gold Conservation Award. From Skipton

# YORKSHIRE

take B6265 to Threshfield then B6160 for 100yd. Turn L after garage into Skirethorns Lane. Entrance clearly SP at 300yd and 600yd. Open: 1 March - 31 December. ★★★★ BH&HPA 20🚐 20🏕 35A 3⛺

## Slingsby

(0.5m). **Slingsby Camping & Caravanning Club Site, Railway Street, Slingsby, North Yorkshire YO62 4AN.** *01653 628335.* www.campingandcaravanningclub.co.uk. A 3 acre site with 60 pitches, accepting all units. Site is mainly grass with some hardstanding. Close to the North Yorkshire Moors and several seaside resorts. Non-members welcome. Nearby Malton is a lively and attractive market village. Special deals available for families and backpackers. At Slingsby on B1257 turn downhill to site on R at end of village. 6m from Malton. Open: 1 April - 31 October. ★★★★ NCC 60🚐 60🏕 A

## Sutton-on-the-Forest

**Ponderosa Caravan & Camping, Goose Lane, Sutton-on-the-Forest, North Yorkshire YO61 1ET.** *01347 810744.* Children's play area. Children allowed. Owner supplied copy. B1363 from York (7m), SP on B1363. Site 800yd. Open: All year. 30🚐 A 58⛺

## Tadcaster

(5m). **White Cote Caravan Park, Ryther Road, Ulleskelf, Tadcaster, North Yorkshire LS24 9DY.** *01937 835311.* www.whitecotecaravanpark.co.uk. Sheltered, well maintained site. Licensed bar open weekends. 0.5m to local shop, PO and petrol station selling gas and pub. River fishing 1m. Supermarket, swimming and golf 4m. Owner supplied copy. Off A162 S of Tadcaster, E on B1223 towards Selby. Open: 1 March - 31 January. 20🚐 25🏕 A

## Thirsk

(1.5m). **Carlton Miniott Park, Sandhutton Lane, Carlton Miniott, Thirsk, North Yorkshire YO7 4NH.** *01845 523106.* 7-acre lake for fishing, canoeing, rowing & sailing. NB: pitches are let on a yearly basis ie campers pay one fee and their pitches are reserved for them during the opening season. No overnight/short stay available. Take road for 'Sandhutton' off A61, entrance 400yds on R. Open: 31 March - 31 October. 40🏕

(2.5m). **Scenecliffe Caravan Park, Moor Lane, Bagby, Thirsk, North Yorkshire YO7 2PN.** *01845 597368.* Village of Bagby is 0.25m away with one pub but no shops. ADULTS ONLY. We have 5 pitches available with electric generally available during the season. Fishing sites within 2-3m. Gliding club 3m, golf courses 3m & 10m. Thirsk has all facilities ie PO, doctors, cinema, swimming baths, etc. Take A170 from Thirsk (ignore caravan ban sign). 2.5m from Thirsk, turn R at sign marked Bagby. The site is then 0.5m on R. Open: 18 March - 16 October. 28🏕

(1m). **Sowerby Caravan Park, Islebeck Road, Sowerby, Thirsk, North Yorkshire YO7 3AG.** *01845 522753.* www.ukparks.co.uk/sowerby. Quiet rural park with river frontage. AA 3 pennants. Site is 3m follow council signs. Open: 1 March - 31 October. 5🚐 25🏕 80⛺

(3m). **Thirkleby Hall Caravan Park, Thirkleby Park, Thirkleby, Thirsk, North Yorkshire YO7 3AR.** *01845 501360.* www.greenwoodparks.com. Manager lives on park. Lovely park built within grounds of a former stately home with lake and extensive woods. Children's play area. Bar. Games room. Bottled gas. Fishing lake on park. Playground. Golf course 3m, weekly market in Thirsk 3m, York 16m. AA 3 pennants. Telephone for free brochure 01243 514433. On A19 York to Thirsk, road lies E of A19, 3m from Thirsk. Open: 1 March - 31 October. 50🚐 50🏕 A 195⛺

(0.25m). **Thirsk Racecourse Caravan Club Site, Thirsk, North Yorkshire YO7 1QL.** *01845 525266.* www.caravanclub.co.uk. On this site you are pitched within sight of the main stand and with the famous turf before you, and only a 5 mins walk to the market town of Thirsk. Toilet blocks and laundry facilities, vegetable preparation area and gas/Gaz. Dog walk on site, golf and NCN route nearby. Facilities for disabled. Non-members and tent campers welcome. Ideal for families. See website for standard directions to site. Open: 30 March - 8 October. NCC 60🚐 60🏕 A

(2.6m). **York House Holiday Park (Bagby), Balk, Bagby, Thirsk, North Yorkshire YO7 2AQ.** *01845 597495.* www.yhlparks.co.uk. Beautiful location on the edge of the North York Moors National Park. Local pub and meals nearby. Shopping and cinema 3m. Golf 6m. David Bellamy Gold Conservation Award. Travelling from Thirsk on A19 take L turn signed Bagby, Balk, Kilburn. Go through Bagby to T Junction, turn R go 500yd down hill, park is on the L. Open: 1 March - 30 November. ★★★★ BH&HPA 160⛺

## Wetherby

(4m). **Maustin Park (Adults only), Kearby, Wetherby, North Yorkshire LS22 4DA.** *01132 886234.* www.maustin.co.uk. South facing, sheltered in Lower Wharfe Valley between Harrogate (5m) and Wetherby, close to Harewood House. The park offers a peaceful haven for people without family responsibilities. Flat green bowling. Restaurant/bar on the park. Brochure on request. Lots to do including Harewood House nearby. Telephone for directions or see website. Open: 1 March - 28 January. ★★★★★ BH&HPA NCC 5🚐 20🏕 A 75⛺

## Whitby

(9m). **Abbots House Farm, Goathland, Whitby, North Yorkshire YO22 5NH.** *01947 896270.* www.abbotshouse.org.uk. Moorland scenery and North Yorkshire Moors Steam Railway. 'Heartbeat' country. Facilities include showers, toilets, freezer pack exchange. Under-5s free. Awnings, hot showers free. From Whitby S on A169, take Goathland sign. Site 0.5m along lane beside Goathland Hotel. Open: 1 March - 31 October. 90🚐 90🏕

(9m). **Brow House Farm, Goathland, Whitby, North Yorkshire YO22 5NP.** *01947 896274.* Shops, PO within 0.5m. Takeaway meals, doctor 4m. Fishing, golf 7-8m. Swimming 9m. York-Pickering-Goathland or Middlesbrough-Whitby-Goathland. Open: 1 March - 31 October. ★ 10🚐 30🏕 A

(7m). **Burnt House Holiday Park, Ugthorpe, Whitby, North Yorkshire YO21 2BG.** *01947 840448.* Free showers. Play area. Hardstanding or grass. Well lit site, country pubs nearby. Owner supplied copy. A171 Whitby to Guisborough road signed to Ugthorpe village, 275yd on R. Open: 1 April - 31 October. BH&HPA 50🚐 74⛺

(8m). **Grouse Hill Caravan Park, Fylingdales, Nr Robin Hood's Bay, Whitby, North Yorkshire YO22 4QH.** *01947 880543.* www.grousehill.co.uk. Quiet, family site situated in moorland valley with extensive moorland walks. AA 3-pennant and star award. 40 new hardstandings with electric and water. Level terrace grass pitches, 5mins walk to locay country inn. Off A171 between Scarborough and Whitby, highway sign N of Flask Inn. Open: 16 March - 12 October. 175🏕 A

(5.5m). **Ladycross Plantation, Egton, Whitby, North Yorkshire YO21 1UA.**

# YORKSHIRE

01947 895502. www.ladycrossplantation.co.uk. Peaceful sheltered site in N.Y.Moors National Park. AA 4 pennants. David Bellamy Gold Conservation Award. Off A171. Whitby-Guisborough road. Turning at sign post to Egton. About 5m from Whitby. Open: 18 March - 30 October. ★ ★ ★ ★ ★ BH&HPA ⌂ ⌂ ⊁ ⋈ ⌘ ♞ 🜨 ⚿ ⚒ 6🚐 100⌂

**(4.5m). Low Moor Caravan Club Site, Sneaton, Whitby, North Yorkshire YO22 5JE.** 01947 810505. www.caravanclub.co.uk. Relax on this tranquil site set in the North Yorkshire Moors National Park and very much in Heartbeat country. No sanitation. Pitching areas are pleasantly open and spacious. Non-members welcome. No tents. Boules pitch, mini-golf. Information room. MV service point. See website for standard directions to site. Open: 30 March - 5 November. ★ ★ ★ ★ NCC ⌂ ⊁ ⋈ ⌘ ♞ 🜨 96🚐 96⌂

**(5.5m). Middlewood Farm Holiday Park, Middlewood Lane, Fylingthorpe, Robin Hood's Bay, Whitby, North Yorkshire YO22 4UF.** 01947 880414. www.middlewoodfarm.com. Magnificent views and walking country. Fantastic new facilities, hardstandings. Adventure playground. 10mins walk to beach. Pub and shop 5mins walk. Whitby 5m. Gas & Camping Gaz. Luxury caravans for hire. Rose Award. Fishing nearby. David Bellamy Gold Conservation Award. Open all year for statics. Scarborough/Whitby A171 turn for Robin Hood's Bay and Fylingthorpe. At Fylingthorpe crossroads and PO turn on to Middlewood Lane. Follow official brown signs. Open: 1 March - 31 October. ★ ★ ★ ★ ★ BH&HPA ⌂ ⌂ ⊁ ⋈ ⌘ ♞ 🜨 ⚿ ⚒ 30🚐 20⌂ ▲ 30⌂

**(3m). Northcliffe Holiday Park, Bottoms Lane, High Hawsker, Whitby, North Yorkshire YO22 4LL.** 01947 880477. www.northcliffe-seaview.com. Whitby's top 5 star award winning park. Fabulous sea views. Seasonal touring park only. Luxury caravans for sale. 4 star new holiday cottage available to hire. David Bellamy Gold Conservation Award. 3m S Whitby (A171) L on to (B1447), 0.5m L on to private road. Open: 11 March - 7 November. ★ ★ ★ ★ ★ BH&HPA ⌂ ⌂ ⊁ ⋈ ⌘ ♞ 🜨 ⚿ ⚒ 62⌂ 163⌂

**(4m). Rigg Farm Caravan Park, Stainsacre, Whitby, North Yorkshire YO22 4LP.** 01947 880230. www.riggfarmcaravanpark.co.uk. Small, quiet site in National Park with scenic views. Separate site for tourers. Children allowed. Separate tent pitches also available. AA 3 pennants. Approaching Whitby on A171 take B1416. 1.5m S of Ruswarp, turn into unclassified road SP Sneatonthorpe, Hawksker. Stainsacre (and Rigg Farm). Site about 2m on L. Open: 1 March - 31 October. BH&HPA ⌂ ⌂ ⊁ ⋈ ⌘ ♞ 🜨 14⌂ ▲ 24⌂

**(1m). Sandfield House Farm Caravan Park, Sandsend Road, Whitby, North Yorkshire YO21 3SR.** 01947 602660. www.sandfieldhousefarm.co.uk. Quiet, friendly park surrounded by undulating countryside. 0.25m from long, sandy beach. 0.5m from shops and hotel. Adjacent golf course. 1m N of Whitby centre on A174 coast road, next to Whitby Golf Club. Open: 1 March - 7 November. ★ ★ ★ ★ ★ BH&HPA ⌂ ⌂ ⊁ ⋈ ⌘ ♞ 🜨 60⌂

**(8m). Serenity Touring Caravan & Camping Park, High Street, Hinderwell, Whitby, North Yorkshire TS13 5JH.** 01947 841122. www.serenitycaravanpark.co.uk. Refurbished toilet and shower block and new wash and laundry room. Marvellous coastal, country and moorland walks. Village shops, public telephone and pubs all nearby. Situated 8m N of Whitby on A174, Cleveland Way 1m. A very quiet, sheltered, secure predominately adult site with lovely country views. 0.5m from the sea. Open: 1 March - 31 October. ★ ★ ★ ★ BH&HPA ⌂ ⊁ ⋈ ⌘ 20⌂ ▲ 2⌂

**(8m). The Flask Inn Holiday Home Park, Robin Hoods Bay, Whitby, North Yorkshire YO22 4QH.** 01947 880592. www.flaskinn.com. Small family run site, for over 30 years. Ideal for walkers. All caravans super luxury with central heating, double glazing and freeview TV, DVD player, outside decking with seating. Free Wi-Fi. On A171 Scarborough to Whitby, 4m from Robin Hoods Bay. Open: 19 March - 11 November. ★ ★ ★ ★ BH&HPA ⌂ ⌂ ⊁ ⋈ ⌘ 62⌂

**(8m). Ugthorpe Lodge Caravan & Camping Site, Guisborough Road, Whitby, North Yorkshire YO21 2BE.** 01947 840518. www.whitby-hotel-bed-and-breakfast-inn-accommodation.co.uk. Quiet, family site with full services. Beautiful views. Pub and restaurant on site. Separate field for rallies. B&B facilities. Children's play area. Fishing 2m. Golf, beach 5m. Owner supplied copy. On A171 Guisborough to Whitby. Open: 1 March - 31 October. ⌂ ⌂ ⊁ ⋈ ⌘ ♞ 🜨 20⌂ 20⌂ ▲ 70⌂

**(1.5m). Whitby Holiday Park, Saltwick Bay, Whitby, North Yorkshire YO22 4JX.** 01947 602664. www.whitbypark.co.uk. Clifftop location. Path to secluded beach. Club, pub (serves food) & playground. Golf nearby. One of the closest holiday parks to Whitby. No tents. S of Whitby following signs for Whitby Abbey. Turn R at T-junction. Open: 1 March - 31 October. ★ ★ ★ ★ BH&HPA NCC ⌂ ⌂ ⊁ ⋈ ⌘ ♞ 🜨 ⚿ ⚒ 200⌂ 25⌂

**(3.5m). York House Caravan Park (Whitby), Hawksker, Whitby, North Yorkshire YO22 4LW.** 01947 880354. www.yorkhousecaravanpark.co.uk. Golf course, shopping all within 3.5m. Children's play area. Hotel guest house, bar on site. Beach, bike hire nearby David Bellamy Silver Conservation Award. Off A171 Scarborough to Whitby. Open: 4 February - 4 January. ★ ★ ★ BH&HPA ⌂ ⌂ ⊁ ⋈ ⌘ ♞ 🜨 ⚿ ⚒ 10⌂ 39⌂ ▲

## York

**(3m). Beechwood Grange Caravan Club Site, Malton Road, York, North Yorkshire YO32 9TH.** 01904 424637. www.caravanclub.co.uk. In open countryside outside York, screened with trees and hedges, the site is ideal for reaching this fascinating city and for discovering Yorkshire's varied attractions. Toilet block and baby/toddler washroom, laundry facilities, vegetable preparation area, MV service point, play area and dog walk on site. Non members welcome. No tents. See website for standard directions to site. Open: All year. ★ ★ ★ ★ ★ NCC ⌂ ⌂ ⊁ ⋈ ⌘ ♞ 🜨 127⌂ 127⌂

**(3.5m). Chestnut Farm Holiday Park, Acaster Malbis, York, North Yorkshire YO23 2UQ.** 01904 704676. www.chestnutfarmholidaypark.co.uk. Family run park in pretty village by river Ouse 3.5m from York. Ideal for touring Dales, Coasts and Moors. All modern facilities. Rose Award caravans. 3m from centre of York. Off A64 at Acaster Malbis. Open: 1 March - 30 November. ★ ★ ★ ★ ★ BH&HPA ⌂ ⌂ ⊁ ⋈ ⌘ ♞ 🜨 55⌂

**(8m). Elvington Fisheries Camping and Caravanning Site, Lake Cottage, Wheldrake Lane, Elvington, York, North Yorkshire YO41 4AZ.** 01904 607504. www.elvingtonfisheries.co.uk. Coarse and game fishing on site - carp a speciality. Wild fowl. Nature reserves. Golf club. Toilet block, hot & cold showers. Gas, milk and papers available. Bus service picks up at site for town. Booking and deposit advised. Level site excellent for disabled anglers (wheelchair approach to fishery). Wild fowl nature reserve 3m. Civic bus stops at gate. Booking recommended. Dogs allowed but rules apply. No loud music, good behaviour expected at all times. Off A1079 and B1228. 3m on the right hand side. Open: 1 April - 30

# YORKSHIRE

October. ★★★★★ 13 13

**(8m). Fangfoss Park, Fangfoss, York, North Yorkshire YO41 5QB.** 01759 380491. www.fangfosspark.co.uk. Quiet park at the foot of the Wolds. Laundry facilities. Play area. AA 3-pennant. Close to York, seasonal and touring pitches available. 2m from A1079 at Wilberfoss. Open: 1 March - 27 November. BH&HPA 75 75

**(8m). Goose Wood Caravan Park, Sutton-on-the-Forest, York, North Yorkshire YO61 1ET.** 01347 810829. www.goosewood.co.uk. Quiet and peaceful park, convenient for York yet enjoying the peace of the countryside. All hardstanding pitches with patio and electric hook up. Fishing on site. David Bellamy Gold Conservation Award. From A1237 (York outer ring road) take B1363 N, pass the Haxby-Wigginton junction, take next R, and follow signs or when coming from the N, take first L after 2nd Easingwold roundabout (A19) into Huby then Sutton-on-the-Forest. Open: 4 March - 2 January. ★★★★★ BH&HPA 75 40

**Hollybrook Lodges, Penny Carr Lane, Easingwold, York, North Yorkshire YO61 3EU.** 01347 821906. www.hollybrooklodges.co.uk. Now lodge hire only. WP. Pleasant well-equipped, secluded, level grass site. Regret no children. AA 3 Pennants. Fishing, golf nearby. Owner supplied copy. Off A19 York to Thirsk road. Approaching Easingwold take first R, SP Stillington, in 0.5m turn R into Pennycarr Lane. Site on R after third of a mile. Open: 14 March - 16 December.

**(3m). Lakeside Adult Touring Park and Coarse Fishery (York), Lakeside, Bielby, Nr Pocklington, York, North Yorkshire YO42 4JP.** 01759 318100. www.lakesidewebsite.com. 6 acre fishing lake on site, well stocked with a variety of coarse fish. Distance to nearest shops 2m. Designated dog walking area on site. Owner supplied copy. From A1079 take the Lakeside/Bielby turning, opposite the Pocklington turn off, follow Lakeside signs to Lakeside Caravan Park. Open: 1 March - 31 October. ★★★★★ 10 42

**(4m). Moor End Farm, Acaster Malbis, York, North Yorkshire YO23 2UQ.** 01347 706727. www.moor-end-farm.co.uk. Small well appointed park in nice location for York and Yorkshire as well as York/Selby cycle track. AA 3 pennants. RAC Approved. Off A64 York (4m) to Tadcaster, turn off at Copmanthorpe and follow signs to Acaster Malbis. Open: 1 April - 31 October. ★★★★ BH&HPA 2 10 6

**(6m). Moorside Caravan Park, Lords Moor Lane, Strensall, York, North Yorkshire YO32 5XJ.** 01904 491208. www.moorsidecaravanpark.co.uk. Washing-up area and laundry facilities. Free hot showers. Fishing on site. No children. Dogs must be kept on lead at all times. Golf course nearby. Take Strensall turn off A1237 and head towards Flaxton. Opposite York golf course. Open: 15 March - 31 October. ★★★★★ 10 40

**(3.5m). Rawcliffe Manor Caravan Park (Adults only), Manor Lane, Shipton Road, York, North Yorkshire YO30 5TZ.** 01904 640845. www.lysanderarms.co.uk. ADULTS ONLY. 13 super pitches with water, drainage, foul waste, electric and sat TV. Club. Gas available on site. Tesco's Superstore. 12 screen cinema. Bowling alley and shopping complex next to site. New PH with entertainment built on site, also a la carte restaurant which also has a Sunday carvery. Owner supplied copy. Off A19 at junction with A1237 (new bypass). Open: All year. ★★★★★ BH&HPA 13

**Robin Hood Caravan Park, Green Dyke Lane, Slingsby, York, North Yorkshire YO62 4AP.** 01653 628391. www.robinhoodcaravanpark.co.uk. In the heart of picturesque Ryedale, this privately owned park offers peace and tranquility, an ideal centre for York, the Moors, Heartbeat country, and the seaside resorts of Scarborough, Whitby and Filey. Situated on B1257 Malton to Helmsley Road. Open: 1 March - 4 November. ★★★★★ 48 48 80 55

**Rowntree Park Caravan Club Site, Terry Avenue, York, North Yorkshire YO23 1JQ.** 01904 658997. www.caravanclub.co.uk. A popular site, level and on the banks of the Ouse. MV waste. Advance booking essential. Non-members and tent campers welcome. Privacy cubicles. Laundry facilities. Veg prep. Information room. Ideal for families. Local attractions include Jorvik Viking centre and York Minster. Golf nearby. See website for standard directions to site. Open: All year. ★★★★★ NCC 102 102

**(1m). South Lea Caravan Park, The Balk, Poklington, York, North Yorkshire YO42 2NX.** 01759 303467. www.south-lea.co.uk. Park is set in 15 acres of flat grassland. 1m from Pocklington. Heated shower/toilet facilities, large play area, security barrier. Golf and fishing within 5m. Ideally situated for visiting York, the East Coast and Yorkshire moors. David Bellamy Gold Conservation Award. Turn off A1079 (York-Hull) at the Yorkway Motel on to B1247. Park is situated 400yd on L. Open: 1 March - 31 October. ★★★★ BH&HPA 72

**(6m). Swallow Hall Touring Caravan Park, Crockey Hill, York, North Yorkshire YO19 4SG.** 01904 448219. www.swallowhall.co.uk. Pleasant, secluded 5-acre site. Forest walks. Golf (18-hole par 3 adjoining). Driving range. New tennis court. Hot showers etc. AA 2 pennants. Owner supplied copy. Situated E off A19 between York and Selby signed Wheldrake. Open: 22 April - 31 October. 5 25

**(10m). The Alders Caravan Park, Home Farm, Monk Green, Alne, York, North Yorkshire YO61 1RY.** 01347 838722. www.alderscaravanpark.co.uk. Tennis courts and children's playground nearby. Pub with restaurant in the village. Golf courses and fishing within 3m. 3m S of Easingwold. Located in centre of village. Open: 1 March - 31 October. ★★★★★ BH&HPA 30

**Tollerton Holiday Park, Station Road, Tollerton, York, North Yorkshire YO61 1RD.** 01347 838313. www.greenwoodparks.com. Children's playground. Shop, PO in Tollerton 0.5m. Golf, fishing within 3m. Good shopping in York and Easingwold. Telephone for free brochure 01243 514433. AA 3 pennants. Owner supplied copy. Situated off A19 between York and Easingwold, Tollerton and Linton-on-Ouse turn-off. Open: 1 March - 31 October. 18

**(8m). Weir Caravan Park, Stamford Bridge, York, North Yorkshire YO41 1AN.** 01759 371377. www.yorkshire-holidayparks.co.uk. Peaceful site, 5 mins walk to village, shops and pubs. Buses into York City centre. Fishing on park. David Bellamy Silver Conservation Award. On A166 Bridlington to York. Open: 1 March - 31 October. ★★★★★ BH&HPA 15 15 87

**(3m). Willow House Caravan Park, Wigginton Road, Wigginton, York, North Yorkshire YO32 2RH.** 01904 750060. www.willowhouseyork.co.uk. Coarse fishing. Exclusively for adults. Owner supplied copy. From A1237 north side of York outer ring road, take B1363 SP Wigginton. 1m

# YORKSHIRE

on R. Open: All year. 15🆔 15🆔 A

(3m). **Wrens Of Ryedale Touring Park, Gale Lane, Nawton, York, North Yorkshire YO62 7SD.** *01439 771260.* www.wrensofryedale.co.uk. A delightful, small, family run site in the heart of the Ryedale countryside. Ideal for N Yorkshire moors, dales, coast and York. Within walking distance of village pub, restaurant, takeaway and major bus route. 3m E of Helmsley on the A170. At Beadlam turn R on to Gale Lane after the Spice Desi restaurant. We are on the R 600yd from the village. Open: 1 April - 31 October. ★★★★ 20🆔 5 A

(5m). **York Touring Caravan Park (Towthorpe), Greystones Farm, Towthorpe Moor Lane, Towthorpe, York, North Yorkshire YO32 9ST.** *01904 499275.* www.yorkcaravansite.co.uk. On-site golf range and 9 hole pay & play course. 3 golf courses within 5m. Strensall village 2m away (shops, PO, doctor). All new park facilities (showers, toilets, laundry room). Take Strensall/ Haxby, turn off the A64. Park is 1m on L. Open: 4 February - 3 January. ★★★★ BH&HPA 20🆔 20🆔 A

## SOUTH YORKSHIRE
### Barnsley

(3m). **Greensprings Touring Park, Rockley Abbey Farm, Rockley Lane, Barnsley, South Yorkshire S75 3DS.** *01226 288298.* Award winning site nestling in picturesque wood and farmland in the Pennine foothills. Suitable for a relaxing break on journeys north and south or for touring the Peak District and Pennine Yorkshire. Off M1 J36, A61 towards Barnsley left after 0.25m, park 1m down hill on L. Open: 1 April - 31 October. **BH&HPA** 10🆔 60🆔 A

### Doncaster

(8m). **Hatfield Water Park, Old Thorne Road, Hatfield, Doncaster, South Yorkshire DN7 6EQ.** *01302 841572.* www.doncaster.gov.uk. Site incorporates a lake with water sports facilities. Centre is recognised by RYA for sailing & windsurfing and BCU for canoeing & kayaking. Fishing also available by day ticket. Residential accommodation in bunkhouse style dormitories available for organised groups. Children's playground. Hot & cold drinks, snacks, ice creams available from visitor centre. Local shops 10mins walk. Superstore (Tesco/ Sainsbury's) 10mins by car. Situated about halfway between Doncaster and Thorne on the A18. Leave M18 at J5 onto M180 then leave at J1, for A18 and follow signs for Hatfield. Open: 1 April - 1 November. ★★★ 75🆔 A

**Woodcarr Park, Sandtoft Road, Belton, Doncaster, South Yorkshire DN9 1PN.** *01427 873487.* Holiday home site with 11 months license. Quiet secluded site. Over 50+ site no facilities for children. Leisure centre, swimming, indoor bowls, etc. cinema (8m). Museums, shopping e-coast 30mins. Fishing, golf nearby. David Bellamy Gold Conservation Award. Owner supplied copy. J2, M180 for Gainsborough A161. Turn right at mini roundabout. Sandtoft Road. Park on L alongside garden centre. 8m from Scunthorpe. Open: 1 March - 31 October. **BH&HPA** 5🆔 35🆔

### Sheffield

(4m). **Fox Hagg Farm, Lodge Lane, Rivelin, Sheffield, South Yorkshire S6 5SN.** *01142 305589.* Quiet country caravan park on working farm. Between Sheffield and Peak District. Wash room. Free showers. No hire caravans. Bus 51 every 15mins to town. 0.25m to shops and doctor. Near rock climbing, golf, nature reserve and country park walks. On edge of Peak District, about 2m. Owner supplied copy. W of Sheffield on A57, near Rivelin PO. Open: 1 April - 31 October. 10🆔 10🆔 A 30🆔

## WEST YORKSHIRE
### Elland

(0.5m). **Elland Hall Farm Caravan Park, Exley Lane, Elland, West Yorkshire HX5 0SL.** *01422 372325.* www.ellandhallfarm.co.uk. Family run park, in a quiet & peaceful setting. Located in the Calder Valley with lots of walks. Plenty of towns & attractions nearby. 2 miles from the M62, junction 24. Open: 1 March - 31 October. **BH&HPA** 10🆔 A

### Haworth

(1.5m). **Upwood Holiday Park, Blackmoor Road, Haworth, West Yorkshire BD22 9SS.** *01535 644242.* www.upwoodpark.co.uk. Situated close to Yorkshire Dales National Park with panoramic views over Bronte country. Bar with family room/food and play area. Camping pods now available. David Bellamy Gold Conservation Award. A629 to B6141 Denholme Oxenhope. Turn into Blackmoor Road. Site 0.5m. Open: 1 March - 4 January. ★★★★ BH&HPA 7🆔 68🆔 A 2🆔

### Hebden Bridge

(2.5m). **Lower Clough Foot Caravan Club Site, Cragg Vale, Hebden Bridge, West Yorkshire HX7 5RU.** *01422 882531.* www.caravanclub.co.uk. A site for the discerning, tucked away off the road, well screened and gently sloping. Motorhome service point and gas/gaz exchange. Fishing, golf, water sports and NCN route nearby. Good area for walking. Quiet and peaceful off-peak. Own sanitation required. Non-members welcome. No tents. See website for standard directions to site. Open: 30 March - 5 November. ★★★★ NCC 45🆔 45🆔

(3m). **Pennine Camp & Caravan Site, High Greenwood House, Heptonstall, Hebden Bridge, West Yorkshire HX7 7AZ.** *01422 842287.* Golf course, shops, garages, doctor 3m. PO, fishing and climbing within 3m. Early bookings required. Owner supplied copy. From Hebden Bridge take Heptonstall Road. Then follow camping and caravan signs. We are in the Camping and Caravan Club site. Open: 1 March - 31 October. 5🆔 5🆔 A

### Holmfirth

(1.5m). **Holme Valley Caravan & Camping Park, Thongsbridge, Holmfirth, West Yorkshire HD9 7TD.** *01484 665819.* www.holmevalleycamping.com. In delightful setting in the heart of the beautiful 'Last of the Summer Wine' country and on the fringe of the Peak District National Park. Laundry room. On site angling. Enclosed play area. David Bellamy Gold Conservation Award. Halfway between Holmfirth & Honley in the valley bottom off the A6024 (turn off main road by the bottle banks). Open: All year. ★★★★ BH&HPA 62🆔 62🆔 A

### Ilkley

**Clarion Lodge Campsite, West Chevin Road, Menston, Ilkley, West Yorkshire LS29 6BL.** *01943 871619.* www.clarionlodgecampsite.co.uk. Small family run campsite with spectacular views over attractive countryside. Leeds & Harrogate are close by, as are many walks. Accessed from the A65 & A660. Open: 1 March - 30 November. 2🆔 20🆔 A

(3m). **Olicana Caravan Park, High Mill, Addingham, Ilkley, West Yorkshire LS29 0RD.** *01943 830500.* olicana-caravan-park.com. Fishing. Dogs on lead. Bottled gas sales. Owner supplied copy. On B6160. Open: 1 April - 31 October. 5🆔 50🆔

# YORKSHIRE / EAST MIDLANDS

## Keighley

**(5m). Brown Bank Caravan Park, Brown Bank Lane, Silsden, Keighley, West Yorkshire BD20 0NN.** 01535 653241. Peaceful site on edge of Ilkley Moor. Fantastic views. Ideal for the Dales with many local walks. Golf courses 1-2m, pony trekking, cinema, swimming, fishing, shopping within 2-5m. Off A6034 from Silsden (2m) or Addingham (2m). Open: 1 April - 31 October. ⛺🚽♿ 5🚿 6🚻 ▲ 100⚡

**(1m). Dalesbank Holiday Park, Low Lane, Silsden, Keighley, West Yorkshire BD20 9JH.** 01535 653321. Licensed bar. Cafe. Games/function room. Lodge rooms. 6 B&B also available. Doctor 1m, hospital 3m. Golf 3m, 1m to Silsden. Horse riding 1m. Owner supplied copy. Off A65, Bolton Road from Silsden tophill. L Cringles Lane, keep L for 2m. Open: 1 April - 31 October. ⛺🚽♿ 10🚿 52🚻 ▲

## Leeds

**(7m). Glenfield Caravan Park, Blackmoor Lane, Bardsey, Leeds, West Yorkshire LS17 9DZ.** 01937 574657. Quiet, country site, surrounded by golf courses and lovely country inns. Ideal touring base for Wetherby, Harrogate and Knaresborough etc. AA 3 pennants. Walking in nearby Nature Reserve. Owner supplied copy. Off A58 at Bardsey. From Wetherby A1. Church Lane 1.5m up hill on R. From Leeds A58. L at Shadwell, follow R fork then 1m down hill on L. Open: All year. BH&HPA ⛺🚽♿ 30⚡ ▲

**(7m). Haighfield Caravan Park, Blackmoor Lane, Bardsey, Leeds, West Yorkshire LS17 9DY.** 01937 574658. www.haighfieldcaravanpark.co.uk. Very pretty immaculately kept park with holiday homes for sale and hire. Excellent location from which to explore Yorkshire and only 7m to Leeds. 28 day camping field and Loo Award Shower Block. Close to 10 golf courses, 3m to Emmerdale set. No pets in hire caravans. Rose Award. Owner supplied copy. Turn off at A58 Leeds to Wetherby, turn at Bardsey into Church Lane, past the Bingley Arms to the top of hill, park 50yd on L. Open: All year. ★★★★★ BH&HPA ⛺🚽♿ 4🚿 4🚻 ▲ 37⚡

**(7m). Moor Lodge Caravan Park (Adults only), Blackmoor Lane, Bardsey, Leeds, West Yorkshire LS17 9DZ.** 01535 572424. www.moorlodgecaravanpark.co.uk. 1.5m to shops. Adults only. Immaculate grounds and new shower block with private hand basins, close to Harewood House, Dales, York and Leeds City 7m. Owner supplied copy. Off A58, 7m from Leeds, L at Shadwell sign then follow caravan signs. Open: All year. ★★★★ BH&HPA ⛺🚽♿ 12⚡ 12🚿 ▲ 60⚡

**(3m). St Helena's Caravan Park R (Adults only), Otley Old Road, Horsforth, Leeds, West Yorkshire LS18 5HZ.** 01132 841142. www.st-helenas.co.uk. Well kept site with full toilet block. Close to local amenities and attractions. Walks, dales and market towns. Bookings necessary. 1.5m from the A658, 2.5m from Leeds/Bradford airport. Open: 1 April - 31 October. ★★★★ BH&HPA ⛺🚽♿ 10⚡ 40🚿 ▲

## Shipley

**(1m). Crook Farm Caravan Park Ltd, Glen Road, Baildon, Shipley, West Yorkshire BD17 5ED.** 01274 584339. www.dalescaravanparks.co.uk. Children's play area. Launderette, shower block & toilets. 3 holiday apartments for hire. Golf adjacent, shops 0.5m, cinema & public pool 2m. Bronte country. Owner supplied copy. BH&HPA ⛺🚽 208⚡

**(4m). Dobrudden Caravan Park, Baildon Moor, Baildon, Shipley, West Yorkshire BD17 5EE.** 01274 581016. www.dobrudden.co.uk. Mob: 07999 870581. Bronte country. Golf, shops 2m. Horse riding 3m. Owner supplied copy. 3m N of Baildon. Close to Ilkley Moor and Haworth. Open: 1 March - 31 January. BH&HPA ⛺🚽♿ 10⚡ 10🚿 ▲ 115⚡

# DERBYSHIRE

## Alfreton

**Golden Valley Camping & Caravan Park, Coach Road, Golden Valley, Riddings, Alfreton, Derbyshire DE55 4ES.** 01773 513881. preview.hosts.co.uk/~goldenvalleycaravanpark.co.uk. Gym, fishing. Bar. Pool table. Kids games indoor and outdoor. Bike hire and Fort adventure. Disco room, new showers block. Golf course 1m. Shopping centre 5m. Cinema 10m. Butterley Railway free and half price on train. 120 metre zip slide: the 'flying dragon'. Wood sculptures, electric security gates. Donkeys from beach for children's donkey rides. David Bellamy Gold Conservation Award. M1, J26 A610 bypass to Codnor, turn R. R again on to Alfreton Road, follow for 1.5m, sign on L on to Coach Road, L on to park. Open: All year. ★★★★ BH&HPA ⛺🚽♿ 10⚡ 40🚿 ▲ 120⚡

## Ashbourne

**(3.5m). Ashbourne Camping & Caravanning Club Site, Belper Road (A517), Bradley, Ashbourne, Derbyshire DE6 3EN.** 01335 370855. www.campingandcaravanningclub.co.uk. PO and petrol station 1m. Pubs, fishing lakes and golf available a short drive away from site. Perfect for exploring the Peak District and Derbyshire Dales. From Ashbourne site on R off A517. From Belper site on L off A517 Belper Road. Open: 16 February - 12 November. ★★★★ NCC ⛺🚽♿ 50⚡ 50🚿 ▲

**(3m). Ashbourne Heights (North Dales), Fenny Bentley, Ashbourne, Derbyshire DE6 1LE.** 01335 350228. www.northdales.co.uk. 13m away from Alton Towers. Tissington Trail runs along the side of the park. Well stocked shop, heated indoor swimming pool. Large play area. Playground. Rally fields. Booking advisable at peak periods. Take A515 out of Ashbourne, towards Buxton, through Fenny Bentley, turning by Green Bridge over road. Open: 4 March - 31 October. BH&HPA ⛺🚽♿ 4🚿 100⚡ ▲ 7🚻

**(6m). Blackwall Plantation Caravan Club Site, Kirk Ireton, Ashbourne, Derbyshire DE6 3JL.** 01335 370903. www.caravanclub.co.uk. Set in a pine plantation, convenient base for walkers with beautiful scenery of Dovedale and surrounding countryside. Carsington Water 15mins walk away. Advance booking essential. Dog walk. Non-members welcome. Toilet block with privacy cubicles, laundry facilities and baby/toddler washroom. MV service point. Play equipment. Ideal for families. No tents. See website for standard directions to site. Open: 23 March - 1 November. ★★★★ NCC ⛺🚽♿ 130⚡ 130🚿 ▲

**(0.5m). Callow Top Holiday Park, Buxton Road, Ashbourne, Derbyshire DE6 2AQ.** 01335 344020. www.callowtop.co.uk. Full facilities including heated pool, games room, restaurant and pub etc. Flat pitches. Adjacent to Tissington Trail cycle path. Family site in beautiful countryside. Alton Towers 20mins. Fishing on site. David Bellamy Gold Conservation Award. On A515 Buxton road, 0.5m from Ashbourne town centre. Open: 15 April - 6 November. ★★★★ BH&HPA ⛺🚽♿ 100⚡ 150▲ 2🚿

**(5m). Carsington Fields Caravan Park, Millfields Lane, Nr Carsington Water, Ashbourne, Derbyshire DE6 3JS.** 01335 372872. www.carsingtoncaravaning.co.uk. 400yd from Carsington water. 1.5m from nearest shop/PO/pub. Fishing, water sports, boats for hire 1m. Turn R off A517 Belper to Ashbourne within 0.25m past

# EAST MIDLANDS

Hulland Ward into Dog Lane in 0.75m turn R SP Carsington. The site is on the R within 0.75m o/s 119251493. Open: 22 April - 30 September.

 (6m). **Rivendale Caravan & Leisure Park**, Buxton Road, Alsop-en-le-Dale, Ashbourne, Derbyshire DE6 1QU. 01335 310311. www.rivendalecaravanpark.co.uk. 25 acres of pasture and woodland. Close to Tissington Trail. Hardstanding with 16 amp supplies. New underfloor heated toilet and shower block. Cafe & bar now open. Static holiday homes for sale. Alan Rogers recommended. B&B rooms, yurts and hot tubs for hire. David Bellamy Gold Conservation Award. Heading N from Ashbourne, take the A515 towards Buxton. Find Rivendale after 6m on the right hand side. Open: 1 February - 2 January. ★★★★ BH&HPA

### Bakewell

(3m). **Bakewell Camping & Caravanning Club Site**, Hopping Farm, Youlgreave, Bakewell, Derbyshire DE45 1NA. 01629 636555. www.campingandcaravanningclub.co.uk. In the heart of the Peak National Park. 100 pitches in 14 acres. Local attractions include Speedwell Cavern in Castleton and Chatsworth House. Accepts all units. Non-members welcome. Own sanitation essential. Special deals available for families and backpackers. A6/B5056 after 0.5m turn R to Youlgreave, turn sharp L after church down Bradford lane, opposite George Hotel. 0.5m to sign turn R. Open: 1 April - 31 October. ★★★★ NCC

(4m). **Chatsworth Park Caravan Club Site**, Baslow, Bakewell, Derbyshire DE45 1PN. 01246 582226. www.caravanclub.co.uk. Set in an old walled garden on 1000-acre Chatsworth Estate with views of surrounding countryside. No entrance through Chatsworth Estate. Please arrive after 1pm due to congestion and bottleneck in area. Playground. Advance booking essential. Dog walk. Non-members welcome. Toilet block with privacy cubicles and laundry facilities. Baby/toddler washroom. MV service point. Service pitches available at a supplement. No tents. See website for standard directions to site. Open: All year. ★★★★★ NCC

(1m). **Greenhills Holiday Park**, Crowhill Lane, Bakewell, Derbyshire DE45 1PX. 01629 813052. www.greenhillsholidaypark.co.uk. Club house. Shop. Golf course 1m, shopping centre 12m, cinema 15m. From A6 (Buxton-Matlock), 0.25m E at Ashford-in-the-Water, turn S into Crowhill Lane, SP. Open: 1 February - 30 November. BH&HPA

### Belper

(1m). **The Firs Caravan Club Site**, Crich Lane, Belper, Derbyshire DE56 2JH. 01773 852913. www.caravanclub.co.uk. Level pitches and charming rural atmosphere. Good touring base for Derbyshire Dales and Peak District. Non-members and tent campers welcome. See website for standard directions to site. Open: 30 March - 5 November. ★★★★★ NCC

### Biggin by Hartington

(4m). **Waterloo Inn**, Main Street, Biggin by Hartington, Derbyshire SK17 0DH. 01298 84284. Inn on site. Shops 2m, railway 1m. Bus stop at the gates. PO, doctors, golf course and fishing nearby. About 0.25m from M5 J27. On Wellington to Willand road at Waterloo Cross. Open: All year.

### Bradwell

**Eden Tree House Caravan Park**, Eccles Lane, Bradwell, Derbyshire S33 9JT. 01433 623444. www.edentreecaravanpark.co.uk. Electric hook-ups. Free hot showers. All grass site. Within easy walking distance of shops. Booking advisable. Dogs on leads allowed on touring field only. Shops & PO 0.5m. Doctors 2m. Fishing, golf course 3m. Static caravans are privately owned and are not let out. Off B6049 at The Samuel Fox Inn in Bradwell. 9m from Bakewell and 8m Buxton. Open: 1 March - 31 October. BH&HPA

### Buxton

(6m). **Beech Croft Farm Camping and Caravan Park**, Beechcroft, Blackwell-in-the-Peak, Buxton, Derbyshire SK17 9TQ. 01298 85330. www.beechcroftfarm.net. Small quiet family run park located on the Pennine bridleway, between Buxton and Bakewell in Derbyshire. Ideal base for exploring the Peak District National Park. Off A6 midway between Buxton and Bakewell. SP. Open: All year. ★★★ BH&HPA

(0.75m). **Cold Springs Farm**, Manchester Road, Longhill, Buxton, Derbyshire SK17 6SS. 01298 22762. www.coldspringsfarm.co.uk. Working farm close to Buxton. Lovely views across Buxton & surrounding countryside. Ten minutes from Goyt Valley with walks & reservoir. Take the A5004 from town centre. Open: All year.

(2m). **Grin Low Caravan Club Site**, Grin Low Road, Ladmanlow, Buxton, Derbyshire SK17 6UJ. 01298 77735. www.caravanclub.co.uk. Landscaped site set in heart of Peak District National Park. Advance booking advised. Play area and play frame. Tents accepted. Most pitches are hardstanding. Dog walk nearby. Non-members welcome. Toilet block, laundry facilities, baby/toddler washroom. Motorhome service point. Golf nearby. See website for standard directions to site. Open: 23 March - 5 November. ★★★★★ NCC

(1m). **Lime Tree Park**, Dukes Drive, Buxton, Derbyshire SK17 9RP. 01298 22988. www.limetreeparkbuxton.co.uk. In a rural valley setting, though within 20mins walk of Buxton. Friendly site located on the edge of the historic spa town of Buxton, in the heart of the Peak District. Ideal walking and cycling. Off A515, 1m S of Buxton. Duke's Drive links A515 to A6. Open: 1 March - 31 October. ★★★★ BH&HPA

(7m). **Longnor Wood Caravan and Camping Park** (Tranquil Adults-only), Longnor, Buxton, Derbyshire SK17 0NG. 01298 83648. www.longnorwood.co.uk. Peaceful site in the heart of the country and central for many Peak District attractions including Chatsworth House, Hartington, Bakewell and the beautiful dales. Putting green, boules court and croquet. A site just for adults. Pubs, cafe/restaurants/takeaway meals nearby. David Bellamy Gold Conservation Award. On reaching Longnor crossroads follow site signs for 1.25m to site. Open: 1 March - 10 January. ★★★★ BH&HPA

(9m). **Newhaven Caravan Park**, Newhaven, Buxton, Derbyshire SK17 0DT. 01298 84300. www.newhavencaravanpark.co.uk. Modern, 30-acre site in the heart of the Peak National Park. Restaurant adjacent. Playroom. AA 3 pennants. Close to the High Peak Trail and Tissington Trail, historic house and the Derbyshire Dales. At junction A5012 and A515 halfway between Ashbourne and Buxton, entrance on A5012. Open: 1 March - 31 October. ★★★ BH&HPA NCC

# EAST MIDLANDS

(5m). **The Pomeroy Caravan and Camping Park**, Street House Farm, Pomeroy, Flagg, Buxton, Derbyshire SK17 9QG. 01298 83259. H&C to wash basins and showers. Hand and hairdryers and shaver points. Site fully lit. Adjoins 'High Peak Trail'. Central for Peak District National Park. The Caravan Club and The Camping & Caravanning club members are welcome. Owner supplied copy. On A515 adjoining High Peak Trail central site for Peak National Park. Ashbourne 16m. Open: 22 April - 31 October. ★★ 🏠🐕 6⚡ 30⛺ ⛺

## Castleton

(0.5m). **Losehill Caravan Club Site**, Castleton, Derbyshire S33 8WB. 01433 620636. www.caravanclub.co.uk. Features 81 hardstanding pitches and separate tent area. Facilities include a toilet block with privacy cubicles & a drying room. See website for directions. Open: All year. ★★★★★ NCC 🏠🐕 🚿♿ 81⚡ 81⛺ ⛺

(2.5m). **Rowter Farm**, Hope Valley, Castleton, Derbyshire S33 8WA. 01433 620271. www.peakdistrict-nationalpark.com. Flat field, partly sheltered overlooking Man Tor. Excellent for walkers and touring the Peak District. In Castleton (2.5m) 6 hotels, good range of shops and tearooms. Parking alongside units, reasonable rates. Owner supplied copy. W of Castleton off B6061. Open: 22 April - 31 October. 🏠🐕 5⚡ 5⛺ ⛺

## Chesterfield

**Poolsbrook Caravan Club Site**, Poolsbrook Country Park, Staveley, Chesterfield, Derbyshire S43 3LS. 01246 470659. www.caravanclub.co.uk. Set in the heart of 165 acre country park. Children's adventure play area, fishing lakes. Non-members welcome. No tents. See website for standard directions to site. Open: 30 March - 5 November. ★★★★★ NCC 🏠🐕 🚿♿ 86⚡ 86⛺

## Derby

(0.25m). **Beechwood Park**, Main Road, Elvaston, Thulston, Derby, Derbyshire DE72 3EQ. 07973 562689. www.beechwoodparkleisure.co.uk. Situated in 30 acres of idyllic green belt. 5 fishing lakes. Children's go-kart track. Shop on site and just 1m to village shops. Follow signs for Elvaston Castle, on B5010. Beechwood Park is 300yd from Castle entrance on opposite side of road. Open: All year. 🏠🐕 20⚡ 50⛺ ⛺

**Cavendish Caravan & Camping Site**, Derby Road, Doveridge, Derby, Derbyshire DE6 5JR. 01889 562092. Pub and food 100yd. Entrance to site is through double open gates across a closed garage forecourt. Dogs allowed on leads. On A50 in Doveridge midway between Derby and Stoke-on-Trent. 1.5m E of Uttoxeter. Open: Contact site direct. 🏠🐕 🚿♿ ⛺

(4m). **Elvaston Castle Caravan Club Site**, Borrowash Road, Elvaston, Derby, Derbyshire DE72 8WB. 01332 573735. www.caravanclub.co.uk. Very attractive site in well-kept 200-acre country park. Families will enjoy the castle, lake and large play area in the castle grounds. Advance booking essential. Toilet block. Non-members and tent campers welcome. Fishing and golf nearby. Ideal for walkers. Local attractions include Alton Towers, American Adventure, Tales of Robin Hood and Denby Pottery. Battery charging, gas, dog walk nearby. See website for standard directions to site. Open: 30 March - 5 November. ★★★ NCC 🏠🐕 44⚡ 44⛺ ⛺

## Glossop

**Crowden Camping & Caravanning Club Site**, Woodhead Road, Crowden, Glossop, Derbyshire SK13 1HZ. 01457 866057. www.campingandcaravanningclub.co.uk. 🏠🐕 ⛺

## Hayfield

**Hayfield Camping & Caravanning Club Site**, Kinder Road, Hayfield, Derbyshire SK22 2LE. 01663 745394. www.campingandcaravanningclub.co.uk. Site set on the banks of the River Sett, ideal for fell and moorland walkers. The National Trust Kinder Round Walk is ideal for the bird watcher and botanist. NO TOWED CARAVANS permitted. Non members welcome. Special deals available for families and backpackers. A624 - Glossop to Chapel en le Frith. Hayfield by-pass, follow wooden carved signs to site. 4m N of Chapel en Le Frith. 12m from Stockport. 5m from Glossop. Open: 1 April - 31 October. ★★★ NCC 🏠🐕 🚿♿ 90⚡ ⛺

## High Peak

(0.75m). **Ringstones Caravan Park**, Yeardsley Lane, Furness Vale, High Peak, Derbyshire SK23 7EB. 01663 732152. Beautifully situated, quiet site with lovely views of the Peak District. Small shop, PO, train station and bus stop all within 0.75m. Tennis, bowling, football pitch, 3 pubs within walking distance. 2m to supermarket, swimming pool, leisure centre. Golf, rock climbing nearby. Owner supplied copy. From Whaley Bridge, A6 to Furness Vale. Turn off A6 at Cantonese restaurant by pelican crossing then 0.75m up Yeardsley Lane. 10m from Buxton. 2m from Whaley Bridge. Open: 1 March - 31 October. 🏠🐕 🚿♿ 5⚡ 10⛺ 44⛺

## Hope Valley

**Coopers Camp & Caravan Site**, New Fold Farm, Hope Valley, Derbyshire S33 7ZD. 01433 670372. Turn R at Hope Church off A6187-5m to centre of Edale village. Open: All year. 🏠🐕 🚿♿ 120⚡ 15⛺ 11⛺

**Highfield Farm (Edale)**, Nr Upper Booth, Edale, Hope Valley, Derbyshire S33 7ZJ. 01433 670245. Convenient site for hill walking. Fees on application. Shops, PO, cafe & restaurant, golf within 2m. Doctor 7m. Owner supplied copy. Turn off A6187 (previously A625) at Hope Church. Take minor road to Edale, past turn for Edale Village. At bottom of hill turn R under viaduct and past picnic area. Open: All year. 🏠🐕 🚿♿ ⛺

**Laneside Caravan Site**, Laneside, Hope, Hope Valley, Derbyshire S33 6RR. 01433 620215. www.lanesidecaravanpark.co.uk. Level, riverside site surrounded by hills bordering village (shopping and 3 pubs). Laundry room. Central heated shower block. Boules courts, golf courses, horse riding and rock climbing close by. No aggressive breeds. No single sex or unaccompanied teenagers. Owner supplied copy. On A6187 Hathersage to Castleton. On Eastern border of Hope Village (200yd). 11m from Buxton. 8m from Bakewell. Open: 16 March - 11 November. 🏠🐕 🚿♿ 15⚡ 70⛺ 28⛺

(12m). **Stocking Farm Caravan Site**, Calver, Hope Valley, Derbyshire S32 3XA. 01433 630516. Shop, PO: 0.5m. Doctors: 2m. Dogs on leads allowed. Golf courses, Co-op Bakewell 5m. Morrison's Chesterfield 10m. Owner supplied copy. 5m from Bakewell. On A623. Follow the first two signs to Calver Mill then straight ahead. Open: 1 April - 31 October. 🏠🐕 🚿♿ 2⚡ 8⛺ 10⛺

(0.5m). **Swallowholme Caravan Park**, Station Road, Bamford, Hope Valley, Derbyshire S33 0BN. 01433 650981. Fishing and golf nearby. Shop 0.25m. Site unsuitable for children. Owner supplied copy. On A6013. 2m S of Ladybower Reservoir. Open: 1 March - 31 October. 🏠🐕 🚿♿ 25⚡ 45⛺

(5m). **Waterside Farm**, Barber Booth Road, Edale, Hope Valley, Derbyshire S33 7ZL. 01433 670215. Small quiet

# EAST MIDLANDS

family run site in the Peak District with wonderful views. Cafe, shop, pub and PO within 1m. Owner supplied copy. Off the A6 bypass at Chapel-en-le-Frith, SP Rushop Edge, Edale. Open: 22 April - 30 September.

### Isley Walton

(8m). Donington Park Farmhouse Hotel & Caravan Park, Melbourne Road, Isley Walton, Derbyshire DE74 2RN. 01332 862409. www.parkfarmhouse.co.uk. Golf course and Donington Park Grand Prix Collection half mile away. Open all year except Christmas. At exit 23A & 24 of M1, take the A453 past East Midlands airport. Turn right at Isley Walton, site is 0.5 mile on right hand side. Open: All year.

### Matlock

(5m). Barn Farm, Barn Farm, Birchover, Matlock, Derbyshire DE4 2BL. 01629 650245. Catering van weekends only. Working farm site. Sauna, a lot of walks, luxury 2 person suite, marquee for hire, caravan storage. Recommended by Peak District online, 4 luxury camping barns. Off B524 and A6. Bakewell 5m. Shop, restaurant and pub in village of Birchover 250yd from site. Open: 1 April - 31 October.

(4m). Birchwood Farm, Wirksworth Road, Whatstandwell, Matlock, Derbyshire DE4 5HS. 01629 822280. www.birchwoodfcp.co.uk. Showers, H&C wash basins, shaver point. Hairdryer point. Launderette. Calor Gas sales. Milk, eggs and confectionery for sale. Leave A6 at Whatstandwell, take B5035 Wirksworth Road. 1.25m. Open: 25 March - 31 October. ★★ BH&HPA

(6m). Haytop Country Park, Whatstandwell, Matlock, Derbyshire DE4 5HP. 01773 852063. 65-acre country park with river and woodland. 1m of river frontage. Fishing, boating and canoeing. Long stay sites available. Near train station. 2.5m to PO, general stores and garage. Owner supplied copy. Entrance at Whatstandwell Bridge off A6, from North Cross Bridge and turn L, do not pass telephone kiosk, from South Cross pass telephone kiosk then R before bridge. Open: All year. BH&HPA

(2.5m). Lickpenny Touring Park, Lickpenny Lane, Tansley, Matlock, Derbyshire DE4 5GF. 01629 583040. www.lickpennycaravanpark.co.uk. Fishing

nearby. Cafe/garden centre 500yd. Local shops, doctor, PO 3m. Bus service at end of lane. Train station in Matlock. M1, J28. A38 SP Derby, take Alfreton exit and immediately L turn to A615 for 8m, turn R on to Lickpenny Lane SP on R. Open: All year. ★★★★ BH&HPA

(3m). Pinegroves Caravan Park, High Lane, Tansley, Matlock, Derbyshire DE4 5BG. 01629 534815. Mainly adult site - peaceful and quiet. Sailing, golf, shopping all within 3m. New static caravans for sale also good quality second hand statics. Seasonal pitches for tourers available. Via M1 J28, A38 and A615 towards Matlock through Wessington; 2m, 2nd L at crossroads. Or via A6 Matlock-A615 Alfreton through Tanasley, 1m, 2nd R at crossroads. Open: 1 April - 31 October.

### Shardlow

Shardlow Marina Caravan Park, London Road, Shardlow, Derbyshire DE72 2GL. 01332 792832. www.shardlowmarina.co.uk. 35 mixed pitches in total. Bar, restaurant and shower block. Fishing. Doctor, hospital within 5m. PO in village. Shop in village. AA 3 pennants. Static holiday homes for sale. Max 1 child per unit only. Owner supplied copy. Leave M1 on exit 24 on to A50, exit J1 at Roundabout take exit to Shardlow. Cavendish Bridge, site 1m on R on A6. 5m from Derby. Open: 1 March - 31 January. BH&HPA

### Swadlincote

(5m). Beehive Woodland Lakes, Woodland Lakes, Rosliston, Swadlincote, Derbyshire DE12 8HZ. 01283 763981. www.beehivefarm-woodlandlakes.co.uk. Situated in 66 acres of woodland. Modern amenity block. Offers: fishing, walks, conservation areas, animal farm, playgroup/play area and tea room. Local services within 0.5m: PO, village pubs, grocery store, newsagent. Local attractions: Alton Towers, ski centre, Uttoxeter Racecourse, Donington Park. Follow brown signs from Linton Road. Open: 10 January - 18 December.
★★★ BH&HPA

(5m). Conkers Camping & Caravanning Club Site, 50 Bath Lane, Moira, Swadlincote, Derbyshire DE12 6BD. 01283 224925. www.campingandcaravanningclub.co.uk. Our club site at Conkers is in the heart of the country's youngest forest. Next door to the award winning attraction of the same name. Walkers and cyclists see The Ashby

Woulds Heritage Trail. Located just off the A444 Conkers is accessible from the M42, A50 and also the M1. Open: 1 January - 31 December. ★★★★ NCC

## LEICESTERSHIRE

### Barrow upon Soar

(4m). Meadow Farm Marina and Caravan Park, Huston Close, Sileby Road, Barrow upon Soar, Leicestershire LE12 8NB. 01509 812215. Picturesque site in 32 acres by the river Soar. Licensed Club house/free membership. Hot showers. Centrally heated toilet and showers. Free fishing when on site. Supermarket close by. Take A6 from Loughborough or Leicester then four left turns off the dual carriageway for Mountsorrel, Sileby and Barrow, turnoff brings you to gates 1.5m from A6. Open: All year.

### Hinckley

(5m). Wolvey (Villa Farm) Caravan Park, Wolvey, Hinckley, Leicestershire LE10 3HF. 01455 220493. www.wolveycaravanpark.itgo.com. AA 3 pennants 75%. Fishing on site, putting green. Owner supplied copy. A46 Coventry to Leicester then B4065 (old A46). 0.5m W of Wolvey, M6 exit 2, M69 exit 1. Open: All year.

### Lutterworth

(4.5m). Stanford Park Caravan Site, Stanford Hall, Lutterworth, Leicestershire LE17 6DH. 01788 860250. www.stanfordhall.co.uk. No sanitation. MV service point. Fishing and golf nearby. Designated dog walk through Estate Woodland. Visitors staying on the site have free admission to Stanford Hall Grounds during the normal opening times, except on some Event Days. Leave M1 J20 on to A427. At traffic lights turn L on to A426, in 0.15m turn L SP Swinford, in 3.2m at B5414 junction, turn R, then L into Stanford Road. OS map ref - 140: SP582790. Open: All year.

### Whetstone

(6m). Whetstone Gorse Farm, Whetstone Gorse East, Whetstone, Leicestershire LE8 6LX. 01162 773796. www.whetstonegorse.co.uk. Hardstanding for winter/grass pitches summer all with electric points. Laundry facilities (washing machine & dryer). Good ladies, gents and showers/wet room with toilet for disabled people.

Fishing on site (coarse fishing), 4 pools, 5 acres of water. Golf, shops inc PO 2m. Swimming 4m. Good eating out pubs close by. Rally field 400 van capacity with entertainment licence. Owner supplied copy. 6m from Leicester, on A426 to Blaby then L for Countesthorpe, take Willoughby Road out of Countesthorpe in about 2m turn R down Farm Track. Open: All year. **6 20**

## NOTTINGHAMSHIRE

### Edwinstowe

**(5m). Sherwood Forest Holiday Park, Gorsethorpe, Edwinstowe, Nottinghamshire NG21 9HW.** *01623 823132.* www.sherwoodforestholidaypark.co.uk. A quiet retreat in the heart of Robin Hood country. Good facilities. Special area for dog exercising on leads. Close to many places of interest. Privately owned and managed with a resident warden. 4m NE of Mansfield via B6030 and N to Warsop. Open: All year. **BH&HPA** **30 150**

### Gunthorpe

**(3m). Riverdale Park, Gunthorpe Bridge, Gunthorpe, Nottinghamshire NG14 7EY.** *01332 810818.* From Nottingham take A612 to Lowdham, turn R on to A6097 to village of Gunthorpe, by river Trent. Nottingham 6m. Radcliffe-on-Trent 3m. GS. Open: 1 March - 6 January. **BH&HPA** **5 14**

### Holme Pierrepont

**(3.5m). Holme Pierrepont (NWSC) Caravan & Camping Park, National Water Sports Centre, Adbolton Lane, Holme Pierrepont, Nottinghamshire NG12 2LU.** *01159 824721.* www.nwsc-notts.com. 270 acres country park, water sports available if pre-booked; site is 28 acres of flat grass. Rallies welcome. Close to river, fishing in river and ponds. Owner supplied copy. 3.5m SE of Nottingham via A52 Grantham road. Site SP National Water Sports Centre. Open: All year. **360**

### Mansfield

**(1.5m). Redbrick House Hotel, Peafield Lane, Edwinstowe, Mansfield, Nottinghamshire NG20 0EW.** *01623 846499.* Adult only site. Secluded site at the rear of the hotel with its public bars and restaurant. Set in the heart of Sherwood Forest on the A6075, 4m from Edwinstowe visitors centre. Open: All year. **10 50**

**(1m). Tall Trees Park CL, Tall Trees, Old Mill Lane, Forest Town, Mansfield, Nottinghamshire NG19 0JP.** *01623 626503.* www.talltreestouringpark.co.uk. Mains services. Pubs, restaurants, takeaways, shops all within walking distance. From Mansfield, take A60 Worksop Road for about 0.5m then turn R at traffic lights into Old Mill Lane. Open: All year. ★★★ **BH&HPA** **15 15**

### Newark-on-Trent

**Carlton-on-Trent Caravan and Camping Park, Ossington Road, Carlton-on-Trent, Newark-on-Trent, Nottinghamshire NG23 6NU.** *01530 835662.*

**(5m). Milestone Caravan Park, Great North Road, Cromwell, Newark-on-Trent, Nottinghamshire NG23 6JE.** *01636 821244.* www.milestonepark.co.uk. Level site with hard standings. On site calor gas, laundry, showers, telephone, dishwashing facilities, razor sockets, tourist information. 2 mins walk to local shop. Fishing on site. Golf 5m. Owner supplied copy. From the north on the A1, approx 7m south of Markham Moor service area. From the south 5m further on the A1 from Newark. Open: All year. ★★★★★ **BH&HPA NCC** **120**

**(1m). Smeaton's Lakes Touring Caravan Park, Great North Road, South Muskham, Newark-on-Trent, Nottinghamshire NG23 6ED.** *01636 605088.* www.smeatonslakes.co.uk. 90 acres parkland. 1m to nearest town for PO, doctor, restaurant etc. Takeaway meals delivered to site. On A616 close to A46 to A1. Open: All year. **120**

### Nottingham

**(3m). Hayes Farm, Hucknall Road, Newstead, Nottingham, Nottinghamshire NG15 0BD.** *01159 632755.* www.hayesfarm.co.uk. Club. Bar. Entertainment. Playground. Adjacent river Crouch and boating. Off A132 Wickford to South Woodham Ferrers. Open: 1 March - 31 October. **NCC** **70**

### Radcliffe-on-Trent

**(5m). Thornton's Holt Camping Park, Stragglethorpe, Radcliffe-on-Trent, Nottinghamshire NG12 2JZ.** *01159 332125.* www.thorntons-holt.co.uk. Family camping park with a rural atmosphere. Indoor heated swimming pool. Play area. 35 hardstandings. 150 metre to pub and restaurant and local bus stop. SP from A46 and A52. Open: All year. **BH&HPA** **155**

### Ratcliffe-on-Soar

**(1m). Redhill Marina, Red Hill Marine Ltd, Ratcliffe-on-Soar, Nottinghamshire NG11 0EB.** *01509 672770.* www.redhill-marina.co.uk. Adjoining marina. Fishing. Next to East Midland Parkway Railway Station. Owner supplied copy. 3m from Kegworth. Open: All year. **BH&HPA** **5**

### Retford

**(0.75m). Hallcroft Fishery & Caravan Park, Hallcroft Road, Retford, Nottinghamshire DN22 7RA.** *01777 710448.* www.hallcroftfishery.co.uk. The park is 80 acres. There are 5 lakes for coarse fishing totalling 380+ pegs. A fully equipped and stocked tackle shop on site. Cafe/restaurant and licensed bar. Also cater for larger corporate events including large rallies. Open all year for tourers, 11 months for statics. M1, J30 take Worksop Road, then to Retford, Retford centre. A638 to Bawtry. Pass Honda garage on L and King/Miller PH on R. Turn R Hallcroft Industrial Estate. Open: All year. **15 15** **22**

### Sutton-in-Ashfield

**(3m). Teversal Camping & Caravanning Club Site, Silverhill Lane, Teversal, Sutton-in-Ashfield, Nottinghamshire NG17 3JJ.** *01623 551838* . www.campingandcaravanningclub.co.uk. Set in 6 acres of glorious countryside Teversal gives you the chance to explore both


**Tall Trees Touring Park Mansfield, Nottinghamshire**
Quiet Park in rural location just 1 mile from Mansfield
Caravans, Motorhomes and Tents £12.50 per night
**Tel: 01623 626503 Website: www.talltreestouringpark.co.uk**
TALL TREES TOURING PARK

# EAST MIDLANDS / WEST MIDLANDS

Nottinghamshire and neighbouring Derbyshire. The Silverwood Country Park is opposite the site, wireless internet is available and car hire. M1, J29 follow A6175 L on to B6039, on to 36014, then L at Carnarvon Arms. Open: All year. ★★★★★ NCC ⌂ ♨ ↻ ⚐ ♘ ☼ ✤ ⚒ ⚠ ⚓ ⚐ 126⛺ 126⛟ ⛁

### Tuxford

(16m). **Greenacres Caravan & Touring Park (Tuxford), Lincoln Road, Tuxford, Nottinghamshire NG22 0JN.** *01777 870264.* www.greenacres-tuxford.co.uk. Retford 6m. Ideal for night halts and for touring Robin Hood country. Tourist info centre. Euro payments accepted. Local shops, pubs etc. (nearest pub 100yd). Static holiday homes for sale and hire. A1(N) leave at Tuxford sign. At village centre turn R (church opposite). After Fountain PH, site on L in 50yd. (A6075). A1(S) leave at Tuxford local services sign follow slip road to 'T' junction, turn R, SP Lincoln (A57). After Fountain PH site on L in 50yd (A6075). Open: 16 March - 31 October. ★★★ BH&HPA ⌂ ♨ ⚒ ⚠ ⚓ ⚐ ✤ ⚒ ⚠ ⚓ 40⛺ ⛁ 39⛟

(12m). **Orchard Park Touring Site (Tuxford), Marnham Road, Tuxford, Nottinghamshire NG22 0PY.** *01777 870228.* www.orchardcaravanpark.co.uk. Quiet, sheltered, level site. Ideal for Sherwood Forest. Modern amenities block with facilities for disabled. AA 3 pennants. David Bellamy Silver Conservation Award. 1.25m SE of A1, off A6075 Lincoln road. Turn R in 0.75m on to Marnham Road. Site on R in 0.75m. Open: 17 March - 17 November. BH&HPA ⌂ ♨ ⚒ ⚠ ⚓ ⚐ ✤ ⚒ ⚠ ⚓ 10⛺ 50⛟ ⛁

### Worksop

(4.5m). **Clumber Park Caravan Club Site, Lime Tree Avenue, Clumber Park, Worksop, Nottinghamshire S80 3AE.** *01909 484758.* www.caravanclub.co.uk. 20-acre site set in 4000 acres of parkland where you can walk, cycle or ride. Barbecues with permission only. Dog walk. Advance booking essential Bank Holidays and weekends. MV waste. Play equipment. Toilet blocks. Laundry facilities. Baby/toddler washroom. Veg prep. Ideal for families, quiet and peaceful off peak. Significant interest nearby. Golf, fishing and NCN cycle path all within 5m. Good area for walking. Non-members welcome No tents. See website for standard directions to site. Open: All year. ★★★★★ NCC ⌂ ♨ ⚒ ⚠ ⚓ ⚐ ✤ ⚒ ⚠ ⚓ 180⛺ 180⛟

(0.25m). **Riverside Caravan Park (Worksop), Central Avenue, Worksop, Nottinghamshire S80 1ER.** *01909 474118.* www.riversideworksop.co.uk. A level site with waterside walks. Secluded yet adjacent to town centre. Everything within walking distance up to 0.5m. Dogs allowed on short lead only. Owner supplied copy. At roundabout JA57/A60 Mansfield, follow international site signs to town centre onto Newcastle Ave. 1st L onto Stubbing Lane, R onto Central Avenue, next L to site. Open: All year. ★★★★ BH&HPA ⌂ ♨ ⚒ ⚠ ⚓ ⚐ ✤ ⚒ ⚠ 60⛟ ⛁

## RUTLAND
### Oakham

(4m). **Greendale Farm Caravan and Camping Park (Tranquil adults-only), Pickwell Lane, Whissendine, Oakham, Rutland LE15 7LB.** *01664 474516.* www.rutlandgreendale.co.uk. Small, quiet ADULT ONLY site, set in rolling countryside. 6m from Rutland Water and 0.5m from village of Whissendine with 2 pubs and bistro. Ideal for walking, cycling, bird watching. Wi-Fi. Amazing facilities for such a small park! England in Excellence awards 06/07/08. David Bellamy Gold Conservation Award. Caravans must approach from A606. Take the 3rd turning to Whissendine from Melton Mowbray or the 2nd from Oakham or bypass opposite brown signs, then 0.5m on R. Open: 10 April - 25 September. ★★★★ BH&HPA ⌂ ♨ ⚒ ⚠ ⚓ ⚐ ✤ ⚒ ⚠ ⚓ 7⛺ 13⛟ 3⛁

(2m). **Ranksborough Hall Caravan Park, Hillground Park, Langham, Oakham, Rutland LE15 7JR.** *01572 722984.* www.ranksboroughhall.com. PO, picnic area on site. Free bus to local supermarket. Medical practice/hospital/pharmacy 2m. Bowling green 2m. 3 golf courses nearby. Fishing, bird watching, sailing, cycling 4m. On A606 Melton to Oakham. In village of Langham. Open: All year. BH&HPA ⌂ ♨ ⚒ ⚠ ⚓ ⚐ ✤ ⚒ ⚠ ⚓ 40⛺ ⛁

(5m). **PREMIER PARKS 2011. Rutland Caravan And Camping Park, Greetham, Oakham, Rutland LE15 7FN.** *01572 813520.* www.rutlandcaravanandcamping.co.uk. Wireless Internet site coverage. Site next to Greetham village with 3 pubs all serving food, shop, garage, garden centre, walk to from site and Viking Way footpath. Golf course, fishing, horse riding all within 1m; Rutland water 4m with fishing, cycling, rock climbing, butterflies. AA graded 3 pennants. From A1 N or S bound turn off on to B668 towards Greetham village. Turn R at crossroads before the village and take 2nd L to site. Open: All year. ⌂ ♨ ⚒ ⚠ ⚓ ⚐ ✤ ⚒ ⚠ ⚓ ⛟ ⛁

## HEREFORDSHIRE
### Brilley

(6.5m). **Penlan Caravan Park, Brilley, Herefordshire HR3 6JW.** *01497 831485.* www.penlancaravanpark.co.uk. A small, secluded site with magnificent views, peace and space. National Trust farm. Advanced notice of arrival essential. Brochure available. 3m to nearest shops. 4.5m to Kington (golf course, market town). Site situated 0.5m from Kington to Whitney on Wye by road, 4.5m SW of Kington. Open: 6 April - 31 October. ★★★★ ⌂ ♨ ⚒ ⚠ ⚓ ⚐ ✤ ⚒ ⚠ ⚓ 10⛺ 10⛟ 10⛁

### Bromyard

(1m). **The Rock Caravan Park, Tenbury Road, Bromyard, Herefordshire HR7 4LP.** *01885 482630.* www.therockcaravanpark.co.uk. Ideally situated for walking, fishing, golf, bowls, tennis, archery or exploring the heart of the country. Take Tenbury road out of Bromyard, 1m and park is on right. Open: 1 February - 31 December. BH&HPA ⌂ ♨ ⚒ ⚠ ⚓ ⚐ ✤ ⚒ 4⛺ 6⛟ ⛁ 50⛁

### Craswall

**Old Mill Camp Site (Craswall), Craswall, Herefordshire HR2 0PN.** *01981 510226.* Quiet camping site near river and the Offa's Dyke path. At the foot of the Black Mountains. Owner supplied copy. 8m off the A465 at Pandy. Open: 1 March - 31 October. ⌂ ♨ ⚒ ⚠ ⚓ ⚐ ✤ ⚒ ⚠ ⛟ ⛁

### Golden Valley

(2m). **Poston Mill Park (Best of British), Peterchurch, Golden Valley, Herefordshire HR2 0SF.** *01981 550225.* www.bestparks.co.uk. Award winning quality park for touring, walking, fishing. Restaurant and shop on site. Shops, PO, doctor 1m. Bus stops at entrance. Environmentally friendly, sustainable business. Dogs welcome. David Bellamy Gold Conservation Award. On B4348 midway Hereford and Hay-on-Wye. Open: All year. ★★★★★ BH&HPA NCC ⌂ ♨ ⚒ ⚠ ⚓ ⚐ ✤ ⚒ ⚠ ⚓ 30⛺ ⛁ 117⛟

### Hereford

(4m). **Cuckoo's Corner Campsite, Moreton-on-Lugg, Hereford, Herefordshire HR4 8AH.** *01432 760204.* www.cuckooscorner.com. ADULTS ONLY SITE. 15 hardstandings of which 5 are 45 feet long. Free wireless broadband. (Takeaway food and shop 0.5m). Fishing on Lugg and Wye. Easily accessible off A49. 4m N of Hereford. Open: All year. ⌂ ♨ ⚒ ⚠ ⚓ ⚐ ✤ ⚒ ⚠ ⚓ 19⛺ 19⛟ ⛁

# WEST MIDLANDS

**(5m). Lucksall Caravan And Camping Park, Lucksall, Mordiford, Hereford, Herefordshire HR1 4LP.** *01432 870213.* www.lucksallpark.co.uk. Level, non-commercialised. Fishing, walking, shop. Canoeing (hire). New static caravans for sale. David Bellamy Gold Conservation Award. Off B4224. Between Hereford and Ross on Wye. Bordered by river Wye. Open: 1 March - 30 November. ★★★★★ BH&HPA ♦ ♣ ♠ ♥ ♪ ♫ ◘ ♠ ♣ × ♠ ♣ ♦ 120⛺ 120⛿ △ 25⛽

**(10m). Moorhampton Caravan Club Site, The Old Station, Moorhampton, Hereford, Herefordshire HR4 7BE.** *01544 318594.* www.caravanclub.co.uk. A quiet little site in heart of Herefordshire countryside. Dog walk on site. Toilet blocks. Privacy cubicles. Laundry facilities. Veg prep. MV service point. Golf nearby. See website for standard directions to site. 10m from Hereford. Open: 30 March - 1 October. NCC ♦ ♣ ♠ ♥ ♪ ♫ ◘ ♠ ♣ 47⛺ 47⛿

**(2.5m). The Old Post Office, Withington, Hereford, Herefordshire HR1 3NN.** *01432 820600.* Small level touring site beside the river Irt. Fishing on site. Bridge Inn/Hotel nearby. Close to miniature railway and ancient castle. 2.5m from Wasdale Lake, 5m from sea, golf and doctor. 3m from PO, shops, riding, diving. Laundry, washer, dryer available. AA 3 pennants. A595 to Holmbrook, 2.5m to Santon Bridge, over bridge from Bridge Inn. Open: All year. ♦ ♣ ♠ ♥ ♪ ♫ ◘ ♠ ♣ ♦ 10⛺ 5⛿ △

## Leominster

**(5m). Arrow Bank Holiday Park (Adults only), Nun House Farm, Eardisland, Leominster, Herefordshire HR6 9BG.** *01544 388312.* www.arrowbankholidaypark.co.uk. River fishing on site. Quiet & peaceful landscaped park, 4mins walk to 'Black & White' Tudor village. Supermarket, golf courses, swimming pool 4-5m. Cinema 15m. Sales of private caravans & country lodges. David Bellamy Silver Conservation Award. Off A44 Leominster to Rhayader, R fork at Barons Cross garage continue for about 4m, 100yd after Eardisland sign turn R along private drive to junction, park opposite. Open: 1 March - 7 January. ★★★★★ BH&HPA ♦ ♣ ♠ ♥ ♪ ♫ ◘ ♠ ♣ 6⛺ 30⛿ △ 3⛽

**(6m). Pearl Lake Leisure Park, Shobdon, Leominster, Herefordshire HR6 9NQ.** *01568 708326.* www.bestparks.co.uk/PearlLake. Set in 80 acres of parkland, surrounded by beautiful countryside, this family-run, 5 star park has something for everyone. Exclusive 9-hole, 2,300 yard golf course, 15 acres fishing lake, woodland walks, children's play area, bar and restaurant. Short walk to village shop. Award winning park. David Bellamy Gold Conservation Award. On the B4362, on the Presteigne edge of the village of Shobdon, NW of Leominster. Open: 1 March - 30 November. ★★★★★ BH&HPA ♦ ♣ ♠ ♥ ♪ ♫ ◘ ♠ ♣ × ♠ ♣ ♦ 5⛺ 15⛿ △ 202⛽

 **Townsend Touring Park, Townsend Farm, Pembridge, Leominster, Herefordshire HR6 9HB.** *01544 388527.* www.townsendfarm.co.uk. Spacious 12 acre 60 pitch park. Luxurious facilities block showers, wash cubicles, toilets, disabled bathroom, family bathroom, laundry room. All fully serviced pitches. Lake, amenity and picnic area. On site farm shop and butchery. Off the A44 at Pembridge. Open: 1 March - 17 January. ★★★★★ NCC ♦ ♣ ♠ ♥ ♪ ♫ ◘ ♠ ♣ 60⛺ 60⛿ △

## Little Tarrington

**(7m). Hereford Camping & Caravanning Club Site, Little Tarrington, Herefordshire HR1 4JA.** *01432 890243.* www.campingandcaravanningclub.co.uk. Set in idyllic rural location and perfect spot for relaxing, fishing, walking and exploring the Malvern Hills and Wye Valley. David Bellamy Gold Conservation Award. M50, J2, Ledbury A438 SP Tarrington (about 7m). Second turning R. Site 200yd on R. Open: 3 March - 31 October. ★★★★★ BH&HPA NCC ♦ ♣ ♠ ♥ ♪ ♫ ◘ ♠ ♣ 102⛿ △

## Ross-on-Wye

**(0.25m). Broadmeadow Caravan & Camping Park, Broad Meadows, Ross-on-Wye, Herefordshire HR9 7BW.** *01989 768076.* www.broadmeadow.info. Coarse fishing available on site. Supermarket within 4mins walk from site. Town about 10mins from site, where pubs and refreshments are open. PO in town centre. Local hospital and doctors are nearby. Adjacent to A40 relief road. Access is obtained from the Pancake roundabout off the relief road turning into Ross and taking 1st R into Ashburton Estate Road, following road and turning R just before the roundabout. Open: 25 March - 2 October. ★★★★★ BH&HPA ♦ ♣ ♠ ♥ ♪ ♫ ◘ ♠ ♣ 150⛺ 150⛿ △

**(6m). Sterrett's Caravan Park, Symonds Yat (West), Ross-on-Wye, Herefordshire HR9 6BY.** *01594 832888.* Rural location. Boat trips. Traditional country pub. Adjacent recreation area. Fishing. Laundrette. Holiday homes for sale and for hire. For brochure: 01594 832888. No pets in hire caravans. A40 midway Monmouth to Ross-on-Wye turn off at Whitchurch, SP Symonds Yat (W). Open: 1 February - 30 November. ★★★★★ BH&HPA ♦ ♣ ♠ ♥ ♪ ♫ ◘ ♠ ♣ 8⛺ △ 86⛽

**(2m). The Yew Tree Park R, Peterstow, Ross-on-Wye, Herefordshire HR9 6JZ.** *01625 599545.* BH&HPA ♦ ♣ ♠ ♥

# SHROPSHIRE
## Bishops Castle

**(5m). The Green Caravan Park, Wentnor, Bishops Castle, Shropshire SY9 5EF.** *01588 650605.* www.green-caravanpark.co.uk. Long Mynd is unsuitable for caravans. Peaceful riverside park set in the Shropshire hills, an Area of Outstanding Natural Beauty. Superb walks. Excellent birdlife. Dog walk on site. Pub at site entrance. Within easy reach of Shrewsbury, Ludlow and Ironbridge. David Bellamy Gold Conservation Award. Follow brown tourist signs from A488 and A489. Open: 30 March - 31 October. BH&HPA ♦ ♣ ♠ ♥ ♪ ♫ ◘ ♠ ♣ × ♠ ♣ ♦ 10⛺ 60⛿ △ 21⛽

## Bridgnorth

**(2m). Stanmore Hall Touring Park (Caravan Club Affiliated Site), Stourbridge Road, Bridgnorth, Shropshire WV15 6DT.** *01746 761761.* www.morris-leisure.co.uk. CARAVAN CLUB AFFILIATED SITE. Set in beautiful grounds, the park takes full advantage of the mature trees and two-acre lake with its water lilies and resident peacocks. Toilet blocks, laundry facilities and MV service point. Play area, shop and dog walk on site. Fishing and golf nearby. Facilities for disabled. Ideal for families. Quiet and peaceful off-peak. From Bridgnorth on A458 to Stourbridge. Open: All year. ★★★★★ BH&HPA NCC ♦ ♣ ♠ ♥ ♪ ♫ ◘ ♠ ♣ ♦ 131⛿ △

**(1m). The Riverside Caravan Park, Kidderminster Road, Bridgnorth, Shropshire WV15 6BY.** *01746 765858.* www.theriversidecaravanpark.co.uk. Quiet park 10mins walk from low town Bridgnorth. Tourers park right on River Bank with views of the river Severn and Severn Valley Railway. Club-pub on the park open weekends during the season. Owner supplied copy. On A442 Kidderminster to Bridgnorth. Open: 1 March - 31 January. NCC ♦ ♣ ♠ ♥ ♪ ♫ ◘ 8⛺ 218⛿

## Church Stretton

**(2m). Small Batch Camping Site, Little Stretton, Church Stretton, Shropshire**

# WEST MIDLANDS

SY6 6PW. *01694 723358*. www.small-batch-camping.webeden.co.uk. 2 pubs nearby. Shop, PO, doctor 2m. Dogs must be on lead. N to S turn R of A49 for Little Stretton A49-B5477 second L. Then R through stream to site. Open: 1 April - 30 September.

### Craven Arms

(3m). **Engine & Tender Inn**, Broome, Craven Arms, Shropshire SY7 0NT. *01588 660275*. Pub food and children's room. Shower. Owner supplied copy. B4368 W from Craven Arms for 2m then S on B4367 for 1m. Open: All year.

### Ellesmere

(4m). **Fernwood Caravan Park**, Lyneal, Ellesmere, Shropshire SY12 0QF. *01948 710221*. www.fernwoodpark.co.uk. Site 22 acres with 40 acres of woodland adjacent, open to caravanners. Own lake with wildfowl & fishing. AA 4 pennants. RAC. David Bellamy Gold Conservation Award. Off B5063. Open: 1 March - 30 November. ★★★★★ BH&HPA NCC

### Ludlow

(1m). **Ludlow Caravan Park**, Overton Road, Ludlow, Shropshire SY8 4AD. Brand new 20 acre well-screened site located on the banks of the River Teme. Good access to the A49, within walking distance of Ludlow town. Off the A49 near Richards Castle. Open:

(5m). **Orleton Rise Holiday Home Park**, Green Lane, Orleton, Ludlow, Shropshire SY8 4JE. *01584 831617*. Immaculately kept, quiet, spacious, set in 10 acres of parkland with open countryside all around. Full facilities. Take B4361 Ludlow to Leominster road to Orleton. Turn R at Maidenhead Inn. Green Lane, continue up to Park. Open: 1 March - 31 January. ★★★★ BH&HPA

(6m). **Westbrook Park**, Little Hereford, Ludlow, Shropshire SY8 4AU. *01584 711280*. www.bestparks.co.uk. A beautiful kept traditional quiet touring campsite in a cider orchard on the banks of the river Teme, with 0.5m fishing, local pub with walking distance. Lovely walks off park. Every pitch has its own full services. Special rates for mid week and longer stays. Just off A456 first on L up lane between Little Hereford Bridge and large house. A beautiful kept traditional quiet touring campsite in a cider orchard on the banks of the river Teme, with 0.5m fishing, local pub with walking distance. Lovely walks off park. Every pitch has its own full services. Special rates for mid week and longer stays. Open: 1 March - 30 November. BH&HPA

### Much Wenlock

(2.5m). **Presthope Caravan Club Site**, Stretton Road, Much Wenlock, Shropshire TF13 6DQ. *01746 785234*. www.caravanclub.co.uk. Set in beautiful countryside ideal for naturalists with abundant wildlife on site. Own sanitation required. Chemical toilet disposal point. Advance booking essential all Bank Holidays. Non-members welcome. No tents. Some hardstandings. Steel awning pegs required. Gas and Gaz. Fishing nearby. Good area for walking. See website for standard directions to site. Open: 30 March - 1 October. ★★★ NCC

### Newport

**King's Head Park Homes R**, Green Lane, Newport, Shropshire TF10 7LG. *01952 812661*. Located in Newport. 12m to Stafford and 10m to Telford. Open: All year. BH&HPA

### Oswestry

(8m). **Oswestry Camping & Caravanning Club Site**, Cranberry Moss, Kinnerley, Oswestry, Shropshire SY10 8DY. *01743 741118*. www.campingandcaravanningclub.co.uk. Once a vital frontier between England and Wales, Oswestry is now a vibrant market town. Local attractions include Whittington Castle, Shrewsbury Abbey and Wroxeter Roman city. Wi-Fi available. Turn off the A5 at the roundabout at the north end of the dual carriageway, signed B4396 (Knockin). Open: All year. ★★★★★ NCC

(10m). **Royal Hill Caravan Park** (Adults only), Edgerley, Oswestry, Shropshire SY10 8ES. *01743 741772*. royalhillcaravanpark.co.uk. Public telephone. Features within easy reach. Rivers Severn and Vyrnwy, Llangollen and Welsh Hills, Offa's Dyke, Towns of Shrewsbury, Oswestry and Welshpool. Owner supplied copy. Off A5. Open: All year

### Shrewsbury

(1.5m). **Beaconsfield Farm**, Upper Battlefield, Shrewsbury, Shropshire SY4 4AA. *01939 210370*. www.beaconsfield-farm.co.uk. ADULTS ONLY. Traditional A La Carte restaurant. Indoor swimming pool & steam room, coarse fishing pool. AA 5 pennant, Best of British Park. Golf 3m. 0.5m N of Shrewsbury on A49. Open: All year. ★★★★★ BH&HPA NCC

**Brow Farm Campsite**, Ratlinghope, Shrewsbury, Shropshire SY5 0SR. *01588 650641*. www.browfarmcampsite.co.uk. Quiet farm site. Pub 1m. PO, doctors, shops in Church Stretton 4m. Gliding field 3m. 4m west of Church Stretton. 12m south of Shrewsbury. Next to Ratlinghope Church. Open: All year.

(6m). **Cartref Caravan Park**, Ford Heath, Shrewsbury, Shropshire SY5 9GD. *01743 821688*. www.cartrefcaravansite.co.uk. Small, level site. Peaceful countryside. Dogs allowed on leads. Dish washing area. Free showers. Hot water in basins. Cafe/restaurant, shop available nearby. From Shrewsbury bypass A5, take A458 Welshpool for 2 miles. SP from Ford village or take B4386 Montgomery road for 2m to Cruckton crossroads (site signposted). Now SP from A5 Shrewsbury by-pass on Montgomery junction B4386. Open: 22 April - 31 October.

**Ebury Hill Camping & Caravanning Club Site**, Ring Bank, Haughton, Shrewsbury, Shropshire SY4 4GB. *01743 709334*. www.campingandcaravanningclub.co.uk. Non-members welcome and may join at site. All units accepted. Own sanitation required. Some all weather pitches available. Site is set upon an ancient Iron Age Hill Fort. Fishing is available from site which is close to Telford Park. Site is 6m from Shrewsbury and well situated for the Severn Valley and Welsh Borders. Nearby is the Shropshire Way footpath. Special deals available for families and backpackers. 2.5m through Shrewsbury on A53. Turn R signed Haughton and Upton Magna. Continue 1.5m site on R. Open: 1 April - 31 October. ★★★★ NCC

(12m). **Mill Farm Caravan Park** (Shrewsbury), Hughley, Shrewsbury, Shropshire SY5 6NT. *01746 785208*. www.millfarmcaravanpark.co.uk. Horse riding, fishing on park. Shopping 5m, golf course 4m. Restaurant 2m. No single sex partioo. David Bellamy Gold Conservation Award. On A458 Bridgnorth to Shrewsbury. SP from Harley. 5m from Much Wenlock. Open: 1 March - 30 January. ★★★ BH&HPA NCC

(2m). **Oxon Hall Touring Park**, Welshpool Road, Shrewsbury, Shropshire SY3

# WEST MIDLANDS

5FB. *01743 340868*. www.morris-leisure. co.uk. Access to Park and Ride. Children welcome. Pubs within walking distance. Close to hospital and doctors. Golf, fishing within 3m. Adjacent to park & ride bus service. 2m from Shrewsbury Town Centre on A458 Welshpool Road. 1m from A5. Open: All year. ★★★★★ BH&HPA 🏠🐕♿♿🚿⚡🔌 ⚡🚿♿🏠 30💷 120💷 A 60💷

(7m). **Seven Oaks Caravan Holiday Home Park, Crew Green, Shrewsbury, Shropshire SY5 9BU.** *01743 885080*. www.sevenoaksholidayhomepark.co.uk. One of Shropshire's premier parks, developed to the highest standard with elevated views of the river Severn. Excellent fishing - river and pool. Golf course and health club nearby. Ideal for retired people as a holiday retreat. A458 Shrewsbury to Welshpool, road turn R on B4393, SP Lake Vyrnwy, about 6m to Seven Oaks. Open: 1 March - 14 January. ★★★★★ 🏠🐕⚡🚿 75💷

### Telford

**Severn Gorge Park (Adults-only), Bridgnorth Road, Tweedale, Telford, Shropshire TF7 4JB.** *01952 684789*. www.severngorgepark.co.uk. Level, sheltered site set amongst woodland. All modern facilities. Ideal for exploring Ironbridge and the rest of Shropshire. From M54 J4, take A442 for 1m, then A442 SP Kidderminster for 1.6m. Follow SP for Madeley then Tweedale. Open: All year. ★★★★★ BH&HPA NCC 🏠♿🐕⚡🔌🚿♿🏠🚿 10💷 10💷 A 3💷

### Wem

(1m). **Lower Lacon Caravan Park, Lower Lacon, Wem, Shropshire SY4 5RP.** *01939 232376*. www.llcp.co.uk. AA 3 pennants. Quiet rural site. Heated outdoor swimming pool. Licensed lounge. Food. Golf course 3m. Cinema, shopping centre 10m. Off A49. On to B5065. Open: All year. 🏠♿🐕♿⚡🔌🚿♿🏠🚿♿🏠 270💷 270💷 270 A 5💷

### Whitchurch

(4m). **Green Lane Farm, Green Lane, Prees, Whitchurch, Shropshire SY13 2AH.** *01948 840460*. www.greenlanecaravanpark.co.uk. 3 spacious acres full of flowers. Games green. Children's play area. One mile to local PO, shop and doctor. 4m to swimming pool, 2m to fishing. Golf & horse riding nearby. Central for all local attractions. Owner supplied copy. Whitchurch-Newport A41. 4m S of Whitchurch turn R to Hodnet (park SP), after 150yd turn R for Prees. Site is first farm house on R. Open: 1 March - 31 October. 🐕⚡🔌🚿♿ 20💷 22💷 A 🚿

## STAFFORDSHIRE
### Burton-on-Trent

(10m). **Kingfisher Holiday Park (Alrewas), Fradley Junction, Alrewas, Burton-on-Trent, Staffordshire DE13 7DN.** *01283 790407*. www.kingfisherholidaypark.co.uk. Picturesque setting at junction of 2 busy canals. Always plenty of narrowboat activity. Our own cafe and shop on site. Holiday homes for hire and sale. Alton Towers and Drayton Manor Park nearby. Free fishing on canal. Local village 2m (pubs, take-away, etc.). Golf club 2.5m. Shopping centre 3m. David Bellamy Silver Conservation Award. From A38 dual carriageway take A513 for Kings Bromley. 2m down that road, turn L. Just before canal bridge, turn R along canal bank (tarmac road). Park is past Swan Inn on R. 3.5m from Lichfield. Open: 1 March - 31 October. ★★★★★ BH&HPA 🏠🐕✖♿🚿♿🏠🚿 105💷

### Cheadle

(0.5m). **Hales Hall Caravan and Camping Park, Oakamoor Road, Cheadle, Staffordshire ST10 4QR.** *01538 753305*. www.haleshallcaravanandcampingpark.com. Bar and bar meals. Rally field. New children's play area with football field. Fishing lake 0.5m away. 5m from Alton Towers. From Cheadle take B5417 to Alton Towers & Oakamoor. Site on L about 0.5m. Open: 1 March - 31 October. BH&HPA NCC 🏠♿🐕⚡🔌🚿♿🏠🚿♿ 🏠♿✖🚿♿🏠🚿 30💷 50💷 A

### Leek

(2.75m). **Blackshaw Moor Caravan Club Site, Leek, Staffordshire ST13 8TW.** *01538 300203*. www.caravanclub.co.uk. Attractive site with tempting views of the Staffordshire Climbs. Ideal site for families. All hardstandings. Play equipment. Dog walk. Toilet blocks. Privacy cubicles. Laundry facilities. Baby toddler washroom. Veg prep. MV service point. Gas and Gaz. Golf, fishing and water sports nearby. Advance booking required Bank Holidays and weekends. Non-members welcome. No tents. No late night arrivals. See website for standard directions to site. Open: 23 March - 3 January. NCC 🏠♿🐕⚡🔌🚿♿ 🏠🚿 89💷 89💷

(3.5m). **Glencote Caravan Park, Station Road, Cheddleton, Leek, Staffordshire ST13 7FF.** *01538 360745*. www.glencote.co.uk. Small family run park adjacent to Heritage Steam Railway in the beautiful Churnet Valley. Canalside pub nearby. Winner of the Middle England 2007. David Bellamy Gold Conservation Award. Sign off A520 Leek to Stone road. Open: 1 February - 31 December. ★★★★★ BH&HPA NCC 🏠♿🐕⚡🔌🚿♿ 🚿♿🏠🚿♿ 60💷 60💷 60 A

(2m). **Leek Camping & Caravanning Club Site, Blackshaw Grange, Blackshaw Moor, Leek, Staffordshire ST13 8TL.** *01538 300285*. www.campingandcaravanningclub.co.uk. An ideal site to enjoy the beautiful Peak District, visit Alton Towers. Leek town centre is full of interesting shops and markets. The potteries of Staffordshire are close to the site. Fly and coarse fishing available locally. The Tissington Trail is within easy reach for walkers and cyclists. Caravans, motorcaravans and tents accepted. Non-members welcome. Special deals available for families and backpackers. Visit Heart of England Bronze Award. On the main A53 Leek to Buxton Road. The site is located 200yd past the sign for 'Blackshaw Moor' on the left hand side of the road. Open: All year. ★★★★ NCC 🏠♿🐕⚡🔌🚿♿🏠 ♿🏠♿🐕⚡🚿♿🏠🚿 70💷 70 A

### Rugeley

(3m). **Cannock Chase Camping & Caravanning Club Site, Old Youth Hostel, Wandon, Rugeley, Staffordshire WS15 1QW.** *01889 582166*. www.campingandcaravanningclub.co.uk. Non-members welcome. All units welcome. Loo Of The Year (5 stars). Site is a peaceful haven of heath and forest. The site is ideal for the avid walker with 17,000 acres of Chase to explore. Cannock boasts many shops, a leisure centre and an attractive market place. Special deals available for families and backpackers. From Rugeley take A460, turn L at 'Hazelslade' SP and R in 1m for site. Open: 1 April - 31 October. ★★★★★ NCC 🏠♿🐕⚡🔌🚿♿ 🏠♿🚿♿🏠 60💷 60💷 A

(2m). **Silver Trees Holiday Park, Stafford Brook Road, Penkridge Bank, Rugeley, Staffordshire WS15 2TX.** *01889 582185*. www.silvertreesholidaypark.co.uk. Quiet holiday park on Cannock Chase. New or pre-owned holiday homes for sale, indoor swimming pool, tennis, forest walks. Laundry. Golf 1m. Shopping 2m. Cinema 3m. Rose Award Park. NO TOURING, NO CAMPING. Dogs allowed except in hire fleet. David Bellamy Gold Conservation Award. Owner supplied copy. 2m W of Rugeley off A51 on to unclassified road towards Penkridge turn R by white fence; follow brown signs 'Silver Trees Holiday Park'. Open: 5 March - 17 December. ★★★★ BH&HPA 🐕⚡🚿 🏠♿🚿 100💷

### Stafford

(7.75m). **High Onn Caravan Club Site, Church Eaton, Stafford, Staffordshire**

# WEST MIDLANDS

ST20 0AX. *01785 840141.* www.caravanclub.co.uk. Peaceful and rural site with views into Shropshire and towards Wales. Own sanitation required. Chemical closet emptying points. Dog walk adjacent. Part hardstanding. Steel awning pegs required. Gas. MV service point. Local attractions include Ironbridge. Members only. No tents. See website for standard directions to site. Open: 30 March - 1 October. NCC ⚑ ⛺ ✈ ⚙ ♿ ♨ 70🚐 70⛺

(12m). **White Pump Farm, Ivetsey Bank, Weston-Under-Lizard, Stafford, Staffordshire ST19 9QU.** *01785 841153.* www.whitepumpfarm.com. This is a 5 van site situated on a small working farm. Ideally located for Weston Park, RAF Cosford. Equal distance from Telford, Stafford, Cannock and Wolverhampton. Situated alongside the A5 road, from M6, J12, 5m E. From W, 3m from Weston-under-Lizard. Open: All year. ⚑ ⛺ ✈ ❄ ♿ 5🚐 5⛺ ▲

### Stoke-on-Trent

(10m). **The Cross Inn Caravan Park, Cauldon Low, Stoke-on-Trent, Staffordshire ST10 3EX.** *01538 308338.* www.the-crossinn.co.uk. Pub/restaurant on site. Carvery all day Sunday. Families welcome. Family room with pool and football tables. Alton Towers 3m. Owner supplied copy. On A52 Stoke-Ashbourne road. Alton Towers 3m, Peak Park 5mins. Open: 19 March - 31 October. ★★★★★ ⚑ ⛺ ✈ ⚙ ♿ ♨ × ✉ ⚒ ♳ ♨ 20🚐 ▲ 6⛺

(4m). **The Star Caravan & Camping Park, Star Road, Cotton, Nr Alton Towers, Stoke-on-Trent, Staffordshire ST10 3DW.** *01538 702219.* www.campingandcaravaninclub.co.uk. Static caravans for hire. Calor Gas. Facilities for disabled. Fishing within 2m, golf course within 1m. Extra shops, PO, doctor all within 2-3m. Central location to Alton Towers, market towns of Cheadle, Leek, Uttoxeter, Ashbourne, the Potteries and the Peak District. AA 4 pennants. Rose Award. Family Welcome Award. David Bellamy Silver Conservation Award. Situated 1.25m from Alton Towers (closest site) within easy reach of Peak Park and Matlock Bath. 15m from the Potteries, about 9m from market town of Ashbourne, Leek and Uttoxeter. We are on Star Road B5417. Open: 19 March - 31 October. ★★★★★ BH&HPA ⚑ ⛺ ✈ ⚙ ♿ ♨ ⚒ ♳ ♨ 195🚐 195⛺ ▲ 58⛺

### Tamworth

(3m). **Drayton Manor Park, Fazeley, Tamworth, Staffordshire B78 3TW.** *0844 4721950.* www.draytonmanor.co.uk. Theme park camping & caravan site for families only. Over 100 rides and attractions. Telephone or email for more information. Owner supplied copy. On A4091, near J9 & 10, M42, exit T2, M6 toll. Open: 21 March - 31 October. ⚑ ⛺ ✈ ⚙ ♿ ♨ × ✉ ⚒ ♳ ♨ 75🚐 ▲

### Uttoxeter

(0.5m). **Uttoxeter Racecourse Caravan Club Site, Wood Lane, Uttoxeter, Staffordshire ST14 8BD.** *01889 564172.* www.caravanclub.co.uk. Situated on the National Hunt Racecourse with beautiful views over open countryside and golf course adjacent. Racing free to site users. Dog exercise area. Advance booking advised Bank Holidays, weekends and race days. Non-members and tent campers welcome. Privacy cubicles. Veg prep. MV service point. Play area. Ideal for families. Local attractions include Alton Towers. See website for standard directions to site. Open: 16 March - 5 November. ★★ NCC ⚑ ⛺ ✈ ⚙ ♿ ♨ ⚒ ♳ 76🚐 76⛺ ▲

## WARWICKSHIRE
### Alcester

**Cottage of Content, Welford Road, Barton, Bidford-on-Avon, Alcester, Warwickshire B50 4NP.** *01789 772279.* 24-pitch site to the rear of the Cottage of Content Inn within the village of Barton. Toilet/shower facilities in the pub. Off B4085, behind Cottage of Content Inn. Open: 1 March - 31 October. ⚑ ⛺ ✈ ⚙ ♿ ♨ × ✉ ⚒ ♳ ♨ ▲

### Bidford-on-Avon

(1.5m). **Dovecote Riverside Caravan Park, Welford Road, Barton, Bidford-on-Avon, Warwickshire B50 4NP.** *07590 700718.* www.bartonmoorings.com. Quiet, tranquil site, stunning river views - site does not flood. Owner supplied copy. Off A439, Bidford-on-Avon in the village of Barton. Open: 23 March - 31 October. BH&HPA ⚑ ⛺ ✈ ⚙ ♿ 32⛺ ▲

### Birmingham

(1m). **Chapel Lane Caravan Club Site, Chapel Lane, Wythall, Birmingham, Warwickshire B47 6JX.** *01564 826483.* www.caravanclub.co.uk. Non-members welcome. No tents. Convenient for the NEC. All hardstandings. Toilet blocks. Privacy cubicles. Laundry facilities. Veg prep. MV service point. Gas & gaz. Playframe. Local attractions include Cadbury World. Storage pitches. Fishing, golf and NCN cycle path within 5m. Quiet and peaceful off peak. See website for standard directions to site. Open: All year. ★★★★★ NCC ⚑ ⛺ ✈ ⚙ ♿ ♨ 108🚐 108⛺

### Halesowen

(1m). **Clent Hills Camping & Caravanning Club Site, Fieldhouse Lane, Romsley, Halesowen, Warwickshire B62 0NH.** *01562 710015.* www.campingandcaravanningclub.co.uk. Hidden away site has peaceful, tranquil atmosphere with 7.5 acres suitable for all units. In the heart of the country. Close to the Welsh Borders and Birmingham. Play area. Birmingham and attractions such as the National Sealife Centre, Millennium Point and the Botanical Gardens are only 15m away. Local attractions include Black Country Museum in Dudley. Steam train enthusiasts will enjoy the nearby Seven Valley Railway. Non-members welcome. Special deals available for families and backpackers. David Bellamy Bronze Conservation Award. M5, J3, take A456 then L on B4551 to Romsley, turn R past Sun Hotel take 5th L, SP Bell End and Broughton. Site is 330yd on L. Open: 1 April - 31 October. ★★★★ NCC ⚑ ⛺ ✈ ⚙ ♿ ♨ ⚒ ♳ 95🚐 95⛺ ▲

### Henley-in-Arden

(4m). **Island Meadow Caravan Park, Mill Lane, Aston Cantlow, Henley-in-Arden, Warwickshire B95 6JP.** *01789 488273.* www.islandmeadowcaravanpark.co.uk. Quiet, rural park on the River Alne in historic and picturesque village close to Stratford. Fishing free to guests. Booking essential at peak periods. David Bellamy Gold Conservation Award. Off A3400 and A46 NW of Stratford (6m) in the village of Aston Cantlow. 3m W of Alcester. Open: 1 March - 31 October. ★★★ BH&HPA ⚑ ⛺ ✈ ⚙ ♿ ♨ ⚒ ♳ 24🚐 24⛺ 12▲ 5⛺

### Meriden

(0.6m). **Somers Wood Caravan Park, Somers Road, Meriden, Warwickshire CV7 7PL.** *01676 522978.* www.somerswood.co.uk. Exclusively adults only. Adjacent to golf course with clubhouse and coarse fishery. Shops 0.5m, 3m from the National Exhibition Centre. 7 nights for the price of 5 on selected weeks, 4 nights for the price of 3. Please enquire for further details. From A45 take A452, SP Meriden/Leamington. 1m at next roundabout turn L onto B4102 (Hampton Lane) site 0.5m on left hand side. 4m from Solihull. Open: All year. ★★★★★ BH&HPA ⚑ ⛺ ✈ ⚙ ♿ ♨ ⚒ ♳ 48🚐 48⛺

### Nuneaton

**Bosworth Water Trust Caravan Site, Far Coton Lane, Wellsborough Road,**

# WEST MIDLANDS

Nuneaton, Warwickshire CV13 6PD. *01455 291876.* www.bosworthwatertrust.co.uk. Windsurfing, sailing, canoeing, crazy golf, fishing. Lakeside snack bar on site. Bosworth Water Trust is situated on the B585, 0.5m W of Market Bosworth. Open: All year. ★★★ BH&HPA 56

### Rugby

**(7m). Lairhillock Touring Park (Adults only), Sandy Lane, Marton, Rugby, Warwickshire CV23 9TP.** *01926 632119.* www.lairhillocktouringpark.co.uk. ADULTS ONLY PARK. Easy access. Level site set in beautiful rural countryside. 6 hardstanding pitches. Toilet and free shower facilities, chemical waste. Also washing up facility. Good centre for touring many places of interest. Dogs are free. On A423 1m S of Marton. 6m from Leamington Spa, 7m from Rugby and Coventry. 15m from Banbury. The turning is on the L, and is signed to Lairhillock Touring Park. Open: All year. BH&HPA 26 26

### Stratford-upon-Avon

**(2m). Dodwell Park, Evesham Road, Stratford-upon-Avon, Warwickshire CV37 9SD.** *01789 204957.* www.dodwellpark.co.uk. Country walks to Luddington village and river Avon. Ideal for visiting the Cotswolds, Warwick Castle and Shakespeare properties. From Stratford-upon-Avon take the B439 towards Bidford-on-Avon for 2m. The park is on the L and is SP. Open: All year. ★★★ BH&HPA 55 55

**(1m). Riverside Caravan Park (Stratford), Tiddington Road, Stratford-upon-Avon, Warwickshire CV37 0NS.** *01789 292312.* www.stratfordcaravans.co.uk. No tents or trailer tents. Riverside location with river taxi service to Stratford town centre. Bar, clubhouse on adjacent park, offers entertainment on Saturday nights throughout the season. Children's play area and coffee shop on site. 1.5m of free fishing. Golf course, cinema, leisure centre, restaurants all nearby. David Bellamy Gold Conservation Award. Take B4086 Tiddington Road from the bridge in Stratford. As you enter the village of Tiddington the park entrance is on the left hand side opposite the NFU. Open: 1 April - 31 October. BH&HPA NCC 50 50 80

**(1m). Stratford-upon-Avon Racecourse Touring Park, Luddington Road, Stratford-upon-Avon, Warwickshire CV37 9SE.** *01789 201063.* www.stratfordracecourse.net. Combine the Sport of Kings with a visit to our friendly Touring Park close to the heart of Shakespeare's country. Facilities for over 100 vans and tents. Level grass with tarmac access road, shower block, launderette, limited disabled facilities, Premium pitches with electric, chemical disposal and water points & small permanent play area. 400yd to shop, 1m walk into town. M40, J15, S on A46, follow signs to Racecourse. From SW leave M5 for Evesham N on A46. Open: 9 March - 31 October. 50 150 50

### Studley

**(3m). Outhill Caravan Park, Hardwick Lane, Outhill, Studley, Warwickshire B80 7DY.** *01527 852160.* Undeveloped quiet country park. No electricity. Please book in advance. £5 per caravan per night. Owner supplied copy. Off A4189, Outhill Farm is first house on L after turning off A4189 on to lane towards Studley. Turning is at top of hill 3.5m from Henley-in-Arden and 1.5m from Mappleborough Green, SP, Morton Bagot 1.5m. Open: 1 April - 31 October. BH&HPA 4 14

### Sutton Coldfield

**(7m). Kingsbury Water Park Camping & Caravanning Club Site, Bodymoor Heath Lane, Sutton Coldfield, Warwickshire B76 0DY.** *01827 874101.* www.campingandcaravanningclub.co.uk. Surrounding the site are 600 acres of Kingsbury Water Park with lakes and countryside to explore. The park is ideal for walking, cycling, bird watching and fishing. Gold award for excellence in tourism by the Heart of England Tourist Board. All units accepted. Non-members welcome. Water sports available at the Water Park complex. Nearby attractions include Drayton Manor Family Theme Park, Twycross Zoo, National Sea Life Centre, Cadbury World and the city museum art gallery. Try skiing and snowboarding on real snow at Snowdrome at nearby Tamworth. Special deals available for families and backpackers. Attained Silver Visit Britain Tourism in Excellence Award. Loo Of The Year (5 stars). Leave M6 at J4 and follow A446 N, turn R at junction with A4097. After 1.5m turn L at Water Park sign, continue for 0.5m then turn R at C&CC sign. Open: All year. ★★★★★ NCC 150 150

### Warwick

**(4m). Newlands Caravan Park, Loxley Lane, Wellesbourne, Warwick, Warwickshire CV35 9EN.** *01789 841096.* www.newlandscaravans.co.uk. The site has hardstanding, electric hook ups and a shower & toilet block. 5mins walk to a licensed cafe. Ideally situated to explore the Cotswolds, Warwick Castle, and the many National Trust properties in the area. Theatres, restaurants, shopping and Shakespeare properties can be enjoyed at nearby Stratford upon Avon. From M40/A46 Junction take A429 through Barford. Turn R go through Charlecote to crossroads. Straight over past all flying schools. Newlands is second bungalow on R, opposite helicopter school. Open: All year. 20 35

---

**STRATFORD TOURING PARK** — Luddington Road, Stratford-upon-Avon, Warks, CV37 9SE

Open Mar 16th - Oct 31st

Stratford Touring Park is close to the River Avon, about a mile from the heart of Stratford-on-Avon. The rural site offers pitches for motorhomes/caravans & tents. You may wish to combine the 'sport of kings' with your visit to the area, or you may just want to enjoy the historic county of Warwickshire from a central base with easy access to junction 15 of M40 & junction 7 of the M5.

Tel: 01789 201063 • www.stratfordtouringpark.com

---

## DODWELL PARK

Evesham Road, Stratford-upon-Avon, Warwickshire CV37 9SR
*OVER 50 YEARS AS A FAMILY BUSINESS!!*    Telephone: 01789 204957
e-mail: enquiries@dodwellpark.co.uk    web: www.dodwellpark.co.uk

A family run, clean, quiet touring park in the countryside, two miles south-west of Stratford-upon-Avon. An ideal location for visiting Shakespeare's birthplace, Warwick Castle and the Cotswolds. We have a well-provisioned shop and off-licence, free showers and country walks to the river Avon. Open all year. Free brochure on request.

# WEST MIDLANDS

(0.5m). **Warwick Racecourse Caravan Club Site**, Hampton Street, Warwick, Warwickshire CV34 6HN. *01926 495448*. www.caravanclub.co.uk. The site is set on grass and tarmac in the racecourse enclosure, and is only a 6 mins walk from the centre of Warwick. Free access to racing. Non-members welcomed. No tents. Toilet blocks. Privacy cubicles. Laundry facilities. Veg Prep. MV Service point. Gas. No late night arrivals area. See website for standard directions to site. Open: 23 March - 4 January. ★★★ NCC 55 55

## WORCESTERSHIRE
### Bewdley

(9m). **Bank Farm Holiday Park**, Bank Farm, Arley, Bewdley, Worcestershire DY12 3ND. *01299 401277*. www.bankfarmholidaypark.co.uk. David Bellamy Gold Conservation Award. Take B4194 out of Bewdley. 3.5m turn for Arley. At New Inn pub bear L follow for 1m to park. Open: 1 May - 30 September. ★★★ BH&HPA 9

### Bringsty

**Boyce Caravan Park**, Stanford Bishop, Bringsty, Worcestershire WR6 5UB. *01886 884248*. www.boyceholidaypark.co.uk. Peaceful park with showers, laundry etc. Farm walks and 3 coarse fishing pools on premises. No flooding. Shopping 3m, golf 7m, cinema and swimming pool 12m. Turn R off A44 Bromyard to Worcester on to B4220 SP Malvern. After 1.75m turn sharp L SP Linley Green. Then first R or follow the caravan signs. (About 3.5m from Bromyard). 14m from Worcester. Open: 1 March - 31 October. BH&HPA 14 14 5

### Broadway

(0.5m). **Broadway Caravan Club Site**, Station Road, Broadway, Worcestershire WR12 7DN. *01386 858786*. www.caravanclub.co.uk. Landscaped on two levels, the site is on the edge of one of the loveliest of the golden-stoned villages of the Cotswolds. Toilet blocks, laundry facilities, baby and toddler washroom and MV service point. Good area for walking, dog walk on site and golf nearby. Facilities for the disabled. Ideal for families. Members only. No tents. See website for standard directions to site. Open: All year. BH&HPA 115 115

### Evesham

(4m). **Abbot's Salford Caravan Park**,

**Abbot's Salford**, Evesham, Worcestershire WR11 8UN. *01386 870244*. www.allens-caravans.com. Club/bar, laundrette, shop and cafe. Outdoor swimming pool, private club, fishing, boating. Playground. Private boat moorings. Shops, restaurants, etc. in nearby towns of Evesham and Stratford. David Bellamy Silver Conservation Award. Owner supplied copy. On A46 take the turning to Abbot's Salford. The lane to the park is opposite the PH in the village. Open: 6 March - 8 January. BH&HPA NCC 350

(2m). **Evesham Vale Caravan Park**, Boston Lane, Hinton-on-the-Green, Evesham, Worcestershire WR11 2RD. *01386 860377*. Farm 0.75m on double bend. Off A44 Pershore to Evesham SP Charlton. Open: 1 March - 31 October. 20 40 A

(5m). **Long Carrant Park**, Cheltenham Road, Ashton-under-Hill, Evesham, Worcestershire WR11 7QP. *01386 881724*. 45 mixed pitches in total. Nestled at the base of Bredon Hill and only 7m from Tewkesbury, 11m from Cheltenham. 24hrs restaurant/shop opposite park. S of Evesham on A46, opposite the Vale services. Open: 1 March - 31 October. BH&HPA 45

**Pippins Green Holiday Caravan Park**, Waterside, Evesham, Worcestershire WR11 6BU. *01386 860063*. Off A44. Open: 1 March - 31 January. BH&HPA 4 A 16

(6m). **Ranch Caravan Park**, Honeybourne, Evesham, Worcestershire WR11 7PR. *01386 830744*. www.ranch.co.uk. Licensed club. Heated outdoor swimming pool, gym and leisure centre on park. Contact: Mr Andy Attridge. Golf 4m, fishing 5m, shopping 6m. David Bellamy Gold Conservation Award. From Evesham take B4035 to Badsey and Bretforton, turn L to Honeybourne. Site SP. Open: 1 March - 30 November. ★★★★★ BH&HPA NCC 100 200

**Weir Meadow Holiday And Touring Park**, Lower Leys, Evesham, Worcestershire WR11 3AA. *01386 442417*. www.allens-caravans.com. Tourer section on river bank. Seasonal moorings. One caravan is especially adapted for the disabled. Free fishing for patrons. Shops, restaurants, cinema etc in Evesham. David Bellamy Silver Conservation Award. Turn off A44 by Workman Bridge into Port Street, then L into Burford Road, Evesham. The Park is at the bottom of the road on the R. Open: 1 March - 31 December. BH&HPA NCC 24 10 2

### Hanley Swan

(1m). **Blackmore Camping & Caravanning Club Site**, No 2, Hanley Swan, Hanley Swan, Worcestershire WR8 0EE. *01684 310280*. www.campingandcaravanningclub.co.uk. Splendid centre for touring the countryside of the Malvern Hills and Severn Valley, 40sq miles of walking around the site. All units accepted. Loo Of The Year (5 stars). Non-members welcome. Ball games area available. The site is conveniently situated for Tewkesbury and Great Malvern. Special deals available for families and backpackers. David Bellamy Silver Conservation Award. From J7, M5. Watch for Blackmore Camp sign at junction of B4211. All approaches to the site are well signposted. 4m from Malvern. Open: 1 January - 31 December. ★★★★★ NCC 180 180 A

### Hawford

(3m). **Mill House Caravan and Camping Site**, Mill House, Hawford, Worcestershire WR3 7SE. *01905 451283*. 90 mixed pitches in total. Level, grassy site surrounded by small river. Dogs to be exercised off site, kept on leads and cleaned up after. Arrivals before 7pm. Coarse fishing (small river). Restriction of size of unit. No commercial vehicles or trailers. On A449 N from centre of Worcester. Open: 6 April - 31 October. 90 90 90 A

### Holt Heath

**Holt Fleet Farm**, Holt Fleet, Holt Heath, Worcestershire WR6 6NW. *01905 620512*. Doctor and PO in village 1.5m, local shops 100yd. Club on site. Owner supplied copy. On A4133. 5m from Droitwich. Open: 1 April - 31 October. 75 A 99

### Kidderminster

**Shorthill Caravan & Camping Centre**, Worcester Road, Crossway Green, Kidderminster, Worcestershire DY13 9SH. *01299 250571*. www.kidderminstercaravans.co.uk. Small family site in heart of beautiful Worcestershire countryside. Ideal base for sightseeing. New rally site available. Fees on application. Owner supplied copy. Mid-way between Kidderminster & Worcester on A449, next to Little Chef. Open: All year.

(2m). **Wolverley Camping & Caravanning Club Site**, Brown Westhead Park, Wolverley, Kidderminster, Worcestershire DY10 3PX. *01562*

# WEST MIDLANDS

850909. www.campingandcaravanning-club.co.uk. A quiet and secluded site with peaceful ambience. Children's play area. Close to Severn Valley Railway. All units accepted. Non-members welcome. The site is adjacent to the Staffordshire and Worcestershire Canal, ideal for walking or cycling. Golf and horse riding available locally. Birmingham and its attractions are just a short drive away. Special deals available for families and backpackers. From Kidderminster A449 to Wolverhampton, turn L at lights on to B4189 signed Wolverley. Follow brown camping signs, turn R. Site on L. Open: 1 April - 31 October. ★★★★ NCC 120 120

### Malvern

**Kings Green Caravan Park**, Kings Green, Berrow, Malvern, Worcestershire WR13 6AQ. 01531 650272. A small, family run campsite with grass & hardstanding pitches. Close-cut grass, well-maintained, beautiful site. Modern, clean facilities. Close to the M50 & A438 Ledbury Road. Open: 1 March - 31 October.

(3.5m). **Riverside Caravan Park** (Malvern), Little Clevelode, Malvern, Worcestershire WR13 6PE. 01684 310475. www.riverside-park.co.uk. Club. Fishing. Tennis. Play area. Laundrette. AA 3 pennants. Newly developed riverside plots available. Halfway between Worcester and Upton-on-Severn on B4424. Open: 1 March - 31 October. ★★★ BH&HPA 70 135

### Pershore

**Comberton Golf Club Campsite**, Great Comberton, Pershore, Worcestershire WR10 3DU. 01386 710738. Adjacent to river Avon free fishing (licence needed). Beautiful country pubs and walks over Bredon Hill. 18-hole, starter golf course adjacent to site plus club room. Club house. Fully licensed. Large function room for hire, catering facilities available for functions. 30 hardstanding with electric. Open all year. Rally field open March-October, for up to 200 vans. Off B4084. Open: All year. 50 200

### Shrawley

**Brant Farm Caravan Park**, Shrawley, Worcestershire WR6 6TD. 01905 621008. 3m from Stourport. Shrawley Woods within 5mins walking distance. Fishing nearby. 2 Pubs within 5mins walking distance. Owner supplied copy. On B4196 Worcester to Stourport on left-hand side in the centre of Shrawley between Rose and Crown and New Inn public houses. Open: 1 February - 31 December. 25

### Stourport-on-Severn

(1m). **Greenlawns Caravan Park**, Worcester Road, Stourport-on-Severn, Worcestershire DY13 9PB. 01243 606080. www.bunnleisure.co.uk. A4025 Stourport to Worcester. Rear of Cooks Garden Centre. Open: 1 March - 31 December. BH&HPA 30

(1m). **Lickhill Manor Caravan Park**, Stourport-on-Severn, Worcestershire DY13 8RL. 01299 871041. www.lickhillmanor.co.uk. Riverside position, level ground, superb 5 star 'Loo of Year', washrooms. Fishing, many attractions in the area to suit all ages. Town centre, leisure centre 1m. Golf 2m. West Midlands Safari Park and Severn Valley Railway 3m. David Bellamy Gold Conservation Award. SP at crossroads with traffic lights on the B4195 Bewdley to Stourport road, then R at park signs. Open: All year. ★★★★★ BH&HPA 15 100 124

(0.75m). **Lincomb Lock Caravan Park**, Titton, Stourport-on-Severn, Worcestershire DY13 9QR. 01299 823836. www.hillandale.co.uk. Alongside the River Severn with fishing. Local shop at park entrance. Golf 0.5m. Town and leisure centre 1m. Owner supplied copy. Take A4025 out of Stourport. After 0.75m turn R on left hand bend at sign posts. Open: All year. BH&HPA 6 14 118

(0.25m). **Redstone Caravan Park**, The Rough, Stourport-on-Severn, Worcestershire DY13 0LD. 01299 871711. Fully licensed club with music. Laundrette. Play area. Takeaway. Club open at weekends. Owner supplied copy. A451 from Kidderminster to Stourport, through town centre, over bridge 2nd L into The Rough. Alongside river Severn. Open: 1 March - 31 October. BH&HPA 6 34 290

(1.5m). **Severnside Caravan Park**, Sandy Lane, Titton, Stourport-on-Severn, Worcestershire DY13 9PY. 01299 824976. www.allenscaravans.com. Own river frontage, private fishing. Clubhouse. Play area. Heated outdoor swimming pool. Golf course about 2m, shopping centre about 1.5m. Owner supplied copy. On A4025 (Worcester road) turn R into Sandy Lane. Open: 1 March - 31 December. BH&HPA NCC 142

**Walshes Farm Caravan Park Ltd**, The Rough, Off Dunley Road, Stourport-on-Severn, Worcestershire DY13 0AA. 01299 877577. www.walshesfarmcaravanpark.co.uk. Off A451. Situated virtually in the town centre. Open: 1 February - 18 December. BH&HPA 262

### Tenbury Wells

(2m). **Orchard Holiday Park (Tenbury)**, New House Farm, St Michaels, Tenbury Wells, Worcestershire WR15 8TW. 01568 750618. www.orchardholidaypark.co.uk. Idyllic location, amongst beautiful countryside and pools, ideal for the fishing or walking enthusiasts. 9 & 18 hole golf courses nearby. Village pubs and restaurants. Severn Steam railway, Bewdley Safari Park. Owner supplied copy. On A4112 between Leominster and Tenbury Wells. Open: 1 March - 31 December. 5 33

(6m). **Wigley Orchard Caravan Park**, Stoke Bliss, Tenbury Wells, Worcestershire WR15 8QH. 01885 410331. www.wigleyorchard.co.uk. Good fishing. Lots of peace and quiet. Lovely views. Holidays booked through Hoseasons. Golf, pub 2m. Fish & Chips 6m. Good base for touring holiday - visit Severn Valley Steam Railway, Ironbridge Industrial Heritage Museum, Cadbury World and Worcester, Hereford, Ludlow. Owner supplied copy. W off B4203 Bromyard to Witley, near Upper Sapey golf club. Open: 17 March - 3 November. BH&HPA 86

### Worcester

**Blackmore Caravan Club Site**, Blackmore End, Hanley Swan, Worcester, Worcestershire WR8 0EE. 01684 310505. www.caravanclub.co.uk. The Malvern Hills overlook the site which is level, open, blissfully quiet & recommended for a peaceful holiday. Toilet blocks. Privacy cubicles. Laundry facilities. Veg prep. MV Service point. Gas & gaz. Play equipment. Dog walk. Good area for walking. Ideal family site. Mums and toddlers room, small football pitch. Members only. No tents. See website for standard directions to site. 2.5m from Great Malvern. Open: 23 March - 3 January. NCC 217 217

**Bromyard Downs Caravan Club Site**, Brockhampton, Bringsty, Worcester, Worcestershire WR6 5TE. 01885 482607. www.caravanclub.co.uk. This woodland site is well situated in the beautiful countryside between the cathedral cities of Worcester and Hereford. The site is ideal for those

# WEST MIDLANDS / EAST OF ENGLAND

seeking a rural holiday. Walking is a pleasure from the site, over Bromyard Downs, Bringsty Common or in the National Trust estate at Brockhampton with its lovely timbered moated manor house. Some hardstandings and dog walk nearby. No toilet block. Non-members welcome, no tents. See website for standard directions to site. Open: 30 March - 15 October. ★ ★ ★ ★ NCC

**(1.5m). Ketch Caravan Park & Boat Moorings, Bath Road, Broomhall, Worcester, Worcestershire WR5 3HW.** 01905 820430. Fishing on site. Supermarket, pharmacy, Chip Shop 1m, Indian and Chinese takeaways delivered to site. 1.5m from Worcester city centre (Bath road A38) on route to Tewkesbury. Open: 1 April - 30 October.

**(3m). Seaborne Leisure Caravan Park, Court Meadow, Kempsey, Worcestershire WR5 3JL.** 01905 820295. www.seaborneleisure.co.uk. As well as touring and statics, Seaborne also offer luxurious log cabins and lodges in their exclusive gated development next to the river Severn, overlooking the wonderful Malvern Hills. Owner supplied copy. Off A38 Worcester to Tewkesbury, 3m S of Worcester in Kempsey village. Turn opposite Crown Inn, SP St Mary's Church, follow road round until church is behind you then L into Court Meadow. Open: 1 March - 31 October. BH&HPA

## BEDFORDSHIRE
### Pavenham

**Riverside Holiday Home Park (Pavenham), Bedford Road, Pavenham, Bedfordshire MK43 7JN.** 01255 821190. www.amberleisure.com.

### Ridgmont

**Rose & Crown, 89 High Street, Ridgmont, Bedfordshire MK43 0TY.** 01525 280245. www.roseandcrownridgmont.co.uk. Beautiful Bedfordshire countryside with a friendly old-fashioned English country pub and restaurant. 'Stables' function rooms available for camping groups. Situated at the rear of the Rose and Crown PH, Ridgmont, just off A507, 1m from M1, J13. Near Woburn Abbey and Safari Park. 5m from Milton Keynes. Open: All year.

## CAMBRIDGESHIRE
### Brampton

**(2m). The Willows Caravan Park, Bromholme Lane, Brampton, Cambridgeshire PE28 4NE.** 01480 437566. www.willowscaravanpark.com. Park on R turn opposite country park. Pub-restaurant, boating, fishing and attractive walks, historical Huntingdon town, Country Park and Grafham Water nearby. Dogs allowed under strict supervision. Shop nearby. Tents welcome. Children's playground (under 7s). Washing machine. AA 3 pennants. Leave A1 N join B1514, SP Brampton, follow signs for Huntingdon. Leave A1 S join A14 then B1514 follow signs for Huntingdon. Open: All year.

### Burwell

**(8m). Stanford Park (Adults-only), Weirs Road, Burwell, Cambridgeshire CB5 0BP.** 01638 741547. www.stanfordcaravanpark.co.uk. Quiet adult only site. Ideally situated for exploring Cambridge and Newmarket. Shaver points. Hairdryers. Playground. Shops, restaurants only 15 mins walk. RAC appointed. AA 4 pennants. Caravan site signs at main junctions in village. Open: All year. ★ ★ ★ BH&HPA

### Cambridge

**(2.5m). Cherry Hinton Caravan Club Site, Lime Kiln Road, Cherry Hinton, Cambridge, Cambridgeshire CB1 8NQ.** 01223 244088. www.caravanclub.co.uk. Imaginatively landscaped site ideally located for exploring Cambridge. Dog walk on site. Non-members and tent campers welcome. Advance booking essential Bank Holidays and weekends June-August. Some pitches limited in size and shape. MV service point. Shops, garage, PO, doctor etc within 1m. Fishing, golf within 10m. See website for standard directions to site. Open: All year. ★ ★ ★ ★ ★ NCC

**(5m). Highfield Farm Touring Park (Cambridge), Long Road, Comberton, Cambridge, Cambridgeshire CB23 7DG.** 01223 262308. www.highfieldfarmtouringpark.co.uk. Iron. Hairdryers. Razor points. Baby changing facilities. Washing up sinks. Public telephone. Post box. Hardstandings. Golf course, PO, shops, doctor available nearby. From Cambridge take A428 (Bedford) and A1303 for 3m then follow signs for Comberton. From M11 leave J12 take A603 (Sandy) then B1046 to Comberton. Open: 25 March - 31 October. ★ ★ ★ ★ ★ BH&HPA

### Ely

Riverside Caravan & Camping Park (Adults only) (Ely), 21 New River Bank, Littleport, Ely, Cambridgeshire CB7 4TA. 01353 860255. www.riversideccp.co.uk. ADULTS ONLY. Quiet lawned riverside site. 2 dogs maximum. Wi-Fi. Calor gas sales. Fishing adjacent. Good pub 400yds serving food, well stocked village 15 mins walk. Ely 4m away. A10 northbound past Littleport, cross River Ouse. Turn R at roundabout. Site 1m on L. Open: All year.

### Great Shelford

**(3m). Cambridge Camping & Caravanning Club Site, 19 Cabbage Moor, Great Shelford, Cambridgeshire CB22 5NB.** 01223 841185 . www.campingandcaravanningclub.co.uk. Ideal for exploring the city and surrounding attractions. Plenty of space for children's ball games, play area. All units accepted. Non-members welcome. Special deals available for families and backpackers. M11, J11 on to A1309 SP Cambridge. At first set of lights turn R, SP 'Skelford'. After 0.5m follow sign on L, pointing down the lane. Open: 1 April - 31 October. ★ ★ ★ ★ NCC

### Huntingdon

**(0.5m). Crystal Lakes Touring Park, Low Road, Fenstanton, Huntingdon, Cambridgeshire PE28 9HU.** 01480 497728. www.crystallakesleisure.co.uk. Picturesque, secluded site just outside village of Fenstanton. Spacious shower facilities. Fishing on site, car boot fair every Sunday. Children's indoor and outdoor activity centre available. Fenstanton is situated just off A14 between Cambridge and Huntingdon, 8m from the top of M11-S and 8m from the A1 at A14 junction-N. 8m from A45. Open: 1 March - 31 October. ★ BH&HPA

**(5.25m). Grafham Water Caravan Club Site, Church Road, Grafham, Huntingdon, Cambridgeshire PE28 0BB.** 01480 810264. www.caravanclub.co.uk. 6 acres with 75 pitches separated by trees in idyllic surroundings. Excellent facilities inc. play area & picnic benches. No tents allowed. Off A14 Huntingdon to Kettering road. Open: 23 March - 5 November.

**(2m). Houghton Mill Caravan Club Site, Mill Steet, Houghton, Huntingdon, Cambridgeshire PE28 2AZ.** 01480 466716. www.caravanclub.co.uk. Set on the bank of the river Great Ouse with spectacular views across the river to the

# EAST OF ENGLAND

National Trust's Houghton Mill. Non-members and tent campers welcome. Toilet blocks with privacy cubicles and laundry facilities. Dog walk nearby, fishing and with 5m of National Cycle network. See website for standard directions to site. Open: 30 March - 5 November.
★★★★ NCC

(5m). **Quiet Waters Caravan Park, Hemingford Abbots, Huntingdon, Cambridgeshire PE28 9AJ.** 01480 463405. www.quietwaterscaravanpark.co.uk. Riverside park. Angling on site. Golf, shop 1m. A14, J25. 1m off A14, 13m from Cambridge. Open: 1 April - 31 October.
★★★★ BH&HPA

(2m). **Wyton Lakes Holiday Park (Adults only), Banks End, Wyton, Huntingdon, Cambridgeshire PE28 2AA.** 01480 412715. www.wytonlakes.com. Adults Only Park. Quality fishing on site. Boating, golfing, riding all nearby. Restaurants, shops, pubs within 1m. Doctor, PO within 2m. Marina next door, rural retreat in delightful scenery, river frontage, woodland and lakes. Each pitch with electric and water. Free showers, some hardstandings. David Bellamy Silver Conservation Award. A14, exit 23, follow A1123 to St Ives. 1m down pass Hartford Marina. Wyton Lakes is next door on right hand side. Open: 1 April - 30 October.
★★★★ BH&HPA

## Little Thetford

(2m). **Two Acres Camping, Ely Rd, Little Thetford, Cambridgeshire CB6 3HH.** 01353 648570. www.twoacrescaravan.com. Small family-run site within easy reach of Cambridge, Newmarket, Norfolk Broads, the Fens and East Coast. Electronic security gate, swings side park. Fishing nearby. Adjacent to A10 at Little Thetford junction. Open: All year.
BH&HPA

## March

(5m). **Floods Ferry Marina Park, Staffurths Bridge, March, Cambridgeshire PE15 0YP.** 01354 677302. www.floodsferrymarina.co.uk. Tranquil park in the heart of Fenland, on site marina, fishing, licensed club house with bar food and occasional live music, all touring pitches, located on river bank. Static caravans and lodges for sale. A141 bypass of March town, turn for Floods Ferry for 3m. Look for brown signs. Open: All year. ★★★ BH&HPA

## Peterborough

(2m). **Ferry Meadows Caravan Club Site, Ham Lane, Peterborough, Cambridgeshire PE2 5UU.** 01733 233526. www.caravanclub.co.uk. Ideal family site, level and open, located in country park with water sports, golf, fishing and cycling facilities. Non-members and tent campers welcome. Dogs must be exercised off site. Advance booking essential Bank Holidays. MV service point. Grass and hardstanding pitches. See website for standard directions to site. Open: All year. ★★★★★ NCC

**Northey Lodge, Northey Lodge, North Bank, Peterborough, Cambridgeshire PE6 7YZ.** 01733 223918. www.northeylodge.co.uk. Adjacent to the river Nene and within easy reach of Peterborough. Well-behaved dogs welcome but must be kept on a lead when on site. Off A1139. Open: 2 January - 24 December. BH&HPA

(8m). **Sacrewell Farm & Country Centre, Thornhaugh, Peterborough, Cambridgeshire PE8 6HJ.** 01780 782254. www.sacrewell.org.uk. The farm and country centre admission included in caravan fees: working watermill, bygones, animals. Children's play area. Farm trail. Nearest village with pubs, PO, doctor within 1m. Located off A47 just E of A1/A47 junction near Wansford, Peterborough. Open: 3 January - 23 December.

## Pidley

**Stroud Hill Park, Fen Road, Pidley, Cambridgeshire PE28 3DE.** 01487 741333. www.stroudhillpark.co.uk. CARAVAN CLUB AFFILIATED SITE. Adults only. This quiet, attractive and rural site provides a five star location. Toilet blocks and laundrette. Shop, cafe, bar and restaurant on site. Good area for walking. Fishing and golf nearby. Quiet and peaceful off peak. 4m from St Ives. Open: All year. ★★★★★ BH&HPA NCC

## St Neots

(0.5m). **St Neots Camping & Caravanning Club Site, Hardwick Road, Eynesbury, St Neots, Cambridgeshire PE19 2PR.** 01480 474404. www.campingandcaravanningclub.co.uk. On the banks of the Great Ouse. Ideal for boating and fishing. St Neots within easy reach. Non-members welcome and may join at site. All units accepted. Some all-weather pitches available. All facilities nearby eg shops, pubs, restaurants, doctors, dentist in St Neots. Fishing is available from this site. Paxton Pits Nature Reserve, just 2m away is a paradise for birdwatchers. Special deals available for families and backpackers. From A1 take A428 to Cambridge, 2nd roundabout L to Tesco's, past sport centre, site SP. Open: 1 April - 31 October.
★★★★ NCC

## Willingham

(8m). **Roseberry Tourist Park, Earith Road, Willingham, Cambridgeshire CB4 5LT.** 01954 260346. www.roseberrytouristpark.co.uk. 9 acre orchard site amid pear trees. Ideal for touring Cambridge, Ely or St Ives en route to Felixstowe or Harwich Ferry. Hardstandings. Golf/fishing nearby. Shops 1m. From A14 take B1050 at Bar Hill. Site 1m N of Willingham on L of B1050. Open: All year. BH&HPA

# ESSEX

## Brightlingsea

**Lakeside Touring Caravan and Camping site, Promenade Way, Brightlingsea, Essex CO7 0HJ.** 01206 303421. Located next to Brightlingsea Creek, 50 pitches, each with electric hook-up. Shops, cafés & restaurants just a walk away. Off B1029, 50yd from town. Open: 1 March - 31 October.

## Burnham-on-Crouch

(1.5m). **Creeksea Caravan Park, Ferry Road, Burnham-on-Crouch, Essex CM0 8PJ.** 01621 782387. Tucked away in a rural location, this small site offers 60 hook-up pitches, although seasonals are parked on touring pitches (call first). Off B1010. Open: 1 March - 30 November. BH&HPA

(0.5m). **Sea End Caravan Park, Sea End Boathouse, Burnham-on-Crouch, Essex CM0 8AN.** 01621 782063. www.riceandcole.co.uk. Quiet and secluded park like setting. A selection of new and used caravan holiday homes for sale. Warden on site 24hrs. Friendly atmosphere. 10mins walk to town. Owner supplied copy. At end of Burnham High Street, turn R into Belvedere Road. Follow road for about 0.5m along sea wall. Open: 1 April - 30 November. BH&HPA

## Canvey Island

**Thorney Bay Park Ltd, Thorney Bay Road, Canvey Island, Essex SS8 0DB.** 01268 691500. www.thorneybay.co.uk. On B1014. Open: All year.

# EAST OF ENGLAND

## Clacton-on-Sea

**(3m). Ashley Holiday Park,** London Road, Little Clacton, Clacton-on-Sea, Essex CO16 9RN. 01255 860200. Well run, quiet family park for those long weekends. Owner supplied copy. On A133 Colchester to Clacton. Open: 1 April - 31 October. BH&HPA ✱ ⚐ 118⚑

**(2m). Highfield Grange Holiday Park** (Clacton), London Road, Clacton-on-Sea, Essex CO16 9QY. 01255 424344. www.park-resortstouring.com. Water resorts programme, FREE kids club, FREE family evening entertainment. All weather sports court, adventure playground, amusements, shop on site, indoor and outdoor swimming pool complex, laundrette, cafe and takeaway, pool, darts. Clacton pier: amusements, stalls and shops. David Bellamy Silver Conservation Award. Follow A12 to Colchester and take A120 Harwich road, leading to A133 direct to Clacton on Sea. Highfield is situated on B1441 on left hand side. Open: 20 March - 2 November. ★★★ BH&HPA ⚐ 900⚑

**(5m). Hutleys Caravan Park,** St Osyth Beach, Clacton-on-Sea, Essex CO16 8TB. 01255 820712. www.hutleyscaravans.co.uk. Adjacent to beach. Indoor heated swimming pool. A12 to Colchester. A120 to Clacton then A133 to Clacton. On to St Osyth. Open: 18 April - 31 October. BH&HPA 18⚐ 18⚑

**(2m). Martello Beach Holiday Park,** Belsize Avenue, Jaywick, Clacton-on-Sea, Essex CO15 2LF. 01255 820372. www.park-resortstouring.com. Indoor and outdoor swimming pool complex. On site store, cafe, FREE kids clubs, amusements, multi sports court. Outdoor play area, FREE family entertainment. Pool table. Darts. Takeaway. Clacton-on-sea pier: amusements, stalls and fun fair. Follow A12 from London to Clacton. Take A133 to Clacton-on-sea. Turn R on to the B1077. Continue for 1.5m then turn L on to Jaywick lane. Continue for 3m then follow signs for the park. Open: 1 April - 31 October. BH&HPA ⚐ 100⚑ 70⚐ 30⚑ 332⚑

**(4m). Oaklands Holiday Park (Clacton),** Colchester Road, St Osyth, Clacton-on-Sea, Essex CO16 8HW. 01255 820432. www.ParkHolidaysUK.com. Fishing lake. Family club/bar. Kids club. Clacton-On-Sea: shopping, cinema, restaurants. 5m from town centre. 1.5m to local St Osyth village, pubs and restaurants. David Bellamy Silver Conservation Award. B1027 from Colchester on main road, 100yd before St Osyth turning. Open: 1 March - 31 October. ★★★ BH&HPA NCC 400⚑

**(6m). Seawick Holiday Park,** Beach Road, St Osyth, Clacton-on-Sea, Essex CO16 8SG. 0845 8159775. www.ParkHolidaysUK.com. Disabled 3 bedroom chalet on hirer system. 500yd from beach. Heated indoor pool. New outdoor swimming pool in 2009. Entertainment and leisure centre, gym, sauna and spa bath. Dogs allowed in home owners only. Clacton-on-Sea: shopping, restaurants, cinema, beach. David Bellamy Bronze Conservation Award. Owner supplied copy. Off B1027. Flat ground. Open: 19 March - 4 January. ★★★ BH&HPA NCC 625⚑

**(2m). Silver Dawn Touring Park,** Jaywick Lane, Clacton-on-Sea, Essex CO16 8BB. 01255 421856. www.silverdawntouringpark.co.uk. Golf course, fishing and shops within 0.5-2m. David Bellamy Silver Conservation Award. Off B1027. Open: 1 April - 31 October. BH&HPA 10⚐ 40⚑ 56⚑

**(6m). St Osyth Beach Holiday Park,** Beach Road, St Osyth Beach, Clacton-on-Sea, Essex CO16 8SG. 01255 820247. www.ParkHolidaysUK.com. Owners only park. Convenience store. Evening entertainment. Kids club & play park. Indoor swimming pool. Family club. Fishing lake. All weather sports pitch. Boat storage area. Cinema, shopping outlet, take away, leisure centre all within 2m radius. David Bellamy Bronze Conservation Award. Off B1027. Open: 1 March - 10 January. ★★★ BH&HPA NCC 504⚑

**(5m). The Orchards Holiday Village (Haven),** Point Clear Road, St Osyth, Clacton-on-Sea, Essex CO16 8LJ. 01255 820651. www.caravancamping.co.uk. Indoor and outdoor swimming pool, bowling greens and multi sports area. Family entertainment. Kids clubs. A mini market, fishing lakes, golf course. 7m to shopping centre/cinema. Pitch n putt, play areas, children's paddling area. Mash & Barrel cafe bar. David Bellamy Gold Conservation Award. From Clacton-on-Sea, take B1027 out of Clacton (SP Colchester), turn L after the 'Save' petrol station, then over the crossroads in St Osyth. Follow signs to Point Clear. Travel 3m to the park entrance. Open: 18 March - 31 October. ★★★★ BH&HPA NCC 54⚐ 1520⚑

**(1m). Valley Farm Caravan Park,** Valley Road, Clacton-on-Sea, Essex CO15 6LY. 01255 422484. www.park-resorts.com. Indoor pool and heated outdoor pool, soft play area, FREE kids clubs, FREE evening entertainment, amusements, crazy golf, store, laundrette. Clacton Pier with amusements, stalls and funfair. David Bellamy Gold Conservation Award. Follow A12 to Colchester then take A120 and A133 to Clacton. On entering town, SP for B1032 towards Frinton. Valley is 1m from the town on your L. Open: 3 April - 2 November. ★★★★ BH&HPA NCC 54⚑

## Colchester

**Bentley Country Park,** Flag Hill, Great Bentley, Colchester, Essex CO7 8RF. www.bentleypark.co.uk/. Bentley country park offer the latest model holiday homes and log cabins for sale.

**(0.75m). Colchester Camping and Caravanning Park,** Colchester Holiday Park Ltd, Cymbeline Way, Colchester, Essex CO3 4AG. 01206 545551. www.colchestercamping.co.uk. CARAVAN CLUB AFFILIATED SITE. Non-members and tent campers welcome. Ideal for visiting Britain's oldest town or base for East Anglia and Constable country. Stop-over for ferry ports. Heated shower block. Secure storage available. Shop on site, golf course nearby. At junction of A12 and A133 Colchester Central, follow tourist signs. Colchester 5mins by car, 30mins walk Colchester. CARAVAN CLUB AFFILIATED SITE. Non members and tent campers welcome. Ideal for visiting Britain's oldest town or base for East Anglia and Constable country. Stop-over for ferry ports. Heated shower block. Secure storage available. Shop on site, golf course nearby. Open: All year. ★★★★ BH&HPA 165⚑

**(7m). Coopers Beach Holiday Park,** East Mersea, Mersea Island, Colchester, Essex CO5 8TN. 0844 0502559. www.park-resorts.com. Indoor swimming pool, tennis court, cafe and takeaway, laundrette, multi sports court, bar, FREE kids entertainment, FREE family evening entertainment. Pony trekking 7m. David Bellamy Silver Conservation Award. Take A12 towards Colchester. Follow signs to Colchester Zoo - look for signs to Mersea Island. Follow the Mersea road on to the Island. Bear L into East Mersea. Park is 50yd on R from PO. Open: 1 April - 31 October. ★★★ BH&HPA NCC 600⚑

**Debden House Centre,** 59 Straight Road, Boxted, Colchester, Essex CO4 5QY. 020 8508 3008. www.debdenhouse.com. London Tube 1.5m. Central line to

# EAST OF ENGLAND

Debden. Access from site into Epping Forest. Bottled gas sales. Laundry and cafe on site. Shop on site, PO 10mins walk. Golf nearby. No bottle gas sale. Off A121. M25 exit J26, A121 to Loughton, left A1168, second left Pyrles Lane, T-junction R then second L. M11, 2m. Open: 1 May - 30 September. ★★ 🏕️ ⛺ 🐕 ⚙️ ✉ 🔥 🚿 🛁 🚻 ♿ 🏊 100⚡ 125🔌 ♿

(8m). **Fen Farm Caravan Site**, Moore Lane, East Mersea, Colchester, Essex CO5 8FE. *01206 383275*. www.fenfarm.co.uk. Quiet, rural site, close to beach and country park. Village shop & PO 1m. Supermarket, doctor 4m. Showers. Shaver points. Play area. Family shower room. Laundry room + iron. Mobile shop calls. Safe swimming. Wi-Fi. David Bellamy Gold Conservation Award. Off B1025, take L fork over causeway, follow road to Dog and Pheasant PH -1st turning R. Open: 16 March - 31 October. ★★★★ BH&HPA 🏕️ ⛺ ⚙️ ✉ 🔥 🚿 🛁 🚻 ♿ 65⚡ 65🔌 65♿

(3m). **Gosfield Lake Resort**, Moore Lane, Colchester, Essex CO5 8FE. *01787 475043*. www.gosfieldlake.co.uk. Flat, sheltered site with picnic area and adjacent to large lake. Waterskiing and fishing on site. M11 Turn off for Stansted A120 towards Braintree A120. Follow to High Garrett then 1017 to Gosfield. Open: All year. **BH&HPA** 🏕️ ⛺ 🐕 ♿ ✉ 🔥 ⚙️ 🚿 🛁 🚻 25⚡ ♿

(10m). **Waldegraves Holiday and Leisure Park**, Mersea Island, Colchester, Essex CO5 8SE. *01206 382898*. www.waldegraves.co.uk. Rose Award. Private beach, golf, pitch & putt, fishing. Family entertainment. All weather sports area, swimming pool, children's play area. Shop & restaurant on site and nearby. David Bellamy Gold Conservation Award. Off B1025 from Colchester, follow tourist signs on island. Open: 1 March - 30 November. ★★★★ BH&HPA NCC 🏕️ ⛺ 🐕 ⚙️ ✉ 🔥 🚿 🛁 🚻 ♿ 60⚡ 60🔌 ♿ 25⚡

### Doddinghurst

(5m). **Kelvedon Hatch Camping & Caravanning Club Site**, Warren Lane, Doddinghurst, Essex CM15 0JG. *01277 372773*. www.campingandcaravanningclub.co.uk. Located between London and Chelmsford with plenty of sporting activities within easy reach. The site is peaceful and quiet surrounded by trees with 90 pitches. Caravans, motorcaravans and tents accepted. Non-members welcome. Area for ball games available with volleyball net. Special deals available for families and backpackers. David Bellamy Gold Conservation Award. M25 J28 Brentwood 2m L on A128 SP Ongar. 3m turn R, SP. Open: 1 April - 31 October. ★★★★ NCC 🏕️ ⛺ 🐕 ⚙️ ✉ 🔥 🚿 🛁 🚻 ♿ 90⚡ 90🔌 ♿

### Saffron Walden

**Hawthorn House CL**, Walden Road, Great Chesterford, Saffron Walden, Essex CB10 1PS. *0845 6521697*. www.chesterford.org.uk/caravan-site.htm. This 5-pitch CL is near the village of Great Chelmsford, spread over half an acre within a 2 acre site. Good access. Level, grassed pitches. Open: All year. 🏕️ ♿ ♿ ✉

**Home Farm Fishery**, Saffron Walden, Essex CB10 1XE. *01799 524038*. www.homefarmfishery.co.uk. A little tricky to locate – make sure you take the cul-de-sac Petts Lane not Petts Lane at the Crown Public House. The private approach road is narrow so won't take the bigger rigs. However, when you do get there, the site is an absolute gem. A three-acre site with an excellent fishing lake. The five CS pitches are grassed and somewhat sloping so be prepared to use your levelling blocks. No showers, only one toilet and no hook-up. Open: All year. 🏕️ 🚻 ♿ ✉

# EAST OF ENGLAND

**(5m). Steeple Bay Holiday Park, Steeple, Southminster, Essex CM0 7RS.** *0845 8159765.* www.ParkHolidaysUK.com/mmc. Situated next to river Blackwater with slipway. Heated outdoor swimming pool, nearest PO in the village of Steeple 3m away. David Bellamy Bronze Conservation Award. Turn off A12 on to A414 on to B1010-1012 to Latchingdon follow signs through Mayland, then Steeple Village, turn L after Steeple sign. 1m down lane. Open: 18 March - 30 November. ★★ BH&HPA NCC

**(6m). Waterside Holiday Park, Main Road, St Lawrence Bay, Southminster, Essex CM0 7LY.** *01621 779248.* www.park-resortstouring.com. Indoor swimming pool, sauna and spa pool, cafe, fast food takeaway, outdoor play area, amusements, pub, FREE kids entertainment, FREE family evening entertainment. David Bellamy Gold Conservation Award. A12 towards Chelmsford take the A414 to Maldon. Follow signs to Latchingdon on B1010. Drive through village and follow signs for St Lawrence. Pick up signs for Waterside Holiday Park. Open: 1 April - 31 October. BH&HPA NCC

### St Lawrence Bay

**St Lawrence Holiday Home Park, 10 Main Road, St Lawrence Bay, Essex CM0 7LY.** *01621 779434.* www.slcaravans.co.uk. Welcome Host. Wi-Fi access available. Driving range 3m. Golf, cinema 8m. Shopping centre 11m. David Bellamy Silver Conservation Award. Owner supplied copy. Off B1021 at Latchingdon, follow brown and white tourism signs on road to Bradwell. At St Lawrence Bay turn L into Main Road, park about 1m on R. Open: 5 March - 22 November. ★★ BH&HPA

### Walton-on-the-Naze

**(0.25m). Naze Marine Holiday Park, Hall Lane, Walton-on-the-Naze, Essex CO14 8HL.** *01255 682410.* www.park-resortstouring.com. Water resorts programme, FREE kids clubs, FREE family entertainment, amusements, adventure playground, cafe, takeaway, shop. Indoor swimming pool. Laundrette, bar, darts, pool tables. David Bellamy Gold Conservation Award. Take A12 to Colchester - follow A120 Harwich Road as far as A133. On the A133 take the B1033 all the way to Walton Seafront. Park is on L. Open: 20 March - 29 October. ★★★ BH&HPA NCC 667

### West Mersea

**(1m). Seaview Holiday Park (West Mersea), Seaview Avenue, West Mersea, Essex CO5 8DA.** *01206 382534.* Located on the seafront with beach huts and lodges available for purchase. Facilities: clubhouse, boat launch, hardstandings with electric & water. 20mins walk from village centre. B1025 Colchester to Mersea. Open: 1 April - 31 October. BH&HPA 80 200

## HERTFORDSHIRE
### Baldock

**Ashridge Farm Caravan Club Site, Ashwell Street, Ashwell, Baldock, Hertfordshire SG7 5QF.** *01462 742527.* www.caravanclub.co.uk. This small and pretty site with its many trees and shrubs is the perfect place to relax and unwind. Toilet blocks, laundry facilities and MV service point. Good area for walking and within 5m of NCN route. Facilities for disabled. Quiet and peaceful off-peak. Member only. No tents. See website for standard directions to site. Open: All year. NCC 40 40

**(1.5m). Radwell Mill Lake Caravan Site (CS), Radwell Mill, Radwell, Baldock, Hertfordshire SG7 5ES.** *01462 730242.* www.radwellmill.com. A Camping and Caravanning Club certificated site. Small site with lake and bird reserve. Takeaway meals, shop, cafe/restaurant available nearby at Motorway Services 0.5m. See website for description and further details. Open April 1-October 31. A507 from Baldock and A507 from Shefford. Turning marked Radwell only on A507. Exit 10 A1 (M). Open: 1 April - 31 October.

### Bishops Stortford

**(11m). Three Horseshoes, Mole Hill Green, Takely, Bishops Stortford, Hertfordshire CM22 6PQ.** *0871 4329005.* www.threehorseshoesmolehillgreen.co.uk. The Three Horseshoes is a public house, literally next to Stansted airport - ideal for plane spotting or catching a plane. No services. 7m from Ludlow. On B4364 road. Adjoining the Country Inn with bar meals available during Inns opening hours and Sunday roasts. Open all year but no hard standing so access in wet weather may only be possible with 4WD. Lovely views and walking country (alongside the Shropshire Way). Historic Ludlow and Bridgnorth nearby. Open: All year. 50 50

### Hertford

**(1m). Hertford Camping & Caravanning Club Site, Mangrove Road, Hertford, Hertfordshire SG13 8AJ.** *01992 586696.* www.campingandcaravanningclub.co.uk. Sports field. Non-members welcome. Local attractions include Lea Valley Park, Paradise Wildlife Park and the gardens of Benington Lordship. Special deals available for families and backpackers. All units accepted. Loo Of The Year (3 stars). David Bellamy Gold Conservation Award. From the A1, avoid town centre signs at Hertford and follow A414. From A10 take A414 to Hertford, cross first roundabout, then first L into Mangrove Road. Site on L. Open: All year. ★★★★ NCC 250 250

### Royston

**Appleacre Park, London Road, Fowlmere, Royston, Hertfordshire SG8 7RU.** *01763 208354.* www.appleacrepark.co.uk. 3m to Imperial War Museum, Duxford. 9m S of Cambridge on B1368 through Fowlmere village, entrance on L. Open: All year. ★★ BH&HPA 20

### Waltham Cross

**(2m). Theobalds Park Camping & Caravanning Club Site, Theobalds Park, Bulls Cross Ride, Waltham Cross, Hertfordshire EN7 5HS.** *01992 620604.* www.campingandcaravanningclub.co.uk. Plenty of open space for children's games. All units accepted. Non-members welcome. Site is tree screened and there is plenty of wildlife to see from the site. Recreation hall and play area on site. There is boating, sailing, swimming pools and sports in nearby Lee Valley. Special deals available for families and backpackers. Park is situated in Hertfordshire just 13m from Central London, 10mins drive from M25, leaving at J25. A10 towards London keep in R lane, R at first lights, R at T-junction, R behind dog kennels. Site 250yd towards top of lane on R. Open: 1 April - 31 October. ★★★ NCC 90 90

### Welwyn Garden City

**(2m). Commons Wood Caravan Club Site, Ascots Lane, Welwyn Garden City, Hertfordshire AL7 4HJ.** *01707 260786.* www.caravanclub.co.uk. Pleasantly green, flat and rural site

# EAST OF ENGLAND

within easy reach of London by public transport. Toilet blocks. Privacy cubicles. Laundry facilities. Veg prep. MV service point. Golf, fishing and water sports nearby. Member only. No tents. See website for standard directions to site. Open: All year. BH&HPA NCC ☐ ☐ ✱ ♿ ♘ ✻ ✿ ✤ ⛔ ❄ ⚓ ⛱ ✽ 74🚐 74⛺

## LINCOLNSHIRE

### Alford

(3m). **Woodthorpe Hall Leisure Park**, Woodthorpe, Alford, Lincolnshire LN13 0DD. *01507 450294*. www.woodthorpehallleisure.co.uk. Affiliated 18 hole golf course and fishing lake, garden centre and aquatic centre within the grounds. Woody's Bar and Restaurant with family room serving food. Snooker & pool tables. Access via Louth to Mablethorpe A157 or Alford, A1104 then B1373. Open: 1 March - 1 January. BH&HPA ☐ ☐ ✱ ♘ ♿ ✽ ✤ ⛔ ❄ ⚓ ⛱ 10🚐 50⛺ ⛺ 105⛺

### Barton-on-Humber

(0.5m). **Silver Birches Holiday Home Park**, Waterside Road, Barton-on-Humber, Lincolnshire DN18 5BA. *01652 632509*. www.silverbirches-holidayhomepark.co.uk. AA 4 pennants recommended. Owner supplied copy. On A15 or 1077. Follow signs for Humber Bridge Viewing Area. Site just past the Sloop Public House. Follow viewing area signs to Waterside Road. Site situated next to Humber Bridge only 250yd from viewing area and nature reserves. Open: All year. ★★★ BH&HPA ☐ ☐ ✱ ♘ ♿ ✽ ✤ ⛔ ❄ ⚓ ⛱ ✻

### Boston

(1.5m). **Pilgrims Way Caravan and Camping Park**, Church Green Road, Fishtoft, Boston, Lincolnshire PE21 0QY. *01205 366646*. www.pilgrimswaycaravanandcamping.com. A relaxing and peaceful site in the heart of the Lincolnshire countryside. Your home from home. Family park. Pilgrims Way is only 1.5m from Boston Centre, 20mins drive to Skegness and Spalding. Take A52 out of Boston towards Skegness there are two signs first on Bargate Bridge. Second on Wainfleet Road or take any road to Fishtoft. Open: All year. ★★★★ BH&HPA NCC ☐ ☐ ✱ ♘ ♿ ✽ ✤ ⛔ ❄ ⚓ ⛱ ✻ 24🚐 28⛺ 30⛺

(5m). **Walnut Lake Lodges and Camping**, Main Road, Algakirk, Boston, Lincolnshire PE20 2LQ. *01205 460482*. www.walnutlakes.co.uk. Lakeside log cabins and camping park within walking distance to Public House, Burger King, Little Chef. 1.5m to village, bus stop, shop, restaurant, Dr surgery, caravan spares shop. Fishing on site. Dogs allowed on touring park only. Bus to Boston or Spalding. Just off the A16 - A17. Sutterton roundabout, heading for Kings Lynn on A17 about 500yd. 6m from Spalding/Boston. Open: 6 April - 30 September. ★★★★ BH&HPA NCC ☐ ☐ ✱ ♘ ♿ ✽ ✤ ⛔ ❄ ⚓ ⛱ ✻ 10🚐 10⛺ 3⛺ 2⛺

(8m). **White Cat Caravan & Camping, The Cottage**, Old Leake, Boston, Lincolnshire PE22 9LQ. *01205 870121*. www.whitecatpark.com. Free showers. Swings. PO & pub nearby. Ideal base for Skegness and touring the Fens. Seasonal pitches for tourers. Limited facilities for disabled. Children's play area. Restaurant/pub nearby. AA 3 pennants. Equestrian centre 2m. Golf, cinema, swimming, shopping 6m. On A52 Boston to Skegness Road. Turn R opposite B1184 Sibsey road. Open: 1 April - 31 October. BH&HPA ☐ ☐ ✱ ♘ ♿ ✽ 40🚐 40⛺ ⛺

### Caistor

(1m). **Caistor Fisheries Ltd**, 99a Brigg Road, Caistor, Lincolnshire LN7 6RX. *01472 852032*. www.caistorfisheries.co.uk. Mob: 077529 15555. Three fishing lakes on site. 10mins walk to town centre which offers shops and takeaways. Viking Way 500yd away. Humberside airport 5m. Caistor is situated on the edge of the Lincolnshire Wolds with breathtaking scenery. 12m from Grimsby. Caistor is situated off the A46 and the site is on the A1084 to Brigg Road. Other routes include the M180 to Brigg and then the A1084 to Caistor Road. Open: All year. ☐ ☐ ✱ ♘ ♿ ✽ ✤ ⛔ ❄ ⚓ ⛱ ✻ 20🚐 30⛺ 13⛺ 4⛺

### Chapel St Leonards

(1m). **Eastfields Leisure Park**, Chapel Point, Chapel St Leonards, Lincolnshire PE24 5UX. *01754 874499*. www.eastfieldspark.co.uk. Excellent quiet park, next to beach, static caravans for sale (non letting site). Fishing, golf courses nearby. Within 1m: shop, doctor, PO (open March-October). Owners occupiers only - no letting. Owner supplied copy. Turn off A52 on to Skegness road, take first L then very first R onto St Leonards Drive, second L after Trafalgar club. Open: 9 April - 16 October. ☐ ☐ ✱ ♘ ♿ ✽ ✤ ⛔ ❄ ⚓ ⛱ ✻ 5⛺ 66⛺ 133⛺

### Cleethorpes

(2m). **Thorpe Park Holiday Centre (Haven)**, Anthony's Bank Road, Cleethorpes, Lincolnshire DN35 0PW. *0871 2310891*. www.caravancamping.co.uk. Heated indoor pool, adventure Splashzone, family entertainment, kids' clubs, multi sports court, fishing & golf. Two mini markets, bakery. Investor in People. Outdoor family Funzone with bouncy castle, trampolines, adventure crazy golf, orbiters and much more. David Bellamy Gold Conservation Award. From M180 take A180 and follow signs for Cleethorpes town centre. Follow signs for Holiday Parks and Pleasure Island. Open: 18 March - 31 October. ★★★★ BH&HPA NCC ☐ ☐ ✱ ♘ ♿ ✽ ✤ ⛔ ❄ ⚓ ⛱ ✻ 120🚐 120⛺ ⛺ 1700⛺

### Grantham

(8m). **Woodland Waters Holiday Park**, Willoughby Road, Ancaster, Grantham, Lincolnshire NG32 3RT. *01400 230888*. www.woodlandwaters.co.uk. 72 acre picturesque park set in a beautiful wooded valley with five fishing lakes on site. AA 3 pennants. 4 golf courses nearby. The historic city of Lincoln close by and the local market towns of Grantham, Newark and Sleaford a short drive away. Go-karting, golf, paint balling and horse riding venues close by. Bar/restaurant on site and function room, garage with shop at entrance of park. On A153 between Grantham and Sleaford, from S leave A1 at Colsterworth to B6403 to Ancaster. From N leave A1 at Newark to A17 to Sleaford, leave just before RAF Cranwell R to B6403 to Ancaster. Open: All year. ★★★ ☐ ☐ ✱ ♘ ♿ ✽ ✤ ⛔ ❄ ⚓ ⛱ ✻ 24🚐 60⛺ 50⛺ 14⛺

### Horncastle

(1.5m). **Ashby Park**, West Ashby, Horncastle, Lincolnshire LN9 5PP. *01507 527966*. Touring site of 70 acres with 7 fishing lakes. The site has been awarded a David Bellamy Conservation Gold award for the last 10 years. Lincolnshire environmental trophy. Golf 1m, Horncastle and shops 1.5m. Holiday statics for sale. David Bellamy Gold Conservation Award. 1.5m N of Horncastle between the A153 and A158. Open: 1 March - 30 November. ★★★★ BH&HPA ☐ ☐ ✱ ♘ ♿ ✽ ✤ ⛔ ❄ ⚓ ⛱ ✻ 10🚐 100⛺ ⛺

### Lincoln

(2m). **Hartsholme Country Park Camp Site**, Skellingthorpe Road, Lincoln, Lincolnshire LN6 0EY. *01522 873578*. www.hartsholmecountrypark.com. Sheltered, level site beautifully situated in a country park with woods, meadows and lakes. Perfect for exploring the historic City of Lincoln. Open for Lincoln's Christmas market - 5 nights special opening. 26 touring pitches for caravans or motorhomes. SP from A46, 3m S of Lincoln. Open: 1 Mar - 31 Oct (& Lincoln

64 CARAVAN & HOLIDAY PARKS 2012

# EAST OF ENGLAND

Xmas Market). ★★★ 🏠🐕🏊🛶⛵🎣
🍴🚗🚌✕🍽️♿ 25🏕️25🚐 8👤

**(9m). Lowfields Country Holiday Fishing Retreat, Eagle Road, North Scarle, Lincoln, Lincolnshire LN6 9EN.** 01522 778717. www.lowfields-retreat.co.uk. Welcome pets. Rose award. 8 exclusive fishing lakes, laundrette, satellite TV, small children's play area. Golf course, horse riding, swimming, pubs, shops, historic town of Lincoln 9m away. David Bellamy Gold Conservation Award. Owner supplied copy. Turn off A1 and take A46 to Lincoln. Turn on to the A1133 to Gainsborough. Stay on road until turn SP North Scarle. Follow road, take R turn over hump backed bridge, turn again then first L. Follow road for 1m. Park is on right hand side after log cabin. Open: 15 February - 14 January.
★★★★ BH&HPA 🏠🐕🏊🛶⛵
🚗🚌♿🚐 146🛶

**(1.5m). Oakhill Leisure, Norton Disney, Lincoln, Lincolnshire LN6 9QG.** 01522 868771. www.oakhill-leisure.co.uk. Children's play area, fishing lake, woodland, country walks. Pub 1m, shops 4m. A46 Newark to Lincoln - signed Thurlby, at roundabout, R at t-junction, round S-bend, straight in front sign for Oakhill Leisure. Turn R then L into park. 6m from Newark. Open: All year. 🏠🐕🏊🛶⛵
✱🚗🍴♿🚐 10🏕️60🚐 👤

**(6m). Shortferry Caravan Park, Ferry Road, Fiskerton, Lincoln, Lincolnshire LN3 4HU.** 01526 398021. www.shortferry.co.uk. Fishing and tackle shop. Outdoor heated (seasonal) swimming pool. Tents welcome except on Bank Holiday weekends. Pub and restaurant on site. Entertainment most weekends. Some park homes have private fishing. Coarse and carp lakes. GS. Off A158 Lincoln to Skegness about 5m. Open: All year. 🏠🐕
🏊🛶⛵🎣🍴♿ 🚗🍽️✕🏕️
♿♿ 10🏕️ 40🚐 👤 250🛶

**(1.5m). Willow Holt Caravan & Camping Park, Lodge Road, Tattershall, Lincoln, Lincolnshire LN4 4JS.** 01526 343111. www.willowholt.co.uk. Well-drained, family run parkland with woods, lakes and abundant wildlife. New facilities block. Fishing on site. Golf, Swimming, horse riding, tennis, bowls and water-skiing nearby. Dogs on leads allowed. Leave A153 road at Tattershall market place SP Woodhall Spa. Site on L in 1.5m. Open: 15 March - 31 October. 🏠🐕🏊🛶⛵🎣🍴🚗🚌
♿♿♿ 70🏕️ 90🚐 30👤 3🛶

## Louth

**(10m). Lakeside Park (Louth), North Somercotes, Louth, Lincolnshire LN11 7RB.** 0845 4565268. www.donamottparks.com. Heated indoor pool. Takeaway. Amusements. Indoor leisure complex.

Sauna. Laundrette. Water front club. Tennis courts, golf course, bowling green, fitness suite, steam room. A1031 Cleethorpes to Skegness road. Open: 15 March - 30 November. NCC 🏠🐕🏊🛶⛵🎣♿
🚗✕♿♿♿ 100🏕️ 150🚐

## Mablethorpe

**(1m). Golden Sands Holiday Park (Haven), Quebec Road, Mablethorpe, Lincolnshire LN12 1QJ.** 0871 2310884. www.caravan-camping.co.uk. 210 mixed pitches in total. Indoor and outdoor pools, go-karts, crazy golf, playground. Supermarket. Bakery. Coffee shop. Fish & chip shop. Children's Funzone. Free kids' club. Daytime and evening entertainment. Multi sports court, fishing lake, amusements. Touring site 10-15mins - touring has a large play area and its own shop located in touring reception as well as 2 fishing lakes. David Bellamy Gold Conservation Award. Head towards Mablethorpe located between Cleethorpes and Skegness on the Lincolnshire coast. From Mablethorpe town centre, turn L on to the seafront road towards the North End. Golden Sands is situated along this road on the L. Open: 18 March - 31 October.
★★★★ 🏠🐕🏊🛶⛵🎣♿
🍴🚗🚌✕🍽️♿♿ 210🚐
👤 1750🛶

**(2m). Grange Leisure Park, Alford Road, Mablethorpe, Lincolnshire LN12 1NE.** 01507 472814. www.coastfieldsleisureltd.co.uk. Tranquil campsite offering holiday homes and touring pitches. Two miles from beach. Set in 170 acres with six fishing lakes. On-site bar. Located on A1104 between Maltby Le Marsh and Mablethorpe. Open: 1 March - 30 November. BH&HPA 🏠🐕🏊🛶⛵
🍴🚗✕♿♿ 🏕️ 8🛶

**(1m). Greenfield Caravan Park (Mablethorpe), Sutton Road, Trusthorpe, Mablethorpe, Lincolnshire LN12 2PU.** 01507 441203. www.greenfieldcaravanpark.com. Greenfield Caravan Park is a well kept privately owned caravan park situated on the main A52 coastal road, between Mablethorpe and Sutton-On-Sea with its own access to the golden beaches of Trusthorpe. Owner supplied copy. On A52 Mablethorpe to Sutton-on-Sea. Open: 2 March - 19 November. BH&HPA 🏠🐕🛶
♿♿ 🚐 117🛶

**Hawthorn Farm Caravan Club Site, Crabtree Lane, Sutton-On-Sea, Mablethorpe, Lincolnshire LN12 2RS.** 01507 441503. www.caravanclub.co.uk. An ideal site for family holidays with excellent facilities, only 0.75m from safe bathing beach. Dog walk. Advance booking advised Bank Holidays, July and

August. Toilet blocks. Privacy cubicles. Laundry facilities. Veg prep. MV service point. Golf, fishing and water sports nearby. Members only. No tents. See website for standard directions to site. 1.25m from Sutton-On-Sea. Sutton-on-Sea 1.25m. Open: 30 March - 5 November. NCC 🏠🐕🏊🛶⛵🎣🍴
♿♿ 113🏕️ 113🚐

**(0.8m). Holivans Ltd, Quebec Road, Mablethorpe, Lincolnshire LN12 1QH.** 01507 473327. www.holivans.co.uk. Wireless network available for computers. David Bellamy Gold Conservation Award. Owner supplied copy. Take A1031 into Mablethorpe, 0.75m along Quebec Road. Adjacent to sand dunes. Open: 15 March - 31 October. ★★★ BH&HPA 🏠🐕
🛶♿♿♿♿ 6🏕️ 15🚐 165🛶

**(1m). Mablethorpe Camping & Caravanning Club Site, Highfield, 120 Church Lane, Mablethorpe, Lincolnshire LN12 2NU.** 01507 472374. www.campingandcaravanningclub.co.uk. All units accepted. Non-members welcome. Located in a flat surrounding area, perfect for cyclists. The site is conveniently situated 10-15mins walk from both town and shore. Skegness is not far away, this pretty seaside resort area is always winning awards for its beaches. The Lincolnshire Wolds are a haven for birds and animals. Special deals available for families and backpackers. Take A157 from Louth to Mablethorpe, then A1104 N and follow the sign to site is on the R just 1m from beach. Open: 1 April - 31 October. ★★★★ NCC 🏠🐕
🏊🛶⛵🎣♿♿♿♿ 105🚐
👤

**(1m). Seacroft Holiday Estate (Trusthorpe) Ltd, Sutton Road, Trusthorpe, Mablethorpe, Lincolnshire LN12 2PN.** 01507 472421. seacroftcaravanpark.com. Shop, bar and restaurant, fishing lake. Direct beach access. Golf 3m. Shops and cinema 1-2m. David Bellamy Gold Conservation Award. Between Mablethorpe and Sutton on Sea on the A52. Open: 1 March - 31 October.
★★★★ BH&HPA 🏠🐕🏊🛶⛵♿
♿♿♿♿ 13🚐 275🛶 👤

## Market Deeping

**(2m). Deepings Caravan Park, Outgang Road, Market Deeping, Lincolnshire PE6 8LQ.** 01778 344335. www.thedeepings.com. Family run site. Children's play area. Club house and fishing on site. Follow A15 signs to Market Deeping. At roundabout go straight over, at Towngate Inn turn R, site 2m. Open: All year. BH&HPA NCC 🏠
🐕🏊🛶⛵🎣♿♿🚗🚌♿♿
♿ 🚐 50🚐 👤

Visit www.caravanclub.co.uk

# EAST OF ENGLAND

### Market Rasen

**(10m). Lincolnshire Lanes Camp Site, Manor Farm, East Firsby, Market Rasen, Lincolnshire LN8 2DB.** 01673 878258. www.lincolnshire-lanes.com. Quiet site 10m N of Lincoln. Neighbouring Saxon reconstruction. Pet exercise area. 2 golf courses within 2m. Good cycling. Cycles, tandem hire. One field for families, one field more tranquil. Hook ups. 3 bed log cabins. Small shop on site. Some facilities for the disabled. Owner supplied copy. N from Lincoln on A15. 2.5m after RAF Scampton turn R on to minor road sp Spridlington. At Spridlington church turn L sp Normanby. Site is 0.75m on L. Follow brown signs from A15. Open: All year. ★ ★ ★ 🏠 🐕 🐾 🎉 🏕 💰 ♿ 15🚐 15🅿 Ⓐ

**(1m). Market Rasen Racecourse Caravan Park, Legsby Road, Market Rasen, Lincolnshire LN8 3EA.** 01673 842307. www.marketrasenraces.co.uk. Caravan Club affiliated site. Set on the edge of the lovely, rolling Lincolnshire Wolds. Children's play area. There's a pay and play golf course adjacent to the site, and within a short distance another golf course. Non-members and tent campers welcome. Good area for walking. See website for directions. Open: All year. ★ ★ ★ NCC 🏠 🐕 🐾 🎉 🏕 ♿ 55🅿 Ⓐ

### Saltfleet

**(10m). Sunnydale Holiday Park, Sea Lane, Saltfleet, Lincolnshire LN11 7RP.** 01507 338100. www.park-resortstouring.com. Indoor heated pool, on site store, bar, cabaret bar, play zone for kids. Outdoor play area, FREE kids clubs, FREE family evening entertainment. Sandy beach 2m, 18 hole golf course 9m. Fishing pond. Amusements. Darts. Pool table. David Bellamy Silver Conservation Award. Head towards Louth on the B1200 through Manby & Saltfleet. Sea Lane is on R in Saltfleet. The park is about 400yd on the left hand side. Open: 20 March - 31 October. ★ ★ ★ ★ BH&HPA NCC ♀ 🏠 🐕 🐾 🎉 🏕 💰 ♿ 48🚐 48🅿 367🛏

### Scunthorpe

**(4m). Brookside Caravan & Camping Park, Stather Road, Burton-Upon-Stather, Scunthorpe, Lincolnshire DN15 9DH.** 01724 721369. www.brooksidecaravan-park.co.uk. Set in an area of outstanding beauty with views over the river Trent and woodland. Our family run cuporbly equippod park with 35 hardstanding, spacious pitches, is ideal for summer and winter touring. From Scunthorpe take the B1430 to Burton Stather 4m. Turn L in front of Sheffield Arms Pub. New entrance 250yds on R. Open: All year. ★ ★ ★ ★ ★ ★ 🐕 🐾 🎉 🏕 35🚐 35🅿 Ⓐ

### Skegness

**Barham Park, Walls Lane, Ingoldmells, Skegness, Lincolnshire PE25 1JE.** 01754 762231. www.barhamcaravan.co.uk. Swimming pool, Laundrette. Dogs on leads only. Owner supplied copy. On A152. Open: 1 March - 31 October. BH&HPA 🏠 🐕 🐾 290🅿

**(4m). Bridge End Touring Site, Bolton's Lane, Ingoldmells, Skegness, Lincolnshire PE25 1JJ.** 01754 872456. www.bridgeendsite.co.uk. A small, quiet family run site. Some hard standing plots Catering for families only. Walking distance to Fantasy Island and markets and numerous pubs, clubs and seaside amenities. Short distance to the beach. Plenty of fishing and golf in the proximity. Owner supplied copy. Junction A52 and Boltons Lane, Ingoldmells. Open: 22 April - 31 October. 🐕 🐾 🎉 🏕 10🚐 35🅿 Ⓐ

**(5m). Coastfields Holiday Village, Roman Bank, Ingoldmells, Skegness, Lincolnshire PE25 1JU.** 01754 872592. www.coastfieldsleisureltd.co.uk. Indoor heated swimming pool. Adventure playground. Free kids club. Family entertainment club and bar. Very close to beach and within walking distance to Fantasy Island. 2m N of Skegness on A52. Open: All year. ★ ★ ★ NCC ♀ 🏠 🐕 🐾 🎉 🏕 💰 ♿ 70🅿

**(4m). Country Meadows Holiday Park, Anchor Lane, Ingoldmells, Skegness, Lincolnshire PE25 1LZ.** 01754 874455. www.countrymeadows.co.uk. Play area. Fishing available. Families only. Close to beach, Hardys Animal farm and 10mins to Fantasy Island. 4m N of Skegness on A52 to Ingoldmells, follow A52 through Ingoldmells and take first R on leaving village down Anchor Lane. Park 0.5m on L follow signs to Animal Farm. 300yd past animal farm. Open: 6 April - 31 October. ★ ★ ★ ★ BH&HPA 🏠 🐕 🐾 🎉 🏕 40🚐 120🅿 60Ⓐ

**(1.5m). Croft Bank Holiday Park, Croft Bank, Skegness, Lincolnshire PE24 4RE.** 01754 763887. www.croftbankholidaypark.co.uk. Quiet, peaceful non-letting park under personal supervision of the proprietors. Laundrette. Play area. New and used caravan sales. Lodges for sale. Fishing on site and golf nearby. Holiday apartment to rent. Owner supplied copy. Out of Skegness on A52 towards Boston, park is on the R 1.5m from Skegness. Open: 1 March - 11 November. BH&HPA 🏠 🐕 🐾 🎉 🏕 💰 ♿ 112🅿

**(7m). Golden Palm Resort (Robin Hood Leisure Park), South Road, St Leonards, Skegness, Lincolnshire PE24 5TR.** 01754 874444. www.robinhoodleisure.com. Family-oriented touring site with large indoor pool centre, Maid Marian pub, Sherwood restaurant & cafe. Amusement arcade, Chinese takeaway. Off A52 near Chapel St Leonards. Open: 1 March - 31 October. ★ ★ ★ ★ ♀ 🏠 🐕 🐾 🎉 🏕 💰 ♿ 70🚐 840🅿

**(0.5m). Goodwin Caravan Park, Trunch Lane, Chapel St Leonards, Skegness, Lincolnshire PE24 5UA.** 01754 873930. www.goodwincaravanpark.co.uk. BH&HPA 🏠 🐕 🐾 🎉 🏕 💰 ♿ 12🅿

**(7m). Happy Days Leisure, Trunch Lane, Chapel-St-Leonards, Skegness, Lincolnshire PE24 5TU.** 01754 872341. www.happydaysleisure.com. Caravan sales and hire. Happy Days family club for entertainment and kids club. Arches pub. Arcade. Outdoor heated pool. Licensed restaurant. Private beach access. Good public transport links. Owner supplied copy. From Skegness take the A52 and follow signs to Ingoldmells and Mablethorpe. Take first R sign to Chapel on to Trunch Lane. Open: 20 March - 31 October. 🐕 🐾 🎉 🏕 💰 ♿ 580🅿

**(4m). Hardy's Tourer Site, Sea Lane, Ingoldmells, Skegness, Lincolnshire PE25 1PG.** 01754 874071. All facilities including laundrette. Next door to Fantasy Island. Close to all the holiday entertainment. Market 200yd. Sea 0.5m. Golf 1m. Cinema 4m. Owner supplied copy. A52 N from Skegness to Ingoldmells. Turn R at Ship pub in Ingoldmells, into Sea Lane, 0.5m on R next to Fantasy Island. 5mins from the village centre and the sea. 0.5m down Sea Lane on R. Open: 22 April - 31 October. BH&HPA 🏠 🐕 🐾 🎉 🏕 20🚐 150🅿

**(10m). Homelands, Sea Road, Anderby, Skegness, Lincolnshire PE24 5YB.** 07989 435641. Small quiet secluded site in peaceful countryside yet within 1.5m of beautiful sandy beaches. Free showers. Fishing adjacent. Golf course 2m. Shops, PO, doctors etc 2.5m at Chapel St Leonards. Owner supplied copy. Take A52 (Skegness to Mablethorpe). Halfway between villages of Mumby and Huttoft, turn off on sharp bend SP Anderby. Go through village (about 1.5m). Site on left hand side by post box. 2m NW of Chapel St Leonards. Open: 1 March - 1 November. 🏠 🐕 🐾 🎉 🏕 10🅿

**Jackson's Caravan Site, 92 Burgh Road, Skegness, Lincolnshire PE25 2RJ.** 01754 763910. On A52. Open: 15 March - 30 September. BH&HPA 🏠 🐕 215🅿

**(1.5m). Kings Chalet & Caravan Park, Trunch Lane, Chapel St Leonards,**

# EAST OF ENGLAND

**Skegness, Lincolnshire PE24 5TA.** 01754 872540. kingscacp.co.uk. Licensed club, hairdressing salon. Fish & Chip restaurant and takeaway. Bingo and amusement arcade. Bottled gas. Owner supplied copy. A52 from Skegness. Open: 1 April - 31 October.

**Manor Farm Caravan Park (Skegness), Sea Road, Anderby, Skegness, Lincolnshire PE24 5YB.** 01507 490372. www.manorfarmcaravanpark.co.uk. New site. Small, family run. Family bathroom. Along the A16 to Ulceby Cross, follow the A1104 to Alford, turn R at the windmill to Bilsby. Turn R in Bilsby at the Three Tuns Pub onto B1449. Follow the road to join A52, turn L. Take next R into Anderby. Site is 1.5m through village on L. Open: 1 March - 31 October. ★ ★ BH&HPA

**(0.5m). North Shore Holiday Centre, Elmhirst Avenue, off Roman Bank, Skegness, Lincolnshire PE25 1SL.** 01754 763815. www.northshore-skegness.co.uk. Family holidays catered for. Very close to seaside and all amenities of Skegness, but set back from the main road. On site plenty to do during peak season. Sorry no tents. Off A52 road between Skegness and Ingoldmells. Open: 1 March - 30 November. BH&HPA

**(0.5m). Richmond Holiday Centre, Richmond Drive, Skegness, Lincolnshire PE25 3TQ.** 01754 762097. www.richmondholidays.com. The ideal holiday base a short walk from the resort of Skegness with its funfairs, sandy beaches and donkey rides. Nightly entertainment June to August, indoor heated pool, shop, laundrette, amusement arcade, fish and chip shop, cafe, children's play area, chiropodist and alternative therapies surgery. Gas available. Payment required for dogs. Some facilities may not be available out of peak season - please check. On approach to Skegness follow signs for Richmond Coach Park. When on one-way system keep R until you have Lumley Hotel on your immediate right. Bear L on to Richmond Drive, site is about 0.5m on right hand side. Open: 5 March - 31 October. ★ ★ ★ BH&HPA

**(6m). Riverside Caravan Park (Skegness), Wainfleet Bank, Wainfleet, Skegness, Lincolnshire PE24 4ND.** 01754 880205. Secluded caravan site with limited space for tents. Hot & Cold to washbasins. Fishing nearby. Shops, PO, doctor, rail, bus all within 1m. Golf 1m. Owner supplied copy. Leave bypass on to B1195, follow signs. A52 Boston to Skegness. Open: 15 March

- 31 October. BH&HPA NCC

**(0.5m). Rose Villa, 18 Burgh Road, Skegness, Lincolnshire PE25 2RA.** 01754 763820. One of the closest sites to Skegness town centre with the town's amenities and beach within easy walking distance. Shops 0.25m. PO, doctors 0.5m. Fishing, golf 1m. Owner supplied copy. A158 from Lincoln on L. Just before traffic lights. Close to the junction with A52 Roman Bank Coast Road. Open: 1 April - 24 October.

**(1.75m). Skegness Sands (CC Affiliated), Winthorpe Avenue, Skegness, Lincolnshire PE25 1QZ.** 01754 761484. www.skegness-sands.com. CARAVAN CLUB AFFILIATED SITE. A site for the classic bucket and spade holiday, with its own private access to the promenade and not far from the centre of Skegness. Toilet blocks and laundry facilities. Playground and swimming pool on site. Fishing, golf and water sports nearby. Facilities for disabled. Ideal for families. NCC

**(2m). Skegness Water Leisure Park, Walls Lane, Ingoldmells, Skegness, Lincolnshire PE25 1JF.** 01754 899400. www.skegnesswaterleisurepark.co.uk. On site facilities: fishing, cable tow water skiing, coffee shop, the Barn Inn (pub). Children's play area. David Bellamy Gold Conservation Award. North from Skegness on A52, turn L on to Walls Lane, opposite Butlins. SP 'Water Leisure Park'. Open: 3 March - 28 October. ★ ★ ★ BH&HPA

**(4m). Stevenson Golden Sands Estate, Anchor Lane, Ingoldmells, Skegness, Lincolnshire PE25 1LX.** 01754 872483. www.goldensands.gb.com. Family owned park situated next to the beach at the quieter end of Ingoldmells. Licensed club house with family room, amusement arcade, laundrette and shop. David Bellamy Silver Conservation Award. Owner supplied copy. North of Skegness, near Fantasy Island. Open: 2 March - 25 November. BH&HPA

**(3m). Sycamore Farm, Chalk Lane, Burgh-Le-Marsh, Skegness, Lincolnshire PE24 5HN.** 01754 810533. www.sycamorefarm.net. The park is situated 1m from the village of Burgh-Le-Marsh which offers all local amenities, shops, PO etc. There are a number of golf courses nearby and the seafront only 3m away. We have a private fishing lake on site (small charge). No children. An oasis of tranquility (to rest and relax in picturesque surroundings). 2 cottages also available. Owner supplied copy. Travelling on A158 towards the coast, proceed through the village of Burgh-Le-Marsh. Before leaving village, turn L, SP to Addlethorpe and Ingoldmells. Continue for about 1.5m then turn L into Chalk Lane. Site is about 300 yds on R. T Open: All year. NCC

**(3m). The Elms, Orby Road, Addlethorpe, Skegness, Lincolnshire PE24 4TR.** 01754 872266. www.elmstouringcaravansite.co.uk. Fishing on site. Golf course next door. Shops, PO, doctor within 1m. Owner supplied copy.

## Sleaford

**(9m). Low Farm, Spring Lane, Folkingham, Sleaford, Lincolnshire NG34 0SJ.** 01529 497322. www.lowfarmpark.com. Quiet family-run park situated within walking distance of conservation village with all amenities, ie shop, PO and public house. Fishing available nearby. Situated just off A15, midway between Bourne and Sleaford. Open: 5 April - 14 October. ★ ★ ★ BH&HPA

## Spalding

**(9m). Delph Bank Touring Caravan and Camping Park (Tranquil Adults-Only), Old Main Road, Fleet Hargate, Spalding, Lincolnshire PE12 8LL.** 01406 422910. www.delphbank.co.uk. Quiet site in centre of village - Exclusively for Adults. Pubs, shop and eating places all within easy walking distance. David Bellamy Gold Conservation Award. 550yd off A17 between Kings Lynn and Sleaford. Open: 15 March - 15 November. ★ ★ ★ ★ BH&HPA

**(12m). Foremans Bridge Caravan Park, Sutton Road, Sutton St James, Spalding, Lincolnshire PE12 0HU.** 01945 440346. www.foremans-bridge.co.uk. 4 star country park, with great bird watching, fishing, riverbank walks, peace and quiet place to get away from it all. David Bellamy Gold Conservation Award. From A17 take B1390 to Sutton St James Park on L after 2m. Open: 15 March - 15 January. ★ ★ ★ ★ BH&HPA

**(15m). Orchard View Caravan and Camping Park (Spalding), 102 Broadgate, Sutton St Edmund, Spalding, Lincolnshire PE12 0LT.** 01945 700482. www.orchardviewholidays.com. Rural site close to fishing, horse riding, golf and Hull to Harwich cycle route. Licensed clubhouse. Peaceful location. Excellent escape from the madness! Just wildlife to enjoy. Campfire facility pre booked. A47 Peterborough to Wisbech.

# EAST OF ENGLAND

After McDonalds roundabout turn L at 3rd roundabout, follow road 2.5m, turn R, then 3rd L. Open: 17 March - 30 November. ★★★★ ♿ ... 35 ... 35 ... 67 ...

### Spilsby

(3m). **Meadowlands Lodge Park, Monksthorpe Road, Great Steeping, Spilsby, Lincolnshire PE23 5PP.** 01754 830794. www.meadowlandslodgepark.co.uk. Quiet country park suitable semi-retired. Aviation heritage, NT properties nearby. Handy Skegness and the Wolds, local fishing, cycleways, walking or just relaxing. Golf, cinema, seaside nature reserves, all within 10m. Wide range of local shopping, garden centres, etc. Pets at owners discretion. No children. Owner supplied copy. From A16 to Spilsby town centre, follow Wainfleet road, B1195, passing the Bell PH at Halton Holegate, then about 1m turn L. Park is then 0.5m on R. Open: All year. BH&HPA NCC ... 5 ... 16 ...

### Stamford

(4m). **Tallington Lakes, Barholm Road, Tallington, Stamford, Lincolnshire PE9 4RJ.** 01778 347000. www.tallington.com. 260-acres water sports park. Dry ski slope. Licensed bar and restaurant. Cinema, shopping 4m. Golf course 6m. On the Barholm road, off A16 between Stamford and Market Deeping. 260-acres water sports park. Dry ski slope. Licensed bar and restaurant. Cinema, shopping 4m. Golf course 6m. Open: All year. ... 100 ... 397 ...

### Sutton on Sea

(1.5m). **Cherry Tree Site (Tranquil adults-only), Huttoft Road, Sutton on Sea, Lincolnshire LN12 2RU.** 01507 441126. www.cherrytreesite.co.uk. Now exclusively for adults. Family run site close to safe, sandy beaches and delightful Wolds villages. Perfect for touring Lincolnshire. Golf, horse riding & fishing nearby. 60 pitches in total. All hardstanding pitches. 10 fully serviced. Cafe/restaurant nearby. 1.5m S of Sutton on Sea on left-hand side of road (A52). Entrance via lay-by. Open March-October. Open: 12 March - 31 October. ★★★★★ BH&HPA ... 60 ...

(1m). **Kirkstead Holiday Park, North Road, Trusthorpe, Sutton on Sea, Lincolnshire LN12 2QD.** 01507 441343. www.kirkstead.co.uk. Club house with bar food, children's room and snooker room. Laundry room. Shower block, children's adventure playground. 10mins walk to beach, fishing watercourse at rear of site, rod licence required. Shopping 0.5m. Golf, cinema 3m. Doctors, PO 1m. Owner supplied copy. Take A52 coast road to Trusthorpe, turn sharp from Mablethorpe R at 1 BT telephone kiosks, go 300yd down North Road. Open: 1 March - 1 November. ... 3 ... 40 ... 81 ...

### Tattershall

(0.25m). **Tattershall Lakes Country Park, Sleaford Road, Tattershall, Lincolnshire LN4 4LR.** 01526 348800. www.tattershall-lakes.com. Indoor pool with spa facilities including hot tub and beauty treatments and fitness studio. Other facilities on park include 18 hole golf course, jet ski lake, water ski lake and fishing lakes. David Bellamy Silver Conservation Award. Join the A153 at Sleaford and follow the signs for Horncastle. Travel about 12m. Open: 30 March - 5 November. ★★★★ BH&HPA NCC ... 150 ... 150 ... 265 ... 20 ...

### Woodhall Spa

(1.5m). **Bainland Country Park, Horncastle Road, Woodhall Spa, Lincolnshire LN10 6UX.** 01526 352903. www.bainland.co.uk. The park of over 40 acres is classified as one of the top parks in Lincolnshire. 18 hole, par 3 golf course. All weather bowling green, indoor/outdoor tennis, heated indoor swimming pool, sauna, Jacuzzi, children's adventure playground, trampoline and many more facilities on site, including bar and restaurant. From Woodhall Spa travel E towards Horncastle on the B1191, 1.5m on R next to petrol station. Open: All year. ★★★★★ BH&HPA NCC ... 150 ... 150 ... 10 ...

(1m). **Jubilee Park Caravan Site, Stixwould Road, Woodhall Spa, Lincolnshire LN10 6QH.** 01526 352448. www.woodhallspa.org. Park surrounded by woods, with all amenities close by. Fees on application to Park Manager. On site facilities include a heated outdoor swimming pool (May-September), bowls, putting, tennis and cycle hire. Near centre of town junction B1191 and B1192. Open: 2 April - 31 October. ★★★ ... 88 ...

(3m). **Woodhall Spa Camping & Caravanning Club Site, Wellsyke Lane, Kirkby-on-Bain, Woodhall Spa, Lincolnshire LN10 6YU.** 01526 352911. www.campingandcaravanningclub.co.uk. Non-members welcome. All units accepted. Parent and baby room. A nature lovers dream with woodpeckers, kestrels and kingfishers often seen from the site. The lake on site is not for fishing. The town of Woodhall Spa set in a magnificent pine and birch wood is just 3m away. The site is peaceful and relaxing with a friendly atmosphere. Lincoln is not far away and is well worth a visit. Special deals available for families and backpackers. From Sleaford or Horncastle take A153 to Hailsham. At garage turn on to side road, over bridge, L towards Kirkby on Bain. First turn R signed. Open: 1 April - 31 October. ★★★★ NCC ... 90 ... 90 ...

## NORFOLK
### Attleborough

(0.5m). **Oak Tree Park, Norwich Road, Attleborough, Norfolk NR17 2JX.** 01953 455565. www.oaktreepark.co.uk. Quiet, restful, family run park on the outskirts of Attleborough. 15min drive from Norwich. Close to many attractions inc. Norfolk Broads. Turn R off A11 (Thetford-Norwich) SP Attleborough, in 2m continue through Attleborough passing Sainsbury's, fork L immediately past church at T junction, site on R in 0.5m. Open: 1 April - 31 October. ★★★★ BH&HPA ... 30 ... 30 ...

### Bacton

**Cable Gap Holiday Park, Coast Road, Bacton, Norfolk NR12 0EW.** 01692 650667. www.cablegap.co.uk. Rose Award. Golf 3m, shopping centre, railway station 5m, cinema 11m & 23m. All accommodation non smoking, double glazed and centrally heated. Easy access cottage with level 2 accessibility and level 3 self catering. David Bellamy Silver Conservation Award. 5m from North Walsham. Following the B1159 we can be found on the L, between the Coast Road and the sea, as you enter Bacton. Open: 1 March - 1 November. ★★★★★ BH&HPA ... 65 ... 1 ...

**Castaways Holiday Park, Paston Road, Bacton, Norfolk NR12 0JB.** 01692 650436. castawaysholidaypark.net. Set in quiet, peaceful village of Bacton with direct access to fine sandy beach and ideal for discovering Norfolk and The Broads. Modern caravans, pine lodges and flats. Licensed club, entertainment, children's play area. Pets welcome. On B1159 Mundesley to Bacton. 5m from North Walsham. Open: 1 March - 1 January. ★★★★ BH&HPA ... 35 ...

(1m). **Red House Chalet and Caravan Park, Paston Road, Bacton, Norfolk**

# EAST OF ENGLAND

NR12 0JB. *01692 650815*. www.redhousechalets.co.uk. Caravans, chalets and flats on small quiet family run coastal park with direct beach access via steps. Good location for sea fishing, nearby golf course, horse riding and fishing lakes. Ideal for touring the Broads and North Norfolk. Owner supplied copy. On B1159 Bacton to Mundesley. Open: All year. ★★★★ BH&HPA ♀ ♂ ⚑ ⚐ ✿ ⚒ ⚓ ⚔ 26⚕

### Banham

(18m). **Applewood Caravan & Camping Park**, The Grove, Banham, Norfolk NR16 2HE. *01953 715319*. www.banhamzoo.co.uk. Choice of restaurants. Hairdressing. Craft courtyard and access to Banham Zoo. Clothes washing and drying. Caravan accessories shop. Freezer service. Local pub and PO. Between Attleborough and Diss. Open: 13 February - 31 October. ★★★★ BH&HPA ♀ ♂ ⚑ ⚐ ✿ ⚒ ⚓ ⚔ 100⚕ 100⚖ A

### Clippesby

(9m). **Clippesby Hall**, Clippesby, Norfolk NR29 3BL. *01493 367800*. www.clippesby.com. Perimeter parking. Woodland and parkland setting in 6 different areas. Quiet, family owned. Grassy, sheltered. Surrounded by rivers, Broads, nature reserves and tourist attractions. Lots to do. Colour brochure. Norfolk Broads 2m. Norwich 8m. Great Yarmouth 9m. David Bellamy Gold Conservation Award. In Norfolk Broads National Park between Acle and Potter Heigham off B1152, turn opposite Clippesby Village sign. Open: All year. ★★★★ BH&HPA ♀ ♂ ⚑ ⚐ ✿ ⚒ ⚓ ⚔ 10⚕ 100⚖ 100A

### Cromer

(1m). **Forest Park Caravan Park Site**, Northrepps Road, Cromer, Norfolk NR27 0JR. *01263 513290*. www.forest-park.co.uk. Indoor heated pool. Laundrette. Clubhouse. Children's play area. Well stocked shop. Adjacent to Cromer Golf Course. Award winning Touring and Holiday Home haven. Golf course 0.5m. Cinema, shopping centre 1m. David Bellamy Gold Conservation Award. Off B1159. Open: 15 March - 15 January. ★★★ BH&HPA ♀ ♂ ⚑ ⚐ ✿ ⚒ ⚓ ⚔ 50⚕ 350⚖ A

(1m). **Gap Caravan Park**, Beach Road, East Runton, Cromer, Norfolk NR27 9PA. *01263 513292*. www.gapcaravanpark.co.uk. Close to shops and beach. 4m to Sheringham. Sea and freshwater fishing close by. 2 golf courses within 1m. Owner supplied copy. On A149 Cromer to Sheringham. Open: 22 April - 1 November. BH&HPA ♀ ♂ ⚑ ⚐ ✿ 185⚕

(2m). **Incleboro Fields Caravan Club Site**, Station Close, West Runton, Cromer, Norfolk NR27 9QG. *01263 837419*. www.caravanclub.co.uk. Located in a hillside area of 21 acres with sea views, woodlands, walks and wild flowers. 1m from sea. 9-hole golf course adjacent. Play area. Dog walk. Toilet blocks. Privacy cubicles. Laundry facilities. Baby/toddler washroom. Veg prep. MV service point. Ideal for families. Members only. No tents. See website for standard directions to site. Open: 30 March - 5 November. NCC ♀ ♂ ⚑ ⚐ ✿ ⚒ ⚓ ⚔ 260⚕ 260⚖

(1m). **Manor Farm Caravan & Camping Site (Cromer)**, East Runton, Cromer, Norfolk NR27 9PR. *01263 512858*. www.manorfarmcaravansite.co.uk. Secluded, family-run site situated on traditional mixed farm. Showers, washbasins, razor points. Hairdryer points. Laundry and washing-up sinks. Calor Gas. Two supermarkets within 0.25m. No motorcycles. 1m W of Cromer turn off A148 at brown and white Manor Farm signs. Open: 20 April - 31 October. ♀ ♂ ⚑ ⚐ ✿ ⚒ ⚓ 30⚕ 110⚖ A

(0.5m). **Seacroft Caravan Club Site**, Runton Road, Cromer, Norfolk NR27 9NJ. *01263 514938*. www.caravanclub.co.uk. Seacroft has a great location within walking distance of Cromer's sandy beaches. Ideal for a family holiday with so much to do on site and nearby. Non members and tent campers welcome. See website for standard directions to site. Open: 23 March - 3 January. ★★★★★ NCC ♀ ♂ ⚑ ⚐ ✿ ⚒ ⚓ ⚔ 101⚕ 101A

(3m). **West Runton Camping & Caravanning Club Site**, Holgate Lane, West Runton, Cromer, Norfolk NR27 9NW. *01263 837544*. www.campingandcaravanningclub.co.uk. 1m from sea and sandy beaches, 3m to Cromer where golf and fishing are available. All units accepted. Non-members welcome. Visit nearby Cromer with its church tower and lighthouse. Kids will love the Seal Reserve at Blakeney Point and the Shire Horse Centre at West Runton. Panoramic views of the surrounding countryside can be enjoyed from the site. Special deals available for families and backpackers. Loo Of The Year (4 stars). From King's Lynn on A148 towards Cromer, turn L at Roman Camp Inn. Site track on R at Crest of Hill, 0.5m to site. Open: 1 April - 31 October. ★★★★ NCC ♀ ♂ ⚑ ⚐ ✿ ⚒ ⚓ ⚔ 200⚕ 200⚖ A

**PREMIER PARKS 2011** (1m). **Woodhill Park**, Cromer Road, East Runton, Cromer, Norfolk NR27 9PX. *01263 512242*. www.woodhill-park.com. 275 pitches in total which can take tourers / tents / motorcaravans. High quality park offering peace and tranquillity. Magnificent views of the coastline and countryside. Rose Award. David Bellamy Gold Conservation Award. Clifftop location with sandy beach below between Cromer and Sheringham on A149. Open: 19 March - 31 October. ★★★★ BH&HPA NCC ♀ ♂ ⚑ ⚐ ✿ ⚒ ⚓ ⚔ 275⚕ 62A 16⚖

NORTH NORFOLK... *naturally* — Woodhill Park

Relax in your touring caravan or tent enjoying peace and tranquillity with magnificent views of the sea and surrounding North Norfolk countryside. Multi-service, electric pitches and amenity buildings available. Luxurious centrally heated holiday homes for hire.

Bookings or brochure **01263 512242**
or online **www.woodhill-park.com**
Cromer Road, East Runton, Cromer, Norfolk NR27 9PX

# EAST OF ENGLAND

**(0.5m). Wyndham Holiday Park, Cromer Road, East Runton, Cromer, Norfolk NR27 9NH.** 01263 512304. wyndham-holidaypark.com. Clifftop position. Paddling pool, sand pit, swings, barbecue area. Dog walk. Owner supplied copy. 0.5m W of Cromer on A149 Cromer/Sheringham coast road. Open: 20 March - 1 November. BH&HPA NCC 157

## Diss

**(1.5m). The Willows Caravan & Camping Park, Diss Road, Scole, Diss, Norfolk IP21 4DH.** 01379 740271. On Norfolk/Suffolk county boundary. Level, peaceful site on the banks of the river Waveney, surrounded by conservation area. Walking distance to historical Saxon village of Scole. Fishing, golf driving range and golf course nearby. 1.50m E of Diss on A1066, 250yd from Scole A140 roundabout. Open: 1 April - 31 October. 32

## East Harling

**(20m). The Dower House Touring Park, Thetford Forest, East Harling, Norfolk NR16 2SE.** 01953 717314. www.dowerhouse.co.uk. Family run touring park set deep in Thetford Forest. Heated swimming pool. Very large pitches. David Bellamy Gold Conservation Award. From Thetford take A1066 E for 5m fork L at Camping and East Harling sign, site on L after 2m, set in Thetford Forest. Open: 20 March - 3 October. ★ ★ ★ BH&HPA 100 100

## Fakenham

**(0.75m). Fakenham Racecourse, Pudding Norton, Fakenham, Norfolk NR21 7NY.** 01328 862388. www.fakenhamracecourse.co.uk. Set in beautiful countryside. Ideally located for visiting Norfolk's coastal resorts, stately homes, wildlife and many other attractions. Sports centre adjacent. Dog walk. Free access to racing for caravan/camping guests. Non Caravan Club members and tents welcome. Toilet blocks with showers and privacy cubicles. Laundry facilities. Veg prep. MV service point. Bar & restaurant at sports centre on site. Golf, fishing, tennis. Ideal for families. From Norwich A1067. At roundabout follow brown signs to Racecourse Caravan/Camping. From A1065 and A148 on approach to Fakenham follow signs as above. Open: All year. ★ ★ ★ 120

**(7m). The Old Brick Kilns Caravan & Camping Park, Little Barney Lane, Barney, Fakenham, Norfolk NR21 ONL.** 01328 878305. www.old-brick-kilns.co.uk. Quiet, family park for the discerning caravanner or camper. Mostly flat, open or shaded all weather pitches. Clean modern facilities. Family games areas. Licensed restaurant. Fishing pond. AA 4 pennants. David Bellamy Gold Conservation Award. Off A148, at B1354 to Melton Constable follow brown Tourist Board signs to Barney. Turn L down Little Barney Lane. Park at end of lane (0.75m). Quiet, family park for the discerning caravanner or camper. Mostly flat, open or shaded all weather pitches. Clean modern facilities. Family games areas. Licensed restaurant. Fishing pond. AA 4-pennants. David Bellamy Gold Conservation Award. Open: 15 March - 2 January. ★ ★ ★ ★ ★ BH&HPA 60 60

## Gorleston

**(5m). Breydon Water, Butt Lane, Burgh Castle, Gorleston, Norfolk NR31 9QB.** 01493 780357. www.park-resortstouring.com. Yare village: heated outdoor pool, water resorts programme, FREE kids clubs, tennis court, amusements, laundrette, shop, restaurant and takeaway, FREE family evening entertainment. Bure village: indoor pool, adventure playground, crazy golf, gym, solarium, on park store, laundrette, fish & chip shop, FREE family evening entertainment. David Bellamy Silver Conservation Award. From Great Yarmouth on A12 towards Lowestoft go straight over 2 roundabouts. Take next exit and turn L at the bottom of the slip road. At roundabout take 1st exit and straight over next. Turn L at next T-junction and R at the next. Park is 0.5m from here. Open: 1 March - 31 October. ★ ★ ★ BH&HPA NCC 49

## Great Yarmouth

**Broadlands Caravan Club Site, Johnson Street, Ludham, Great Yarmouth, Norfolk NR29 5NY.** 01692 630357. www.caravanclub.co.uk. A tranquil open site in the midst of the Broads. Toilet blocks, laundry facilities, baby and toddler washroom and MV service point. Playground and boules pitch. Fishing and water sports nearby. Ideal for families. Quiet and peaceful off-peak. Facilities for disabled. Members only. No tents. See website for standard directions to site. Open: 23 March - 5 November. NCC 110 110

**(12m). Bureside Holiday Park, Boundary Farm, Oby, Great Yarmouth, Norfolk NR29 3BW.** 01493 369233. Heated swimming pool, launching slipway and fishing. Play area. Dogs allowed. Close to river and near Thurnemouth. Open: 30 April - 13 September. 85

**(5m). Burgh Castle Marina & Caravan Park, Butt Lane, Burgh Castle, Great Yarmouth, Norfolk NR31 9PZ.** 01493 780331. www.burghcastlemarina.co.uk. Pontoon moorings. Generous space, quiet, rural setting. Spectacular views and walks to Roman ruins. Information and exhibition centre with permanent displays of Roman ruins and marshland heritage. Riverside pub and restaurant. Swimming pool. Disabled suite. Green Tourism Business Scheme Silver award. Golf course 3m. Horse riding 7m. Holiday homes for sale. No pets. David Bellamy Gold Conservation Award. Off A143 Yarmouth to Beccles 3m W of Gorleston on Sea. Follow signs for marina to Belton. Turn R after 1m for Burgh Castle. Park entrance on left hand side, another 0.75m. Open: 6 April - 31 October. ★ ★ ★ BH&HPA 40 40 25

**(3m). Caister Holiday Park (Haven), Ormesby Road, Great Yarmouth, Norfolk NR30 5NQ.** 0871 4680496. www.haven.com. Investor in People. Indoor pool. Mini golf. On site stores. Restaurants and takeaways. Self catering caravans and chalets available. Kids clubs. Daytime and evening entertainment. Direct beach access, fun palace, kiddie cars. David Bellamy Gold Conservation Award. A47 into Great Yarmouth and at 1st roundabout as you enter town take 2nd exit continuing on A47 for 0.5m. At next roundabout take exit towards Caister on A149. Follow bypass around Caister taking 1st exit at 1st roundabout, 2nd exit at 2nd roundabout and 3rd exit at 3rd roundabout. Caister Park is 1m along on the left hand side. Open: 18 March - 31 October. ★ ★ ★ BH&HPA NCC 500

**(6m). Drewery Caravan Park, California Road, California, Great Ormesby, Great Yarmouth, Norfolk NR29 3QW.** 01493 730845. Clubhouse and amusements on site. Pub, restaurant close by, fish and chips and takeaways close to site. Tent site overlooking beach. Owner supplied copy. Off B1159. Open: 22 April - 31 October. 10 25 80

**(2m). Elm Beach Caravan Park, Manor Road, Caister-on-Sea, Great Yarmouth, Norfolk NR30 5HG.** 01493 721630. www.elmbeachcaravanpark.com. Adjoining sandy beach. Pets allowed. All caravans fully equipped and heated. Quiet park. Manager: Mr T Bolger. Off A149 Stalham to Yarmouth. Follow signs to Caister, 3rd L off Beach Road, 2nd caravan park on R. Open: 1 March - 31 January. ★ ★ ★ ★ BH&HPA 58

70 CARAVAN & HOLIDAY PARKS 2012

# EAST OF ENGLAND

(3m). Grasmere Caravan Park, Bultitude's Loke, Yarmouth Road, Caister-on-Sea, Great Yarmouth, Norfolk NR30 5DH. *01493 720382.* www.grasmere-wentworth.co.uk. Small family site with no entertainment, local shops, pubs, cafes and takeaways within 0.5m. David Bellamy Bronze Conservation Award. A149 from Great Yarmouth enter Caister at roundabout. Past Yarmouth Stadium. After 0.5m turn sharp L just before bus stop. Open: 1 April - 31 October. ★ ★ ★ BH&HPA 40 74

(1.5m). Great Yarmouth Caravan Club Site, Great Yarmouth Racecourse, Jellicoe Road, Great Yarmouth, Norfolk NR30 4AU. *01493 855223.* www.caravanclub.co.uk. An open site in excellent position next to racecourse and golf course. 300yd from seafront, at its quieter, northern end. Dogs must be exercised off site. Advance booking essential BH. Non-members welcome. No tents. Toilet blocks. Privacy cubicles. Laundry facilities. Veg prep. MV service point. Play area. Golf, fishing and water sports nearby. Ideal for families. Within 5m of new cycle route. See website for standard directions to site. Open: 30 March - 5 November. ★ ★ ★ ★ ★ NCC 115 115

(4m). Hopton Holiday Village (Haven), Hopton-on-Sea, Great Yarmouth, Norfolk NR31 9BW. *0871 4680496.* www.haven.com. Heated indoor and outdoor swimming pool. Club. Entertainment. Supermarket. Direct beach access. Multi sports, 9 hole golf course, bowling green, crazy golf, bouncy castle. Restaurants. Sauna, cycle hire. David Bellamy Gold Conservation Award. Open weekends Nov & Dec + 10 days either side of Christmas. Off A12 between Lowestoft and Great Yarmouth. Open: 18 March - 31 October. ★ ★ ★ ★ BH&HPA NCC 1246

(5m). Long Beach Estate Caravan Park, Long Beach Estate, Hemsby, Great Yarmouth, Norfolk NR29 4JD. *01493 730023.* www.long-beach.co.uk. Club. Laundrette. Cafe. Supermarket. Private sandy beach. PO 1m, doctor 0.75m. Turn E off B1159 Hemsby on Beach Road. Then 2nd L (Kings Loke), SP Long Beach. Open: 16 March - 3 November. 20 12

(6m). Newport Caravan Park, Newport Road, Hemsby, Great Yarmouth, Norfolk NR29 4NW. *01493 730405.* newportcaravanpark.co.uk. 6m Norfolk Broads for boat hire, fishing. Licensed club with entertainment. Shop, diner, amusements, chippy, 500yds from sandy beach. Tourer, campers, caravan for hire. Golf 3m. No pets. No all male or female parties under 25 years of age. On B1159 coast road between Great Yarmouth and Cromer, 6m N of Great Yarmouth. Open: 1 April - 31 October. ★ ★ ★ ★ BH&HPA 90 200

(4m). Rose Farm Touring Park (Yarmouth), Stepshort, Belton, Great Yarmouth, Norfolk NR31 9JS. *01493 780896.* www.rosefarmtouringpark.co.uk. Swings. AA 4 pennants. GS. Local transport. From the A143 turn into new road, SP Belton and Burgh Castle first R at Stepshort, site first on R. Great Yarmouth 4m, Gorleston 2m. Open: All year. BH&HPA 80 145 65

(5m). Scratby Hall Caravan Park, Scratby, Great Yarmouth, Norfolk NR29 3SR. *01493 730283.* www.scratbyhall.co.uk. Rural location, level and grassy. Children's play area. Gas supplies. Washing up and food preparation room. 2m N of Caister via A149 and B1159. Site is about 1m from junction. Open: 2 April - 30 September. ★ ★ ★ ★ BH&HPA 85

(1m). Seashore Holiday Park (Haven), North Denes, Great Yarmouth, Norfolk NR30 4HG. *0871 4680496.* www.haven.com. Adjacent to racecourse with beach frontage. Fun pool. Adventure playground. Mini golf. On site shops and bakery. Kids club. Daytime and evening entertainment for all the family. Sports & leisure programme, indoor soft play area. Racecourse 3mins from park. Shops only 1m from park. David Bellamy Silver Conservation Award. From Great Yarmouth take A149 Northwards towards Caister. Turn R at 2nd set of traffic lights, SP to seafront and racecourse. Continue to the sea and turn L. Seashore is on the L. Open: 18 March - 31 October. ★ ★ ★ BH&HPA NCC 1300

(4m). The Grange Touring Park, Yarmouth Road, Ormesby St. Margaret, Great Yarmouth, Norfolk NR29 3QG. *01493 730306.* www.grangetouring.co.uk. 1m to beach; golf course, riding nearby and close to Norfolk Broads. Telephone bookings can be taken with a credit, debit or switch card. Internet reception & Wi-Fi to all pitches. PO, doctor, shop and garage in Ormesby Village. Restaurant next door. On B1159 N of Caister-on-Sea. Open: 16 March - 1 October. ★ ★ ★ ★ BH&HPA 70

(1m). Vauxhall Holiday Park, 2 Acle New Road, Great Yarmouth, Norfolk NR30 1TB. *01493 857231.* www.vauxhall-holiday-park.co.uk. Free entertainment. Heated indoor pool. Disco. Kids' Club. Adventure playground. Restaurant. Arcade. Supermarket. Multi-sport arena. On A47 Norwich to Gt Yarmouth. Open: 2 April - 4 November. ★ ★ ★ ★ ★ BH&HPA 200 385

(4m). Wild Duck Holiday Park (Haven), Howard's Common, Belton, Great Yarmouth, Norfolk NR31 9NE. *0871 2310876.* www.caravancamping.co.uk.

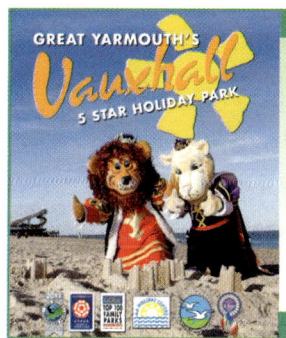

## GREAT YARMOUTH AND THE NORFOLK BROADS
### GREAT TOURING

**5 STAR TOURING FACILITIES**
- Over 220 all electric sites • Free car parking
- Grass & hard standings • Baby changing facilities
- Gas cylinder refills on site • Hair dryers
- Heated shower & toilet blocks • Awnings FREE
- Night security for late arrivals
- SUPER PITCH: Full mains service pitch with hedged, landscaped and awning areas

**FREE WITH YOUR HOLIDAY**
- ★ Star Studded Entertainment ★ Kid's Club
- ★ Sport & Fitness Fun ★ Electricity
- ★ Indoor Tropical Waterworld
- ★ T.V. Selected Freeview Channels (super pitch only)
- ★ Louie's Treehouse Adventure Playground
- ★ Wi Fi access ★ V-Lounge over 18's only
- ★ Hideout Club for 12-17'

Call Now For a Free Colour Brochure
**01493 857231**

Vauxhall Holiday Park, 10 Acle New Road, Great Yarmouth, Norfolk NR30 1TB Ref: 10

great touring savers at www.vauxhall-holiday-park.co.uk

# EAST OF ENGLAND

Park set in 98 acres of woodland. Heated indoor pool. Bar and cafe. Jamboree club with visiting cabarets, games room, amusement arcade, takeaway. Children's clubs, playground, crazy golf, bike hire, mini bowling. Golf courses nearby. Family entertainment. David Bellamy Gold Conservation Award. A47 to Great Yarmouth then pick up A143 for Beccles. Straight over mini roundabout, SP Belton & Burgh Castle. Follow this road to a T-junction and turn L. The park is a further 200yd on the R. Open: 18 March - 31 October. ★★★★ BH&HPA NCC 130 130 120

## Harleston

(2m). **Little Lakeland Caravan Park**, Wortwell, Harleston, Norfolk IP20 0EL. 01986 788646. www.littlelakeland.co.uk. Quiet, family touring park with fishing lake and library. Modern toilet block. AA Award for Environment. Turn off A143 (Diss to Bungay) at roundabout SP Wortwell. In village turn R 350yd past Bell pub. Open: 15 March - 31 October. ★★★★ BH&HPA 22 22 16

## Holt

(1m). **Kelling Heath Holiday Park**, Sandy Lane, Weybourne, Holt, Norfolk NR25 7HW. 01263 588181. www.kellingheath.co.uk. 300 pitches in total which can take tourers/tents/motorcaravans. A 250 acre estate of woodland and heathland. Nature trails and woodland walks. Health club. Bars and restaurants. David Bellamy Gold Conservation Award. From A148 turn N at site sign at Bodham. From A149 turn S at Weybourne Church, then turn L again following the camping sign & NN Railway, Kelling is at the top of the hill. Open: 10 February - 2 January. ★★★★★ BH&HPA 300 460

## Hunstanton

**Manor Park Holiday Village** (Hunstanton), Manor Road, Hunstanton, Norfolk PE36 5AZ. 0843 3092591. www.park-resorts.com. Club. Swimming pool. Laundrette. Dogs allowed except in hire vans. Local shops 0.5m. 9 hole golf course in nearby site. Owner supplied copy. On A149. Open: All year. ★★★★ 64 925

(0.5m). **Searles Leisure Resort**, South Beach Road, Hunstanton, Norfolk PE36 5BB. 01485 534211. www.searles.co.uk. 200yds from award winning beach. Indoor & outdoor pools. Air-conditioned club and health club. Tennis courts. Hire shop. Environmental award park. 9 hole golf course and driving range, fishing lake, hair and beauty salon. New kids soft play area. Colour brochure on request. On B1161 off A149, 14m N of Kings Lynn. Open: 26 December - 23 December. ★★★★★ BH&HPA 222 222 600

(3m). **Sunnymead Holiday Park** (Hunstanton), Kirkgate, Holme-next-Sea, Hunstanton, Norfolk PE36 6LH. 01485 525381. www.sunnymeadcorner.co.uk. Approved caravan holiday home. 3 flint cottages for hire. Owner supplied copy. Off A149. Open: 26 March - 31 October. ★★★★ BH&HPA 14

## King's Lynn

 **Grange Farm Touring Park** (Adults only), Whittington Hill, Whittington, King's Lynn, Norfolk PE33 9TF. 01366 500075. www.grangefarmtouringpark.co.uk. Adults only. Tranquil riverside location on the river Wissey with excellent access. Level grassed pitches with hook-ups. Modern facilities with small shop on site open April-September with petrol station and mini market opposite. Their own catering wagon operates on a Friday and Saturday evening. South of Downham Market, off the A134. Open: 1 February - 31 December. ★★★ 9 20

(4m). **Greenwoods Campsite**, Fakenham Road, Tattersett, King's Lynn, Norfolk PE31 8RS. 01485 529212. www.greenwoodscampsite.co.uk. 2m from East Rudham on A148 with PO, shops, butcher, PH. Doctors 5m to Fakenham or Massingham. From King's Lynn A148 Fakenham (14m). Open: 13 March - 3 October. ★★★ NCC 14

**Heacham Beach Holiday Park**, South Beach Road, Heacham, King's Lynn, Norfolk PE31 7BD. 0844 0502561. www.park-resorts.com. Sports resorts programme court. Free kids club. Children's adventure playground. Tavern with family entertainment. Shops, PO, doctors 0.5m. David Bellamy Bronze Conservation Award. Off A149 from Kings Lynn to Hunstanton (3m). Heacham first village after Snettisham. Turn L at sign for Heacham beach and fork L about 1m along this road. Open: 1 March - 31 October. ★★★★ BH&HPA NCC 460

(2.5m). **King's Lynn Caravan & Camping Park**, New Road, North Runcton, King's Lynn, Norfolk PE33 0QR. 01553 840004. www.kl-cc.co.uk. Well situated for King's Lynn, inland market towns and the north Norfolk coast. Park is in 5.5 acres of pleasant parkland. Good local pubs, Tesco's (1.5m). Site is used and recommended by most of the caravan clubs. Clubs welcome. Fishing, golf course nearby. PO & shop 1m, doctor 3m. 1.5m from the A17, A10, A47, A149 main King's Lynn Hardwick roundabout, on the R of the A47 going towards Swaffham. Open: All year. ★★★ BH&HPA 100 100 3

Enjoy the beauty of Kelling Heath from your touring pitch set amongst rare open heathland with backdrops of pine and native woodland. A magnificent range of facilities and environmental activities await you. Lodges and holiday homes available for hire.

**Bookings** or **brochure** **01263 588181** or online www.kellingheath.co.uk
Kelling Heath, Weybourne, Holt, Norfolk NR25 7HW

Escape the normal routine...

# EAST OF ENGLAND

(9m). **Pentney Park Caravan & Camping Site, Main Road, Pentney, King's Lynn, Norfolk PE32 1HU.** 01760 337479. www.pentney-park.co.uk. 170 mixed pitches in total. 2 heated swimming pools (indoor/outdoor), gym, spa and sauna. Shop, cafe/bar. Play area. Fishing within 1m. Golf 8m, shopping & cinema 9m. On A47 Swaffham to King's Lynn. At junction with B1153. Open: 14 February - 14 January. ★★★★ BH&HPA 170 3

(16m). **The Rickels Caravan and Camping Park, Bircham Road, Stanhoe, King's Lynn, Norfolk PE31 8PU.** 01485 518671. ADULTS ONLY. Quiet, friendly, high quality, family run offering a peaceful and relaxed atmosphere. Fishing, shop, PO, doctor 2m, golf course 6m. From Kings Lynn take A148 to Hillington L on to B1153, fork R on to B1155 site on L 100yd over crossroads. Open: 1 April - 31 October. ★★★★★ 30

### Mundesley

(0.5m). **Kiln Cliffs Caravan Park, Cromer Road, Mundesley, Norfolk NR11 8DF.** 01263 720449. www.kilncliffsholiday-homesmundesley.co.uk. Peaceful, clifftop site with private access to sandy beach, no bar or clubhouse. Well behaved pets welcome. Discounts for off-peak bookings. Owner supplied copy. On B1159 Mundesley to Cromer Road. Open: 20 March - 31 October. BH&HPA 167

(0.5m). **Sandy Gulls Caravan Park Ltd, Cromer Road, Mundesley, Norfolk NR11 8DF.** 01263 720513. www.parklandsleisure.co.uk/norfolk/sandygulls. Adults only touring park. Managed by the owning family for 30 years. Clifftop location overlooking the sea within easy reach of the Norfolk Broads National Park. Sheringham, Cromer, Great Yarmouth. TV hook ups. David Bellamy Gold Conservation Award.

5m S of Cromer, on A148 Cromer to Mundesley main coast road. Open: 1 March - 30 November. ★★★ BH&HPA 30 30 102

### North Walsham

(1m). **Two Mills Touring Park (Best of British), Yarmouth Road, North Walsham, Norfolk NR28 9NA.** 01692 405829. www.twomills.co.uk. Adults only. 2 dogs per pitch. Shops, doctors, PO etc within 1m. AA 4 pennants. David Bellamy Gold Conservation Award. From N Walsham follow old Yarmouth road 1m SE past police station and hospital to park on L opposite Scarborough Hill hotel. Open: 1 March - 3 January. ★★★★★ BH&HPA 81 81 81

(1m). **Two Mills Touring Park (Tranquil adults-only), Yarmouth Road, North Walsham, Norfolk NR28 9NA.** 01692 405829. www.twomills.co.uk. Adults only. 2 dogs per pitch. Shops, doctors, PO etc within 1m. AA 4 pennants. David Bellamy Gold Conservation Award. From N Walsham follow old Yarmouth road 1m SE past police station and hospital to park on L opposite Scarborough Hill hotel. Open: 1 March - 3 January. ★★★★★ BH&HPA 55 55

### Norwich

**Deer's Glade Caravan & Camping Park, White Post Road, Hanworth, Norwich, Norfolk NR11 7HN.** 01263 768633. www.deersglade.co.uk. Fishing on site. Pitch and store facilities. David Bellamy Gold Conservation Award. From Norwich, take the A140 towards Cromer. 5m beyond Aylsham, turn R towards Suffield Green SP White Post Road. The site is 0.5m on the R. Open: All year. ★★★★★ BH&HPA 125

(18m). **Golden Beach Caravan Park, Sea Palling, Norwich, Norfolk NR12 0AL.** 01692 598269. www.goldenbeachpark.co.uk. Quiet family park in peaceful village 200yds from award winning golden sandy beaches, cafes, village store, PO and pubs. Ideal location for exploring the Norfolk Broads, Norwich and Great Yarmouth. On B1159 Stalham to Sea Palling, turn L down beach road. Site is on L. Open: 20 March - 31 October. ★★★ BH&HPA 133

(0.5m). **Norwich Camping & Caravanning Club Site, Martineau Lane, Norwich, Norfolk NR1 2HX.** 01603 620060. www.campingandcaravanningclub.co.uk. Site 150yd on R. A 2.5 acre site overlooking beautiful open countryside with some shade. Within easy reach of the Norfolk Broads, perfect for boating, bird watching and walking. Non-members welcome. All units accepted. 2mins to pub/restaurant. 5mins walk to local shops and bus into city every 20mins. Norwich city 30mins walk away. Fishing in season. Special deals available for families and backpackers. From A47, join the A146 towards city centre. L at lights to next lights, under Low Bridge to the Cock Pub, turn L. Open: 1 April - 31 October. ★★★ NCC 50 50

(5m). **Pampas Lodge Holiday Park, The Street, Haddiscoe, Norwich, Norfolk NR14 6AA.** 01502 677765. Broads holiday centre. Fishing, golf nearby. Shops, PO 2m. Doctor 5m. 8m from Great Yarmouth & Gorleston. Owner supplied copy. 5m N of Beccles and 10m SW of Great Yarmouth on A143. Site behind Haddiscoe Tavern PH. Open: 1 March - 31 October. BH&HPA 54 6

(15m). **Reedham Ferry Caravan Park, Ferry Road, Reedham, Norwich, Norfolk NR13 3HA.** 01493 700429. www.archerstouringpark.co.uk. Flat, landscaped site adjacent to 17th century pub. Modern

# EAST OF ENGLAND

toilet facilities. Tumble dryer. Barbecue. Fishing close by. Moorings and slipway for trailed boats. A47 to Acle. Reedham is well-signposted from Acle 7m S. Open: 1 March - 31 October. ★★★ 🛁 🚻 ♿ 🐕 🅿 ⚓ ⛴ 🎣 🚣 🍴 🛒 🐟 ⛱ 🔌 10🚐 10🏠 👤

**(7m). Swans Harbour**, Barford Road, Marlingford, Norwich, Norfolk NR9 4BE. *01603 759658*. www.swansharbour.co.uk. Modern underfloor heated toilet block. Designated as unspoilt area of river valley. Park & Ride 1m. PO 2m. Fishing on site. Golf course, golf driving range, supermarket within 1-2m. Owner supplied copy. Turn R off B1108 (Norwich-Watton) in Barford SP Marlingford. After 350yd turn R at T-junction. Site on L after 0.75m (immediately past river bridge). Open: All year. NCC 🛁 🚻 ♿ 🐕 🅿 🎣 ⚡ ✳ 🔌 🚻 ♿ 10🚐 25🏠 👤

**(6m). Walcott Caravan & Chalet Park**, Coast Road, Walcott-on-Sea, Norwich, Norfolk NR12 0AP. *01692 650020*. www.walcottpark.co.uk. Park is adjacent to beach. Good beach fishing. PO and general store + mini supermarket, next to site. Chip shop, cafe, pub all within a few hundred yards. Wonderful sea views. Nearest doctor at Stalham. Local bus service. Holiday and residential (over 50's) units available. Owner supplied copy. 6m from North Walsham and/or Stalham. Open: 26 March - 24 October. 🛁 🚻 🐕 🎣 🚐 27⛴

## Potter Heigham

**(10m). Causeway Cottage Holiday Park**, Potter Heigham, Norfolk NR29 5JB. *01692 670238*. www.causewaycottage.webs.com. Holiday caravans and touring meadow. Small, family site 250yd from river, shops, pubs and entertainment. Fishing, boating. All modern conveniences. Beach 6m. Buses pass park. Gas bottle agent. Off A149 at Potter Heigham. Open: 1 March - 31 October. BH&HPA NCC 🛁 🚻 🐕 ♿ 🐾 🎣 🚣 🔌 🚿 ⚓ ☯ ✳ 🔌 ♿ 5🚐 5🏠 👤 4⛴

**(0.5m). Willowcroft Camping & Caravan Park**, Staithe Road, Repps with Bastwick, Potter Heigham, Norfolk NR29 5JU. *01692 670380*. www.willowcroft.net. Within 2m walk of river, with access for fishing and safe walk along riverbank into Potter Heigham. Flat site with good amenities, boasting peace and tranquility in abundance. Beautiful new, modern toilets for ladies open Easter 2009. Off A149 into Church Road at Repps then R into Staithe Road. About 10/15m from Norwich/Great Yarmouth/Wroxham. Open: 1 March - 31 October. 🛁 🚻 🐕 ♿ 🎣 🐾 🍴 🚿 20🚐 20🏠 👤

## Sandringham

**(2m). Sandringham Camping & Caravanning Club Site, The Sandringham Estate**, Double Lodges, Sandringham, Norfolk PE35 6EA. *01485 542555*. www.campingandcaravanningclub.co.uk. Sitenestles among trees of the Royal Sandringham Estate. Site just a few miles from the beach. All units accepted. Non-members welcome. Sandringham House, grounds and museum are well worth a visit. The historic port of Kings Lynn is within easy reach. The area has some of the most unspoilt country in the UK. Special deals available for families and backpackers. Visit Britain Caravan Holiday Park of the Year, East England winner. Loo Of The Year (5 stars). From A148 turn L on to B1440 signed West Newton. Follow signs to site or take A149 turning L and follow signs to site. 7.5m from Kings Lynn. Open: 10 February - 14 November. ★★★★ 🛁 🐕 ⚡ 🐾 🎣 🚻 ♿ 🔌 🛒 ⚓ 275🚐 275🏠 👤

**Sandringham Estate Caravan Club Site**, Glucksburg woods, Sandringham, Norfolk PE35 6EZ. *01553 631614*. www.caravanclub.co.uk. Prestigious site on royal estate. Comprehensive facilities with 136 pitches (127 hardstanding). Excellent dog walks & small shop are nearby. See website for standard directions to site. Open: All year. 🛁 🚻 ♿ 🐕 🔌 ☯ ✳ 🔌 🐾 🚐 🏠 👤

## Snettisham

**Diglea Caravan & Camping Park**, Beach Road, Snettisham, Norfolk PE31 7RA. *01485 541367*. Friendly family-run park in rural setting. Children's playground. Cafe/restaurant and takeaway available a few yards away. Rally field available. Dogs on leads welcome. Fees on application. 10.5m N of King's Lynn on A149 Hunstanton Road. Turn L at sign marked 'Snettisham Beach'. Park 1.5m on L. 0.25m from beach and RSPB Reserve. Open: 30 March - 30 September. ★★★★ 🍴 🐕 🎣 🚣 🔌 ☯ ✳ 🐾 🚻 ⚓ 🚐 👤

## Swaffham

**(0.5m). Breckland Meadows Touring Park**, Lynn Road, Swaffham, Norfolk PE37 7PT. *01760 721246*. www.brecklandmeadows.co.uk. ADULTS ONLY. Small, friendly and very clean. Three-acre site about 0.5m W of Swaffham with walkway adjacent linking with Peddars Way. Central for touring Norfolk. Heated amenity block with free showers. Hardstandings if required. 3 AA pennants. Take Swaffham turn-off from the A47 between King's Lynn and Norwich. Open: All year. BH&HPA 🛁 🚻 🐕 ♿ 🎣 🐾 ⚡ 🔌 ♿ 45🚐 45🏠 👤

## Thetford

**Brick Kiln Farm Caravan Park**, Brick Kiln Farm, Swaffham Road, Thetford, Norfolk IP25 7BT. *01760 441300*. Set in 15 acres of farmland with large wooded area, ideal for walking. Facilities include free use of showers in immaculate toilet block, electric hook up if required. Dogs welcome on leads. Graded 4 stars by East Anglian Tourist Council. Ideal location to visit Norfolk, the coast and Thetford forest. Swimming pool, golf courses and fishing close by. 4 miles from both Watton and Swaffham. Open: All year. ★★★★ 🛁 🚻 🐕 ♿ 🐾 🎣 ✳ 🔌 ⚓ ☯ 🚻 ♿ 50🚐 50🏠 50👤

**Lowe Caravan Park**, Ashdale, 134 Hills Road, Saham Hills, Thetford, Norfolk IP25 7EZ. *01953 881051*. www.lowecaravanpark.co.uk. Small friendly park mainly suited to the over 50's. Open all year except Christmas and New Year. Owner supplied copy. 2.5m from Watton. Open: 5 January - 21 December. ★★★★ 🛁 🐕 ♿ 🐾 🎣 20🚐 4⛴

**The Covert Caravan Club Site**, High Ash, Hilborough, Thetford, Norfolk IP26 5BZ. *01842 878356*. www.caravanclub.co.uk. Set in Forestry Commission woodland, a quiet, secluded site with pitching areas in little open glades, ideal for the wildlife observer. Market town nearby. Dog walk. Restricted use of barbecues. Advance booking essential Bank Holidays. Non-members welcome. No toilet block. MV service point. No tents. See website for standard directions to site. 7.5m from Swaffham. Open: 30 March - 5 November. ★★★★ NCC 🛁 🚻 🐕 ♿ 🐾 103🚐 103🏠

**(6m). Thetford Forest Camping & Caravanning Club Site**, Puddledock Farm, Great Hockham, Thetford, Norfolk IP24 1PA. *01953 498455*. www.campingandcaravanningclub.co.uk. Our club site at Thetford Forest is surrounded by natural history. Right next to the site, the forest itself is home to rare butterflies and plants and you might spot red, roe or muntjac deer. Accessible via the A134, the A11 when you reach the A1075, SP. Open: All year. ★★★★ BH&HPA NCC 🛁 🚻 🐕 ♿ 🐾 ✳ ⚡ 🔌 🎣 ♿ 160🚐 160🏠 👤

**(5m). Thorpe Caravan and Camping Site**, Shadwell, Thetford, Norfolk IP24 2RX. *01842 751042*. www.forestholidays.co.uk. A secluded site in Thetford Forest Park ideal for visiting the Norfolk Broads. No shower or toilet facilities at this site. Bookings and brochure requests on 0845 1308224. Shops, PO, doctor 3.5m. Fishing in season on site or local; golf course 10m. Off A1066 Thetford to Diss.

# EAST OF ENGLAND

After 5m bear L to East Harling. The site is 0.25m on the L. Open: All year. **BH&HPA** 460

**(10m). Warren House Caravan Site, Brandon Road, Methwold, Thetford, Norfolk IP26 4RL.** *01366 728238*. Quiet site surrounded by forestry. Good central location for touring East Anglia. Owner supplied copy. 1m from Methwold on the B1112 towards Brandon-5m. Open: 1 April - 31 October. 40

### Wells-next-the-Sea

**(0.75m). Pinewoods Holiday Park, Beach Road, Wells-next-the-Sea, Norfolk NR23 1DR.** *01328 710439*. www.pinewoods.co.uk. Good facilities on north Norfolk coast beside national nature reserve. Ideally placed to explore. Boating, pitch and putt, laundrette, and coffee shop/takeaway. 2mins to the safe sandy beach. Cinema, golf courses 10m, shopping centre 30m. David Bellamy Gold Conservation Award. Open until January 2 for winterised homes. Off A149 and B1105 at Wells Quay. Open: 15 March - 31 October. ★★★★ **BH&HPA** 150 596

### West Runton

**(0.75m). Beeston Regis Caravan Park, Cromer Road, West Runton, Norfolk NR27 9NG.** *01263 823614*. www.beeston-regis.co.uk. 41 touring pitches all with 16-amp hook-ups & on well-cut grass. There is a small shop on site, and a Portacabin toilet block & laundry. On A149 Cromer to Sheringham road, from Sheringham proceed to West Runton. The entrance is on the left hand side after 0.75m. Need to proceed over the railway line, please follow directions. Tourers must proceed over the railway line to our main entrance. Open: 24 March - 31 October. 41

### Wortwell

**(2m). Waveney Valley Lakes, Wortwell, Norfolk IP20 0EJ.** *01986 788676*. www.waveneyvalleylakes.com. Peaceful 60 acre site with 11 lakes. Shop and tackle shop on site. Fishing on site. Dogs allowed. Golf 10m. Cinema, coast, Norfolk Broads 20m. David Bellamy Gold Conservation Award. On A143 Diss to Bungay. Turn off into Wortwell village. Access road between two bungalows. Open: All year. **BH&HPA** 82

## NORTHAMPTONSHIRE

### Corby

**Top Lodge Caravan Club Site, Fineshade, Corby, Northamptonshire NN17 3BB.** *01780 444617*. www.caravanclub.co.uk. Tranquil, open meadowland site surrounded by woodland. Good walks, ideal for wildlife enthusiasts. Dog walk adjacent. Advance booking essential Bank Holidays and weekends. No toilet block. MV waste. Non-members welcome. No tents. Fishing and golf nearby. See website for standard directions to site. Open: 30 March - 5 November. ★★★★★ **NCC** 83 83

### Kettering

**(1m). Wicksteed Park, Barton Road, Kettering, Northamptonshire NN15 6NJ.** *01536 512475*. www.wicksteedpark.co.uk. Set in 147 acres of lakes and parklands, with facilities that include 35 rides and attractions including fishing, year round events programme, narrow gauge railway, daytime entertainment shows and much much more. Call for opening times details. From North leave M1, J19 and join the A14. Exit at J10 and follow brown signs. From South leave M1, J15 and join A43 then take A14 (J8) E to J10. Open: Contact site direct. **BH&HPA** 250

### Northampton

**(3m). Billing Aquadrome, Crow Lane, Great Billing, Northampton, Northamptonshire NN3 9DA.** *01524 781453*. www.billingaquadrome.com. Set in 235 acres of beautiful parkland with nine lakes. Excellent facilities include: jet ski lake, fishing, licensed bars, supermarket, funfair, dining and takeaway food and full events programme. Off A45, 3m from Northampton, 7m from M1 exit 15. Open: 7 February - 7 January. ★★★ **BH&HPA** 800 800 10

### Peterborough

**(8m). Yarwell Mill Caravan Park, Mill Road, Yarwell, Peterborough, Northamptonshire PE8 6PS.** *01780 782344*. www.yarwellmill.co.uk. Boating and fishing on site. River Nene flows through site. Old stone town of Stamford 6m. Nene Way walks lead from site. Local shop, PO, doctor, medical centre within 1m. Off A1 and A47 intersection. At Wansford church follow Yarwell signs. Open: 1 March - 31 October. ★★★ **BH&HPA** 13 20 2

## SUFFOLK

### Beccles

**(7.5m). Ilketshall The Garage Campsite,** Halesworth Road, Ilketshall St. Lawrence, Beccles, Suffolk NR34 8LB. *01986 781241*. Level grass, surrounded by trees. Ideal touring area, 20m S of Norwich. On A144, 4m N of Halesworth, 5m S of Bungay. Open: 18 April - 30 September.

**(6m). Waveney River Centre, Staithe Road, Burgh St Peter, Beccles, Suffolk NR34 0BT.** *01502 677343*. www.waveneyrivercentre.co.uk. Indoor leisure centre with swimming pool and spa, restaurant and PH. Adjacent to River Waveney, fishing during open season, rowing boats and day cruisers for hire. Play area, well stocked shop. Golf course 6m. David Bellamy Gold Conservation Award. Follow brown signs from A143 at Haddiscoe. Turn down Wiggs Road. After 2.3m turn L into Burgh Road, site is another 2m. (Site is 4m from A143). Open: 13 April - 31 December. ★★★★ **BH&HPA** 16 16 30 46 46

### Bungay

**(0.3m). Outney Meadow Caravan Park, Outney Meadow Caravan Park, Bungay, Suffolk NR35 1HG.** *01986 892338*. www.outneymeadow.co.uk. Canoe trail. Bike hire, fishing and golf. Off A143 between Bungay golf course and river Waveney. Open: 1 April - 31 October. ★★★ **BH&HPA** 45

### Bury St Edmunds

**Henry's Lake, High Town Green, Rattlesden, Bury St Edmunds, Suffolk IP30 0SZ.** *01449 736600*. www.henryslake.co.uk/home. 1.5 acre family run site with views over fishing lake & farm land. Set in rural Suffolk, surrounded by villages, close to amenities.

**(1m). Round Plantation Caravan Club Site, Brandon Road, Mildenhall, Bury St Edmunds, Suffolk IP28 7JE.** *01638 713089*. www.caravanclub.co.uk. A very pleasant carefully landscaped site in woodland setting. The woodland attracts all kinds of birds so good for bird watchers. Own sanitation required. Good area for walking, dog walk on site. Quiet and peaceful off-peak. Non-members welcome. No tents. See website for standard directions to site. Open: 23 March - 8 October. **NCC** 95 95

**(5m). The Dell Camping And Caravanning Park, Beyton Road, Thurston, Bury St Edmunds, Suffolk IP31 3RB.** *01359*

# EAST OF ENGLAND

270121. www.thedellcaravanpark.co.uk. Excellent clean toilet blocks. Dogs welcome. Follow A14 take J46 for Beyton/Thurston, follow signs for park. Less than 1hr from coast. Open: All year. ★★★ BH&HPA 10

## East Bergholt

(8m). The Grange Country Park, Straight Road (East End Road), East Bergholt, Suffolk CO7 6UX. *0800 014 8248*. www.thegrangecountrypark.co.uk. Offers luxury lodges and static caravans for sale on an 11-acre site set in the beautiful Constable Countryside. Facilities are comprehensive and include an outdoor heated swimming pool, together with a clubhouse with restaurant and bar, providing regular entertainment. There's also a children's play area, a general store on-site, as well as an outdoor BBQ area, nature trails and woodland walks. On A120 Colchester to Harwich turn north at Horsley Cross onto B1035 for 1.5m then right to Bradfield and enter the site. Leave A12 at junction 31, then turn left onto the B1070 (East Bergholt), turn left onto East End Road which merges to Straight Road. The entrance to the park is on the left hand side. Open: 1 February - 31 December. ★★★★

## Felixstowe

(1m). Felixstowe Beach Holiday Park, Walton Avenue, Felixstowe, Suffolk IP11 2HA. *0845 8159775*. www.ParkHolidaysUK.com. Indoor pool, children's facilities. Golf, bird watching, fishing, walking. Slide, sports field, pool, snacks. Felixstowe: shopping, restaurants. Golf 2m. David Bellamy Bronze Conservation Award. Off A14. Felixstowe is 200yd down from second roundabout - SP. Open: 1 March - 14 January. ★★★ BH&HPA NCC 385

(1m). Peewit Caravan Park, Walton Avenue, Felixstowe, Suffolk IP11 2HB. *01394 284511*. www.peewitcaravanpark.co.uk. Family owned and operated. Laundry, children's play area, bowls green. Boules/petanque. Shops nearby. Town centre 1m, seafront 900yd. David Bellamy Gold Conservation Award. A14 to Felixstowe Port roundabout. Entrance to park on L, 100yd along Walton Avenue towards Town Centre. Open: 1 April - 31 October. ★★★★ 10 50

(1m). Suffolk Sands Holiday Park, Carr Road, Felixstowe, Suffolk IP11 2TS. *0845 8159775*. www.ParkHolidaysUK.com. Situated on seafront. Family entertainment. Licensed club. Laundrette. Dogs charged for. Felixstowe: restaurants, shopping, cinema. David Bellamy Silver Conservation Award. Owner supplied copy. Off A14 just S of Felixstowe. Open: 1 March - 5 January. BH&HPA NCC 334

## Ipswich

(3m). Low House Touring Caravan Centre, Bucklesham Road, Foxhall, Ipswich, Suffolk IP10 0AU. *01473 659437*. 3.5 acres of lawns and trees. Situated between Felixstowe and Ipswich. Pets corner, play area. Tourist Board member. PO, shops, golf course 2m; doctor 4m. Turn off A14 Ipswich ring road S via slip road onto A1156 go over bridge second R and site is on L now, SP. Open: All year. ★★★ 30

(4m). Orwell Meadows Leisure Park, Alnesbourne Priory, Nacton, Ipswich, Suffolk IP10 0JS. *01473 726666*. www.orwellmeadows.co.uk. Luxury caravans for hire. Modern showers. Swimming pool. Clubhouse. Family run site adjacent to country park. 1m from A14 Ipswich bypass follow sign for Ransomes Europark and Orwell Country Park. Open: 1 March - 14 January. ★★★★ BH&HPA 80 7

## Relax..... Unwind.....
### Enjoy the quieter life.....

Sheltered by pines and oaks, catching every moment of the sun. Priory Park is a unique and magnificent property. Set in the middle of an area of outstanding natural beauty, its 100 acres of the south facing wooded parkland enjoys panoramic views over the river Orwell estuary.

Within the secure gated grounds of Priory Park we are pleased to offer a selection of lodges and new caravan holiday homes for sale enabling you to own your own country retreat.

The tranquility of Priory Park is an ideal location to escape the rigours of everyday life!

If you would like further details or to make an appointment to view, please contact either Lisa or James at:
**Priory Park, Ipswich, Suffolk IP10 0JT**
**01473 727393 • www.priory-park.com**

# EAST OF ENGLAND

**Priory Park**, Priory Park, Nacton, Ipswich, Suffolk IP10 0JT. *01473 727393*. www.priory-park.com. New developments available with choice of plots & holiday homes to buy. Private 9 hole golf course, south facing landscaped grounds, river views, gated community, exclusive park maintaining very high standards. Open all year. Leave A14 Ipswich southern bypass at Nacton interchange. Follow signs towards Ipswich Town Centre. After 300yds turn L and follow road into Priory Park. Open: All year. BH&HPA 60⚡ ▲ 3⛺

**Shotley Caravan Park**, Gate Farm Road, Shotley Gate, Ipswich, Suffolk IP9 1QH. *01473 787421*. Adults only. 9-acre site with panoramic views of the river Orwell with walks along the river. Electric hook-up points. Shop and PO in village seven minutes walk. Rallies welcome. Marina nearby. A45 to Ipswich, take B1456 to Shotley through village of Shotley Gate Farm road on L. Open: All year. 10⚡ 30⛺

(4.5m). **The Oaks Caravan Park** (Adults-only), Chapel Road, Bucklesham, Ipswich, Suffolk IP10 0BT. *01394 448837*. www.oakscaravanpark.co.uk. Age 18 years and over. Very quiet in countryside. Free use of following: BBQs, on site quoits, boules, hot & cold wash up sinks. Patio area, local fishing lake, pay & display golf, on site cycle hire, local restaurants and pubs nearby. A14 E towards Felixstowe exit L, SP Bucklesham/ Brightwell continue for about 1m turn R to Kirton, site on right hand side. Open: 1 March - 15 January. 100⚡

### Leiston

(1m). **Cakes and Ale Caravan Park**, Abbey Lane, Leiston, Suffolk IP16 4TE. *01728 831655*. www.cakesandale.net. Quiet low key well maintained grounds and facilities. Most sites hardstanding super pitch. Club. Tennis courts. Play area. Recreation area with golf driving range and practice nets. Volleyball, petanque. AA 3-pennant. Leave A12 turn on to B1121 to Saxmundham. Turn E on to B1119 towards Leiston. After 3m turn N to Theberton and follow camping park signs. 2m W of Minsmere bird sanctuary. Convenient Aldeburgh, Dunwich, Southwood. Open: 1 April - 31 October. 50⚡ 50⚡ ▲

(2m). **Cliff House Camping & Caravan Park**, Sizewell Common, Leiston, Suffolk IP16 4TU. *01728 830724*. www.cliffhousepark.co.uk. Great for cycling. From A12 take signs to Snape, follow road to Leiston then Sizewell beach. Open: 16 March - 16 December. BH&HPA 60⚡ ▲ 3⛺

### Lowestoft

(2m). **Azure Seas Holiday Village**, The Street, Corton, Lowestoft, Suffolk NR32 5HN. *01502 731403*. www.azureseas.co.uk. Luxury caravan holiday homes for sale with sea views. Very close to Pleasurewood Hills American theme park. Adjoining beach. Gas. Shops near. Booking advisable July and August. Fishing, swimming pool within 0.25m. Off A12 2m N of Lowestoft on to Corton Long Lane, L then immediately R. Open: 8 March - 1 November. NCC 50⚡ 50⚡ ▲ 72⛺

(2m). **Beach Farm Residential & Holiday Park**, Arbor Lane, Pakefield, Lowestoft, Suffolk NR33 7BD. *01502 572794*. www.beachfarmpark.co.uk. Few minutes walk from sea. Licensed clubroom. Laundry. Swimming pool. 5mins from large supermarket. Peaceful, sheltered site. Seasonal entertainment, takeaway food. On A12 Kessingland to Yarmouth. Off Pakefield roundabout (Water Tower). Open: 1 March - 31 October. ★★★ BH&HPA 3⚡ 2⚡ ▲ 28⛺

(3m). **Broadland Sands Holiday Park**, Coast Road, Corton, Lowestoft, Suffolk NR32 5LG. *01502 730939*. www.broadlandsands.co.uk. Close to Oulton Broad and 7m from Gt Yarmouth. 46 level acres. 100ft heated pool with 45 metre flume. Children's pool. Large walled sun terrace. Family club complex with live entertainment. Tennis. Playground. Pitch and putt etc. Restaurant, separate bar and vast conservatory, snooker lounge, sports bar with TV. Arcade. Private coast access. 7m from Gt Yarmouth. Off A12 Yarmouth Road. Open: 1 March - 31 October. ★★★★ 420⚡

(2m). **Carlton Manor**, Chapel Road, Carlton Colville, Lowestoft, Suffolk NR33 8BL. *01502 561100*. www.carltonmanorpark.co.uk. On A146.

Open: 1 March - 15 January.

(3.5m). **Chestnut Farm Touring Park**, Gisleham, Lowestoft, Suffolk NR33 8EE. *01502 740227*. 3 acres, level grassy site. Private fishing. Pubs & restaurants 1.5m; shops, golf & beaches within 3m. AA 2 pennants. W off A12 at southern roundabout on Kessingland bypass (opposite Suffolk Wildlife Park) SP Rushmere, Mutford and Gisleham, then 2nd turning on L, then 1st drive on L. Open: 1 April - 31 October. NCC 20⚡ 20⚡ ▲

(4m). **Heathland Beach Caravan Park**, London Road, Kessingland, Lowestoft, Suffolk NR33 7PJ. *01502 740337*. www.heathlandbeach.com. Three heated outdoor pools. Tennis. Private beach access. Play area. Bar. Fishing. David Bellamy Gold Conservation Award. Off A12 on B1437, North of Kessingland village. Open: 1 April - 31 October. ★★★★★ BH&HPA 63⚡ 63⚡ ▲ 183⛺

(4m). **Kessingland Beach Holiday Park**, Beach Road, Kessingland, Lowestoft, Suffolk NR33 7RW. *01502 740636*. www.park-resortstouring.com. Indoor and outdoor heated pools. Laundrette. On site store. Tennis courts. Free kids club. Free evening entertainment for all the family. Amusements. Takeaway and restaurant. Bar. Mini ten pin bowling. Soft play area. Adventure playground. All weather sports court. David Bellamy Gold Conservation Award. Kessingland is on A12 Ipswich to Lowestoft Road. About 4m S of Lowestoft, take the Kessingland beach exit from the roundabout near the Wildlife Park on to Whites Lane. Follow road for about 1.5m to the beach. Park is 400yd further on. Open: 20 March - 31 October. ★★★ BH&HPA NCC 90⚡ ▲ 465⛺

(4m). **Kessingland Camping & Caravanning Club Site**, Whites Lane, Kessingland, Lowestoft, Suffolk NR33 7TF. *01502 742040*. www.campingandcaravanningclub.co.uk. All units accepted. Non-members welcome. Great Yarmouth and Lowestoft are close by and boast excellent beaches. Special deals available for families and backpackers. Loo Of The Year (5 stars). Follow Wildlife Park signs off

---

**CAKES AND ALE**
*THE CENTRE FOR COASTAL SUFFOLK*
Open 1st March to 15th January
For a free brochure call **01728 831655** or email alternatively try our **web site www.cakesandale.net** or just come and visit us

Set amongst the beautiful Suffolk scenery between Aldeburgh and Southwold, Cakes and Ale is an oasis of tranquillity and quality. Just minutes from Minsmere bird sanctuary and the ancient monument of Leiston Abbey. Cakes and Ale the ideal place to explore the Suffolk Heritage Coast (or just relax and put your feet up). New holiday homes available from £30,000

CAKES AND ALE ABBEY LANE THEBERTON SUFFOLK IP16 4TE

# EAST OF ENGLAND

A12 from Lowestoft towards London. After leaving A12 at roundabout SP Kessingland, turn R to site entrance. Adjacent to Suffolk Wildlife Park and within easy reach of east coast resorts. Open: 1 April - 31 October.
★★★★ NCC 90 90

(1.5m). Pakefield Caravan Park, Arbor Lane, Lowestoft, Suffolk NR33 7BE. 01502 561136. www.pakefieldpark. co.uk. A quiet, select site situated on a cliff with a family club house, heated outdoor pool, shop, laundry and play area. Close to the beach 7 bus stop. From A12 northbound, at Pakefield McDonald's roundabout take 3rd exit - London Road, past water tower, 2nd R onto Clifftonville Road then 1st R - Grayson Avenue. Park Sraight ahead. From A1117 take 1st exit at McDonald's roundabout then as above. Open: 1 March - 31 October.
★★★ BH&HPA 393

(5m). White House Beach Caravan Club Site, Kessingland, Lowestoft, Suffolk NR33 7RW. 01502 740278. www.caravanclub.co.uk. 7 acre site with 117 pitches (20 have their own toilet block and dishwashing facility) and 80 hardstandings. Small children's play area. Members only. Off A12. Open: 23 March - 5 November. NCC 117 117

### Polstead

(4m). Polstead Camping & Caravanning Club Site, Holt Road, Bower House Tye, Polstead, Suffolk CO6 5BZ. 01787 211969 . www.campingandcaravanningclub.co.uk. Set on the edge of a beautiful conservation area. Long Melford, Sudbury, Lavenham & the Stour valley are within easy reach of the site. When on the A1071 either in the direction of Sudbury or the direction of Ipswich, follow the brown Camping signs & ignore Sat Nav. Open: 14 February - 14 January.
★★★ NCC 50 50

### Saxmundham

(1.5m). Carlton Meres Country Park, Rendham Road, Saxmundham, Suffolk IP17 2QP. 01728 603344. www.carltonmeres.co.uk. Beauty salon, gym, tennis court. Sauna and steam room. Wi-Fi connections. Brown tourist info signs from A12. Turn W off A12 on to B1119 then follow signs. Open: 28 March - 1 November. BH&HPA 100 10

(8m). Cliff House Holiday Park, Minsmere Road, Dunwich, Saxmundham, Suffolk IP17 3DQ. 01728 648282. www.cliffhouseholidays.co.uk. Country house in 30-acres, beach frontage between Southwold (8m) and Aldeburgh adjoining National Trust and RSPB. Free House bar and informal restaurant. Shower block. Games room and playground. Golf courses, beach. David Bellamy Gold Conservation Award. From A12 at Yoxford turn off to Westleton. Turning L at T junction. Turn R to Dunwich Heath and after 1.5m turn R again. The park is 0.75m on the L. 6 miles from Southwold. Open: 1 March - 31 October. ★★★★ BH&HPA 87 59

(6m). Haw Wood Farm Caravan Park, Darsham, Saxmundham, Suffolk IP17 3QT. 01986 784248. www.haw-woodfarm.co.uk. The perfect site for discovering the Suffolk coast and countryside. Quiet site with showers and play area. Fishing and golf nearby. Little Chef 0.5m, nearest pub about 1.5m. Darsham station 2m. Owner supplied copy. Off A12. Turn R off A12 1.5m N of Darsham level crossing at Little Chef. Park 0.5m on R. 8m from Southwold. Open: 1 March - 14 January. BH&HPA 100 55

(2m). Marsh Farm Caravan Site, Marsh Farm, Sternfield, Saxmundham, Suffolk IP17 1HW. 01728 602168. 30-acre site in tranquil rural setting. Coarse fishing lakes adjoining. Close to Snape Maltings and Aldeburgh. From A12 after Farnham take 1st R sp Aldeburgh A1094. In 1.5m turn L sp Sternfield proceed 1m then follow farm signs. 30-acre site in tranquil rural setting. Coarse fishing lakes adjoining. Close to Snape Maltings and Aldeburgh. Open: All year. 45

(1m). Whitearch Touring Caravan Park, Main Road, Benhall, Saxmundham, Suffolk IP17 1NA. 01728 604646. One acre coarse fishing lake. Tennis court. 50 pitches electric hook-ups, TV points. Great base for sightseeing. J A12 and B1121. Open: 1 April - 30 September. ★★★ 50

### Southwold

(1m). Southwold Camping and Caravan Park, Southwold, Suffolk IP18 6ND. 01502 722486. www.waveney.gov.uk. Enquiries to the manager. No booking necessary. Off A12. Turn towards Southwold at Wrentham. Go through towards harbour mouth. Open: 18 April - 31 October. 500 330

### Stowmarket

(5m). Stonham Barns Caravan & Camping Park, Pettaugh Road, Stonham Aspal, Stowmarket, Suffolk IP14 6AT. 01449 711901. www.stonhambarnsleisure.co.uk. A warm welcome awaits you at Stonham Barns Caravan & Camping Park, which is set in a peaceful tree lined corner of Stonham Barns Leisure & Retail Park that offers: fisheries, Suffolk owl sanctuary, restaurant, shopping, jewellery, pottery, kitchenware. Golf range & course. Leave A14, Stowmarket to Ipswich road at Jct 51. At roundabout take A140 Norwich. R on to A1120 SP Stonham Aspal and Stonham Barns. Follow brown signs. Open: All year. 60 60

## Holiday Homes For Sale

Quiet beautifully landscaped parkland, woodland and meadows. Sandy beach, golf, tennis, restaurant.

### MOON & SIXPENCE

Newbourn Road, Waldringfield, Woodbridge, Suffolk IP12 4PP.
Tel: 01473 736650
www.moonandsixpence.eu
email: info@moonandsixpence.eu

# EAST OF ENGLAND / SOUTH EAST

## Sudbury

(2m). **Willowmere Camping Park**, Little Cornard, Sudbury, Suffolk CO10 0NN. *01787 375559*. Has 40 touring pitches (24 with electric) in 3 acres surrounded by trees. Food shop & restaurant within 0.5 mile. Nearest takeaway 1 mile. Take B1508 from Sudbury. Open: 1 March - 31 October. ★★★ BH&HPA 🚻♿🏕🚐⚡🛁🍴🏪🛒 ⚘🔥📶🎣 40⚡ 👤

## Woodbridge

(4m). **Moon And Sixpence**, Newbourn Road, Waldringfield, Woodbridge, Suffolk IP12 4PP. *01473 736650*. www.moonandsixpence.eu. AA 5 pennant premier park. Superb loos and bathrooms, lounge bar and restaurant. 2 acre, deep water lake with private fishing mid-September and mid-October, golden sand beach. Adventure play area. 3 hard tennis courts, volley & basketball, petanque. 9 hole compact golf course. Quietness essential from 9pm - 8am. 18 hole golf 0.5m away. Sailing, water sports 2m. Indoor pool 4m. No groups. Turn off Ipswich eastern bypass A12 taking minor road towards Waldringfield. Park is SP. Open: 8 April - 31 October. 🍴🚻♿🏕🚐⚡🛁🍴🏪🛒⚘🔥📶🎣✕🐕📶 90⚡ 90⚡ 👤

**Steadings Park Caravan Park**, Ipswich Road, Newbourne, Woodbridge, Suffolk IP12 4NS. *01473 736505*. www.steadingspark.co.uk. A small touring park within ten minutes of Woodbridge in the heart of rural Suffolk. In a tranquil setting the park borders Newbourne Springs Nature Reserve and the river Deben with its peaceful yacht harbour is only a short walk. A quiet retreat that provides the perfect base for walkers, cyclists and holidays makers alike to explore glorious Suffolk and the Heritage coast. Great village pub & restaurant 5 minutes walk. Children's playground. Travelling from the west take jct 58 off the A14 - signposted A12N Woodbridge. At bottom of slip road turn left onto the A12. Follow the A12 until you see tourist signs for 'Katie's Garden'. At R/A take the third exit towards Newbourne. After approx half a mile turn right - signposted 'Fox Inn & Katie's Garden'. When you see Newbourne village signs the site is approx 500m past these on the left. Open: Contact site direct. 🚻♿🏕🚐⚡🛁🍴🏪🛒⚘🔥📶🎣 30⚡ 👤

## BERKSHIRE

### Lambourn

**Farncombe Farm CS**, Baydon Rd, Lambourn, Berkshire RG17 7BN. *01488 71833*. Rural site with good views. Open: All year. 🏕🚐⚡🛁🍴

## Hurley

(1m). **Hurley Riverside Park**, Hurley, Berkshire SL6 5NE. *01628 823501*. www.hurleyriversidepark.co.uk. Family run park alongside River Thames. Over 1km of private river frontage for picnics, BBQs & fishing. Accepts tourers, motorhomes, RVs & tents. Grass, hardstanding & premium multi-service pitches. Holiday Park has four separate fields of individual Caravan Holiday Homes in their own unique garden, some with a river view. Set in picturesque Hurley village. Good access to major roads. M40 J4 & M4 J8/9. Take A404(M) then exit A4130 Henley-on-Thames. Park 1km past Hurley village. Open: 1 Mar - 31 Oct. ★★★★ BH&HPA 🚻♿🏕🚐⚡🛁🍴🏪🛒⚘🔥📶🎣 ♿ 138⚡ 138⚡ 62🔺 10⚡

**Hurleyford Farm Holiday Home Park**, Park Office, Mill Lane, Hurley, Berkshire SL6 5ND. *01628 829009*. Child free park (children may visit occasionally), south bank of River Thames. Fishing on park. All mains facilities. Own private gardens, working farm. Shop 200yd, pubs & restaurants in village. 0.5m of river frontage. 11 months licence (closed February). David Bellamy Gold Conservation Award. From M4, J8/9 take A404 N then A4130 towards Henley on Thames. After 1.5m turn R into Hurley High Street. Take R fork by village green into Mill Lane. From M40 J5 take A404 S, 3rd exit A4130 towards Henley on Thames, then as above. 4m from Maidenhead. Open: 1 Mar - 31 Jan. ★★★★ BH&HPA 🚻🏕🍴 🚐⚡🛁 109⚡

# SOUTH EAST

## Maidenhead

(3m). **Amerden Caravan and Camp Site, Old Marsh Lane, Dorney Reach, Maidenhead, Berkshire SL6 0DZ.** *01628 627461.* www.amerdencaravanpark.webs.com. Small riverside site. River fishing in season. Supermarket 1.5m. Train station to London 1.25m. Ideal base for visiting Windsor, London and Legoland. Leave M4 J7 (Slough West) turn L along A4 towards Maidenhead, 3rd turn L Marsh Lane, 1st turn R Old Marsh Lane. Open: 1 April - 31 October.
★★★★ ♿ ♿ ⚲ ⚲ ⚲ ⚲ ⚲ ⚲ ⚲ 20🚐 20🛻 20A 2⛽

## Newbury

(2m). **Oakley Farm Caravan Park, Andover Road, Wash Water, Newbury, Berkshire RG20 0LP.** *01635 36581.* www.oakleyfarm.co.uk. Not suitable for caravans over 22 foot long or motorcaravans over 24 foot long. 30-pitch, 3-acre site surrounded by beautiful countryside. 2.5m S of Newbury off A343. From A34 Newbury bypass, take exit marked Highclere/Wash Common. Turn L towards Newbury on A343. After 400yd turn R into Penwood Road. Open: 1 March - 31 October. ♿ ♿
⚲ ⚲ ⚲ ⚲ ⚲ ⚲ 30🚐 30🛻 30A

## Reading

◆ (6m). **Wellington Country Park, Riseley, Reading, Berkshire RG7 1SP.** *01189 326444.* www.wellington-country-park.co.uk. Beautiful campsite set within woodland glades, just off A33 between Reading and Basingstoke, 4m S of M4, J11. Campers have FREE access to Country Park with children's play areas, crazy golf, animal farm and miniature railway. Cafe and gift shop. Open: 16 March - 4 November. ★★★★ BH&HPA ♿ ♿
⚲ ⚲ ⚲ ⚲ ⚲ ⚲ ⚲ ⚲ ⚲ ⚲ 44🚐 58🛻 27A

## BUCKINGHAMSHIRE
### Beaconsfield

(3m). **Highclere Farm Park, Newbarn Lane, Seer Green, Beaconsfield, Buckinghamshire HP9 2QZ.** *01494 874505.* www.highclerefarmpark.co.uk. Only 20m from London. Local train service to Marylebone 35mins. Station 1m. Windsor 10m. A peaceful site well situated for touring Buckinghamshire. A355 Beaconsfield to Amersham, R to Seer Green then follow tourist signs. Open: 1 March - 31 January.
★★★★ BH&HPA ♿ ♿ ⚲ ⚲ ⚲ ⚲
⚲ ⚲ ⚲ ⚲ ⚲ 45🚐 45🛻

### Emberton

(0.5m). **Emberton Country Park, Olney Road, Emberton, Buckinghamshire MK46 5FJ.** *01234 711575.* www.mkweb.co.uk/embertonpark. 200 acres of beautiful parkland. 5 all year fishing lakes and river Ouse (closed season observed on river). Rallies welcome, special rates. On A509 Newport Pagnell to Olney. Open: 1 April - 31 October. ★★ ♿ ♿ ⚲ ⚲ ⚲
⚲ ⚲ ⚲ 30🚐 50🛻 A

### Milton Keynes

**Cosgrove Leisure Park, Cosgrove, Milton Keynes, Buckinghamshire MK19 7JP.** *01908 563360.* www.cosgrovepark.co.uk. Swimming pool, grocery shop, fishing, tackle & bait, water skiing, children's play area, mini golf, tennis, amusement park, cafe, takeaway food, fishing. Golf course 4m, central Milton Keynes shopping centre 7m. Owner supplied copy. 2.5m from Stony Stratford, off A508 through village of Cosgrove. Open: 1 April - 1 November. ⚲ ⚲ ⚲ ⚲ ⚲ ⚲ ⚲ ⚲ ⚲
⚲ 50🚐 350🛻 391🛻

(3m). **Gullivers Milton Keynes Camping & Caravanning Club Site, Livingstone Drive, Milton Keynes, Buckinghamshire MK15 0DT.** *02476 475580.* www.campingandcaravanningclub.co.uk. 90 mixed pitches in total. Site popular with families and children with a theme park next door. Camping pods available on site. Main attractions close to site and central Milton Keynes 3m away. From M1 take A509 towards Milton Keynes follow signs to Gullivers then park. Open: 1 April - 31 October. ★★★★ ♿ ♿ ⚲ ⚲ ⚲ ⚲ ⚲
⚲ ⚲ ⚲ ⚲ 90🚐 90🛻 A

### Newport Pagnell

(0.5m). **Lovat Meadow Caravan Park, London Road, Newport Pagnell, Buckinghamshire MK16 0AE.** *01908 610858.* newport-pagnell.org.uk. Secluded riverside site close to Milton Keynes, Silverstone, Woburn Abbey and Safari Park. Heated swimming pool adjacent. Limited facilities. Resident warden. Owner supplied copy. M1 J4 (1.5m) A509-B526 Newport Pagnell by-pass 0.25m. Open: 5 April - 31 October. ⚲ ♿ ⚲ 40🛻

### Uxbridge

(1m). **Wyatts Covert Caravan Club Site, Tilehouse Lane, Denham, Uxbridge, Buckinghamshire UB9 5DH.** *01895 832729.* www.caravanclub.co.uk. Very conveniently placed not far from both the M25 and M40, but surprisingly green, and screened by good trees. MV service point. Fishing, golf and NCN route nearby. Facilities for disabled. Members only. No tents. See website for standard directions to site. Open: All year. NCC ⚲ ♿ ⚲ ⚲
⚲ ⚲ ⚲ ⚲ ⚲ 50🚐 50🛻

## EAST SUSSEX
### Battle

(2.5m). **Crazy Lane Tourist Park, Whydown Farm, Sedlescombe, Battle, East Sussex TN33 0QT.** *01424 870147.* www.crazylane.co.uk. A small, secluded park situated in a suntrap valley in the heart of 1066 country. Within easy reach of beaches and historical sites. S on A21 turn L 100yd past junction B2244 opposite Blackbrooks Garden Centre. Open: 1 March - 31 October. ★★★ BH&HPA
♿ ⚲ ⚲ ⚲ ⚲ ⚲ 20🚐 36🛻 A

(3m). **Normanhurst Caravan Club Site, Stevens Crouch, Battle, East Sussex TN33 9LR.** *01424 773808.* www.caravanclub.co.uk. Located in a former garden with specimen trees and shrubs. Views of distant downs. Dog walk. Advance booking essential Bank Holidays, July, August and weekends. Toilet blocks with privacy cubicles and laundry facilities. MV service point. Hardstandings. Playground. Fishing and golf nearby. Ideal for families. Shops within 3m. Non-members welcome. No tents. See website for standard directions to site. Open: 30 March - 5 November.
★★★★ NCC ⚲ ♿ ⚲ ⚲ ⚲ ⚲ ⚲
⚲ ⚲ ⚲ ⚲ 149🚐 149🛻

(2m). **Senlac Wood Holiday Park, Catsfield Road, Catsfield, Battle, East Sussex TN33 9LN.** *01424 773969.* 5 mins drive from Battle, 15 mins Hastings. 20 acres of woodland walks and all the usual facilities on quiet site. Riding, golf and fishing nearby. Historic sites and walks. 3 pennants. From Battle take A271 (Bexhill/Catford) past Squirrel Pub, take next L (B2204), Senlac Wood is on this road on L. Open: 1 March - 31 October. ⚲
♿ ⚲ ⚲ ⚲ ⚲ ⚲ ⚲ ⚲ ⚲ ⚲ ⚲ ⚲
⚲ 16🚐 24🛻 20A

### Bexhill-on-Sea

(1m). **Cobbs Hill Farm Caravan & Camping Park, Watermill Lane, Bexhill-on-Sea, East Sussex TN39 5JA.** *01424 213460.* www.cobbshillfarm.co.uk. Quiet, farm site with level sheltered pitches and within easy reach of Battle, Hastings and Eastbourne. Rally field and tent field available. From Bexhill take A269, turn R into Watermill Lane. Site 1m on L, SP. Open: 1 April - 31 October. ★★★★ BH&HPA NCC ♿ ⚲ ⚲ ⚲ ⚲ ⚲ ⚲ ⚲ ⚲
⚲ ⚲ 45🚐 45🛻 A 2⛽

(4m). **Kloofs Camping & Caravan Park, Sandhurst Lane, Bexhill-on-Sea, East Sussex TN39 4RG.** *01424 842839.* www.kloofs.com. Quiet country site about 2m from sea. Ultra modern all year pitches. Facilities, play area. From Bexhill take A259 west to Little Common roundabout,

# SOUTH EAST

turn R into Peartree Lane, 1m turn L to Whydown, signs to site. Open: All year. ★★★★★ BH&HPA ⛺ ♿ 🚿 ... 50⚡ ⛺ 75💰

## Brighton

**Sheepcote Valley Caravan Club Site, East Brighton Park, Brighton, East Sussex BN2 5TS.** *01273 626546.* www.caravanclub.co.uk. Ideally located 2m E of Brighton, a short distance inland from the marina and adjacent to extensive recreation grounds. Baby/toddler washroom. MV service point, gas/gaz and vegetable preparation area. Golf, water sports and NCN route nearby. Facilities for disabled. Playground, ideal site for families. Non-members and tent campers welcome. See website for standard directions to site. Open: All year. ★★★★★ NCC ... 269⚡ 269⚡

## Crowborough

**(0.5m). Crowborough Camping & Caravanning Club Site, Goldsmith Recreation Ground, Crowborough, East Sussex TN6 2TN.** *01892 664827.* www.campingandcaravanningclub.co.uk. A great view from the site across the Weald to the North Downs. Indoor swimming pool nearby with concession rates for campers. A peaceful relaxing atmosphere. Non-members welcome. All units accepted. Special deals available for families and backpackers. Leave M25 at exit 5 take A21 to Tonbridge, then A26 through Tunbridge Wells to the northern outskirts of Crowborough. Turn L off A26 into entrance to Goldsmiths Grand signed Leisure Centre. At top of road turn R into site lane. Open: 1 April - 31 October. ★★★★ NCC ... 90⚡ 90⚡ ⛺

## Crowhurst

**(0.5m). Brakes Coppice Park, Forewood Lane, Crowhurst, East Sussex TN33 9AB.** *01424 830322.* www.brakescoppicepark.co.uk. A small, quiet, secluded park in a beautiful, sheltered position. Close to the beaches of Bexhill and Hastings. Washing up and laundry facilities. Coarse fishing on site. Off A2100. 2m from Battle. Open: 1 March - 31 October. DII&HPA ... 30⚡ 30⚡ 30⛺

## Eastbourne

**(1m). Fairfields Farm Caravan & Camping Park, Eastbourne Road, Westham, Pevensey, Eastbourne, East Sussex BN24 5NG.** *01323 763165.* www.fairfieldsfarm.com. An attractive touring park on a family run working farm (60 pitches in all). Close to Eastbourne and an ideal base for exploring the many attractions of the region. Peaceful location with free fishing. Situated on B2191 in Westham. 3m from Eastbourne. Open: 1 April - 31 October. ★★★★ ... 60⚡ ⛺

## Hailsham

**The Old Mill Caravan Park, Chalvington Lane, Golden Cross, Hailsham, East Sussex BN27 3SS.** *01825 872532.* www.jasminewindmill.com. ...

## Hastings

**(5m). Coghurst Hall Holiday Park, Ivyhouse Lane, Ore, Hastings, East Sussex TN35 4NP.** *0845 8159775.* www.ParkHolidaysUK.com. Indoor leisure pool, children's club. Golf, horse riding, fishing, bird watching. Nature trail round the park, suitable for children. Woodland walks. Natural waterfall. Coghurst Hall is all about total relaxation in a superb countryside setting surrounding an impressive fishing lake and is just a short drive from Hastings seafront. David Bellamy Gold Conservation Award. 3m NE of Hastings located midway between Ore and Three Oaks. Open: 1 March - 31 January. ★★★ BH&HPA NCC ... 600💰

**(6m). Fairlight Wood Caravan Club Site, Watermill Lane, Pett, Hastings, East Sussex TN35 4HY.** *01424 812333.* www.caravanclub.co.uk. A small and intimate site in flower-rich woodland. Dog walk. Shop 0.5m. Toilet blocks with privacy cubicles and laundry facilities. MV service point. Ideal for families. Members only. No tents. See website for standard directions to site. Open: 23 March - 5 November. NCC ... 42⚡ 42⚡

**(1.5m). Spindlewood Country Park, Bricklands Farm, Rock Lane, Ore, Hastings, East Sussex TN35 4JN.** *01424 720825.* www.spindlewood.co.uk. Fully licensed clubhouse. Laundry facilities. Lake fishing. Golf course 3m. 1.5m to Hastings town centre, cinema, theatre, shopping centre, attractions. Owner supplied copy. M25 J5 towards Hastings on A21 Turn R into Junction Road, then R on to B2093 to Ore. Turn L at traffic light on to A259. Turn L after B&Q store, straight on for 200yd into Rock Lane. Park on L. Open: 1 March - 30 November. BH&HPA ... 92⚡

**(2.5m). Stalkhurst Caravan Park, Ivyhouse Lane, Hastings, East Sussex TN35 4NN.** *01424 439015.* Sites available for owner-occupied holiday static caravans. Good access. Gently sloping, well sheltered. Indoor heated swimming pool. New and used caravans for sale. Golf and fishing nearby. 2.5m to Hastings town centre and beach. 1m to nearest shops and PO. A259 from seafront towards Rye. Turn L on to B2093. After about 0.5m Ivyhouse Lane is on R. From A21 at the boundary take road SP A259 Folkestone. After 2.5m turn L into Ivyhouse Lane. Open: 1 March - 15 January. ★★★ BH&HPA ... 11⚡ ⛺ 22💰

## Heathfield

**(1.5m). Greenviews Caravan Fields, Burwash Road, Broad Oak, Heathfield, East Sussex TN21 8RT.** *01435 863531.* Licensed club on site (weekends). Spar shop and PO 0.5m away, pub and restaurant 500yd. Owner supplied copy. On A265 between Board Oak and Heathfield. Open: 1 April - 31 October. BH&HPA ... 10⚡ ⛺ 51💰

**(0.25m). Horam Manor Touring Park, Horam, Heathfield, East Sussex TN21 0YD.** *01435 813662.* www.horam-manor.co.uk. A tranquil, rural setting in an Area of Outstanding Natural Beauty. Nature trails, farm museum, cafe, horse riding, fishing on the estate. All local services within 5 mins walking distance. On A267 3m S of Heathfield and 10m N of Eastbourne. Open: 1 March - 31 October. ★★★★ BH&HPA ... 90⚡

## Lewes

**(7m). Broomfield Farm Caravan Club Site, Stalkers Lane, East Hoathly, Lewes, East Sussex BN8 6QS.** *01825 872242.* www.caravanclub.co.uk. A peaceful, rural site set in Sussex countryside. Own sanitation required. Dog walk. MV service point. Boules pitch. Golf and fishing nearby. Members only. No tents. See website for standard directions to site. 1.5m from East Hoathly. Open: 23 March - 22 October. NCC ... 78⚡ 78⚡

## Pevensey

**(17m). Castle View Caravan & Camping Site, Eastbourne Road, Pevensey, East Sussex BN24 6DT.** *01323 763038.* Licensed shop. Fast food. Laundry. Beach 10 mins. Eastbourne 3m. Free hot water, baths & showers. Calor Gas. TV Room. Owner supplied copy. On A259. Open: 1 March - 31 October. ... 75⚡ ⛺ 62💰

**(3m). Norman's Bay Camping & Caravanning Club Site, Norman's Bay,**

# SOUTH EAST

**Pevensey, East Sussex BN24 6PR.** *01323 761190* . www.campingandcaravanningclub.co.uk. Quiet, family run site with laundry facilities. Private beach, free boat park. Non-members welcome. New and second-hand caravan sales. S of A259 roundabout at Pevensey, situated in village. Open: 1 April - 31 October. ★★★★ BH&HPA

## Pevensey Bay

**(1m). Bay View Park, Old Martello Road, Pevensey Bay, East Sussex BN24 6DX.** *01323 768688*. www.bay-view.co.uk. Award winning park next to beach. On site 9 hole par 3 golf course. Adjacent to Sovereign Harbour Marina with its range of bars and restaurants. David Bellamy Gold Conservation Award. On A259 Eastbourne to Pevensey Bay. Open: 4 March - 31 October. ★★★★★ BH&HPA 49 49 9

## Polegate

**Peel House Farm Caravan Park, Sayerlands Lane (B2104), Polegate, East Sussex BN26 6QX.** *01323 845629*. peelhocp@tesco.net. Quiet country site with views to Downs, many places of interest within 20m. Walks. Heated toilet block with showers and free hot water to basins and sink. Games room with TV, pool table tennis and darts. Fishing, riding nearby. Footpath to Cuckoo Trail. Hailsham to Stonecross 1.75m on B2104. Open: 1 April - 31 October. ★★★★ BH&HPA 20 11

## Robertsbridge

**(5m). Lordine Court Caravan Park, Staplecross, Ewhurst, Robertsbridge, East Sussex TN32 5TF.** *01580 830209*. www.lordine-court.co.uk. Laundry room. Showers. Two bars. Playground. Amusement room. Swimming pool. Restaurant, takeaway. Payphones. Separate pets enclosure. Fishing lake under parks control (off site). Woodland walks. In countryside but only 10m to south coast resort. A21 towards Hastings. L to Hawkhurst B2244 to Cripps corner. B2165 to Northiam left hand side. Open: 1 March - 31 October. BH&HPA NCC 60 160

**Park Farm (Bodiam) Caravan Site, Bodiam, Robertsbridge, East Sussex TN32 5XA.** *01580 831982*. www.parkfarmcamping.co.uk. Beautiful rural site near river and Bodiam Castle. Children's play area. Free fishing in river Rother. Barbecues allowed. Many walks around farm. Owner supplied copy. 3m S of Hawkhurst on B2244. Open: 1 April - 31 October.

## Rye

**(4m). Camber Sands Holiday Park, New Lydd Road, Rye, East Sussex TN31 7RT.** *01797 222000*. www.park-resortstouring.com. 4 indoor pools, spa bath, adventure playground, multi-sports court, amusements, FREE kids clubs, FREE family evening entertainment. Sauna, solarium. David Bellamy Gold Conservation Award. From M25 take M20 come off at J10. Come on to A2070, follow signs to Hastings and Rye, staying on A259, take a L before Rye, SP Camber. The park is 3m along on this road. Open: 20 March - 31 October. ★★★★ BH&HPA NCC 45 90

**(2m). Frenchmans Beach Holiday Park, Rye Harbour, Rye, East Sussex TN31 7TX.** *0845 8159775*. www.parkholiday-suk.com. Family site with indoor leisure complex, pool. Jacuzzi, sauna, clubhouse, pool & cafe. Close to several beaches. Rye: shopping, restaurants. David Bellamy Bronze Conservation Award. 0.25m W of Rye on A259 Hastings road, SP for Rye Harbour. Open: 1 March - 4 January. ★★★ BH&HPA NCC 280

**(7m). Rother Valley Caravan Park, Station Road, Northiam, Rye, East Sussex TN31 6QT.** *01797 253997*. www.rother-valley.com. Fishing 0.5m. Garage, shops, PO, doctor all available nearby. Golf course within 7m. Owner supplied copy. On A28 Hastings to Tenterden road, 50yd from Kent & East Sussex Steam Railway. Open: 1 March - 31 October. 5 10 12

**(3m). The Cock Inn (CS), Main Street, Peasmarsh, Rye, East Sussex TN31 6YD.** *01797 230281*. www.thecockinnatpeasmarsh.co.uk. Quiet site located near Rye, 10m to Camber Sands. Traditional 17th century pub serving good food, large children's play equipment and large sunny gardens, darts, pool and boules pitch. Owner supplied copy. On A268 London to Rye, next door to Jempsons Superstore. Open: 1 March - 31 October. 5 20

**(3.5m). Winchelsea Sands Holiday Park, Pett Level Road, Winchelsea Beach, Rye, East Sussex TN36 4NB.** *0845 8159775*. www.ParkHolidaysUK.com. Outdoor fun pool. Lounge bar and family entertainment club. Free kids club. Rye: shopping, restaurants, 4m away. Local grocery store next door to park. David Bellamy Bronze Conservation Award. Owner supplied copy. Take Rye to Hastings road (A259) turn L into Sea road. Follow for 1m - turn R opposite church in Winchelsea Beach. Open: 2 March - 6 January. ★★★ BH&HPA 386

## Seaford

**(1m). Buckle Caravan And Camping, Marine Parade, Seaford, East Sussex BN25 2QR.** *01323 897801*. www.buckleholidaypark.co.uk. Quiet family run park adjacent to beach. Cross-Channel ferry five minutes by car. Seasonal and storage pitches available. Adult only field if required, disabled facilities. AA 3 stars. A259 between Newhaven and Seaford. Open: All year. BH&HPA 150 150

## St Leonards on Sea

**(3m). Combe Haven Holiday Park (Haven), Harley Shute Road, St Leonards on Sea, East Sussex TN38 8BZ.** *0871 4680496*. www.haven.com. Welcome Host Award. Hastings In Bloom Award. Indoor and outdoor fun pool. Sports and leisure facilities. Restaurant. Kids club. Daytime and evening entertainment. Burger King. Roller disco, sports drome, playground, 9 hole pitch n putt, bowling green, amusements. Play area. Papa John's Pizza. David Bellamy Gold Conservation Award. A21 from London and in Hastings take A259 towards Bexhill. Between Hastings and Bexhill, turn R at Harley Shute Road, Combe Haven is on L, about 200yds. Open: 18 March - 2 November. ★★★★ BH&HPA 450

## Uckfield

**(8m). Heaven Farm, Furners Green, Uckfield, East Sussex TN22 3RG.** *01825 790226*. www.heavenfarm.co.uk. A 1.5m nature trail with wallabies, ponds and parkland which surrounds this ancient farm with many surprises. Fishing on site. Shop, PO 1m. Golf courses nearby. Doctor 5m. Hospital 8m. AA 2 pennants. Owner supplied copy. On A275 1m Sof Danehill. 1m N of Sheffield park, Bluebell Railway. Open: All year (tents May - October). 25 25

**(4m). Honeys Green Caravan Park, Easons Green, Framfield, Uckfield, East Sussex TN22 5GJ.** *01732 860205*. Small friendly privately owned site in stunning rural location. Modern facilities block. Telephone. Walks. Own coarse fishing lake. At Halland roundabout (A22) turn on to B2192 Heathfield road. Site is 0.25m on L. Open: 1 April - 31 October. ★★★ BH&HPA 22 22 22 5

# SOUTH EAST

## HAMPSHIRE
### Andover

(3m). **Wyke Down Touring Caravan & Camping Park**, Picket Piece, Andover, Hampshire SP11 6LX. 01264 352048. www.wykedown.co.uk. 50 electric hook ups (26 of which are hard stand/water/drainage/electric). Dogs allowed but please check breed. Swimming pool. Country pub and restaurant. Limited bus service. Golf driving range. PO, bottle gas 0.75m. Supermarket 2.5m. Town 3m. Fishing & horse riding close by. Camping Park signs from A303 trunk road, follow signs to Wyke Down. Open: All year. ★★★ BH&HPA ♀☐☒♨♠✿ ↯☼⊞⇌✕☐⑤☒⊞☐ 69↯ ⌂

### Ashurst

(5m). **Ashurst Caravan & Camping Site**, Lyndhurst Road, Ashurst, Hampshire SO40 7AR. 02380 292097. www.forestholidays.co.uk. Attractive site set in woodland glade. Level campsite in mainly open ground with some shaded areas of oakwood. Dog free site. Bookings and brochure request on 0845 1308224. David Bellamy Silver Conservation Award. SW of Southampton on A35 sp. 2m from Ashurst. Open: 14 April - 26 September. BH&HPA ⌂ ☐⊞♠⇌♨☐☒ 280↯ ⌂

### Brockenhurst

(1m). **Aldridge Hill Caravan & Camping Site**, Brockenhurst, Hampshire SO42 7QD. 01590 623152. www.forestholidays.co.uk. An attractive level site on the edge of Blackwater stream, close to Brockenhurst village. No toilet facilities. Booking and brochure request on 0845 1308224. Off A337,1m NW of Brockenhurst village. Open: 26 May - 5 Sep (closed 7 - 22 Jun). BH&HPA ⌂ ♠ ↯ 170↯ ⌂

(1m). **Black Knowl (New Forest) Caravan Club Site**, Aldridge Hill, Brockenhurst, Hampshire SO42 7QD. 01590 623600. www.caravanclub.co.uk. Located in the midst of the ancient royal hunting forest of William the Conqueror within walking distance of Brockenhurst. Toilet blocks, laundry facilities & MV service point. Good area for walking, golf & NCN route nearby. Facilities for disabled. Ideal for families. Members only. No tents. Accessed from A35 & A337. Open: 23 March - 19 November. NCC ⌂ ♠ ⌂ ♠ ↯☼⊞♠⇌☒ 127↯ 127↯ ⌂

(2m). **Roundhill Caravan & Camping Site**, Beaulieu Road, Brockenhurst, Hampshire SO40 7QL. 01590 624344. www.forestholidays.co.uk. A spacious site with plenty of room and lots to do. Minimum stay of 2 nights. Refurbished toilets and showers. Booking and brochure requests on 0845 1308224. David Bellamy Gold Conservation Award. B3055, SE of Brockenhurst, off A337 SP. Open: 14 April - 26 September. ★★★ BH&HPA ⌂ ☐♠⇌♨☒☐ 500↯ ⌂

### Christchurch

**New Forest Caravan Club Site**, Forest Road, Bransgore, Christchurch, Hampshire BH23 8EB. 01425 673638. www.caravanclub.co.uk. Set amidst beautiful countryside, close to Christchurch, Poole and Bournemouth. Dog walk, play equipment. Great base to explore area on foot or bicycle. Members only. No tents. See website for standard directions to site. Open: 2 March - 31 October. NCC ⌂ ♠ ⇌♨☐⊞ ♠ ☐☒☐ 261↯ 261↯ ⌂

### Fareham

(2m). **Ellerslie Touring Caravan & Camping Park**, Down End Road, Fareham, Hampshire PO16 8TS. 01329 822248. Bar, squash, hairdresser, sauna, steam room and gymnasium at extra cost. Off A27 (exit 11off M27) north at Cams Hall traffic lights, signposted. Open: 1 March - 31 October. ★★ BH&HPA ⌂ ♠ ↯ 10↯ 20↯ ⌂

(4m). **Rookesbury Park Caravan Club Site**, Hundred Acres Road, Wickham, Fareham, Hampshire PO17 6JR. 01329 834085. www.caravanclub.co.uk. Splendid setting in parkland on edge of the Forest of Bere. Good walking from site and convenient for Portsmouth and Isle of Wight. Privacy cubicles. Baby washroom. Veg prep. MV service point. Play equipment. Good area for walking. Ideal for families. Members only. No tents. See website for standard directions to site. Open: 23 March - 31 October. NCC ⌂ ♠ ↯☼⊞♠⇌☐☒ 165↯ 165↯ ⌂

### Fordingbridge

(1.5m). **Sandy Balls Holiday Centre**, Godshill, Fordingbridge, Hampshire SP6 2JY. 0845 270 2248. www.sandyballs.co.uk. Over 200 pitches nestled in the New Forest National Park, with 120 acres of woodland to enjoy and explore. Fishing on site, nearby stables, hair and beauty suite, full leisure club and gym. Also offers a cycle centre, gift shop, tourist info, together with the Woodside Inn and Pizza in the Piazza restaurant. AA campsite of the year 2011 regional winner. From Salisbury A338 to Fordingbridge, turn off on to B3078 signposted Godshill, situated at the Western end of Godshill village. Open: All year. ★★★★★ BH&HPA ♀☐⊞♠⇌✿♨☐☒♠ ☼⊞♠⇌✕☐☒⊞☒☐ 233↯ 233↯ ⌂ 180↯

### Gosport

(3m). **Kingfisher Caravan Park** (Gosport), Browndown Road, Stokes Bay, Gosport, Hampshire PO13 9BE. 02392 502611. www.kingfisher-caravan-park.co.uk. Kingfisher Caravan Park is situated very close to Stokes Bay in Gosport, Hampshire. Just a short stroll to the pebble beach. Open all year for tourers. March-Jan for hire & owners. M27 motorway junction 9 or 11 to Gosport. Open: All year. ★★★★ BH&HPA NCC ♀☐⊞♠☐♨♠⇌☒☐⊞✿✕ ☒☐☒☐ 130↯ ⌂

Surrounded by breathtaking scenery, the heart of the ancient New Forest is the perfect place for your escape to nature.

Explore the forest by foot, bike or horseback; unwind by the pool, in the sauna or Jacuzzi; dine out in Pizza in the Piazza or the Woodside Inn.

For a brochure or to make a booking call **0845 2702248** or visit our website.

www.sandyballs.co.uk
Email: post@sandyballs.co.uk
Godshill, Fordingbridge, The New Forest, Hants SP6 2JZ.

make it... Sandy Balls

# SOUTH EAST

### Hayling Island

**(0.25m). Fishery Creek Touring Park, 100 Fishery Lane, Hayling Island, Hampshire PO11 9NR.** 02392 462164. www.keyparks.co.uk. Fishery Creek is an award winning park set in a beautiful and quiet location adjoining a tidal creek of Chichester Harbour; an Area Of Outstanding Natural Beauty. David Bellamy Gold Conservation Award. From A27 cross bridge to Hayling Island and follow camping signs. Open: 1 March - 31 October. ★★★★ BH&HPA NCC 160

**(2m). Fleet Farm Caravan & Camping Park, Yew Tree Road, Hayling Island, Hampshire PO11 0QE.** 02392 463684. www.haylingcampsites.co.uk. Storage and rallies catered for. Long term parking on site. Site on tidal creek with full use of slipway for small craft. Handy touring area for Portsmouth, New Forest. Family pub very close. Fishing, tennis. Nice beach very close. 3 golf courses within 2m, of which one is a famous Links course. Owner supplied copy. Follow A3023 over road bridge onto island. About 1.5m on island then turn L into Copse Lane, then R into Yew Tree Road, site on L. Open: 1 March - 1 November. 75

**(2m). Hayling Island Holiday Park, Manor Road, Hayling Island, Hampshire PO11 0QS.** 0844 3353450. www.parkdean.com. Surrounded by picturesque countryside and close to 4m of peaceful shores and the historic cities or Portsmouth and Chichester. Stay in a choice of holiday homes and enjoy our heated indoor pool with Jacuzzi, gymnasium, evening entertainment, restaurants, and nearby visitor attractions. David Bellamy Bronze Conservation Award. A302 to Hayling Island. After 3m take 2nd exit on roundabout to Manor Road, Hayling Island Holiday Park will be on your L after 0.5m. Open: 1 March - 1 November. ★★★★ BH&HPA NCC 530

### Lymington

**Carrington Caravan Park, New Lane, Milford on Sea, Lymington, Hampshire SO41 0UQ.** 01590 642654. Carrington Caravan Park holiday homes are all privately owned and not available for holiday lets. The park is in an ideal location 500m from the seafront, Sturt Pond, Hurst Spit and Keyhaven Marshes. Ideal for bird watching and relaxing. Milford village is a 500m level walk. An excellent family run park if you are thinking of buying a holiday home by the sea. Reached from the B3058 (off the A337) Lymington Road. Open: 1 March - 2 January. ★★★★★★

**(2m). Downton Holiday Park, Shorefield Road, Milford-On-Sea, Lymington, Hampshire SO41 0LH.** 01425 476131. www.downtonholidaypark.co.uk. All units have water and main drainage, all with showers and TV. Near New Forest, beach and Bournemouth nearby. Swimming, sailing, riding and golf close by. Pets welcome by arrangement. We have safe children play equipment, games room and a laundry. On B3058. Open: 1 March - 31 October. ★★★★ BH&HPA 100

**(2m). Shorefield Country Park, Shorefield Road, Downton, Lymington, Hampshire SO41 0LH.** 01590 648356. www.shorefield.co.uk. Rose award. Club. Heated indoor and outdoor swimming pool. Reflection day spa. 800yd from beach. Golf 2m. 3m from the New Forest. David Bellamy Gold Conservation Award. Owner supplied copy. From M27 take Lyndhurst exit 1on to A337 to Downton. Turn L at Royal Oak pub. 3m from Lymington, 12m from Bournemouth. Open: All year. ★★★★★ BH&HPA 823

### Lyndhurst

**Denny Wood (Forest Holidays), Beaulieu Road, Lyndhurst, Hampshire SO32 7FZ.** 02380 293144. www.forestholidays.co.uk. Peaceful grassland site among

84 CARAVAN & HOLIDAY PARKS 2012

# SOUTH EAST

scattered oaks. Dog free site. No toilet or shower facilities. Booking and brochure request on 0845 1308224. On B3056, 3m SE of Lyndhurst. Open: 14 April - 26 September. **BH&HPA** ⛺🐕🚐 170🏕️ ⛺

**(2m). Matley Wood (Forest Holidays), Beaulieu Road, Lyndhurst, Hampshire SO43 7FZ.** 02380 293144. www.forestholidays.co.uk. Small secluded site in a beautiful woodland setting. No toilet or shower facilities. Permits from nearby Denny Wood campsite. Booking and brochure requests on 0845 1308224. On B3056, 2m SE of Lyndhurst. Open: 26 March - 27 September. **BH&HPA** ⛺🐕🚐 70🏕️ ⛺

**Ocknell & Longbeech Caravan & Camping Site, Fritham, Lyndhurst, Hampshire SO43 7HH.** 02380 812740. www.forestholiday.co.uk. Ocknell is a heathland site whilst Longbeech is in an ancient beech wood. Longbeech: temporary WC facilities, no hot water. Both sites: no showers, no premium pitches. Booking and brochure requests on 0845 1308224. David Bellamy Silver Conservation Award. B3079 off A31 at Cadnam, then B3078 via Brook and Fritham. Open: 14 April - 26 September. ★ ★ ★ **BH&HPA** ⛺🐕🚐 ♿ 🚐 480🏕️ ⛺

### Milford on Sea

**(3m). Lytton Lawn Touring Park, Lymore Lane, Milford on Sea, Hampshire SO41 0TX.** 01590 648331. www.shorefield.co.uk. Well-drained site, 1m from beach and close to New Forest. Shop. Full access to the facilities of sister park 2.5m away: indoor & outdoor pool, gym, bars and eateries, day spa. David Bellamy Bronze Conservation Award. S of Lymington via A337 to Everton, then B3058 to site. Second turning on L. Open: 5 February - 2 January. ★ ★ ★ ★ **BH&HPA** ⛺🐕🚐 ♿🚐 ⛺ 136🏕️ 136🏕️ ⛺

### New Milton

**(1.25m). Glen Orchard Holiday Park, Walkford Lane, New Milton, Hampshire BH25 5NH.** 01425 616463. www.glenorchard.co.uk. Recreational facilities, fishing, golf, riding nearby. Close to forest and beaches. Lymington 7m with ferry to Isle of Wight. Recreation centre and fishing 0.75m. Golf, shopping 1.25m. Wi-Fi available. Off A35 Christchurch to Lyndhurst, at Hinton turn to Walkford after 0.75m turn to New Milton, further 0.75m turn L for park. Open: 1 March - 30 November. ★ ★ ★ ★ **BH&HPA** ⛺🐕🚐 19🏕️ ⛺

**(1m). Hoburne Bashley, Sway Road, New Milton, Hampshire BH25 5QR.** 01425 612340. www.hoburne.com. Free hot showers. Laundrette. Licensed club. Seasonal entertainment. Indoor leisure pool. Two 18m circular outdoor pools. 9-hole par 3 golf course. Hard court tennis. Playground. Football field. Snooker. Pool. England for Excellence Silver Award and Rose Award. David Bellamy Gold Conservation Award. On B3058 N of New Milton. Open: 28 February - 1 November. ★ ★ ★ ★ **BH&HPA NCC** ⛺🐕🚐 307🏕️ 307🏕️ 434🏕️ ⛺

**(1m). Hoburne Naish, Christchurch Road, New Milton, Hampshire BH25 7RE.** 01425 273586. www.hoburne.com. Indoor & outdoor pools. Tennis courts, kids adventure playground. Restaurant. Seasonal entertainment. Licensed club. Laundrette. Cliff top position. Children allowed in park homes. Rose Award Park. One pet per owner allowed. Themed bar and restaurant with mini 10 pin bowling. GS. David Bellamy Gold Conservation Award. On A337 between New Milton & Highcliffe. Open: 1 March - 5 November. ★ ★ ★ ★ ★ **BH&HPA NCC** ⛺🐕🚐 490🏕️ ⛺

**(3m). Setthorns Forest Holidays Site, Wootton, New Milton, Hampshire BH25 5WA.** 01590 681020. www.forestholidays.co.uk. Pitch amongst the pines and oaks in a beautiful forest setting. Select pitches available. No toilet or shower facilities. Bookings and brochure requests on 0845 1308224. David Bellamy Gold Conservation Award. SP from A35 Lyndhurst - Christchurch Road, 7m SW of Lyndhurst. Open: All year. **BH&HPA** ⛺🐕🚐 207🏕️ 207🏕️ 30⛺

### Ringwood

**(3m). Forest Edge Touring Park, Boundary Lane, St Leonards, Ringwood, Hampshire BH24 2SD.** 01590 648331. www.shorefield.co.uk. Well located on the edge of the New Forest only 9m from sandy beaches. Guests also have use of Oakdene's facilities, just 1m away. David Bellamy Bronze Conservation Award. Access off A31, turn L at 2nd roundabout, W of Ringwood into Boundary Lane. Park is on L. Open: 4 February - 2 January. ★ ★ ★ ★ **BH&HPA** ⛺🐕🚐 62🏕️ 62🏕️ 14🏕️ ⛺

**(3m). Oakdene Forest Park, St Leonards, Ringwood, Hampshire BH24 2RZ.** 01590 648331. www.shorefield.co.uk. Licensed club. Entertainment. Cafeteria. Takeaway. Adventure playground. Bordering Avon Forest. Indoor and outdoor pools, gym, sauna, steam room, flume. Lodges with hot tubs. See website for detailed tariff. David Bellamy Gold Conservation Award. Off A31, W of Ringwood. Bournemouth 9m. Open: 1 February - 2 January. ★ ★ ★ ★ **BH&HPA** ⛺🐕🚐 504🏕️ ⛺

**(4m). Red Shoot Camping Park, Toms Lane, Linwood, Ringwood, Hampshire BH24 3QT.** 01425 473789. www.redshootcampingpark.com. Set in the heart of the New Forest and close to Bournemouth and Ringwood, children's play area and adjacent to Red Shoot Inn. Owner supervised to a high standard. AA 3 pennants. David Bellamy Gold Conservation Award. Off A31 (M27) at exit 1. Follow signs for New Forest and Linwood or minor road off A338 2m N of Ringwood, SP Linwood. Open: 1 March - 31 October. **BH&HPA** ⛺🐕🚐 100🏕️ 30🏕️ ⛺

**(2m). Shamba Holidays, Ringwood Road, East Moors Lane, St Leonards, Ringwood, Hampshire BH24 2SB.** 01202 873302. www.shambaholidays.co.uk. Family run park, which is always friendly and clean. Clubhouse (inc bar, and large screen TV). Heated indoor & outdoor swimming pool, play area. Modern toilet/shower facilities. Winter storage. Seasonal pitches. David Bellamy Gold Conservation Award. W of Ringwood, located directly off the main A31 Ringwood to Wimborne road (sign on roadside). Open: 1 March - 31 October. ★ ★ ★ ★ **BH&HPA** ⛺🐕🚐 150🏕️ 150🏕️ ⛺

### Romsey

**(4m). Green Pastures Farm, Ower, Romsey, Hampshire SO51 6AJ.** 02380 814444. www.greenpasturesfarm.com. Family run site on working farm in New Forest National Park. Convenient ferries for Europe and Isle of Wight. Space for children to play safely. Local pub with good food and real ales. Fishing

# SOUTH EAST

(3m), golf and swimming pool nearby. Day kennelling available. SP from J2 off M27 (Salisbury direction) and A36 and A3090 at Ower. Open: 15 March - 31 October. ★★★ BH&HPA 🏠🏕🏊⚡🚿🍴🍽🍺 10⛺ 45🚐 ▲

### Southampton

(5m). Dibles Park, Dibles Road, Warsash, Southampton, Hampshire SO31 9SA. *01489 575232.* www.diblespark.co.uk. Shops, PO, doctor available within 0.5m. Fishing and golf courses nearby. Warsash (a yachting centre) lies on the East bank of the river Hamble. Close by are the Hook Nature Reserve, Brownwich Country Park and Solent Way. Excellent location for walking and cycling. Ideal for cross-channel ferries. Owner supplied copy. At the 3rd roundabout, take 1st exit into Brook Lane, continue along going straight across 3 roundabouts. At 4th roundabout (min) take 2nd exit. Park entrance on L 500yds. Open: All year. ★★★★ BH&HPA NCC 🏠🏕🏊⚡🚿🍴🍽🍺 7⛺ 74🚐 ▲

(1m). Riverside Holidays (Southampton), Satchell Lane, Hamble, Southampton, Hampshire SO31 4HR. *02380 453220.* www.shambaholidays.co.uk/riverside-holidays. Close to the New Forest, Portsmouth and Winchester. Bar/restaurant on Hamble Marina (2mins walk). Excellent walking, cycling, fishing and sailing. Boat hire, supermarket, pubs/restaurants (Hamble 1m). Golf 5m. Dogs welcome when touring. David Bellamy Bronze Conservation Award. J8, M27 (Southampton) then B3397 to Hamble, turn L into Satchell Lane. Site is adjacent to marina overlooking the river. Open: 1 March - 31 October. ★★★ BH&HPA NCC 🏠🏕🏊⚡🚿🍴🍽🍺 77⛺ ▲ 52🚐

(5m). Solent Breezes Holiday Village, Hook Lane, Warsash, Southampton, Hampshire SO31 9HG. *0845 8159775.* www.ParkHolidaysUK.com. Excellent facilities including outdoor heated pool. Private slipway, boat moorings. Tennis court. Village store. Cafe. Sun terrace and lounge bar. Free kids club. Rose Award. Southampton: restaurants, shopping, cinema, theatre. David Bellamy Bronze Conservation Award. Exit 9 from M27 take last exit at large roundabout, proceed to second roundabout and turn sharp L into Hunts Pond Road. Turn R at junction with Warsash Road first L in to Hook Lane and L into Chilling Lane. Open: 1 March - 1 January. ★★★ BH&HPA NCC 🏠🏕🏊⚡🚿🍴🍽🍺 252🚐

### Southbourne

(0.5m). Chichester Camping & Caravanning Club Site, Main Road, Southbourne, Hampshire PO10 8JH. *01243 373202.* www.campingandcaravanningclub.co.uk. Ideally located for Chichester, South Downs, Bosham and Portsmouth. Close to sea and shops. The site is set in an ancient orchard. Attractions in nearby Portsmouth include HMS Victory and the huge maritime museum. The area is full of history with Iron Age hill forts, Roman remains and Norman castles. Non-members welcome. All units accepted. Special deals available for families and backpackers. 6m W of Chichester, 3m E of Havant, site is well marked on north side of A259, off A27. Follow signs Nutbourne or Southbourne. Site on R past Inlands Road. Open: 3 February - 21 November. ★★★ NCC 🏠🏕🏊⚡🚿🍴🍽🍺 58⛺ 58🚐 ▲

### Southsea

(5m). Southsea Leisure Park, Melville Road, Southsea, Hampshire PO4 9TB. *02392 735070.* www.southsealeisurepark.com. Playground and room, organised activities in season. Heated outdoor swimming pool, free hot showers. Restaurant and bar. Direct access to beach. 10 mins from cross-channel ferries. From M27, A27 and, A3M take Southsea exit (A2030 south) and follow signs along Eastern Road. Open: All year. ★★★ BH&HPA 🏠🏕🏊⚡🚿🍴🍽🍺 188🚐 ▲ 51🏕

### Winchester

(3m). Morn Hill Caravan Club Site, Morn Hill, Winchester, Hampshire SO21 1HL. *01962 869877.* www.caravanclub.co.uk. Set on the outskirts of Winchester, convenient for ferries and exploring the New Forest. Advance booking essential Bank Holidays and July and August. Non-members and tent campers welcome. MV service point, play frame, laundry facilities. Toilet/shower block with privacy cubicles. Veg prep area. Shop 3m away. Fishing, golf and cycling routes all within 5m. See website for standard directions to site. Open: 23 March - 5 November. ★★★ NCC 🏠🏕🏊⚡🚿🍴🍽🍺 120⛺ 120🚐 ▲

## ISLE OF WIGHT

### Adgestone

(1.5m). Adgestone Camping & Caravanning Club Site, Lower Adgestone Road, Adgestone, Isle of Wight PO36 0HL. *01983 403432.* www.campingandcaravanningclub.co.uk. Site is adjacent to River Yar, beneath the Brading Downs in an area of natural beauty close to Sandown. Non-members welcome. Caravans, motor-caravans and tents accepted. Fishing on site at river and lake. Adventure playground. Outdoor heated swimming pool and take-away on site. 270 pitches set in 22 acres. Golf course, Blackgang Chine theme park nearby and the marine heritage museum. Special deals available for families and backpackers. Formerly listed as one of Caravan Magazine 101 top sites. Turn off A3055 at The Fairway by Manor House pub in Lake, which is between Sandown and Shanklin, past golf course on L, turn R at T-junction, park 200yd on R. 1m from Sandown. Open: 14 April - 30 September. ★★★★ NCC 🏠🏕🏊⚡🚿🍴🍽🍺 270⛺ 270🚐 ▲

### Bembridge

(1.5m). Whitecliff Bay Holiday Park, Hillway Road, Bembridge, Isle of Wight PO35 5PL. *01983 872671.* www.whitecliff-bay.com. Heated swimming pools. Licensed clubs. Entertainment. Restaurant. Leisure centre. Snack bar with takeaway, play zone, coffee shop, fitness studio. David Bellamy Gold Conservation Award. Off the A3055 Ryde to Sandown on to B3395 to Bembridge and Whitecliff Bay. Open: 30 March - 5 November. ★★★★ BH&HPA NCC 🏠🏕🏊⚡🚿🍴🍽🍺 400🚐 ▲ 230🏕 3

### Brighstone

(0.75m). Grange Farm, Brighstone, Isle of Wight PO30 4DA. *01983 740296.* www.brighstonebay.fsnet.co.uk. 2-acre level site on small family run farm having many unusual friendly animals including llamas, kune-kune pigs, goats, pony, horse, water buffalo etc. Ideal for children. Easy access to our sandy beach (1min). Safe swimming. Walkers paradise, fossil hunting. An ideal family holiday for camping or self catering in our static caravans or converted barns. A3055 coast

**Relax & explore the beautiful south**
Beautiful views over the Marina and River Hamble
• Excellent sailing, walking, fishing and horse riding nearby • Serviced touring pitches • Superior pine lodges and static caravans available to hire all year.

Riverside Holidays
Satchell Lane, Hamble, Hampshire SO31 4HR
Please call: 02380 453220
or visit our website: www.riversideholidays.co.uk

# SOUTH EAST

road midway between Freshwater Bay and Chale. Open: 1 March - 31 October. ★★★ BH&HPA NCC 🏠🐕♿☕♨ ♪🚿🍴🏪❌🛒🚻♿ 30🚐 30🚗 ▲ 10⚡

### Brook

(2m). **Compton Farm, Brook, Isle of Wight PO30 4HF.** 01983 740215. www.comptonfarm.co.uk. Working farm. Flush toilets and water in each caravan all with showers. 10mins to clean sandy beach. Golf nearby, riding 3m, shops 2m. National Trust Area of Outstanding Natural Beauty. Owner supplied copy. Just off A3055. 10m from Newport. 1m from Freshwater Bay. Open: 15 May - 15 September. ★★ BH&HPA 🏠🐕🛒🚻 🚐 ▲ 12⚡

### Chale

(7m). **Chine Farm Camping Site, Military Road, Atherfield Bay, Chale, Isle of Wight PO38 2JH.** 01983 740901. www.chine-farm.co.uk. Situated on the south side of the Isle of Wight at Cowleaze Chine which is midway between the villages of Chale (3m) and Brighstone (2.5 m) on the A3055 crossroad. 120 mixed pitches in total. Friendly family run site. Outstanding scenery. Fishing, sea at site, coarse 2m away. Good walking area. Large spacious pitches including electric hook-ups. Local amenities in village 2m. Situated on the south side of the Isle of Wight at Cowleaze Chine which is midway between the villages of Chale (3m) and Brighstone (2.5 m) on the A3055 crossroad. Open: 22 April - 30 September. ★★★ 🏠 🐕♿♪🍴🛒🚻 🚐 120🚗 ▲

### Cowes

(1m). **Comforts Farm Camping Park, Pallance Road, Northwood, Cowes, Isle of Wight PO31 8LS.** 01983 293888. www.comfortsfarm.co.uk. Motorhome, caravan & tent pitches close to the beach & ideally located for the Isle of Wight Music Festival. Off A3020. Open: 1 May - 30 September. 🏠🐕♿♪🍴🛒🚻🏪 🚻♿ 🚐 20🚗 ▲

(4m). **Thorness Bay Holiday Park, Thorness Lane, Thorness, Cowes, Isle of Wight PO31 8NJ.** 01983 523109. www.park-resortstouring.com. Showbars. Food court/takeaway. Indoor pool. Excellent fun all round fun and entertainment absolutely free. Free kids club. Multi sports court, playground, darts, pool table. David Bellamy Gold Conservation Award. From East Cowes and Fishbourne, follow signs to Newport and take A3054 towards Yarmouth. After 1m take first turning on R and follow signs to Thorness Bay. From Yarmouth, take A3054 towards Newport. After Shalfleet take first L and follow signs to Cowes. After about 5m, Thorness Bay will be on the L. Open: 20 March - 31 October. ★★★★ BH&HPA NCC ♀🏠 🐕♿♪🎵🍴♨🛒🏪❌🚻♿ 🚻 130🚐 ▲ 606🚗

**Waverley Park Holiday Centre, 51 Old Road, Cowes, Isle of Wight PO32 6AW.** 01983 293452. www.waverleypark.co.uk. 45 mixed pitches in total. Friendly family run site. Open air heated pool, entertainment, bar and evening meals in high season (Spring Bank Holiday - Early September). Panoramic views across Solent and Cowes Harbour with constant movement of shipping and leisure craft. Within walking distance of mainland car ferry connections, Cowes and Osborne House. David Bellamy Gold Conservation Award. Owner supplied copy. 600 metres from Red Funnel Ferry Terminal, East Cowes to park. Open: All year. ★★★★ BH&HPA 🏠🐕♿♪ ♨🛒♿❌🍴🚻 🚐 45🚗 ▲ 46⚡

### Freshwater

(0.5m). **Heathfield Farm Camping, Heathfield Road, Freshwater, Isle of Wight PO40 9SH.** 01983 407822. www.heathfieldcamping.co.uk. Family camping on level field with sea and downland views. Excellent modern shower facilities. Ideal walking area. David Bellamy Gold Conservation Award. 2m from Yarmouth ferry port off A3054 road at Freshwater. Open: 1 May - 30 September. ★★★★ BH&HPA 🏠🐕♿♪🛒 🐕♿ 50🚐 60🚗 60▲

### Newbridge

(4m). **The Orchards (Newbridge), Main Road, Newbridge, Isle of Wight PO41 0TS.** 01983 531331. www.orchards-holiday-park.co.uk. Beautiful rural situation with excellent views all round. Indoor and outdoor heated pools with poolside coffee shop. Takeaway food, shop, table tennis, play areas and dog walk. New facilities centre. Excellent cycling and walking from the park. Bird watching at Newton Creek . Green Island Gold award and Best of British member. Complete car ferry booking service available. Nearest town Yarmouth. David Bellamy Gold Conservation Award. E of Yarmouth and 6m W of Newport on B3401. Entrance opposite Newbridge PO. Open: 18 February - 2 January. ★★★★★ BH&HPA 🏠🐕♿♪ ♨🛒🍴🏪❌🚻♿ 175🚐 175▲ 65⚡

### Ryde

(2.5m). **Beaper Farm, Brading Road, Ryde, Isle of Wight PO33 1QJ.** 01983 615210. www.beaperfarm.com. 150 mix units (tourers, motorcaravans, tents). Family site with play area in 13 acres of countryside. Phone for brochure. Two large closely mown camping fields offering plenty of space for children to play. No regimental marked pitches, 2 toilet blocks with toilet for disabled. Shower block, laundry room, dishwashing room, chemical toilet point. 3m S of Ryde on A3055 towards Sandown. Open: 22 April - 30 September. ★★★ BH&HPA 🏠🐕♿ ♪🛒♿🍴🏪 🚻 🚐 ▲

(3m). **Carpenters Farm Campsite, St Helens, Ryde, Isle of Wight PO33 1YN.** 01983 874557. www.carpentersfarm.co.uk. Small on site shop, milk, eggs, bread, ice creams, bottle gas, newspapers, etc. Off B3330. Open: All year. ★★★ 🏠🐕♪♪ 🛒♿🚿🍴🚻 🚐 100🚗 ▲

(3.25m). **Kite Hill Farm Camping Park, Kite Hill Farm, Wootton Bridge, Ryde, Isle of Wight PO33 4LE.** 01983 882543. www.kitehillfarm.co.uk. Village shops 10mins walk away including doctor. 3 pennants AA site. Off A3054. Open: All year. 🏠🍴🐕♿♪ ♪🛒♿❌🚻 🚻 60🚐 60🚗 ▲

(3m). **Nodes Point Holiday Park, Nodes Road, St. Helens, Ryde, Isle of Wight PO33 1YA.** 01983 872401. www.park-resortstouring.com. Indoor fun pool with waterslide. Kids' clubs. Sports programme. Launderette. Evening entertainment for all the family. Amusements. Diner and takeaway. Playground. Darts. Pool tables. Horse riding nearby. David Bellamy Gold Conservation Award. From Fishbourne on A3054 E towards Ryde. At junction with A3055, then L on to B3330 to St Helens. Nodes Point is on the L. From Cowes on A3021, then as above. Open: 3 April - 31 October. ★★★ BH&HPA ♀ 🏠🐕♿♪🎵🍴♨🛒🏪❌ 🛒🍴🚻♿ 240🚐 ▲ 242⚡

(2m). **Pondwell Camping Site, Pondwell Hill, Ryde, Isle of Wight PO34 5AQ.** 01983 612330. www.seaview-holidays.co.uk. TV lounge. Offer holiday bungalows (available for long-term rental) and touring pitches. The touring area covers 14 acres and is on gently sloping ground in peaceful countryside. Electric hook-ups available. Walking distance to sea. Set near Wishing Well public house which offers traditionally cooked British food. 24-hour security on site. Childrens play area, TV room and well-stocked shop that sells gas. On B3340. Open: 7 April - 30 September. ★★★ BH&HPA 🏠🐕♪♪ 🛒🍴🚻♿ 🚻 60🚗 ▲

# SOUTH EAST

■ **Woodside Beach Holiday Park, Lower Woodside Road, Wooton Bridge, Ryde, Isle of Wight PO33 4JT.** *0844 272 9506* www.woodsidebeachpark.co.uk. A peaceful site with its own private sandy beach. Bounded by protected woodland with walking routes. Located between Cowes and Ryde, next to the picturesque Wooton Creek. The park is a short journey from the Wooton Ferry which connects the island to the mainland. BH&HPA

## Sandown

**(2m). Cheverton Copse Holiday Park, Scotchells Brook Lane, Sandown, Isle of Wight PO36 0JP.** *01983 403161.* www.cheverton-copse.co.uk. Family park in delightful, wooded parkland. Licensed club and games room, entertainment in high season. Play area. Bus 300yd. Supermarket near. Lovely walking area 1.5m to beach. 1.5m W of town on A3056. Open: 20 March - 5 November. ★★★★ BH&HPA 57

**(1m). Fairway Holiday Park, The Fairway, Sandown, Isle of Wight PO36 9PS.** *01983 403462.* www.fairwayholidaypark.co.uk. Modern caravans with showers. Snack bar. Licensed club. Laundrette. Arcade. Play area. Outdoor heated pool. Off A3055. Open: 1 March - 1 October. ★★★ BH&HPA 30 100 216

**(0.25m). Fort Holiday Park, Avenue Road, Sandown, Isle of Wight PO36 8BD.** *01983 402858.* www.fortholidaypark.co.uk. A secluded family park with countryside views. We are within easy level walking distance of all Sandown's facilities and beach. David Bellamy Gold Conservation Award. On A3055 and B3329 just two minutes from beach and town. Open: 1 March - 31 October. ★★★ BH&HPA 45

**(1.5m). Old Barn Touring Park, Cheverton Farm, Newport Road, Apse Heath, Sandown, Isle of Wight PO36 9PJ.** *01983 866414.* www.oldbarntouring.co.uk. Lovely downland views. Super pitches available. David Bellamy Gold Conservation Award. 500yd S of Apse Heath on A3056 Newport to Sandown. 2m to sandy beaches of Shanklin and Sandown. Open: 1 May - 30 September. ★★★★ BH&HPA 60 60

**(3m). Queen Bower Dairy Caravan Park, Alverstone Road, Queen Bower, Sandown, Isle of Wight PO36 0NZ.** *01983 403840.* www.queenbowerdairy.co.uk. 60 acre National Trust copse nearby. Dogs must be exercised off site. PO 1m, superstore 2m. AA 1 pennant. Off A3056 Sandown to Newport turn in to Alverstone Road at Apse Heath, entrance 1m on L. Open: 1 May - 31 October. ★★★ 20 20

**(3m). Southland Caravan Club Site, Winford Road, Newchurch, Sandown, Isle of Wight PO36 0LZ.** *01983 865385.* www.caravanclub.co.uk. Level site within in easy reach of Sandown and Shanklin. Sandy beaches and safe bathing nearby. Local activities including fishing, golf, swimming, horse riding and sailing. David Bellamy Gold Conservation Award. See website for standard directions to sire. Open: 23 March - 31 October. ★★★★ NCC 120

**(1.5m). Village Way Camping & Caravanning Park, Newport Road, Apse Heath, Sandown, Isle of Wight PO36 9PJ.** *01983 863279.* www.villagewaypark.co.uk. Hot water and showers. Power points in toilet block. Free carp fishing on site. On A3056, follow Sandown sign from Newport. Open: All year. ★★★ BH&HPA 14 12

## Shanklin

**(0.5m). Landguard, Landguard Manor Road, Shanklin, Isle of Wight PO37 7PJ.** *01983 863100.* www.park-resortstouring.com. Bookings from non-family parties will be at the discretion of the management. Large outdoor pool and paddling pool, indoor fun pool and slide, oasis pool bar, licensed club, entertainment for all ages, restaurant, takeaway meals, amusement and games room, shop, children's play area, laundrette, kids club. Beach 0.5m, fishing and boat hire 0.5m, supermarket, swimming pool, sports centre, tennis 1m. Golf 3m, horse riding 8m. Shopping centre 0.5m. From Cowes - take A3021 and then the A3054 to Ryde. Take the A3055 SP Brading and Sandown and continue on this road to lake. Turn R at the traffic lights SP to Newport and then turn L after 0.75m into Whitecross Lane. After 0.5m turn R into Landguard Holidays. Open: 20 March - 2 November. ★★★★ BH&HPA 50 100 153

**(0.3m). Lower Hyde Holiday Park, Landguard Road, Shanklin, Isle of Wight PO37 7LL.** *01983 866131.* www.park-resortstouring.com. Within walking distance of Shanklin. Outdoor fun pool. Adventure playground. Multi sports court. Laundrette. Amusements. Takeaway and restaurant. Free kids clubs. Free family entertainment. Advance booking advisable. Darts. Pool table. Spa pool. David Bellamy Gold Conservation Award. From Ryde follow A3055 to Shanklin via Sandown and Lake. At Lake turn R at the traffic lights towards Newport (A3056). After about 1m turn L into Whitecross Lane. Lower Hyde is 1m down on the R. Open: 20 March - 31 October. ★★★★ BH&HPA NCC 128 450

**(1m). Ninham Country Holidays, Shanklin, Isle of Wight PO37 7PL.** *01983 864243.* www.ninham-holidays.co.uk. Country park setting overlooking wooded valley with small lakes. Coarse fishing. Play areas. Laundrette. Leisure centre 1m. Water sport school 1m. Advance booking advisable. Outdoor heated swim-

**Stunning Solent views await you at this peaceful caravan holiday park on the Isle of Wight**

- Stunning accommodation and sea views.
- Private sandy beach for guests.
- Set in an area of outstanding natural beauty.
- Excellent walking and cycling routes from the park.
- Short distance from the Wooton Ferry.

**20% off your booking Quote CHP20**

*Terms and conditions apply.*

To book call **0844 272 9506** or visit **www.woodsidebeachpark.co.uk**

# SOUTH EAST

ming pool. Games room. Ideal base for cycling. Discounted ferry tickets issued. Online booking. Off A3056, W of Lake. Newport to Sandown road, 400 metres W of Morrisons superstore, use postcode PO36 9PJ in Sat Nav. Open: 1 April - 1 October. ★★★★★ 🏠🎾🐕🛁🚿🏊‍♂️🎣 30🚐 50🚐 ⛺ 12🛖

### St Helens

**Old Mill Holiday Park Ltd (Isle of Wight)**, Mill Road, St Helens, Isle of Wight PO33 1UE. *01983 872507*. www.oldmill.co.uk. Sheltered, peaceful location ideal for bird watchers and everyone needing a relaxing holiday. Solent shipping can be watched from the park. No new pets allowed. Accommodation includes pine cabins and apartments. NO TOURERS OR TENTS. Rose Award Park. Golf 3m. Tesco 3.5m. Shops 0.5m. Fishing 100yd. David Bellamy Gold Conservation Award. Owner supplied copy. Turn off to St Helens the B3330, Mill Road is off Lower Green Road. Open: All year. ★★★★★ BH&HPA 🏠🍴♿♲ 🚻♿ 60🛖

### Ventnor

(2m). **Appuldurcombe Gardens Holiday Park**, Appuldurcombe Road, Wroxall, Ventnor, Isle of Wight PO38 3EP. *01983 852597*. www.appuldurcombegardens.co.uk. Very pretty family holiday site in tranquil unspoilt countryside, a few minutes by car from beaches of Shanklin, Sandown and Ventnor. Ideal for walkers and cyclists. One of the Island's most beautiful holiday hideaways! David Bellamy Gold Conservation Award. Situated just slightly inland, between Shanklin and Ventnor, in the village of Wroxall. Open: 1 March - 1 November. ★★★★ BH&HPA  100🚐 ⛺ 40🛖

## KENT
### Ashford

(3m). **Broadhembury Caravan & Camping Park**, Steeds Lane, Kingsnorth, Ashford, Kent TN26 1NQ. *01233 620859*. www.broadhembury.co.uk. Lovely Kentish park with first class facilities (65 mixed units). Plenty to do regardless of weather. Central to 100s of interesting places, Channel Ports and Eurotunnel. Ideal location for walking and cycling. Good fishing and golf course with driving range only 5mins away. Shops, PO 1.5m. From M20, exit 10 take A2070 to 2nd roundabout, SP following signs for Kingsnorth L at second crossroad in village. Open: All year. ★★★★★ BH&HPA 🏠🍴♿🎾 70🚐 70🚐 70⛺ 3🛖

**Dunn Street Farm**, Westwell, Ashford, Kent TN25 4NJ. *01233 712537*. www.caravancampingsites.co.uk. Quiet farm site within easy reach of Canterbury, Chilham, Sissinghurst etc. Dishwashing facilities. Cafe/restaurant nearby. Owner supplied copy. On North Downs Way, 4m NW of M20 J19, 2m N of A20 at Hothfield. Open: 1 April - 31 October. 🏠🍴🛁♿🎾 🚻♿ 🚐⛺ ⛺

### Biddenden

(3m). **Woodlands Park (Biddenden)**, Tenterden Road, Biddenden, Kent TN27 8BT. *01580 291216*. www.leisurepark-suk.co.uk. Touring, lodges & residential. Perfectly placed in the heart of the Kent countryside. Offers a quiet & tranquil environment to enjoy. From A1 Wansford, A47 to Leicester, 12m to Morcott, turn R then first L to Wing 2.5m outside village by 400yd. Open: 1 March - 31 October. BH&HPA 🏠🍴♿🎾♲🛁🚿🎣🛎 🚻♿ 🚐⛺ 6🛖 ⛺

### Birchington

(1m). **Quex Caravan Park**, Park Road, Birchington, Kent CT7 0BL. *01843 841273*. www.keatfarm.co.uk. Wi-Fi internet on whole park. Golf course, cinema 2m. Shopping centre 3m. David Bellamy Silver Conservation Award. Off A28 and B2049 follow road signs to Margate, when in Birchington turn R at mini roundabout after 100yd take first turning on R and R again, follow Tourist Board signs. Open: 7 March - 7 November. ★★★★★ BH&HPA NCC 🏠🍴♿🎾♲🛁🚿🎣 🚻♿ 🚐 42🚐 165⛺

(1m). **Quex Caravan Park (Best of British)**, Park Road, Birchington, Kent CT7 0BL. *01843 841273*. www.keatfarm.co.uk. Wi-Fi internet on whole park. Golf course, cinema 2m. Shopping centre 3m. David Bellamy Silver Conservation Award. Off A28 and B2049 follow road signs to Margate, when in Birchington turn R at mini roundabout after 100yd take first turning on R and R again, follow Tourist Board signs. Open: 7 March - 7 November. ★★★★★ BH&HPA NCC 🏠🍴♿🎾♲🛁🚿🎣 42🚐 165⛺

(3m). **St Nicholas Camping Site**, Court Road, St Nicholas-at-Wade, Birchington, Kent CT7 0NH. *01843 847245*. Level site within reach of five major towns: Canterbury, Margate, Herne Bay, Ramsgate & Broadstairs. Gas sales only. From M2 follow onto A299. At the sign to St Nicholas turn L over bridge into village. Off A28 at St Nicholas sign. Open: 1 March - 31 October. ★★★ 🐕🎾 🚻♿ 5🚐 12⛺ ⛺

(1.5m). **Two Chimneys Caravan Park**, Shottendane Road, Birchington, Kent CT7 0HD. *01843 841068*. www.twochimneys.co.uk. Licensed bar. Heated enclosed pool. Tennis court. Children's play area, amusement arcade. Golf, cinema, beaches, sea, horse riding, sports centre, water sports, fishing, theme park all within 3m. Near lovely sandy beaches of Margate, Ramsgate and Broadstairs. From A299, turn R into Park Lane (B2048) at Birchington Church. L fork B2050 'RAF Manston'. 1st L on to B2049. Site 0.5m on R. Open: 1 March - 31 October.

---

## Appuldurcombe Gardens Holiday Park

Appuldurcombe Road, Wroxall, Isle Of Wight PO38 3EP
Tel: 01983 852597
www.appuldurcombegardens.co.uk

Award winning 4 star family owned Holiday Park located within an area of outstanding natural beauty. The site has 40 static caravans situated within a traffic free walled orchard. There are also 100 touring and camping pitches varying from grass, super or handstanding pitches. Close proximity to beaches, towns and attractions.

• Bar with function room and games room
• Sheltered outdoor heated pool
• Shop
• Cafe
• Laundrette
• Children's play area

*One of the islands most beautiful holiday hideaways*

# SOUTH EAST

★★★★ BH&HPA NCC
20 200 10

## Canterbury

**(1m). Canterbury Camping & Caravanning Club Site, Bekesbourne Lane, Canterbury, Kent CT3 4AB.** *01227 463216* . www.campingandcaravanningclub.co.uk. Great stopover when travelling to or from France, or to explore Kent. Canterbury itself is a bus ride away or less than 30mins on foot. Off the A257 from Canterbury. Open: All year. ★★★★ NCC
200 200

**(4m). Yew Tree Park, Stone Street, Petham, Canterbury, Kent CT4 5PL.** *01227 700306*. www.yewtreepark.com. Small, picturesque country park overlooking beautiful Chartham Downs. Ideally situated for exploring local heritage and Kent. Large open-air heated swimming pool. Canterbury 4m. On B2068 4m from Canterbury and 9 m from J11 of M20. Turn by The Chequers Inn, park entrance on L. Open: 26 March - 11 September. ★★★★ BH&HPA
15 8

## Deal

**(1m). Clifford Park Caravan Site, Thompson Close, Dover Road, Walmer, Deal, Kent CT14 7PB.** *01304 373373*. Shop 3mins walk. Country walks. Sea 1m, Channel ports 4.5m. Calor gas. Leisure centre 4m. Swimming pool 1m. Owner supplied copy. A2 to Dover. Last roundabout before docks. A258 to Deal. About 4.5/5m turn L, 0.5m past second hand car sales and hand car wash. Open: 1 March - 30 October. BH&HPA
15 15 160

## Dover

**(3m). Hawthorn Farm (Premier Park), Station Road, Martin Mill, Dover, Kent CT15 5LA.** *01304 852658*. www.keatfarm.co.uk. Showers, toilets, laundry, washing up facilities. Disabled toilet and shower room. Mother/toddler room. Shop. Cafe. Wi-Fi Internet. Fishing and golf nearby. David Bellamy Gold Conservation Award. Situated off main road between Deal and Dover A258. Well SP. Open: 1 March - 31 October. ★★★★★ BH&HPA NCC
147 176

## Dymchurch

**(1m). New Beach Touring Park, Hythe Road, Dymchurch, Kent TN29 0JX.** *0845 8159721*. www.ParkHolidaysUK.com/mmc. Indoor pool, children's facilities, restaurant, shops, entertainment. Visit Britain Holiday Park (4 stars). David Bellamy Silver Conservation Award. On the coastal road A259 between Hythe and Dymchurch. Open: 1 March - 31 October. ★★★ BH&HPA NCC
250 790

## Faversham

**(3m). Country View Park, Cleve Hill, Graveney, Faversham, Kent ME13 9EE.** *01227 275022*. www.countryviewpark.co.uk. Small quiet country park with five twin unit holiday lodges. 1m to beach, 7m to Canterbury. Follow Graveney signs from A299 - right through village - past Graveney church, 0.25 mile left hand side. Open: 1 March - 2 January. ★★★★ BH&HPA 5

## Folkestone

**(4m). Black Horse Farm Caravan Club Site, 385 Canterbury Road, Densole, Folkestone, Kent CT18 7BG.** *01303 892665*. www.caravanclub.co.uk. Set in the heart of farming country in the Kentish village of Densole on the Downs. Quiet and relaxed country site, ideally suited for families. Non-members and tent campers welcome. Toilet blocks. Hardstandings. Privacy cubicles. Laundry facilities. Veg prep. MV service point. Playground. Golf, fishing nearby. Good area for walking. Baby/toddler washroom. Dog walk. See website for standard directions to site. Open: All year. ★★★★★ NCC
140 140

**(4m). Folkestone Camping & Caravanning Club Site, The Warren, Folkestone, Kent CT19 6NQ.** *01303 255093*. www.campingandcaravanningclub.co.uk. This cliff site is situated in an Area of Outstanding Natural Beauty, adjacent to a pebble beach. On a clear day you can see France from this club site. Non-members welcome. NO TOWED CARAVANS permitted. Folkestone harbour is very picturesque with its own clifftop promenade. Sea fishing is available from the beach. Special deals available for families and backpackers. Loo Of The Year (5 stars). Visit Britain Tourism in Excellence Award - SE runner up. From M2 and Canterbury join A260, take L at island into Folkestone, Hill Road, straight on over crossroads into Wear Bay Road and second L turn before Martello Tower, site 0.5m on R. Open: 1 April - 31 October. ★★★★★ NCC
80

**(2.5m). Little Satmar Holiday Park, Winehouse Lane, Capel-le-Fene, Folkestone, Kent CT18 7JF.** *01303 251188*. www.keatfarm.co.uk. Quiet, well-maintained park convenient for ferries and Channel Tunnel. Wi-Fi Internet on whole park. David Bellamy Gold Conservation Award. Inland off B2011 Folkestone to Dover. Open: 1 March - 31 October. ★★★★ BH&HPA NCC
40 25 75

**(1.5m). Little Switzerland Camping and Caravanning Site, Wear Bay Road, Folkestone, Kent CT19 6PS.** *01303 252168*. Small family run site. Shop 0.25m. Licensed restaurant. Booking advisable. Off A20. Follow signs Country Park. Open: 1 March - 31 October.
16 16

**(4m). Varne Ridge Caravan Park, 145 Old Dover Road, Capel-le-Ferne, Folkestone, Kent CT18 7HX.** *01303 251765*. www.varne-ridge.co.uk. Clifftop location overlooking the English Channel. Small secluded and exclusive family run S E England Tourist 5 stars holiday park, situated near to the cliffs and having panoramic views over the Channel to the coastline of France. Ideal location to visit the Kentish attractions. Midway between Folkestone and Dover. Clifftop road marked 'Old Dover Road' runs off the B2011 at Capel-le-Ferne. Open: 1 April - 31 October. ★★★★★ BH&HPA
6 6 11

## Herne Bay

**(3m). Waterways Caravan Park, Reculver, Herne Bay, Kent CT6 6ST.** *01227 372620*. www.waterwayscaravanpark.co.uk. Children's play area, club house, amusement arcade: open seasonal from March 1-October 31. 100yd from the Stone beach and sea fishing. Fishing and golf course 3m away. Owner supplied copy. 9m from the cathedral city of Canterbury and 45mins to Dover ferry. Open: 1 March - 31 January. BH&HPA
197

## Hythe

**(4m). Daleacres Caravan Club Site, Lower Wall Road, West Hythe, Hythe, Kent CT21 4NW.** *01303 267679*. www.caravanclub.co.uk. Attractive, level site. Play area. Dog walk. Toilet blocks. Privacy cubicles. Laundry facilities. Veg prep. MV service point. Play equipment. Golf, fishing and water sports nearby. Good for walking. Ideal for families. Member only. No tents. See website for standard directions to site. Open: 23 March - 2 November. NCC
130 130

# SOUTH EAST

### Isle of Sheppey

**(1m). Ashcroft Coast Holiday Park, Plough Road, Minster-on-Sea, Isle of Sheppey, Kent ME12 4JH.** *0843 3092591.* www.park-resorts.com. Heated indoor & outdoor pool. Kids club, adventure playground. Water and sports resorts programmes. Takeaway. Entertainment. Amusements. Sports court. Spa bath. Laundrette. David Bellamy Gold Conservation Award. Take the A249 towards Sheerness Once on the Island turn R onto B223 into Eastchurch (about 4m). Turn L at the Church and follow road into Plough Lane. Ashcroft is on R. Open: 1 March - 31 October. ★★★★★ BH&HPA 🏕 385

**(7m). Harts Holiday Village, Leysdown Road, Leysdown-on-Sea, Isle of Sheppey, Kent ME12 4RG.** *0845 8159775.* www.ParkHolidaysUK.com. Leisure complex with heated swimming pool, paddling pool and slide. Jacuzzi. Play areas and amusement arcade. Clubhouse with free entertainment. 5mns from beach. Hire fleet on site. Bistro which are open for breakfast, lunch and dinners. Good location as a base if people want to travel to London. Owner supplied copy. M2, J5 to A249 then pick up B2231 to Leysdown. 9m from Sheerness. Open: 1 March - 1 January. **BH&HPA NCC** 267

**Shurland Dale Holiday Park, Warden Road, Eastchurch, Isle of Sheppey, Kent ME12 4EN.** *0844 0502572.* www.park-resorts.com. Indoor pool, adventure playground, kids club, sports field, amusements. Darts, pool table. Family evening entertainment. Howletts Wild Animal Park nearby. David Bellamy Gold Conservation Award. M20 or M2 to A249 to Sheerness. Turn R at the roundabout on the B2231 towards Leysdown. Follow road into Eastchurch and turn L at the church into Warden Road, then first R, second L. Open: 1 April - 30 October. ★★★★ **BH&HPA** 375

**(6m). Warden Springs Holiday Park, Thorn Hill Road, Warden Point, Isle of Sheppey, Kent ME12 4HF.** *01795 880088.* www.park-resortstouring.com. Outdoor heated swimming pool, club house, FREE kids clubs, FREE family evening entertainment. Restaurant, bar, playground. David Bellamy Gold Conservation Award. From M25 take A2, J2. Then take M2, till J5. Follow A249 for 8m then R, on to B2231 to Eastchurch. Turn L following signs for park. Open: 30 March - 31 October. ★★★★ **BH&HPA NCC** 48 19

### Maidstone

**(3m). Bearsted Caravan Club Site, A20 Ashford Road, Bearsted, Maidstone, Kent ME17 1XH.** *01622 730018.* www.caravanclub.co.uk. Tranquil site in the heart of Kent. Historic Leeds Castle nearby. Easy reach of Maidstone and coastal towns of Whitstable and Margate. Non members welcome. No tents. See website for standard directions to site. Open: 23 March - 1 November. ★★★★★ NCC 69 69

**(3m). Cold Blow Farm, Cold Blow Lane, Thurnham, Maidstone, Kent ME14 3LR.** *01622 730439.* www.coldblow-camping.co.uk. Small quiet park. 60 beds in bunkhouses and disabled accommodation. Fishing nearby. From M20: if towing or driving a coach or lorry DO NOT use J7. Leave the motorway at J8 (Leeds Castle) and follow signs to Maidstone A20, carry on for 1m, take first turning on R onto Roundwell. Then take first R onto Water Lane, go to end of Water Lane, passing under 3 bridges. At crossroads straight over onto Coldblow Lane. Entrance within 0.5m on R. Open: All year. 5 5

**The Finches International Olympic Camping & Caravan Park, Chartway Street, Kingswood, Maidstone, Kent ME17 3DN.** *01622 844538.* www.caravansatkingswood.co.uk. Farm shop and cafe adjacent. General store/post office 0.5 mile. Golf course 0.5 mile. Five pubs within 2 miles. Doctor 2 miles. Leeds Castle 2 miles. 10 tourers for hire on site. M20 J8. Follow signs to Leeds Castle. Take B2163 to A276. L. First L. 1 mile on L. Open: All year. 20 20

**(1m). Yew Tree Mobile Home Park, Maidstone, Kent CT5 3AR.** *01233 713551.* www.yewtreepark.com. Mobile home park. A20 main trunk road to Folkestone. Open: 26 March - 11 September. ★★★★ **BH&HPA** 20 50

### Marden

**(10m). Tanner Farm Touring Caravan & Camping Park, Goudhurst Road, Marden, Kent TN12 9ND.** *01622 832399.* www.tannerfarmpark.co.uk. CARAVAN CLUB AFFILIATED SITE. Extremely peaceful setting in centre of attractive family farm. Mainly flat and grass. Farm animals. B&B also available in Tudor farmhouse. David Bellamy Gold Conservation Award. 3m from Marden, 10m Maidstone from either A229 or A262 on to B2079, midway between Goudhurst & Marden. Open: All year. ★★★★★ **BH&HPA** 

40 100

### Minster-on-Sea

**(1.5m). Lazy Days Holiday Park (Minster), Bell Farm Lane, Minster-on-Sea, Kent ME12 4JB.** *01795 874000.* www.lazyholidays.co.uk. Please ring. Quiet tranquil park for discerning adults, no clubs nor bingo. All pitches have superb sea views across the Thames estuary. Owner supplied copy. M20, J7 take A249 N towards Sittingbourne and Sheerness. B2231 towards Minster. Straight after traffic lights and next roundabout. Take second L, then R (by phone box) after mini roundabout: Plough Road. Immediately on L is Bell Farm Lane, follow road till entrance of park. Open: 1 March - 31 October. **BH&HPA** 12 8

### New Romney

**(0.25m). Marlie Holiday Village, Dymchurch Road, New Romney, Kent TN28 8UE.** *0845 8159750.* www.ParkHolidaysUK.com/mmc. About 10mins drive to beach. Leaflets on display in reception. Club house, indoor leisure complex with pool. Jacuzzi, play area and cafe. Horses, donkeys, ducks and rabbits. New Romney has bars. David Bellamy Silver Conservation Award. On A259 coast road. Open: 18 March - 5 January. ★★ **BH&HPA NCC** 30 222

**(3m). Romney Sands Holiday Park, The Parade, Greatstone-on-Sea, New Romney, Kent TN28 8RN.** *0843 3092591.* www.park-resorts.com. Indoor heated pool, FREE kids club, FREE family entertainment, adventure playground, amusements, laundrette, diner, takeaway, tennis courts. Bar, family club room, pool, darts. Southbeach Club. David Bellamy Silver Conservation Award. From London, take M20 to Ashford. Exit at J10, and follow signs to Brenzett. Follow signs to New Romney taking 1st R past Shell garage to the seafront. Turn R on coast road. Open: 1 April - 31 October. ★★★★ **BH&HPA NCC** 660

### Ramsgate

**(2.5m). Manston Caravan And Camping Park, Manston Court Road, Manston, Ramsgate, Kent CT7 0HD.** *01843 823442.* www.manston-park.co.uk. 100 mixed pitches in total. Play area. Golf within 1m; supermarket, PO within 2m. Ramsgate, Margate and Broadstairs 3m away. M2 motorway follow A299

# SOUTH EAST

to Monkton roundabout, follow Kent International Airport signs to join B2050. 1st L after airport first L, park 400yd on R. Open: 1 April - 31 October. ★★★★
BH&HPA ⌂ ⌐ ♀ ⍺ ⌂ ⌂ ⌂ ⌂ ⌂
⛺ 100⛺ ▲ 40⛺

**Nethercourt Touring Park**, Nethercourt Hill, Ramsgate, Kent CT11 0RX. 01843 595485. www.barrowcliffe.net. 52 mixed pitches in total. Limited facilities for the disabled. Fees on application. Follow A253 into Ramsgate. At Nethercourt Circus roundabout. Bear L to site entrance 150yd on L. 0.5m from beach and 1m to yacht marina and ferry. Open: All year. ⌂ ⌂ ⌂ ⌂ ⌂ ⌂ ⌂ ⌂ ⌂ ⌂ ⌂ ⌂ ⌂ ⌂ 52⛺ ▲

(1m). **Pegwell Bay Caravan Park**, Pegwell Road, Ramsgate, Kent CT11 0NJ. 01843 592222. www.pegwellcaravanpark.co.uk. Take A299 Thanet Way to A253. L at double roundabout and R immediately at second roundabout into Chilton Lane. Open: 5 March - 31 October.
BH&HPA ⌂ ⌂ ⌂ ⌂ 95⛺

(5.5m). **The Foxhunter Park**, Monkton, Ramsgate, Kent CT12 4JG. 01843 821311. www.saunderssparkhomes.co.uk. Club. Swimming pool. Beauty Spa. Restaurant. Putting Green, bowls, children's adventure land. Golf courses, fishing, shopping centre etc close by, beaches. Winner of Calor 'Best Park' and ETB 'England for Excellence'. Q. Owner supplied copy. Off A299. From London take A2, on to M2, on to A299. At Monkton roundabout, take 3rd exit Willetts Hill. Turn L at small roundabout. We are up on R. Open: 2 April - 15 October. ★★★★★
BH&HPA NCC ⌂ ⌂ ⌂ ⌂ ⌂ ⌂ ⌂ ⌂ ⌂ ⌂ ⌂ ⌂ 360⛺

### Rochester

(9m). **Allhallows Leisure Holiday Park (Haven)**, Allhallows on Sea, Rochester, Kent ME3 9QD. 0871 4680496. www.haven.com. Welcome Host Award Investor in People. Bars. Indoor and outdoor heated pools. Multi sports court. Nightly entertainment. Playground. Amusement arcade. Fishing lake, stables and bowling green. Laundrette. Tennis court, 9 hole golf course, kid's clubs, horse riding, crazy golf, inflatable slide by outdoor pool, trampolines and a new Papa Johns. David Bellamy Gold Conservation Award. M25 J2 SP Canterbury. Take A2 until signs for Gillingham A289/(Grain A228). Follow A289 until roundabout then first exit for A228 Grain. Allhallows is SP from the A228. Open: 10 March - 31 October. ★★★★ BH&HPA NCC ⌂ ⌂ ⌂ ⌂ ⌂ ⌂ ⌂ ⌂ ⌂ ⌂ ⌂ ⌂ ⌂ ⌂ ⛺ 1000⛺

### Sandwich

(0.2m). **Sandwich Leisure Park**, Woodnesborough Road, Sandwich, Kent CT13 0AA. 01304 612681. www.sandwich-leisurepark.co.uk. Relaxed park with excellent shower and WC facilities. Town 5 mins on foot. Laundry, phone, playground. David Bellamy Gold Conservation Award. Follow A257 to Sandwich then follow caravan park brown signs. Open: 4 March - 31 October. ★★★★★
BH&HPA ⌂ ⌂ ⌂ ⌂ ⌂ ⌂ ⌂ ⌂ ⌂ ⌂ ⛺ 187⛺ ▲ 106⛺

### Sevenoaks

(9m). **Gate House Wood Touring Park**, Ford Lane, Wrotham Heath, Sevenoaks, Kent TN15 7SD. 01732 843062. www.gatehousewoodtouringpark.com. 12 month licence for winter rallies, etc. American RVs welcome. M26, J2A take A20 S towards Maidstone, through traffic lights at Wrotham Heath take first L, SP Trottiscliffe, L at next junction. Gate House Wood is 100yd on L. Open: 1 March - 31 October. ★★★★★ BH&HPA ⌂ ⌂ ⌂ ⌂ ⌂ ⌂ ⌂ ⌂ ⌂ ⌂ ⛺ 56⛺ ▲

(4m). **Oldbury Hill Camping & Caravanning Club Site**, Styants Bottom, Seal, Sevenoaks, Kent TN15 0ET. 01732 762728. www.campingandcaravanningclub.co.uk. A 4 acre site. Levelling ramps required. Ideal site for exploring the delights of the Garden of England. All units accepted. Non-members welcome. Site is located in National Trust land surrounded by woodland walks. Convenient for Channel Ports at Dover and Folkestone. Special deals available for families and backpackers. 0.5m off the A25 between Sevenoaks and Borough Green. Turn L just after Crown Point Inn. Down narrow lane to Styants Bottom, site on L. Open: 1 April - 31 October. ★★★★ NCC ⌂ ⌂ ⌂ ⌂ ⌂ ⌂ ⌂ ⌂ ⌂ 60⛺ 60⛺ ▲

**Thriftwood Holiday Park**, Plaxdale Green Road, Stansted, Sevenoaks, Kent TN15 7PB. 01732 822261. www.thriftwoodholidaypark.com. Gas supplies & refills. Bar. Shaver points. Tennis nearby. Play area. Outdoor swimming pool. Licensed club house. From M25, take M20 towards Dover, J2. Follow A2 Northbound and Thriftwood signs. M26 J2A follow A20 Northbound towards West Kingsdown. Open: 1 March - 31 January. ★★★★ BH&HPA ⌂ ⌂ ⌂ ⌂ ⌂ ⌂ ⌂ ⌂ ⌂ ⌂ ⌂ ⌂ 150⛺ ▲ 5⛺

(0.5m). **To The Woods**, Botsom Lane, West Kingsdown, Sevenoaks, Kent TN15 6BN. 01322 863751. Small, quiet park with limited facilities. Ideal for quiet weekends. Idyllic setting close to mainline to London (19m from Central London). The site is high on the North Downs, but sheltered by trees and well-drained. Brands Hatch circuit 1m, Shops & pub 0.75m. 4m NW of Wrotham. Turn L at Botsom Lane off A20. Site (800yd). Open: All year. ⌂ ⌂ ⌂ ⌂ ⌂ ⌂ ⌂ ⌂ ⌂ ⌂ ⛺ 30⛺ ▲

### Sheerness

(0.5m). **Priory Hill Holiday Park**, Wing Road, Leysdown, Sheppey, Sheerness, Kent ME12 4QT. 01795 510267. www.prioryhill.co.uk. Clubhouse entertainment, swimming pool (indoor heated) and lots more. See our website. M2/M20-A249 to Isle of Sheppey, B2231 to Leysdown follow brown signs to Priory Hill. Open: 1 March - 28 October. BH&HPA ⌂ ⌂ ⌂ ⌂ ⌂ ⌂ ⌂ ⌂ ⌂ ⌂ ⌂ ⌂ ⌂ ⌂ 35⛺ ▲ ⛺

(3m). **Sea Cliff Caravan Park**, Oak Lane, Minster, Sheerness, Kent ME12 3QS. 01795 872262. www.leisureretreats.co.uk. On site: club, restaurant, bingo, entertainment, playground, playing field. Within 3-4m: golf, shops, Leysdown amusements. Owner supplied copy. Off A249, through Minster village, tourist sign on L. Open: 19 March - 30 October. BH&HPA ⌂ ⌂ ⌂ ⌂ ⌂ ⌂ ⌂ ⌂ ⛺ 154⛺

(1.5m). **Sheerness Holiday Village**, Halfway Road, Minster-on-Sea, Sheerness, Kent ME12 3AA. 0845 8159760. www.ParkHolidaysUK.com/mmc. Club. Indoor pool. Children's club. Amusements, sports & leisure facilities, playground, on site shop, takeaway & cafe. David Bellamy Silver Conservation Award. Off M2 and A2 following signs to Sheerness, 0.5m from town on R. Open: 18 March - 31 October. ★★★ BH&HPA NCC ⌂ ⌂ ⌂ ⌂ ⌂ ⌂ ⌂ ⌂ ⌂ ⌂ ⌂ ⌂ ⌂ ⌂ ⛺ 50⛺ ▲ 320⛺

(0.5m). **Willow Trees Holiday Park**, Oak Lane, Minster on Sea, Sheerness, Kent ME12 3QR. 01795 875833. Children welcome. Accessed from A249. Open: All year. BH&HPA ⌂ ⌂ ⌂ ⛺

### Sutton-by-Dover

(3m). **Sutton Vale Caravan Park**, Vale Road, Sutton-by-Dover, Kent CT15 5DH. 01304 374155. www.sutton-vale.co.uk. Licensed club. Pool. Restaurant. Play area. Sports field. Horse riding next door. Sea fishing 4m. Lake fishing 2m. 4 golf courses radius 3m - local pub, traditional ales and 5 mins walk. Car ride 2 mins. A2, 4m from Dover Whitfield roundabout turn R, 20yd opposite MacDonalds into Archers Court Road, exactly 4m on R. Open: All year. ★★★★ BH&HPA NCC ⌂ ⌂ ⌂ ⌂ ⌂ ⌂ ⌂ ⌂ ⌂ ⌂ ⌂ ⌂ ⌂ ⌂ ⌂ ⌂ 10⛺ 14⛺ ▲ 90⛺

# SOUTH EAST

### Swalecliffe

**(1.5m). Seaview Holiday Park (Park Holidays UK) (Swalecliffe)**, St John's Road, Swalecliffe, Kent CT5 2RY. *0845 8159755*. www.ParkHolidaysUK.com/mmc. AA 3 pennants. Bar, bar snacks. New complex bar and cafe integral, heated outdoor swimming pool. Canterbury: shopping, restaurants. Amenities, golf, swimming pool, fishing all within 1m David Bellamy Silver Conservation Award. Off A299 for Whitstable, continue along A2990, at double roundabout L under railway bridge, mini roundabout turn R 600yd on L, lane down to park (SP). Open: 1 March - 31 October.
★★★★ BH&HPA NCC ♀☐☐♠☐
♫♪♣♂♠♂☐♣♠✖☐♣♿
♨ 171⚏ 171⚐ ▲ 527⚑

### Tonbridge

**(5m). The Hop Farm Family Park**, Paddock Wood, Tonbridge, Kent TN12 6PY. *01892 838161*. www.thehopfarm.co.uk/touring. Delightfully situated in over 500 acres at one of Kent's most popular family attractions: The Hop Farm's World of Activities. Overlooking fields, woodlands and the spectacular oast village - the ideal base for exploring Kent's Garden of England. Situated on a A228 Paddock Wood, 30mins from J5, M25, 10mins from J4, M20. Open: 1 March - 31 October. BH&HPA ♀☐☐♠♫♪♣♂♠
⚏✖☐♣♿ 40⚏ 60⚐ 300▲

### Whitstable

**(2m). Alberta Holiday Park**, Faversham Road, Seasalter, Whitstable, Kent CT5 4BJ. *01227 274485*. www.ParkHolidaysUK.com. Close to beach. Good position for touring Kent countryside and sea. Laundrette, cafe, public phone, licensed club, takeaway, food shop. Heated outdoor swimming pool. Play area. Many sporting activities. Bus outside park. Canterbury: shopping, restaurants. David Bellamy Gold Conservation Award. Turn off M2 on to A299, L after 2m to Seasalter. Site 1m. Open: 1 March - 30 November.
★★★ BH&HPA NCC ☐☐♠♣♂☐♣
✖☐♣♿ ⚐ 330⚑

**(2m). Homing Leisure Park**, Church Lane, Seasalter, Whitstable, Kent CT5 4BU. *01227 771477*. www.homingpark.co.uk. Licensed club. Laundrette, playground, phone, outdoor pool, tennis court. Shops, cinema within 8m. 1m from beach. Holiday caravans for sale. David Bellamy Silver Conservation Award. Owner supplied copy. Follow A299, turn L into Church Lane towards Seasalter. Park is 300yd on the L. Open: 30 March - 29 October.
★★★★★ BH&HPA ☐♀✉☐✖
☐♣ 43⚏ 43⚐ ▲ 198⚑

**(1.5m). Meadow Farm Caravan Park**, 64 Herne Bay Road, Swalecliffe, Whitstable, Kent CT5 2LT. *01227 792534*. Off A299. Open: 1 March - 31 October. ☐♠⚐ 82⚑

**(1m). Primrose Cottage Caravan Park**, Golden Hill, Whitstable, Kent CT5 3AR. *01227 273694*. 18 mixed pitches in total (12 elec hook-ups). A quiet park with no clubhouse. Superstore nearby. 1m to Whitstable town and 7m to Canterbury. 1m E of Whitstable roundabout on A2990 (Thanet Way), next to Tesco supermarket. Open: 1 March - 31 October. BH&HPA ☐
☐♠♣♫♪♂☐♣⚏♣♣♿
18⚐ ▲ 54⚑

## LONDON
### Chingford

**(2m). Lee Valley Campsite Sewardstone**, Sewardstone Road, Chingford, London E4 7RA. *020 8529 5689*. www.leevalleypark.org.uk. Close to M25 and Epping Forest. Play area. Bus stops on site for connection to London. Fishing, open form and parks all close by. Site is on A112 between Chingford and Waltham Abbey to the S of M25, leave M25 at J26. Open: 1 March - 31 January. ★★★★ ☐☐♠♣♫♪
☐☐♣♣♣♿ ⚏ 200⚐ ▲ ⚑

### Edmonton

**(1m). Lee Valley Camping & Caravan Park**, Meridian Way, Edmonton, London N9 0AR. *020 8803 6900*. www.leevalleypark.org.uk. Golf course, and Odeon cinema on complex. Shops 0.5m away. M25 J25, follow signs for A10 (City). At first set of traffic lights turn L, continue on this road for 6m. At Odeon cinema turn L into leisure centre complex, camping is SP. Open: 2 January - 23 December.
★★★★★ ☐☐♠♣♫♪♂☐♣⚏
✖☐♣♿ ⚏ 100⚐ ▲

### London

**Abbey Wood Caravan Club Site**, Federation Road, Abbey Wood, London, London SE2 0LS. *020 8311 7708*. www.caravanclub.co.uk. Only 35mins by train to central London yet retaining a rural atmosphere. Playframe. Advance booking essential bank holidays, July and August. Hardstandings. Heated toilet blocks. Privacy cubicles. Laundry facilities. Baby changing facilities. Veg prep. MV service point. Golf, water sports and cycling all within 5m. Non-members welcome. Tent campers admitted. See website for standard directions to site. Open: All year.
★★★★★ NCC ☐☐♠♣✉☐
✿♣⚏☐♣♣♿ ⚏ 210⚏ 210⚐ ▲

**Crystal Palace Caravan Club Site**, Crystal Palace Parade, London, London SE19 1UF. *020 8778 7155*. www.caravanclub.co.uk. Adjacent to pleasant park with many attractions for children. Next to National Sports Centre. Excellent facilities. Mainline railway stations to central London within walking distance. Hardstandings. Advance booking necessary. Toilet blocks. Privacy cubicles. Laundry facilities. Veg prep. MV service point. Non-members welcome. See website for standard directions to site. Open: 9 February - 7 January. ★★★★★ NCC ☐☐♠♣
♫♪☐♣♣♿ ⚏ 126⚏ 126⚐ ▲

### Loughton

**The Elms Caravan & Camping Park**, Lippitts Hill, High Beach, Loughton,

**Homing Park**
Touring and Camping
Caravan holiday homes for sale
Close to the beach and harbour
Tennis court & swimming pool
Family owned and run
Licensed bar

Church Lane, Seasalter, Whitstable, Kent CT5 4BU
t: 01227 771477 e: info@homingpark.co.uk

www.homingpark.co.uk

# SOUTH EAST

London IG10 4AW. 020 8502 5652. www.theelmscampsite.co.uk.

## OXFORDSHIRE

### Abingdon

(4m). Bridge House Caravan Site (Oxford), Clifton Hampden, Abingdon, Oxfordshire OX14 3EH. 01865 407725. Fishing on site. Shops, PO, doctor within 0.25m. Off A415. Open: 1 April - 31 October. BH&HPA 4⚡12⚡ 44⚡

### Banbury

(4m). Anita's Touring Caravan Park, The Yews, Banbury, Oxfordshire OX17 1AZ. 01295 750731. 36 pitches with hook-ups. Set in farmland on the edge of Mollington village. Groceries one mile. Good for walking & cycling. Camping and camping pods. Leave Jct 11 M40, follow sign to Chipping Norton over 2 roundabouts to 3rd roundabout turn R, SP to Southam. Travel 4 miles to Mollington, stay on A423 go 200yds, on left. Open: All year. ★★★★

(3m). Barnstones Caravan & Camping Park, Great Bourton, Banbury, Oxfordshire OX17 1QU. 01295 750289. Golf course 2.5m. Fishing, doctor, PO, shop 1m. Pub serving food 150yd. Garage 0.5m. Leave Banbury on A423 SP Southam. After 3m turn R, SP Great Borton. Site on R in 100yd. If using M40 leave J11 Banbury and follow sign to Chipping Norton, over 2 roundabouts. At 3rd roundabout turn R, SP Southam on to A423. Open: All year. ★★★★ BH&HPA 40⚡ 55⚡ A

(3.5m). Bo Peep Caravan Park, Aynho Road, Adderbury, Banbury, Oxfordshire OX17 3NP. 01295 810605. www.bo-peep.co.uk. Tranquil 13 acre touring site set in 85 acres of farmland. River frontage and woodland walks. Excellent facilities. Central for Oxford, Blenheim, Stratford-on-Avon and Warwick Castle. Year round caravan storage available. Situated on B4100 0.5m E of Adderbury and 3m S of Banbury. Access via M40, J10. Open: 1 March - 31 October. ★★★★ BH&HPA 112⚡

Fir Tree Farm Caravan Site, Warmington, Banbury, Oxfordshire OX17 1JL. 07983 144681.

### Bicester

(5m). Godwins Ice Cream Farm, Northampton Road, Weston-on-the-Green, Bicester, Oxfordshire OX25 3QL. 01869 351647. Home-made ice cream made on the farm. Cafe, bar/restaurant and shop. Golf course nearby. Nationwide cycle track linking Oxford to Milton Keynes (route 51). Oxfordshire way footpath. PO, shops, pub/restaurants 10mins walk away. Situated 2mins from J9M40, midway Oxford and Bicester. Open: 1 March - 31 October. 16⚡ 16⚡

(4m). Heyford Leys Camping Park, Heyford Leys, Upper Heyford, Bicester, Oxfordshire OX25 5LX. 01869 232048. www.heyfordleyspark.co.uk. Washing facilities. Play area. GS. Off B4030 Chipping Norton to Bicester. 2m from M40. Open: All year. ★ BH&HPA 10⚡ 20⚡ A 16⚡

### Burford

(2m). Burford Caravan Club Site, Bradwell Grove, Burford, Oxfordshire OX18 4JJ. 01993 823080. www.caravanclub.co.uk. An attractive and spacious site opposite Cotswold Wildlife Park. Some hardstanding pitches, toilet block with privacy cubicles and laundry facilities. MV service point, playground, shops within 2m and dog walk on site. Non-members welcome. No tents. See website for standard directions to site. Open: 23 March - 5 November. ★★★★ NCC 119⚡ 119⚡

### Charlbury

(1m). Cotswold View Caravan & Camping Site, Enstone Road, Charlbury, Oxfordshire OX7 3JH. 0800 0853474. www.cotswoldview.eu. High standard. Children's recreation area. Site is on a working farm. Situated on the B4022, 1m N of Charlbury on the road to Enstone. Open: 1 April - 31 October. ★★★★

### Chipping Norton

(2.5m). Chipping Norton Camping & Caravanning Club Site, Chadlington, Chipping Norton, Oxfordshire OX7 3PE. 01608 641993. www.campingandcaravanningclub.co.uk. Set in lovely spot in Cotswolds countryside. Site has children's play area and a woodland walk adjacent to the site. Local villages such as Stow-on-the-Wold and Bourton-on-the-Water are well worth a visit. Oxford and Stratford are both only 20m away. Non-members welcome. Special deals available for families and backpackers. Take Oxford ring road the A3400 to Stratford-upon-Avon, then A44 in Chipping Norton take A361 for Burford. In 1.5m bear L at fork SP Chadlington. Open: 1 April - 31 October. ★★★★ NCC 105⚡ 105⚡ A

### Henley-On-Thames

(0.75m). Four Oaks Caravan Club Site, Marlow Road, Henley-On-Thames, Oxfordshire RG9 2HY. 01491 572312. www.caravanclub.co.uk. Shops 0.5m. Pleasantly green and level site with mature trees. Within walking distance of Henley. Hardstandings. Toilet blocks. Privacy cubicles. Laundry facilities. Baby/toddler washroom. Veg prep. MV service point. Dog walk on site. Playground. Ideal for families. Members only. No tents. See website for standard directions to site. Open: 23 March - 5 November. NCC 87⚡ 87⚡ A

(0.5m). Swiss Farm International Touring and Camping Park, Marlow Road, Henley-on-Thames, Oxfordshire RG9 2HY. 01491 573419. www.swissfarmcamping.co.uk. Friendly, international, family run site. Excellent facilities including open air swimming pool, fishing lake, licensed bar and games room. Quiet park, no groups please. On A4155 near river. Once in Henley follow signs out towards Marlow. We are on the L just outside town centre after rugby club. Open: 1 March - 31 October. ★★★ BH&HPA 20⚡ 120⚡ A 6⚡

### Kidlington

(1m). Greenhill Farm Caravan & Camping Park, Station Road, Bletchingdon, Kidlington, Oxfordshire OX5 3BQ. 01869 351600. www.greenhill-leisure-park.co.uk. Quiet and spacious farm site. Pets corner, farm animals. Riverside walks, fishing on site. Rally field. Heated toilet block. Games room and playground. Ideal for touring the Cotswolds, 4m from Blenheim Palace. From Oxford on A34 N, turn on to B4027. Bletchingdon site 0.5m after village. 4m from Woodstock. Open: All year. 70⚡ 70⚡ A

### Oxford

(0.5m). Benson Waterfront Holiday Park, Benson Cruiser Station, Benson, Oxford, Oxfordshire OX10 6SJ. 01491 838304. www.bensonwaterfront.com. Close to Benson village and its facilities. Restaurant. Children allowed. Boat hire available. On A4074 Oxford to Henley at T-junction B4009. On River Thames. Open: 1 April - 31 October. BH&HPA 20⚡ 25⚡

(1m). Oxford Camping & Caravanning Club Site, 426 Abingdon Road, Oxford,

# SOUTH EAST

Oxfordshire OX1 4XG. *01865 244088*. www.campingandcaravanningclub.co.uk. This site is 1.5m from the historic city centre. Makes an ideal touring base. Good access to M4/M40. Non-members welcome. All units accepted. This university city offers more than 650 listed buildings. Special deals available for families and backpackers. South side of Oxford take A4144 to city centre from ring road, SP from A34. Open: All year. ★ ★ NCC ⌂ ⚘ ⚒ ⚑ ⚒ ⚘ ⚘ ⚘ ⚘ 85⚒ 85⚒ ♿

## Wallingford

(0.25m). **Bridge Villa Camping & Caravan Park, Crowmarsh Gifford, Wallingford, Oxfordshire OX10 8HB.** *01491 836580*. www.tiscover.co.uk/bridge.villa. Disabled facilities. Washroom. Hot showers and wash basins. Electric shaver & hairdryer points. Gas supplies. Laundrette within 220yd. Ironing room available. Many sporting facilities within 2m of site. Information on request. Perfect location for visiting Oxford, Henley and Windsor. Off A4130 in the village of Crowmarsh Gifford, nr Wallingford Bridge. Open: 1 February - 31 December. BH&HPA ⌂ ⚘ ⚘ ⚘ ⚘ ⚘ ⚘ ⚘ ⚘ 111⚒ ♿

## Witney

(4.5m). **Hardwick Parks, Downs Road, Standlake, Witney, Oxfordshire OX29 7PZ.** *01865 300501*. www.hardwickparks.co.uk. Fishing. Golf course 4m. Horse riding 0.5m. Air conditioned shower and toilets. Air conditioned clubhouse. Wi-Fi access. Water skiing, ware boarding, lessons and tows. David Bellamy Silver Conservation Award. Off A415, S of Witney. Open: 30 March - 31 October. ★ ★ ★ BH&HPA ⚘ ⌂ ⚘ ⚘ ⚘ ⚘ ⚘ ⚘ 50⚒ 164⚒ ♿ 160⚒

(5.5m). **Lincoln Farm Park Oxfordshire, High Street, Standlake, Witney, Oxfordshire OX29 7RH.** *01865 300239*. www.lincolnfarmpark.co.uk. Situated in village, 2 pubs serving food, village PO, shop. 2 indoor swimming pools, spa pools and saunas on site, kids pool all indoors. Fitness centre. Fishing nearby in private lake. GS. From A40 take Witney exit, follow signs for Standlake 4m, turn by Village Petrol Station, park is 300yds. Open: 1 February - 11 November. ★ ★ ★ ★ ★ BH&HPA ⌂ ⚘ ⚘ ⚘ ⚘ ⚘ ⚘ ⚘ 25⚒ 90⚒ ♿

 (5.5m). **Lincoln Farm Park Oxfordshire (Premier Park), High Street, Standlake, Witney, Oxfordshire OX29 7RH.** *01865 300239*. www.lincolnfarmpark.co.uk. Situated in village, 2 pubs serving food, village PO, shop. 2 indoor swimming pools, spa pools and saunas on site, kids pool all indoors. Fitness centre. Fishing nearby in private lake. GS. From A40 take Witney exit, follow signs for Standlake 4m, turn by Village Petrol Station, park is 300yds. Open: 1 February - 11 November. ★ ★ ★ ★ ★ BH&HPA ⌂ ⚘ ⚘ ⚘ ⚘ ⚘ ⚘ ⚘ 25⚒ 90⚒ ♿

## Woodstock

(0.75m). **Bladon Chains Caravan Club Site, Bladon Road, Woodstock, Oxfordshire OX20 1PT.** *01993 812390*. www.caravanclub.co.uk. Level site surrounded by magnificent trees. Toilet blocks, laundry facilities and MV service point. Significant areas of interest and NCN route nearby. Facilities for disabled. Members only. No tents. See website for standard directions to site. Open: 23 March - 5 November. NCC ⌂ ⚘ ⚘ ⚘ ⚘ ⚘ ⚘ 92⚒ 92⚒ ♿

# SURREY

## Chertsey

(1m). **Chertsey Camping & Caravanning Club Site, Bridge Road, Chertsey, Surrey KT16 8JX.** *01932 562405*. www.campingandcaravanningclub.co.uk. Picturesque site on banks of the Thames. Good access to London and surrounding areas. Fishing is permitted from the riverbank with the holiday site managers' permission. Local attractions include Thorpe Park, Windsor Castle and Legoland. Non-members welcome. All units accepted. Special deals available for families and backpackers. Leave M25 exit 11. Follow signs (A317) to Chertsey. At roundabout take first exit to lights. Straight over at next lights. Turn R 400yd turn L into site. Open: 1 January - 31 December. ★ ★ ★ ★ NCC ⌂ ⚘ ⚘ ⚘ ⚘ ⚘ ⚘ ⚘ ⚘ ⚘ 200⚒ 200⚒ ♿

## East Horsley

(2m). **Horsley Camping & Caravanning Club Site, Ockham Road North, East Horsley, Surrey KT24 6PE.** *01483 283273*. www.campingandcaravanningclub.co.uk. Recreation hall and play area. Next to Horsley Lake, ideal for fishing. Non-members welcome. The site has an abundance of wildlife, with foxes, deer, rabbits and ducks often spotted. Special deals available for families and backpackers. All units accepted. M25, J10 on to A3. Take B2039, exit marked Ockham, East Horsley, look for post box on R at Green Lane, access road to site SP on R. Open: 1 April - 31 October. ★ ★ ★ ★ NCC ⌂ ⚘ ⚘ ⚘ ⚘ ⚘ ⚘ ⚘ ⚘ 130⚒ 130⚒ ♿

## Farnham

**Tilford Woods, Tilford Road, Tilford, Farnham, Surrey GU10 2DD.** *0844 272 9507*. www.tilfordwoods.co.uk. A country retreat offering lodge accommodation in the heart of rural Surrey. Bordered by woodland and open fields, the park lies within the Surrey Hills Area of Outstanding Natural Beauty. The historic market town of Farnham, which has excellent transport links into London, is just a few miles away. Exclusive lodges with a private outdoor hot tub, sauna or jacuzzi bath. Guests can enjoy the neighbouring pub and restaurant where there is a children's play area. A golf club is directly opposite the park. See website for full directions to park. Open: All year. ★ ★ ★ ★ BH&HPA ⚘ ⚘ ⚘ ⚘ ⚘

**A stunning country retreat offering lodge accommodation in the heart of beautiful rural Surrey**

- Exclusive lodge accommodation
- Set in an area of outstanding natural beauty
- Private outdoor hot tub, sauna and jacuzzi bath
- Complete with all your creature comforts
- Local pub and restaurant including children's play area
- Golf course opposite the park

**20% off your booking Quote CHP20**

*Terms and conditions apply

Pet Friendly

To book call **0844 272 9507** or visit **www.tilfordwoods.co.uk**

# SOUTH EAST

### Godalming

(3m). **The Merry Harriers, Hambledon, Godalming, Surrey GU8 4DR.** 01428 682883. www.merryharriers.com. Shower and shaver point. Fishing nearby. Owner supplied copy. Off A3 on to A283, L to Hambledon after Wormley. 2m S of Milford. Milford or Whitley station 1.5m. Open: All year.

### Lingfield

(1.5m). **Long Acres Caravan & Camping Park, New Chapel Road, Lingfield, Surrey RH7 6LE.** 01342 833205. www.longacres-camping.co.uk. Clean site, ideal for visiting London, Surrey, Kent and Sussex. Set in 40 acres. Plenty to see and do. 1hr from London by train, 1hr from South Coast. Many local attractions, Hever, Chartwell, Chessington, various gardens. Local fishing and golf. Off J6, M25 S on A22 towards East Grinstead turn L on B2028 towards Lingfield. Open: All year. ★★★ BH&HPA

### Mytchett

**Canal Visitor Centre, Mytchett Place Road, Mytchett, Surrey GU16 6DD.** 01252 370073. www.basingstoke-canal.co.uk. Beautiful canalside setting. WC, showers and water point on site. 45mins away from London. M3, J4, follow A331 S and turn L to Mytchett. 2.5m from Farnborough. 3m from Camberley. Open: All year.

### Redhill

(4m). **Alderstead Heath Caravan Club Site, Dean Lane, Merstham, Redhill, Surrey RH1 3AH.** 01737 644629. www.caravanclub.co.uk. Non-members admitted. A quiet site surrounded by rolling, wooded countryside with marvellous views. Dog walk on site. Shops 3m. Toilet blocks. Privacy cubicles. Laundry facilities. Veg Prep. MV Service point. Gas & Gaz. Playframe. Fishing and golf nearby. Ideal for families. Local attractions include Chessington World of Adventures, Thorpe Park, Bluebell Line Steam Railway. Some hardstandings. Baby and toddler washroom. Quiet and peaceful off peak. Good area for walking. NCN cycle path within 5m. See website for standard directions to site. Open: 1 April - ★★★★★ NCC

### Staines

**Laleham Park Camping Site, Thameside, Laleham, Staines, Surrey TW18 1SS.** 01932 564129. www.lalehamcampingclub.co.uk.

Riverside site. Owner supplied copy. From Staines or Shepperton (B376 and B377). Take turning opposite Three Horseshoes Inn to riverside. Site is 500yd down river along tow path road. From Chertsey, cross Chertsey Bridge (B375), on to tow path road. Open: 1 April - 30 September.

### Walton on Thames

(3m). **Walton on Thames Camping & Caravanning Club Site, Fieldcommon Lane, Walton on Thames, Surrey KT12 3QG.** 01932 220392. www.campingandcaravanningclub.co.uk. Camped beside the river Mole under a weeping willow - it's hard to believe London is just 15m away! Club members only. Own san essential. Fishing is available from this site. Caravans, motorcaravans and tents accepted. Golf, horse riding and swimming close by, also Kempton Park Racecourse and Hampton Court. Special deals available for families and backpackers. From M25 J13 to Staines and then to Walton, turn L at traffic lights, SP Molesey at the end of Rydens Road, turn L and turn sharp R into Fieldcommon Lane. Open: 1 April - 31 October. ★★★ NCC

## WEST SUSSEX

### Arundel

(0.75m). **Maynards Caravan and Camping Park, Crossbush, Arundel, West Sussex BN18 9PQ.** 01903 882075. Places to visit include Arundel Castle, bird sanctuary and large Sunday market. Also scenic walks on the downs at Burpham, Warningcamp and Wepham. Owner supplied copy. A27 Arundel to Worthing after 0.75m turn L into Beefeater pub and restaurant. Open: All year. BH&HPA

(2m). **Ship & Anchor Marina, Ford, Arundel, West Sussex BN18 0BJ.** 01243 551262. Pub and restaurant. Shaver points. Boating. AA 2 pennants. David Bellamy Gold Conservation Award. Owner supplied copy. On road W of river Arun, S off A27 in Arundel or N off A259 at Climping. Open: 1 March - 31 October. BH&HPA

(6m). **Slindon Camping & Caravanning Club Site, Slindon Park, Arundel, West Sussex BN18 0RG.** 01243 814387. www.campingandcaravanningclub.co.uk. Within the National Trust property of Slindon Park. Non-members welcome. Caravans, motorcaravans & tents accepted. The site is set in an orchard within 3500 acres of Slindon Park with 40 pitches. Nearby is Goodwood Racecourse. Fishing, swimming & golf close by at Chichester. The area is a walkers' paradise with many footpaths & bridleways. Special deals available for families & backpackers. NO TOILETS OR SHOWERS ON SITE. From A27 Fontwell to Chichester turn R at SP Brittons Lane & second R to Slindon, site is on this road. Open: 1 April - 26 September. ★★ NCC

### Billingshurst

(1.5m). **Limeburners Arms Camping, Newbridge, Billingshurst, West Sussex RH14 9JA.** 01403 782311. Showers. Chemical toilet disposal point. Licensed bar. Toilets. H&C water to basins. AA 2 pennants. 1.5m W of Billingshurst on A272, turn L on to B2133, site 300yd on the L. Open: 1 March - 31 October.

### Bognor Regis

(2m). **Copthorne Caravans, Rose Green Road, Bognor Regis, West Sussex PO21 3ER.** 01243 262408. www.copthornecaravans.co.uk. Small, family park with 4 star accommodation. Games room and launderette. Ideal base for many attractions. Shops, takeaway 50yd from entrance. Rose award. Bognor Regis centre 2m. Chichester 6m, multiplex cinema, bowling, etc. A29 turn R just before dual carriageway, after 2m and two crossroads Copthorne on R opposite Texaco station. Open: 1 April - 31 October. ★★★★

(1.5m). **Riverside Caravan Centre (Bognor), Shripney Road, Bognor Regis, West Sussex PO22 9NE.** 01243 865823. www.rivcentre.co.uk. NO TOURERS. Club. Indoor swimming pool. On A29 Pulborough to Bognor. Open: 1 March - 31 October. ★★★★★ BH&HPA NCC

(1.25m). **Rowan Park Caravan Club Site, Rowan Way, Bognor Regis, West Sussex PO22 9RP.** 01243 828515. www.caravanclub.co.uk. An attractive site screened by trees and with views of downs. 1m from beach. Shops 0.5m. Advance booking advised Bank Holidays, July and August. Non-members and tent campers welcome. Privacy cubicles. Veg Prep. Motorhome service point. Play frame. Dog walk, some hardstanding, shop 50yds, golf, and NCN cycle path within 5m. Water sports nearby. See website for standard directions to site. Open: 23 March - 5 November. ★★★★★ NCC

(4m). **The Lillies Caravan Park, Yapton Road, Barnham, Bognor Regis, West**

# SOUTH EAST

Sussex PO22 0AY. 01243 552081. www.lilliescaravanpark.co.uk. Showers, razor point, chemical toilet disposal point and telephone on site. Gas sales. Close to shops and railway station. Laundrette. Park set in 3 acres of secluded countryside, easy reach of Goodwood, Car & Horse racing, beaches and leisure amenities. Touring/Holiday Homes Hire: all year - tents: March-October. Owner supplied copy. Take A29 from Bognor Regis to Eastergate then the B2233 to the park. Or A29 off A27 towards Fontwell then B2233. Open: All year. ★★★★ 🚐 24 🚗 24 ⛺ 40

## Chichester

(5m). **Bell Caravan Park, Bell Lane, Birdham, Chichester, West Sussex PO20 7HY.** 01243 512264. Local shop and pub serving food within walking distance. Bus service nearby. Fishing, riding, sailing and golf course all within 5m. Beaches 2m away. From Chichester take A286 SP Wittering to Birdham, opposite garage turn L into Bell Lane, park on L. Open: 1 March - 31 October. ★★ BH&HPA 🐕 🚐 15 🚗 15 ⛺

(2m). **Chichester Lakeside Park, Vinnetrow Road, Chichester, West Sussex PO20 1QH.** 0845 8159745. www.ParkHolidaysUK.com/mmc. Set in 220 acres of scenic parkland with a nature reserve with over 150 acres of water covering 12 lakes. Outdoor heated leisure pool, fishing. Bar, bistro. Chichester: shopping, restaurants. David Bellamy Gold Conservation Award. Accessible from A259 and B2166. Take A27 to Chichester until Bognor road roundabout take Pagham exit which leads to Lakeside. Open: 11 March - 31 October. 🚐

(4m). **Church Farm Holiday Village (Haven), Church Lane, Pagham, Chichester, West Sussex PO21 4NR.** 0871 4680496. www.haven.co.uk. Newly refurbished indoor and outdoor pool with sun terrace. Sports and leisure activities plus kids clubs. Welcome Host Award. Daytime and evening entertainment for all the family. Mini market. Bakery. 9 hole golf course. Crazy golf. Family entertainment. Beaches nearby. Nature reserve. David Bellamy Gold Conservation Award. Where A27 roundabout crosses A259 on the eastern outskirts of Chichester, take the Pagham exit and continue to the roundabout (1m). Turn L and follow road for 3-4m to the end, Park entrance is directly in front of you. Open: 18 March - 31 October. ★★★★ BH&HPA NCC 🚐 225

(4m). **Ellscott Park, Sidlesham Lane, Birdham, Chichester, West Sussex PO20 7QL.** 01243 512003. www.ellscottpark.co.uk. Quiet country site. Cafe and bus service nearby. Nearest shop, PO 0.75m. Booking essential July and August. AA 3 pennants. Owner supplied copy. From Chichester take the A286 to Bracklesham and Wittering, turn L, SP to Butterfly Gardens. Open: 1 April - 14 October. 🚐 50 ⛺

(7m). **Itchenor Caravan Park, Shipton Green Lane, Itchenor, Chichester, West Sussex PO20 7BZ.** 01243 514433. www.greenwoodparks.com. Manager lives on this secluded park overlooking farmland and close to Chichester Harbour. Good shops & PO, doctor and great beach within 2m. 2 golf courses 5m. Free brochure 01243 514433. 2 month winter licences available. Owner supplied copy. Off A27, on A286 to Birdham, at Birdham bear R on B2179, next turning on R 400yd. Park entrance on R. Open: 1 March - 31 October. 🚐 182

**Nunnington Farm Campsite, Nunnington Farm, West Wittering, Chichester, West Sussex PO20 8LZ.** 01243 514013. www.camping-in-sussex.com. Flat site 1m from sea and 1.5m from Itchenor for sailing. 125 units in total (tourers, motorcaravans, tents). Shop in village 300yd. Friendly, family site. Small animal park free for our customers. From Chichester A286 on to B2179. Open: 18 April - 15 October. 🚐 125 ⛺

(7m). **Red House Farm, Bookers Lane, Earnley, Chichester, West Sussex PO20 7JG.** 01243 512959. www.rhfcamping.co.uk. Flat, level. Site 1m from sea and village, car recommended. Takeaways, shops and cafe/restaurant available nearby. Ideal for Marina, 8m to Goodwood. Booking advised at peak periods. No single sex groups (4 and over). Owner supplied copy. Take road A286 to Witterings from Chichester, 5m fork L at Total garage towards Bracklesham on B2198, 0.5m at sharp bend turn L into Bookers Lane, site 500yd on L. Open: All year. 🚐 25 🚗 25 ⛺

(8m). **Walnut Tree Caravan Park, Rookwood Road, West Wittering, Chichester, West Sussex PO20 8NB.** 01243 513084. www.islandmeadow.co.uk. Beautiful park close to magnificent beach at West Wittering and overlooking Chichester Harbour. Telephone 01246 670207 for free brochure. Demonstration caravans available for inspection at the park. Ancient cathedral city of Chichester. Golf, horse racing (Goodwood/Fontwell), Roman Palace at Fishbourne, Chichester shops. Cathedral, theatre, golf driving range at Hunston. Owner supplied copy. Follow signs to Chichester on A27. At Stockbridge roundabout follow A286 to Birdham. Then bear R, follow signs to West Wittering. Park entrance is on R before West Wittering village. Open: 1 March - 31 October. 🚐 184

(1m). **Warner Farm Touring Park, Warner Lane, Selsey, Chichester, West Sussex PO20 9EJ.** 01243 604499. www.warnerfarm.co.uk. Use of 3 entertainment venues and leisure complex included in your booking. A27 to Chichester, take B2145 to Selsey SP from Chichester, turn R at school lane and follow the signs. Open: 1 March - 31 October. ★★★★ NCC 284

(6m). **Wicks Farm Camping Park, Redlands Lane, West Wittering, Chichester, West Sussex PO20 8QE.** 01243 513116. www.wicksfarm.co.uk. Children's play areas. Outdoor table tennis, basketball, shop. Beach 2m, shopping 3m, cinema/bowling 6m. David Bellamy Gold Conservation Award. Off A27 at Chichester, take A286/B2179 from Chichester for 6m towards West Wittering, turn R into Redlands Lane. 1m before West Wittering village. Open: 1 March - 28 November. ★★★★★ BH&HPA 🚐 40 ⛺ 40

## Crawley

(2m). **Amberley Fields Caravan Club Site, Charlwood Road, Lowfield Heath, Crawley, West Sussex RH11 0QA.** 01293 524834. www.caravanclub.co.uk. Marvellous for plane spotters, also a storage site. Toilet blocks. Privacy cubicles. Laundry facilities. MV Service point. Gas. Dog walk. Local attractions include Thorpe Park and Bluebell Line Steam Railway. Members only. No tents. See website for standard directions to site. Open: All year. NCC 26 🚗 26

## Graffham

(2m). **Graffham Camping & Caravanning Club Site, Great Bury, Graffham, West Sussex GU28 0QJ.** 01798 867476. www.campingandcaravanningclub.co.uk. The site is set in 20 acres with secluded pitches dispersed in trees and rhododendrons. In the heart of the South Downs, an Area Of Outstanding Natural Beauty. Excellent for walkers and bird watchers will find many varieties of bird living around the site. Non-members welcome. Special deals available for families and backpackers. 2m from Petworth off the A285. Take a L at sign for Selham Graffham. 1m turn L, SP Graffham. 400yd, site entrance on L, just past house. Open: 1 April - 31 October. ★★★★ NCC 🚐 90 ⛺ 90

# SOUTH EAST / SOUTH WEST

## SOUTH EAST

### Henfield

(2m). **Farmhouse Caravans & Camping**, Tottington Drive, Small Dole, Henfield, West Sussex BN5 9XZ. *01273 493157*. Small, quiet, farm site near South Downs and 10m from Brighton. Peaceful setting with panoramic views and well away from the main roads. Ideal for families and walkers. Shop and pub nearby. Turn off A2037 in Small Dole. Site SP in village. Open: 1 March - 1 November.

### Horsham

(10m). **Honeybridge Park**, Honeybridge Lane, Dial Post, Horsham, West Sussex RH13 8NX. *01403 710923*. www.honeybridgepark.co.uk. Spacious touring, camping and caravan park on outskirts of woodlands in Area Of Outstanding Natural Beauty. Large hardstanding and grass pitches, electric hook-ups, heated amenity blocks, licensed shop, games room, play area. Ideal base for Brighton and the coast, South Downs, Gatwick and London. Tourer storage available. Holiday homes for sale. 10m S of Horsham on A24. Outside Dial Post village turn at the 'Old Barn Nurseries', 300yd on R. Open: All year.

(4.5m). **Slinfold Caravan Club Site**, Spring Lane, Slinfold, Horsham, West Sussex RH13 0RT. *01403 790269*. www.caravanclub.co.uk. Imaginatively landscaped site with silver birch, rowan and flowering cherry at the end of a country lane, close to a pretty village. No sanitation. Dog walk. Shop 0.5m. Hardstandings. Steel awning pegs advised. MV Service point. Members only. No tents. See website for standard directions to site. Open: 23 March - 22 October. NCC

### Littlehampton

(1.5m). **Brookside Caravan Park**, Lyminster Road, Lyminster, Littlehampton, West Sussex BN17 7QE. *01903 713292*. www.brooksideuk.com. Lovely family-run park established over 50 years. Small well maintained and central to all South Coast attractions. Swings, play area, sand pit, rocking horse and springers for children. Small games room with table tennis, bar football and pool table. Wi-Fi. Shops 0.5m. Open to caravan owners 01/03/10 to 07/01/11. Due south from A27, on A284 between Littlehampton and Arundel. Open: 1 March - 31 October. ★★★ BH&HPA

(1.5m). **Daisyfields Touring Park**, Cornfields Close, Worthing Road, Littlehampton, West Sussex BN17 6LD. *01903 714240*. www.camping-caravaning.co.uk. Free showers and hairdryers. Gas. Ball game area and badminton courts. Nature areas. Level, well-drained site. Fishing, golf, horse riding, boating all nearby. Open all year weather permitting - appointment only November to April. Owner supplied copy. On A259 Worthing to Bognor Regis road. Open: All year.

(1m). **Littlehampton Caravan Club Site (White Rose Touring Park)**, Mill Lane, Wick, Littlehampton, West Sussex BN17 7PH. *01903 716176*. www.caravanclub.co.uk. Set on the outskirts of delightful resort but within walking distance of the town & beach. Excellent base from which to explore Arundel & the South Downs. Accessed from A284. Open: 23 March - 7 January. ★★★★★ BH&HPA

### Washington

**Washington Caravan & Camping Park**, London Road, Washington, West Sussex RH20 4AJ. *01903 892569*. www.washcamp.com. Walking, cycling. Close to many places of interest. N of Washington on A283 E of roundabout with A24, SP. Halfway stop on South Downs Way below Chanctonbury Ring. Open: All year. ★★★★

### Worthing

(2.5m). **Northbrook Farm Caravan Club Site**, Titnore Way, Worthing, West Sussex BN13 3RT. *01903 502962*. www.caravanclub.co.uk. An attractive, grassy site in open countryside with good trees and only 2m from the coast. Non-members welcome. No tents. Storage pitches and hardstandings, shops 0.25m. Privacy cubicles. Veg Prep. MV Service point. Gas & Gaz. Playground. Dog walk. Water sports and golf nearby. Ideal for families. Quiet and peaceful off peak. Good area for walking. See website for standard directions to site. Open: 23 March - 2 November. ★★★★ NCC

(4m). **Onslow Caravan Park**, Onslow Drive, Ferring by Sea, Worthing, West Sussex BN12 5RX. *01903 243170*. www.islandmeadow.co.uk. Fishing, golf, horse racing, bowls, walking all nearby. Theatres, cinemas, shops, doctor, all within easy reach. Quiet park. Demonstration caravans available for inspection at the park. Owner supplied copy. Follow A27, sp Ferring, turn into Onslow Drive, drive along to park entrance. Open: 1 March - 31 October. ★★★★

## SOUTH WEST

### CORNWALL

#### Bodmin

(4m). **Ruthern Valley**, Ruthernbridge, Bodmin, Cornwall PL30 5LU. *01208 831395*. www.ruthernvalley.com. Quiet site in unspoilt valley. Touring centre or overnight stop. No dogs July/August period. Close to Camel Trail. Eden Project 10m. David Bellamy Gold Conservation Award. 1.5m from Salisbury on the A345. Large open field next to Old Sarum. Open: 1 April - 31 October. ★★★★ BH&HPA

#### Boscastle

(2.5m). **Lower Pennycrocker Farm**, St Juliot, Boscastle, Cornwall PL35 0BY. *01840 250257*. www.pennycrocker.com. 40 mixed pitches in total. Owner supplied copy. 2.5m N of Boscastle on B3263 SP Pennycrocker. Open: 22 April - 31 October.

#### Bude

(9m). **Bude Camping & Caravanning Club Site**, Gillards Moor, St. Genny's, Bude, Cornwall EX23 0BG. *01840 230650*. www.campingandcaravanningclub.co.uk. Excellent position for touring the region. Near coastal paths in the heart of King Arthur's country. Cyclists are well catered for, with 42m of signposted traffic-free routes stretching from Bude to Bodmin. All units accepted. Non-members welcome. The site has some of the best surfing beaches nearby. Special deals for families & backpackers. From Wadebridge heading N on the A39 towards Bude. Site on L, SP. 10m from Camelford. Open: 1 April - 26 September. ★★★★ NCC

(1m). **Bude Holiday Park**, Maer Lane, Bude, Cornwall EX23 9EE. *01288 355955*. www.budeholidaypark.co.uk. Large heated swimming pool. Clubhouse with nightly entertainment. Two bars. Arcade, pool room, TV room. Restaurant. Play area. Off A39, through town centre and follow signs to park. Open: 12 March - 31 October. ★★★ BH&HPA

(3m). **Budemeadows Touring Park**, Widemouth Bay, Bude, Cornwall EX23 0NA. *01288 361646*. www.budemeadows.com. Family run site with heated outdoor pool, licensed bar, shop, large children's play area and games room. Private wash facilities, free hot water and hairdryers, disabled toilet and shower facilities. Bath room and baby bath.

# cornwall's finest parks

independent, top graded parks, offering fabulous facilities, superb locations and superior service - especially for families and couples - choose a great holiday from cornwall's finest quality parks

Get in touch ▶

www.**hendra-holidays**.com
BOOKING HOTLINE **01637 875778**

## Hendra
### HOLIDAY PARK
camping ★ touring ★ holiday homes

CELEBRATING **40** YEARS

01637 875778
www.hendra-holidays.com
Hendra Holidays, Newquay, Cornwall, TR8 4NY

◀ Check out our latest special offers online

★ five star park ★ five star facilities ★ five star holiday ★ five star fun ★

## Mother Ivey's Bay Holiday Park

Situated in an area of outstanding natural beauty and adjoining our own private beach, Mother Ivey's really is the perfect location for you to relax and enjoy your wonderful family holiday

### Mother Ivey's Bay Holiday Park
Trevose Head, Nr Padstow, Cornwall PL28 8SL
Tel: (01841) 520990   Fax: (01841) 520550
Email: info@motheriveysbay.com
www.motheriveysbay.com

NO CLUBS!    NO BARS!    NO DISCOS!

www.cornwallfinestparks.co.uk

# cornwall's finest parks

independent, top graded parks, offering fabulous facilities, superb locations and superior service - especially for families and couples - choose a great holiday from cornwall's finest quality parks

## Porth Beach
### Tourist Park • Newquay

Only 100m from the beach...

**Porth, Newquay, Cornwall, TR7 3NH**
t: 01637 876531  e: info@porthbeach.co.uk
www.porthbeach.co.uk

## Trevella Park
### CARAVAN AND CAMPING PARK
CRANTOCK   NEWQUAY   CORNWALL TR8 5EW

### One of Cornwall's Finest Parks

* 5* award winning park set in beautiful landscaped parkland
* Ideal base for Crantock and Newquay's beaches
* Perfect for walking, fishing, surfing and exploring the local area
* Heated outdoor swimming & paddling pools, fishings lakes, free fishing and nature reserve
* Play areas, TV & games room, cafe & takeaway and launderette
* Luxury caravans for hire & for sale
* Superb touring facilities
* Well maintained/spacious pitches
* Special rates available - quote 'Best Caravan 2012'

**For 2012**
✓ 'Ready Tents'
✓ Own your own Holiday Home at Trevella
✓ Leave your caravan and go home 'tow free'!

Tel: 0844 870 6031
Email: holidays@trevella.co.uk
Follow us on Facebook
**www.trevella.co.uk**

## Treloy
### Touring Park

The friendly park in beautiful Cornwall

**Telephone: 01637 872063**
**Website: www.treloy.co.uk**
Email: treloy.tp@btconnect.com
Newquay, Cornwall TR8 4JN

| Heated swimming pool | Licensed family bar | Free entertainment |
|---|---|---|

| Adventure playground | Electric hook-ups | On site shop |
|---|---|---|
| TV and games room | Café/takeaway | Treloy golf course nearby |

## Tehidy
### HOLIDAY PARK

"...a green champion" David Bellamy

A family owned and run, award winning park, nestled in a wooded valley near broad, sandy beaches, hidden coves and the crystal clear ocean. Safe, quiet, natural surroundings located in central Cornwall.

Caravan Holiday Park and Holiday Village of the Year 2010
Visit Cornwall - Bronze

Holiday Park of the Year 2008
Shires Magazine

Top 10 Best Holiday Parks in Cornwall
Cornwall Today 2009

**COTTAGES, HOLIDAY CARAVANS, TOURERS & WIGWAM CAMPING CABINS**

☎ **01209 216489**
**www.tehidy.co.uk**
✉ holiday@tehidy.co.uk

Tehidy Holiday Park, Harris Mill, Illogan, Redruth, Cornwall. TR16 4JQ

www.cornwallfinestparks.co.uk

# cornwall's finest parks

independent, top graded parks, offering fabulous facilities, superb locations and superior service - especially for families and couples - choose a great holiday from cornwall's finest quality parks

## trevornick holiday park

ESCAPE
EXPLORE
DISCOVER

CORNWALL'S FINEST FIVE STAR HOLIDAY PARK

www.trevornick.co.uk · 0843 453 5531    Holywell Bay  Nr. Newquay  Cornwall  TR8 5PW

·· TOURING  ··  CAMPING  ··  EUROTENTS  ··

### Welcome to Cosawes Touring & Camping Park...

Secluded and quiet, Cosawes nestles in a beautiful 100 acre sheltered valley near the village of Perranarworthal in South West Cornwall. Open all year round, campers benefit from the natural shelter of the surrounding woodland and valley in the worst of the winter weather and a sun-trap during the warm summer months. Dogs welcome provided they are kept under strict control. Nearby attractions:

- Water sports
- New heated Shower & Toilet Block
- Golf course
- Good sailing waters nearby
- Horse riding
- Launderette
- Plenty of country walks
- Cycle hire
- Situated between the Cathedral City of Truro and the harbour-side town of Falmouth
- Asda Supermarket (24hr)
- Pubs offering good food and drink

01872 863724 (9am-1pm Mon-Fri)
info@cosawes.com  ·  www.cosawestouringandcamping.co.uk

### A park for all seasons
## Trethiggey Holiday Park

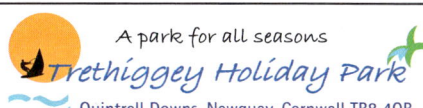

Quintrell Downs, Newquay, Cornwall TR8 4QR

Set in beautiful countryside, Trethiggey is an award-winning touring park just minutes from Cornwall's "Coast of Dreams" and some of the finest beaches in Europe.

Centrally positioned for top attractions including the Eden Project, we're only seven miles from Newquay International Airport.

Tel: 01637 877672
E-mail: enquiries@trethiggey.co.uk
Online booking: www.trethiggey.co.uk

www.cornwallfinestparks.co.uk

# SOUTH WEST

Pitches arranged in small groups separated by hedges and picket fences. Open all year (takeaway, bar, shop and pool May to September). A39 S from Bude for 3m. Site on L after Widemouth turn off. Open: All year. ★★★★★ BH&HPA ⚲ 🏠🚿♿🐕♨🍴⚽🏊🍽🛒🚌🅿️🚲 ⛳📶👶 25🚐 60🅿️ ⛺

**(5m). Cornish Coasts Caravan & Camping Park, Middle Penlean, Poundstock, Widemouth Bay, Bude, Cornwall EX23 0EE.** *01288 361380.* www.cornishcoasts.co.uk. Peaceful, family run, friendly site with wonderful sea views and level terraced pitches. Close to beaches and SW coastal path, ideal touring location. Play area. On A39 5m S of Bude. Open: 1 March - 31 October. BH&HPA 🏠🚿♿🐕♨🍴⚽🛒🚌🅿️🚲 ⛳📶 10🚐 45🅿️ ⛺ 4⛺

**Coxford Meadow, Crackington Haven, Bude, Cornwall EX23 0NS.** *01288 230707.* www.north-cornwall-accommodation.com/coxford_meadow. 1-acre field with easy access. Shops, cafe 1m away. Above quiet wooded valley leading to sea. Owner supplied copy. 1m from Crackington Haven. Open: 22 April - 30 September. 🏠♿🚿🅿️📶 🚐🅿️ ⛺

**(5m). East Thorne Touring Park, Kilkhampton, Bude, Cornwall EX23 9RY.** *01288 321654.* www.eastthornecamping.co.uk. Family run site set in quiet farmland. Games room. Playground. 5m N of Bude on A39. Take B3254 0.5m to site. Open: 1 April - 31 October. 🏠🐕♿🍴🚐 📶🚿 29🚐 29🅿️ ⛺

**(9m). Edmore Tourist Park, Wainhouse Corner, Jacobstow, Bude, Cornwall EX23 0BJ.** *01840 230467.* www.cornwallvisited.co.uk. Free hot showers, washing up sinks. Play area. Dogs allowed on lead. Owner supplied copy. Site off A39 (250yd) SP at Wainhouse Corner. Open: 22 April - 31 October. 🏠🐕♿🍴📶 28🚐 ⛺ 2🅿️

**(10m). Hentervene Holiday Park,**

**Crackington Haven, Bude, Cornwall EX23 0LF.** *01840 230365.* www.hentervene.co.uk. Quiet meadow park near sandy surfing beach and coastal path. An ideal base for exploring Cornwall and North Devon. Luxury lodges and modern well equipped caravans to hire/buy. (OS grid SX155944). Off A39. Bude-Camelford road at Otterham station. Open: All year. ★★★ BH&HPA 🏠🚿♿🐕♨🍴⚽🛒🚌 ⛳📶👶 9🚐 12🅿️ 4🛖 3⛺

**(3m). Ivyleaf Camping Sites, Ivyleaf Hill, Bush, Bude, Cornwall EX23 9LD.** *01288 321442.* Quiet, family owned site. Sheltered site with beautiful views; one of the cheapest sites in Bude. N of Bude on A39, turn R at Willow campsite up Ivyleaf Hill site halfway up hill on the R. Open: All year. 🏠🐕♿🚿🍴⚽🛒🚌 5🚐 10🅿️ ⛺

**(5m). Penhalt Farm Holiday Park, Widemouth Bay, Bude, Cornwall EX23 0DG.** *01288 361210.* www.penhaltfarm.co.uk. Splendid sea views. Close to coastal path, 1.5m from sandy beach. Laundry. Play area. Telephone, gas. Spectacular sea views from site. Widemouth Bay well known surfing beach. Garage and PO in Widemouth Bay. All amenities in Bude. Owner supplied copy. 4m S of Bude on A39, take 2nd turn R for Widemouth Bay, turn L at the bottom by W B Hotel. Family site 2/3m along on R. Open: 22 April - 31 October. ★★★ BH&HPA 🏠🐕♿🚿🍴⚽📶🅿️ 🚌🚐🅿️ 100🅿️ ⛺ 2⛺

**(4m). Penstowe Caravan and Camping Park, Stibb Road, Kilkhampton, Bude, Cornwall EX23 9QY.** *01288 321601.* www.penstoweholidays.co.uk. Family owned park in a peaceful countryside location with views to the sea. Walking distance to Kilkhampton village with shops. PO and pub nearby. Sandymouth beach 2m. Bude about 4m. Six local beaches within 6m. Owner supplied copy. Situated on A39, N of Bude. Open: 8 January - 17 December. ★★★★ BH&HPA NCC 🏠🐕♿🚿🍴⚽🛒🚌📶 🅿️⛺

**(3m). Red Post Inn & Holiday Park, Launcells, Bude, Cornwall EX23 9NW.** *01288 381305.* www.redpostinn.co.uk. Good, level, well sheltered family site. An ideal base for touring North Devon and Cornwall. Sporting facilities nearby. E of Bude off A3072. Open: 1 April - 30 September. ⚲ 🏠🐕♿🚿🍴⚽🛒🚌🅿️ ⛳📶👶 20🚐 20🅿️ ⛺

**(4m). Sandymouth Holiday Park, Stibb, Bude, Cornwall EX23 9HW.** *0844 272 9530.* www.sandymouthbay.co.uk. Extensive coastal and countryside views. Licensed clubhouse with entertainment. Shower block, play area, Laundrette. Gas sales. Indoor swimming pool. Crazy golf. Restaurant. On the Bude to Kilkhampton road (A39), 3m from Bude. Open: 15 March - 5 November. ★★★★★ BH&HPA NCC ⚲ 🏠🐕♿🚿🍴⚽🏊🛒🚌🅿️🛖⛳📶👶 23🚐 ⛺ 247🅿️

**(0.5m). Upper Lynstone Camping & Caravan Park, Lynstone, Bude, Cornwall EX23 0LP.** *01288 352017.* www.upperlynstone.co.uk. Quiet, family site situated within walking distance of town, sandy beach, bars and restaurants. Coastal footpath from park along beautiful Cornish coast. Fishing available nearby. S of Bude on coastal road to Widemouth Bay. Open: 1 April - 30 September. ★★★★ BH&HPA NCC 🏠🐕♿🚿🍴⚽🛒🅿️ 45🚐 25🅿️ ⛺ 63⛺

**(4m). Widemouth Bay Caravan Park, Poundstock, Bude, Cornwall EX23 0DF.** *01288 361208.* www.johnfowlerholidays.com. A modern, family park a few minutes from a lovely beach. Licensed club with entertainment and children's club. New tropical heated pool, crazy golf, bistro and takeaway. Off A39. Open: 9 April - 31 October. BH&HPA ⚲ 🏠🐕♿🚿🍴⚽🏊🛒🚌📶👶 327🚐 327🅿️ ⛺

**Widemouth Fields Caravan & Camping Park, Park Farm, Poundstock, Bude, Cornwall EX23 0NA.** *01288 361351.*

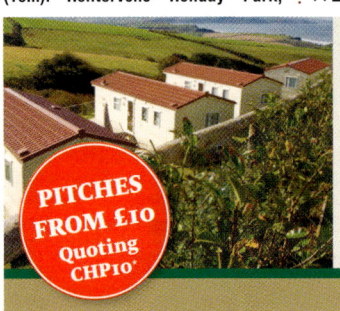

- Stunning caravan, lodge and bungalow accommodation.
- Indoor heated pool.
- Licensed bar and restaurant.
- On-site mini-market.
- Crazy golf, arcade and bouncy castle.
- Adventure play area with full size pirate ship.
- Touring guest facilities.

**Family friendly, relaxed 5* holiday park just minutes from the beaches in Bude, Cornwall**

PITCHES FROM £10 Quoting CHP10

*Terms and conditions apply

To book call 0844 272 9530 or visit www.sandymouthbay.co.uk

# SOUTH WEST

www.widemouthbaytouring.co.uk. Located 1m from the beach at Widemouth Bay. We provide a bus to take you to the bay beaches and Bude. Opened in 2008 we are proud of our facilities and we welcome touring caravans, motorhomes and tents to this super park where you are surrounded by the cream of Cornish Countryside. AA 5 pennants. Exit M5 at j27 (SP Barnstaple). A361 to roundabout before Barnstaple. Take A39 (SP Bideford, Bude). Do not leave A39 at Stratton for Bude, continue south for 3 miles. Just past crossroads to Widemouth Bay, entrance in lay-by on L. Open: 15 April - 25 September. 5 ★ ↑ ∕ ⊘ ▣ ♨ ✕ ⚑ ♿ ⚐ ♿

 **(1.5m). Wooda Farm Holiday Park, Poughill, Bude, Cornwall EX23 9HJ.** *01288 352069.* www.wooda.co.uk. Family run park 1.25m from sandy beaches. Adventure playground, woodland walks, well-stocked coarse fishing lake, licensed restaurant, off-licence, take-away, farmyard friends, fun golf course. Tennis, badminton, fitness suite, Wi-Fi throughout the park. Splash indoor pool is nearby. David Bellamy Gold Conservation Award. From A39 North of Stratton, take Poughill/Coombe Valley Road for 1m. Through crossroads Wooda is 200yd on your R. Open: 1 April - 31 October. ★ ★ ★ ★ BH&HPA ♀ ⚑ ↑ ∕ ⚐ ♿ ∕ ⚑ ⊘ ▣ ♨ ✕ ⚑ ♿ ⚐ § ⚑ ♿ & 80⚑ 120⚑ 20⚐ 55⚑

### Bush

**(2m). Willow Valley Holiday Park, Dye House, Bush, Cornwall EX23 9LB.** *01288 353104.* www.willowvalley.co.uk. Small, sheltered site in beautiful Strat valley. Friendly atmosphere. Modern facilities block with 6 family showers open for 2009. Write or telephone for colour brochure or visit our website. N of Bude on A39. 3m S of Kilkhampton. Open: 15 April - 30 September. BH&HPA ⚑ ↑ ∕ ⚐ ♿ ∕ ⊘ ▣ ♨ ⚑ ♿ & 45⚑ ⚐

### Camborne

**(2m). Magor Farm Caravan Site, Tehidy, Camborne, Cornwall TR14 0JF.** *01209 713367.* www.magorfarm.co.uk. Sheltered site with wooded surroundings within easy reach of all Cornwall's famous beauty spots and beaches. SP from cliff Portreath road near Hells Mouth cafe. Play area. Laundrette, free showers. Electric shaving points. Country park nearby. RAC and Caravan Club. Tehidy golf club 2 miles, leisure centre, local coarse fishing, Camborne, Redruth, Mining Heritage Centres. Owner supplied copy. Take Camborne (west) exit off A30. Turn R over A30 bridge in approx. 0.5m go straight

across, blind left hand corner. Site is 1.5m further on down over hill. Open: 22 April - 31 October. ⚑ ↑ ∕ ⚐ ▣ ♨ ⚑ ♿ 40⚑ ⚐

### Camelford

**(1m). Juliot's Well Holiday Park, Camelford, Cornwall PL32 9RF.** *01840 213302.* www.juliotswell.com. Swimming pool. Tennis court. Pub garden, play area. Badminton. Licensed bar. Restaurant. Also available 10 pine lodges and 5 cottages. Through Camelford on A39, take second turning R, then first L. Site 400yd down lane on R. Open: All year. ★ ★ ★ BH&HPA ♀ ⚑ ↑ ∕ ⚐ ♿ ∕ ⊘ ▣ ♨ ✿ ⚑ ✕ ⚑ ♿ ⚐ ♿ 39⚑ ⚐ 42⚑

**(1m). Lakefield Caravan Park, Lower Pendavey Farm, Camelford, Cornwall PL32 9TX.** *01840 213279.* www.lakefieldequestriancentre.co.uk. We now run a full riding school alongside park. A30 from Exeter to Launceston and shortly after A395 to join the A39 to Camelford. In 2m turn right on to B3314 and the L on to B3266 park is 100yd on the R. Open: 1 April - 31 October. ★ ★ ★ ⚑ ↑ ∕ ⊘ ▣ ♨ ⚑ ✕ ⚑ ♿ ⚐ ♿ 40⚑ ⚐

**Valley Truckle Caravan Club Site, Camelford, Cornwall PL32 9RF.** *01840 212206.* www.caravanclub.co.uk. A small, attractive site, quiet and peaceful off-peak. An adjacent tennis course and a championship golf course within easy walking distance. MV service point. Dog walk nearby. Good area for walking, NCN route nearby. Ideal for families. Members only. No tents. See website for standard directions to site. Open: 30 March - 1 October. NCC ⚑ ↑ ∕ ⚐ ⊘ ▣ ♨ ⚑ ♿ & 60⚑ 60⚑

### Delabole

**(0.2m). Planet Caravan Park, Westdown Road, Delabole, Cornwall PL33 9DT.** *01840 213361.* Quiet park, wonderful views. Touring centre. Shop 300yd. Fees on application. 4m W of Camelford and 6m S of Tintagel. SW end of village on B3314 off A39 road. Open: All year. BH&HPA ⚑ ↑ ∕ ⚐ ♿ ⊘ ▣ ♨ ✿ ⚑ ♿ 40⚑ 40⚑ ⚐

### Falmouth

**(2m). Pennance Mill Farm, Maenporth, Falmouth, Cornwall TR11 5HJ,** *01326 317431.* www.pennancemill.co.uk. Private cycle and footpath to Maenporth beach 20mins, 0.5m. Whitsun and summer holiday games nights and events in barn. Approach Falmouth via A39 continue to Hillhead roundabout. Turn R towards Maenporth. Along road for 2m. Pennance Mill is on your L at bottom of hill. Open:

18 April - 1 November. ★ ★ ★ BH&HPA NCC ⚑ ↑ ∕ ⚐ ♿ ∕ ⚐ ⊘ ▣ ♨ ⚑ ♿ ⚐ ♿ 75⚑ 75⚑ ⚐

**(2.5m). Tregedna Farm, Maenporth, Falmouth, Cornwall TR11 5HL.** *01326 250529.* Laundry sinks. Play area. Telephone on site. Close to golf, fishing. Distance to PO & garage, doctor 2.5m. Swimming pool 3m. From Truro A39 to Falmouth. 0.5m from sandy beach. Open: 1 April - 31 October. ★ ★ ⚑ ↑ ∕ ⚐ ♿ ∕ ⚐ ⚑ ♿ ⚐ ♿ 40⚑ ⚐

### Fowey

**(1.5m). Penhale Caravan and Camping Park, Penhale Farm, Fowey, Cornwall PL23 1JU.** *01726 833425.* www.penhale-fowey.co.uk. Close to lovely walks and sandy beaches. Splendid views. No overcrowding. David Bellamy Bronze Conservation Award. On A3082 Par to Fowey road. Open: 1 April - 31 October. ★ ★ ★ ★ BH&HPA ⚑ ↑ ∕ ⚐ ♿ ∕ ⊘ ▣ ♨ ✿ ⚑ ♿ ⚐ ♿ 10⚑ 45⚑ ⚐ 25⚑

**(1m). Penmarlam Caravan and Camping Park, Boddinnick, Fowey, Cornwall PL23 1LZ.** *01726 870088.* www.penmarlampark.co.uk. Level, grassy site with outstanding views. Quay, slipway and storage for small boats. Modern amenities block, shop and off licence on site, Wi-Fi and Internet access. From Liskeard take A38, then A390 turn L on to B3359. Follow signs to Bodinnick. Open: 1 April - 31 October. ★ ★ ★ BH&HPA ⚑ ↑ ∕ ⚐ ♿ ∕ ⚐ ⊘ ▣ ♨ ⚑ ♿ ⚐ ♿ & 63⚑ 63⚑ ⚐

**(0.5m). Polruan Holidays - Camping & Caravanning, Polruan-by-Fowey, Fowey, Cornwall PL23 1QH.** *01726 870263.* www.polruanholidays.co.uk. Select park in an area of outstanding natural beauty surrounded by sea. National Trust farmland, coastal path and beautiful Fowey estuary. Personal service guaranteed. Dogs must be kept on lead. No single sex groups of three or more. David Bellamy Gold Conservation Award. Owner supplied copy. 12m SE of St Austell off the A390 between Fowey and Polperro. Open: 6 April - 30 September. ★ ★ ★ BH&HPA ⚑ ↑ ∕ ⚐ ♿ ∕ ⊘ ▣ ♨ ⚑ ♿ ⚐ ♿ 7⚑ 7⚑ ⚐ ⚐ 20⚑

### Hayle

**(1.5m). Atlantic Coast Holiday Park, 53 Upton Towans, Hayle, Cornwall TR27 5BL.** *01736 752071.* www.atlanticcoastpark.co.uk. Situated on the edge of St Ives Bay, nestling in the sand dunes. Licensed shop. Dogs allowed at a small charge (beach allows dogs all year). Bus stop at gate. David Bellamy Gold Conservation

# SOUTH WEST

Award. Take B3301 off A30 at double roundabout. Site is on L after about 1m. Open: 1 March - 6 January. ★★★★ BH&HPA NCC 15⚏ 15⚐ 15A 19⛺ 2⚑

**(0.75m). Beachside Holiday Park (Hayle), Hayle, Cornwall TR27 5AW.** 01736 753080. www.beachside.co.uk. Beside the sea, amidst sand dunes in St Ives Bay. Heated swimming and paddling pool. Leave A30 at Hayle, turn R opposite Jet petrol station, entrance 0.5m on R. Open: 31 March - 29 September. ★★★★ BH&HPA 90⚏ 116A

**Calloose Caravan & Camping Park, Leedstown, Hayle, Cornwall TR27 5ET.** 0800 3287589. www.calloose.co.uk. Sheltered, family park. Swimming pool. Licensed bar. Snacks. Skittle alley. Bar meals. Pay phone. Play area. Tennis courts. Trout fishing. Crazy golf. Rose Award Park. AA 4 pennants. Leave A30 at the roundabout N of Hayle and drive through the town until you see the large viaduct. Drive under the first arch and turn L at the small roundabout and take B3302 road towards Helston. Leedstown is 3.5m along this road. Park SP on the L as you enter the village. Open: 28 Mar - 3 Oct & 15 Dec - 3 Jan. ★★★★ 4 BH&HPA 96⚏ 19⚐

**(3m). Godrevy Park Caravan Club Site, Upton Towans, Hayle, Cornwall TR27 5BL.** 01736 753100. www.caravanclub.co.uk. Quiet and peaceful off peak. A spacious site only 1m from beautiful sandy beach. Dog walk adjacent. Shop 200yd. Advance booking advised in June and essential July and August. Toilet block with privacy cubicles and laundry facilities plus baby and toddler washroom. MV service point. Boules pitch. Fishing nearby. Good area for walking. Ideal for families. Veg prep area, gas and gaz. NCN cycle route within 5m. Members only. No tents. See website for standard directions to site. Open: 23 March - 5 November. NCC 115⚏ 115⚐

**(3m). Higher Trevaskis Caravan Park, Gwinear Road, Connor Downs, Hayle, Cornwall TR27 5JQ.** 01209 831736. www.highertrevaskiscaravanpark.co.uk. Friendly, secluded, family run countryside park in a great location. Ideally situated for visiting local beaches and attractions of West Cornwall. Touring only. Spacious level pitches in small enclosures. Designated play areas & our renowned spotlessly clean facilities. 'Big enough to cope - Small enough to care'.

Leave A30 dual carriageway at Camborne West exit. Follow signs to Connor Downs (A3047), L at crossroads entering village. Park is 0.75m on right hand side. Open: 14 April - 1 October. ★★★★ BH&HPA 82⚏ A

**(3m). Parbola Holiday Park, Wall, Gwinear, Hayle, Cornwall TR27 5LE.** 01209 831503. www.parbola.co.uk. Large well-spaced pitches in woodland or parkland. Showers. Swimming pool. Adventure playground. Crazy golf. Games room. Table tennis. Laundrette. Washing up facilities. Mother and baby room. Under fives play area. Local pub providing meals lunchtime and evening. PO, shop in nearby village. Comprehensive tourist information available for all visitors. Short driving distance to glorious sandy beaches. Off A30. At Hayle roundabout take first exit to Connor Downs, at end of village turn R to Carnhell Green. Go over railway crossing and continue to T Junction, turn R. Park is located 1m on left hand side. Open: All year. BH&HPA 6⚏ 110⚐ A

**(0.3m). Riviere Sands Holiday Park (Haven), Riviere Towans, Hayle, Cornwall TR27 5AX.** 0871 4680496. www.haven.com. Indoor and outdoor pool complex. On site store. Fish & Chip shop. Sports and leisure facilities. Kids clubs. Daytime and evening entertainment for all the family. 20mins from Tate Gallery, 30-40mins from Eden Project and Minack Theatre. Situated on one of Cornwall's whitest sandy bays. David Bellamy Gold Conservation Award. Off A30 at Hayle . At Jet garage turn R, park is at top of hill on R overlooking sea. Open: 18 March - 31 October. ★★★★ BH&HPA NCC 308⚐

**(1m). St Ives Bay Holiday Park, 73 Loggans Road, Upton Towans, Hayle, Cornwall TR27 5BH.** 01736 752274. www.stivesbay.co.uk. In sand dunes running down to huge sandy beach. Good offers for couples and young families. Many sea views. Huge choice of accommodation. Indoor heated swimming pool. Takeaway. Hire shop. Brochure on application. No pets allowed. No single sex groups. Owner supplied copy. Take Hayle exit off A30 at mini-roundabouts turn R on to B3301, SP 'Portreath'. 600yd along B3301. Open: 14 April - 27 September. ★★★★ BH&HPA 200⚐ A

## Helston

**(6m). Boscrege Caravan and Camping Park, Ashton, Helston, Cornwall TR13 9TG.** 01736 762231. www.caravanpark-cornwall.com. Flat and sheltered park. Washing up room and laundry. TV, microwave. Top 100 parks GB. Most facilities available in Helston and Penzance. Centrally situated for visiting West Cornwall. Off A394 Penzance to Helston. 0.5 m along lane at side of PO in Ashton. Open: 1 March - 1 November. ★★★ 50⚏ 50⚐ A 26⛺

**(10m). Chy Carne Chalet Caravan & Camping Park, Kennack Sands, Kuggar, Ruan Minor, Helston, Cornwall TR12 7LX.** 01326 290200. www.chycarne.co.uk. Gas supplies. Near coastal path, 10mins walk to clean, safe beach. AA 3 pennant. Owner supplied copy. Turn R off B3293 Helston to St Keverne at Traboe Cross. Open: All year. 3 30⚏ 60A 15⛺

**(3m). Gunwalloe Caravan Park, Helston, Cornwall TR12 7QP.** 01326 572668. Holiday site. Cafe/restaurant nearby. 40 mixed pitches in total. Owner supplied copy. S of Helston via A3083 to Lizard. 2m from Helston road for Gunwalloe. Site is SP. Open: 1 April - 31 October. 40⚏ 40⚐ A

**(10m). Gwendreath Farm Holiday Park, Kennack Sands, Ruan Minor, Helston, Cornwall TR12 7LZ.** 01326 290666. www.tomandlinda.co.uk. AA 3 pennants. David Bellamy Silver Conservation Award. Owner supplied copy. From Helston take A3083, turn L on B3293 SP St Keverne, continue for 4m to Goonhilly Earth Station, take next R, then next L. At end of lane turn R over cattle grid and drive through Seaview and stop at second reception. Open: 21 May - 17 September. 3 BH&HPA 17⛺

**(10m). Henry's Camp Site, Caerthillian Farm, The Lizard, Helston, Cornwall TR12 7NX.** 01326 290596. www.henryscampsite.co.uk. Sea views. Beaches close by. Near amenities in village centre but secluded. Owner supplied copy. Take B3083 from Helston. Enter village take first R across village green then second R. Open: All year. 10⚏ 10⚐ A

**(10m). Little Trevothan Caravan Park, Coverack, Helston, Cornwall TR12 6SD.** 01326 280260. www.littletrevothan.com. Spacious family site with level, grassy pitches. Free hot showers Children's playground. Beautiful walks. No noisy club. Modern holiday caravans for sale or hire. AA 3 pennants. Colour brochure available. No cats. Owner supplied copy. SP from B3293 at Zoar garage, turn R follow road, take 3rd L site on right hand

104 CARAVAN & HOLIDAY PARKS 2012

# SOUTH WEST

side. 0.75m from picturesque fishing village of Coverack. Open: 1 March - 31 October. 3 BH&HPA 25 25 34

**(3m). Lower Polladras Touring Park, Carleen, Helston, Cornwall TR13 9NX.** *01736 762220.* www.lower-polladras.co.uk. Tranquil and beautiful surroundings set in a small hamlet. Quiet family run site. AA 3 pennant. Take B3302 off A394 Helston to Penzance. Turn L to Carleen village, after 0.75m from A30 take B3303 after junction with B3302 take 1st R to Carleen. Open: 6 April - 2 January. 3 BH&HPA NCC 60 60

**(1.5m). Mullion Holiday Park, Ruan Minor, Helston, Cornwall TR12 7LJ.** *01326 240428.* www.parkdeanholidays.co.uk. Close to golden sandy beaches and secret coves, spectacular cliffs and coastline and family attractions. Free all weather facilities including indoor swimming pool, live entertainment and children's clubs. Choose your accommodation from our wide range of fully equipped holiday homes and bungalows. Touring & camping facilities also available. David Bellamy Silver Conservation Award. Follow the road to The Lizard from Helston, A3083. After about 7m we are on the L. Open: 23 March - 2 November. ★★★★ BH&HPA NCC 150 327

**(3m). Penmarth Farm, Coverack, St Keverne, Helston, Cornwall TR12 6SB.** *01326 280389.* Woodland walk and pond. Picnic area. Short walk to Coverack village - shops, PO and doctor. Owner supplied copy. Off B3293. Open: 1 April - 31 October. 6 16 4

**(2.5m). Poldown Caravan Park, Carleen, Helston, Cornwall TR13 9NN.** *01326 574560.* www.poldown.co.uk. Secluded site ideal for exploring west Cornwall. 3m to superb sandy coves and beaches. Shopping centre, attraction park, fishing trips 2m, golf 2.5m, surfing 3m. Owner supplied copy. Follow Penzance road from Helston (A394) for about 1m. Turn R at Hilltop garage on to B3302 to Hayle. Take 2nd L, site 0.75m down lane. Open: 6 April - 30 September. ★★★★ 2 10 8 7

**(3m). Retanna Holiday Park, Edgcumbe, Helston, Cornwall TR13 0EJ.** *01326 340633.* www.retanna.co.uk. A peaceful green holiday park, ideal for couples and families with reception, takeaway 3 nights a week and shop in main season. AA 3 pennants. Owner supplied copy. On A394

midway Falmouth-Helston. Open: 1 March - 31 October. 3 BH&HPA 24 A 46

**(9m). Sea Acres Holiday Park, Ruan Minor, Kennack Sands, Helston, Cornwall TR12 7LT.** *01326 290064.* www.parkdean.com. Enjoy the spectacular views over Kennack Sands plus the indoor heated pool, family club house, restaurant and takeaway. Mini supermarket, crazy golf, PADI dive station, kids' club. David Bellamy Silver Conservation Award. Owner supplied copy. A39 to Truro, through Truro and head for Helston on A394. B3293 to Kennack Sands - head towards beach. Open: 1 April - 30 October. ★★★★ BH&HPA NCC 132

**(10m). Silver Sands Holiday Park, Gwendreath, Near Kennack Sands, Helston, Cornwall TR12 7LZ.** *01326 290631.* www.silversandsholidaypark.co.uk. 800yds walk to award winning sandy beach. On edge of The Lizard National Nature Reserve. Take A3083 from Helston, then B3293. After Goonhilly turn R. In 1.50m turn L, signed 'Gwendreath'. Open: 15 March - 15 November. ★★★★ BH&HPA 15 15 20 14 1

### Isles of Scilly

**St Martin's Campsite, Middle Town, St Martin's, Isles of Scilly, Cornwall TR25 0QN.** *01720 422888.* www.stmartinscampsite.co.uk. Level, grassy, sheltered site on quiet, unspoilt island. Booking essential. Owner supplied copy. Ferry, helicopter or plane from Penzance/Lands End. Launch from St Mary's to St Martin's. Open: 14 March - 8 October. ★★★★

### Land's End

**(4.5m). Cardinney Caravan & Camping Park, Main A30, Crows-An-Wra, Land's End, Cornwall TR19 6UX.** *01736 810880.* www.cardinney-camping-park.co.uk. Quiet family-run site in peaceful surroundings. Spacious pitches. Hardstandings. Serviced pitches ie: electric hook up, water hook up and grey water soak-a-way, Wireless internet access. Golf, beaches 3.5m. Penzance 5m. Conveniently situated for local attractions. On A30 between Penzance and Lands End. 4.5m from Penzance. Open: All year. ★★★★ 105

**(6m). Lower Treave Caravan And Camping Park, Crows-An-Wra, Land's End, Cornwall TR19 6HZ.** *01736 810559.* www.lowertreave.co.uk. Quiet family site

at the heart of the Land's End peninsula. Panoramic rural views to the sea. Sheltered grass terraces. Internet and free Wi-Fi. Sennen Blue Flag beach 2.5m. David Bellamy Gold Conservation Award. 6m W of Penzance on A30. Open: 1 April - 31 October. ★★★★ BH&HPA 5 35 5

### Lanlivery

**(1.5m). Eden Valley Holiday Park (Powderham Castle), Lanlivery, Cornwall PL30 5BU.** *01208 872277.* www.edenvalleyholidaypark.co.uk. Quiet uncommercialised select park. Ideal location for touring all Cornwall and near to the Eden Project. Children's activity centre, indoor badminton, soft tennis. TV room. Laundrette. Seasonal pitches and storage. Holiday homes for sale or hire. AA 4 pennants. David Bellamy Bronze Conservation Award. Off A390,1.5m SW of Lostwithiel, turn R at SP Powderham Castle N 400m. Open: 1 April - 31 October. BH&HPA 12 56 56 2 11

### Launceston

**(7m). Chapmanswell Caravan Park, Chapmanswell Well, St-Giles-on-the-Heath, Launceston, Cornwall PL15 9SG.** *01409 211382.* www.chapmanswellcaravanpark.co.uk. Quiet, country park supervised by the owner. Hardstanding and grass pitches. Central for touring Devon and Cornwall. Caravan storage available. Fishing, golf, water sports on reservoir within 7m. Off A388, Launceston to Holsworthy Road, at Chapmanswell take left turning to Boyton-200yd along on L. Open: All year. BH&HPA 35 40

### Liskeard

**Colliford Tavern Campsite, Colliford Lake, St Neot, Liskeard, Cornwall PL14 6PZ.** *01208 821335.* www.colliford.com. Quiet, family-run, sheltered site near Colliford Lake. Tavern and restaurant. Modern hot showers. Dishwashing. Laundry and baby care facilities. AA-4 pennant. Please ring for brochure. Off A30 2m W of Bolventor on Bodmin Moor. 10m from Bodmin. Open: All year. ★★★ 10 15 30

**(3m). Great Trethew Manor Caravan Park, Horningtops, Liskeard, Cornwall PL14 3PY.** *01503 240663.* www.greattrethew-manor.co.uk. Small, well-drained site in 30 acres of woodlands and gardens with use of adjoining park facilities. Play areas, fishing, tennis court. Owner sup-

# SOUTH WEST

plied copy. Situated E of Liskeard, turn off A38 on to B3251 follow for 0.25m to drive entrance. Open: 1 March - 31 October. 55

**(2m). Hoburne Doublebois**, Doublebois, Liskeard, Cornwall PL14 6LD. *08442 451074*. www.hoburne.co.uk/park-details/hoburne-doublebois. Facilities on the park include hard court tennis, a games room with snooker, pool, skittles, table football and more (some activities are chargeable), children's adventure playground, crazy golf and a laundrette. 9 hole par 3 golf course. David Bellamy Bronze Conservation Award. Off A38. Open: 1 March - 2 January.

**(4m). Pine Valley Caravan Park**, Doublebois, Liskeard, Cornwall PL14 6LE. *01579 320183*. Wardens on site. Golf course nearby. Shop, PO 2m. Doctor 3m. 4m W of Liskeard via A38 through Dobwalls towards Bodmin, turn L on to the B3360 at Doublebois, peaceful, wooded park 150yd on the R. Open: All year. ★★★★ BH&HPA 45 45 

### Looe

**(2m). Camping Caradon Touring Park**, Trelawne, Looe, Cornwall PL13 2NA. *01503 272388*. www.campingcaradon.co.uk. 3.5 acres of level ground with easy access. 22 hardstandings, 16amp hook up for all pitches. AA 3 pennants. Green Tourism Business Scheme Silver Award. 2m W of Looe via A387 to Polperro, park is off B3359. Rural location between Looe & Polperro, close to Talland Bay. Open: All year. 4 50 50 50A

**(4m). Killigarth Manor Holiday Park**, Polperro, Looe, Cornwall PL13 2JQ. *01271 866766*. www.johnfowlerholidays.com. Situated in an area of outstanding beauty. Indoor pool. Entertainment daily. Adventure playground. Tennis court. Club. Takeaway. Fishing, golf course and Eden project nearby. Cross Tama bridge A38, turn L at roundabout signed Looe. R A387, cross over bridge in Looe. 3.5m out turn L, SP Killigarth. Open: 13 March - 31 October. ★★★★ BH&HPA NCC  190

**(1m). Looe Bay Holiday Park**, St Martins, East Looe, Looe, Cornwall PL13 1NX. *01503 263737*. www.parkdeanholidays.co.uk. Set in SE Cornwall's beautiful countryside where winding lanes lead you to sandy beaches and unspoilt fishing villages. All weather facilities including multi sports court, indoor heated swimming pool and free children's clubs. For tots to teens, great nightly entertainment. Choose from a selection of fully equipped holiday homes. David Bellamy Gold Conservation Award. From Plymouth A38 towards Liskeard, L at Trerulefoot on to A374 then R on A377. Park on B3253 1.5m from Looe. Open: 1 March - 31 October. ★★★★ BH&HPA NCC  269

**(1.5m). Looe Caravan Club Site**, St Martin, Looe, Cornwall PL13 1PB. *01503 264006*. www.caravanclub.co.uk. Open air heated swimming pool. Mini-golf. Tennis courts. Play area. Public phone. Dog walk. Some hardstandings, part sloping, levelling blocks required. Storage pitches. MV service point. Toilet blocks and laundry facilities. Volleyball area. Golf and water sports nearby. Good area for walking. Ideal for families. NCN cycle route within 5m. Members only. No tents. See website for standard directions to site. Open: 23 March - 5 November. 217 217

**(2m). Oaklands Park (Looe)**, Polperro Road, Looe, Cornwall PL13 2JS. *01503 262640*. www.oaklands-park.co.uk. Perfect location between Looe and Polperro. Wonderful views over countryside. Peaceful park. Pets welcome with designated dog walk area. Laundrette and play area. Development for holiday caravans, leisure lodges & lodges. Beach, sailing, fishing, horse riding. No hire caravans. David Bellamy Gold Conservation Award. Open March-September (tourers), March-January (statics). Owner supplied copy. A38 to Plymouth. Cross Tamar bridge and through tunnel at Saltash. Straight across roundabout on A38. Next roundabout exit L on A374. 1m turn R on to A387 to Looe. Go through town centre over bridge follow road to Polperro and Pelynt for 2.5m. Park on R. Open: 1 March - 31 January. BH&HPA  135

**(2.5m). Polborder House Caravan & Camping Park**, Bucklawren Road, St Martins-by-Looe, Looe, Cornwall PL13 1NZ. *01503 240265*. www.peaceful-polborder.co.uk. Small select and peaceful caravan and camping park nestling in the sleepy hamlet of Bucklawren, set in beautiful countryside surroundings with stunning views. 2.5m E of Looe off B3253, follow signs for Polborder and Monkey Sanctuary. Open: All year. ★★★★ BH&HPA  31 5

**(2m). Seaview Holiday Village (Looe)**, Polperro, Looe, Cornwall PL13 2JE. *01503 272335*. www.seaviewholidayvillage.co.uk. Club. Nightly entertainment, children's club, indoor, outdoor pool, sauna, steam room & leisure facilities. Golf 4m. Plymouth 24m. Off A387. Between Looe & Polperro. Open: 1 April - 31 October. ★★★★ BH&HPA  133

**(1.25m). Tencreek Holiday Park**, Polperro Road, Looe, Cornwall PL13 2JR. *01503 262447*. www.dolphinholidays.co.uk. Family park overlooking sea. Newly built toilet and shower facilities. Heated indoor swimming pool with 45m water flume. Play area, amusement arcade. Takeaway meals. Licensed club with entertainment. On A387, Looe to Polperro road. Open: All year. ★★★★ BH&HPA  50 200 43

**(2m). Trelawne Manor Holiday Park**, Looe, Cornwall PL13 2NA. *01503 272151*. www.johnfowlerholidays.com. Set around stately manor house with family entertainment and children's clubs. Indoor and outdoor pools with flume. Tennis court. Table tennis, Arcade and games room. David Bellamy Silver Conservation Award. Owner supplied copy. Off the B3359 from Looe. Open: 13 March - 28 October. ★★★★ BH&HPA NCC  350

**(3m). Trelay Farmpark**, Pelynt, Looe, Cornwall PL13 2JX. *01503 220900*. www.trelay.co.uk. Small, uncommercialised, family run park surrounded by farmland. Superb washing facilities/laundry/disabled suite. New children's play area. Shops/restaurants etc. in Pelynt (10 mins walk). Amazing Eden Project 12m W. Looe and Polperro 3m. Fishing, golf, diving all nearby. 0.5m S of Pelynt on B3359. Open: 1 December - 31 October. NCC  50 24

### Marazion

**Mounts Bay Caravan Park**, Green Lane, Marazion, Cornwall TR17 0HQ. *01736 710307*. www.mountsbay-caravan-park.co.uk. Families and couples only. Laundry. Heated outdoor pool. Penzance, cinema 3m. Horse riding 7m. Leisure centre/indoor pool 8m. Rose award. Owner supplied copy. Off A394. 500yd from Marazion. About 50yd from beach, opposite St Michael's Mount. Open: 15 March - 15 November. ★★★★  18

**(0.5m). Wheal Rodney Holiday Park**, Gwallon Lane, Marazion, Cornwall TR17 0HL. *01736 710605*. www.whealrodney.co.uk. Showers, laundry facilities. Solarium. Heated indoor swimming pool free of charge to guests. Shop on site. Holiday bungalows for hire. AA 3 pen-

# SOUTH WEST

nants. Fishing, horse riding nearby. Half mile to St Michaels mount and beaches. Owner supplied copy. Off A30. At Crowlas take road SP Rospeath, we are 1.5m on R. Open: 1 March - 31 October. 3 BH&HPA ✿ ⛺ ✵ ⬛ ♨ ⬛ WC ♿ 12🚐 12⛺ ▲ 10📅

## Mevagissey

**(4m). Pentewan Sands Holiday Park, Pentewan, Mevagissey, Cornwall PL26 6BT.** 01726 843485. www.pentewan.co.uk. Large, safe, sandy private beach, boat launching facilities. Clubhouse, shop, restaurant and takeaway. Free showers. Laundrette. Large level pitches. No jet skis. Traditional family site (no single sex bookings). Caravan and boat storage. On B3273. 4m S of St Austell towards Mevagissey. Look for the large site beside the beach on your left. You are there. Open: 1 April - 31 October. ★★★★ BH&HPA ♀ ✿ ⛺ ✵ ♨ ⬛ ❖ ◊ ✡ ⛲ ⚒ ⧖ ⛒ ♿ ✕ ♿ WC ♿ 🚐 420⛺ ▲ 121📅

## Mullion

**(5m). Franchis Holiday Park, Cury Cross Lanes, Mullion, Cornwall TR12 7AZ.** 01326 240301. www.franchis.co.uk. Quiet, family run park in an Area of Outstanding Natural Beauty. Wonderful sandy coves, pubs and shops a short drive away. Perfectly placed for touring the Lizard and West Cornwall. On A3083 Helston to Lizard. Open: 1 April - 31 October. ★★★ BH&HPA ✿ ⛺ ✵ ♨ ♀ ⬛ ⌂ ⛒ ⚒ ⛖ ❖ WC 🚐 65⛺ ▲ 4📅

## Newquay

**(4m). Cottage Farm Touring Park, Treworgans, Cubert, Newquay, Cornwall TR8 5HH.** 01637 831083. www.cottagefarmpark.co.uk. Small, quiet family site. Families and couples only. Dogs welcome April to mid July and September. Owner supplied copy. 5m SW of Newquay. S from Newquay on A3075. At Rejerrah crossroads, turn W for Cubert, then turn N towards Crantock for 0.75m. Open: 1 April - 30 September. ✿ ⛺ ✵ ♨ ⬛ WC 5🚐 20⛺ ▲ 📅

**(3.5m). Crantock Beach Holiday Park, Crantock, Newquay, Cornwall TR8 5RH.** 0844 3353450. www.parkdean.com. Quiet, peaceful park with magnificent views across a sandy, family beach which is a short walk away. Light evening entertainment, bar, children welcome, play areas, pitch and putt, takeaway food, laundrette. Follow M4/M5 to Exeter then A30 to Newquay. Take exit signed A392 to Newquay. Follow road through Quintrell Downs past Morrisons, turn for A3075 Redruth then Crantock Beach. Follow brown signs for Crantock Beach & Quarryfields. Open: 1 April - 31 October. ★★★★ BH&HPA NCC ✿ ⛺ ✵ ♨ ♀ ⬛ ⚒ ⧖ ⛒ ✕ ♿ WC ♿ 🚐 169⛺

**(3m). Crantock Plains Touring Park, Crantock, Newquay, Cornwall TR8 5PH.** 01637 830955. www.crantock-plains.co.uk. 1.5m from beach. PO 1.5m, fishing and golf 3m. Families and couples only, children's' play area. Cornwall's best kept secret! Owner supplied copy. S of Newquay via A3075 Redruth road. After lake on R, garage on L. Continue over mini roundabout. Site is 0.5m down second SP lane to Crantock on R. Open: 21 April - 30 September. ★★★ NCC ✿ ⛺ ✵ ♨ ⬛ WC ♿ 🚐 40⛺ 40📅 ▲

**(2m). Hendra Holiday Park, Newquay, Cornwall TR8 4NY.** 01637 875778. www.hendra-holidays.com. A family run park for couples and families. Heated outdoor pool and indoor fun pools with waterslide. Food bar. Sauna. Bars. Children's complex and club. Entertainment. Restaurant. (Riding, fishing and golf within 2m). Freephone brochure line: 0500 242523. David Bellamy Gold Conservation Award. From M5 at Exeter, take A30 to the Highgate Hill junction, follow the sign for the A392 to Newquay. At Quintrell Downs go straight across the roundabout and on for 0.5m. Hendra Holiday Park is on the L (1.5m from Newquay town centre). Open: 1 April - 31 October. ★★★★★ BH&HPA ♀ ✿ ⛺ ⚒ ✵ ♨ ♿ ⧖ ⛒ ❖ ⌂ ⛖ ✕ ⬛ ⛲ ⚕ WC ♿ 🚐 725⛺ ▲ 308📅

**(3m). Holywell Bay Holiday Park, Holywell Bay, Newquay, Cornwall TR8 5PR.** 0844 3353450. www.park-deanholidays.co.uk. 39 mixed pitches. Peaceful valley with a sandy, family beach a short walk away. Children club, free nightly entertainment, heated pool with 300ft slide, amusements. Pool open between May-September only. David Bellamy Silver Conservation Award. 6m W of Newquay off A3075 SP Cubert and Holywell Bay. Open: 27 March - 2 November. ★★★★ BH&HPA NCC ♀ ✿ ⛺ ✵ ♨ ⚒ ⬛ ❖ ⛒ ✕ ⧖ WC 🚐 39⛺ ▲ 162📅

**(6m). Magic Cove Touring Park, Mawgan Porth, Newquay, Cornwall TR8 4BD.** 01637 860263. www.magiccove.co.uk. Level site 300yd from the beach, shops and pub. Water and drain adjacent to each pitch. TV, hook up points. Well maintained facilities. Free Wi-Fi. Situated halfway between Newquay and Padstow on the north Cornish coast. Open: 9 April - 2 October. ✿ ⛺ ✵ ♨ ⬛ WC ♿ 25⛺ ▲

**Marver Holiday Park, Mawgan Porth, Newquay, Cornwall TR8 4BB.** 01637 860493. www.marverholidaypark.co.uk. Small, level, quiet, family run site. Families and couples only. 200yd level walk to sandy beach. Dogs allowed on beach & nearby beach. Takeaway meals, shop, cafe/restaurant all available nearby. See website for directions. Open: All year. ✿ ⛺ ✵ ♨ ♀ ⬛ ❖ ⛒ ⧖ ⬛ ⚒ WC ▲ 🚐

**(6m). Mawgan Porth Holiday Park, Mawgan Porth, Newquay, Cornwall TR8 4BD.** 01637 860322. www.mawganporth.co.uk. Countryside location. Cornish coast path very close by. Families and couples only. Outdoor heated pool (late May-September) Children's playground. Bed linen hire available. David Bellamy Gold Conservation Award. Owner supplied copy. Off B3276. Newquay to Padstow coast road, 400yd in land. 400yd to sandy beach. Open: All year. ★★★★ BH&HPA ✿ ⛺ ♨ ❖ ⛒ ⚒ WC 🚐 27⛺ ▲

**(4m). Monkey Tree Holiday Park, Scotland Road, Hendra Croft, Newquay, Cornwall TR8 5QR.** 01872 572032. www.monkeytreeholidaypark.co.uk. Set in ideal surroundings only a short distance from Cornwall's popular surfing beaches. Lounge bar. Cafe. Heated swimming pools. Clubhouse with entertainment, restaurant, shop. David Bellamy Gold Conservation Award. From M5, A30 to Exeter, Bodmin, Redruth off at Boxheater junction B3285, after 0.5m turn R, after 1m turn L to Monkey Tree. Open: 26 March - 29 October. BH&HPA ♀ ✿ ⛺ ✵ ♨ ⚒ ⧖ ⛒ ❖ ⌂ ✕ ♿ WC ♿ 🚐 450⛺ ▲ 48📅

**(4m). Newperran Holiday Park, Rejerrah, Newquay, Cornwall TR8 5QJ.** 01872 572407. www.newperran.co.uk. Spacious family park in elevated position with countryside and sea views. Level perimeter pitching surrounded by Cornish hedges and farmland with no road noise. Fees on application. Crazy golf. Off-licence. Cottage Inn and cafe. 5m S of Newquay via A3075 towards Redruth. Turn R to Newperran, 1m after garage. Open: 26 March - 29 October. ★★★★★ BH&HPA ♀ ✿ ⛺ ✵ ♨ ♀ ⬛ ⚒ ⧖ ⛒ ✕ ♿ WC ♿ 🚐 371⛺ ▲ 31📅

**(2m). Newquay Holiday Park, Newquay, Cornwall TR8 4HS.** 01637 871111. www.parkdeanholidays.co.uk. A short drive from Newquay and its fabulous beaches. Children's club, free nightly entertainment, 3 heated swimming pools, water slide, amusements, pool, snooker, pitch & putt, crazy golf, playground, restaurant, takeaway food. David Bellamy Gold Conservation Award. Off A3059. Direction

# SOUTH WEST

Newquay - after 4m- park is SP at bottom of the hill. Open: 23 March - 1 November. ★★★★ BH&HPA NCC ⚑ 🛏 🏠 🌳 ♪♫♪ ♨ ⌂ ⛱ ⚿ ⛺ ✕ 🅿 🛌 🚽 259🚐 259⚡ ⛺ 335🚿

**Perran Quay Tourist Park, Hendra Croft, Rejerrah, Newquay, Cornwall TR8 5QP.** *01872 572561* . www.perran-quay.co.uk. Bar and restaurant. Play area. Outdoor heated swimming pool. Quality shower and toilet facilities, modern launderette. On A3075 midway between Newquay & Perranporth. Open: All year. ⚑ 🛏 🏠 🌳 ♪♫♪ ♨ ⌂ ⛱ ⚿ ⛺ ✕ 🅿 🛌 🚽 ♿ & 🚐 66⚡ ⛺ 40🚿

 **(1.5m). Porth Beach Tourist Park, Porth, Newquay, Cornwall TR7 3NH.** *01637 876531*. www.porthbeach.co.uk. Close to beach. Playground. Shops near. Riding, fishing and boating 1m. Turn R off A30 at Indian Queens on to A392 to Quintrell Downs roundabout. A3058 to Newquay. At Porth, Four Turnings turn R on to B3276, coast road to Padstow. Open: 5 March - 29 October. ★★★★ BH&HPA 🛏 🏠 🌳 ♪ ♨ ⌂ ⛱ ⚿ ⛺ ✕ 🅿 🛌 🚽 ♿ & 200🚐 200⚡ ⛺ 176🚿 18🏕

**(3m). Quarryfield Caravan & Camping Park, Crantock, Newquay, Cornwall TR8 5RJ.** *01637 872792*. www.quarryfield.co.uk. Overlooking Crantock Beach - 10mins walk to beach. 5mins walk to village. Licensed bar. Outdoor heated pool. Dogs allowed and cared for. PO and shop in village. AA 3 pennants. Owner supplied copy. Off A3075 Redruth to Newquay road to Crantock village, turn R by telephone booth and R into road opposite. Open: 16 April - 29 October. 3 BH&HPA 🛏 🏠 🌳 ♨ ⌂ ✕ 🅿 🛌 🚽 & 15🚐 15⚡ ⛺ 40🚿

**(2.5m). Riverside Holiday Park (Newquay), Gwills Lane, Newquay, Cornwall TR8 4PE.** *01637 873617.* www.riversideholidaypark.co.uk. On site: games room, bar, cafe/takeaway, swimming pool, showers, laundry. Short drive: amusements and other amenities. Newquay town centre, pony trekking 2m.

Golf course, beaches 3m. Owner supplied copy. Off A392 at Quintrell Downs go straight across at roundabout, then take second turning on L, SP 'Gwills' past Lane Theatre and follow signs. Open: 6 April - 31 October. ★★★★ BH&HPA 🛏 ♪ ⚑ ♨ ⌂ ⛱ ⚿ ⛺ ✕ 🅿 🛌 🚽 & 🚐 60⚡ ⛺ 70🚿 4🏕

**(1m). Rosecliston Park, Trevemper, Newquay, Cornwall TR8 5JT.** *01637 830326*. www.rosecliston.co.uk. Good recreational facilities in a pleasantly designed park. Singles and couples only. Owner supplied copy. On A3075 Newquay-Redruth road. Open: 27 May - 29 August. BH&HPA 🛏 🏠 🌳 ♪ ♨ ⌂ ⛱ ⚿ ⛺ 🅿 🛌 🚽 & 🚐 ⚡ ⛺

★ **(5m). Summer Lodge Holiday Resort, Whitecross, Newquay, Cornwall TR8 4LW.** *0844 2721138*. www.summerlodge.co.uk. Ideally situated for touring. Facilities include heated swimming pool, cafe, takeaway, club with live entertainment. Golf, horse riding and full range of water sports locally. From M5 take A30 then turn on to A392 to Newquay. SP at Whitecross. Open: 9 February - 9 January. BH&HPA 🛏 🏠 🌳 ♪ ♨ ⌂ ⛱ ✕ 🅿 🛌 🚽 & 🚐 100⚡ ⛺ 157🚿 🏕

**(5.5m). Sun Haven Valley Holiday Park, Mawgan Porth, Newquay, Cornwall TR8 4BQ.** *0800 6346744*. www.sunhavenvalley.com. Fishing next to site. Golf 1m. Bus to Newquay and Padstow stops at gate. Beach 0.5m. Silence at 10.30pm enforced by wardens. David Bellamy Bronze Conservation Award. Turn R off B3276 Newquay to Padstow coast road, park on L 0.75m from coast. Open: 31 March - 30 October. ★★★★ BH&HPA 🛏 ♪ ♨ ⌂ ⛱ ⚿ ⛺ ✕ 🅿 🛌 🚽 & 7🚐 32⚡ ⛺ 71🚿 33⚡ 5🏕

**(5m). Treago Farm Park, Crantock, Newquay, Cornwall TR8 5QS.** *01637 830277*. www.treagofarm.co.uk. Site is in sheltered valley 0.5m from the sea and surrounded by National Trust land.

Footpath to two sandy beaches. Off A3075 2m S of Newquay follow signs to Crantock and the Treago, West Pentire signs. Open: 18 April - 31 October. BH&HPA ⚑ 🛏 🏠 🌳 ♪ ♨ ⌂ ⛱ ⚿ ⛺ ✕ 🅿 🛌 🚽 90🚐 90⚡ ⛺ 14🚿

**(3m). Trebarber Farm Camping Park, Trebarber, St Columb Minor, Newquay, Cornwall TR8 4JT.** *01637 873007*. www.trebarberfarmholidays.com. 4 cottages for rent, static caravans for hire, touring caravan hook-ups and camping facilities. Level site 3m from beach. Coarse fishing & golf nearby. Owner supplied copy. Off A3059 Newquay to St Columb road. Open: 1 May - 15 October. 🛏 🏠 🌳 ♪ ♨ ⌂ 🅿 🛌 🚽 🚐 ⚡ ⛺ 2🚿

**(5m). Tregurrian Camping & Caravanning Club Site, Tregurrian, Newquay, Cornwall TR8 4AE.** *01637 860448* . www.campingandcaravanningclub.co.uk. The nearby beach at Watergate Bay is always popular with youngsters and excellent for surfers. Non-members welcome. All units welcome. Fishing, horse riding, golf, PO, shops, cycle routes, doctor, hospital, swimming pool, zoo, Eden Project etc all within easy reach by car or public transport. Special deals available for families and backpackers. Ideal base for exploring North Cornwall. Loo Of The Year (4 stars). From A3059 to Newquay. 1.5m on after service station, R to Newquay airport, continue to J, then L at Tregurrian. Follow Watergate Bay signs. Open: 1 April - 31 October. ★★★★ NCC 🛏 🏠 🌳 ♪ ♨ ⌂ ⛱ ⚿ ⛺ ✕ 🅿 🛌 🚽 & 90🚐 90⚡ ⛺

**(3m). Tregustick Holiday Park, Porth, Newquay, Cornwall TR8 4AR.** *01637 872478*. www.thpark.co.uk. Off B3276. Open: 22 April - 31 October. BH&HPA 🛏 🚽 25🚐 ⚡ ⛺ 26🚿

**(6.5m). Trekenning Tourist Park, Newquay, Cornwall TR8 4JF.** *01637 880462*. www.trekenning.co.uk. Swimming pool. Licensed bar. Family bathrooms and free showers. Hot and cold washing up

**Just minutes from the golden beaches in Newquay - the perfect base for your family holiday in Cornwall**

- Stunning accommodation in landscaped park.
- Club and restaurant.
- Outdoor heated pool.
- Sports Bar and family entertainment area.
- Children's play park.
- Laundrette.
- Touring guest facilities.
- Caravan holiday homes for sale

**20% off your booking Quote CHP20***

*Terms and conditions apply

**To book call 0844 272 11687 or visit www.summerlodge.co.uk**

# SOUTH WEST

basins. Dogs by arrangement. Just off A39 0.5m S of St Columb. 10mins Newquay, 4m Watergate and Mawgan Porth beaches. Open: All year. ★★★★ BH&HPA NCC ⚘ ♿ ♨ ♫ ♪ ♣ ⚙ ❄ ✱ ♠ ✗ ✉ ☂ ☕ ♿ 🚐 75💷 ⛺

**(3m). Treloy Touring Park, Newquay, Cornwall TR4 4JN.** 01637 872063. www.treloy.co.uk. Heated swimming pool, licensed bar, family room, entertainment. Free showers. Adventure playground. Coarse fishing nearby. Golf course 500yds concessionary green fees. David Bellamy Silver Conservation Award. Just off A3059 Newquay road. Open: 1 April - 17 September. ★★★ BH&HPA ⚘ ♨ ⛱ ♫ ♪ ♣ ⚙ ❄ ✱ ♠ ✗ ☂ ☕ ♿ 🚐 20💷 140💷 ⛺

**(0.5m). Trenance Holiday Park, Edgecumbe Avenue, Newquay, Cornwall TR7 2JY.** 01637 873447. www.trenance-holidaypark.co.uk. Games room. Restaurant and takeaway. Nearest park to Newquay town centre. No dogs. No single sex groups or mixed groups. Owner supplied copy. On main A3075 Newquay Truro road, situated about 0.5m from Newquay Town Centre. Open: 6 April - 6 October. ★★★ BH&HPA ⚘ ♨ ♫ ♪ ♣ ⚙ ❄ ✱ ♠ ✗ ☂ ☕ ♿ 🚐 50💷 ⛺ ⛺ 134💷

**(2m). Trethiggey Holiday Park, Quintrell Downs, Newquay, Cornwall TR8 4QR.** 01637 877672. www.trethiggey.co.uk. Family site with excellent facilities and wonderful country views. Level pitches. Adventure playground. Caravan storage. Dog walk area. Fishing and local pub a few minutes walk. 15m from Eden project. David Bellamy Gold Conservation Award. Off A3058. Open: 2 March - 2 January. ★★★ BH&HPA ⚘ ♨ ♫ ♪ ♣ ⚙ ❄ ✱ ♠ ✗ ☂ ☕ ♿ 🚐 157💷 ⛺ 12💷

**(4.5m). Trevarrian Holiday Park, Mawgan Porth, Newquay, Cornwall TR8 4AQ.** 01637 860381. www.trevarrian.co.uk. Flat, well-drained site with fine views; about 1m from beach. Level grassy site. Heated pool. Bar. Tennis court. Pitch and putt. Sports field. Special offers. N of Newquay via B276 Padstow road. Open: 1 April - 31 October. BH&HPA ⚘ ♨ ⛱ ♫ ♪ ♣ ⚙ ❄ ✱ ♠ ✗ ☂ ☕ ♿ 🚐 185💷 ⛺

**Trevelgue Holiday Park, Porth, Newquay, Cornwall TR8 4AS.** 0845 1301515. www.trevelgue.co.uk. ⚘ ♨ ♫ ♪ ♣ ⚙ ❄ ✱ ♠ ✗ ☂ ☕ 🚐 ⛺ ♿

**PREMIER PARKS 2011** **(1.5m). Trevella Caravan & Camping Park, Crantock, Newquay, Cornwall TR8 5EW.** 01637 830308. www.trevella.co.uk. Heated swimming pool, crazy golf, adventure playground, cafe, own fishing lake. Ideally situated to visit the Eden Project. David Bellamy Gold Conservation Award. Off A3075, on the road to Crantock. Open: 1 April - 29 October. ★★★★★ BH&HPA ⚘ ♨ ⛱ ♫ ♪ ♣ ⚙ ❄ ✱ ♠ ✗ ☂ ☕ ♿ 270💷 ⛺ 75💷

**PREMIER PARKS 2011** **(4m). Trevornick Holiday Park, Holywell Bay, Newquay, Cornwall TR8 5PR.** 01637 830531. www.trevornick.co.uk. Large level pitches most with electric hook-ups. Heated pool, 18 hole golf course and 18 hole pitch and putt course, and fishing ponds. Full programme of free entertainment with disco and cabaret. Children's club. Great places to eat and Holywell Bay Fun Park and wonderful beach right next door. Also 68 euro tents. David Bellamy Gold Conservation Award. Off A3075 Newquay to Perranporth road. Open: 21 May - 17 September. ★★★★★ BH&HPA ⚘ ♨ ⛱ ♫ ♪ ♣ ⚙ ❄ ✱ ♠ ✗ ☂ ☕ ♿ 250💷 250💷

**(4m). Watergate Bay Touring Park, Tregurrian, Newquay, Cornwall TR8 4AD.** 01637 860387. www.watergatebaytouringpark.co.uk. Heated pool, licensed bar, evening entertainment, cafeteria, adventure playground, sports field, dog exercise area, free minibus to beach and access to coastal footpath. Fishing available 0.5m, golf 2m. David Bellamy Silver Conservation Award. Follow airport signs of A30 continue on to B3276, SP Watergate Bay. The site is situated at Tregurrian 0.5m from the bay. Open: 1 March - 31 October. ★★★★ BH&HPA ⚘ ♨ ⛱ ♫ ♪ ♣ ⚙ ❄ ✱ ♠ ✗ ☂ ☕ ♿ 170💷 170💷 ⛺ 2💷

**(6m). White Acres Country Park, White Cross, Newquay, Cornwall TR8 4LW.** 01726 862100. www.parkdeanholidays.co.uk. White Acres boasts 13 tranquil fishing lakes amongst 184 acres of stunning countryside plus a range of facilities to keep everyone happy including indoor pool and kids clubs. David Bellamy Gold Conservation Award. A392 to Newquay, travel over first roundabout. Park entrance on the right hand side. Open: 14 March - 7 November. ★★★★ BH&HPA NCC ⚘ ♨ ⛱ ♫ ♪ ♣ ⚙ ❄ ✱ ♠ ✗ ☂ ☕ ♿ 186💷

## Otterham

**St Tinney Farm Holidays, St Tinney Farm, Otterham, Cornwall PL32 9TA.** 01840 261274. www.st-tinney.co.uk. Good touring centre. Four coarse fishing lakes. Farm animals. Pony rides. Dogs allowed on touring site only. Outdoor swimming pool. Pub on site. 10m to Bude, 6m to Boscastle, 4m to Crackington Haven. AA 3-pennant. Owner supplied copy. 10m S of Bude, just off A39. Open: 2 April - 6 November. 3 BH&HPA ⚘ ♨ ♣ 20💷 ⛺ 16💷 ⛺

## Padstow

**Atlantic Bays Holiday Park, St Merryn, Padstow, Cornwall PL28 8PY.** 01841 520855. www.atlanticbaysholidaypark.co.uk. The park is set amidst 27 acres of peaceful parkland. 2m from the dramatic North Cornwall coast. Children's play area adjacent to the amenities centre. Please see website for things to do & discounted attractions. Off A389. Open: 1 March - 2 January. ⚘ ♨ ♫ ♪ ♣ ⚙ ❄ ✱ ☂ ☕ ♿ 50💷 ⛺ 150💷

**(4m). Carnevas Holiday Park, Carnevas Farm, St Merryn, Padstow, Cornwall PL28 8PN.** 01841 520230. www.carnevasholidaypark.co.uk. Beach 0.5m. Family run site. Showers, family bathrooms, laundry, children's play area, games room, club, Wi-Fi, bar. Rose Award Park 2009. Fishing, golf course nearby. From St Merryn take B3276 towards Porthcothan Bay (about 2m), turn R opposite Tredrea Inn. Open: 1 April - 31 October. ★★★★ BH&HPA ⚘ ♨ ⛱ ♫ ♪ ♣ ⚙ ❄ ✱ ☂ ☕ ♿ 🚐 195💷 ⛺ 9💷

**(0.25m). Dennis Cove Camping Ltd, Dennis Lane, Padstow, Cornwall PL28 8DR.** 01841 532349. www.denniscove.co.uk. Quiet family site. Advance booking necessary. Adjacent to Camel estuary and Camel trail cycle track. 10mins walk to Padstow harbour. Supermarket, cafes and restaurants, fishing, sailing nearby. Owner supplied copy. At S side of town. Approaching A389, turn R at Tesco supermarket, turn R into Dennis Lane, campsite straight ahead. Open: 5 April - 30 September. ⚘ ♨ ♫ ♪ ♣ ⚙ ❄ ✱ ☂ ☕ ♿ 10💷 5💷 ⛺

**(3m). Harlyn Sands Caravan Park, Lighthouse Road, Trevose Head, St Merryn, Padstow, Cornwall PL28 8SQ.** 01841 520720. www.harlynsands.co.uk. Licensed bar. Reception area. Play park. Holiday caravans for hire. 300yd from superb beaches. Families only. Shop, restaurant, children's games room. Before reaching Padstow, turn off for St Merryn, follow signs for Harlyn Sands. If towing a caravan when you reach St Merryn, head for Constantine, then turn for Trevose Golf Course. Come through golf course, turn L for Harlyn Sands. Open: 9 April - 30 October. BH&HPA ⚘ ♨ ♫ ♪ ♣ ⚙ ❄ ✱ ☂ ☕ ♿ 150💷 ⛺ 290💷

**(3m). Higher Harlyn Park, St Merryn, Padstow, Cornwall PL28 8SG.** 01841

# SOUTH WEST

520022. www.higherharlynpark.co.uk. Licensed bar. Outdoor heated swimming pool. Children's play area. Laundrette. Diner. St Merryn village is only a 5mins flat walk away. No under 25s permitted unless with their families. No groups. Owner supplied copy. Off B3276. Open: 1 March - 31 October.

**(3m). Maribou Holiday Park, St Merryn, Padstow, Cornwall PL28 8QA.** 01841 520520. www.maribouholidaypark.co.uk. Licensed bar. Takeaway. Shaver points. Laundry. Showers. Club house on site. Fees on application. Indian restaurant and shop at 100yds. Fishing 1.5m. Golf 3m, surfing beaches 2m. WE NO LONGER ACCEPT TOURING CARAVANS OR TENTS. Owner supplied copy. Take B3274 off A30, second road L after roundabout to St Merryn. Open: 31 March - 31 October.

**(4m). Mother Ivey's Bay Holiday Park, Trevose Head, Padstow, Cornwall PL28 8SL.** 01841 520990. www.motherriveysbay.com. Outstanding coastal location. Private beach. Golf, fishing and water sports available nearby. Perfect for traditional family holidays with beautiful landscape grounds and immaculate facilities. David Bellamy Gold Conservation Award. 4m from Padstow signed off the B3276 Padstow to Newquay coast road (Trevose Head). Open: 1 April - 6 November.

**(5m). Old MacDonald's Farm, Porthcothan Bay, Padstow, Cornwall PL28 8LW.** 01841 540829. www.old-macdonalds.co.uk. Quiet park ideal for families. Free entrance to farm park during stay. Showers. Play area. Pony rides on site. Sporting facilities nearby. Half mile from beach, ideal for surfing and swimming. Advance booking accepted. Colour brochure. Owner supplied copy. On B3276 coast road between Padstow and Newquay, look for signs. Open: All year.

**(1m). Padstow Holiday Park, Cliff Downe, Padstow, Cornwall PL28 8LB.** 01841 532289. www.padstowholidaypark.co.uk. Near to several sandy beaches. Quiet family run park in countryside setting. Footpath to Padstow. Level, well-maintained. Uncrowded and friendly. Owner supplied copy. On main A389 Padstow road, on right hand side 1.5m before Padstow. Open. All year.

**(1m). Padstow Touring Park, Padstow, Cornwall PL28 8LE.** 01841 532061. www.padstowtouringpark.co.uk. Quiet family park. Easy access. 2m to sandy beach. Panoramic views with public footpath to Padstow. Some en suite pitches. David Bellamy Silver Conservation Award. On A389 1m S, SW of Padstow. If towing or large motorhome, avoid A389 through St Issey, take B3274. Open: All year.

**(2m). Tregavone Touring Park, Tregavone Farm, St Merryn, Padstow, Cornwall PL28 8JZ.** 01841 520148. www.tregavonefarm.co.uk. 4 acres, 40 mixed pitches, quiet, family run site with unspoilt country views. Kept to a high standard of cleanliness, ideal for sandy beaches and touring Cornwall. 2m to picturesque Padstow, fishing and golf course. AA 2 pennants. SW of Padstow on A389. Open: 1 March - 31 October.

**(4m). Trethias Farm Caravan Site, Treyarnon Bay, St Merryn, Padstow, Cornwall PL28 8PL.** 01841 520323. Quiet family run park for couples and families only. Environmentally friendly site. Recycling point for all customers. Shop and beach nearby. Golf course 2m, PO, doctor 1.5m. David Bellamy Gold Conservation Award. Off B3276 from St Merryn past Farmers Arms, 3rd turning R, park SP from here. Open: 1 April - 30 September.

**(4m). Trevean Caravan and Camping Park, St Merryn, Padstow, Cornwall PL28 8PR.** 01841 520772. www.trevean-caravanandcamping.net. An ideal family site, situated near sandy surfing beaches. Coastal footpaths with spectacular scenery of the north Cornish coast. No pets allowed in caravans for hire. Owner supplied copy. From St Merryn village take the B3276 Newquay road for 1m, turn L for Rumford, site 0.25m on R. Open: 1 April - 31 October.

**(4m). Treyarnon Bay Caravan & Camping Park, Treyarnon Bay, Padstow, Cornwall PL28 8JR.** 01841 520681. www.treyarnonbay.co.uk. Ideal family site 200yds from beach overlooking Treyarnon Bay. Coastal walks and surfing. Dogs not allowed on touring site main summer weeks. Off B3276 Newquay to Padstow road, turn off for Trevarnon Bay follow lane into beach car park. Holiday park adjacent. Open: 1 April - 25 September.

## Penryn

**(2.5m). Calamankey Farm, Longdowns, Penryn, Cornwall TR10 9DL.** 01209 860314. www.calamankey.com. Mob: 07831 797723. Working farm campsite in open countryside with views to St Mawes and Roseland Peninsula beyond. Centrally situated (Truro 10m, Helston 9m, Redruth 9m, Falmouth 4m) ideal for exploring Lizard and Helford river. Many family attractions nearby (Flambards Theme Park, Seal Sanctuary, Poldark Mine). Local shop/PO and PH 20yd from drive entrance, large ASDA just 1.5m away. Golf, boating, fishing, tennis, scuba diving, riding, sailing & swimming all available nearby. No pets. On A394 opposite Texaco filling station in Longdowns village. Open: 1 February - 15 December.

## Penzance

**(1m). Bone Valley Caravan & Camping Park, Heamoor, Penzance, Cornwall TR20 8UJ.** 01736 360313. www.bonevalleyholidaypark.co.uk. Quiet family run park. Very sheltered, clean and friendly. Supervised 24hrs. Limited disabled facilities in holiday caravans. TV room, laundry facilities, kitchen with microwave and electric kettle, shower/toilet block. Baby changing facilities. Bottled gas Calor/camping gaz, battery charging. Cornwall Tourist Board quality member. All amenities in local village. Follow A30 Penzance bypass, turn off at Heamoor roundabout, continue through Heamoor to caravan and camping sign on R. Continue down hill to next sign on L, SP Bone Valley, site is 200yd on L. Open: All year.

**(7m). Kelynack Caravan and Camping Park, St Just, Penzance, Cornwall TR19 7RE.** 01736 787633. www.kelynackholidays.co.uk. Close to the coast. 1m from shops, pubs, PO, doctors. 2m from golf course. David Bellamy Gold Conservation Award. Owner supplied copy. On B3306 St Ives to Land's End. 1m S of St Just alongside stream in secluded valley. Open: 14 March - 1 November.

**(6m). Kenneggy Cove Holiday Park, Higher Kenneggy, Rosudgeon, Penzance, Cornwall TR20 9AU.** 01736 763453. www.kenegaycove.co.uk. Set in an Area of Outstanding Natural Beauty with the Rose Award for excellence, this immaculate park offers spacious lawned pitches with a beautiful garden setting with panoramic sea views. 50 pitches in total. Freshly baked bread and home-made meals to take away. 15mins walk to SW

# SOUTH WEST

coast path and safe secluded beach. NB: this is a quiet site operating a policy of no noise after 10pm or before 8am. Off A394 Helston to Penzance, 3m E of Marazion on the south coast. Open: 12 May - 30 September. ★★★★ BH&HPA 20 A 16

**(4m). River Valley Country Park, Relubbus, Penzance, Cornwall TR20 9ER.** *01736 763398.* www.surfbayholidays.co.uk. Quiet, rural, family park on banks of clear shallow stream. Short or long stays welcome. Large level pitches. David Bellamy Silver Conservation Award. Open March-January for statics. From A30 at St Michaels Mount roundabout, take A394 SP Helston. At the next roundabout turn L on to B3280 SP Relubbus. Travel for about 3m, then just over a small bridge, River Valley Country Park is on L. Open: 25 February - 4 January. ★★★★★ BH&HPA 87

**(4.5m). Roseland's Caravan & Camping Park, Dowran, St Just, Penzance, Cornwall TR19 7RS.** *01736 788571.* www.roselands.co.uk. Games room, play area, showers, laundrette. Breakfast and evening meals served in our new conservatory. Sea views, level pitches. Ideal base for walking, water activities and local attractions including golf course. Eden project 75mins drive, Maritime Museum 30mins drive. Dog friendly. David Bellamy Silver Conservation Award. From Penzance on A3071 to St Just - 6m, SP on R 800yd. Open: 1 January - 31 October. ★★★ BH&HPA 7 7 A 30

**(8m). Seaview Holiday Park (Penzance), Sennen, Penzance, Cornwall TR19 7AD.** *01736 871266.* www.seaview.org.uk. 140 pitches in total which can take tourers, tents and motorcaravans. Family park. Outdoor swimming pool, cafe and BBQ area on site. Bike hire. Crazy golf, extended play area, play train, table tennis. Cinema in Penzance. 2 lane 10-pin bowling alley, space maze, bar, restaurant, play zone. Minack open air theatre. Golf 3m. Tennis court on site, trampolines, pizza takeaway. Dogs welcome by agreement only. On A30 Penzance to Lands End. Open: 1 April - 31 October. ★★★★ BH&HPA 140 A 170 10

**(7m). Sennen Cove Camping & Caravanning Club Site, Higher Tregiffian Farm, St Buryan, Penzance, Cornwall TR19 6JB.** *01736 871588.* www.campingandcaravanningclub.co.uk. A 4 acre site with 75 pitches accepting all units. Sennen Cove Blue Flag beach within easy reach. Non-members welcome. Ball game area and playing field available. Situated on a farm in peaceful countryside in an area of spectacular coastline. Special deals available for families and backpackers. Follow A30 towards Lands End. Turn R on to the A3306 St Just/Pendeen Road. Site 200yd on L. Open: 14 April - 26 September. ★★★★ NCC 72 72

**(2m). Threeways Caravan Club Site, St Hilary, Goldsithney, Penzance, Cornwall TR20 9DU.** *01736 710723.* www.caravanclub.co.uk. A very attractive site in parkland setting with beautiful views. Quiet and peaceful off peak. Levelling blocks required, steel awning pegs required. No sanitation. Dog walk. MV service point. Golf and water sports nearby. Ideal for families. NCN cycle route within 5m. Members only. No tents. See website for standard directions to site. Open: 30 March - 1 October. NCC 60 60

**(5m). Tower Park Caravans and Camping, St. Buryan, Penzance, Cornwall TR19 6BZ.** *01736 810286.* www.towerparkcamping.co.uk. 36 EHU pitches and 66 standard pitches. Peaceful, family run campsite with level grass and sheltering hedges. Static caravans for hire. 5mins walk to village pub and shop. Near unspoilt beaches and coves, ideal for Minack Theatre. From A30 Lands End road turn L on B3283 SP St Buryan. 300yd from village on St Just road. Open: 7 March - 31 October. ★★★★ BH&HPA 102 A 5

**(6m). Trevair Caravan Park, South Treveneague, St Hilary, Penzance, Cornwall TR20 9BY.** *01736 740647.* www.trevairtouringpark.co.uk. Set in 3 secluded acres surrounded by fields and woodland. A well maintained friendly family site. Very clean facilities. Caravans to let. AA 3 pennants. Owner supplied copy. 2m NE Marazion B3280. Open: 6 April - 31 October. 3 10 10 A 2

**(0.5m). Trevaylor Caravan and Camping Park, Botallack, St Just, Penzance, Cornwall TR19 7PU.** *01736 787016.* www.trevaylor.com. Graded AA 3 pennants. Trevaylor is situated in an Area of Outstanding Natural Beauty and only 500yds from the coastal path and the sea. The golf course is 3m away and horse riding is 200yds away from the site. The nearest swimming pool is at the golf course and the bus stops at the entrance to the site; regular service to Penzance, St Ives and Lands End. 0.5m from St Just on B3306 to St Ives. Open: 31 March - 4 November. 3 55 A

**(7m). Trevedra Farm Caravan Club Site (Affiliated Site), Sennen, Lands End, Penzance, Cornwall TR19 7BE.** *01736 871835.* www.caravanclub.co.uk. CARAVAN CLUB AFFILIATED SITE. AA 3 pennants. Non-members and tent campers welcome. Certain areas for members only. Takeaway meals available in peak season only. Public telephone. Calor and Camping Gaz. Shower block. Laundrette. Footpath to Gwenver Beach and coastal path. Brochure available (with SAE). Turn R off A30 just after B3306 junction. 2.5m from Lands End. Open: 1 April - 31 October. 3 60 A

**(6m). Treverven Touring Caravan & Camping Park, St Buryan, Penzance, Cornwall TR19 6DL.** *01736 810200.* www.chycor.co.uk/camping/treverven. Quiet, farm site with excellent sea views. Easy access to coves and beaches. Well situated for touring west Cornwall. Shaver points. Hairdryer units. Deep freeze. Children's play area, lovely walks. AA 3 pennant site. Rock fishing, course fishing nearby, golf course about 6m away. On B3315 coastal road. Open: 22 April - 31 October. 3 BH&HPA 75 75 A

**(5m). Wayfarers Caravan Park (Tranquil adults-only), St Hilary, Penzance, Cornwall TR20 9EF.** *01736 763326.* www.wayfarerspark.co.uk. Adult only park. Two village pubs within 1m. Tranquil award winning park beautifully landscaped, marked, level pitches. Excellent facilities. Graded excellent by English Tourist Council. Golf, horse riding. Coastal walks, water sports. Fishing 1m. From Penzance A30 roundabout, L on to A394. First roundabout L on to B3280 proceed for 1.5m. Wayfarers on left hand side or road. 2m from Marazion. Open: 5 May - 29 September. ★★★★ BH&HPA 5 40 A 3

## Perranporth

**(1m). Perran Sands Holiday Park (Haven), Perran Sands, Perranporth, Cornwall TR6 0AQ.** *0871 2310871.* www.caravancamping.co.uk. Heated indoor pool, daytime and evening entertainment for all the family. All-weather multi sports court. Adventure playground. Very near beach, golf course nearby. Near the Eden Project. David Bellamy Gold Conservation Award. From Exeter take A30 through Devon and Cornwall. 1m beyond Wind Farm roundabout (Mitchell) turn R on to B3285 towards Perranporth. Perran

# SOUTH WEST

Sands is on the R before going down hill into Perranporth. Open: 18 March - 31 October. ★★★★ BH&HPA 346 1000

**(2.5m). Perran Springs Holiday Park, Goonhavern, Perranporth, Cornwall TR4 9QG.** *01872 540568.* www.perransprings. co.uk. Award winning, friendly, quiet family park, 22 acres 120 units in total (for tourers or tents). Private stocked coarse fishing lakes, nature trail and pond, shop, caravan holiday homes to hire and buy, eurotents, spacious level pitches, hook-ups, play area, laundrette, panoramic countryside views. David Bellamy Gold Conservation Award. Owner supplied copy. Leave A30 turn R on to the B3285 'Perranporth'. Follow brown tourism signs marked 'Perran Springs' for 1.5m. Entrance to park on right hand side. Open: 27 May - 17 September. ★★★★ BH&HPA 120 12

**(1m). Perranporth Caravan Holidays, Perran Sands, Perranporth, Cornwall TR6 0AE.** *01872 572385.* www.caravans-cornwall.co.uk. All facilities of adjacent Perran Sands Holiday Village are available to holiday makers, including shop, club, heated swimming pool etc. Some charges apply. 5mins drive to golf. 10mins drive to shops in village. 20mins drive to cinema. A30, follow signs to Perranporth and from The New Inn the park entrance is 1.25m on the R. Open: 1 April - 31 October. ★★★ BH&HPA 16

### Polzeath

**Tristram Caravan & Camping Park, Polzeath, Cornwall PL27 6UG.** *01208 862215.* www.polzeathcamping.co.uk. 150 mixed pitches in total. On clifftop overlooking beach with own private access. Site is fenced off for safety. Booking advisable in school holidays. Fishing, surfing, boating, skiing, golf, potholing, all nearby. AA 3 pennants. Owner supplied copy. 7m N of Wadebridge via B3314 road signs to Polzeath. Open: 6 April - 31 October. BH&HPA 150

### Portscatho

**(14m). Treloan Coastal Holidays, Treloan Lane, Gerrans, Portscatho, Cornwall TR2 5EF.** *01872 580349.* www.treloancoastalholidays.co.uk. Child and dog friendly, petting corner, Daily Telegraph No 1 family friendly campsite. Overlooking a spectacular panorama of the south coast, Treloan provides basic touring facilities in peaceful surroundings. Three secluded coves, the coastal footpath and villages with shops all within few minutes walk. Also self catering static vans and tourers. Winter storage, season pitches. 60 mixed pitches in total. A30 take A3076 to Truro then A390 to St Austell. Take A3078 to St Mawes. At Trewithian turn to Gerrans/Portscatho until church where Treloan Lane runs alongside the 'Royal Standard' pub. Open: All year. NCC 60 60 60A 5 1

### Redruth

**(6m). Caddy's Corner Lodges, Carnmenellis, Redruth, Cornwall TR16 6PH.** *01209 860275.* www.caddyslodges.org.uk. Static caravans occupy a small sheltered garden site with picnic tables and BBQ. Overlook open moorland and fields with views towards Falmouth and The Lizard. Showers. Laundry room. Owner supplied copy. 6m from Helston. A30 to Redruth then B3297 towards Helston. After 1m turn L towards Stithians. After 4m turn R opposite Carnmenellis PO. Open: 22 April - 31 October. 5

**(2m). Cambrose Touring Park, Portreath Road, Redruth, Cornwall TR16 4HT.** *01209 890747.* www.cambrosetouring-park.co.uk. Small, family run park. Heated outdoor pool from May to September. Adventure playground, mini football pitch away from camping area. Wet weather room. Shops, doctor, golf within 2m. Off B3303 Redruth to Portreath. Pass Treasure Park, first R, SP Porthtowan 100yd on L. Open: 22 April - 31 October. ★★★ 60

**(2m). Lanyon Holiday Park, Loscombe Lane, Four Lanes, Redruth, Cornwall TR16 6LP.** *01209 313474.* www.lanyon-holidaypark.co.uk. Lovely family run park set in beautiful Cornish countryside looking out towards the sea. Heated covered pool, games room, bar and restaurant, play park, laundrette, 3 modern toilet and shower blocks, pets welcome - large dog walking paddock. Village 10mins walk with pubs, shops and bus stop. Within 2m fishing, water sports, horse riding, walking, cycling path. Cinema, market indoor/outdoor, leisure centre 3m. Beach 5m. Sorry no young groups. On B3297 Redruth to Helston road within the confines of Four Lanes village. Open: 1 April - 31 October. ★★★★ BH&HPA NCC 105 105 15 2

**(2m). St Day Holiday Park, St Day, Redruth, Cornwall TR16 5LE.** *01209 820459.* www.stday.co.uk. Small, quiet site central for south Cornwall. Open close-mown meadow screened by hedging. Owner supplied copy. E of Redruth on B3298, site SP. Open: 1 April - 31 October. BH&HPA 15 35 A 43

**(1.5m). Tehidy Holiday Park, Harris Mill, Illogan, Redruth, Cornwall TR16 4JQ.** *01209 216489.* www.tehidy.co.uk. A quiet multi award family site. Close to sandy beaches, gardens and major attractions. Woodland, walks from site. Laundrette. Showers. Games room. Shops, doctors 0.5m, PO 1m. Playground, payphone, off licence. David Bellamy Gold Conservation Award. Take B3300 out of Redruth, L at fork, L again at Cornish Arms pub. Open: 24 March - 3 November. ★★★★ BH&HPA 11 11 19A 20 4

### Saltash

**(4m). Dolbeare Park, Landrake, Saltash, Cornwall PL12 5AF.** *01752 851332.* www.dolbeare.co.uk. We are located in beautiful countryside but just 1m from A38. Flat and gently sloping. Hardstanding with electric. Plymouth, Looe, Eden project in 20mins. Children's play area. Dog walk. David Bellamy Silver Conservation Award. 4m W of Saltash via A38 to Landrake. Then R just after footbridge. We are 1m on right hand side. Open: All year. ★★★★★ BH&HPA 54 54 30A

### St Agnes

**(2m). Beacon Cottage Farm, Beacon Drive, St Agnes, Cornwall TR5 0NU.** *01872 552347.* www.beaconcottagefarmholidays.co.uk. Small secluded park. 5mins walk to sandy beach. Spectacular coastal scenery. Ideal for touring Cornwall. Razor points. Telephone. Free showers and hot water. Laundry and dishwashing facilities. Gas available. Play area. Dog exercise field. Leave A30 at roundabout and follow B3277 to St Agnes at mini-roundabout turn L towards Chapel Porth and follow signs to park. Site is SP. Open: 1 April - 30 September. ★★★★ BH&HPA 70 70 70A

**(1m). Presingoll Farm, Penwinnick Road, St Agnes, Cornwall TR5 0PB.** *01872 552333.* www.presingollfarm.co.uk. The site is 2m from the north coast surfing beaches. The fully serviced village is only a walking distance of about 0.75m. Many leisure facilities are within 2-3m. Dairy produce available. AA 3 pennants. Owner supplied copy. Off A30. At Chyverton Cross roundabout take B3277 for St Agnes. Park about 3m on the right hand side. Open: 1 April - 31 October. 3 90

# SOUTH WEST

**(0.75m). St Agnes Beacon Caravan Club Site, Beacon Drive, St Agnes, Cornwall TR5 0NU.** 01872 552345. www.caravanclub.co.uk. Panoramic views of Cornish coastline from this gently sloping site. Quiet and peaceful off peak. Conveniently located for some of the best beaches in Cornwall, good area for walking. Dog walk on site. Tradesman calls. Advance booking advised mid-June to August. No sanitation. Recycling facilities. MV service point. Bathing off this coastline can be dangerous, please note local notices. Members only. No tents. See website for standard directions to site. Open: 30 March - 1 October. NCC ⚐ 🐕 ♿ ✎ ⊟ ☼ 🚗 112⛺ 112🚐

## St Austell

**(3m). Carlyon Bay Caravan & Camping Park, Cypress Avenue, Carlyon Bay, St Austell, Cornwall PL25 3RE.** 01726 812735. www.carlyonbay.net. Path to beach. 1.5m from the Eden Project. SP off the A3082. Turn off A390 at Britannia Inn roundabout then first R to Cypress Avenue. Open: 1 April - 1 October. ★★★★★ ⊟ ⚐ 🐕 ♿ ✎ ⊘ ⊟ ☼ 🚗 ≈ ✖ ⛱ 🏊 ⚽ 50⛺ 130🚐 A

**(4m). Carnmoggas Holiday Park, Little Polgooth, St Austell, Cornwall PL26 7DD.** 01726 74170. www.carnmoggas.com. Small family park. Licensed club house. Heated indoor pool. Snooker, skittles and pool. Pets welcome. Indoor bowling greens. Sandy Pentewan beach 3m and weekly markets at St Austell. Owner supplied copy. Between A390 and B3273. Open: All year. BH&HPA ⚐ 🐕 ♿ ❋ ⛱ ♿ 🚐 30⛺

**(10m). Croft Farm Holiday Park, Luxulyan, St Austell, Cornwall PL30 5EQ.** 01726 850228. www.croftfarm.co.uk. Quiet, sheltered park conveniently located close to St Austell Bay with its spectacular coastline and the beautiful Luxulyan Valley. Children allowed. 1m from the Eden Project. GS. David Bellamy Gold Conservation Award. Follow directions to Eden Project from Tywardreath Highway, then follow road signs to Luxulyan village. Park is on the L, 0.75m from village. Open: 21 March - 21 January. ★★★★ BH&HPA ⊟ 🐕 ♿ ✎ ⚐ ♿ ⊘ ⊟ ☼ 🚗 ≈ ✖ ⛱ 🏊 ⚽ 🎾 9⛺ 5A 3🚐 1🏠

**(1m). Holigan Woods Holiday Park, St. Ewe, St Austell, Cornwall PL26 6EZ.** 01726 842714. www.heliganwoods.co.uk. 12 acres, grassy site with mature trees and bushes. Part sloping and sheltered overlooking Mevagissey Bay. Close by the Lost Garden of Heligan. Facilities of Pentewan sands including own private beach freely available to customers of Heligan Woods. No single sex groups, no jet skis. On site warden. Secure caravan and boat storage available. 6m S of St Austell, W off B3273 (Gorran) road. Open: 10 January - 21 November. ★★★★ BH&HPA ⊟ ⚐ 🐕 ✎ ⊟ ☼ 🚗 ≈ ⛱ ♿ ⚽ 85⛺ 85🚐 30A

**(5m). Meadow Lakes (was Trencreek), Hewas Water, St Austell, Cornwall PL26 7JG.** 01726 882540. www.meadow-lakes.co.uk. Also available 4 lodges and 9 bungalows. Many farmyard animals. Perfect for families with young children. Coarse fishing. Lakes. Playgrounds. Tennis court. David Bellamy Silver Conservation Award. On B3287, A390 take Taragony turn off - we are 1m off this road. Open: 15 March - 15 January. ★★★★ BH&HPA NCC ⊟ ⚐ 🐕 ♿ ✎ ⚐ ♿ ⊘ ⊟ ☼ 🚗 ≈ ⛱ ☼ 🚗 S 200🚐 A 37⛺ 6🏠

**(1.5m). River Valley Holiday Park, London Apprentice, St Austell, Cornwall PL26 7AP.** 01726 73533. www.rivervalleyholidaypark.co.uk. A quiet family park set in the Pentewan Valley with an off-road cycle trail to the beach. No under 21s. Just off B3273, 1.5m from St Austell in the small hamlet of London Apprentice. Open: 16 April - 7 October. ★★★★★ BH&HPA ⊟ ⚐ 🐕 ✎ ⚐ ♿ ⊟ ☼ 🚗 ≈ ⛱ ♿ 40🚐 A 80⛺

 **(10m). Seaview International Holiday Park (St Austell), Boswinger, St Austell, Cornwall PL26 6LL.** 01726 843425. www.seaviewinternational.com. Large, level pitches for touring caravans, motorhomes and tents alike. With views across the bay. Close to the Eden Project, Lost Gardens of Heligan, and several beautiful beaches. With centrally heated facilities, extensive children's play area, award winning caravans, and a heated outdoor pool. It's no wonder this is a multi award winning park. Four times 'Best in Britain', AA Five Pennant and Five Star Rose Award, it's certainly something to write or email home about. For a free brochure write, phone or email ( holidays@seaviewinternational.com). From St Austell, take B3273, signed Mevagissey. Prior to village, turn R following brown signs (avoids narrow streets). 3.5m from Mevagissey. Open: 31 March - 27 October. ★★★★★ 5 BH&HPA ⊟ 🐕 ♿ ✎ ⚐ ♿ ⊘ ⊟ ☼ 🚗 ≈ ⛱ ♿ 201⛺ 201🚐 174A 25⛺ 3🏠

**(2m). Sun Valley Holiday Park, Pentewan Road, St Austell, Cornwall PL26 6DJ.** 01726 843266. www.sunvalleyholidays.co.uk. Ideal touring centre situated in wooded valley 1m from the sea. Licensed club and indoor swimming pool. Tennis courts, indoor & outdoor play facilities, on site entertainment. Rabbitland, resident donkeys and goats. From St Austell take B3273 to Mevagissey. Park 2.5m on R. Open: 1 April - 30 October. ★★★★ BH&HPA ⚐ 🐕 ♿ ✎ ⚐ ♫ ♿ ⊘ ⊟ ☼ 🚗 ≈ ✖ ⛱ 🏊 ♿ 🎾 28🚐 A 130⛺

**(7m). Tregarton Park, Gorran, Mevagissey, St Austell, Cornwall PL26 6NF.** 01726 843666. www.tregarton.co.uk. Large hedged pitches (125 mixed in total), either grass or hardstanding, situated in a beautiful sheltered park with glimpses of the sea through the valley. On site - shop, takeaway, large heated swimming pool. 2 mins from fabulous beaches and the 'Lost Gardens of Heligan', 20 mins from the 'Eden Project'. Sports facilities nearby including golf and fishing. Travel S on B3273. Turn R at top of Pentewan Hill, 3m on right hand side. Open: 1 April - 30 October. ★★★★ BH&HPA ⊟ ⚐ 🐕 ♿ ✎ ⚐ ⊘ ⊟ ☼ 🚗 ≈ ✖ ⛱ ♿ 🎾 21⛺ 109🚐 109A

**(10m). Trelispen Caravan & Camping Park, Gorran Haven, St Austell, Cornwall PL26 6NT.** 01726 843501. www.trelispen.co.uk. Level & sheltered park, near beaches and cliffs (0.5m) with private nature reserve. Hot showers and hot water to basins. Shop & PO 0.5m. Doctors 2m. Cafe/restaurant, bottled gas supply, dairy produce all available nearby. Golf course 10m. Take B3273 from St Austell, for Mevagissey then road for Gorran Haven. Open: 1 April - 31 October. ★★ BH&HPA ⚐ 🐕 ♿ ✎ ⚐ 🚗 ≈ ⛱ 10⛺ 10🚐 40A

**(9m). Treveor Farm Caravan & Camping Park, Gorran, St Austell, Cornwall PL26 6LW.** 01726 842387. www.treveorfarm.co.uk. Coarse fishing. Village shop, PO, pub, coastal path and beaches within 1m. Lost Gardens of Heligan - 3m, Mevagissey - 5m, Railway Station - 10m, Eden Project is 12m. Take B3273 from St Austell having passed Pentewan beach, go up hill and turn R to Gorran. After about 4m turn R at sign boards. Open: 1 April - 16 October. ⊟ ⚐ 🐕 ✎ ⚐ ⊟ ☼ 🚗 50🚐 A

## St Austell Bay

**Par Sands Holiday Park, St Austell Bay, Cornwall PL24 2AS.** 01726 812868. www.chycor.co.uk/parsands. Level site with large friendly beach within 2mins walk of reception. Crazy golf and children's playground. Indoor heated pool with aquaslide. Tennis. Bowls. Pets welcome. Takeaway meals, cafe/restaurant available nearby. 0.5m E of Par off A3082. Open: 27 March - 30 October. ★★★★ BH&HPA ⊟ 🐕 ♿ ✎ ⚐ ♿ ⊘ ⊟ ☼ 🚗 ≈ ⛱ ♿ 🎾 280⛺

# SOUTH WEST

## St Columb Major

**Gnome World Touring Park, Indian Queens, St Columb Major, Cornwall TR9 6HN.** 01726 860812. summerlaneparks.co.uk. 5 acre quiet, level, relaxing park with beautiful views over Goss Moor and beyond. Central for touring Cornwall. No bars or amusements. Pay phone. Owner supplied copy. Situated off the new by-pass at Indian Queens. CS984. Open: 1 March - 31 December. 50 25

**(1m). Southleigh Manor Naturist Holiday Park, St Columb Major, Cornwall TR9 6HY.** 01637 880938. www.southleigh-manor.com. Licensed bar and dining area. Heated outdoor swimming pool, sauna and spa bath. Play area. Shop opens in high season only. Very family orientated. Member of CCBN. Only open to naturist couples and families. E of St Columb Major. A3059 SP Springfield park centre. Open: 16 April - 31 October. 5 30 15 4 2

**(1m). Trewan Hall Camping & Caravanning Club site, Trewan Hall, St Columb Major, Cornwall TR9 6DB.** 01637 880261. www.campingandcaravanningclub.co.uk. Camping and Caravanning Club members only. All units accepted. Showers, hot snacks available, telephone, chemical toilet disposal points, swimming pool. The site is set in the midst of 36 acres of woodland. The Eden Project is just 13m away. David Bellamy Gold Conservation Award. From intersection A3059 and A39 go N on A39 for 1.5m, turn L, site 0.5m on L. Open: 8 May - 14 September. NCC 200 200

## St Ives

**(0.5m). Ayr Holiday Park, Ayr, St Ives, Cornwall TR1 1EJ.** 01736 795855. www.ayrholidaypark.co.uk. The only holiday park in St Ives itself - 10 min walk to beaches, harbour & town centre. Beautiful coastal views. Family-friendly campsite. Dogs allowed with permission. 0.5m from town centre turn off B3306 into Bullans Lane or Carnellis Road and then to Ayr Terrace. Open: All year. ★★★★ BH&HPA 15 35 A 43

**(2.5m). Balnoon Camping Site, Halsetown, St Ives, Cornwall TR26 3JA.** 01736 795431. Sheltered site 2m from sea. Facilities nearby, public house, horse riding, golf course, fishing, coastal footpath. AA 2 pennants. From A30 take A3074 SP St Ives, L at second mini-roundabout. SP Tate St Ives (B3311) and second R SP (Balnoon) about 3m from A30. Open: 22 April - 31 October. 2 5 8

**(1m). Hellesveor Caravan & Camping Site, St Ives, Cornwall TR26 3AD.** 01736 795738. Riding, fishing and golf course nearby. Doctors surgery 1m. Owner supplied copy. On B3306 Land's End to St Ives. 1m to town centre and beaches. 0.5m to shop and PO. Open: All year. 8 A 27

**(2m). Little Trevarrack Holiday Park, Laity Lane, Carbis Bay, St Ives, Cornwall TR26 3HW.** 01736 797580. www.little-trevarrack.co.uk. A well maintained and spacious landscaped park, ideal for family holidays with a range of superb modern facilities. Some pitches with sea views. About 1m from the stunning Carbis Bay beach and the coastal footpath into St Ives. High season bus service from the site into St Ives. David Bellamy Silver Conservation Award. From A30 take A3074 to St Ives. SP L opposite turning for Carbis Bay Beach. Straight across at next crossroads. About 500 metres on R. Open: 1 April - 30 September. ★★★★ BH&HPA 235 235

**(2.5m). Penderleath Caravan & Camping Park, Towednack, St Ives, Cornwall TR26 3AF.** 01736 798403. www.penderleath.co.uk. Set in classified area of outstanding natural beauty with unrivalled views. Peaceful, family run and supervised park. Quiet 'Olde Worlde' licensed bar on site. 2m to St Ives local bus service, shop. Own bus in high season. Off B3311 from St Ives take 1st R turn after Halsetown. After 0.25m take L fork, second L. Open: 1 April - 31 October. ★★★★ BH&HPA 25 25

**(2m). Polmanter Touring Park, Halsetown, St Ives, Cornwall TR26 3LX.** 01736 795640. www.polmanter.com. Family park with lovely sea views, within walking distance of St Ives & beaches. Swimming pool. Tennis courts. Family lounge. Games room. Lounge bar. TV. Golf & fishing 2m. Off B3311, take HR route off the A30 to St Ives. Open: 1 April - 3 November. ★★★★★ BH&HPA 210 210 43

**(4.5m). Sunny Meadow Holiday Park, Lelant Downs, Hayle, St Ives, Cornwall TR27 6LL.** 01736 752243. www.sunnymeadowholidaypark.co.uk. Small family run site, quiet and ideally placed for touring Cornwall. Close to premier tourist attraction. Coach route. Owner supplied copy. Off A30 by-pass, sign for St Ives (B3311). Open: All year. BH&HPA 7

## St Mabyn

**(5m). St Mabyn Holiday Park, Longstone Road, St Mabyn, Cornwall PL30 3BY.** 01208 841677. www.stmabynholidaypark.co.uk. At St Mabyn Holida Park you can enjoy idyllic touring or self-catering holidays (holida homes for sale) away from the hustle and bustle of normal everyday life. David Bellamy Silver Conservation Award. A389 to Wadebridge. Turn R to Camelford on B3266. After 5m, take 2nd L to St Mabyn. Park is on R. Open: 15 March - 1 November. 130 130 20

## Tintagel

**(0.25m). The Headland Caravan & Camping Site, Atlantic Road, Tintagel, Cornwall PL34 0DE.** 01840 770239. www.headlandcaravanpark.co.uk. All types of fishing, golf, horse riding available within 6m. 15 mins walk to local beach. From B3263 through village to site, follow brown signs. 3mins walk to centre of Tintagel. 2mins walk from coastal path. Open: 22 April - 31 October. BH&HPA 20 20 A 30

**(1.5m). Trewethett Farm Caravan Club Site, Trethevy, Tintagel, Cornwall PL34 0BQ.** 01840 770222. www.caravanclub.co.uk. The views from here are breathtaking as the site boasts a clifftop setting, overlooking Bossiney Cove with its safe sandy beach. Fishing, golf and NCN route nearby, good area for walking. Facilities for disabled. Non-members and tent campers admitted. See website for standard directions to site. Open: 23 March - 5 November. ★★★★★ NCC 142 142

## Torpoint

**(10m). Carbeil Holiday Naturist Park, Trelliddon Lane, Downderry, Torpoint, Cornwall PL11 3LS.** 01503 250636. www.carbeil.co.uk. Sheltered, flat, easily accessible family run park under new ownership. 500yd from shingle and rocky beach. Swimming pool and table tennis. Ideal for coastal walks along National Trust footpaths. Off B3247 near Downderry. Open: 1 March - 31 October. BH&HPA 10 A 16

**(6m). Whitsand Bay Holiday Park, Millbrook, Torpoint, Cornwall PL10 1JZ.** 01752 822597. www.whitsandbay-holidays.co.uk. 8m from Plymouth with panoramic views. South-east Cornwall's award winning park. Full range of facilities including heated pool. Club with entertainment. Free colour brochure. Off

# SOUTH WEST

B3247. Open: All year. **BH&HPA** [icons] 20 [icons]

## Truro

**(2.5m). Carnon Downs Caravan Park Affiliated Caravan Club Site,** Carnon Downs, Truro, Cornwall TR3 6JJ. *01872 862283*. www.carnon-downs-caravanpark.co.uk. Very easy access. Restaurant nearby. David Bellamy Gold Conservation Award. Between Truro and Falmouth off A39 at Carnon Downs roundabout. Open: All year. ★★★★★ **BH&HPA** [icons] 120 [icons]

**(6m). Chacewater Park (Adults only),** Cox Hill, Chacewater, Truro, Cornwall TR4 8LY. *01209 820762*. www.chacewaterpark.co.uk. Flat, grassy, quiet caravan park central for touring west Cornwall. Exclusively for adults over 30. Dogs allowed on touring pitches by prior agreement only. From A30 take A3047 to Scorrier, L at Crossroads Hotel take B3298 1.25m, L to Chacewater 0.75m, SP to park. Open: 22 April - 2 October. ★★★★ **BH&HPA** [icons] 20 [icons] 100 [icons] 5A

**(5m). Chiverton Caravan & Touring Park,** Blackwater, Truro, Cornwall TR4 8HS. *01872 560667*. www.chivertonpark.co.uk. Limited facilities for the disabled. Dogs allowed. Quiet family run park. Shop, laundry room, children's play area. PO and shop in Blackwater, doctors in St Agnes/Chacewater. Swimming, surfing, golf, fishing, horse riding within 5m. Sauna, steam room, gym. Fully heated toilet and shower block. Free Wi-Fi. From A30 Chiverton roundabout take B3277 to St Agnes, 0.5m turn L. Park 200yd on L. Open: 5 March - 1 November. **BH&HPA** [icons] 100 [icons]

[PREMIER PARKS 2011] **(6m). Cosawes Touring and Camping Park,** Perran-ar-Worthal, Truro, Cornwall TR3 7QS. *01872 863724*. www.cosawestouringandcamping.co.uk. Tents, tourers, motorhomes, RVs welcome. New toilet/shower block. 100 acre wooded valley between Truro and Falmouth. Safe, peaceful, friendly. Wi-Fi, hardstandings. GS. AA 4 pennants. David Bellamy Silver Conservation Award. Off A39 midway between Truro and Falmouth. Open: All year. 4 **BH&HPA** [icons] 25 [icons] 25 [icons] 20A

**(6m). Killiwerris Touring Park (Tranquil adults-only),** Penstraze, Chacewater, Truro, Cornwall TR4 8PF. *01872 561356*. www.killiwerris.co.uk. ADULTS ONLY PARK. Smartly kept. Central for sightseeing. Horse riding, golf course, fishing, local shops all within 1m. Travelling W along A30. At Chiverton Cross roundabout, (about 6m E of Redruth) take 3rd exit SP St Agnes, then 1st exit SP Blackwater. In 500yd turn L, into Kea Downs Road. Site on R in 1m. Open: All year. ★★★★ **BH&HPA** [icons] 10 [icons] 20 [icons]

**(17m). Merrose Farm Caravan Club Site,** Portscatho, Truro, Cornwall TR2 5EL. *01872 580380*. www.caravanclub.co.uk. Set in 14 acres with 178 16 amp hook-ups (and 37 hardstandings). Immaculate toilet block. Children's play area & dog walk. Small shop. Accessed from A3078. Open: 23 March - 5 November. **NCC** [icons] 178 [icons] 178 [icons]

**(2m). Penrose Holiday Park,** Goonhavern, Nr Perranporth, Truro, Cornwall TR4 9QF. *01872 573185*. www.penroseholidaypark.com. No club or bar. Quiet family run park for families & couples. Beautifully landscaped gardens, shop, takeaway, off licence. Peaceful site in ideal location for touring. 1 RV pitch in with tourers. 2m from Perranporth. Open April 1-October 31 (tourers), all year (statics). From the A30 turn R on to the B3285 Perranporth. Site 1.5m on L. 2.5m from Perranporth beach. Open: 1 April - 31 October. ★★★★ **BH&HPA** [icons] 100 [icons] 12 [icons]

**(8m). Porthtowan Tourist Park,** Mile Hill, Porthtowan, Truro, Cornwall TR4 8TY. *01209 890256*. www.porthtowantouristpark.co.uk. Quiet family site with level grass pitches. 1m from Blue Flag beach & village. Ideal for touring Cornwall, close to Coastal Path & Mineral Tramway Trail. David Bellamy Silver Conservation Award. Drive along A30 until you reach the exit 'Redruth to Porthtowan'. Cross the A30, and continue through North Country to 'T' junction, turn R up the hill. About 0.5m park entrance on L. Open: 1 April - 2 October. ★★★★ **BH&HPA** [icons] 10 [icons] 40 [icons]

**(1.5m). Roseville Holiday Park,** Goonhaven, Truro, Cornwall TR4 9LA. *01872 572448*. www.rosevilleholidaypark.co.uk. 2m from Perranporth, ideal surfing/ walking beach. 10m from Eden Project. Excellent location for touring all sites in Cornwall. 3 pennants. Recommended for mature and young families. 8m from New Quay, 10m from Truro. On B3285. Open: 6 April - 31 October. **BH&HPA NCC** [icons] 85 [icons] A 12 [icons]

**(2.5m). Silverbow Park,** Goonhaven, Truro, Cornwall TR4 9NX. *01872 572347*. www.chycor.co.uk. No noisy clubs or bars. All weather & grass tennis & badminton courts, short mat bowls. Covered heated swimming pool. Games room. Laundry. Bath. Showers. Shops, PO, doctor, dentist in Perranporth (2.5m). Silverbow is different, tranquillity and space, very central. Renowned for cleanliness and courteous service. 90% repeats. No single sex groups. David Bellamy Gold Conservation Award. Owner supplied copy. 0.5m S Goonhavern Village. On A3075 Newquay to Redruth. Open: 24 April - 25 September. ★★★★★ **BH&HPA** [icons] 90 [icons] A 15 [icons]

**(2m). Summer Valley Touring Park,** Shortlandsend, Truro, Cornwall TR4 9DW. *01872 277878*. www.summervalley.co.uk. Quiet, family run site with excellent facilities. Site bordered by mature trees but allowing rural views. Close to County Town and superb beaches. David Bellamy Silver Conservation Award. Site SP on B3284 2.5m from Truro, 1.5m from A30. Open: 1 April - 31 October. ★★★★ 3 **BH&HPA** [icons] 20 [icons] 25 [icons] 15A

**(1.5m). Treamble Valley Caravan Club Site,** Rose, Truro, Cornwall TR4 9PR. *01872 573675*. www.caravanclub.co.uk. MV service point. Golf and water sports nearby. Facilities for walking disabled. Ideal for families. Some hardstanding, privacy cubicles, dog walk on site, storage pitches, quiet and peaceful off peak, good area for walking, beach and NCN cycle route within 5m. Members only. No tents. See website for standard directions to site. Open: 23 March - 5 November. **NCC** [icons] 135 [icons] 135 [icons]

[PREMIER PARKS 2011] **(3m). Trethem Mill Touring Park,** St Just-In-Roseland, Nr St Mawes, Truro, Cornwall TR2 5JF. *01872 580504*. www.trethem.com. Small, clean, family park. Ideal location for beaches, water sports, country walks and exploring Cornwall. Still the only 5 star park on the Roseland Peninsula. David Bellamy Gold Conservation Award. Follow brown signs on A3078 for Trethem Mill. 3m N pf St Mawes. Open: 30 March - 7 October. ★★★★★ **BH&HPA** [icons] 55 [icons] 84 [icons] 30A

**(6m). Trevarth Holiday Park,** Blackwater, Truro, Cornwall TR4 8HR. *01872 560266*. www.trevarth.co.uk. A small, family run park in an excellent location for N & S coast resorts. PO 0.5m, doctor, fishing 2.5m. Golf, cinema, leisure centre 5m. No dogs. No single sex groups. Rose Award. Leave A30 at Chiverton roundabout, on to B3277 SP

# SOUTH WEST

St Agnes. At next roundabout, take road signed Blackwater, site on R in 200yd. Open: 1 April - 15 October. ★★★★ BH&HPA 🏠🚐🏕🚶🐕🍴🛒🚿🚻 35🚐 ▲ 40🛖

**Truro Caravan and Camping Park (Liskey), Greenbottom, Truro, Cornwall TR4 8QN.** 01872 560274. trurocaravanandcampingpark.co.uk. 🐕🚶🏕🐾❄ 🏠♿🐕🚐🛖▲

**(10m). Veryan Camping & Caravanning Club Site, Tretheake, Veryan, Truro, Cornwall TR2 5PP.** 01872 501658. www.campingandcaravanningclub.co.uk. Set in 9 acres with on-site facilities including: laundrette, coarse fishing, playground, games room, TV room. Beach and coastal path 1.5m. Holiday lodge to let on site. Close by is the Eden Project. The Cornish coast near the site is dotted with unspoilt beaches and tiny fishing villages. A little paradise on the Roseland Peninsula. All units accepted. Non-members welcome. Special deals available for families and backpackers. 2m S of Tregony on A3078 turn L for Veryan after petrol station and follow international signs. Site on L. Open: 1 April - 31 October. ★★★★ NCC 🏠🐕🚶🏕🐾🍴🛒🚿🚻♿ 150🚐 150🛖 ▲

## Wadebridge

**(3m). Dinham Farm Caravan & Camping Park, St Minver, Wadebridge, Cornwall PL27 6RH.** 01208 812878. www.dinhamfarm.co.uk. Lovely, secluded family park overlooking the river Camel. Surrounded by trees and shrubs. Near Rock, Polzearth and Daymer bays. Heated swimming pool. Owner supplied copy. Off B3314. Open: 1 April - 15 October. 🏠🐕🚶🏕 40🚐 ▲ 27🛖

**(4.5m). Gunvenna Touring Caravan & Camping Park, St Minver, Polzeath, Wadebridge, Cornwall PL27 6QN.** 01208 862405. www.chycor.co.uk/gunvenna. Within easy reach of safe, sandy beaches. Play area. Laundry facilities. Shower blocks. Shaver points. Hair-dryers. Indoor heated swimming pool. Wi-Fi available. Golf, cinema and shops in Wadebridge 4m. AA 4 pennants. No cats or dogs. No single sex groups. On the B3314. Easy access. Open: 9 May - 15 October. 4 BH&HPA 🏠🚐🐕🚶🏕🍴🚿🚻♿ 75🚐 ▲ 40🛖

**(0.5m). Little Bodieve Holiday Park, Bodieve Road, Wadebridge, Cornwall PL27 6EG.** 01208 812323. www.little-bodieve.co.uk. Heated outdoor swimming pool, waterslide. Club house with live entertainment in high season. Bar meals. Nearest to Camel Trail. 25mns car drive to Eden project. Club rallies welcome to

Luxury caravans for hire or sale. 1m N of Wadebridge. Take A39 at Camelford turn N at second roundabout in Wadebridge on B3314. Site is SP 600yd R. 4m from beach. Open: 1 April - 31 October. ★★★★ BH&HPA 🏠🚐🐕🚶🏕🐾🍴🛒🚿🚻 195🚐 ▲ 95🛖

**(3m). Little Dinham Woodland Caravan Park, St Minver, Rock, Wadebridge, Cornwall PL27 6RH.** 01208 812538. www.littledinham.co.uk. Children's play area. Heated indoor swimming pool. The site looks on to Dinham Creek and is excellent for bird watchers/nature lovers. 3m away from Wadebridge and Rock. Owner supplied copy. Take A30 to Cornwall. Exit at Bodmin Junction. Proceed through Bodmin to Wadebridge. At Wadebridge, take B3314 to Rock/Polzeath, follow the road and after 3m SP Little Dinham Caravan park on the L. Open: 19 March - 31 October. ★★★★ BH&HPA 🏠🐕🚶🏕🐾 60🚐 ▲

**(7m). Lundynant Caravan Site, Polzeath, Wadebridge, Cornwall PL27 6QX.** 01208 862268. www.lundynant.co.uk. 🏠🐕 20🚐 ▲ 50🛖

**(4m). Music Water Touring Park, Rumford, Wadebridge, Cornwall PL27 7SJ.** 01841 540257. Fees on application. Pets corner inc donkeys. Beautiful views. 3m from sea, sailing, golf. Dogs allowed, swimming pool, games room, bar on site. Fishing, shops, riding available all nearby. AA 3 pennants. 4m S of Padstow from A39 Wadebridge to St Columb road. Turn N on B3274 for 2m the W for 500yd to site. Open: 1 April - 31 October. 3 🏠🐕🚶🏕🐾🍴🚿🚻♿ 20🚐 70🚐 ▲ 2🛖

**(7m). Polzeath Beach Holiday Park, Trenant Nook, Polzeath, Wadebridge, Cornwall PL27 6ST.** 01208 863320. www.polzeathbeachholidaypark.com. 18 hole golf course 1.5m, swimming fitness centre, club house open to non-members. Shops and PO are 500-600yd away. Owner supplied copy. From roundabout at Wadebridge boundary take B3314 to Polzeath. In Polzeath turn R, opposite Spar shop and carry on through car park and over Ford into caravan park. Open: 2 April - 29 October. ★★★★ BH&HPA 🐕 66🛖

**(1m). Southwinds Touring Caravan & Camping Park, Polzeath, Wadebridge, Cornwall PL27 6QU.** 01208 863267. www.polzeathcamping.co.uk. Quiet and peaceful with beautiful sea and panoramic rural views yet only 1m from the beach. Flat and well-drained with showers and laundry. Shop, cafe/restaurant, farm produce available next to site. Booking advisable in school holidays. AA 3 pennants.

Owner supplied copy. N of Wadebridge via B3314 road signs to Polzeath. Open: 1 May - 15 September. 3 BH&HPA 🏠🐕🚶🏕🐾🍴🛒🚿🚻♿ 50🚐 100🛖 ▲

**(3m) St Minver Holiday Park, St Minver, Wadebridge, Cornwall PL27 6RR.** 01208 862305. www.parkdeanholidays.co.uk. Set in beautiful woodland, park facilities include indoor pool, kids' club and amusements. Bar, takeaway and live family entertainment. Golf 1m. Wadebridge, shops & cinema 3m. A389, then A39 - follow signs for Port Isaac. Open: 14 March - 13 November. ★★★★ BH&HPA NCC 🏠🐕🚶🏕🐾🍴🚿🚻♿ 343🛖

**(2m). The Laurels Holiday Park, Padstow Road, Whitecross, Wadebridge, Cornwall PL27 7JQ.** 01209 313474. www.thelaurelsholidaypark.co.uk. Just 6m from Padstow & an ideal base for exploring N Cornwall, this site offers grassy pitches with hook-up available. Kids' play area. Situated between Wadebridge & Padstow, off A389 Padstow Road, at its junction with A39. Open: 1 April - 31 October. ★★★★ BH&HPA NCC 🏠🚐🐕🚶🏕🐾🍴🛒 4🚐 50🚐 50🛖

**(3.5m). Trewince Farm Holiday Park, St Issey, Wadebridge, Cornwall PL27 7RL.** 01208 812830. http://www.trewince-farm-holidaypark.co.uk. Quiet family site, 4m from Padstow. Shop on site high season. Nearby St Issey offers pubs. Wetsuit washing facilities. BBQ on site weekly. Off A389 Wadebridge to Padstow. Open: 1 April - 31 October. ★★★★ BH&HPA 🏠🐕🚶🏕🐾🍴🛒🚿🚻♿ 61🚐 61🛖 100▲ 16🛖

**(7m). Valley Caravan Park, Old Polzeath, Wadebridge, Cornwall PL27 6SS.** 01208 862391. www.valleycaravanpark.co.uk. From Wadebridge take B3314, follow signs to Polzeath, upon descending into village take turning opposite beach between the shops. Open: 1 April - 31 October. 🐕 5🚐 60🚐 ▲ 100🛖

## DEVON
### Ashburton

**(2m). Parkers Farm Holiday Park, Higher Mead Farm, Ashburton, Devon TQ13 7LJ.** 01364 654869. www.parkersfarm.co.uk. Friendly family park. Set in beautiful countryside with spectacular open views. Children's and pets paradise. Regular farm visits to feed the animals. Dogs welcome. Short breaks available. 12m to coast. David Bellamy Silver Conservation Award. From Exeter, take the A38 to Plymouth. When SP 'Plymouth 26', take the second L, SP to Woodland

# SOUTH WEST

and Denbury. Friendly family park. Set in beautiful countryside with spectacular open views. Children's and pets paradise. Regular farm walks to feed the animals. Dogs welcome. Short breaks available. 12m to coast. David Bellamy Silver Conservation Award. Open: 26 March - 29 October. ★★★★ BH&HPA ♀⊟⛺🐎 ⚓🎵🍴⚙🏊🚗✖🚻🏪🛒♿ 20⚡ 100⚡ ⛺ 45⛽

## Axminster

(3m). **Andrewshayes Holiday Park, Dalwood, Axminster, Devon EX13 7DY.** 01404 831225. www.andrewshayes. co.uk. Bar and takeaway. Heated outdoor swimming pool (June-September). Play park. Games room. Laundrette. Fishing 3m. Golf course 6m, cinema 8m. Beach 6m. Lovely countryside views. David Bellamy Gold Conservation Award. Off A35, 6m Honiton, 3m Axminster. Turn N at Taunton Cross (by garage/ Little Chef) signed Stockland/Dalwood. 150yd to park. Open: 31 March - 31 October. ★★★★ BH&HPA ♀⊟🐎 ⚓🎵🍴⚙🚗⚡🚻🏪🛒♿ 5⚡ 145⚡ ⛺ 100⛽

(5m). **Hawkchurch Country Park, Hawkchurch, Axminster, Devon EX13 5UL.** 0844 272 9502. www.hawkchurchpark.co.uk. Hawkchurch Country Park boasts a serene rural setting in mature woodland with dramatic views across the Axe Valley. Turn off A35 near Axminster on to B3165 turn L on to Wareham Road. Park on L. Open: 15 February - 4 January. ★★★★ BH&HPA ♀⊟🐎⚓🎵⚙🍴🚗✖ 🏪🛒🚻♿ 168⚡ ⛺ 43⛽

## Barnstaple

(2m). **Brightlycott Barton, Barnstaple, Devon EX31 4JJ.** 01271 850330. www. brightlycottbarton.co.uk. Central touring site with panoramic views of moor and estuary. Leisure centre in Barnstaple. Fishing, golf, horse riding, swimming and tennis all available nearby. Games room, play area. Water heated via solar panels in ablution block. 2m NE of Barnstaple off A39. Road to farm site is SP Brightlycott and Roborough. Open: 15 March - 15 November. ★★★ BH&HPA ⊟🐎 ♀⚓🎵🍴⚙🚗⚡🚻🏪🛒♿ 20⚡ ⛺

(4m). **Chivenor Caravan Park, Chivenor Cross, Barnstaple, Devon EX31 4BN.** 01271 812217. www.chivenorcaravanpark.co.uk. All amenities either on site or within close proximity. Centrally located for touring. Easy access off A361 Barnstaple to Ilfracombe. Small family-run site. 100yd from Tarka Trail. Open: 15 March - 15 January. ⊟🐎♀🍴⚓⚙ ⚡🚗🚻🏪🛒 30⚡ ⛺ 9⛽

**Combe Martin Beach Holiday Park, Woodlands, Combe Martin, Barnstaple, Devon EX34 0AS.** 01271 866766. www. johnfowlerholidays.com. Set in beautiful steeply sloping landscaped grounds and woodland, Combe Martin Holiday Park overlooks our private Newberry Beach (opposite) and Combe Martin public beach. Well stocked shop and lovely children's play area. On A399. Open: 1 March - 31 October. ♀⊟🐎🎵⚓🍴 ✖🏪🛒🚻♿ ⚡ 63⛽

(10m). **Greenacres Touring Caravan Park (Barnstaple), Bratton Fleming, Barnstaple, Devon EX31 4SG.** 01598 763334. Family-run park-separate part of working farm on edge of Exmoor National Park. Coast only 5m away. AA 3-pennants. Easy access from A399, M5, J27, take A361 at Little Chef (North roundabout) turn R (A399) to Blackmoor Gate about 10m. Open: 10 April - 1 October. ★★★★ 3⊟🐎♀⚓🎵⚙ 🍴🏪🛒♿ ⚡ 30⚡

(2m). **Tarka Holiday Park, Braunton Road, Ashford, Barnstaple, Devon EX31 4AU.** 01271 343691. www.tarkapark. co.uk. Sheltered grass parkland site on A361. Quality graded by the West Country Tourist Board. AA 3 pennants. Close to Tarka Trail - bike hire available. David Bellamy Gold Conservation Award. Take A361 Barnstaple to Ilfracombe road. Site is on R from Barnstaple. Open: All year. BH&HPA ♀⊟🍴🐎⚓🎵⚙⚓🌟 ⚡🚗✖🚻🏪🛒 18⚡ 35⚡ ⛺ 144⛽

### Berrynarbor

(3.5m). **Napps Caravan Site, Old Coast Road, Berrynarbor, Devon EX34 9SW.** 01271 882557. www.napps. co.uk. Modern ablution blocks. Tennis court. Heated swimming pool, paddling pool. Takeaway food. Family bar, bistro, beer garden. Adventure playground. Laundrette. Beach. Winter and summer storage. Shop, off license, games room. Nearest shops, PO, doctors, restaurants 1.5m. Fishing 0.5m; golf 2m; horse riding 3.5m. 'The 5 star site by the sea'. Situated on the edge of Exmoor. M5, J27 on to A391 for about 20m, turn R at Aller Cross roundabout, follow signs to Combe Martin (about 17m), drive through Combe Martin, Napps is 1.5m past Combe Martin beach, SP on R. Open: 3 March - 31 October. ♀ ⊟🐎⚓🎵🍴⚙🚗✖♿ 🛒🏪🚻🛁⚡ 100⚡ 100⚡ ⛺

### Bideford

(8m). **Bideford Bay Holiday Park, Bucks Cross, Bideford, Devon EX39 5DU.** 0844 0502549. www.park-resorts.com. Bar. Club. Heated outdoor & indoor pools. Laundrette. Entertainment. Fancy golf. Playground. Restaurant. Mini assault course. Sauna. Darts. Pool table. Riding stables. David Bellamy Gold Conservation Award. Leave M5 at J27 (Tiverton) and follow signs marked A361 Barnstaple. At Barnstaple take A39 - Bude, continue on this road bypassing Bideford. The park is on the right hand side in the village of Buck's Cross, about 8m W of Bideford. Open: 1 April - 31 October. ★★★★ BH&HPA NCC ⚓🐎♀✖🚻🏪🛒♿⚡ 250⛽ 🏠

(9m). **Dyke Green Farm, Clovelly, Bideford, Devon EX39 5RU.** 01237

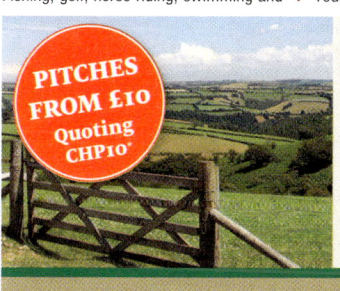

A tranquil camping and touring holiday park minutes from Lyme Regis in beautiful East Devon

- 4* holiday park.
- Licensed bar and restaurant.
- Convenience shop and childrens play area.
- Seasonal pitches.
- Mains electricity and waste disposal points.
- Caravan holiday homes for sale

PITCHES FROM £10 Quoting CHP10

*Terms and conditions apply

To book call 0844 272 9502 or visit www.hawkchurchpark.co.uk

# WOOLACOMBE BAY
### HOLIDAY PARKS · NORTH DEVON

**PITCHES FROM JUST £9 PER NIGHT**

## North Devon family escapes...

Set within North Devon's breathtaking countryside next to Woolacombe's three miles of golden Blue Flag sandy beach.

- **Level Pitches & Easy Access**
- **400 All-Weather Pitches**
- **16 amp Electric Hook-ups**

- Four Award Winning Holiday Parks • Outstanding Leisure Facilities
- Sea View Touring & Supersite Pitches • Modern Amenity Blocks
- Grass and Hard Standing Pitches • Activities For All Ages

**Call 0844 7700 386 or visit woolacombe.com/cs**

# SOUTH WEST

431699. www.dykegreenfarm.co.uk. Sheltered, level site just off roundabout at Clovelly Cross. Breakfast available at farm also bed and breakfast. Dogs under control welcome. About 1.5m S of Clovelly at junction of B3237 & A39. Open: 1 March - 31 October. 40 40

**(13m). Hartland Caravan and Camping Park, South Lane, Hartland, Bideford, Devon EX39 6DG.** 01237 441876. www.hartlandcamping.co.uk. Quiet, family run site set in 6 acres of well maintained meadows, 4mins walk to shops/PH/takeaway meals, cafe/restaurant. New toilet/shower block. Baby changing/family/disabled room. Laundry facilities. Small fishing lake. Convenient for coastal footpath, beaches and woodland walks. 2 holiday homes 6/7 berth to let, set in own gardens. Caravan storage. Open all year weather permitting. From A39 through Clovelly X roundabout, take first R. SP Hartland B3248. On entering village, site is on L. Open: All year. 20 20 A 2

**(5m). Steart Farm Touring Park, Horns Cross, Bideford, Devon EX39 5DW.** 01237 431836. www.steartfarmtouringpark.co.uk. Set in 17 acres overlooking Bideford Bay. 1m from sea. Dog exercise field. Children's playing field. From Bideford follow A39 W (signed Bude). 2m after Horns Cross, site entrance on R. Open: 4 April - 30 September. ★★★ 10 60 A

## Braunton

**(5m). Bay View Farm Caravan and Camping Park, Croyde Bay, Braunton, Devon EX33 1PN.** 01271 890501. www.bayviewfarm.co.uk. 70 mixed pitches in total. A few minutes walk to sandy beach and olde worlde village. Dogs allowed by arrangement. One week only, Saturday to Saturday limited. Golf 2m. M5, J27, take A361 then on to B3231 at Braunton. On RT approaching Croyde Village. Open: 18 April - 31 October. ★★★ BH&HPA 70 A 3

**(1m). Lobb Fields Touring and Camping Park, Saunton Road, Braunton, Devon EX33 1HG.** 01271 812090. www.lobbfields.com. Large grassy park 1.5m from Saunton beach faces S with panoramic views. Takeaway meals at weekends and high season. Golf, all shops, doctor, garages, Tarka Trail for cycling and walking 1m. Fishing 3m. All water sports nearby. From Barnstaple W on A361, 6m to Braunton. In Braunton take B3231 towards Croyde, park on R, 1m.

Open: 23 March - 28 October. ★★★★ BH&HPA 20 80 100 A

## Brixham

**(0.5m). Centry Touring Caravan & Tent Site, Centry Road, Brixham, Brixham, Devon TQ5 9EY.** 01803 856389. www.centrytouring.co.uk. Small site close to town and beaches. Showers. Milk & papers available. Shop nearby. Advance booking July and August. SAE for brochure. Approaching Brixham on 3022 follow signs for Berry Head Country Park. From Paignton follow signs for Berry Head. Open: 1 April - 30 October. ★★ BH&HPA 30 A

**(3m). Galmpton Touring Park, Greenway Road, Galmpton, Brixham, Devon TQ5 0EP.** 01803 842066. www.galmptontouringpark.co.uk. Family park with spectacular views of river Dart and close to beaches and all Torbay attractions. Immaculate facilities. Good access. No dogs in peak period. Two self-catering cottages and two studios available. A380 Torbay ring road then A379 towards Brixham, park SP on the R through Galmpton village. Open: 6 April - 7 October. ★★★★ BH&HPA 30 60 30 A

**(2m). Hillhead Caravan Club Site, Hillhead, Brixham, Devon TQ5 0HH.** 01803 853204. www.caravanclub.co.uk. This site offers some of the finest facilities on the Caravan Club network. Non-members and tent campers welcome, part sloping, toilet blocks, privacy cubicles, baby and toddler washroom, baby changing facilities, laundry, MV service pt, veg prep area, battery charging, gas and gaz, games room. Information room, club, bar, restaurant, takeaway, playground, play area, play equipment, dog walk on site, swimming pool, fishing, golf and water sports nearby. Ideal for families, good area for walking. See website for standard directions to site. Open: 23 March - 2 January. ★★★★★ NCC 239 239 A

**(1m). Landscove Holiday Park, Gillard Road, Berry Head, Brixham, Devon TQ5 9EP.** 0845 8159775. www.ParkHolidaysUK.com Indoor and outdoor heated pools. Full entertainment program including kids club. Swings and play area, walk along the coastal path to Brixham. Golf, fishing with 4m. Owner supplied copy. A380 from Exeter to Torquay, then A380 follow signs for Paignton/Brixham. Take A3022 at Paignton roundabout, follow signs for

Brixton. Turn R at traffic lights, follow signs for Berry Head. Park is located at the end of Gillard Road. Open: 30 March - 4 November. ★★★ BH&HPA NCC 27

**(1m). South Bay Holiday Park, St Mary's Road, Brixham, Devon TQ5 9QW.** 01271 866766. www.johnfowlerholidays.com. Laundrette. Indoor and outdoor pool complex. Takeaway. Convenience store. Free kids club. Sports and leisure facilities. Family club and bar. Coastal walks. Rose Award park. Owner supplied copy. From Exeter take the A38/A380/A3022 to Brixham. Just after 'Welcome to Brixham' sign follow brown sign to Upton Manor Farm (reception to South Bay HP) bringing you to the gates. Open: 13 March - 30 October. ★★★★ BH&HPA NCC 360

## Buckfastleigh

**(1.5m). Beara Farm, Colston Road, Buckfastleigh, Devon TQ11 0LW.** 01364 642026. Site is situated in an idyllic position, close by the River Dart. It is also within easy reach of the sea and Dartmoor. Fishing nearby. Steam railway and butterfly and otter park. Buckfast Abbey, Pennywell Farm all within short distance of site. From Exeter leave A38 at Dart Bridge. Follow signs to South Devon Steam Railway and Butterfly Farm. Take first L after passing entrance. SP Old Totnes Road. After 0.5m turn R, site 1m. Also SP. Open: All year. 10 10 A

## Budleigh Salterton

**Ladram Bay, Otterton, Budleigh Salterton, Devon EX9 7BX.** 01395 568398. www.ladrambay.co.uk. Family holiday park. Private beach, indoor heated pool, live entertainment 7 days a week. 2 restaurants, take away. Arcade. Beautiful countryside. 12m from motorway. David Bellamy Silver Conservation Award. Off A3052 follow signs to Ladram Bay. Open: 16 March - 28 October. ★★★★ BH&HPA 152 152 100 A 117 1

## Chudleigh

**(1m). Holmans Wood Caravan Park, Harcombe Cross, Chudleigh, Devon TQ13 0DZ.** 01626 853785. www.holmanswood.co.uk. Ideally situated for Dartmoor, Exeter and Torquay. Chudleigh town centre 1m. Seasonal pitches & storage available. Tents welcome in our meadow. Neat and level park in beautiful countryside setting. Excellent toilets/showers. David Bellamy

# SOUTH WEST

Gold Conservation Award. Follow M5 to Exeter. A38 towards Plymouth. From top of Haldon Hill, past racecourse. Park is 100yd on L. Open: 15 March - 31 October. ★★★★ BH&HPA

### Colyton

**(2m). Ashdown Caravan Park, Colyton, Devon EX24 6HY.** 01297 20292. www.ashdowncaravanpark.co.uk. Family-run park in a spacious, quiet position, no bars or clubs. Several coastal resorts within easy reach. Level pitches. Owner supplied copy. Off A3052 Lyme Regis Exeter road 3m W of Seaton, at Stafford Cross turn N towards Colyton, site 0.5m on the L. Open: 1 April - 31 October.

**(2m). Leacroft Touring Park, Colyton Hill, Colyton, Devon EX24 6HY.** 01297 552823. Quiet, peaceful site in open countryside with views to Lyme Bay. Picturesque villages and woodland walks nearby. Ideal for touring. Hardstandings. Storage facilities. SP from A3052 Sidmouth to Lyme Regis, at Stafford Cross, do not go into Colyton. Open: 20 March - 12 October. ★★★★ BH&HPA 8 118

### Combe Martin

**(1m). Manleigh Holiday Park, Rectory Road, Combe Martin, Devon EX34 0NS.** 01271 883353. www.manleighpark.co.uk. Children's play area. Outdoor pool. Dog exercise area. Bistro serving delicious home made food. Chalet, log cabins and caravans for hire. Sea 1m. Golf, cinema, indoor swimming pool within 5-6m. Owner supplied copy. M5, leave at J27 towards Barnstaple. 3rd roundabout turn R to Combe Martin. In village L turn towards Barnstaple (Church Street), 0.75m on L. Open: 28 February - 22 December. ★★★★ BH&HPA 30

**(0.25m). Newberry Valley Park, Woodlands, Combe Martin, Devon EX34 0AT.** 01271 882334. www.newberryvalleypark.co.uk. Quiet and peaceful countryside location on North Devon Coast. Combe Martin village with beach, shops, cafés, pubs within 5mins walk, just off SW coastal path. Small shop with essentials and delightful coarse fishing lake and woodland walks. David Bellamy Gold Conservation Award. On A399. NW edge of Combe Martin. Open: 1 April - 31 October. ★★★★ BH&HPA 60 60

**(4m). Stowford Farm Meadows, Berry Down, Combe Martin, Devon EX34 0PW.** 01271 882476. www.stowford.co.uk. AA 4 pennant site. Caravan service & accessories. Horse riding, mini zoo, crazy golf, indoor pool, bar. Cycle hire, shop, takeaway, restaurant, awnings and tents. Award winning caravan centre supplying Elddis, Coachman and Bailey. David Bellamy Gold Conservation Award. Leave M5, exit 27, then follow N Devon link road to Barnstaple, then A39 through Barnstaple town centre. 1m from Barnstaple turn L on to B3230. Turn R at garage. At Lynton Cross, on to A3123. Stowford Farm Meadows is 1.5m on the R, down its own private road. Open: All year. ★★★★ 4 BH&HPA 29 721

### Crediton

**(0.25m). Umberleigh Camping & Caravanning Club Site, Over Weir, Crediton, Devon EX37 9DU.** 01769 560009. www.campingandcaravanningclub.co.uk. Situated in beautiful and sheltered Taw valley. Within easy reach of beaches, surfing and swimming. Fishing on site, also games room, skittle alley, pool table, table tennis, public phone, ice-pack freezing, launderette, new tennis court with free tennis coaching for children during high season, non-members welcome. All units accepted. Special deals available for families and backpackers. Loo Of The Year (4 stars). On A377 from Barnstaple turn right, onto B3227 at Umberleigh sign, site on R in 0.2m. 8m from Barnstaple. Open: 1 April - 31 October. ★★★★ NCC 60 60

**(14m). Yeatheridge Farm Caravan & Camping Park, East Worlington, Crediton, Devon EX17 4TN.** 01884 860330. www.yeatheridge.co.uk. Indoor heated swimming pool. Coarse fishing. Working farm. Horse riding. Panoramic views. About 2.5m of woodland, nature and riverbank trails. Wi-Fi. Off B3137 (old A373) Witheridge and A377 on B3042. Open: 15 March - 3 October. ★★★★ BH&HPA NCC 85 4

### Croyde

**Ruda Holiday Park, Croyde, Devon EX33 1NY.** 0870 4580943. www.parkdeanholidays.co.uk. Enjoy direct access to famous Croyde Bay beach and learn to surf with the school on park or make use of the excellent on park facilities. David Bellamy Gold Conservation Award. Park is off B3231. Open: 16 March - 1 November. ★★★★ BH&HPA NCC 93 93 505

### Cullompton

**(5m). Forest Glade Holiday Park, Cullompton, Devon EX15 2DT.** 01404 841381. www.forest-glade.co.uk. Flat, sheltered, secluded park in forest situated on the Blackdown Hills AONB. Free heated indoor pool. Adventure play area. All-weather tennis court. Free colour brochure on request. Touring caravans must phone for access route. Golf 6m, cinema 11m, shopping centre 20m. David Bellamy Gold Conservation Award. See website for specific routes dependent on vehicle size. Open: 19 March - 1 November. ★★★★ BH&HPA 4 70 10 42

### Dartmouth

**Dartmouth Camping & Caravanning Club Site, Dartmouth Road, Stoke Fleming, Dartmouth, Devon TQ6 0RF.** 01803 770253. www.campingandcaravanningclub.co.uk. Village shop 0.5m from site. Beach, fishing 5m. Golf and country club 5m. Boat launching in Dartmouth. From A3122 turn R on to A379. Follow on, site on R after B3205 Weeke Hill. Open: 15 March - 15 November. ★★★★ NCC 95

**(2.5m). Leonards Cove, Stoke Fleming, Dartmouth, Devon TQ6 0NR.** 01803 770206. www.leonardscove.co.uk. Within village of Stoke Fleming, walking distance Blackpool Sands. Sea views from the camping/touring field. Village PO/stores. Golf & Country Club 3m. Owner supplied copy. On A379 Dartmouth to Kingsbridge. Open: 25 May - 19 Sep (tents). All year (statics). 53

**(2m). Little Cotton Caravan Park, Dartmouth, Devon TQ6 0LB.** 01803 832558. www.littlecotton.co.uk. Seven acres, level and gently sloping, some sheltered with scenic outlook. Park and ride service adjacent. Ideal touring area. Luxurious toilet and shower facilities. Golf course nearby. Leave A38 at Buckfastleigh, A384 to Totnes, from Totnes to Halwell on A381, at Halwell take A3122 Dartmouth Road. Park on R of entrance to town. Open: 13 March - 31 October. BH&HPA 10 95

**(5m). Woodlands Grove Caravan & Camping Park, Blackawton, Dartmouth, Devon TQ9 7DQ.** 01803 712598. www.woodlands-caravanpark.com. AA Campsite of the Year. Spacious pitches and tranquil surroundings. 5m to South Devon coast. Ideal for a relaxed adult break during term time - enquire for 'Adults midweek special'. Families have

# SOUTH WEST

the option of free entry into 90 acre theme park for the perfect family holiday. SP from A38 and Totnes, on A3122. Open: 30 March - 4 November. ★ ★ ★ ★ ★ BH&HPA ⛺🚐🏠♿♣♪🎣∅⛳🏊🍴× ⛱🐕⛔🍽♿¿ 50🚐 175🚐 125🏕

## Dawlish

(2m). **Cofton Country Holidays, Starcross, Dawlish, Devon EX6 8RP.** *01626 890111.* www.cofton-holidays.co.uk. Set in a secluded valley surrounded by rolling meadows, mature woods, fishing lakes and only a short drive to Dawlish Warren's Blue Flag beach. Fantastic facilities in clean tidy surroundings. David Bellamy Gold Conservation Award. Leave M5, J30, take A379 towards Dawlish for 10m. Park is on L, 0.5m after Cockwood Harbour. Open: All year. ★ ★ ★ ★ BH&HPA ⛺ ⛱🐕⛔♿♣♪🎣∅⛳🏊🍴× ⛱🐕⛔🍽♿¿🚐450🚐 🏕66

(1m). **Golden Sands Holiday Park, Week Lane, Dawlish, Devon EX7 0LZ.** *0845 8159797.* www.ParkHolidaysUK.com/mmc. Heated indoor and outdoor pool. Licensed club and free entertainment. 0.5m to safe, sandy beach. Run for families. Ideally located for a holiday in South Devon. From M5 Exeter take A379 to Dawlish. 2m after Starcross the park is SP on the L. Week Lane is second L past garage on R. Open: 1 March - 31 October. ★ ★ ★ ★ BH&HPA NCC ⛺⛱🐕♿ ♣♪∅⛳🏊🍴×⛱🐕⛔🍽♿ ¿🚐 28🏕 270

(1m). **Lady's Mile Holiday Park, Exeter Road, Dawlish, Devon EX7 0LX.** *01626 863411.* www.ladysmile.co.uk. Indoor and outdoor heated swimming pools with 100ft water chutes. Play area and games room. Takeaway food. Bar. Laundrette. Showers. Short distance Dawlish Warren beach and town. On A379 Exeter to Dawlish road. Easy access from J30, M5. Open: 31 March - 28 October. ★ ★ ★ ★ BH&HPA ⛺⛱🐕 ♣♪∅⛳🏊🍴×⛱🐕⛔🍽♿¿460🚐 460🚐 🏕100

(2m). **Leadstone Camping, Warren Road, Dawlish, Devon EX7 0NG.** *01626 864411.* www.leadstonecamping.co.uk. Rolling grassland in natural secluded bowl 0.5m from Dawlish Warren beach and nature reserve. One night stopovers welcome. Ideal base for 'day-touring' Devon. The park is licensed for a total of 137 mixed units (tourers, tents, motorhomes). M5, J30. Take A379 to Dawlish. On approaching Dawlish turn L on brow of hill signed Dawlish Warren. Site 0.5m on R. Open: 8 June - 3 September. ★ ★ ★ BH&HPA ⛱🐕⛔🍽♿¿🚐🏕

## Dawlish Warren

(2m). **Dawlish Sands Holiday Park, Warren Road, Dawlish Warren, Devon EX7 0PG.** *0845 8159775.* www.ParkHolidaysUK.com. Indoor heated leisure pool, outdoor leisure pool. Sundowner Club, kids club, amusements pool tables. Bar, bar snacks, takeaway. City of Exeter, Model Village, Torquay Harbour, Paignton Zoo, Quaywest water pool. Leave M5 Exeter, take A379 Dawlish, at Cockwood harbour L over bridge signed Dawlish Warren, park on L after 1m. Open: 1 March - 1 November. ★ ★ ★ BH&HPA NCC ⛺ ⛱🐕⛔♿♣∅⛳🏊🍴×⛱🐕🍽🚐 360

(0.5m). **Lee Cliff Park, Mount Pleasant Road, Dawlish Warren, Devon EX7 0NE.** *01626 864263.* Small, select family run site. 14 chalets for hire. 1mins to bakers, grocers, fish & chips shop, chinese takeaway, 4 pubs with restaurants. Arcades, cafes, go karts, small fairground, golf course, 3mins to blue flag beaches and nature reserve. 30/40mins to Dartmoor. Owner supplied copy. Take A379 from Exeter towards Dawlish. At Cockwood turn L, over bridge and follow road into Dawlish Warren. About 9m from Exeter. Open: All year. ⛺⛱🐕⛔♿🍽🚐

(3m). **Peppermint Park, Warren Road, Dawlish Warren, Devon EX7 0PQ.** *01626 863436.* www.ParkHolidaysUK.com/mmc. Dog exercise enclosure. Stunning views and surroundings. Play area. Games room. Licensed club. Coarse fishing lake. Golf course 0.25m. Bars and live shows at sister parks nearby (Dawlish Sands & Golden Sands). Swimming pool at both parks. David Bellamy Silver Conservation Award. Leave M5 at Exeter. A379 to Dawlish. Then follow signs to Dawlish Warren and continue down steep hill and follow road round to the L. Park is then 200yd on L. Open: 25 March - 31 October. ★ ★ ★ ★ BH&HPA ⛺⛱🐕⛔♿♣∅ ⛱🐕⛔🍽♿¿🚐80🚐 🏕85

(2m). **Welcome Family Holiday Park, Warren Road, Dawlish Warren, Devon EX7 0PH.** *0845 165 5265.* www.welcomefamily.co.uk. Extensive facilities including four super indoor pools and entertainment. Lots for children to do. Level walk to sandy beach. Pets welcome. Golf courses, fishing 0.5m - beach 600yd. Owner supplied copy. Off A379 Exeter to Teignmouth. 2m from Dawlish. Open: 2 April - 31 October. ★ ★ ★ ★ ⛱🐕⛔🍽 ♿¿🚐 690

---

## Leadstone Camping... *a great little site*

**"Only at Dawlish Warren"** 38 years of our family's experience has gone into the making of Leadstone. Friendly, quiet and uncommercialised it is absolutely unique in this area. Situated 1/2 mile from Dawlish Warren's Blue Flag beach. One nighters welcome. Ideal for touring Devon

**Leadstone Camping** Warren Road, Dawlish, S. Devon EX7 0NG
**Tel: 01626 864411** www.leadstonecamping.co.uk

---

**Cofton Country** HOLIDAYS

**Superb family-run four star park in a Glorious Corner of Devon**

- swimming pools · Swan pub · play areas · take-away
- fishing lakes · blue flag beach five minutes · shop
- WiFi · gold awards for conservation · super pitches
- woodland walks · camping orchard · holiday homes

**0800 085 8649** www.coftonholidays.co.uk

# SOUTH WEST

### Drewsteignton

**(4m). Woodland Springs Touring Park (Tranquil adults-only), Venton, Drewsteignton, Devon EX6 6PG.** 01647 231695. www.woodlandsprings.co.uk. ADULTS ONLY. Quiet, peaceful, natural site within Dartmoor National Park. Ideal for touring Devon, Cornwall and the south west. Special offers available, seasonal pitches. Wi-Fi. Day kennels. 18m from cathedral city Exeter. From A30 Whiddon Down junction follow A382 Moretonhampstead. Then brown tourist signs. 8m from Okehampton. Open: All year. ★★★★ BH&HPA

### Exeter

**(4m). Browns Farm Caravan Park, Browns Farm, Woodbury Salterton, Exeter, Devon EX5 1PS.** 01395 232895. BH&HPA

**(6m). Castle Brake, Castle Lane, Woodbury, Exeter, Devon EX5 1HA.** 01395 232431. www.castlebrake.co.uk. Grassy, level park between Exeter and Exmouth. Medium size park with lovely facilities. Centrally heated holiday caravans for hire. Shower blocks, sauna, steam, bar and restaurant. Hotel quality shower rooms. Adventure playground. Extensive heathland 500yds. Sandy beach 6m. Caravan storage and seasonal pitches available. Good area for walking and attractions. David Bellamy Gold Conservation Award. Rose Award. M5, J30. Take A3052 to Halfway Inn. Turn R B3180 to Exmouth. Turn R after golf/caravan site sign. 4m from Exmouth. Open: 1 March - 30 November. ★★★★ BH&HPA

**(11m). Dartmoor Barley Meadow Camping & Caravanning Club Site, Crockernwell, Exeter, Devon EX6 6NR.** 01647 281629. www.campingandcaravanningclub.co.uk. AA 4 pennants. 63 mixed pitches in total. Grassy site with very good access. Refurbished heated shower block. Seasonal pitches available. Hardstanding pitches. Garage, shop, PO, doctors all 2m away. Okehampton 7m. Fishing, golf course nearby. Within Dartmoor National Park. Walkers very welcome. Children's play area. Turn off A30 towards Cheriton Bishop. Continue through Crockernwell, past crossroad, campsite on L. Open: 10 March - 7 November. ★★★★ BH&HPA NCC

**(6m). Exeter Racecourse Caravan Club Site, Kennford, Exeter, Devon EX6 7XS.** 01392 832107. www.caravanclub.co.uk. An excellent base for exploring Exeter and Dartmoor. Advance booking essential Bank Holidays and advised June-August. Excellent site for dogs. Non-members and tent campers welcome. Free access to racing. Toilet block and laundry facilities. Motorhome service point. Veg prep area, gas and gaz, fishing nearby. Quiet and peaceful off peak, good area for walking. From Plymouth on A38 turn L immediately past Little Chef at top of Haldon Hill into underpass, SP Exeter racecourse. Follow Racecourse signs then caravan club signs. Located at top of Haldon Hill with superb views. Open: 23 March - 29 October. ★★★★ NCC

**(4m). Kennford International Caravan Park, Kennford, Exeter, Devon EX6 7YN.** 01392 833046. www.kennfordinternational.co.uk. Family run park. Individually hedged pitches. 10% discount on holiday bookings for over 50s and Tamba members. Ideal touring centre for Dartmoor, Torquay and the benefits of south Devon. Full facility park near villages and country walks. 1m from end of M5 alongside A38. Open: All year. ★★★★ BH&HPA

**(8m). Springfield Holiday Park, Tedburn Road, Tedburn St Mary, Exeter, Devon EX6 6EW.** 01647 24242. www.springfieldholidaypark.co.uk. Ideal for touring Dartmoor. Superb views. Excellent site facilities. Wi-Fi. Golf courses nearby, shops and PO very close. Selection of pubs and restaurants 0.5m. From J31 of M5 travel W on A30. 2nd exit SP Cheriton Bishop - follow signs to park. Sat Nav users use postcode EX6 6JN. Open: 15 March - 15 November. ★★★★ BH&HPA

**Torquay Holiday Park, Kingskerswell Road, Torquay, Exeter, Devon TQ2 8JU.** 0844 3353450. www.parkdean.com. Indoor fun pool. Crazy golf. Tennis. Adventure playground. Ten-pin bowling. On site store. Laundrette. Restaurant and takeaway. Free children's clubs. Free daytime and evening entertainment. Rose award park. David Bellamy Silver Conservation Award. Owner supplied copy. Off A380 Exeter to Torquay road. 3m from Torquay. Open: 19 March - 1 November. ★★★★ BH&HPA NCC

**(4m). Webbers Caravan & Camping Park, Castle Lane, Woodbury, Exeter, Devon EX5 1EA.** 01395 232276. www.webberspark.co.uk. A friendly, family park close to Woodbury village. Breathtaking countryside views. Lots of space to relax. Ideal for beaches, golf, fishing, walking, cycling and exploring East Devon. All year caravan storage. Please call for a brochure. From M5 J30 take A376 then B3179 to Woodbury, then follow brown and white signs. Open: 24 March - 27 October. ★★★★ BH&HPA

### Exmouth

**(3m). Devon Cliffs Holiday Park (Haven), Sandy Bay, Exmouth, Devon EX8 5BT.** 0871 2310870. www.caravan-camping.co.uk. Indoor and outdoor fun pools. Free kid's clubs. Adventure playground. All weather multi sports court. Daytime and evening entertainment. Spa complex. 3 family bars, great choice of eating areas, shopping arcade. Direct access to Blue Flag beach. Town 3m, golf courses 5m. Exeter 12m. David Bellamy Gold Conservation Award. M5 exit 30 after Exeter and take A376 for Exmouth. At Exmouth follow the brown tourism signs to Sandy Bay and this will bring you directly on to the park. Open: 18 March - 31 October. ★★★★ BH&HPA NCC

### Great Torrington

**(1m). Greenways Valley, Caddywell Lane, Great Torrington, Devon EX38 7EW.** 01805 622153. www.greenwaysvalley.co.uk. Small peaceful park set on south facing ground above a beautiful wooded valley. Walking distance to town. Fishing, walking, cycling. Beach 20mins. Heated outdoor pool. Short tennis court, children play area. Holiday lodges for sale. Holiday caravans and spacious chalets for hire. David Bellamy Silver Conservation Award. Owner supplied copy. M5, J27, A361 to Barnstaple. L along B3227 for South Molton and Great Torrington. Turn L down borough road by first pedestrian crossing. Open: 13 February - 31 October.

**(2m). Smytham Manor, Little Torrington, Great Torrington, Devon EX38 8PU.** 01805 622110. www.smytham.co.uk. 23 acres of beautiful gently undulating grounds with ponds. Heated facilities block with showers, shaver points. Play area. Heated outdoor swimming pool and sun terrace. Licensed bar. Putting green, direct access to Tarka Trail. Booking advisable. Close to Moors and beaches. RHS Rosemoor and Dartington Crystal 1.5m. David Bellamy Gold Conservation Award. S of Torrington towards Okehampton on A386. Open: 25 March - 1 November. ★★★★ BH&HPA

# SOUTH WEST

### Holsworthy

**(5m). Hedley Wood Caravan & Camping Park, Bridgerule, Holsworthy, Devon EX22 7ED.** *01288 381404.* www.hedley-wood.co.uk. Woodland, family run site with outstanding views and a laid-back atmosphere. Pets welcome, daily kennelling, dog walk and nature trail. Clubroom, bar, and all amenities. Adventure area. Open and sheltered areas. Caravan storage. Take A3072 Holdsworth to Bude, midway turn S on to B3254 to Launceston. 2.5m turn R 500yd on R. Open: All year. ★★★ BH&HPA ♀ ❶ ♒ ♿ ♣ ♁ ♒ ♿ ♠ ✕ ✍ ♞ ✉ ♿ ♑ 40⛺ 80⛺ Å 15⛺

**(2.5m). Noteworthy Caravan & Camping Site, Bude Road, Holsworthy, Devon EX22 7JB.** *01409 253731.* www.noteworthy-devon.co.uk. Touring centre for moors and beaches. Quiet family run site. Takeaway meals nearby. AA approved & Quality in Tourism on a working farm. Owner supplied copy. W of Holsworthy on A3072. 1m past golf course. Open: All year. ★★ BH&HPA ⌂ ❶ ✍ ❄ ✉ ♿ ⛺ ⛺ Å ⛺

### Ilfracombe

**(1m). Beachside Holiday Park (Ilfracombe), Beach Road, Hele Bay, Ilfracombe, Devon EX34 9QZ.** *0844 272 9500.* www.beachsidepark.co.uk. Quiet park. No clubhouse or bar but good small amenities. Spectacularly positioned right next to the beach in a peaceful cove designated as an area of outstanding natural beauty. All caravan holiday homes have sea views. Regret no touring or camping facilities. Cinema 1m. Golf course 5m. About 1m from Ilfracombe on A399 to Combe Martin. Open: 15 March - 31 October. ★★★★ BH&HPA ⌂ ❶ ✍ ⛺ ⛺ 50⛺

**(2.5). Brook Lea Caravan Club Site, West Down, Ilfracombe, Devon EX34 8NE.** *01271 862848.* www.caravanclub. co.uk. 3m inland from Ilfracombe with superb views to north and west coasts and Dartmoor. No sanitation. Advance booking advised July and August. MV service point. Playfield. Golf, fishing and water sports nearby. Good area for walking. Ideal for families. Gas and Gaz, dog walk on site. Storage pitches, quiet and peaceful off peak. Volunteer run site. Recycling facilities, within 5m of NCN cycle route. Non-members welcome. No tents. See website for standard directions to site. Open: 30 March - 1 October. ★★★★ NCC ⌘ ❶ ✍ ♒ ♿ ♣ ⛺ 103⛺

**(1m). Hele Valley Holiday Park, Hele Bay, Ilfracombe, Devon EX34 9RD.** *01271 862460.* www.helevalley.co.uk. Just 1m from Ilfracombe, 10-min walk from Hele, this site is in Hele Valley. Quiet, peaceful & well-established. Excellent facilities. Easily accessed from M5 or A39. Open: 1 April - 31 October. ★★★★ BH&HPA ⌂ ❶ ✍ ♒ ♿ ♣ ⛺ ⛺ ♿ ♣ 8⛺ 10⛺ Å 100⛺

**(5m). Hidden Valley Touring Park, West Down, Ilfracombe, Devon EX34 8NU.** *01271 813537.* www.hiddenvalleypark.com. Secluded site in wooded valley. National award winner 2009. Sheltered pitches and five star facilities with coffee shop on site, plus woodland walks. Dog and family friendly. David Bellamy Gold Conservation Award. J27, M5 take A361 to Barnstaple, continue A361 towards Ilfracombe. 8m from Barnstaple, park entrance is on L side of A361. Open: All year. ★★★★★ 5 BH&HPA ⌂ ❶ ✍ ♒ ♿ ♣ ⛺ ♿ ♣ ⛺ ♿ 70⛺ 120⛺ 58Å

**(2.5m). Little Meadow Camping & Caravan Site, Ilfracombe, Devon EX34 9SJ.** *01271 866862.* www.littlemeadow. co.uk. A small, tranquil, uncommercialised site with one of the most spectacular views of the Bristol Channel. Shop on site. Golf course, sea fishing, trips to Lundy Island, horse riding available. On the SW coastal footpath. 2m E of Ilfracombe on A399. Open: 1 April - 30 September. ⌂ ❶ ✍ ♒ ♿ ♣ ♑ ♿ ♣ ⛺ ⛺ 50⛺ 50⛺ 50Å 3⛺

**(3m). Mill Park Touring Site, Berrynarbor, Ilfracombe, Devon EX34 9SH.** *01271 882647.* www.millpark-limited.co.uk. Picturesque, level park in unique woodland setting with waterfall and stream-fed coarse fishing lake. Free hot water and showers. Well-stocked shop. Bar, hot meals. Off-licence. Phone. Laundry. Play area. Dog walks. Between Ilfracombe and Combe Martin, take turning off A399, opposite Sawmills Restaurant for pretty Berrynarbor. Open: 1 March - 31 October. ⌂ ❶ ✍ ♒ ♿ ♣ ♑ ♿ ♣ ⛺ 119⛺ 119⛺ 103Å

**(2m). Mullacott Farm CS, Mullacott Farm, Ilfracombe, Devon EX34 8NA.** *01271 866877.* www.mullacottfarm.co.uk. Gently sloping with views over Bristol Channel. On main A361 road, S of Ilfracombe. Open: 18 April - 31 October. ⌂ ❶ ✍ ♒ ♿ ♣ ⛺ ♿ ♣ ⛺

**(5m). Sandaway Beach Holiday Park, Coombe Martin, Ilfracombe, Devon EX34 9ST.** *01271 866766.* www.johnfowlerholidays.com. Club. Heated pool. Family site with private beach. Children's club. Licensed club with entertainment. Close Exmoor National Park. AA 4 pennant & Rose Award Park. On A399 Ilfracombe to Combe Martin. Open: 10 April - 31 October. ★★★★ ⌂ ❶ ✍ ♒ ♿ ♣ ♑ ♿ ♣ ⛺ 23⛺ 23⛺ Å 86⛺

**(2.5m). Watermouth Cove Holiday Park, Berrynarbor, Ilfracombe, Devon EX34 9SJ.** *01271 862504.* www.watermouthcoveholidays.co.uk. Family management. Swimming pools. Club with entertainment. Bar meals, takeaway, outside play area, laundry, free hot water. Outstanding headland walks. Adjacent to harbour. Private beach and caves. Shop and arcade. Sea fishing. Luxury chalets. M5, J27 take A361 signs Barnstaple to Ilfracombe. Open: 30 March - 28 October.

---

### A tranquil 5* holiday park nestled between the cliffs at beautiful Hele Bay in North Devon

- 5* holiday park.
- Stunning caravan accommodation.
- Right on the beach.
- Nearby cafe overlooking the bay.
- Golf course and indoor swimming pool just minutes from the park.

To book call **0844 272 9500** or visit **www.beachsidepark.co.uk**

*Terms and conditions apply

Visit www.caravanclub.co.uk

# SOUTH WEST

★★★ BH&HPA 🏠⚡🚿🐕🏊♿🎵🍴
🍺🎣🎱🛒🎯🚲🍽️🛁🚻♿ 90⚡
90🛏 ▲ 10🚐

**(2.5m). Watermouth Valley Camping Park, Watermouth, Berrynarbor, Ilfracombe, Devon EX34 9SJ.** *01271 862282.* www.bigmeadow.co.uk. Family site on the coastline between Combe Martin and Ilfracombe. Watermouth Harbour and beach 200yds. Children's play area. The Old Sawmill Inn and restaurant adjoins Watermouth Valley Camping Park. Situated on the coast road A399, between Ilfracombe and Combe Martin. Open: 6 April - 30 September. 🍴🚐♿🍽️
⚡🎣🍺🎱🏊🛒🎯🚲🛁🚻♿ 160🛏
125⚡ ▲

### Ivybridge

**(8m). Broad Park Caravan Club Site, Higher East Leigh, Modbury, Ivybridge, Devon PL21 0SH.** *01548 830714.* www.caravanclub.co.uk. Situated between moor and sea, an excellent base from which to explore south Devon. Toilet blocks with privacy cubicles & laundry facilities. Some hardstanding, veg prep area, gas and gaz. Dog walk on site, quiet and peaceful off peak. Good area for walking. MV service point. Playfield and play equipment. Boules pitch. Ideal for families. Non-members welcome. No tents. See website for complete directions to site. Open: 23 March - 5 November. ★★★★★ NCC 🍴🚐♿
🐕⚡🍽️🎣🎱🚲🛁🚻♿ 112🛏 112⚡

### Kingsbridge

**(9m). Challaborough Bay Holiday Park, Challaborough Beach, Bigbury-on-Sea, Kingsbridge, Devon TQ7 4HU.** *01548 810771.* www.parkdean.com. Laundrette, on site store. Play area and free children's clubs. Diving and fishing. Sports and leisure facilities. Takeaway. Family club and bar. Coastal walks, beautiful surroundings and places of interest nearby. There is no public transport. David Bellamy Silver Conservation Award. Off A379 Plymouth to Kingsbridge. Take B3392 towards Challaborough. Open: 1 April - 31 October.
★★★★ BH&HPA NCC 🐕🍴⚡🛒🍽️
🚿🎣🍺🎱🚲🛁🚻♿ 270🚐

**(1m). Island Lodge Caravan & Camping Site, Stumpy Post Cross, Kingsbridge, Devon TQ7 4BL.** *01548 852956.* www.islandlodgesite.com. Within walking distance of a golf course & historic castle town of Caernarfon. Fishing, sailing & water sports facilities very close. 5mins walk to Menai Straits. 20mins away from the foot of Snowdon. Children can watch milking & feeding calves. Dogs must be kept on lead. Off A381 Open: All year. 🍴🚐
🐕🎣🍽️⚡🚿🛒🎯🛁🚻♿ 10🚐 25⚡ ▲

**(6m). Karrageen Camping and Caravan Park, Bolberry, Malborough, Kingsbridge, Devon TQ7 3EN.** *01548 561230.* www.karrageen.co.uk. Terraced, tree lined pitches with a view - 65 pitches for motorcaravans or tents. NT clifftop walks. Hot takeaway and shop. Beach 1m. First class facilities. AA 3 pennants. Take A381 towards Salcombe. At Malborough turn R, after 0.6m turn R (sp Bolberry). After 0.9m park on R. 4m from Salcombe. Open: 30 March - 30 September. 3 BH&HPA 🍴🐕
▲🍽️🚿🚐⚡🎣🛒🛁🚻♿ 65⚡
20⚡ ▲ 6🚐

**(3m). Mounts Farm Touring Park, The Mounts, East Allington, Kingsbridge, Devon TQ9 7QJ.** *01548 521591.* www.mountsfarm.co.uk. Quiet, family run site, ideal base for touring South Devon. Free showers and hot water. No overcrowding. No charge for awnings, pets and children. Shop with camping accessories. Many beaches and attractions nearby. Free brochure available. Children's play field. AA 3 pennants. N of Kingsbridge on A381. Open: 15 March - 31 October. 🍴🐕
🎣⚡🍽️🚿🛒🛁🚻♿ 10🚐 40⚡ 20▲

**(5m). Old Cotmore Farm Touring Caravan & Camping Park, Old Cotmore Farm, Stokenham, Kingsbridge, Devon TQ7 2LR.** *01548 580240.* www.oldcotmorefarm.co.uk. Picturesque park, 1m from sea and glorious beaches. Holiday cottages available at farm. Dogs allowed. AA 3 pennants. Owner supplied copy. From Kingsbridge, take A379 towards Dartmouth. At Stokenham village turn at mini roundabout to Beesands. Park 1m on right hand side, SP. Open: 15 March - 31 October. 3 🍴🐕🍽️⚡🎣🚿🛒🛁🚻♿
5⚡ 20⚡ ▲

**(1m). Parkland Caravan & Camping Site, Sorley Green Cross, Kingsbridge, Devon TQ7 4AF.** *01548 852723.* www.parklandsite.co.uk. High quality traditional site, set in three acres of level grounds. Free electric hook-ups. Seasonal pitches. Modern facilities, family/disabled suites. Wi-Fi. Views of Salcombe, nearest site to Bantham beach. Storage. A38 S turn off at Totnes junction (A384). At Totnes take A381 for 10m to Stumpy Post Cross junction, follow A381 to the R and follow tourist board signs. Open: All year. 🍴🍽️
🐕⚡🎣🚿🚐♿🛒🛁🚻♿
5⚡ 30⚡ ▲

**(8m). Slapton Sands Camping & Caravanning Club Site, Middle Grounds, Slapton, Kingsbridge, Devon TQ7 2QW.** *01548 580538.* www.campingandcaravanningclub.co.uk. Motorhome and tents, non-members welcome. Caravan owners must be members due to restrictions on numbers. Keen ornithologists will enjoy visiting the wild bird sanctuary at nearby Slapton Ley. Blackpool sands, 4m away, is also popular with families. Sea fishing from the beach near the site. Special deals available for families and backpackers. Loo Of The Year (4 stars). On A379 from Kingsbridge, site entrance is on R 0.25m beyond brow of hill approaching Slapton Village. Open: 1 April - 31 October. ★★★★ NCC 🍴🚐♿🐕
🍽️⚡🎣🚿🛒🛁🚻♿ 115🚐 8⚡ ▲

**(6m). Start Bay Caravan Club Site, Start Bay, Stokenham, Kingsbridge, Devon TQ7 2SE.** *01548 580430.* www.caravanclub.co.uk. A long, gently slop-

**Hope Cove** — **KARRAGEEN**
www.karrageen.co.uk

A Park with character and sea views.
Tree Lined terraces, peaceful with plenty of space. Hope Cove beach 1 mile.
Salcombe 4 miles.
Licensed shop with quality hot takeaway food.
First class toilet facilities.

Special rates for the over 50s
(not high season) from £85.00 week incl ehu

Small fleet of luxury static caravans
for hire, from £280 per week

For colour brochure, please contact:
Phil & Nikki Higgin,
Karrageen Bolberry, Malborough, Kingsbridge,
South Devon
Tel: 01548 561230 Fax: 01548 560192

# SOUTH WEST

ing meadow site screened with well kept shrubs and trees, with the sea only 0.75m away. Toilet blocks, laundry facilities and MV service point. Play equipment and dog walk on site. Fishing and water sports nearby. Good area for walking. Facilities for disabled. Ideal for families. Members only. No tents. See website for standard directions to site. Open: 23 March - 5 November. NCC ⌂ ⟳ ⚭ ⚑ ⌬ ⚙ ⚗ ⚒ ⚐ 90⛺ 90⚏

## Lynton

(2m). **Channel View Caravan Park, Manor Farm, Barbrook, Lynton, Devon EX35 6LD.** *01598 753349.* www.channel-view.co.uk. Licensed pub & restaurant nearby. Fully serviced pitches available, cafe on site. Wi-Fi available. David Bellamy Gold Conservation Award. On A39 Barnstaple to Lynmouth. Open: 1 April - 13 November. ★★★★ BH&HPA ⌂ ⚭ ⚑ ⌬ ⚙ ⚗ ⚒ ⚐ 76⛺ ▲ 5⚏

(2m). **Lynton Camping & Caravanning Club Site, Caffyn's Cross, Lynton, Devon EX35 6JS.** *01598 752379 .* www.campingandcaravanningclub.co.uk. Set in 5.5 acres with pitches accepting all units, superbly situated on the cliff overlooking the Bristol Channel. Non-members welcome. Located very close to Exmoor National Park with an abundance of walks in the surrounding rugged countryside. Very quiet site with stunning views. The area in which the site is located inspired the book Lorna Doone. Special deals available for families & backpackers. M5, J27 on to A361 to 2nd South Molton roundabout. R on to A399 to Blackmoor Gate. R on to A39 towards Lynton, L after 5m, signed Caffyns, immediately R to site in 1m. Open: 1 April - 26 September. ★★★ NCC ⌂ ⟳ ⚭ ⚑ ⌬ ⚙ ⚗ 105⛺ 105⚏ ▲

(0.25m). **Sunny Lyn Holiday Park, Lynbridge, Lynton, Devon EX35 6NS.** *01598 753384.* www.caravandevon.co.uk. Holiday site, easy reach of coast on edge of Exmoor. On SW coastal path alongside village pub and river. Good freshly cooked breakfast available. Lodge and apartments open all year. Free hot showers. Owner supplied copy. S of Lynton on B3234. Or 1m N of junction of this road with A39 at Barbrook, avoiding the steep hill out of Lynton. Open: 15 March 31 October. BH&HPA ⌂ ⚭ ⚑ ⌬ ⚙ ⚗ ⚒ ⚐ 9⛺ 9⚏ ▲ 14⚏ ⚒

## Modbury

(7m). **California Cross Camping & Caravanning Club Site, California Cross, Modbury, Devon PL21 0SG.** *01548 821297 .* www.campingandcaravanningclub.co.uk. Many beautiful villages are dotted around the site to explore. All units accepted. Non-members welcome. Loo Of The Year (4 stars). Indoor and outdoor swimming pools situated 7m away. Special arrangements for early morning site departure for Plymouth Ferry crossings available. Special deals available for families & backpackers. Leave A38 at Wranton Cross onto A3121 continue on crossroads. Cross over on to B3196. Turn L before filling station, SP Dartmouth, site on R. Situated 8m from Bigbury-on-Sea with sandy beach & golf course. Salcombe 12m, centre for yachting. Open: 1 April - 26 September. ★★★★ NCC ⌂ ⚭ ⚑ ⌬ ⚙ ⚗ 80⛺ 80⚏ ▲

(3m). **Moor View Touring Park (Tranquil adults-only), California Cross, Modbury, Devon PL21 0SG.** *01548 821485.* www.moorviewtouringpark.co.uk. Rural, ADULTS ONLY park backing onto woodland, with panoramic views towards Dartmoor, close to coastal walks and beaches. 68 individual level pitches all with electric hook-up of which 65 are fully serviced, hardstandings pitches. Centrally heated luxury showers, shop, laundry and information room. Dogs welcome. From A38 westbound, leave at Wrangaton Cross (signed Modbury, Ermington) turn L, straight on at crossroads and follow park signs. Rural, ADULTS ONLY park backing onto woodland, with panoramic views towards Dartmoor, close to coastal walks and beaches. 68 individual level pitches all with electric hook-up of which 65 are fully serviced, hardstandings pitches. Centrally heated luxury showers, shop, laundry and information room. Dogs welcome. Open: All year. ★★★★ BH&HPA ⌂ ⚭ ⚑ ⌬ ⚙ ⚗ ⚒ ⚐ 68⛺ 68⚏ 20▲ 18⚏

(2m). **Pennymoor Caravan & Camping Park, Modbury, Devon PL21 0SB.** *01548 830542 .* www.pennymoor-camping.co.uk. Immaculately maintained, peaceful site with panoramic views. An ideal family park. From Exeter leave A38 at Wrangaton Cross turn L for 1m to crossroads, straight across and continue for about 4m to petrol garage then take second L and continue for 1m. Open: 15 March - 31 October. ★★★★ ⌂ ⚭ ⚑ ⌬ ⚙ ⚗ ⚒ ⚐ 35⛺ 119⚏ ▲ 70⚏

## Mortehoe

(1.5m). **Warcombe Farm Camping Park, Station Road, Mortehoe, Devon EX34 7EJ.** *01271 870490.* www.warcombefarm.co.uk. Beautiful sea views. Clean, excellent facilities. Play area. Fishing lake. Close to Woolacombe beach. Warm welcome from helpful staff. Peaceful surroundings in the heart of the countryside. David Bellamy Gold Conservation Award. Turn R off B3343 towards Mortehoe, park on R in less than 1m. Open: 6 April - 31 October. ★★★★ BH&HPA ⌂ ⚭ ⚑ 75⛺ 25⚏ ▲

## Newton Abbot

(2.5m). **Dornafield, Two Mile Oak, Newton Abbot, Devon TQ12 6DD.** *01803 812732.* www.dornafield.com. CARAVAN CLUB AFFILIATED SITE. This site is set in a quiet valley close to an ancient farmhouse and surrounded by beautiful countryside. Toilet blocks, laundry facilities, baby and toddler washroom and MV service point. Games room, play equipment and dog walk on site. Golf and NCN route nearby. Facilities for disabled. Ideal for families. David Bellamy Gold Conservation Award. Take A381 (Newton Abbot to Totnes) in 2m at Two Mile Oak Pub turn R in 0.5m first turn L. Park 100yd on R. Open: 16 March - 2 January. ★★★★★ BH&HPA ⌂ ⚭ ⚑ ⌬ ⚙ ⚗ ⚒ ⚐ 135⛺ 135⚏ 135▲

(3m). **Lemonford Caravan Park, Bickington, Newton Abbot, Devon TQ12 6JR.** *01626 821242.* www.lemonford.co.uk. AA 4 pennants, 'one of Britain's best parks' ('Excellent') facilities for tourers and tents. Friendly, family run park, close to the coast and the moor. Holiday homes for hire. Golf course, cinema, shopping 3m in Newton Abbot. Horse riding 4m. From Exeter along A38 towards Plymouth take A382 turn off, on roundabout take 3rd exit to Bickington. From Plymouth take A383 turn off to Bickington. Open: All year. 4 BH&HPA ⌂ ⚭ ⚑ ⌬ ⚙ ⚗ ⚒ ⚐ 25⛺ 70⚏ ▲ 15⚏

(1m). **River Dart Country Park, Holne Park, Ashburton, Newton Abbot, Devon TQ13 7NP.** *01364 652511.* www.riverdart.co.uk. Camping on this award winning site includes entry into adventure playgrounds: pirate ship surrounded by water, toddlers' beach, scenic walks, Old Sawmill cafe - updated menu. The great outdoors at its best! From Exeter, Plymouth take A38 to Ashburton then follow signs to Two Bridges, entrance 1.25m on L. From Tavistock & Dartmoor take Two Bridges road towards Ashburton, turn R 1m after Holne Bridge. Open: 1 April - 26 September. ★★★★ ⌂ ⚭ ⚑ ⌬ ⚙ ⚗ ⚒ ⚐ 170⚏ ▲

(3m). **Ross Park, Park Hill Farm, Moor Road, Ipplepen, Newton Abbot, Devon TQ12 5TT.** *01803 812983.* www.rosspark-caravanpark.co.uk. One of Devon's most

# SOUTH WEST

beautiful parks with tropical conservatory and garden style pitches. Dog walks. Adventure playground. Free wireless Internet access. Golf course adjacent, fishing within 3m. David Bellamy Gold Conservation Award. On A381 between Newton Abbot and Totnes, follow brown tourist signs at Park Hill Cross roads and Jet filling station. Open: 2 March - 2 January. ★★★★ BH&HPA 110 110 A

(3m). **Stover Caravan Club Site**, Stover, Newton Abbot, Devon TQ12 6QG. *01626 361430*. www.caravanclub.co.uk. A quiet, open site in country park on edge of Dartmoor. Ideal for mature caravanners looking for peace and interesting walking. No sanitation. Some hardstandings. Gas and Gaz, dog walk on site. MV service point. Fishing and golf nearby. Members only. No tents. See website for standard directions to site. Open: 23 March - 5 November. NCC 73 73

(2m). **Twelve Oaks Farm Caravan Park**, Twelve Oaks Farm, Teignrace, Newton Abbot, Devon TQ12 6QT. *01626 352769*. www.twelveoaksfarm.co.uk. Family run site on a working farm of nearly 320 acres. Bordered by the river Teign in the village of Teigngrace. Coarse fishing available. Heated outdoor swimming pool. Rallies welcome. Caravan storage. Self catering holiday cottages. Owner supplied copy. From Exeter follow A38 Plymouth bound. Take turning off L SP Teigngrace (before Drumbridges roundabout), continue for about 1.5m through village and find Twelve Oaks on your left-hand side. Open: All year. ★★★★ BH&HPA 25 25 A

(3m). **Woodville Caravan Park**, Totnes Road, Ipplepen, Newton Abbot, Devon TQ12 5TN. *01803 812240*. www.jinkz.com/woodville/homepagea.html. Quiet location for adults only. Spacious individual 'all weather' pitches with electric hook-ups. Adjacent to Woodville park is 'Fermoy's Garden Centre' selling groceries and other goods. Golf course opposite. 3.5 acre family run site. Open: 1 March - 2 January. ★★★★ BH&HPA 10 26

### Newton Ferrers

**Briar Hill Farm Caravan & Camping Park**, Briar Hill Farm, Newton Ferrers, Devon PL8 1AR. *01752 872252*. A quiet picturesque caravan site in the centre of Newton Ferrers within 250yd to local shops (PO, grocery, butcher and chemist) and pub. Set on the opposite side of Newton Creek to Noss Mayo, which is a branch of the beautiful Yealm estuary. 10m from Plymouth. Open: 1 March - 1 November. 50 A

### Okehampton

(6m). **Bridestowe Caravan Park**, Glebe Park, Bridestowe, Okehampton, Devon EX20 4ER. *01837 861261*. Children allowed. From Okehampton, turn off A30 SP direction Bridestowe, in village follow caravan signs to park. Open: 1 March - 10 December. ★★★ BH&HPA 13 13 A 30

(3m). **Bundu Camping & Caravan Park**, Bundu, Sourton Down, Okehampton, Devon EX20 4HT. *01837 861611*. www.bundu.co.uk. Access good. Level site in Dartmoor National Park. Direct access onto National Cycle Way. Adjacent Inn. Short walk to garage and shop. Golf, fishing and horse riding within a few miles. From A30 take slip road A386 to Tavistock, L at T-junction then L again 100yd. Site 0.5m ahead. Open: All year. BH&HPA 12 20 12 A

(8m). **Lydford Caravan Club (AS) Site**, Lydford, Okehampton, Devon EX20 4BE. *01822 820497*. www.lydfordsite.co.uk. Beautiful site on the edge of Dartmoor. Ideal peaceful base for touring Dartmoor, Devon and Cornwall. Regular buses 100yds. Good TV reception. Pubs and restaurants within walking distance. Free Wi-Fi. David Bellamy Gold Conservation Award. From A30 take A386 to Tavistock, in 5m turn R to Lydford. At War Memorial, turn R. Site signed 200yd. Open: 23 March - 30 October. ★★★★ BH&HPA 70 70

### Paignton

(1.5m).  **Ashvale Holiday Park**, Goodrington Road, Paignton, Devon TQ4 7JD. *01803 843807*. www.beverley-holidays.co.uk. Family run holiday park in the beautiful English Riviera, offering holiday caravan homes for the family. Club, bar, restaurant, playground, table tennis and swimming pool. Beach, golf course 1m. Cinema 1.5m. Torbay in Bloom winner. David Bellamy Silver Conservation Award. Owner supplied copy. 2m S of Paignton on A3022, turn L into Goodrington Road. Open: 30 March - 2 November. ★★★★ BH&HPA A 310

(1.5m). **Beverley Park (Best of British)**, Goodrington Road, Paignton, Devon TQ4 7JE. *01803 661958*. www.beverley-holidays.co.uk. Fabulous sea views overlooking Torbay. Lodges and touring open all year. Runner up Alan Rogers 2006. English Riviera "Best Holiday Park" 2004. SW England Tourism Excellence 'Caravan Park of the Year' 2007/2008. Club. Bar. Heated indoor and outdoor pools. Tennis court. Sauna and fitness suite, playground. Beach, golf course 1m. Cinema, Paignton town 1.5m. David Bellamy Gold Conservation Award. Off A379 Dartmouth to Paignton. Open: All year. ★★★★ BH&HPA NCC 118 118 30 A 185 24

(2m). **Bona Vista Holiday Park**, Totnes Road, Paignton, Devon TQ4 7PY. *01803*

Escape to the perfect seaside resort and rediscover the things that really matter.
- Indoor & outdoor pools
- Great nightly entertainment
- Crazy golf & tennis
- Bar & restaurant
- Children's playground

**Beverley HOLIDAYS**

HOLIDAY CARAVANS  TOURING  LODGES
5 star holidays on the English Riviera
**01803 661938**  www.beverley-holidays.co.uk

# SOUTH WEST

551971. www.bona-vista.co.uk. Small, quiet site, 3 flats to let. Fishing nearby. Owner supplied copy. On A385. Open: All year. ★★★★ BH&HPA ⌂🐕🚫🔌🛁🚬 ❄☕13🛒

**(3m). Byslades International (Lodges only), Totnes Road, Paignton, Devon TQ4 7PY.** 01803 666930. www.byslades.co.uk. Friendly award winning lodge park set in 23 acres of beautiful Devon countryside. Nearby the historic town of Totnes, the South Hams and Dartmoor National Park. 2m W of Paignton situated on A385. Open: 15 March - 31 October. ★★★★ BH&HPA ⌂🐕🚫🔌🛁♫🎵♂🔧🔒🚬 ⛽➤🚗✖🏪♿☕

**(1.5m). Hoburne Torbay, Grange Road, Goodrington, Paignton, Devon TQ4 7JP.** 01803 558010. www.hoburne.com. Licensed club and theme restaurant. Outdoor and indoor pool. Seasonal entertainment. Cafeteria. Shop. Adventure playground. Soft play area and mini bowling. Rose Award. David Bellamy Silver Conservation Award. S on A380 (Paignton Ring Road) for 1m after junction with A385. L into Goodrington Road for 0.75m then L into Grange Road. Park is SP. Open: 28 February - 31 October. ★★★★ BH&HPA NCC ⌂🐕♂🔧🚫♫ ⛽♂🔒🚬🛁🚂⛽🚗✖🏪♿♨☕ 189🎵 189🎵 730🛒

 **(1.5m). Whitehill Country Park, Stoke Road, Paignton, Devon TQ4 7PF.** 01803 782338. www.whitehill-park.co.uk. Countryside and woodland walking, bar, restaurant, takeaway, heated swimming pool, playgrounds, craft room, arcade, shop. Golf course and cinema 2m. 3m to nearest beach. David Bellamy Gold Conservation Award. Off A385 Totnes to Paignton. Open: 5 April - 29 September. ★★★★ BH&HPA ⌂🐕♂🔧🚫♫♂🔒 ⛽🚬➤🚗✖🏪♿☕ 104🎵 137🅰 51🛒 ❄

**(2.5m). Widdicombe Farm (Adults only), The Ring Road, Marldon,** Torquay, Paignton, Devon TQ3 1ST. 01803 558325. www.widdicombefarm.co.uk. 'Adults only' park. Lovely views; park landscaped to provide spacious, level pitches (200 in total). Very easy access, no narrow country lanes. Luxurious facilities including free hot water, ladies' private washrooms, laundrette, shop. Hayloft entertainment bar and Poppy Restaurant. Fully serviced pitches available. Storage and seasonal welcome. Golf, cinema, shopping centre all within 2m. 2.5m from Torquay and Paignton. On the A380 Torquay to Paignton ring road. Open: 15 March - 29 October. ★★★★ BH&HPA ⌂🐕♂🔧🚫♫♂🔒⛽🚬➤🚗✖🏪🅂 ⛽☕♿ 180🎵 180🎵 20🅰 3🛒

**(3m). Widend Touring Park, Berry Pomeroy Road, Marldon, Paignton, Devon TQ3 1RT.** 01803 550116. www.devon-connect.co.uk/camping-touring/widend/. 4m to Torbay seafront, spacious, award-winning, family-run park with views of the sea, countryside and with superb facilities. Friendly atmosphere. Heated outdoor pool, adventure playground, family bar. Couples and families only. No dogs July and August. Seasonal pitches available. Static holiday homes for sale. Storage available. David Bellamy Silver Conservation Award. Follow the A380 Torbay Ring road. Turn towards Marldon at the second roundabout. At the next roundabout turn second L into Five Lanes - Head towards Berry Pomeroy and Totnes through Marldon Village. Park on rh side 0.5m past Marldon. Open: 15 April - 30 September. ★★★★ BH&HPA ⌂🐕♂🔧🚫♫🎵♂🔒⛽☕♿ 🚬➤🚗✖ ⛽🏪♿ 207🎵 207🎵 🅰

## Plymouth

**(5m). Brixton Camping & Caravan Park, Venn Farm, Brixton, Plymouth, Devon PL8 2AX.** 01752 880378. www.vennfarm.co.uk. Quiet site with H&C showers. Restaurant, pub, fish & chip shop, PO. Beach 2.5m. River Yealm 0.5m. On A379 3.5m SE of Laira Bridge 0.5m W of Brixton. Open: 15 March - 31 October. ⌂ ⛽🚗✖🏪♿ 43🎵 🅰

**(6m). Pilgrim's Rest, 41 Knighton Road, Wembury, Plymouth, Devon PL9 0EA.** 01752 863429. www.pilgrimsrest.co.uk. Certificated site for 5 caravans etc, and separate area for tents available at Pilgrim's Rest coastal village of Wembury in an Area of Outstanding Beauty. Sea views. Beautiful walks. 5mins drive from beach. On main bus route. Phone for more details and brochure. Owner supplied copy. See website for details. Open: 1 May - 30 September. ⌂🚫♂🔧🚬 🎵5🎵 🅰

**(5m). Plymouth Sound Caravan Club Site, Bovisand Lane, Down Thomas, Plymouth, Devon PL9 0AE.** 01752 862325. www.caravanclub.co.uk. Within easy reach of the historic port, set on a headland outside Plymouth with broad views over the Sound. Close to the South West Coastal Footpath and lovely beaches. Own sanitation required. Good for walking, dog walk on site. Golf, water sports and NCN route nearby. Ideal for families. Non-members welcome. No tents. See website for standard directions to site. Open: 30 March - 1 October. ★★★★ NCC ⌂🐕🚫 ♂➤ 58🎵 58🎵

**(3.5m). Riverside Caravan Park (Plymouth), Leigham Manor Drive, Marsh Mills, Plymouth, Devon PL6 8LL.** 01752 344122. www.riversidecaravanpark.com. Level site amid tall pines and other trees. Two modern toilet blocks. Heated outdoor pool, bar/restaurant. Children's play area and dog walk. Well signed from main roads. Take Plymouth slip road from A38 to large roundabout, around roundabout, take road to Plymouth, 1st set traffic lights, turn L. Open: All year. ⌂🐕♂🔧🚫♫🎵♂🔒⛽☕➤ ✖🏪♿ 232🎵 232🎵 🅰

**(8m). Smithaleigh Caravan Park, Smithaleigh, Plympton, Plymouth, Devon PL7 5AX.** 01752 893194. Motel

the great outdoors
touring, camping,
caravans, lodges,
and camping pods

- 10 acres of woodland
- walking & cycling
- conservation awards
- outdoor heated pool
- hayloft bar
- children's play areas
- children's craft room
- shop, café & takeaway

01803 782338    countryside holidays by the sea    whitehill-park.co.uk

# SOUTH WEST

and restaurant on site. Off A38. Open: All year. 120

## Putsborough

**Putsborough Sands Caravan Park, The Anchorage, Georgeham, Putsborough, Devon EX33 1LB.** 01271 890230. www.putsborough.com. Booking essential as the site has a unique location overlooking and adjacent to the multi Award Winning Putsborough Sands and is extremely popular. Write, phone or e-mail for details. 4m from Braunton, on B3231. Open: 31 March - 10 October. BH&HPA 25

## Salcombe

**(2m). Alston Farm Camping & Caravan Site, Kingsbridge, Salcombe, Devon TQ7 3BJ.** 01548 561260. www.alstoncampsite.co.uk. Level, sheltered site. RAC 3 pennants. Supermarket 1m, boating & fishing 2m, golf and cinema 3m. Lots of beaches within 5m. Off A381. Open: 15 March - 31 October. 3 15 40 58

**Bolberry House Farm Caravanning & Camping Park, Bolberry, Marlborough, Salcombe, Devon TQ7 3DY.** 01548 561251. www.bolberryparks.co.uk. Quiet, family run park amidst outstanding coastal countryside, good access to superb cliff walks and all boating facilities with safe sandy beaches 1m. Children's play area and barn. Dogs welcome with separate exercising paddock. Low season discounts with special rates for over 50s. AA 3 pennants. Please book early. Do not follow sat nav after Totnes - see website for specific suitable directions. Open: 6 April - 30 September. 3 10

**(1m). Higher Rew Caravan & Camping Park, Malborough, Kingsbridge, Salcombe, Devon TQ7 3BW.** 01548 842681. www.higherrew.co.uk. Rural situation. Good, clean facilities. Close to beaches, Salcombe Estuary and cliff walks. Brochure on application. Level pitches all with rural views. Tennis court for hire. Owner supplied copy. Follow A381 towards Salcombe. At Malborough turn R following signs for Soar. After 1m turn L towards Combe/South Sands. Open: 8 April - 31 October. ★★★★ 50 25

## Seaton

**(0.5m). Axevale Caravan Park, Colyford Road, Seaton, Devon EX12 2DF.** 0845 166 2206. www.axevale.co.uk. A quiet park with 68 caravans overlooking the Axe valley. A3052 to Colyford, turn off S by General Store, then 1.5m on L. Open: 1 March - 31 October. ★★★★ BH&HPA 68

**(2m). Beer Head Caravan Park, Beer, Seaton, Devon EX12 3AH.** 01297 21107. www.beer-head.com. Quiet, peaceful, family-run park with panoramic views. Steep hill side. Established over 40 years. Beer village within walking distance. Good centre for boating, fishing and walking. Calor Gas. Colour brochure on request. Golf course nearby. Axminster/Honiton railway station 10m. Owner supplied copy. Off A3052. Open: 19 March - 31 October. 380

**(5m). Berry Barton Caravan and Camping Park, Berry Hill, Branscombe, Seaton, Devon EX12 3BD.** 01297 680208. www.berrybarton.co.uk. Mains water, drainage and electricity. 1m of coastline on 300 acre dairy and beef farm. Shetland ponies. Fishing, riding, golf, shops within 5m. PO, stores in village. Doctor in village once a week. Surgery in Beer 3m, Seaton 5m twice daily. Off A3052, follow signs Gatedown Lane. Open: 15 March - 15 November. BH&HPA 12 9

**(0.5m). Manor Farm Caravan Site (Seaton), Seaton Down Hill, Seaton, Devon EX12 2JA.** 01297 21524. www.manorfarmcaravansite.com. Glorious views of Lyme Bay and Axe Valley. Spacious, quiet, farm site with good facilities. Animals to see and feed. Good playground. Free showers. Beach 1m. Breakfasts served by the site shop, own lamb, pork and free range eggs sold in shop. Owner supplied copy. Off A3052 at Tower Cross, Seaton clearly signed. Open: 12 March - 31 October. 20 30

## Sidmouth

**(3m). Kings Down Tail Caravan & Camping Park, Salcombe Regis, Sidmouth, Devon EX10 0PD.** 01297 680313. www.kingsdowntail.co.uk. A family run quiet, five-acre park. Level and sheltered just inland from Devon's stunning heritage coastline. A variety of craft, animal and historic attractions close by. Adjacent to A3052 3m E of Sidmouth. Open: 15 March - 15 November. ★★★★ BH&HPA 100

**(3m). Oakdown Holiday Park, Gatedown Lane, Weston, Sidmouth, Devon EX10 0PT.** 01297 680587. www.oakdown.co.uk. 150 pitches in total. Level, closely mown, landscaped park. Play area. Microwave. Deep freeze. Free hot water. Family bathrooms and dishwashing facilities all centrally heated. Field trail to world famous Donkey Sanctuary. Serviced super pitches available. Alarmed caravan storage. Colour brochure available with pleasure. Adjacent 9 hole, par 3 golf course now open, complete with reception/cafe. Near Jurassic Coast. David Bellamy Gold Conservation Award. On the A3052, E of Sidmouth. Turn R at the Oakdown International signs. Open: 18 March - 8 November. ★★★★ BH&HPA 20 100 50A 16

**(5m). Putts Corner Caravan Club Site, Putts Corner, Sidbury, Sidmouth, Devon EX10 0QQ.** 01404 42875. www.caravanclub.co.uk. Quiet site in pretty surroundings. Nearby Sidmouth has pebble beach and donkey sanctuary. Local market Tues/Sat. Non-members welcome. No tents. See website for standard directions to site. Open: 23 March - 5 November. ★★★ NCC 117 117

**(1.5m). Salcombe Regis Camping & Caravan Park, Salcombe Regis, Sidmouth, Devon EX10 0JH.** 01395 514303. www.salcombe-regis.co.uk. Hardstandings for tourers and motor caravans. Nearest park to Sidmouth. Situated in an area of outstanding natural beauty on the Heritage coast. Ideal base for exploring rural East Devon. Brochure available on request. 2m from Sidmouth golf club, cinema, shops. E of Sidmouth SP off A3052. Exeter to Lyme Regis coast road. Open: 21 March - 29 October. ★★★★ BH&HPA 40 40 20

## South Brent

**(1.5m). Cheston Caravan Park, Wrangaton Road, South Brent, Devon TQ10 9HF.** 01364 72586. www.cheston-caravanpark.co.uk. Level site. Showers. Set in Dartmoor National Park. Fishing, golf, shop, PO, doctor, horse riding, leisure centre, all nearby. Holiday caravan to let. Owner supplied copy. A38 Exeter, leave at slip road marked Wrangaton Cross turn R at top of slip road and follow signs. From Plymouth take South Brent, Woodpecker slip road go under A38 rejoin A38 then follow directions from Exeter. Open: 15 March - 31 October. 24

## South Molton

**(4.5m). Romansleigh Holiday Park, Odam Hill, South Molton, Devon EX36 4NB.** 01769 550259. www.romansleigh.com. 5m to nearby facilities. 10m Exmoor, 20m coast. 14 acre secluded, rural site, ideal touring

# SOUTH WEST

base for Devon. Heated pool. Games room. Licensed club and bar. Snooker and pool, skittle alley. TV. Pet animals. On B3137 South Molton to Witheridge road. SP R 2m past Alswear. Open: 15 March - 31 October. BH&HPA 3⚡ 10♿ A 55⚡

(4m). **Yeo Valley Holiday Park, The Blackcock Inn, Molland, South Molton, Devon EX36 3NW.** *01769 550297.* www.yeovalleyholidays.co.uk. Indoor swimming pool on site (Easter-September). Country inn serving meals & real ale. Fishing, clay pigeon shooting and other activities nearby. Follow Blackcock Inn sign on the A361 about 4m E of South Molton. Site located on edge of Exmoor. Open: 1 March - 1 January. 65⚡ 65♿ A

### Tavistock

(2m). **Harford Bridge Holiday Park, Peter Tavy, Tavistock, Devon PL19 9LS.** *01822 810349.* www.harfordbridge.co.uk. Quiet level sheltered park in Dartmoor beside the River Tavy. Camping pitches and self catering holiday homes and lodges. Wi-Fi available. Tennis courts, children's play area, table tennis, ideal for walking and relaxing. Easy for exploring Devon and Cornwall. Nearby golf, horse riding, fishing, cinema/theatre all within 2m. David Bellamy Gold Conservation Award. Off A386 Okehampton to Tavistock Road 2m from Tavistock, take Peter Tavy turn, 100yd on R, easy access. Open: All year. ★ ★ ★ 3 BH&HPA 40⚡ 40♿ 40A 13⚡ 2♿

(2.5m). **Langstone Manor Holiday Park, Moortown, Tavistock, Devon PL19 9JZ.** *01822 613371.* www.langstone-manor.co.uk. 40 pitches in total which can take tourers, tents and motor caravans. Quiet secluded park with direct access on to Dartmoor National Park. Clean facilities and warm welcome. Lounge bar serving evening meals. Games room. National Trust properties, gardens, golf, fishing, horse riding, climbing nearby. Ideal base for exploring Devon and Cornwall. Swimming pool, slide and cinema available nearby. Off A386 near Tavistock, take B3357 road to Princetown. After about 1.5m turn R and at crossroads follow brown signs. Open: 15 March - 31 October. ★ ★ ★ ★ 4 BH&HPA 40⚡ 40A 13⚡

**Tavistock Camping & Caravanning Club Site, Higher Longford, Moorshop, Tavistock, Devon PL19 9LQ.** *01822 618672* . www.campingandcaravanningclub.co.uk. The site is located on the West side of Dartmoor National Park and enjoys fabulous views over the Moor. Tavistock Town has a local market and there are many local attractions. Off A386 L on to B3357, site second R after Batteridge Hill. Open: All year. ★ ★ ★ ★ NCC 90⚡ 90♿ A

(4m). **Woodovis Park, Gulworthy, Tavistock, Devon PL19 8NY.** *01822 832968.* www.woodovis.com. Spacious, peaceful, quiet and rural with outstanding views. Sauna & Jacuzzi, mini golf, games room. Play area. Wi-Fi. Bread/croissants baked on site daily. Tavistock: theatre, cinema, shops 4m. Golf 4m. Fishing 2m. Plymouth 15m. Eden Project about 45mins drive. 3.5m W of Tavistock via A390 Callington and Gunnislake road. Turn R at roundabout SP Lamerton, Chip shop. Park sign 1.5m on L. Open: 23 March - 3 November. ★ ★ ★ ★ ★ BH&HPA 50⚡ 50♿ A 22⚡

### Teignmouth

(1m). **Coast View Holiday Park, Torquay Road, Shaldon, Teignmouth, Devon TQ14 0BG.** *01626 872392.* www.coastview.co.uk. Shop, bar, indoor swimming pool, adventure playground. Holiday chalets and caravans. Superb views of Lyme Bay. Families and couples only. Fees on application. S of Teignmouth, 0.5m through Shaldon on A379. Open: 1 April - 31 October. ★ ★ ★ ★ BH&HPA 40⚡ 20♿ A 22⚡

(2m). **Devon Valley Holiday Village, Ringmore, Shaldon, Teignmouth, Devon TQ14 0EY.** *0844 5575100.* www.devonvalley.biz. Heated, indoor swimming pool. Children's club. Indoor amusements and games. Cafe. Laundrette. Cabaret club, riverside pub and restaurant. Owner supplied copy. A380 towards Torbay then B3195 alongside river. Open: 22 April - 31 October. ★ ★ ★ ★ BH&HPA NCC 88⚡

### Tiverton

(5m). **Minnows Touring Park (Affiliated Caravan Club Site), Sampford Peverell, Tiverton, Devon EX16 7EN.** *01884 821770.* CARAVAN CLUB AFFILIATED SITE. Coarse fishing and canoeing on adjacent Grand Western Canal. 15mins walk to pub, shops, PO, doctor & tennis courts. Non-members welcome. Golf driving range and 9 hole golf course within 0.25m. Public transport nearby. Off road cycling (National Cycle Route 3) and walking on the canal paths. Leave M5, J27. Take A361 SP Barnstaple. After 0.25m take slip road on left and follow brown signs. Open: 7 March - 31 October. BH&HPA 59⚡ 59♿ A

(7m). **Zeacombe House Caravan Park, Elackerton Cross, East Anstey, Tiverton, Devon EX16 9JU.** *01398 341279.* www.zeacombeadultretreat.co.uk. Level, lawned site. Hardstandings. Razor points, hairdryers. Home-cooked food available daily. Good centre for touring Exmoor, Taunton, Minehead and Exeter. Adults only. AA 4 pennants. Coarse and trout fishing 3m; golf 10m. Exit J27 to A361 Tiverton. Turn R next roundabout A396 Minehead Dulverton 5m, Exeter Inn L to B3227. SP S Molton 5m turn L. Open: 25 March - 31 October. ★ ★ ★ ★ BH&HPA NCC 50⚡ 50♿ A

### Totnes

(5m). **Higher Well Farm, Waddeton Road, Stoke Gabriel, Totnes, Devon TQ9 6RN.** *01803 782289.* www.higherwellfarmholidaypark.co.uk. 1m from village of Stoke Gabriel on River Dart, shops, PO. Golf course, leisure centre 3m. Cinema 4m. Central for Torbay beaches and South Devon attractions. Follow A380 from Exeter and Newton Abbot towards Torquay and then turn R on to the ring road. Turn R for Totnes on to A385. Turn L at Parkers Arms pub for Stoke Gabriel and follow direction signs. Open: 31 March - 3 November. ★ ★ ★ ★ BH&HPA 80⚡ 80♿ A 19⚡

**Ramslade Caravan Club Site, Stoke Road, Stoke Gabriel, Totnes, Devon TQ9 6QB.** *01803 782575.* www.caravanclub.co.uk. 2.5m from Paignton. A delightfully situated small park

---

# HIGHER WELL FARM HOLIDAY PARK
## TOURING & MOTOR CARAVANS & TENTS WELCOME

A quiet, secluded farm park, central for touring South Devon, within 4 miles Torbay beaches and 1 mile from River Dart. Facilities include toilet and shower block with dishwashing and family rooms. Launderette, shop and payphone. Electric hook-ups and hard standings.
**31st March to 3rd November • ALSO HOLIDAY CARAVANS FOR HIRE**
John & Liz Ball, Higher Well Farm, Higher Well Farm Holiday Park, Stoke Gabriel TQ9 6RN
**Tel: 01803 782289     www.higherwellfarmholidaypark.co.uk**

Visit www.caravanclub.co.uk                    CARAVAN & HOLIDAY PARKS 2012  **129**

# SOUTH WEST

amid rural surroundings with beautiful hillside views from most pitches. Toilet blocks, laundry facilities and baby and toddler washroom. Play area and dog walk on site. Golf, water sports and NCN route nearby. Ideal for families. Quiet and peaceful off-peak. Member only. No tents. See website for standard directions to site. Open: 23 March - 5 November. NCC

153 153

Steamer Quay Caravan Club Site, Steamer Quay Road, Totnes, Devon TQ9 5AL. *01803 862738*. www.caravanclub.co.uk. Green open site with rural views within a short walk of bustling Totnes. Advance booking essential Bank Holidays. Non-members welcome. Battery charging available. Veg prep area, quiet and peaceful off peak. Beach nearby, good area for walking, recycling facilities, NCN cycle route within 5m. Fishing and golf nearby. Ideal for families. See website for standard directions to site. Open: 30 March - 1 October. NCC

40 40

## Umberleigh

(1.5m). Snapdown Farm Caravans, Snapdown, Chittlehamholt, Umberleigh, Devon EX37 9PF. *01769 540366*. www.snapdown.co.uk. Tiny site - six caravans only, with all facilities in beautiful, peaceful countryside. Outside seating and picnic tables. Woodland walks. Pets welcome. Sea and moors within easy reach. reductions for couples. Owner supplied copy. 6m from South Molton. Directions are sent with booking. Open: 1 April - 4 November.

6

## Westward Ho!

(0.25m). Braddicks Holiday Centre, Merley Road, Westward Ho!, Devon EX39 1JU. *01237 473263*. www.braddicksholidaycentre.co.uk. Selection of self-catering, chalets, apartments and caravans beside blue flag beach. Open all year round with seasonal entertainment in our function suite. On-site bar and restaurant. Ideal location for walking, golfing, surfing and exploring Devon and Cornwall. Small touring tent field. M5, J27 on to the North Devon Link Road (A361). A39 from Barnstaple to Bideford, continue till turning marked Westward Ho! The road will take you down a steep hill called 'Stanwell Hill'. At bottom take immediately L turn into Merley Road. Park located at the end of the road on right hand side. Open: 1 May - 31 October.

60

Surf Bay Holiday Park, Golf Links Road, Westward Ho!, Devon EX39 1HD. *01237 471833*. www.surfbayholidays.co.uk. Own access to beach. Entertainment, golf course nearby. Extensive array of shops and facilities in Westward Ho! Cinema in Barnstaple (7m). Golf course 0.6m. Shopping centre less than 1.25m. Owner supplied copy. M5 to J27, A361 Barnstaple. At Barnstaple, take A39 Bideford/Bude road. Follow the road over the Torridge Bridge, at roundabout head for Westward Ho! At Westward Ho!, take second turning on right Beach Road. Open: 19 March - 30 October. ★★★★ BH&HPA NCC

96

## Widecombe in the Moor

(5m). Cockingford Farm Campsite, Widecombe in the Moor, Devon TQ13 7TG. *01364 621258*. Terraced site in a wooded valley in Dartmoor with great views of Honeybag Tor and Bonehill rocks. Fairly shallow little river runs through. 1.5m S of Widecombe. Open: 1 March - 1 November.

10 5

## Winkleigh

(1m). Four Seasons Village R, Winkleigh, Devon EX19 8DP. *01837 83456*. www.four-seasons-village.co.uk. BH&HPA

92

# SOUTH WEST

## Woolacombe

**(2m). Damage Barton Camping & Caravanning Club Site,** Mortehoe, Woolacombe, Devon EX34 7EJ. *01271 870502* . www.campingandcaravanningclub.co.uk. Overlooking the Bristol Channel, the site is located in an Area Of Outstanding Natural Beauty. The surrounding area contains a number of sandy beaches. Information centre on site and local attractions include a number of golf courses as well as Exmoor. From A361 turn L on to B3343 then R towards Mortehoe, R after Warcombe lane on to site. Open: 13 March - 8 November. **NCC** ★110 ★110 A

**(1m). Easewell Farm Holiday Park & Golf Club (Woolacombe Bay Holiday Parks),** Station Road, Mortehoe, Woolacombe, Devon EX34 7EH. *01271 870343*. www.woolacombe.com. Indoor heated pool, bar, restaurant and takeaway. Bus to beach. Use of facilities at three other nearby holiday parks. Fishing nearby. Affiliated golf course on site and nightly star cabaret. Doctor, shops 10mins by car. PO within 10mins walk. J27 take A361. Turn L at Mullacott Cross to Mortehoe village. Easewell SP on the R before the village. Open: 25 March - 29 October. ★★★★ **BH&HPA NCC** 30 133 A

**Europa Park,** Woolacombe Station Road, Woolacombe, Devon EX34 7AN. *01271 871425*. www.europapark.co.uk. Full facilities with superb camping, surf cabins, luxury wooden lodges, static caravans, licensed club house, sauna, children's play area. Off B3343 near Woolacombe. Open: All year.

**(1m). Golden Coast Holiday Park (Woolacombe Bay Holiday Parks),** Station Road, Mortehoe, Woolacombe, Devon EX34 7HW. *01271 870343*. www.woolacombe.com. Tennis, nightly star cabaret, FREE kids club. Hair & beauty salon. Ten pin bowling, fishing, golf course nearby. Bus to beach. Heated indoor and outdoor pools, restaurant and takeaway, bar, shop, cinema, sauna, solarium, amusements. Ceramic studio. M5 J27, A361 Barnstaple to Mullacott Cross. First exit to Woolacombe. Follow signs. Open: 18 February - 28 November. ★★★★ **BH&HPA NCC** 91 91 A 160

**(1m). Little Roadway Farm Campsite,** Georgeham Road, Woolacombe, Devon EX34 7HL. *01271 870313*. www.littleroadway.co.uk. 0.75m to beach, shops, PO, doctors, fishing, golf course, pubs and restaurants, surf shops and surf hire. J27, M5, A361 Barnstaple towards Ilfracombe. Mullacott Cross roundabout L towards Woolacombe B3343, first L B3231 towards Georgeham, 2m on L. Open: 31 March - 31 October. 200 50 A

**(1m). North Morte Farm Caravan Park,** North Morte Road, Mortehoe, Woolacombe, Devon EX34 7EG. *01271 870381*. www.northmortefarm.co.uk. Quiet, family park in beautiful countryside. Play area. Payphone. Sea 500yd. Shop on site. Off B3343. In Mortehoe village turn off at PO on to North Morte Road, park is 500yd on L. Open: 1 April - 30 October. ★★★★ **BH&HPA** 26 26 150 A 23

**(1m). Twitchen House Holiday Park (Woolacombe Bay Holiday Parks),** Station Road, Mortehoe, Woolacombe, Devon EX34 7ES. *01271 870343*. www.woolacombe.com. 334 mixed pitches in total. Licensed club. Nightly star cabaret and entertainment. Indoor and outdoor pool. Restaurant and bar. Games room, amusement arcade. Shop. Adventure playground. Free children's club. Bus to beach. M5, J27, A361 from Barnstaple L on B3343 1.75m. Keep R, SP Mortehoe for 1.5m. Park on L. Open: 23 March - 5 November. ★★★★ **BH&HPA NCC** 334 334 A 232

**(2m). Willingcott Caravan Club Site,** Willingcott, Woolacombe, Devon EX34 7HN. *01271 870554*. www.caravanclub.co.uk. A spacious site with lovely views over Lundy and only 2m from best sandy beach in the county. Some hardstandings, MV service pt, veg prep area, gas and Gaz, dog walk nearby. Quiet and peaceful off peak. NCN cycle route within 5m. Boules pitch. Play equipment. Fishing, golf and water sports nearby. Ideal for families. Members only. No tents. See website for standard directions to site. Open: 23 March - 5 November. **NCC** 164 164

**PREMIER PARKS 2011** **(0.75m). Woolacombe Bay Holiday Parks,** Station Road, Mortehoe, Woolacombe, Devon EX34 7AH. *08432 080391*. www.woolacombe.com/meg. Indoor & outdoor heated pool, Romano health spa, tennis, golf, free cabaret and kids club. Bus between sites and beach. Shop, restaurant and takeaway, bar, solarium. M5 J27, A361 from Barnstaple then first exit at Mullacott Cross, R turn to Mortehoe. Open: 11 February - 28 November. ★★★★ **BH&HPA NCC** 233

**(0.5m). Woolacombe Sands Holiday Park,** Beach Road, Woolacombe, Devon EX34 7AF. *01271 870569*. www.woolacombe-sands.co.uk. Set in beautiful countryside overlooking Woolacombe's fabulous golden sands. First class amenities including indoor heated pool, club with entertainment. Children's club April-October. New WiFi hotspot for 2011. David Bellamy Silver Conservation Award. M5, J27, N Devon link (361) to Barnstaple, A361 to Ilfracombe, B3343 to Woolacombe. Open: 1 April - 30 October. ★★★★ **BH&HPA** 120 A 60

# SOUTH WEST

## Yelverton

(2m). **Magpie Leisure Park (Dartmoor Country Holidays), Bedford Bridge, Horrabridge, Yelverton, Devon PL20 7RY.** 01822 852651. www.dartmoorcountryholidays.co.uk. 35 mixed pitches in total. Tranquil small park within easy access of local amenities. Bordering Dartmoor National Park. Children's play area. Dogs to be kept on leash. Sailing, fishing, golf, horse riding nearby. Take A386 from Plymouth to Tavistock. Turn R after Horrabridge. Open: 15 March - 15 November. BH&HPA ★★★ 35🏊

## DORSET

### Bere Regis

(0.75m). **Rowlands Wait Touring Park, Rye Hill, Bere Regis, Dorset BH20 7LP.** 01929 472727. www.rowlandswait.co.uk. Private, quiet and select in an area of outstanding natural beauty. Ideal for nature lovers, birdwatchers and quiet family holidays. Modern facilities. AA Award. Open in winter by arrangement. Telephone for free brochure. David Bellamy Gold Conservation Award. From Bere Regis take Wool-Bovington road. Site 0.75m up Rye Hill on R. Open: 15 March - 31 January. ★★★ BH&HPA 71

### Blandford

(2m). **The Inside Park, Fairmile Road, Blandford, Dorset DT11 0HG.** 01258 453719. www.theinsidepark.co.uk. Parkland site surrounded by woodland. Play area. AA 3 pennants. RAC appointed. 2m SW of Blandford on road to Winterborne Stickland, clearly signed from bypass. Open: 30 March - 31 October. ★★★★ BH&HPA 125

### Bridport

(1.5m). **Bingham Grange Touring & Camping Park (Adults-only), Melplash, Bridport, Dorset DT6 3TT.** 01308 488234. www.binghamgrange.co.uk. Adult only, award winning, family run park. Excellent heated modern facilities. Bar/restaurant. Views over Dorset's Brit Valley yet only 4.5m from the coast. Pets welcome - great walking. Turn off A35 in Bridport, at roundabout on to A3066 (SP Beaminster) after 1.5m turn L into farm road. Open: 16 March - 31 October. ★★★★★ 50 60 42

(1.5m). **Eype House Caravan & Camping Site, Eype, Bridport, Dorset DT6 6AL.** 01308 424903. www.eypehouse.co.uk. 200yd to beach, on the Dorset Coastal Path. Owner supplied copy. Off A35 to Honiton take turning to Eype, then the turning to the sea. Follow lane to the bottom, entrance to park on R. Open: 31 March - 27 October. ★★★ BH&HPA 20 70

(2m). **Freshwater Beach Holiday Park, Burton Bradstock, Bridport, Dorset DT6 4PT.** 01308 897317. www.freshwaterbeach.co.uk. Private beach. Amusements. Club. Entertainment. Takeaway food. Swimming pools. Riding. Laundrette. Dogs allowed except in hired vans. Golf course adjoining site. Licensed restaurant, 3 bars. Play area. Coastal walks. David Bellamy Bronze Conservation Award. On B3157. Bridport to Weymouth Coast Road. Open: 18 March - 12 November. ★★★★ BH&HPA 500 535 266 60

(3m). **Golden Cap Holiday Park, Seatown, Chideock, Bridport, Dorset DT6 6JX.** 01308 422139. www.wdlh.co.uk. Overlooked by the famous Golden Cap clifftop and surrounded by National Trust countryside on Heritage coastline. Ideal location for walking the coastal path. Fishing lake on site, leisure facilities available at Highlands End (sister park) about 2m away. Golf course 3m. David Bellamy Gold Conservation Award. Off A35 Lyme Regis to Bridport. Turn off to Seatown from Chideock, follow this road and Golden Cap can be found at the end on the left hand side. Open: 16 March - 4 November. ★★★★★ BH&HPA 86 86 29 1

(3.5m). **Graston Copse Holiday Park, Annings Lane, Burton Bradstock, Bridport, Dorset DT6 4QP.** 01308 422139. www.wdlh.co.uk. Flat, well-drained country site. 8 electric (grass), 40 grass pitches non electric. Very quiet rural park surrounded by farmland, but a short distance (about 1m) from the coast. Golf nearby, pubs and shop in Burton Bradstock (10mins walk away). David Bellamy Gold Conservation Award. In village of Burton Bradstock turn at Anchor Hotel, 2nd R into Annings Lane - park 1m on R. Open: 20 April - 9 September. ★★★ BH&HPA 8 8 40

**Highlands End Holiday Park, Eype, Bridport, Dorset DT6 6AR.** 01308 422139. www.wdlh.co.uk. Select family park with exceptional views of Lyme Bay and the Heritage coastline. Indoor heated swimming pool and leisure complex, lounge bar with meals. Tennis court. Pitch & putt course. Golf course 2m. David Bellamy Gold Conservation Award. Off A35,1m W of Bridport, take sp to Eype, follow the road round and take the brown sign, turning on R, SP to Highlands End. Open: 16 March - 4 November. ★★★★★ BH&HPA 95 95 95 24

(1.5m). **Highlands End Holiday Park (Best of British), Eype, Bridport, Dorset DT6 6AR.** 01308 422139. www.wdlh.co.uk. Select family park with exceptional views of Lyme Bay and the Heritage coastline. Indoor heated swimming pool and leisure complex, lounge bar with meals. Tennis court. Pitch & putt course. Golf course 2m. David Bellamy Gold Conservation Award. Off A35,1m W of

# SOUTH WEST

Bridport, take sp to Eype, follow the road round and take the brown sign, turning on R, SP to Highlands End. Off A35,1m W of Bridport, take sp to Eype, follow the road round and take the brown sign, turning on R, SP to Highlands End. Open: 16 March - 4 November. ★★★★★ BH&HPA ♀ 🐕🐾♿🎣🎿⛳️🍴🚿✕🛝 🔥🏊♿ 95🚐 95🚏 95🅰 24🛖

(4m). **Larkfield Holiday Park, Bredy Lane, Burton Bradstock, Bridport, Dorset DT6 4ND.** 01308 422139. www.wdlh.co.uk/Parks/Larkfield. 4mins walk from beach and village facilities. Unique location. Privately owned caravans and holiday lodges. Golf course 1m. David Bellamy Gold Conservation Award. From Bridport take the coast road towards Weymouth pass through village of Burton Bradstock, the park can be found on the left hand side. Open: 18 March - 6 November. ★★★★ BH&HPA 🐕♿ 🐾♿🏊⛳️♿ 20🚐

(3m). **The Travellers Rest, Dorchester Road, Bridport, Dorset DT6 4PJ.** 01308 459503. Convenient for many places of interest. Panoramic views. Fishing, walking, bird watching. Shops, beach 3m. Winter storage available. E of Bridport via A35 Dorchester road. Open: 1 March - 31 October. 🐕♿🐾♿🎣🍴🅿🛖 ♿🚐🚏🅰

(1.5m). **West Bay Holiday Park, West Bay, Bridport, Dorset DT6 4HB.** 01308 422424. www.parkdeanholidays.co.uk. Shops in Bay include groceries, butchers, fish, newsagents, electrical. On site store, Costa Coffee shop, family entertainment, kids club, cabaret, arcade, pool. David Bellamy Silver Conservation Award. Off A35 Dorchester to Bridport. Follow 'West Bay' to harbour and roundabout. Open: 27 March - 6 November. ★★★★ BH&HPA NCC ♀🐕🐾♿🎣🎿♿ 🍴🔥♿✕🎪♿🏊♿ 131🚐 🅰 55🛖

## Charmouth

**Charmouth Camping & Caravanning Club Site, Scotts Lane, Monkton Wylde Farm, Charmouth, Dorset DT6 6DB.** 08455211915. www.campingandcaravanningclub.co.uk. Situated on the Dorset and Devon border amongst rolling countryside down to the sea. A walker's paradise with a 20m coastal path nearby. Non-members welcome. All units accepted. Visitors strip for miles around to hunt for fossils along Charmouth coast. Local attractions include the Undercliff Nature Reserve near the site and Cobb Harbour. Special deals available for families and backpackers. David Bellamy Gold Conservation Award. On A35 from Dorchester, turn R 0.5m past end of dual carriageway, SP 'Marshwood, B3165'. Site on L. 3m from Axminster. Open: 25 March - 1 November. ★★★★★ NCC 🐕♿🐾♿🎣🍴♿✕🛝♿ ♿ 150🚐 150🚏

(1m). **Dolphins River Park, Berne Lane, Charmouth, Dorset DT6 6RD.** 01297 561322. www.dolphinsriverpark.co.uk. Secluded, quiet 'garden park' on banks of river Char, 1m from beach. Golf, cinema, shopping within 2-5m. 5m W of Bridport on A35, turn R to Whitchurch Cannonilorum (opposite Charmouth slip road) Park 300yd on L. Open: 1 April - 31 October. ★★★★ BH&HPA 🐕♿🐾♿ 🚐🚏 40🛖

(6m). **Manor Farm Holiday Centre (Charmouth), Manor Farm, Charmouth, Dorset DT6 6QL.** 01297 560226. www.manorfarmholidaycentre.co.uk. 400 mixed pitches in total. Licensed bar. Family room. Bar with entertainment. Swimming pool. Fish and chip takeaway. Play area. Riding. Golf and fishing nearby. 10mins level walk to beach. Golf course, cinema 3m. Shopping centre 6m. Open all year - statics mid March-October only. In centre of Charmouth off Charmouth bypass (A35). Open: All year. ★★★🐕🐾 ♿🎣🎿♿⛳️🍴🔥🏊✕🎪🛝 ♿🚿♿ 400🚐🅰 4🛖

(3m). **Newlands Holiday Park, Charmouth, Dorset DT6 6RB.** 01297 560259. www.newlandsholidays.co.uk. 200 pitches in total. Two swimming pools. Indoor and outdoor play areas. Delightful Dorset views. Heritage coast village near Lyme Regis. Short stroll to beach. Ideal for touring, walking and all the family. Golf course 2.5m. Cinema 3m. Sea fishing 1m. David Bellamy Silver Conservation Award. On A35 Bridport to Lyme Regis. Open: 1 February - 30 November. ★★★★★ BH&HPA ♀🐕🐾♿🎣🎿♿🍴 🔥♿✕🎪🛝♿🏊♿ 75🚐 150🚏 80🅰 50🛖 15🏠

(0.5m). **Seadown Holiday Park, Bridge Road, Charmouth, Dorset DT6 6QS.** 01297 560154. www.seadownholidaypark.co.uk. Small, family run park alongside River Char. Access from park to World Heritage fossil beach. 5 min walk to village. Badminton field. A35 Bridport to Axminster, SP to Charmouth main street L into Bridge road. Open: 17 March - 3 November ★★★★★ 🐕♿🐾♿🍴 ♿🎣♿🛝♿ 10🚐 50🚏 🅰 205🛖

(1m). **Wood Farm Caravan Park, Axminster Road, Charmouth, Dorset DT6 6BT.** 01297 560697. www.woodfarm.co.uk. CARAVAN CLUB AFFILIATED SITE. Non-members and tent campers welcome. Best of British Park. World Heritage Coast and spectacular rural scenery - the area is famous for its rugged coastline littered with fossils from the Jurassic age. Walkers are spoilt for choice. Off A35, to Western side of village of Charmouth. Open: 29 March - 28 October. ★★★★ BH&HPA ♀🐕♿ 🐾♿🎣♿⛳️🍴🔥♿✕🛝♿ ♿ 163🚐🅰 3🛖

## Christchurch

(3.5m). **Cobbs Holiday Park, 32 Gordon Road, Highcliffe-on-Sea, Christchurch, Dorset BH23 5HN.** 01425 273301. www.cobbspark.co.uk. Pleasant, family run park with enviable location near New Forest and beaches. Laundrette, play area, licensed club with free entertainment. GS. Owner supplied copy. Leave A35 Lyndhurst to Christchurch road at the Somerford roundabout, take A337 to Highcliffe. Look for brown tourist sign to Cobb's Holiday Park, turn L into Gordon road at traffic lights in the village centre. Open: 22 April - 31 October. ★★★★ BH&HPA ♀🐕♿🎣🎵🍴♿✕♿ 90🛖

(4m). **Harrow Wood Farm, Poplar Lane, Bransgore, Christchurch, Dorset BH23 8JE.** 01425 672487. www.caravan-sites.co.uk. Coarse fishing on site. A35, 10m W of Lyndhurst. Turn R at Cat & Fiddle. Site is SP from Bransgore. Open: 1 March - 6 January. ★★★ BH&HPA 🐾♿🎣🛝🏠 ♿♿ 60🚐🅰

(2m). **Hoburne Park, Hoburne Lane, Christchurch, Dorset BH23 4HU.** 01425 273379. www.hoburne.com. Licensed club. Seasonal entertainment. Indoor leisure pool. Outdoor pool. Restaurant. Playground. Hard-court tennis. New mini bowling. Snooker. Laundrette. David Bellamy Silver Conservation Award. From A35 turn L on to A337. Take first exit off next round about. Park on R. Open: 1 March - 31 October. ★★★★★ BH&HPA NCC 🐕♿♿🎣🍴✕♿ ♿ 260🛖

(8m). **Holmsley (Forest Holidays), Forest Road, Thorney Hill, Christchurch, Dorset BH23 7EQ.** 01425 674502. www.forestholidays.co.uk. Ideally situated for a seaside break, just a short drive from beaches at Bournemouth and Christchurch. Mainly grassland site Great for children. Bookings and brochure requests on 0845 1308224. Located off A35 Lyndhurst-Christchurch road, 8m SW of Lyndhurst. Open: 14 April - 31 October. BH&HPA 🐕♿🐾♿🎣🍴♿♿ ♿♿ 600🚐🅰

(1m). **Meadowbank Holidays, Stour Way, Christchurch, Dorset BH23 2PQ.**

Visit www.caravanclub.co.uk

CARAVAN & HOLIDAY PARKS 2012 133

# SOUTH WEST

01202 483597. www.meadowbank-holidays.co.uk. Tourers welcome, booking necessary in peak season. Adjacent to public golf course and private fishing on river Stour. Swimming pool, beach 2m. Pub, restaurants 1m. Rose Award Park. Take Christchurch exit off A338 follow SP. Open: 1 March - 31 October. ★★★★★ BH&HPA 48 275

(3m). **Mount Pleasant Touring Park, Matchams Lane, Hurn, Christchurch, Dorset BH23 6AW.** 01202 475474. www.mount-pleasant-cc.co.uk. 4 AA pennants. Fishing, golf, swimming. Pony trekking, stock car racing, dry ski slope, New Forest, all nearby. Also closest park to Bournemouth. PO 1m. Playground area. Excellent facilities, shop, cafe. . Take A338 from Bournemouth or Ringwood, turn off at Christchurch-Hurn exit and turn R towards Hurn, at first roundabout take second exit on immediate L into Matchams Lane, park is 1m on R. Open: 1 March - 1 November. ★★★★ 4 BH&HPA 50 175

(3m). **Sandhills Holiday Park, Avon Beach, Mudeford, Christchurch, Dorset BH23 4AL.** 0845 8159775. www.ParkHolidaysUK.com. Playground. Heated outdoor pool. Family club. Takeaway. Bar. Amusements. Laundrette. On site store. Free kids club and evening entertainment. Situated on the seafront. Bournemouth: shopping, restaurants, theatre, cinema. New Forest. David Bellamy Silver Conservation Award. Off A337 Christchurch to Lymington road. Open: 1 March - 31 October. ★★★ BH&HPA NCC 164

## Corfe Castle

**Knitson Farm Tourers Site, Knitson Farm, Corfe Castle, Dorset BH20 5JB.** 01929 425121. www.knitsonfarm.co.uk. Quiet family site on working farm for s/c units. Own sanitation necessary. 1.5m to Swanage Beach, 3m Studland beach, excellent walking area. Near to World Heritage coast. Golf course, tennis, horse riding all nearby. Great mountain biking area. L off A351 just after entering Swanage, Washpond Lane, then L at T-junction. Proceed for 0.5m, site on L and further on on R. Open: 6 April - 27 October. 60 60

## Dorchester

**(8m). Clay Pigeon Caravan Park, Wardon Hill, Evershot, Dorchester, Dorset DT2 9PW.** 01935 83492. www.southerncountiesleisure.com. Ideal centre for touring 'Hardy' country. Level, gently sloping mature site. Cafe, bar and restaurant open 7 days/week. Heated toilet block with showers. Fishing, shooting, karting, golf and riding nearby. Rally field available. Owner supplied copy. On A37 midway between Yeovil and Dorchester. Open: 1 April - 31 October. ★★★ BH&HPA 60

**(5.5m). Crossways Caravan Club Site, Crossways, Dorchester, Dorset DT2 8BE.** 01305 852032. www.caravanclub.co.uk. Imaginatively landscaped site, ideal for touring Dorset. Dog walk. Advance booking essential BH and July and August. Hardstandings. Shower blocks and laundry facilities, with privacy cubicles. MV service point. Non-members welcome. No tents. See website for standard directions to site. 8.5m from Weymouth. Open: 23 March - 15 October. ★★★★ NCC 120 120

**(8m). Giants Head Camping & Caravan Park, Old Sherborne Road, Dorchester, Dorset DT2 7TR.** 01300 341242. www.giantshead.co.uk. Cottage and chalet available. Shops, PO, doctor, fishing, golf all within 2-3m. Good walking and views. Owner supplied copy. From Dorchester, into town avoiding bypass, from top of town roundabout, take Sherborne road after about 500yd, fork R at Loders Garage, SP. From Cerne Abbas take Buckland Newton road. Open: 22 April - 31 October. ★★ BH&HPA 50

**(6m). Gorselands Caravan Park, West Bexington-on-Sea, Dorchester, Dorset DT2 9DJ.** 01308 897232. www.gorselands.co.uk. A peaceful and pretty award winning park overlooking Lyme Bay. An ideal setting for exploring the beautiful West Dorset coast and countryside. David Bellamy Silver Conservation Award. Owner supplied copy. 6m E of Bridport on B3157, turn R at Bull Inn in Swyre Village. Park 100yd on r h side. Open: 17 March - 3 November. ★★★★ BH&HPA 145

**(7m). Moreton Camping & Caravanning Club Site, Station Road, Moreton, Dorchester, Dorset DT2 8BB.** 01305 853801. www.campingandcaravanningclub.co.uk. In a popular holiday area, 7m from Weymouth and Dorchester. 2 holiday bungalows available to let. Local leisure centre has large indoor pool with wave machine. Other local attractions include dry ski slope and cider museum. Visit Dorchester on Wednesday for market day. Special deals available for families and backpackers. Non-members welcome. All units accepted. From Poole on A35, continue past Bere Regis, turn L B3390 SP Alfpuddle. After about 2m site on L before Moreton Station and next to Frampton Arms Pub. Open: 1 April - 9 January. ★★★★ 120 120 2

**(3m). Morn Gate Holiday Park, Bridport Road, Dorchester, Dorset DT2 9DS.** 01305 889284. www.morngate.co.uk. Luxury Scandinavian style chalets, lodges and modern caravans. Small exclusive park set in heart of Thomas Hardy countryside. Children's play area and recreation ground. Communal BBQ areas. Ideal base to tour area. Owner supplied copy. W of Dorchester on main A35. Open: All year. ★★★ BH&HPA 50 30 14

**(6m). Sandyholme Holiday Park, Moreton Road, Owermoigne, Dorchester, Dorset DT2 8HZ.** 01308 426947. www.wdlh.co.uk. Quiet family park situated in Hardy countryside with all amenities. Holiday vans for hire/sale. Games room, play park, duck pond. Central for Weymouth, Dorchester and Lulworth Cove. Golf, cinema, shopping centre within 5m. David Bellamy Gold Conservation Award. Minor road N of A352 6m SE of Dorchester. Site is 1m N of turning. Open: 18 March - 6 November. ★★★★ BH&HPA 43 43 7

**(6m). Warmwell Caravan Park (Adults only), Warmwell Road, Warmwell, Dorchester, Dorset DT2 8JD.** 01305 852313. www.warmwellcaravanpark.co.uk. Enjoy the peace and tranquillity of this adults-only, 15-acre site in an Area of Outstanding Natural Beauty. 6m from Dorchester and Weymouth beaches. Touring area is for adults only. Holiday homes for sale. Owner supplied copy. Park is easy to find on B3390, which joins A35 between Bere Regis and Tolpuddle,

**BOURNEMOUTH ST LEONARDS FARM**
Ringwood Road, West Moors, Ferndown, Dorset BH22 0AQ
Quiet level site near Bournemouth, Poole
Cross-Channel Ferries and New Forest. Easy access off A31. Electric hook-ups, modern shower and toilet block including room for disabled, laundrette, play area with picnic tables. Shops, bars, takeaways, swimming, golf, ridings and windsurfing all nearby. Open April-September. Booking advisable July and August.
Bookings: W.E. Love and Son
Email: enquiries_stleonards@yahoo.com  Tel: 01202 872 637  www.stleonardsfarm.biz

# SOUTH WEST

the A353 from Weymouth, and the A352 Dorchester to Wareham Road. Open: 1 March - 2 January.

### Ferndown

**St Leonards Farm Caravan and Camping Park, Ringwood Road, A31, West Moors, Ferndown, Dorset BH22 0AQ.** 01202 872637. www.stleonardsfarm.biz. Ideal for Bournemouth & Poole. Play area. 3 AA pennants. Owner supplied copy. On A31 Ringwood to Ferndown, 5m W of Ringwood opposite Texaco Garage. Open: 1 April - 30 September. BH&HPA 101 101 A 5

### Gillingham

**(1m). Leela Fields (Thorngrove) Camping & Caravan Park, Common Mead Lane, Gillingham, Dorset SP8 4RE.** 01747 821221. www.osholeela.co.uk. Nice views, only a quick drive into Gillingham town. Touring park, static caravan & chalet homes with views over the Blackmore Vale. Off B3081 near Gillingham. Open: All year.

### Lyme Regis

**(1m). Hook Farm Caravan and Camping Park, Hook Farm, Gore Lane, Uplyme, Lyme Regis, Dorset DT7 3UU.** 01297 442801. www.hookfarm-uplyme.co.uk. Gas sales. AA 3 pennants award. Golf course, cinema, shopping and beach: 1m. 400yd to newsagent and village pub. Leafy river footpath walk to Lyme Regis (about 40mins) No cats. Owner-occupied caravans, from 15/3/11 to 31/10/11. Open for Hire caravans, from 15/3/11 to 31/10/11. Owner supplied copy. Take B3165 off A35 into Uplyme. Turn R opposite Talbot Arms pub into Gore Lane. Off A3052 take directions to Uplyme (Gore Lane) before entering Lyme Regis. Open: 1 March - 4 November. 3 40 3 A 22

**(3m). Shrubbery Touring Park, Rousdon, Lyme Regis, Dorset DT7 3XW.** 01297 442227. www.shrubberypark.co.uk. The Shrubbery is a level site situated in an unspoilt and uncommercialised part of the world heritage coastline of outstanding natural beauty. Ideal base for fossil hunters. AA 4 stars. W of picturesque Lyme Regis on the A3052 coast road. Open: 1 April - 31 October. ★★★★ BH&HPA 10 120

**(1m). Timber Vale Caravan Park, Charmouth Road, Lyme Regis, Dorset DT7 3HG.** 01297 442585. www.timber-vale.co.uk. Family owned and run park. NO TENTS, TOURERS OR MOTOR CARVANS. No commercial sub-letting of caravans. Peaceful park on edge of Lyme Regis. For families use only. Golf 0.5m, shops and cinema 1m. Beach 0.75m. Owner supplied copy. Located on A3052, Lyme Regis to Charmouth road. Less than 1m from A35. Open: 2 April - 29 October. 156

### Poole

**(3m). Beacon Hill Touring Park, Blanford Road North, Poole, Dorset BH16 6AB.** 01202 631631. www.beaconhilltouringpark.co.uk. Heated swimming pool. Fully licensed bar with entertainment and takeaway in high season. All-weather tennis court. Coarse fishing lake on site. Children's play area. Situated 0.25m N from jct. of A35 on A350 towards Blandford, approx 3m N of Poole to Cherbourg and Poole to St Malo and Channel Island Ferries. Open: 6 April - 31 October. ★★★ BH&HPA 50 120

**(4m). Huntick Farm, Lytchett Matravers, Poole, Dorset BH16 6BB.** 01202 622222. Small, level grass site in wooded surroundings. 10% discount for OAPs. Rallies welcome. Convenient for ferry crossings from Poole. Storage for caravans and boats now available. Dogs allowed on leads. Fees according to season. AA 3 pennants. Open Easter-October 31. Owner supplied copy. Just off A350 on Poole-Blandford, take sign to L Matravers. First L and L at Rose & Crown pub. Site 1m on R. Open: 1 April - 31 October. 3 10 20

 **(5m). Merley Court Holiday Park, Merley, Wimborne, Poole, Dorset BH21 3AA.** 01590 648331. www.shorefield.co.uk. A 5 star Best of British park. Direct access off A31 roundabout. Open: 7 February - 2 January. ★★★★★ 5 BH&HPA 170 170

**(4m). Organford Manor Country Park (Open 2012), Organford, Poole, Dorset BH16 6ES.** 01202 625120. www.organfordmanorpark.co.uk. 30 tent pitches available. Shop on site in high season. Take first turning L off A35 after the roundabout at the junction of the A351 and A35. Park is first entrance on R about 0.25m. Open: Contact site direct. ★★★ A 42

**(3m). Rockley Park Holiday Park (Haven), Hamworthy, Poole, Dorset BH15 4LZ.** 0871 2310880. www.caravancamping.co.uk. Heated outdoor & indoor pool. Spa experience & treatment rooms. Restaurants & takeaway. Club, bar and family entertainment. Sailing. Windsurfing. Diving. Nature reserve, bowling green, amusements, tennis courts. New outdoor family Funzone, new multi sports courts, play areas, Rollerblades, crazy golf. No dogs allowed Bank Holidays or school holidays (Touring). Welcome host. David Bellamy Silver Conservation Award. Leave M27 and join A31. Follow signs for Poole town centre. In town centre SP for Rockley Park. Alternatively take Dorchester bypass leading to Poole and follow the signs for Rockley Park. Open: 18 March - 31 October. ★★★★★ BH&HPA NCC 60 60 A 1397

**(3m). Sandford Holiday Park, Holton Heath, Poole, Dorset BH16 6JZ.** 01202 622513. www.parkdeanholidays.co.uk. Set in acres of peaceful Dorset woodland, close to the Jurassic coastline and busting centres of Poole and Bournemouth. Fantastic entertainment, children's clubs, choice of pitches and holiday homes, heated indoor and outdoor pools, restaurants, and plenty of family attractions near to the park. David Bellamy Gold Conservation Award. Open February-November + Xmas & New Year. 1m N of Whitby centre on A174 coast road, next to Whitby Golf Club. Open: 6 March - 1 November. ★★★★ BH&HPA NCC 330 A 710

**(3m).South Lytchett Manor Caravan & Camping Park, Dorchester Road, Lytchett Minster, Poole, Dorset BH16 6JB.** 01202 622577. www.southlytchettmanor.co.uk. Set in 20 acres of stunning parkland of the former Lytchett Manor. Exceptional brand new amenities blocks. Dog walking area. TV hook ups & Wi-Fi. Village pub within walking distance. Bus stop at gates. Three miles to Poole. On B3067 off A35 follow A350 S from junction with A31 turn R, first sign to Lytchett Minster, follow road downhill for 1m, park on R at T-junction with B3067. Open: 1 March - 2 January. ★★★★★ BH&HPA 50 50 A 3

**(3m). Pear Tree Holiday Park, Organford Road, Holton Heath, Poole, Dorset BH16 6LA.** 0844 272 9504. www.peartreepark.co.uk. Pear Tree is a picturesque, tranquil park within easy reach of Dorset's many spectacular sites including the Jurassic coast and the towns of Poole, Bournemouth and Swanage. From A35 take A351 to Wareham, then 1st R to Organford. Open: 1 March - 31 October.

Visit www.caravanclub.co.uk

# SOUTH WEST

### Portland

**(0.5m). The Cove Holiday Park, Pennsylvania Road, Portland, Dorset DT5 1HU.** 01305 821286. www.coveholidaypark.co.uk. Clifftop park offering breathtaking sea views, located in the grounds of a former royal castle. Local shops, country pubs, restaurants, beach all within a short walk away. Cove Park is positioned on the left-hand side, just past Portland Museum and Church Ope Cove, next door to Pennsylvania Castle. Short drive from Weymouth & Dorchester. Open: 1 March - 14 January. ★★★★★ 🚐⛺ ✕ 🐕 🚻 ♿ ⛽ ♨ 🛒 🏪 ⚡ 100🏕

### Salisbury

**(11m). Church Farm Caravan & Camping Park, The Bungalow, High Street, Sixpenny Handley, Salisbury, Dorset SP5 5ND.** 01725 552563. www.churchfarmcandcpark.co.uk. Quiet family farm site, situated in the Cranborne Chase, central position for touring. Ideal for walking and mountain biking. Heated amenities block, free showers. Brochure available. New toilets and shower for 2009/10 season. Owner supplied copy. 1m S of Handley Hill roundabout on A354 turn off for Sixpenny Handley. R by school. Site 300yd by church. Open: All year. ★★★ 🚐⛺ ✕ 🐕 ✱ ♨ 🛒 ⚡ ✕ ♿ ⛽ 35🏕 35⚡ ⚡ 4✓

### Shaftesbury

**(2m). Blackmore Vale Camping & Caravan Park, Sherbourne Causeway (A30), Shaftesbury, Dorset SP7 9PX.** 01747 851523. Close to famous Gold Hill, Saxon abbey ruins and hilltop market town of Shaftesbury. A30, W of Shaftesbury. Open: All year. ⛺ 🚐 ♨ ✱ 🚻 ♿ 🐕 🛒 ⚡ 10🏕 20⚡ ⚡

### St Leonards

**(3.5m). Back of Beyond Touring Park** (Tranquil adults-only)**, Ringwood Road, St Leonards, Dorset BH24 2SB.** 01202 876998. www.backofbeyondtouringpark.

co.uk. ADULTS ONLY. 28 acres of peaceful, unspoilt countryside - well off the beaten track. Easy access to local amenities, coast and New Forest. Adults only. Fishing and golf on site. 3.5m W of Ringwood, 2m E of Ferndown on A31. Open: 1 March - 31 October. ★★★★ 🚐⛺ ✕ 🐕 ♨ ⚡ 🛒 🏪 ♿ 80🏕 80⚡

### Swanage

**(2.5m). Downshay Farm, Haycrafts Lane, Swanage, Dorset BH19 3EB.** 01929 480316. www.downshayfarm.co.uk. Family site with spectacular views. Stunning views of Corfe Castle - working farm, small friendly site, camping open only during school holidays. Check website for exact times and prices. Owner supplied copy. A351 Swanage then turn R at Harmans Cross. 0.5m up Haycrafts Lane. Open: 1 April - 1 November. 🚐⛺ ✕ 🐕 ♨ 🛒 ⚡ 🏪 ♿ 12⚡ ⚡

**(3m). Haycraft Caravan Club Site, Haycrafts Lane, Harmans Cross, Swanage, Dorset BH19 3EB.** 01929 480572. www.caravanclub.co.uk. A delightfully situated site in the heart of the Purbeck countryside and within easy reach of Dorset's beautiful coastline. Toilet blocks with privacy cubicles and laundry facilities. Baby and toddler washroom. Fishing and golf within 5m, dog walk on site. Ideal for families and good area for walking. Non members welcome. No tents. See website for standard directions to site. Open: 23 March - 5 November. ★★★★★ NCC 🚐⛺ ✕ 🐕 ♨ ⚡ 🛒 🏪 ♿ 53🏕 53⚡

**(1.5m). Herston Caravan Park, Washpond Lane, Swanage, Dorset BH19 3DJ.** 01929 422932. www.herstonleisure.co.uk. Eggs and milk available at farm house, mobile shop calls. AA 3 pennants. Off A351 near Swanage. Open: All year. 3 BH&HPA 🚐⛺ ✕ 🐕 ♨ 🎵 🛒 🏪 ♿ ✕ ⚡ 🏪 ⚡ ♿ 10🏕 80⚡ ⚡ 4✓

**(1m). Swanage Coastal Park, Priestway, Swanage, Dorset BH19 2RS.** 01590

648331. www.shorefield.co.uk. The park has lovely views of sea and Purbeck Hills. 1m to beach and town. Pool, gym, shop and restaurant available at the park next door which offers daily membership. David Bellamy Bronze Conservation Award. A351 through Wareham and Corfe Castle, past 'Welcome to Swanage' sign into Herston. Turn R into Bell Street. First L into Priests Road, firs R into Swanage Coastal Park. Open: 1 March - 2 November. ★★★ BH&HPA 🚐⛺ ✕ 🐕 ♨ ⚡ 🛒 🏪 ♿ ⚡ 🏪 ⚡ 145✓

**(1.5m). Ulwell Cottage Caravan Park, Ulwell, Swanage, Dorset BH19 3DG.** 01929 422823. www.ulwellcottagepark.co.uk. Family run park located near sandy beaches, coastal walks and golf. 'Village Inn', heated indoor pool. General shop. David Bellamy Gold Conservation Award. In the lovely Isle of Purbeck, 2m from Studland beach, on Swanage road. Open: 1 March - 7 January. ★★★★ 3 BH&HPA ⚡ 🚐⛺ ✕ 🐕 ♨ ⚡ 🛒 ✕ ♿ 🏪 ⚡ 83⚡ ⚡ 100✓

### Wareham

**(3m). Birchwood Tourist Park, Cold Harbour, Wareham, Dorset BH20 7PA.** 01929 554763. www.birchwoodtouristpark.co.uk. Birchwood Tourist Park is in an ideal position for exploring Dorset. Centrally located for visiting Bournemouth, Poole and The Purbecks. Centrally located within Wareham Forest. Boundaries adjoining the forest give unrivalled direct access for walking, mountain biking or riding. There is a children's paddling pool on the site & all sorts of other activities. Rallies welcome. Bring your dog & take a walk in Wareham Forest. AA-rated 3 pennants. W on A351 at Wareham Railway Station Roundabout, turn R into Bere Road (unclassified) in a N.W. direction toward Bere Regis through Wareham Forest. Open: All year. 3 BH&HPA ⛺ 🚐 ✕ ♿ ⚡ ♨ 🛒 🏪 ⚡ 🐕 ⚡ 🏪 ♿ 175🏕 175⚡ 175✓

**(4m). Corfe Castle Camping & Caravanning Club Site, Bucknowle,**

## A peaceful camping and touring holiday park perfect for exploring the stunning Dorset coastline

**pear tree** holiday park

- Minutes from Poole and beaches.
- Convenience shop and childrens play area.
- Local pub just a short walk away.
- Seasonal pitches.
- Mains electricity and waste disposal points.

PITCHES FROM £10 Quoting CHP10

*Terms and conditions apply

To book call **0844 272 9504** or visit **www.peartreepark.co.uk**

# SOUTH WEST

Wareham, Dorset BH20 5PQ. *01929 480280*. www.campingandcaravanningclub.co.uk. Site lies at the foot of the Purbeck Hills. Excellent base for walkers. Near beaches Studland, Swanage and Lulworth Cove. Also Bournemouth and Poole. Off A351. Open: 1 March - 31 October. ★★★ NCC 日 ★ 丄 ♨ 回 ♨ ⛺ ⛽ ♿ 80 🚐 80 🚗 ⛺

**(8m). Durdle Door Holiday Park, Lulworth Cove, Wareham, Dorset BH20 5PU.** *01929 400200*. www.lulworth.com. On the World Heritage Coast between Weymouth and Swanage, surrounded by stunning countryside close to Lulworth Cove. Durdle Door Holiday Park offers a wide range of facilities and on site amenities including shop, bar, restaurant, laundrette, bike hire in an uncommercialised environment. Direct access to beaches. SW of Wareham via A352 and road S at Wool. Local road W in West Lulworth to site. Open: 1 March - 31 October. ★★★★ BH&HPA 日 ⛽ ★ 丄 ♨ ✗ 🚿 ♿ 34 🚐 24 🚗 50 ⛺ 19 £

**(3m). East Creech Farm, Wareham, Dorset BH20 5AP.** *01929 480519*. www.eastcreechfarm.co.uk. Fishing. 3m to shop, doctor and PO. AA 3 pennants. Owner supplied copy. Take by-pass at Wareham, on third roundabout take Furzebrook-Blue Pool road, site 2m on R. Open: 1 April - 1 November. 3 日 ★ 丄 ♨ ⛽ ♿ ⛺ 80 🚗 ⛺

**Hunter's Moon Caravan Club Site, Cold Harbour, Wareham, Dorset BH20 7PA.** *01929 556605*. www.caravanclub.co.uk. This site provides an excellent base for touring Dorset. Toilet blocks, laundry facilities and MV service point. Fishing, golf and water sports nearby. Play equipment and dog walk on site. Facilities for the disabled. Ideal for families. Quiet and peaceful off-peak. Member only. No tents. See website for standard directions to site. Open: All year. NCC 日 ★ ♨ ⛽ ❄ ♿ 120 🚐 120 🚗

**Lookout Holiday Park, Corse Road, Storborough, Wareham, Dorset BH20 5AZ.** *01929 552546*. www.caravan-sites.co.uk. ★★★★ 日 ⛽ ♨ 🍴 ⛺ ❄ ⛽ 🚐 🚿 ♿ 🚗 ⛺

**(3m). Luckford Wood Caravan & Camping Park, Holme Lane, East Stoke, Wareham, Dorset BH20 6AW.** *01929 463098*. www.luckfordleisure.co.uk. Storage facilities for caravans, boats, motorhomes vans etc. Camp fires and hog roast by arrangement. Open wooded and shaded areas. Close to Heritage Coast, Tank Museum, Monkey World. Fully serviced luxury lodge hire. Pets welcome on site, dog walking lane. Bike hire. Classical farmhouse B&B available. Rally site. Modest showers and toilets, free hot water. From Wareham take A352 towards Wool for 1m then take B3070 to Lulworth for 1m at W Holme, crossroad turn R along Holme Lane site entrance 1m on right hand side. Open: 1 March - 31 October. 日 ⛽ ★ ✗ ♨ ⛺ 25 🚐 50 🚗 ⛺

**(3m). Manor Farm Caravan Park (Wareham), East Stoke, Wareham, Dorset BH20 6AW.** *01929 462870*. www.manorfarmcp.co.uk. 60 mixed pitches in total. Family run, flat, grass touring park surrounded by countryside in an area of 2.5 acres, long and short stay plus winter/summer storage. Small, clean and secluded with showers, toilets and play area. Telephone on site. Resident proprietors. Golf course nearby. Seasonal pitches available. SAE for brochure. Close to Jurassic coast, Monkey World and beaches, walking and cycling. David Bellamy Bronze Conservation Award. From Wareham take A352 turn L at East Stoke redundant church, over railway crossing. Park 0.75m on R. Or A352 T L on to B3070 T R 1st SP East Stoke, crossroad T R SP MFCP - or from WOOL, SP. Open: All year. BH&HPA 日 ⛽ ★ 丄 ♨ ⛽ ❄ ⛺ ✗ 🚿 ♿ 60 🚗 ⛺

**(1.2m). Ridge Farm Camping & Caravan Park, Barnhill Road, Wareham, Dorset BH20 5BG.** *01929 556444*. www.ridgefarm.co.uk. 60 mixed pitches in total. Quiet, secluded family run site. Level pitches. Hot showers and laundrette. Shop in high season. Ideal centre for bird watching, walking, cycling and boating (slipway nearby). Dogs welcome except in July & August. AA 3 pennants. Owner supplied copy. B3075 from Wareham turn L in Stoborough down 'New Road' to village of Ridge. Site is at end of Barnhill Road on L. Open: 1 April - 31 October. 3 日 ⛽ ★ ✗ ♨ ⛺ 🚿 🍴 ❄ ⛽ 60 🚗 ⛺

**Smedmore House (CC Affiliated), Kimmeridge, Wareham, Dorset BH20 5PG.** *01929 480702*. www.smedmore-caravansite.co.uk. AFFILIATED CARAVAN CLUB SITE - MEMBERS ONLY. Manager: B & S Belsten. Prior booking essential. Site is an open, sloping field surrounded by farmland. It has views to the sea and Clavell Tower on one side and the Purbeck Hills on the other. Own sanitation required. Dog walk nearby. Fishing and water sports nearby. Good area for walking. Quiet and peaceful. Owner supplied copy. Off A351. 1m from Kimmeridge. Open: 1 May - 31 October. 日 ★ ✗ ⛺ 42 🚗

**(3m). Wareham Forest Tourist Park, North Trigon, Wareham, Dorset BH20 7NZ.** *01929 551393*. www.warehamforest.co.uk. Spacious, level pitches in secluded woodland setting, with direct access into Wareham Forest, and a friendly, relaxing, family atmosphere. Shop and pool (high season), play area, seasonal pitches and storage. Central location. David Bellamy Gold Conservation Award. Off A35 midway between Wareham & Bere Regis. Open: All year. ★★★★★ BH&HPA NCC 日 ★ 丄 ♨ ⛽ ❄ ✗ 🚿 ⛺ ♿ ⛽ ❄ ⛺ 200 🚗 ⛺

### Weymouth

**Bagwell Farm Touring Park, Chickerell, Weymouth, Dorset DT3 4EA.** *01305 782575*. www.bagwellfarm.co.uk. Tranquil rural setting near Dorset's Jurassic Coastline. Sea views from some

# BIRCHWOOD TOURIST PARK

Family-run park, ideally situated for exploring Dorset. Well stocked shop. Off license. Free hot showers. Children's padding pool. Bike hire. Fully serviced pitches. Hard standing. Wi-fi available.

We accept:

**BIRCHWOOD TOURIST PARK**
**Cold Harbour, Wareham, Dorset, BH20 7PA**
TEL: 01929 554763 Fax: 01929 556635
Web: www.birchwoodtouristpark.co.uk

# SOUTH WEST

pitches. Fully stocked shop. Bar open mid/high season. Green Tourism Business Award. Nearby activities include sailing, horse riding, fishing, water sports, diving, rock climbing and swimming pool. 4m W of Weymouth on B3157. Open: All year. ★★★★ BH&HPA

**(3m). Chesil Holiday Park, Portland Road, Wyke Regis, Weymouth, Dorset DT4 9AG.** 01305 773233. www.chesilholidays.co.uk. Heated indoor fun pool with flume, clubroom and bar, live entertainment, Kids club, convenience store, take-away, laundrette. Families & couples only, no single sex groups. Owner-occupied caravans open from 1/3/10 to 15/1/11. Owner supplied copy. On A354 Portland Road, follow signs to Portland from Weymouth. Open: 19 March - 1 October. ★★★★ BH&HPA NCC 340

**(2m). East Fleet Farm Touring Park, Chickerell, Weymouth, Dorset DT3 4DW.** 01305 785768. www.eastfleet.co.uk. Peaceful and spacious park. On organic farmland overlooking Fleet and Chesil Bank. 400 mixed pitches. David Bellamy Gold Conservation Award. B3157 from Weymouth, L at Chickerell TA Camp. Open: 16 March - 31 October. ★★★★ BH&HPA 400

**(1.5m). Littlesea Holiday Park (Haven), Lynch Lane, Weymouth, Dorset DT4 9DT.** 0871 2310879. www.caravancamping.co.uk. Welcome Host Award. Holiday Park of the Year 2007. Fun indoor and outdoor pools. March & Barrel cafe bar, family entertainment centre, amusements. 2 playgrounds. Mini golf. Bouncy castle and trampolines. Free kids clubs. 10mins drive from town centre. Park is on bus route. David Bellamy Gold Conservation Award. Ring for directions. Open: 18 March - 31 October. ★★★★★ BH&HPA NCC 120 120 993

**(5m). Osmington Holiday Park, Osmington Mills, Weymouth, Dorset DT3 6HB.** 01305 837010. www.osmingtonholidays.co.uk. Superb redeveloped holiday park located near to Weymouth. Fantastic country club with bar, restaurant, heated outdoor pool & play area. From Weymouth take A353 E for 5m. Turn R to Osmington Mills. SP. Open: 1 April - 30 September. ★★★★ BH&HPA NCC 132

**(1.5m). Pebble Bank Holiday Park, 90 Camp Road, Wyke Regis, Weymouth, Dorset DT4 9HF.** 01305 774844. www.pebblebank.co.uk. Play area. Licensed bar. Freephone 0500 242656. From harbour roundabout in Weymouth, follow road for Portland, at mini roundabout turn R on to Wyke road (B3156). Camp Road 1m. Open: 1 April - 4 November. ★★★ BH&HPA 40 110

**(6m). Portesham Dairy Farm Campsite, 7 Bramdon Lane, Portesham, Weymouth, Dorset DT3 4HG.** 01305 871297. www.porteshamdairyfarm.co.uk. Calor Gas and Camping Gaz from farmhouse. Play area. Fishing and horse riding nearby. Abbotsbury 2m away with Swannery Tithe barn and sub tropical gardens. Garage, PO, pub serving food and doctor all nearby. B3157 Weymouth to Bridport coast road. Open: 15 March - 31 October. ★★★★ 30 30

**(5m). Sea Barn Farm, Fleet, Weymouth, Dorset DT3 4ED.** 01305 782218. www.seabarnfarm.co.uk. Probably the most beautiful licensed camping park in Dorset with spectacular views of the Fleet Lagoon, Lyme Bay, and the World Heritage Jurassic Coast. AA 3 pennants. Owner supplied copy. On the road B3157 to Abbotsbury. Turn at the sign to Fleet and Moonfleet Manor Hotel, then next turn L to Sea Barn Farm. Open: 18 March - 30 October. 3 30

**(3m). Seaview Holiday Park (Haven) (Weymouth), Preston, Weymouth,**

138 CARAVAN & HOLIDAY PARKS 2012

# SOUTH WEST

Dorset DT3 6DZ. *0871 2310877. www.caravancamping.co.uk.* Indoor and outdoor pools. Kids club. Daytime and evening entertainment for all the family. All the facilities at neighbouring Weymouth Bay to enjoy. Cafe bar and takeaway. David Bellamy Silver Conservation Award. Take A353 from centre of Weymouth to Preston. Seaview is 0.25m beyond village, uphill on R. Open: 18 March - 31 October. ★★★ BH&HPA 92⚏ ▲ 520⚏

(1.5m). **Waterside Holiday Park, Bowleaze Cove, Weymouth, Dorset DT3 6PP.** *01305 833103.* www.watersideholidays.co.uk. Seasonal pitches available. Holidays and holiday homes for sale. 5 star family park with fantastic facilities. Located right on the beach at Bowleaze Cove. Off A353. Park is situated 100yd from beach at Bowleaze Cove. 1.5m from main Weymouth beach. Open: 20 March - 30 October. ★★★★★ BH&HPA NCC 110⚏

(5m). **West Fleet Holiday Farm, Fleet, Weymouth, Dorset DT3 4EF.** *01305 782218.* www.westfleetholidays.co.uk. Kids love camping at West Fleet Farm. Rural location, play area, outdoor pool and family clubhouse. 5m from Weymouth beach and town. 3 AA pennants. Owner supplied copy. On the B3157 towards Abbotsbury. L at mini roundabout to Fleet. 1m on R. Open: 18 March - 30 September. 3 35⚏ ⚏ ▲

(2.5m). **Weymouth Bay Holiday Park (Haven), Preston, Weymouth, Dorset DT3 6BQ.** *0871 4680496.* www.haven.com. Heated indoor and outdoor fun pools. Daytime and evening entertainment for all the family. Kids clubs. All the facilities of neighbouring park, Seaview Holiday Park, adventure playground. David Bellamy Gold Conservation Award. A35 to Dorchester and turn off on A354 SP Weymouth. From Weymouth centre, take A353 to Preston, the park is on the R, 10mins from Weymouth. Open: 18 March - 31 October. ★★★★ BH&HPA NCC 300⚏

## Wimborne

**Charris Camping & Caravan Park, Candy's Lane, Corfe Mullen, Wimborne, Dorset BH21 3EF.** *01202 885970.* www.charris.co.uk. 45 pitches set in 3 acres on mixed standings, with electric hook-ups available. Terraced site on side of Stour Valley 5 miles from Poole. Just off the A31, west of Wimborne. Open: All year. 45⚏ ▲

(1.5m). **Merley House Holiday Park Ltd, Merley House Lane, Wimborne, Dorset BH21 3AA.** *01202 883823.* www.merleyhouse.co.uk. Select, peaceful park set in Dorset countryside. All private owners. Laundrette. Swimming pool. 2 Play areas. Poole and Bournemouth nearby. Cinema/shopping centre 1.5m, golf 3m. Owner supplied copy. Off A31 Wimborne bypass at the A349 Poole roundabout. Open: 16 March - 15 February. BH&HPA 150⚏ ▲

(1.5m). **Springfield Touring Park, Candy's Lane, Corfe Mullen, Wimborne, Dorset BH21 3EF.** *01202 881719.* www.springfieldtouringpark.co.uk. Family run park. Convenient for New Forest and coastal resorts. Free showers and awnings. Special offers low season. Fishing, golf, horse riding, swimming, leisure activities, boating on the river Stour - all available within 2-3m. Turn L off A31 Ringwood to Dorchester, at roundabout western end of Wimborne bypass after 400yd turn R into Candys Lane. Open: 1 April - 16 October. BH&HPA 45⚏ ▲

**Verwood Camping & Caravanning Club Site, Sutton Hill, Wimborne, Dorset BH21 8NQ.** *01202 822763.* www.campingandcaravanningclub.co.uk. A 12.75 acre site for all types of units. Set on the borders of Dorset, Wiltshire and Hampshire this site offers a varied holiday. Non-members welcome. Play area and recreational hall on site. The site is beautifully situated next to Ringwood Forest. Golf course opposite site. Shops, doctors, vets, PO all within 1m. Special deals available for families and backpackers. David Bellamy Silver Conservation Award. From A31 Ringwood by-pass near Texaco Filling Station. Turn L on to B3081 to Verwood. Site on R 1.5m past Verwood and golf club. Open: 1 April - 31 October. ★★★ NCC 150⚏ 150⚏ ▲

(1m). **Wilksworth Farm Caravan Park, Cranbourne Road, Furzehill, Wimborne, Dorset BH21 4HW.** *01202 885467.* www.wilksworthfarmcaravanpark.co.uk. Heated swimming pool. Games room. Tennis court. Large play area. David Bellamy Gold Conservation Award. N of Wimborne on the B3078. Open: 1 April - 30 October. ★★★★★ BH&HPA 60⚏ 60⚏ ▲

(7m). **Woolsbridge Manor Farm Caravan Park, Ringwood Road, Three Legged Cross, Wimborne, Dorset BH21 6RA.** *01202 826369.* www.woolsbridgemanor-caravanpark.co.uk. Easy access to south coast. Level, semi-sheltered park with good facilities. Take A31 W, 1m past Ringwood take filter and follow signs for Three Legged Cross and Moors Valley Country Park. Park is 2m along on R. Open: 1 March - 31 October. ★★★ BH&HPA NCC 60⚏ ▲

### Wool

(5m). **Whitemead Caravan Park, East Burton Road, Wool, Dorset BH20 6HG.** *01929 462241.* www.whitemeadcaravanpark.co.uk. In 5 acres of woodland. 3m from Lulworth Cove. Shop, laundry, games room & play area. Lake fishing 4m. Shop and games room with pool table and darts. Off A352 Wareham to Dorchester road, N of level crossing in Wool, 200yd on R. 4.5m W of Wareham, 300yd off A352 before Wool level crossing. Open: 15 March - 31 October. ★★★★ BH&HPA 95⚏ 95⚏ ▲

## GLOUCESTERSHIRE

### Bourton-On-The-Water

(4.5m). **Notgrove Caravan Club Site, Cheltenham Road, Bourton-On-The-Water, Gloucestershire GL54 3BU.** *01451 850249.* www.caravanclub.co.uk. Delightful site high up in the Cotswolds surrounded by open countryside and superb views. Chemical toilet disposal point. No toilet block. MV service point. Some hardstandings, gas, dog walk on site, storage pitches, quiet and peaceful off peak. Members only. No tents. See website for standard directions to site. Open: 23 March - 8 October. NCC 70⚏ 70⚏

### Bristol

(2m). **Baltic Wharf Caravan Club Site, Cumberland Road, Bristol, Gloucestershire BS1 6XG.** *01179 268030.* www.caravanclub.co.uk. A waterside site in the heart of Bristol's beautifully redeveloped dockland. Non-members welcome. No tents. 55 pitches in total. Advance booking essential at all times. MV service point. Heated toilet block with laundry facilities. Golf nearby. See website for standard directions to site. Open: All year. ★★★★ NCC 55⚏ 55⚏

### Cheltenham

**Briarfields Motel & Touring Campsite, Gloucester Road, Cheltenham, Gloucestershire GL51 0SX.** *01242*

# SOUTH WEST

235324. www.briarfields.net. Briarfields is a family owned, beautifully landscaped touring caravan & camping park. Our pitches include free Wi-Fi and are hard-standing with electric hook-up alongside well maintained lawns, mature trees and shrubs. Open all year round; situated 2.5 miles from Cheltenham town centre and 6 miles from historic Gloucester with a frequent bus service to both from outside our park. Cheltenham makes an ideal base for touring the Cotswolds and its beautiful surrounding areas inc the Malverns, Forest of Dean, Tewkesbury, and Charming Cotswold villages. We are well placed for just relaxing for an overnight stop whilst breaking up your journey (2 mins from M5, J11); giving good road access to the West Country, Midlands, Wales and Oxfordshire. En-suite rooms available from £33.99. Leave M5, J11, follow A40 Cheltenham, take first L at roundabout on to B4063. Open: All year. 4 BH&HPA 72 72 20

**(1.25m). Cheltenham Racecourse Caravan Club Site**, Prestbury Park, Cheltenham, Gloucestershire GL50 4SH. 01242 523102. www.caravanclub.co.uk. A sophisticated location on the edge of Cheltenham with panoramic views of the Cleeve Hills. Dog walk. Non-members welcome. No tents. Toilet block. Laundry facilities. Veg prep. MV service point. See website for standard directions to site. Open: 30 March - 22 October. ★★★ NCC 75 75

(2.5m). **Folly Farm (Cheltenham)**, Bourton-on-the-Water, Cheltenham, Gloucestershire GL54 3BY. 07906 990434. www.cotswoldcamping.net. Ideal for walkers and cyclists. Site is in an Area of Outstanding Natural Beauty and is deliberately basic with its facilities; ie: no floodlights, playgrounds, shops but does have showers, toilets, chemical disposal points. Ideally situated close to Bourton-on-the-Water and Stow-on-the-Wold. 2.5m from Bourton-on-the-Water on the A436. Open: 31 March - 31 October. 15

## Cirencester

**(1m). Cirencester Park Caravan Club Site**, Stroud Road, Cirencester, Gloucestershire GL7 1UT. 01285 651546. www.caravanclub.co.uk. Set in beautiful grade 1 listed parkland, and forming part of the Bathurst Estate, this site is peaceful, level, with many mature trees and within walking distance of Cirencester. Toilet blocks, laundry facilities, baby and toddler washroom and MV service point. Playground, boules pitch and dog walk on site. Fishing, golf, water sports and NCN route nearby. Facilities for the disabled. Members only. No tents. See website for standard directions to site. Open: 23 March - 7 January. NCC 219 219

(4m). **Hoburne Cotswold**, Broadway Lane, South Cerney, Cirencester, Gloucestershire GL7 5UQ. 01285 860216. www.hoburne.com. Licensed club and seasonal entertainment. Outdoor pool and new indoor leisure pool. New family style restaurant. Fishing. Tennis. Laundrette. Adventure playground. Themed pub style bar with mini 10 pin bowling. David Bellamy Gold Conservation Award. Clearly SP from A419 Cirencester road. Open: 28 February - 31 October. ★★★★ BH&HPA NCC 302 A 235

(2m). **Mayfield Park R**, Cheltenham Road, Perrotts Brook, Cirencester, Gloucestershire GL7 7BH. 01285 831301. www.mayfieldpark.co.uk. The site offers a wide variety of pitches to suit caravan or tent. Small shop available, excellent toilet and shower facilities and is well placed for the Cotswold Hills. Owner supplied copy. On A435, 2m from Cirencester and 13m Cheltenham. Leave new bypass at Burford Road junction. Turn towards Cirencester and follow brown camping and caravan signs. Open: All year. ★★★★ BH&HPA 20 36

## Coleford

**Bracelands Caravan & Camping Site**, Bracelands Drive, Coleford, Gloucestershire GL16 7NN. 01594 837258. www.forestholidays.co.uk. A massive 520 pitches, all on grass and suitable for families or those looking for adventure holidays. Electric hook-ups available. Off B4432. Open: 4 April - 31 October. BH&HPA 520

(2m). **Christchurch Forest Holidays**, Bracelands Drive, Coleford, Gloucestershire GL16 7NN. 01594 837258. www.forestholidays.co.uk. Set in the heart of the Forest of Dean, ideal for Symonds Yat. Bookings and brochure requests on 0845 1308224. N of Coleford on the minor road to Symonds Yat. Open: All year. BH&HPA 280

## Dursley

(5m). **Hogsdown Farm Caravan & Camping Site**, Lower Wick, Dursley, Gloucestershire GL11 6DD. 01453 810224. www.hogsdownfarm.co.uk. Excellent walking and touring country on edge of Cotswold Hills. Fishing and golf nearby. Shops, doctors, hospital, PO within 2m. Owner supplied copy. Off A38, between jcts 13 & 14, M5. Half way between Bristol & Gloucester, SP Lower Wick. Open: All year. 12 40 A 3

## Gloucester

(6m). **Gables Farm**, Moreton Valence, Gloucester, Gloucestershire GL2 7ND. 01452 720331. Overnight stop or local touring site. No shop but essentials are available within 3m. Slimbridge Wildfowl and Wetlands 6m. Owner supplied copy. M5, J12 then 1.5m S on A38 and J13 then 1.5m N on A38. Open: 1 March - 30 November. 10 20

**Red Lion Inn Caravan Park**, Wainlodes Hill, Norton, Gloucester, Gloucestershire GL2 9LW. 01452 731810. www.redlioninn-caravancampingpark.co.uk. A

(2m). **Riverside Caravan Park (Gloucester)**, The George Inn, Nr Dursley, Gloucester, Gloucestershire GL2 7AL. 01453 890270. Pub/restaurant on site. Children's play area. Toilet/shower block. Storage available. The nearest shop, PO, doctors are less than 3m away, there is an on site pub/restaurant, children play area. Storage available. Owner supplied copy. A38 Bristol to Gloucester, exit M5 J13 or J14. From J13 travel S on the A38, from J14 travel N on A38. Open: All year. 26 A

## Lechlade

**(0.25m). Bridge House Campsite (Lechlade)**, Bridge House, Thames Street, Lechlade, Gloucestershire GL7 3AG. 01367 252348. Shops, PO, doctor, restaurants and pubs all within 0.25m. Fishing nearby. Golf 5m. Please note that a £20 refundable cash deposit is required for a barrier fob. On A361, 0.25m S of Lechlade. Open: 1 April - 31 October. BH&HPA 20 20 A

**(0.5m). St Johns Priory Park R**, Faringdon Road, Lechlade, Gloucestershire GL7 3EZ. 01268 511555. www.britanniaparks.com. Residential park close to the banks of the River Thames. Over 50s only. Many historic Cotswold towns within driving distance. Inn over road. Off A417 near Lechlade. Open: 1 March - 31 October. BH&HPA NCC

# SOUTH WEST

### Lydney

**(3m). Whitemead Forest Park, Parkend, Lydney, Gloucestershire GL15 4LA.** 0845 3453425. www.whitemead.co.uk. 32 apartments for self catering too available. Shop, indoor heated swimming pool with sauna, gym, steam room, Jacuzzis. Heated shower and toilet blocks. Laundry x2. Daytime cafe, evening restaurant. Bar, entertainment venue with live entertainment at weekends and all school holidays. Family activities in school holidays. Beauty salon, play park, indoor soft play. Off the A48, follow B4234 to park end. Open: All year. BH&HPA 111
61

### Moreton-in-Marsh

**(0.5m). Moreton-In-Marsh Caravan Club Site, Bourton Road, Moreton-in-Marsh, Gloucestershire GL56 0BT.** 01608 650519. www.caravanclub.co.uk. This attractive site is within walking distance of Moreton-in-the-Marsh. Surrounded by picturesque Cotswold villages. Advance booking essential. Dog walk on site. Non-members welcome. No tents. Toilet blocks. Privacy cubicles. Laundry facilities. Baby/toddler washroom. Veg prep. MV service point. Hardstandings. Play equipment. Boules pitch. Fishing locally. Ideal for families. Shops within 0.25m. See website for standard directions to site. Open: All year. ★★★★★ NCC
183 183

### Slimbridge

**(0.5m). Tudor Caravan Park, Shepherds Patch, Slimbridge, Gloucestershire GL2 7BP.** 01453 890483. www.tudorcaravanpark.com. 75 pitches in total. Quiet, family run park adjacent to famous Slimbridge Wetlands Centre and Gloucester, Sharpness Canal. Separate area for adults only. Pub & restaurant adjoining. Fishing. Tearoom & small convenience shop adjacent. Golf course nearby. AA 4 pennants park. David Bellamy Gold Conservation Award. M5 J13, on to A38, follow signs for Slimbridge WWT Wetlands Centre. 1.5m off A38 at rear of Tudor Arms Pub. 75 pitches in total. Quiet, family run park adjacent to famous Slimbridge Wetlands Centre and Gloucester, Sharpness Canal. Separate area for adults only. Pub & restaurant adjoining. Fishing. Tearoom & small convenience shop adjacent. Golf course nearby. AA 4 pennants park. David Bellamy Gold Conservation Award. Open: All year. BH&HPA 75
75 30

### Tewkesbury

**(1.5m). Croft Farm Leisure And Water Park, Bredon's Hardwick, Tewkesbury, Gloucestershire GL20 7EE.** 01684 772321. www.croftfarmleisure.co.uk. Touring caravan and camping site with own water sports lake and fitness centre. Luxury facilities. Bar and cafe. Winter storage. Tuition available in windsurfing, sailing and canoeing. Free river fishing on site. Take Bredon Road out of Tewkesbury on B4080. 1.5m on L. Open: 1 March - 14 November. ★★★ BH&HPA
76 76

**(2m). Dawleys Caravan Park, Owls Lane, Shuthonger, Tewkesbury, Gloucestershire GL20 6EQ.** 01684 292622. www.dawleyscaravanpark.co.uk. Quiet site in rural surroundings. Good walk and fishing nearby. Ideal for touring the Cotswolds, Malvern and Vale of Evesham. Special offers for 7 nights. Golf, fishing, cinema, swimming pool, shopping all within 2m. M50 J1, take A38 S towards Tewkesbury-turn R after 1m. Open: 1 April - 30 September.

**(0.25m). Mill Avon Holiday Park, Gloucester Road, Tewkesbury, Gloucestershire GL20 5SW.** 01684 296876. www.millavon.com. Slipway for small boats. Shops, PO, pubs, restaurants ad doctors surgery, etc all in town centre, 3 golf courses. On A38 0.25m S from town centre. Views from site across Tewkesbury to the Malvern Hills. Slipway for small boats. Shops, PO, pubs, restaurants ad doctors surgery, etc all in town centre, 3 golf courses. Open: All year. BH&HPA 10

**(2m). Sunset View Touring Park, Churchend, Twyning, Tewkesbury, Gloucestershire GL20 6DA.** 01684 292145. 25 mixed pitches in total. Two level acres. A quiet family run site. Horse riding, fishing and golf nearby; pub with restaurant within 5 mins walk. Seasonal pitches available. 1.5m from J1, M50. 2m N of Tewkesbury on A38, almost opposite Crown Inn turn R. Site 200yd on R. Open: All year. 25

**(0.25m). Tewkesbury Abbey Caravan Club Site, Gander Lane, Tewkesbury, Gloucestershire GL20 5PG.** 01684 294035. www.caravanclub.co.uk. A very impressive site almost in the shadow of the ancient abbey and a short walk from town centre. Dog walk. Tent campers welcome. Advance booking advisable. Non-members welcome. Privacy cubicles. MV service point. Veg prep. Golf nearby. Ideal for families. Shop 0.25m away. Good walking. M5, leave at J9 on to A438 SP Tewkesbury at traffic lights keep R and continue straight. In town centre at mini roundabout keep L, in 200yd turn L into Gander Lane, site on L. Open: 23 March - 29 October. ★★★★ NCC
154 154

**(6m). Winchcombe Camping & Caravanning Club Site, Brooklands Farm, Alderton, Tewkesbury, Gloucestershire GL20 8NX.** 01242 620259. www.campingandcaravanningclub.co.uk. Set amidst the lovely Cotswold countryside with its own fishing lake. Non-members welcome. All units accepted. 80 pitches set in 20 acres. A visit to nearby Cheltenham with its fine shopping is worthwhile. The village of Winchcombe with its pretty antique shops and tea rooms is close to the site. Plenty of room for children's ball games. Special deals available for families and backpackers. On A46 from Tewkesbury keep straight on at roundabout and take B4077 to Stow on the Wold, site on R in 3m. Open: 11 March - 15 January. ★★★★
80 80

## SOMERSET

### Bath

**(9m). Bath Chew Valley Caravan Park (Adults-only), Ham Lane, Bath, Somerset BS39 5TZ.** 01275 332127. www.bathchewvalley.co.uk. 45 mixed pitches in total. Set amongst flowers and shrubs. 800yd from Chew Valley lake, famous for its trout fishing and birdlife. Adults only. Overall 2009 Winner of Practical Caravan Top 100 parks. Ideal base for exploring Bath, Bristol and Mendip Hills. David Bellamy Gold Conservation Award. On A368 Bath to Weston-super-Mare road. At Bishop Sutton turn opposite Red Lion pub. Approach from A38 or A37. Open: All year. ★★★★ BH&HPA NCC
45 45

**(2m). Bath Marina & Caravan Park, Brassmill Lane, Bath, Somerset BA1 3JT.** 01225 424301. www.bathcaravanpark.com. Carefully landscaped park to maximise privacy. 240v and TV hook up to all 88 pitches. Advance online booking advisable all year round. Freezer pack services, laundry, children's play area. Family pub a few minutes walk from park. AA 4 Pennant. The centre of Bath and entrance to Kennet and Avon canal 1m upstream from Weston Lock which lies 1m away. M4, J19 on to A4174, to A4 Bath. Pass through Saltford. At end of dual carriageway fork L towards Bath and Newbridge. Cross over the River Avon and pass the park & ride on your L. On your R is Capricorn Motors. Turn

Visit www.caravanclub.co.uk

# SOUTH WEST

R into Brassmill Lane. Park is 100yd on R. Open: All year. ★★★★ 4 ... 88

**Bury View Farm, Corston Fields, Bath, Somerset BA2 9HD.** 01225 873672. Dogs allowed on leads with tourers. Fishing, golf nearby. 2m to PO and shop, 3m to doctor. On A39 Wells to Bath midway between Wheatsheaf Inn and Corston Car Sales Garage. 3m from Keynsham and 2.5m from Saltford. Open: All year. ... 15 ...

**(2m). Newton Mill Caravan and Camping Park, Newton Road, Bath, Somerset BA2 9JF.** 0844 272 9503. www.newtonmillpark.co.uk. Open all year and lying in a beautiful setting in a hidden valley close to the centre of Bath, the park is an ideal touring centre with a frequent bus service and level traffic-free cycle path to the centre. Relax in our beautiful bar, restaurants and gardens, which lie beside the millstream. Separate tent and caravan park meadows. Heated amenities of the highest standard including bathrooms. AA 4 Pennants. David Bellamy Silver Conservation Award. A4 towards Bristol. At roundabout by Globe PH take exit SP Newton St Loe, park is 1m on L. Open: All year. ★★★★ BH&HPA ... 110 ...

### Brean Sands

**(3m). Holiday Resort Unity, Coast Road, Brean Sands, Somerset TA8 2RB.** 01278 751235. www.hru.co.uk. Choice of bars with entertainment, and food venues. Pool with slides, 18 hole golf course and pitch and putt, riding, fishing, children's club. Fun park with 40 rides, bingo, play area. Fenced gardens. Shopping at Weston-super-Mare 8m. David Bellamy Silver Conservation Award. Off M5 J22. Follow signs for Brean Leisure Park for 4.5m. Open: 10 February - 18 November.
★★★★ BH&HPA ...
... 350 350 150 150 6 ...

### Bridgwater

**Fairways International Touring Caravan Park, Bath Road, Bawdrip, Bridgwater, Somerset TA7 8PP.** 01278 685569. www.fairwaysinternational.co.uk. 5mins from M5, 10mins from Glastonbury. 200 pitches. Toilet/shower block, campers kitchen with freezers, microwaves and ice cube machine. Games room & shop. Pubs within walking distance. Handy for Glastonbury, Street, Wookey Hole & Cheddar Gorge. At the Jct of A39 with B3141. 1.5m from Jct 23 of M5 in Glastonbury direction. Open: All year. ...

**(6m). Mill Farm Caravan & Camping Park, Fiddington, Bridgwater, Somerset TA5 1JQ.** 01278 732286. www.millfarm.biz. Beautiful, sheltered site. Free Wi-Fi around the bar area. Heated swimming pools, riding centre, canoes and boating on shallow lake. Phone for brochure. M5 J23 or 24 to Bridgwater, take A39 (Minehead direction) for 6m. Turn R to Fiddington, follow caravan and camping signs. Open: All year. ★★★★ BH&HPA ... 25 125 ...

### Bristol

**(9m). Brook Lodge Farm Camping & Caravan Park - Bristol, Cowslip Green, Wrington, Bristol, Somerset BS40 5RB.** 01934 862311. www.brooklodgefarm.com. Small family run park. Central countryside location for Bristol, Bath, Cheddar, Wells, Clevedon, bus to Bristol 1m in Wrington, 24/7 shop & petrol 2m, bar/restaurant opposite park, farm shop within walking distance. Fishing 2m, network of country lanes/footpaths. AA 3 pennant, Bronze Green Business Award 2006, 2008. Welcome to Excellence Award. From historic city of Bristol take A38 SW, 9m SP on L. From S A38 3m N of Churchill traffic lights. Open: 1 March - 31 October.
★★★ 3 ... 20 29 ...
A 4 ...

# SOUTH WEST

## Burnham-on-Sea

**(5m). Brean Down Inn, Brean, Burnham-on-Sea, Somerset TA8 2RR.** *01278 751420.* BH&HPA 🏠 ⛺ 🚗 45⚡

**(4m). Brightholme Holiday Park, Coast Road, Brean, Burnham-on-Sea, Somerset TA8 2QY.** *01278 751327.* www.burnham-on-sea.co.uk/brightholme. Licensed bar with restaurant. Play area. Laundry. Direct on to sandy beach. Golf course across road. 5 - 10mins to shops. Doctors in Burnham-on-Sea. Leave M5 at J22. Follow signs to Burnham-on-Sea, Berrow, Brean Down. Park is on L 500yd past Berrow beach entrance. Open: 1 March - 15 November. ★ ★ ★ BH&HPA 🏠 ⛺ 🐕 🍴 ✕ 🚻 🚗 100⚡

**(0.25m). Burnham-on-Sea (Haven), Marine Drive, Burnham-on-Sea, Somerset TA8 1LA.** *0871 2310868.* www.caravancamping.co.uk. Situated on the Esplanade facing the sea and adjoining town centre. 95 acres of level parkland with indoor and outdoor swimming pools. Live entertainment. Mini market. Bakery. Laundrette. Children's play area. Welcome Host Award. David Bellamy Gold Conservation Award. M5, J22. Take L at the roundabout on to A38 to Highbridge. Continue over mini-roundabout and railway bridge. Take next R, B3139 to Burnham. Turn L after the Total garage on to Marine Drive - the park is 400yd on the L. Open: 18 March - 31 October. ★ ★ ★ ★ BH&HPA NCC 🏠 ⛺ 🐕 🍴 ♫ ✕ 🚻 🚗 75⚡ 75⚡ 🏕 900⚡

**Channel View Caravan & Camping Site, Brean Farm, Brean Down Road, Brean, Burnham-on-Sea, Somerset TA8 2RR.** *01278 751055.* 🐕 🍴 ✕ 🚗 ⚡

**(4.5m). Diamond Farm Caravan Park (Brean), Weston Road, Brean, Burnham-on-Sea, Somerset TA8 2RL.** *01278 751263.* www.diamondfarm.co.uk. Working farm. 0.5m to golf, beach. Owner supplied copy. Off A370 Weston-super-Mare to Brean. From Burnham to Brean coast road take junction to Weston and Lympsham, Diamond Farm is 800yd from junction. Open: 30 March - 22 October. ★ ★ ★ BH&HPA 🏠 ⛺ 🐕 🍴 ♫ ✕ 🚻 🚗 50⚡ 50🏕

**(2m). Edithmead Leisure Park, Highbridge, Burnham-on-Sea, Somerset TA9 4HE.** *01278 783475.* www.edithmeadleisureandparkhomes.co.uk. Excellent facilities and beautifully landscaped gardens. On site club house. Bus stop at main gate. We have centrally heated, fully appointed holiday statics and cottages available for holiday hire. Situated 1.5m from Burnham-on-Sea and within easy reach of historic Wells and Taunton. Open: 15 February - 17 January. BH&HPA 🏠 ⛺ 🐕 🍴 ♫ ✕ 🚻 🚗 150⚡

**(1m). Home Farm Holiday Park, Edithmead, Burnham-on-Sea, Somerset TA9 4HD.** *01278 788888.* www.homefarmholidaypark.co.uk. Level site. Heated showers and bathrooms. Gift shop. Adventure playground. Leisure club with spa, gym, indoor pool. Fishing. Licensed bars, live entertainment. Swimming pool. Caravan service and sales. Off M5 at exit 22, take road to Burnham-on-Sea, Edithmead. Open: 10 February - 3 January. ★ ★ ★ ★ ★ BH&HPA 🏠 ⛺ 🐕 🍴 ♫ ✕ 🚻 🚗 50⚡ 650⚡ 185⚡

**(3.5m). Hurn Lane Caravan Club Site, Berrow, Burnham-on-Sea, Somerset TA8 2QT.** *01278 751412.* www.caravanclub.co.uk. Ideal family holiday location only 15mins walk from safe, sandy beach. Play area. No arrivals before 12 noon. Toilet blocks. Privacy cubicles. Laundry facilities. Veg prep. MV service point. Gas and Gaz. Play equipment. Late night arrivals area. Golf, fishing and water sports nearby. Member only. No tents. See website for standard directions to site. Open: 23 March - 7 November. NCC 🏠 ⛺ 🐕 🍴 🚗 139⚡ 139⚡

**(0.5m). Lakeside Holiday Park (Burnham), Westfield Road, Burnham-on-Sea, Somerset TA8 2AE.** *01278 792222.* www.lakesideholidays.co.uk. Short, level walk to beach and town centre. Tree lined 3-acre private fishing lake. Club complex provides live family entertainment, poolside conservatory, bistro/takeaway. Heated swimming pool and walled sun terrace, children's playground, bicycle hire. Exit 22 M5. Follow signs for Burnham and at roundabout by Esso garage, for Berrow. Turn R into Westfield Road, opposite swimming pool. Open: 1 April - 31 October. ★ ★ ★ ★ 🍴 ♫ ✕ 🚻 🚗 275⚡

**Lazy Days Holiday Park (Brean Sands), Brean Sands, South Road, Burnham-on-Sea, Somerset TA8 2RD.** *01278 751283.* Licensed club and bar. Garden with children's play area. Cafe, laundrette. Crazy golf at bottom of drive. Close to all fishing, golf, shops, funfair. Swimming pools within 2m. Owner supplied copy. Off J22, M5. Off B3140 Burnham to Brean. Open: 1 March - 30 October. BH&HPA 🏠 ⛺ 🐕 🍴 ✕ 15⚡

**(6m). Northam Farm Caravan Park, South Road, Brean, Burnham-on-Sea,** **Somerset TA8 2SE.** *01278 751244.* www.northamfarm.co.uk. Attractive well established family run park situated 200metre from 5m of sandy beach. 30 acre park offering children's outdoor play areas, fishing lake, cafe, shop, laundrette and dog walks. Easy access from M5, J22. BOS follow signs to Brean 0.5m past Leisure Park on right hand side. Open: 13 March - 31 October. ★ ★ ★ ★ BH&HPA NCC 🏠 ⛺ 🐕 🍴 ♫ ✕ 🚻 🚗 350⚡ 350⚡ 🏕

**(0.5m). Retreat Caravan Park, Berrow Road, Burnham-on-Sea, Somerset TA8 2ES.** *01278 795006.* www.retreatcaravanpark.co.uk. Beautifully secluded with access to miles of golden sandy beach yet only half a mile from Burnham-on-Sea. Pleasant beach walks. Facilities include laundry, toilets/showers, telephone room, information room and children's play area. An ideal base for visits into the surrounding countryside of the Mendips, Cheddar Gorge, Glastonbury and Wells. The resorts of North and South Devon are within easy reach. Golf, riding and sailing nearby. 2.5 miles from Jct 22 of the M5. At Jct 22, take B3140, follow signs to Burnham-on-Sea and then towards Berrow. Open: Contact site direct. ★ ★ ★ ★ 🏠 ⛺ 🐕 🍴 🚗 ⚡

**(3m). Rose Farm Touring Park (Burnham), Red Road, Berrow, Burnham-on-Sea, Somerset TA8 2RW2.** *01278 785888.* Level seaside site close to Burnham on Sea. Well-kept with modern facilities. Close to Cheddar Gorge, Apex Park (fishing) and Puxton Park. Off B3140. Open: 1 March - 31 October. 🏠 ⛺ 🐕 🍴 ♫ ✕ 🚻 🚗 100⚡

**(3m). Sandy Glade Holiday Park, Coast Road, Berrow, Burnham-on-Sea, Somerset TA8 2QX.** *01278 751271.* www.johnfowlerholidays.com. Cabaret, clubhouse, indoor pool. Shop and takeaway. Children's club. Adventure playground. Laundry. Opposite the beach. Chalets and villas for hire. Owner supplied copy. Follow signs for Brean and Berrow. Open: 13 March - 30 October. ★ ★ ★ ★ BH&HPA 🏠 ⛺ 🐕 🍴 ✕ 🚻 🚗 400⚡

**(4m). Skoorbland Caravan Park, South Road, Brean, Burnham-on-Sea, Somerset TA8 2RF.** *01278 751513.* www.skoorbland.co.uk. Caravans for sale. Private use only, no letting. Adjoining sandy beach. Free membership of club. Owner supplied copy. Off M5. Open: 1 March - 31 October. BH&HPA 🏠 ⛺ 🚗 43⚡

# SOUTH WEST

**(4m). Sunningcrest Caravan Park,** Coast Road, Brean, Burnham-on-Sea, Somerset TA8 2RA. 01278 751221 . www.sunningcrest.co.uk. On site: tennis court, sauna, children's play area, launderette, reception, free Wi-Fi, select park with private access to sandy beach. Within 2m: choice of pubs, eateries, fun fair, golf course, fishing lake, horse riding, swimming pool, 10 pin bowling, garden centre and supermarket. Owner supplied copy. M5, J22 follow signs to Brean for about 5m, pass Berrow Beach entrance, park about 400yd on seaward side. Open: 19 March - 30 October. BH&HPA 136

**(5m). Warren Farm Holiday Centre,** Brean Sands, Burnham-on-Sea, Somerset TA8 2RP. 01278 751227. www.warren-farm.co.uk. Family run park within 100yds of sandy beach. There is a large indoor play area, shops, bar and restaurant, providing a wide range of food and entertainment. Dogs not allowed in hire caravans. Riding, swimming, golf available nearby. Leave M5, J22 and follow B3140 through Burnham-on-sea to Berrow and Brean. We are situated 1.5m past Brean Leisure Park. Open: 30 March - 28 October. ★★★★ BH&HPA 100 400 A 11

### Chard

**(1.5m). Alpine Grove Touring Park,** Alpine Grove, Forton, Chard, Somerset TA20 4HD. 01460 63479. www.alpinegrovetouringpark.com. 8.5 acre park of oaks and rhododendrons. Hardstanding area. Free showers, laundry, swings, outdoor heated pool, trampoline, walking and cycling. NEW log cabin open all year for hire. David Bellamy Silver Conservation Award. 2m from Cricket St Thomas, 10m from coast, follow signs to Forton from A358 onto B3162 and A30 onto B3167. Open: 1 April - 30 September. ★★★★ BH&HPA 15 40 25 A 2

**(4m). Five Acres Caravan Club Site,** Beetham, Chard, Somerset TA20 3QA. 01460  234519. www.caravanclub.co.uk. Pleasant, quiet, peaceful off peak site, slightly sloping and in the most lovely South Somerset countryside. Non-members welcome. No tents. Advance bookings advised, Bank Holidays and July/August. Some hardstandings. Toilet blocks. Laundry facilities. Veg prep. MV service point. Gas and Gaz. Ideal for families. NCN cycle path within 5m. See website for standard directions to site. Open: 30 March - 1 October. ★★★★ NCC 74 74

**(3m). South Somerset Holiday Park, The** Tumpike, Howley, Chard, Somerset TA20 3EA. 01460 66036 . Newly refurbished toilet and shower facilities done to a very high standard. Children's play area. 4-acre dog walk area. All weather pitches. Many local attractions. GS. Country pub 0.75m. Farm shop and restaurant 2m. W of Chard on A30 to Exeter. Open: All year. 110 110 A 42

### Cheddar

**(1m). Broadway House Caravan Park,** Axbridge Road, Cheddar, Somerset BS27 3DB. 0844 272 9501 www.broadwayhousepark.co.uk. Broadway House offers superb family friendly facilities and is set in stunning countryside on the outskirts of the Mendip Hills in an Area of Outstanding Natural Beauty. Exit 22 (M5) follow brown signs for Cheddar Gorge. On A371 midway between Cheddar and Axbridge. Open: 1 March - 31 October. ★★★★ BH&HPA 385 A 35

**(0.25m). Cheddar Bridge Touring Park (Tranquil adults-only),** Draycott Road, Cheddar, Somerset BS27 3RJ. 01934 743048. www.cheddarbridge.co.uk. Adults only. Walking distance to shops, village and Cheddar Gorge. Fishing, PO, doctor, very quiet. Views of Mendips, riverside setting. M5, J22. On A371 through Cheddar Village. Next to football club on R. Open: 1 March - 31 October. ★★★★ BH&HPA 45 A 4

**Cheddar Caravan Club Site, Gas House Lane, Draycott Road, Cheddar, Somerset BS27 3RL.** 01934 740207. www.caravanclub.co.uk. This site is situated on the edge of Cheddar village boasts magnificent views of the Mendips and surrounding countryside. Toilet blocks and laundry facilities. Fishing, golf and water sports nearby. Good area for walking. Quiet and peaceful off-peak. Facilities for the disabled. Members only. No tents. See website for standard directions to site. Open: 9 March - 15 November. NCC 64 64

**(2m). Rodney Stoke Caravan & Camping Park, Cheddar, Somerset BS27 3XB.** 01749 870209. Adults only site. Excellent area for walkers, easy access to many tourist sites. Small quiet park at rear of the Rodney Stoke Inn. On A371 midway between Cheddar and Wells. Open: 1 March - 31 October. 22 22

### Congresbury

**(4m). Oak Farm Touring Park,** Weston Road, Congresbury, Somerset BS49 5EB. 01934 833246. Small dogs allowed with permission. Level orchard site, close to all amenities. Booking advised. Golf course, Cheddar Valley Railway Walk nearby. Cycle way as far as Cheddar. Fishing. Village with shops close by. Next door to Greek restaurant. Total garage almost opposite the park. Mid-way between Bristol and Weston-super-Mare on A370, 4m from J21, M5. Open: 1 March - 31 October. ★ 5 10 A

### Crowcombe

**(10m). Quantock Orchard Caravan**

A fun-filled camping and touring holiday park for all the family in picturesque Somerset

- 4* holiday park.
- Minutes from Cheddar Gorge.
- Licensed bar and restaurant.
- BMX bike track.
- Convenience shop and adventure playground.
- Swimming pool and cafe.
- Seasonal pitches.

**PITCHES FROM £10** Quoting CHP10

*Terms and conditions apply

broadway house holiday park

To book call 0844 272 9501 or visit www.broadwayhousepark.co.uk

# SOUTH WEST

Park, Flaxpool, Crowcombe, Somerset TA4 4AW. *01984 618618.* www.quantock-orchard.co.uk. Award-winning campsite with superb panoramic views of the Quantock Hills. Open all year, fully heated toilet and shower block. Tastefully landscaped with several stunning holiday homes for hire. On the A358 between Williton and Taunton. Behind Flaxpool garage. Open: All year. ★★★★★ 🚐 ⚡🚿👨🚻♿ 19🚐 31⚡ ▲ 16⚑

## Dulverton

**(5m). Exe Valley Caravan Site, Bridgetown, Dulverton, Somerset TA22 9JR.** *01643 851432.* www.exevalleycamping.co.uk. Level site in beautiful wooded valley within Exmoor National Park. Wi-Fi and fly fishing - no charge. Adults only. Tents welcome. All pitches are beside the river or mill stream. Local pub 100yd, good walking from campsite. AA 4 pennants. On A396. From Tiverton to Minehead. Open: 16 March - 15 October. 4🚐 ⚡🚿👨🚻♿ 41🚐 41⚡ ▲ 12⚑

**Exmoor House Caravan Club Site, Dulverton, Somerset TA22 9HL.** *01398 323268.* www.caravanclub.co.uk. Excellent base for exploring Exmoor, this pretty site is overlooked by wooded hillsides and a few hundred yards from village. Shops 200yd. Dog walk. Gas and Gaz. MV waste. Non-members welcome. No tents. Advance booking necessary. Do not arrive before 1.00pm. Some hardstandings. Toilet blocks. Privacy cubicles. Laundry facilities. Veg prep. Fishing, NCN cycle path within 5m. Quiet and peaceful off peak. See website for standard directions to site. Open: 23 March - 2 January. ★★★★ 🚐⚡🚿👨🚻♿ 64🚐 64⚡

**(3m). Lakeside Caravan Club Site, Higher Grants, Exebridge, Dulverton, Somerset TA22 9BE.** *01398 324068.* www.caravanclub.co.uk. Situated in a quiet village with attractive rural views towards Exmoor. Toilet blocks and laundry facilities, gas/gaz package. Good area for walking and dog walk on site. Fishing and NCN route within 5m. Quiet and peaceful site off-peak. Non-members welcome. No tents. See website for standard directions to site. Open: 23 March - 5 November. ★★★★★ BH&HPA 🚐⚡🚿👨🚻♿ 80🚐 80⚡

## Glastonbury

The Isle of Avalon Touring Caravan Park, Godney Road, Glastonbury, Somerset BA6 9AF. *01458 833618.* Flat, level park located in quiet location within easy walking distance of Glastonbury. Excellent facilities. Free family sized showers. Restaurant nearby. Cycle hire. A39 W of Glastonbury. B3151 signed Godney. 500yd on R. Open: All year. 🚐⚡🚻♿

**(3m). The Old Oaks Touring Park (Tranquil adults-only), Wick Farm, Wick, Glastonbury, Somerset BA6 8JS.** *01458 831437.* www.theoldoaks.co.uk. Award winning adult only park offering beautifully landscaped pitches, wonderful views and spotless centrally heated facilities. Peace and tranquillity in an outstanding environment. Fishing on site. David Bellamy Gold Conservation Award. Turn L off A361 Glastonbury to Shepton Mallet road. 2m from Glastonbury at Wick SP. Park on L in 1m. Open: 1 January - 15 November. ★★★★★ BH&HPA 🚐⚡🚿👨🚻♿ 90🚐 90⚡ 10▲ 6⚑

## Langport

**(1.5m). Bowdens Crest Ltd Caravan & Camping Park, Bowdens, Langport, Somerset TA10 0DD.** *01458 250553.* www.bowdenscrest.co.uk. Tranquil, level site. Disabled unit available. Licensed bar, laundry, washing up sinks and free showers. Near fishing, walking, cycling and many local attractions. Walking route from park. Shop & meals available, children & pets welcome. Fishing 1m, cycling routes 2m, golf 4m. Off A372 Bridgwater to Langport. Open: All year. ★★★★ BH&HPA 🚐⚡🚿👨🚻♿ 30🚐 30⚡ ▲ 12⚑

## Lynton

**(1m). Cloud Farm Camping, Oare, Lynton, Somerset EX35 6NU.** *01598 741278.* www.cloudfarmcamping.co.uk. In heart of idyllic Doone Valley by side of river. Well behaved dogs allowed. Camp fires and barbecues allowed on site. Off A39. 6 m W of Porlock. SP from A39 near county boundary of Devon and Somerset. Follow signs for Lorna Doone Farm, then see Cloud Farm on L before river. In heart of idyllic Doone Valley by side of river. Well behaved dogs allowed. Camp fires and barbecues allowed on site. Open: All year 🚐⚡🚿👨🚻♿ 5⚑ ▲

## Martock

**(1m). Southfork Caravan Park, Parrett Works, Martock, Somerset TA12 6AE.** *01935 825661.* www.southforkcaravans. co.uk. Small, peaceful, rural, level site near river Parrett. Clean, modern, heated amenities block (free showers). Play area. AA 4-pennants. Numerous places of interest nearby for all age groups. Approved caravan workshop for repairs/servicing. Caravan accessories/spares. Fishing nearby. Village 1m. David Bellamy Bronze Conservation Award. 8m NW of Yeovil. 2m N of A303. Open: All year. ★★★★ BH&HPA NCC 🚐⚡🚿👨🚻♿ 25⚡ ▲ 6⚑

## Minehead

**(16m). Halse Farm Caravan & Camping Park, Winsford, Minehead, Somerset TA24 7JL.** *01643 851259.* www.halsefarm.co.uk. In Exmoor National Park adjacent to moor on working farm. Peaceful. Spectacular views. Quality toilet block. Shop, pub, garage within 1m. David Bellamy Gold Conservation Award. SP from the A396. In Winsford turn L in front of thatched pub. 1m on, entrance on L immediately after cattle grid. 5m from Dulverton. Open: 19 March - 31 October. ★★★★ BH&HPA 🚐⚡🚿👨🚻♿ 22🚐 22⚡ ▲

**(4m). Hoburne Blue Anchor, Blue Anchor Bay, Minehead, Somerset TA24 6JT.** *01643 821360.* www.hoburne.com. Indoor leisure pool. Self service shop. Laundrette. Adventure playground and crazy golf. Rose Award Park 1991-2005. David Bellamy Silver Conservation Award. From A39 take B3191 for 1.75m. Park is on R. Open: 28 February - 31 October. ★★★★ BH&HPA NCC 🚐⚡🚿👨🚻♿ 103🚐 355⚡

**(1m). Minehead & Exmoor Caravan & Camping Park, Porlock Road, Minehead, Somerset TA24 8SW.** *01643 703074.* www.minehead andexmoor camping.co.uk. AONB, on edge of Exmoor. Calor Gas. Telephone. Clean first class toilet facilities. Off A39 W of Minehead centre, situated in open country. Open: All year. 🚐⚡🚿👨🚻♿ 25🚐 25⚡ ▲

**(2m). Minehead Camping & Caravanning Club Site, Hill Road, North Hill, Minehead, Somerset TA24 5LB.** *01643 704138.* www.campingandcaravanningclub.co.uk. 3.75-acre site with 60 pitches. No towed caravans permitted. Non-members welcome. Site on top of hill giving spectacular views. Walkers will enjoy the coastal path 0.5m from site. There are lakes, rivers, hills and valleys of the Exmoor National park to explore. Special deals for families and backpackers. From A39 towards town centre. At T junction turn R on to duel carriageway. Turn L into Blenheim Road, then L into Martlett Road, L around War Memorial

# SOUTH WEST

into St Michael's Road. Past church into Moor Road, then on to Hill Road, site on R. Open: 14 April - 26 September. ★★★★ NCC 60

**Minehead Caravan Club Site, Hopcott Road, Minehead, Somerset TA24 6DJ.** 01643 704345. www.caravanclub.co.uk. A small, hillside site well screened from the road and with lovely views over the hills behind nearby Minehead. Beach 0.5m. Members are warned that bathing off the coast can be dangerous. Mostly hardstandings. Toilet blocks. Laundry facilities. Veg prep. MV service point. Gas and Gaz. No late night arrivals area. Golf nearby. Good area for walking. Suited for families. Members only. No tents. See website for standard directions to site. Open: All year. ★★★★ NCC 50 50

**(8m). St Audries Bay Holiday Club, West Quantoxhead, Minehead, Somerset TA4 4DY.** 01984 632515. www.staudriesbay.co.uk. Family owned award winning park on the Somerset coast, near Exmoor, in beautiful surroundings with fantastic views & beach access. David Bellamy Gold Conservation Award. Off A39. M5, 15m. away at Taunton or Bridgwater. 2m from Williton. Open: 2 April - 31 October. ★★★★ BH&HPA 20 20 18

**(5m). The Beeches Holiday Park, Blue Anchor Bay, Minehead, Somerset TA24 6JW.** 01984 640391. www.beechespark.co.uk. Panoramic views overlooking Blue Anchor Bay. Situated at the gateway to Exmoor, Quantocks and Brendon Hills. Fishing, pony-trekking, walking and golf nearby. Heated swimming pool. Playground. Rose Award. Owner supplied copy. On B3191 Minehead to Watchet Off A39. Open: 19 March - 29 October. ★★★★ BH&HPA 170

**Westermill Farm, Exford, Minehead, Somerset TA24 7NJ.** 01643 831238. www.westermill.com. This is a beautiful, secluded site beside the river Exe in the heart of Exmoor. 4 waymarked walks over 500 acres. Log cabins for hire. David Bellamy Gold Conservation Award. Leave Exford on Porlock road. After 0.25m fork L. Go 2m along valley. 'Westermill' is on tree fork L. Open: All year.

## Porlock

(5m). Burrowhayes Farm Caravan & Camping Site & Riding Stables, West Luccombe, Porlock, Somerset TA24 8HT.

01643 862463. www.burrowhayes.co.uk. Situated in glorious National Trust scenery in Exmoor National Park. Riding stables on site, so popular with walkers and riders. Telephone, laundrette, free showers, well stocked shop. Cinema, golf course, supermarket all within 5m. 5m W of Minehead turn L off A39 to West Luccombe site 0.25m on the R. Between Minehead and Porlock on the National Trust Estate of Holnicote in Exmoor National Park. Open: 15 March - 31 October. ★★★★ BH&HPA 54 20

(6m). **Porlock Caravan Park, High Bank, Porlock, Somerset TA24 8ND.** 01643 862269. www.porlockcaravanpark.co.uk. Quiet, family run park in Vale of Porlock. Excellent for touring, walking, riding, centre for Exmoor. 2mins to village, beach close by. Children allowed. Phone or write for brochure. David Bellamy Gold Conservation Award. A39 Minehead to Porlock, in Porlock turn R B3225 Weir, park SP. Open: 15 March - 31 October. ★★★★ BH&HPA 14 40 40 54

## Radstock

(4m). **Old Down Touring Park, Emborough, Radstock, Somerset BA3 4SA.** 01761 232355. www.olddowntouringpark.co.uk. AA 3 pennants. Convenient for Bath, Wells, The Mendips and Bath & West Showground, Longleat, Wookey Hole and Cheddar Caves. Opposite the site is a 17th century coaching inn offering good food. Owner supplied copy. From Shepton Mallet 6m N on A37 turn R on B3139, entrance on right opposite the Old Down Inn. 6m NE of Wells via B3139. Open: All year. 3 NCC 30 30

## Rodney Stoke

(3m). **Bucklegrove Caravan and Camping Park, Rodney Stoke, Somerset BS27 3UZ.** 01749 870261. www.bucklegrove.co.uk. Ideal for exploring Wells, Wookey Hole caves & Cheddar Gorge. Open plan site with countryside views. Indoor pool, bar & games room. Woodland walk on site. See website for full directions. Do not rely on Sat Nav as some local lanes not suitable for large/towing vehicles. Open: 2 March - 2 December. ★★★★ BH&HPA 10 70 20 11

## Taunton

(4m). **Ashe Farm Caravan & Camping Site, Ashe, Thornfalcon, Taunton, Somerset TA3 5NW.** 01823 443674.

www.ashefarm.co.uk. Peaceful, family run, farm site with lovely views, central for touring. Washroom, play area, tennis court and dog walk. Golf course within 3m. Leave M5 at J25, south easterly. Take A358 for 2.5m, turn R at Nags Head. Open: 1 April - 31 October. ★★★ 10 20 3

(2m). **Cornish Farm Touring Park, Shoreditch, Taunton, Somerset TA3 7BS.** 01823 327746. www.cornishfarm.com. Level well drained site. Luxury fully tiled and heated toilets and showers. Family room/disabled facilities and laundry. Wi-Fi access. The site has dusk to dawn lighting for our guests' safety. AA 4 pennants. Recently listed in top 100 sites in the country. From M5 follow Taunton/Racecourse signs then brown signs. Open: All year. 4 50

(6m). **Holly Bush Park, Culmhead, Taunton, Somerset TA3 7EA.** 01823 421885. www.hollybushpark.com. Peaceful site set up in the Blackdown Hills, an area of outstanding natural beauty. Fishing, golf, swimming nearby. Surrounded by forestry commission woods, ideal for walking, cycling etc. Country pub 100yd away with good food and beer. No charge for dogs, children under 3 years, shop, telephone, gas and laundrette on site. From J25 on M5 follow directions for Taunton. At first traffic lights turn L and follow signs for racecourse and Corfe. 3.5m after Corfe turn R at crossroads then R again, park on L. Open: All year. ★★★★ 8 15 5

**Lowtrow Cross, Upton, Taunton, Somerset TA4 2DB.** 01398 371199. www.lowtrowcross.co.uk. ADULTS ONLY site. Quiet edge of Exmoor. Shower block. Laundry. Use of freezer and microwave. Small shop essential items only. Inn with restaurant. Fishing, sailing 3m. Shops 6m. From S exit motorway to Tiverton, Bampton follow B3190 (signs to Wimbleball Lake) site 1m Nof Upton, borders Devon and Somerset. 7m from Dulverton. Open: 6 April - 31 October. ★★★★ 5 8 14 2

(12m). **Waterrow Touring Park (Adults only), Waterrow, Wiveliscombe, Taunton, Somerset TA4 2AZ.** 01984 623464. www.waterrowpark.co.uk. Gently sloping site in an attractive river valley. Exclusively for adults. One holiday home for hire. Fly fishing on site. Dog walking field. Landscaped hardstandings all with views. Watercolour painting holidays and fly fishing tuition. Country pub nearby. David Bellamy Gold Conservation Award. 3m SW of Wiveliscombe via B3227.

# SOUTH WEST

300yd past The Rock pub at Waterrow. Open: All year. ★★★★★ BH&HPA 38 38 A

### Watch et

(2m). **Doniford Bay Holiday Park (Haven), Sea Lane, Watchet, Somerset TA23 OTJ.** 0871 4680496. www.haven.com. Investor In People. Heated indoor pool. Kids' clubs. Entertainment for the whole family. Convenience store. Bakery. All weather multi-sports court. Mini golf, go-karts, indoor fun palace. David Bellamy Gold Conservation Award. M5, J23 then take A38 towards Bridgwater. Then take A39 towards Minehead. After about 15m, in West Quantoxhead, fork R after St Audries garage. Doniford bay is about 1m further on the R. Open: 18 March - 31 October. ★★★★ BH&HPA NCC 191

(1m). **Helwell Bay Holidays, Helwell Bay, Watchet, Somerset TA23 OUG.** 01984 631781. www.helwellbay.com. Close to town. Situated on level ground, overlooking the Bristol Channel and adjacent to the West Somerset Steam Railway, about 8mins walk into Watchet. All pitches overlook the sea. Very quiet and relaxing. On B3191, off A39 Bridgwater to Watchet. Open: 1 April - 31 October. ★ BH&HPA 12 40

(1m). **Sunnybank Holiday Park, Doniford, Watchet, Somerset TA23 OUD.** 0844 272 9505. www.sunnybankpark.co.uk. Small, quiet family park. Heated swimming pool. Overlooking the sea. Luxury caravans in a picturesque area. Short breaks. Pets welcome. Bus service nearby. Small shop, ideal for walkers, cyclists and those who want a quiet relaxing break. A39 from Bridgwater at West Quantoxhead turn R on to B3191. Bottom of steep hill turn R at Sunnybank Caravan Park. Open: 5 February - 3 January. ★★★★ BH&HPA 54

(1m). **Warren Bay Holiday Village, Watchet, Somerset TA23 OJR.** 01984 631460. www.pringsholidayparks.co.uk. Less than a mile from the historic seaside town of Watchet. A large holiday complex with a small shop. On B3191 Minehead to Watchet. Open: 1 February - 31 October. 100 A 222

### Wellington

(1m). **Cadeside Caravan Club Site, Nynehead Road, Wellington, Somerset TA21 9HN.** 01823 663103. www.caravanclub.co.uk. This is a well screened rural site with views of the surrounding hills and within a 10mins walk of Wellington. No toilet block, dog walk on site and recycling facilities within 1m. Much of this site has been developed into an all year secure storage area. Non-members welcome. No tents. See website for standard directions to site. Open: All year. NCC 16 16

### Wells

**Cheddar Mendip Heights Camping & Caravanning Club Site, Mendip Heights, Townsend, Priddy, Wells, Somerset BA5 3BP.** 01749 870241. www.campingandcaravanningclub.co.uk. Well landscaped franchised site with large grassy areas. 90 pitches (35 hardstanding). Play area with slide & swings. Holiday home rental. From the A39 take the B3135. Open: 1 March - 15 November. ★★★★ NCC 90 90

### Weston-Super-Mare

(3m). **Country View Holiday Park, Sand Road, Sand Bay, Weston-Super-Mare, Somerset BS22 9UJ.** 01934 627595. www.cvhp.co.uk. 120 pitches (including hardstandings), plus separate camping field. Beach 2mins walk. Bar, outdoor pool & play area. Restaurants nearby. 10mins from Jct 21 of M5. Open: 1 March - 31 January. ★★★★ BH&HPA 90 90 30 A

(5m). **Dulhorn Farm Holiday Park, Weston Road, Lympsham, Weston-super-Mare, Somerset BS24 OJQ.** 01934 750298. www.dulhornfarmholidaypark.co.uk. Working farm set in countryside close to Mendip Hills, sea about 3m. Lots to do within 1hr. Bristol, Bath, Longleat. Ideal for touring. Bus service 1m, railway station 4.5m. Fishing 4m. Open February 10-January 10 (statics). M5, J22, A38 to Bristol, then A370 SP Weston-super-Mare. Through traffic lights on A370, about 0.75m on L. Open: 1 March - 31 October. ★★★★ BH&HPA 20 107 100 A 1 4

(3m). **Netherdale Camping, Sidcot, Winscombe, Weston-Super-Mare, Somerset BS25 1NH.** 01934 843007. 30 mixed pitches in total. Village shops/supermarket/takeaways 1m. Restaurant/pub next door. Pools, sports centres, activity centre, ski slopes 3m. Golf and fishing 4m. Mendip Hills adjoining. Excellent walking area. Dogs allowed on lead only. On A38 road midway between Bristol and Bridgwater and where Weston-super-Mare to Cheddar road (A371) crosses A38. Open: 1 March - 31 October. 10 10 A

(1.5m). **Purn Holiday Park, Bridgwater Road (A370), Bleadon, Weston-super-Mare, Somerset BS24 OAN.** 01934 812342. www.purnholidaypark.com. Licensed club with entertainment, dining and dancing, children allowed. Heated swimming pools, games room etc. Ideally situated in the green belt area of Bleadon, only 2m from the leading holiday resort of Weston super Mare. Purn Holiday Park can be your annual seaside retreat. Leave M5 J21 and take signs for Weston hospital, turn L at hospital roundabout on to A370, park 1m on R. Open: All year. BH&HPA 96 133

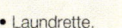

Amazing views of the coastline are enjoyed from each of our caravan holiday homes at Sunnybank in Somerset

- 5* holiday park.
- 1 mile from ancient harbour town of Watchet.
- Superb sea views.
- Outdoor heated pool and sun terrace.
- Laundrette.
- Rambling walks for all abilities.
- Caravan holiday homes for sale

20% off your booking Quote CHP20
*Terms and conditions apply

To book call 0844 272 9505 or visit www.sunnybankpark.co.uk

CARAVAN & HOLIDAY PARKS 2012 **147**

# SOUTH WEST

**West Acres Touring Park**, Westacres Farm, West Wick, Weston-super-Mare, Somerset BS24 7TL. 01934 510796. Park 100yd on L. A quiet, family run park. Secure caravan storage compound situated on site to rear. Owner supplied copy. From Junction 21, M5, follow signs to West Wick, over mini roundabout, L at T-junction. Park 100yd on L. Open: All year.

(2m). **West End Farm Touring Park**, Laneys Drove, Locking, Weston-Super-Mare, Somerset BS24 8RN. 01934 822529. www.westendcaravan.com. Quiet family park. Level and well sheltered. Pub (for food) & shop in local village. Leave M5, J21 follow signs for International Helicopter Museum, first R after museum, site signed. Open: All year. ★★★ BH&HPA

(2m). **Weston-Super-Mare Camping & Caravanning Club Site**, West End Farm, Locking, Weston-super-Mare, Somerset BS24 8RN. 01934 822548. www.campingandcaravanningclub.co.uk. A traditional seaside holiday resort, Cheddar Gorge & Wookey Hole are a short journey away. Club Members only. Fishing, golf and horse riding nearby. Bath, Bristol & Glastonbury are also nearby and well worth a visit. Special deals available for families & backpackers. All units accepted. M5, exit 21, take A370 - W-S-M, follow Helicopter Museum signs - take first turning R after museum entrance - passing mobile home park on L. At the top as you enter West End Farm, turn R into the site. Open: 1 April - 26 September. ★★★ NCC

## Williton

(2m). **Home Farm Holiday Centre**, St. Audries Bay, Williton, Somerset TA4 4DP. 01984 632487. www.homefarmholidaycentre.co.uk. Family run with private beach. Indoor swimming pool (40 mixed pitches). Licensed bar. Play area and dog walk. Bungalows and caravans for hire. Shop and bar closed November-March, pool open all year. 3 AA pennants. A39 Bridgwater towards Minehead for 17m. At West Quantoxhead take B3191 SP Doniford, 1st R in 0.5m. Mile long drive with ramps. 2m from Watchet. Open: All year. 3 BH&HPA

## Wincanton

(0.5m). **Wincanton Racecourse Caravan Club Site**, Wincanton, Somerset BA9 8BJ. 01963 34206. www.caravanclub.co.uk. Attractive location in open countryside with beautiful views to Bruton Forest and Downs. TV and information room. 9 hole golf course within the racecourse. Dog walk. Shops 1m. Shower for disabled. Non-members and tent campers welcome. See website for standard directions to site. Open: 23 March - 1 October. ★★★ NCC

## Yeovil

(3m). **Halfway Caravan & Camping Park**, Halfway, Ilchester Road, Yeovil, Somerset BA22 8RE. 01935 840342. www.halfwaycaravanpark.com. Great food, drinks. Site overlooks the inn's fishing lake. Guests may fish upon inn's permission for free. Close by Ilchester village provides all amenities. AA 2 pennants. Owner supplied copy. From A303, exit at Ilchester, continue on A37 Yeovil Road, after 2m you'll see the Halfway House Inn on your L, we are next door at Trees Cottage. Open: 14 March - 18 October. 2

(7m). **Long Hazel Park**, High Street, Sparkford, Yeovil, Somerset BA22 7JH. 01963 440002. www.longhazelpark.co.uk. ADULTS ONLY. Level site 40 hardstandings. Holiday lodges for sale and hire. Near to Village Inn. Walking distance to shop/garage/McDonalds/PO. Modern facilities. Public Telephone. Wi-Fi available. Bus stop outside. Lots to see and do including Haynes International Motor Museum and Fleet Air Arm Museum at Yeovilton. Just off A303/A359 junction. At Hazlegrove Services roundabout. Follow brown and white tourist signs into the village. Open: All year. ★★★★ BH&HPA

# WILTSHIRE
## Calne

(1.5m). **Blackland Lakes**, Stockley Lane, Calne, Wiltshire SN11 0NQ. 01249 813672. www.blacklandlakes.co.uk. Scenic, sheltered, friendly, natural site with lakes & coarse fishing. 17 acres. Super pitches. Play areas. Good touring & family holiday centre. ADAC & ANWB. RAC appointed & AA 3 pennants. Mother and baby and disabled rooms. No club house. No statics. 1m trail. 6 paddocks. David Bellamy Silver Conservation Award. E of Calne off A4, SP. Open: All year. 3 BH&HPA

## Chippenham

(4m). **Piccadilly Caravan Park**, Folly Lane West, Lacock, Chippenham, Wiltshire SN15 2LP. 01249 730260. Set in open countryside 0.5m from historic National Trust village of Lacock. Ideal touring centre. Turn R off A350 Chippenham to Melksham road SP to Gastard with caravan symbol. Open: 1 April - 31 October. ★★★★★ BH&HPA

(3m). **Plough Lane Caravan Site** (Tranquil adults-only), Plough Lane, Kington Langley, Chippenham, Wiltshire SN15 5PS. 01249 750146. www.ploughlane.co.uk. Adults only. All pitches half-hardstanding and half-grass with 16 amp elec. 25 fully serviced pitches. Good pubs nearby. Bus service from outside site. Very well located for touring Wiltshire, Cotswolds and Bath. Pre booking essential. SP from A350 N of Chippenham (J17, M4). Open: Mid March - 31 October. ★★★★★ BH&HPA

## Devizes

(3m). **The Bell Caravan Park**, Andover Road, Lydeway, Devizes, Wiltshire SN10 3PS. 01380 840230. Swimming pool - not heated. The Bell Caravan park has a covered barbecue area. Fishing lake 3m. SE of Devizes on A342 Andover road. Open: 28 March - 30 September.

## Malmesbury

(0.25m). **Burton Hill Caravan and Camping Park**, Arches Lane, Malmesbury, Wiltshire SN16 0EH. 01666 826880. www.burtonhill.co.uk. Relaxed and friendly, Burton Hill is a level, grassy site overlooking the town and farmland. 5-10mins walk along part of the town's river walk into Malmesbury with pubs, shops, supermarket, restaurants, swimming pool. There are many walks and cycle ways, and shopping at the Outlet Centre, Swindon. Off A429 Chippenham to Malmesbury Road, turn into Arches Lane, by 30/40mph sign. 5m N of M4, J7. Open: 1 April - 31 October. BH&HPA

## Marlborough

(6m). **Hillview Park**, Sunnyhill Lane, Oare, Marlborough, Wiltshire SN8 4JG. 01672 563151. Level site. Free hot showers. SAE for brochure. Advance booking advisable. Shops and station within 2m. Cannot take motor vans over 21ft or caravans overall length 22ft. Tents over 4 berth will incur extra charge. Owner supplied copy. S of Marlborough on A345. Open: 1 April - 30 September. ★★★ BH&HPA

# SOUTH WEST / SCOTLAND

**(1m). Postern Hill (Forest Holidays), Postern Hill, Marlborough, Wiltshire SN8 4ND.** *01672 515195.* www.forestholidays.co.uk. Set in woodland with sheltered pitches and plenty of wildlife to enjoy. Toilets (summer season only) but no shower facilities. Bookings and brochure requests on 0845 1308224. David Bellamy Gold Conservation Award. S of Marlborough on the A346 towards Tidworth. Open: All year. BH&HPA 170

## Marston Meysey

**Second Chance Touring Park, Marston Meysey, Wiltshire SN6 6SZ.** *01285 810675.* Upper Thames riverside location on the edge of the Cotswolds. Fishing on site. Explore the Isis with your own canoe. Golf course nearby. 3.5m to shops, doctor, PO. Close to Roman town Cirencester, capital of Cotswolds. AA 2 pennants. Owner supplied copy. Midway between Cirencester and Swindon along A419. turn off at Fairford/Latton, SP. Proceed 3m. Turn R at brown tourist camping sign. Park is 150yds on R. 3.5m from Fairford. Open: 1 March - 7 November. 26 26

## Melksham

**(2m). Devizes Camping & Caravanning Club Site, Spout Lane, Melksham, Wiltshire SN12 6RN.** *01380 828839.* www.campingandcaravanningclub.co.uk. Non-members welcome. Caravans, motorcaravans and tents accepted. Fishing is available all year round in canal adjacent to site. Special deals available for families and backpackers. Loo of the Year (5 stars). SW Tourism Highly Commended: runner up. On A361 from Devizes turn R on to A365 over canal and next L down the lane beside '3 Magpies' PH, site on R. Bordering the Kennett and Avon Canal, 4m from Devizes. Open: 1 January - 31 December. ★ ★ ★ ★ NCC 90 90

## Salisbury

**(3m). Alderbury Caravan & Camping Park, Southampton Road, Whaddon, Salisbury, Wiltshire SP5 3HB.** *01722 710276.* www.alderburycaravanpark.co.uk. Clean, pleasant site on the edge of village, opposite the Three Crowns inn with excellent food. Free showers, utility room. Excellent location for Stonehenge and New Forest. Take A36 to Southampton and follow signs for Alderbury and Whaddon. Open: All year. 39

**(4m). Coombe Touring Caravan Park, Coombe Nurseries, The Race Plain, Netherhampton, Salisbury, Wiltshire SP2 8PN.** *01722 328451.* www.coombetouringpark.co.uk. Laundrette. Gas supplies. Shop open May to September. SAE for brochure. 2.5m to shops, PO. 4m to doctors. Adjacent to racecourse (flat). Golf course nearby. AA 4 pennants. Take A36 Salisbury to Warminster, 2m from Salisbury outskirts, turn at traffic lights on to A3094. Next to Salisbury racecourse. Open: All year. 4 BH&HPA 5 45 4

**(10m). Green Hill Farm Camping & Caravanning Park, New Road, Landford, Salisbury, Wiltshire SP5 2AZ.** *01794 324117.* www.greenhillholidays.co.uk. ADULT ONLY site (no under 18 years). On Hants/Wilts border within New Forest Heritage area. Two lakes, fishing on site. Shops, PO 1m, Doctors 2.5m. Ideal base for walking or cycling - direct access to New Forest at rear of site. Pubs and eating-houses within easy reach. Dogs must be kept on leads whilst on site and farm areas. Stock calor gas. AA 3 pennants. M27 south bound exit J2. A36 Salisbury road 3m BP garage on L take next L into new road SP Nomansland, site on L 1m along new road. Open: All year. 3 10 100 50

**(9m). Hillside Caravan Club Site, Andover Road, Lopcombe Corner, Salisbury, Wiltshire SP5 1BY.** *01980 862527.* www.caravanclub.co.uk. Set in rolling countryside, most pitches in woodland glades in an Area of Outstanding Natural Beauty. Toilet blocks. Veg prep. Gas. MV service shop 3m. Local attractions include Salisbury Cathedral and Sherbourne Castle. Member only. No tents. See website for standard directions to site. Open: 23 March - 8 October. NCC 46 46

**(1.5m). Salisbury Camping & Caravanning Club Site, Hudson's Field, Salisbury, Wiltshire SP1 3RR.** *01722 320713.* www.campingandcaravanningclub.co.uk. The site is 30mins walk along river Avon from Salisbury. A visit to the city is a must, with its shops and spectacular cathedral. The Iron Age Settlement of Old Sarum, preserved by English Heritage is nearby. Gliding, fishing, horse riding and cycling are all within easy reach of the site. Non members welcome. All units accepted. Special deals available for families and backpackers. 1.5m from Salisbury on the A345. Large open field next to Old Sarum. Open: 1 April - 31 October. ★ ★ ★ ★ NCC 150 150

**(11m). Stonehenge Touring Park, Orcheston, Salisbury, Wiltshire SP3 4SH.** *01980 620304.* www.stonehengetouringpark.com. Quiet, level, country site. Close to Stonehenge. Booking advisable. Dogs on leads for touring site. Children allowed. Off A360 Devizes to Salisbury. Open: All year. ★ ★ ★ 3 BH&HPA 30

## Tilshead

**Brades Acre Caravan Site, The Bungalow, Tilshead, Wiltshire SP3 4RX.** *01980 620402.* Close to places of interest. Shops, PO 1m. Doctor 5m. Salisbury 14m. Devizes 10m. A360 Salisbury to Devizes. Open: 1 April - 31 October. NCC 25 25

## Warminster

**(5m). Longleat Caravan Club Site, Warminster, Wiltshire BA12 7NL.** *01985 844663.* www.caravanclub.co.uk. A beautiful parkland site. Non-members welcome. No tents. Advance booking advised BH and July and August. Toilet block. Privacy cubicle. Laundry facilities. Baby/toddler washroom. Veg prep. Motorhome service point. Gas & gaz. Play equipment. Water sports. Ideal for families. Some hardstanding, dog walk, good area for walking, fishing and NCN cycle path within 5m. See website for standard directions to site. Open: 23 March - 5 November. ★ ★ ★ ★ ★ NCC 165 165

## Westbury

**(3.5m). Brokerswood Country Park, Brokerswood, Westbury, Wiltshire BA13 4EH.** *01373 822238.* www.brokerswoodcountrypark.co.uk. Site set in 80 acres woodlands with lake and Heritage centre. Adventure playground. Narrow gauge railway. Toddlers undercover play area. Coarse fishing. David Bellamy Gold Conservation Award. Follow brown tourist signs from A36 or A361. 3.5m N of Westbury. 5m from Trowbridge. Open: All year. ★ ★ ★ ★ 4 BH&HPA 21 69 50

# ABERDEENSHIRE

## Aboyne

**(0.5m). Aboyne Loch Caravan Park, Aboyne, Aberdeenshire AB34 5BR.** *01339 886244.* Dogs allowed on leads at all times on park. Coarse fishing on loch, boats for hire. Shops, PO, swimming pool, restaurants and bowling within 0.5m of park. Golf beside the park. Dog walk path around the loch. David Bellamy Gold Conservation Award. Off A93. Open: 1 April - 24 October. BH&HPA 15 5 86

# SCOTLAND

## Alford

**Haughton Caravan Park,** Montgarrie Road, Alford, Aberdeenshire AB33 8NA. 01975 562107. www.aberdeenshire.gov.uk/caravanparks. Beautiful country location. Ideal touring base. Fishing and golf on or adjacent to site. Dogs allowed but not in holiday hire caravans. 5 flats and 1 bungalow also for hire. Situated 25m W of Aberdeen. Open: 1 April - 31 October. ★★★★ 170 A 50

## Ballater

(0.25m). **Ballater Caravan & Camping Site,** Anderson Road, Ballater, Aberdeenshire AB35 5QW. 01339 755727. www.aberdeenshire.gov.uk/caravanparks. Magnificent scenery with views from the site. Plenty of shops, bars and restaurants just a few minutes walk away in Ballater. Off A93. Open: 1 April - 31 October. ★★★ 139 A 93

(0.5m). **The Invercauld Caravan Club Site,** Glenshee Road, Braemar, Ballater, Aberdeenshire AB35 5YQ. 01339 741373. www.caravanclub.co.uk. An ideal site for walkers and mountain bikers. Non-members welcome. Tent campers welcome. Some hardstandings. Facilities for skiers, ski rocks, boot store, drying room and community room. Privacy cubicles, MV service point, veg prep area, playground, dog walk. Ideal for families, quiet and peaceful off peak for walking, fishing and golf within 5m. Advance booking essential at all times. See website for standard directions to site. Open: 1 January - 18 October. ★★★★ NCC 97 97

## Banchory

(5m). **Feughside Caravan Park,** Strachan, Banchory, Aberdeenshire AB31 3NT. 01330 850669. www.feughsidecaravanpark.co.uk. Quiet family run park. Caravans well spaced, good toilet facilities. Level, grassy. Hotel adjacent. Fishing nearby, forest walks 1.5m, shops 2m. Several golf courses in area. David Bellamy Silver Conservation Award. Take B974 from Banchory W to Strachan then B976 to Feughside Inn turn R, site is behind Inn. Open: 1 April - 31 October. ★★★★ BH&HPA 10 22 A

(1.5m). **Silverbank Caravan Club Site,** North Deeside Road, Banchory, Aberdeenshire AB31 5PY. 01330 822477. www.caravanclub.co.uk. Close to river Dee. Convenient for walking, pony trekking, golf and fishing. Indoor pool at Banchory. All hardstandings, toilet block (privacy cubicles), laundry facilities, veg prep, MV service point, gas and gaz, shops 0.5m, dog walk. Members only. No tents. See website for standard directions to site. Open: 23 March - 7 January. NCC 62 62

## Banff

(1m). **Banff Links Caravan Park,** Banff Links, Banff, Aberdeenshire AB45 2JJ. 01261 812228. www.aberdeenshire.gov.uk/caravanparks. Popular park set close to the large sandy beach of Banff Bay, a great attraction to surfers. Next to the caravan site is a well equipped newly installed children's play park. Off A98 Cullen to Banff. 1m W of Banff, SP coastal route. Open: 18 April - 31 October. ★★★★ 82 A

(0.25m). **Portsoy Caravan Park,** Maclean Terrace, Portsoy, Banff, Aberdeenshire AB45 2RQ. 01261 842695. www.aberdeenshire.gov.uk/caravanparks. Set overlooking Portsoy Bay near to the 17th century harbour & village shops. Off A98. Open: 1 April - 31 October. ★★★★ 43 A 16

(3m). **Wester Bonnyton Farm,** Gamrie, Banff, Aberdeenshire AB45 3EP. 01343 850223. www.wester-bonnyton.xplodelite.com. All caravans are fully serviced (toilet, shower, fridge and TV). Touring sites with hook-up facilities, play area for children. All caravans and pitches have a view of Moray Firth. Many local tourist attractions. Fishing and golf within 2m. 2m E of Macduff on the B9031 and 1m off A98 (Banff-Fraserburgh road). Open: 1 April - 31 October. ★★★ BH&HPA 8 8 A 7

**Whitehills Caravan Park,** Whitehills, Banff, Aberdeenshire AB4 2JN. 01261 861474. www.whitehillscaravanpark.co.uk. Ideal location for a family holiday. Convenient for golf courses, fishing and right in the heart of castle country. Owner supplied copy. BH&HPA 72

## Fraserburgh

**Rosehearty Caravan Park,** Union Street, Rosehearty, Fraserburgh, Aberdeenshire AB43 7JQ. 01346 510041. www.aberdeenshire.gov.uk. Situated on the seashore within the village, close to shops, hotels & services. On site laundry & toilet/shower facilities. Off B9031 near Rosehearty. Open: 1 April - 31 October. ★★ 40 A

## Huntly

(0.5m). **Huntly Castle Caravan Park,** The Meadows, Huntly, Aberdeenshire AB54 4UJ. 01466 794999. www.huntlycastle.co.uk. CARAVAN CLUB AFFILIATED SITE. Large indoor recreation facility (available weekends, local school holidays) including snooker, large play area and refreshments. 5mins walk to town. Ideal touring base for Whisky castle and coastal trails. Golf course, river fishing, swimming, shops, all within 0.5m. From Aberdeen on A96 (Huntly bypass), at roundabout on outskirts of Huntly continue on A96 (sp Inverness). In about 0.75m turn R then 2nd L (Riverside Dir). Open: 28 March - 30 October. ★★★★★ BH&HPA NCC 66 66 A 37

## Inverurie

(1m). **Hillhead Caravan Park,** Kintore, Inverurie, Aberdeenshire AB51 0YX. 01467 632809. www.hillheadcaravan.com. 24 mixed pitches in total. AA 3-pennant and RAC approved. Well-equipped, high quality, quiet park. Golf, shop, PO, doctor nearby. Castle trail, whisky trail. Aberdeen city 12m, airport 6m. From S leave A96 at Broomhill roundabout 3rd exit. From N stay on A96 past Kintore (Do not enter Kintore), leave at Broomhill roundabout 1st exit. Follow brown/white caravan signs on to B994. Then take second R, 3m along B994. Hillhead is 1m on R. Open: All year. ★★★★ BH&HPA 24

## Laurencekirk

(4m). **Brownmuir Caravan Park,** Fordoun, Laurencekirk, Aberdeenshire AB30 1SJ. 01561 320786. www.brownmuircaravanpark.co.uk. Fishing, golf course in village; cycling, hiking. 1m to shops in village and bowls, tennis. Park has children's play area and is flat and grassy. Off A90, 4m N of Laurencekirk, 10m S of Stonehaven. At Fordoun pass village, 1m on R. Park 1m from village of Fordoun. Open: 1 April - 31 October. ★★★ NCC 11 11 A 3

(5m). **Dovecot Caravan Park,** Northwaterbridge, Laurencekirk, Aberdeenshire AB30 1QL. 01674 840630. www.dovecotcaravanpark.co.uk. Well maintained, sheltered park. Excellent base for touring. Wi-Fi available. David Bellamy Gold Conservation Award. Off A90 Dundee-Aberdeen road, 5m N of Brechin, turn off at Northwaterbridge at Edzell Woods sign 500yd on L. Map reference 045/648663. Open: 1 April - 22 October.

# SCOTLAND

★★★★ BH&HPA 25

## Macduff

(0.5m). **Myrus Caravan Park, Macduff, Aberdeenshire AB45 3QP.** 01261 812845. www.myrusholidaypark.co.uk. Overnight stop for tents. Fees on application. Owner supplied copy. On A947. Open: 1 April - 31 October. BH&HPA 10 14 36

## Maryculter

(5m). **Deeside Holiday Park, South Deeside Road, Maryculter, Aberdeenshire AB12 5FX.** 01224 733860. www.holiday-parks.co.uk. Family-run holiday park at Gateway to Royal Deeside and only short drive to the lively city of Aberdeen. Holiday homes for hire. On A90 follow B9077 for Maryculter. At Bridge of Dee roundabout, park is about 5m next to Old Mill Inn. Open: All year. ★★★★★ BH&HPA 10 40 7

## Peterhead

(8m). **Aden Caravan Park, Mintlaw, Peterhead, Aberdeenshire AB42 8FQ.** 01771 623460. www.aberdeenshire.gov.uk. Set within a woodland area with a heritage centre, which includes a working farm, restaurant and sensory garden. On A950. Open: 18 April - 31 October. ★★★★★ 73 13

**Peterhead Lido Camping Site, South Road, Peterhead, Aberdeenshire AB42 2XX.** 01779 473358. www.aberdeenshire.gov.uk/caravanparks. Council-owned and run site next to an award-winning beach & marina. Situated in Peterhead, well signed from main road. 29 touring pitches. Situated at the Peterhead Lido, the park is next to a busy thoroughfare overlooking the Bay of Refuge, and marina close to the maritime heritage centre, gift shop, cafeteria and play area. Open: 1 April - 31 October. ★★★★ 35 13

## Portsoy

(3m). **Sandend Caravan Park, Sandend, Portsoy, Aberdeenshire AB4 2UA.** 01261 842660. www.sandendcaravanpark.co.uk. Overlooking candy beach in conservation village. Short walk to village harbour. Ideal for children. No single sex groups. Thistle Award. Off A98 between Cullen and Portsoy. Open: 1 April - 8 October. ★★★ NCC 12 30 28

## Tarland

**Tarland Camping & Caravanning Club Site, Tarland, Aberdeenshire AB34 4UP.** 01339 881388. www.campingandcaravanningclub.co.uk. The area is a paradise for walkers and anglers. The site is located in the quiet and pretty village of Tarland. The mountain scenery of Royal Deeside is spectacular. Non-members welcome. Special deals for families and backpackers. Some all-weather pitches available. Several golf courses are available in the area. From Aberdeen on A93 turn R in Aboyne at Struan Hall on to B9094. After 6m take next R and then fork L before bridge, continue for 600yd, site on L. 6m from Aboyne. Open: 1 April - 31 October. ★★★★★ NCC 52 52 14

## Turriff

(10m). **East Balthangie Caravan Park, Cumminestown, Turriff, Aberdeenshire AB53 5XY.** 01888 544261. www.eastbalthangie.co.uk. PO and shop 2m. Secure area for pet owners. Farm walk. Open March-October with CL site all year. From Ellon on A948 to New Deer, road becomes B9170 to Cuminestown. Continue straight on for 2m, then turn R at the junction SP New Byth. Park is 3.5m down this road on left hand side. Open: 1 March - 31 October. 12 12 12

(0.5m). **Turriff Caravan Park, Station Road, Turriff, Aberdeenshire AB53 4ER.** 01888 562205. www.aberdeenshire.gov.uk/caravanparks. Site is adjacent to attractive park with children's play area, crazy golf, bowling and boating pond. Sports centre. Dogs on leads allowed. From Turriff town centre off A947 Aberdeen to Banff road 9m S of Banff. Open: 1 April - 31 October. ★★★★ 57 15

(10m). **Woodlea Caravan Park, New Byth, Turriff, Aberdeenshire AB53 5TY.** 01888 544817. Golf. Tennis. Bowls. Sailing. Croquet. Badminton. Play area. Pony rides. Games room & other attractions. Indoor swimming pool. Sauna, restaurant, bar. On A702 New Galloway Road, 1.5m out of Moniaive. Open: 1 April - 31 October. 8

# ANGUS

## Arbroath

(0.5m). **Red Lion Holiday Park, Dundee Road, Arbroath, Angus DD11 2PT.** 01241 872038. www.redlion-holidaypark.co.uk. Modern laundrette. Licensed bar, cafe, takeaway and children's disco. Swimming pool, toddlers pool, sauna, steam room, spa, family room, amusements, fitness suite, soft play, pool tables. 0.5m to main shopping centre. 1m to golf course. On A92 Dundee to Arbroath. Open: 9 March - 29 October. 31 31 320

## Brechin

(7m). **Glenesk Caravan Park, The Burn Estate, Edzell, Brechin, Angus DD9 7YP.** 01356 648565. An attractive woodland site featuring a small fishing lake. Many local attractions and outdoor activities. Manager: Ms N J Morgan. From A90 Aberdeen-Dundee take B966 to Edzell, 1.5 m N of Edzell turn N, SP Glenesk. Park 1m from junction. Open: 1 April - 31 October. ★★★★ BH&HPA 45 45 14

## Carnoustie

(0.5m). **Woodlands Caravan Park (Carnoustie), Newton Road, Carnoustie, Angus DD7 6GR.** 01241 854430. woodlandscaravanpark.net. All shops, takeaways, restaurants, fishing, golf, swimming pool, sports facilities all within 5-10 mins walk. Take the Carnoustie turn off from A92 turn on to Newton road just before Carnoustie and follow signs. Open: 12 March - 14 October. ★★★★ 46

## Forfar

(2m). **Drumshademuir Caravan Park, Roundyhill By Glamis, Forfar, Angus DD8 1QT.** 01575 573284. www.drumshademuir.co.uk. Well kept family run site. Lunches, evening meals, pub. Putting. Laundry. Woodland walk. Caravan storage. AA 4 pennant. Midway between Glamis Castle and Kirriemuir on the A928. Open: All year. ★★★★ 4 BH&HPA 80 80

(2m). **Foresterseat Caravan Park, Burnside, Arbroath Road, Forfar, Angus DD8 2RY.** 01307 818880. www.foresterseat.co.uk. This modern, peaceful, family run park on the outskirts of Forfar has beautiful views from every hardstanding pitch with water and electricity hookup. Kookaburras fully licensed restaurant next door. From Forfar take A932 toward Arbroath, out of Forfar, and pass Cunninghill golf course on R. Foresterseat is 1m past the course, on R. Open: 23 March - 8 November. ★★★★ BH&HPA 33 33

Visit www.caravanclub.co.uk

# SCOTLAND

**Lochside Caravan Club Site, Craig O'loch Road, Forfar, Angus DD8 1BT.** 01307 468917. www.caravanclub.co.uk. Picturesque parkland location near the bustling centre of Forfar. Adjacent to play area, tennis courts, crazy golf and leisure centre. Non members welcome. No tents. See website for standard directions to site. Open: 23 March - 5 November. ★★★★ NCC 71⛺ 71🚐

### Montrose

**(6m). East Bowstrips Caravan Park, St Cyrus, Montrose, Angus DD10 0DE.** 01674 850328. Delightful quiet park, set in attractively landscaped grounds, close to beach and nature reserve. Ideal touring centre. Facilities for disabled visitors. Fishing 1m, golf 6m. AA 4 pennants. About 6m N of Montrose on A92. From S (Montrose) enter St Cyrus, pass hotel 1st L, 2nd R. From N (Aberdeen) enter St Cyrus 1st R, 2nd R. Open: 1 April - 31 October. ★★★★ BH&HPA 27🚐

**(7m). St Cyrus Park, St Cyrus, Montrose, Angus DD10 0DJ.** 01674 850316. www.welchshomes.co.uk. On A92. N of St Cyrus village. Open: All year. 80⛺

**(8m). Wairds Park Caravan Site, Wairds Park, Beach Road, Johnshaven, Montrose, Angus DD10 0EP.** 01561 362395. www.johnshaven.com. Putting. Bowling. Play area. Multi-sports courts with floodlights. 0.25m to village shops and PO. Confections and refreshments sold in park reception. 6 golf courses within 20m radius. On A92, N of St Cyrus. By the sea. Open: 1 April - 31 October. ★★★★ BH&HPA 20⛺ 20🚐 49

## ARGYLL & BUTE
### Acharacle

**Glenview Caravan Park, Strontian, Loch Sunart, Acharacle, Argyll & Bute PH36 4HZ.** 01967 402123. Laundrette, drying room, on site Pets corner. Shop, takeaway and doctor surgery within 200yd. PO and petrol 0.25m. 23m from Fort William. Owner supplied copy. On A82 take Corran Ferry across Loch Linnhe to Ardgour. Follow A861 to Strontian. Turn R at police station, site 300yd on R. Open: 1 March - 31 January. ★★★★ BH&HPA 14⛺ 4

**(4m). Resipole Farm Caravan And Camping Park, Loch Sunart, Acharacle, Argyll & Bute PH36 4HX.** 01967 431335. www.resipole.co.uk. Laundrette. Pay-phone. Private slip-way. Art gallery and studios. On A861. 8m W of Strontian. Open: 1 April - 31 October. ★★★★ BH&HPA 20⛺ 20🚐 20 2 4

### Alexandria

**Luss Camping & Caravanning Club Site, Luss, Loch Lomond, Alexandria, Argyll & Bute G83 8NT.** 01436 860658. www.campingandcaravanningclub.co.uk. Club members caravans and motorcaravans only. On the banks of Loch Lomond with good views of Ben Lomond. Tents accepted. 90 pitches set in 12 acres. Fishing available on site. Golf, horse riding, rock climbing and swimming pool nearby. Special deals available for families and backpackers. From Erskine Bridge take A82 N towards Tarbet. Turn R at lodge of Loch Lomond and International Camping Sign. Heading S from Tarbet, take first L after site sign and lodge of Loch Lomond sign. Campsite about 200yd. 11m from Dumbarton. Open: 1 April - 31 October. ★★★★ NCC 90⛺ 90🚐

### Ardlui

**Ardlui Holiday Home Park, Hotel, Marina & Holiday Home Park, Ardlui, Argyll & Bute G83 7EB.** 01301 704243. www.ardluiholidayhomepark.com. Situated on the shores of Loch Lomond, in the centre of the Loch Lomond and Trossachs National Park. 16m to Loch Lomond international golf course. On A82, 43m N of Glasgow. 8m to Arrochar. Open: All year. ★★★★ BH&HPA 7⛺

### Arrochar

**(2m). Ardgartan Caravan and Camping Site (Forest Holidays), Ardgarten, Arrochar, Argyll & Bute G83 7AR.** 01301 702293. www.forestholidays.co.uk. On the shores of Loch Long surrounded by the magnificent scenery of the Argyll Forest Park. On A83 Inveray to Arrochar. W of Arrochar. Open: All year. ★★★ BH&HPA 100

**(0.3m). Glenloin House, Arrochar, Argyll & Bute G83 7AJ.** 01301 702239. Permanent snack bar. Open all year except February and November. Owner supplied copy. On A83 Inveray to Arrochar. 200yd past PO behind Gulf petrol station at head of Loch Long. Open: 1 March - 31 January (not Nov). 4⛺ 5 30

**(3m). Loch Lomond Holiday Park, Inveruglas, Arrochar, Argyll & Bute G83 7DW.** 01301 704224. www.lochlomond-caravans.co.uk. Peaceful park on loch-side - ideal for fishing and water sports, walking and touring. On A82 Ardlui to Tarbet. Open: All year. ★★★★★ NCC 18⛺ 58🚐

### Ballachulish

**(1.5m). Glencoe Camping & Caravanning Club Site, Ballachulish, Argyll & Bute PH49 4LA.** 01855 811397. www.campingandcaravanningclub.co.uk. Our glorious club site at Glencoe where all pitches enjoy breathtaking views of the surrounding mountains. The woodlands around the site have streams tumbling over boulders. Excellent site for walkers. David Bellamy Gold Conservation Award. On A82. Crianlarich to Glencoe road. Take sign for Glencoe visitors centre. 18m from Fort William. Open: 1 April - 31 October. ★★★★ NCC 120⛺ 120🚐

### Barcaldine

**(0.5m). Oban Camping & Caravanning Club Site, Barcaldine, Argyll & Bute PA37 1SG.** 01631 720348. www.campingandcaravanningclub.co.uk. Ideally placed for touring Highlands and Islands. Licensed bar on site, also serves bar meals. All units accepted. Non-members welcome. The site is set in 4.5 acres of delightful walled garden. Superb woodland walks are just 5 mins from the site. Special deals available for families and backpackers. N from Connel Bridge on A828 site on right of village. Opposite the Marine Resource Centre proceed through the large iron gates. 12m from Oban. Open: 1 April - 31 October. ★★★★ NCC 75⛺ 75🚐

### Benderloch

**(8m). Seaview Caravan & Camping Park (Benderloch), Seaview, Keil Crofts, Benderloch, Benderloch, Argyll & Bute PA37 1QS.** 01631 720360. www.seaviewcaravanandcamping.co.uk. Couples only. Shop, PO, garage under 1m. Doctor 2.5m. Owner supplied copy. A85 to Connel Cross Connel Ferry Bridge on to the A828 road, N. Seaview is 3m from bridge. Open: 22 April - 30 September.

### Cairndow

**(8m). Strathlachlan Caravan Park, Strachur, Cairndow, Argyll & Bute PA27 8BU.** 01369 860300. www.strathlachlan.co.uk. On B8000. Open: 1 March - 31 October. 95

152 CARAVAN & HOLIDAY PARKS 2012

# SCOTLAND

## Campbeltown

**(5m). Peninver Sands Caravan Park, Peninver, Campbeltown, Argyll & Bute PA28 6QP.** 01586 552262. www.peninver-sands.com. Family run high quality park on beach location with excellent sea views. Ideal base for touring Kintyre. Swimming pool, cinema, shops within 5m. 3 golf courses within 10m. No single sex groups. Owner supplied copy. On B842. On R entering village of Peninver. Open: 15 March - 15 January. ★★★★ BH&HPA 🏕 🐕 ✓ 🎣 🍴 ⛱ 🚻 🚗 6⚡ ⛺ 55🚐

## Dunoon

**Glenfinart Caravan Park, Ardentinny, Dunoon, Argyll & Bute PA23 8TS.** 01369 810256. www.glenfinart-caravan-park.co.uk. Park set in the gardens of the old Glenfinart Mansion House with loch views and close to beach. Superb walking area. Owner supplied copy. From Dunoon take A815 N for 5m, turn right onto A880, after 8m park is on right opposite Fingals Falls. Open: 1 March - 1 December. 🏕 🐕 ⚡ 65🚐

**(2m). Hunter's Quay Holiday Village, Hunter's Quay, Dunoon, Argyll & Bute PA23 8HP.** 0845 4599772. www.argyllholidays.com. A fun and lively park in a scenic location. Ideal for families. Leisure centre on site, golf nearby, restaurant on site. David Bellamy Gold Conservation Award. A815 Hunter's Quay to Dunoon Coast Road. Open: All year. ★★★★★ BH&HPA 🏕 🐕 🎣 ⛱ ✱ ❌ ♨ 🚻 🚗 ⚡ 100🚐

**(4.5m). Invereck Countryside Holiday Park, Invereck, Sandbank, Dunoon, Argyll & Bute PA23 8QS.** 01369 705544. www.invereck.com. Garage 500yd, PO & shop 1.5m, hospital 3.5m, doctor, supermarket 4.5m. Owner supplied copy. Off A815. Open: 1 April - 31 October. 🏕 🐕 ✓ 🎣 🍴 ⛱ 🚻 14🏠 14⚡ ⛺ 15🚐 🏕

## Glencoe

**Red Squirrel Campsite, Glencoe, Argyll & Bute PH49 4HX.** 01855 811256. www.redsquirrelcampsite.com. An easy-going, hill farm campsite on the river Coe. Climbing, walking country. Appeals to naturalists. 12m S of Fort Williams. On the old Glencoe Road. 1.5m through Glencoe village over hump bridge. Parallel with 82. Open: All year. 🐕 ✓ 🍴 ✱ ♨ 🚻 ⛺ ⚡

## Glendaruel

**Glendaruel Caravan & Camping Park, Glendaruel, Argyll & Bute PA22 3AB.** 01369 820167. www.glendaruelcaravanpark.co.uk. Small, peaceful family run park within a 22-acre country estate. Walking, cycling and bird/wildlife watching. Thistle Award. Well stocked shop on park including Loch Fyne Ales, range of wines, Orkney ice cream, venison, books, maps and much more. Good base for touring. Discounts arranged with various local attractions. Off A886. Near Kyles of Bute. 17m from Dunoon. Open: 1 April - 31 October. ★★★★★ BH&HPA 🏕 🐕 ♿ ✓ 🎣 🍴 ⛱ 🚻 🚗 35⚡ ⛺ 27🚐

## Helensburgh

**(15m). Rosneath Castle Park, Rosneath, Helensburgh, Argyll & Bute G84 0QS.** 01436 831208. www.rosneathcastle.co.uk. Water sports centre, children's fun club, pub/bistro, outdoor activity area, indoor soft play area. Owner supplied copy. A82, then A814 for Garelochhead and then follow signs for B833 Kilcreggan. Park is situated 1m beyond Rosneath. GS. Open: 7 March - 31 January. ★★★★★ BH&HPA NCC 🏕 🐕 ✓ ❌ ⛱ ♿ ⚡ 365🚐

## Inveraray

**(2.5m). Argyll Caravan Park, Inveraray, Argyll & Bute PA32 8XT.** 01499 302285. www.argyllcaravanpark.com. Ideal location for relaxing and touring. Many places of interest within easy reach and Oban and Iona ferry 1hr drive away. 2.5m S of Inveraray. Open: 1 March - 31 October. ★★★★★ BH&HPA 🏕 🐕 ✓ 🎣 🍴 ⛱ 🚻 🚗 20⚡ ⛺ 40⚡ 205🚐

## Islay

**Kintra Farm Caravan Park, Kintra Beach, Port Ellen, Islay, Argyll & Bute PA42 7AT.** 01496 302051. www.kintrafarm.co.uk. Snacks, meals and takeaways available. Hot water & showers. Direct access to beach. Exceptional area for walking, bird watching, plant and wildlife study. Port Ellen 4m. Owner supplied copy. Take unclassified road from A846 towards Oa, follow Kintra signs. Open: 22 April - 30 September. 🐕 ♿ ⛺ ⚡

## Isle of Coll

**(5m). Garden House, Isle of Coll, Argyll & Bute PA78 6TB.** 01879 230374. www.visitcoll.co.uk. Peace and quiet to relax. Beautiful island, wildlife and flowers. Natural history; wonderful beaches. Not a lot of people. Home of Kattie Morag. From Ferry, through village, take L fork W for 4m. Between two white cottages at Uig on L private road down to walled garden. In the middle of RSPB Nature Reserve. Open: 1 April - 30 September. 🏕 ✓ ⛺ 🚻 ⛺ 3⚡

## Isle of Mull

**(0.5m). Shieling Holidays, Craignure, Isle of Mull, Argyll & Bute PA65 6AY.** 01680 812496. www.shielingholidays.co.uk. On the sea with views of Ben Nevis. Hot showers, laundry etc, all spotlessly clean. Self-catering Shielings. Hostel beds. Stroll to shop, pub, bistro, buses, ferry and swimming pool. Otters, sometimes dolphins. From ferry pier at Craignure turn L, in 400yd L again, follow signs to reception by the sea. 0.5m from Craignure. Open: 11 March - 31 October. ★★★★★ 4 BH&HPA 🏕 🐕 ✓ 🎣 🍴 ⛱ ♿ 30⚡ 30⚡ 60⚡ 16🚐 1🏠

## Lochgilphead

**Castle Sween Holiday Park, Achnamara, Lochgilphead, Argyll & Bute PA31 8PT.** 01546 850223. www.ellary.com. 15,000 acres of Scottish countryside. Lochside location with safe beaches, walking and wildlife. Restaurant. Bar. Laundrette. Bicycle hire. Slipway. From Lochgilphead take A816 Oban road, then B841 Crinon road at Cairnbarin to Bellonoch. Park signposted from there. Open: 1 March - 30 October. ★★★★ BH&HPA ♿ 🏕 🐕 ✓ ❌ ⛱ 🚻 🚗 250🚐

**(11m). Leachive Caravan Park, Leachive Farm, Tayvallich, Lochgilphead, Argyll & Bute PA31 8PL.** 01546 870206. www.leachive.co.uk. 2 microlodges available for hire. Restaurant, pub and shop in easy walking distance. Open April 1-October 31. A816 N from Lochgilphead, fork L on B841 for 3m, then L and join B8025 to Tayvallich, site on R in village. 2 microlodges available for hire. Restaurant, pub and shop in easy walking distance. Open April 1-October 31. Open: 1 April - 31 October. 🏕 🐕 ✓ 🚻 ♿ 5⚡ 10⚡ ⛺ 39🚐

**(0.3m). Lochgilphead Caravan Park, Bank Park, Lochgilphead, Argyll & Bute PA31 8NX.** 01546 602003. www.lochgilpheadcaravanpark.co.uk. Golf, swimming pool, heritage sites, fishing and beautiful walks close by. Clean heated toilets, laundry and all facilities. At junction A83 and A816. Open: 1 April - 30 September. ★★★★ BH&HPA 🏕 🐕 ♿ ✓ 🎣 🍴 ❌ ⛱ 🚻 🚗 30⚡ 40⚡ ⛺ 40🚐

## Luss

**(4m). Inverbeg Holiday Park, Inverbeg, Luss, Argyll & Bute G83 8PD.** 01436 860267. www.lussestates.co.uk. On Loch Lomond with private beach, good launching facilities and excellent fishing from shore. Award winning caravans and loch front chalets. TV and games room. Play

CARAVAN & HOLIDAY PARKS 2012   153

# SCOTLAND

area. Family restaurant and pub 200yd. Boat trips nearby. Co-ordinator: Elspeth Richardson. Open March-January for statics. On A82. Open: 1 March - 31 October. ★★★★ BH&HPA 115

### Morvern

**Fiunary Caravan & Camping Park,** Morvern, Argyll & Bute PA80 5XU. *01967 421225*. www.campingandcaravanningclub.co.uk. Camping & Caravanning Club Certificated Site. Shop, doctor, PO 4.5m in Lochaline. Own beach. Ideal for launching small craft. Fishing and swimming locally. Forest walks from site. Convenient for Isle of Mull car ferry from Lochaline 4.5m. Passenger ferry straight into Tobermory (6m). Owner supplied copy. Leave A82, 8m S of Fort William. Cross Corran-Ardgour car ferry. Follow sign posts to Lochaline (A884) 31m turn R on B849. 4.5m to site. Open: 1 May - 30 September. 20 A

### Mull of Kintyre

**(15m). Carradale Bay Caravan Park (Caravan Club Affiliated Site),** Carradale, Campbeltown, Mull of Kintyre, Argyll & Bute PA28 6QG. *01583 431665*. www.carradalebay.com. CARAVAN CLUB AFFILIATED SITE. This site is on the wooded east coast of Kintyre, right on the sandy beach, facing the Isle of Arran. Toilet blocks, laundry facilities and vegetable preparation area. Fishing, golf, water sports and NCN route nearby. Good area for walking, dog walk nearby. Quiet and peaceful off-peak. Off B842. Open: 10 April - 30 September. ★★★★ BH&HPA 60 A

**Machrihanish Caravan & Camping Park,** East Trodigal, Machrihanish, Campbeltown, Mull of Kintyre, Argyll & Bute PA28 6PT. *01586 810266*. www.campkintyre.co.uk. A

### Oban

**(8m). Caravans at Highfield,** 3 Kiel Croft, Benderloch, Oban, Argyll & Bute PA37 1QS. *01631 720262*. www.clsite.co.uk. Mob: 07766 303136. Highfield is our 7 acre family run croft, situated in a quiet country location by the sea, about 8m from Oban. 10 pitches suitable for tourers and motorcaravans. Ideal as a base to explore the West Highlands and the Argyll islands. Glencoe and Fort William, Inveraray, Easdale, Kilmartin Glen, Lochgilphead and the Crinan canal are all within 1hr of Highfield. Village shop/PO/garage all within 1m. Owner supplied copy. Turn off A828 in Benderloch village at signpost for Tralee and South Shian, about 800 metres on R (2nd R after restaurant). Open: 15 April - 15 October. 5 5

**(5.25m). North Ledaig Caravan Park (Affiliated Caravan Club Site),** North Ledaig, Connel, Oban, Argyll & Bute PA37 1RU. *01631 710291*. www.caravanclub.co.uk. AFFILIATED CARAVAN CLUB SITE - MEMBERS ONLY with adjacent non-member park. One of the best locations on Scotland's West coast, the 30 acre park has been awarded a David Bellamy Conservation award. Toilet blocks, baby and toddler washroom and MV service point. Fishing, golf, water sports and NCN route nearby. Good area for walking. Quiet and peaceful off-peak. Facilities for disabled. Ideal for families. David Bellamy Silver Conservation Award. From S off A85 on to A828 SP Fort William, park is 1.5m N of Connel Bridge on L. From N off A82 on to A828 SP Connel-Oban. Park is 1m S of Benderloch on R. Open: 25 March - 31 October. ★★★★ BH&HPA NCC 34 120

**(2.5m). Oban Caravan and Camping Park,** Gallanachmore Farm, Gallanach Road, Oban, Argyll & Bute PA34 4QH. *01631 562425*. www.obancaravanpark.com. Family run farm on seafront overlooking the island of Kerrera, an area of outstanding scenic beauty. Showers. H&C basins. Laundrette. Colour brochure available. Follow signs to Gallanach from Oban centre roundabout. Open: 1 April - 5 October. ★★★★ 60 60 150 A 15

**(1.5m). Roseview Caravan Park,** Glenshellach Road, Oban, Argyll & Bute PA34 4QJ. *01631 562755*. www.roseviewoban.co.uk. A family park in a delightful and quiet setting. Golf course, fishing, supermarkets nearby. No groups or commercial vehicles. Owner supplied copy. At traffic island by tourist office, take ferry terminal exit (Albany Street). Then 2nd L, 1st R, 1st L following 'Glenshellach' camping signs. Open: 17 December - 31 October. ★★★★ 10 20 A

**(15m). Sunnybrae Caravan Park,** Southcuan, Isle of Luing, Oban, Argyll & Bute PA34 4TU. *01852 314274*. www.oban-holiday.co.uk. Peaceful park on easily accessible isle of Luing. Nearest shop 2m. Ideal for walking, cycling, diving, wildlife, fantastic scenery. 9 hole golf course and boat trips nearby. Isle of Luing is 16m south of Oban, accessible by ferry from North Cuan, on Seil Island. Seil is connected to the mainland by the famous 'Bridge over the Atlantic'. Open: 1 March - 31 October. ★★★★ 14

**(8m). Tralee Bay Holidays,** Benderloch, Oban, Argyll & Bute PA37 1QR. *01631 720255*. Boat slip, fishing pond, putting green, and woodland walks. Sandy beach on site. Luxury mobile homes and lodges for hire. David Bellamy Gold Conservation Award. 3m north of bridge at Connel off A828. Open: 1 April - 31 October. ★★★★ BH&HPA 80

### Tarbert

**(24m). Killegruer Caravan Park,** Woodend, Glenbarr, Tarbert, Argyll & Bute PA29 6XB. *01583 421241*. Ideally suited for ferry routes to Arran and Inner Hebrides. Level, grassy park overlooking safe, sandy beach. Bottled gas delivery service. Park has now been upgraded to include showers, facilities for the disabled etc. Shop 1m of site. Restaurant, bar within 2m. Walking, golf, horse riding all within reasonable distance from site. On R of A83, 12m N of Campbeltown, 24m S of Tarbert, Loch Fyne. Open: 1 April - 30 September. ★★★★ NCC 10 20 A 44

**(22m). Muasdale Holiday Park,** Muasdale, Tarbert, Argyll & Bute PA29 6XD. *01583 421207*. www.muasdale-holidays.com. Touring park next to beach. Shop 100yd. Caravan holiday homes & tourers have unobstructed view of the Atlantic, islands & wildlife. On main A83 southern end of Muasdale village. 15m from Campbeltown. Open: 1 April - 23 October. ★★★ BH&HPA 10 10 10 A 1

**(17m). Point Sands Caravan Park,** Tayinloan, Tarbert, Argyll & Bute PA29 6XG. *01583 441263*. www.pointsands.co.uk. Beautiful peaceful park. Safe sandy beach. Off A83, S of Tarbert, Loch Fyne. Open: 1 April - 31 October. ★★★ BH&HPA NCC 40 A 60

**(15m). Port Ban Caravan Park,** Port Ban, Kilberry, Tarbert, Argyll & Bute PA29 6YD. *01880 770224*. www.portban.com. Family run park with cycling, tennis and other sports facilities available. Coffee bar and evening meals served during busy season. Shop on site. Fishing, golf course nearby. Kilberry Inn 1m from park. On B8024 off A83. 1m N of Kilberry. 15m S of Ardrishaig situated on the beach with a panoramic view of Islay and Jura. Open: 1 April - 31 October. ★★★★ BH&HPA NCC 15 A 90

# SCOTLAND

## Taynuilt

(2m). Lochawe Holiday Park (Crunachy), Bridge of Awe, Taynuilt, Argyll & Bute PA35 1HT. *01866 822666*. www.argyll-holidays.com. Shower, Laundrette, phone, restaurant, games room and swings. Hotel/bar 300yd. Golf 2m. Fishing, walking, climbing nearby. On A85 Oban to Crianlarich. 14m E of Oban. Open: All year.

## AYRSHIRE

### Ayr

(4m). Craig Tara Holiday Park (Haven), Dunure Road, Ayr, Ayrshire KA7 4LB. *0871 2310866*. www.caravancamping.co.uk. Heated indoor fun pool, Kids' clubs, daytime and evening entertainment, convenience store, bakery, sports court, play area. Go-karts, mini bowling, indoor crazy golf. 9 hole golf course. Climbing wall. David Bellamy Gold Conservation Award. Take A77 towards Stranraer and take 2nd R after Bankfield roundabout, S of Ayr. From Doonholm Road take L at the junction and immediately R into Greenfield Avenue. At next junction take L and follow the Craig Tara signs. Open: 18 March - 31 October. ★★★★ BH&HPA NCC

(0.5m). Craigie Gardens Caravan Club Site, Craigie Road, Ayr, Ayrshire KA8 0SS. *01292 264909*. www.caravanclub.co.uk. Laundry. Baby and toddler washroom. Vegetable preparation area. Motorhome waste point. Gas and Gaz. Information room. Play frame plus play area, dog walk nearby, quiet and peaceful off peak. Toilet block with privacy cubicles. Advance booking essential at all times. All hardstandings. Ideally suited for families. Beach, fishing, golf and NCN cycle route within 5m. Non-members welcome. No tents. See website for standard directions to site. Open: 23 March - 7 January. ★★★★★ NCC

(2m). Crofthead Holiday Park, McNairston Road, Ayr, Ayrshire KA6 6EN. *01292 263516*. www.croftheadholidaypark.co.uk. 45 touring pitches & holiday home hire, surrounded by beautiful rural Ayrshire countryside. Only 2 miles from Ayr town centre. SP off A70. Open: All year. ★★★ BH&HPA

(5m). Heads Of Ayr, Dunure Road, Ayr, Ayrshire KA7 4LD. *01292 442269*. www.headsofayr.com. Located on the Ayrshire coast. 10mins walk to the beach. Family run friendly park for over 40 years. Club.

Numerous golf courses nearby from 2-20m. On A719 Dunure to Ayr. Open: 1 March - 31 October. ★★★★ BH&HPA NCC

(4m). Sundrum Castle Holiday Park, Coylton, Ayr, Ayrshire KA6 5JH. *01292 570057*. www.parkdeanholidays.co.uk. Indoor pool with toddlers' pool and flume. Kids' club, amusements and adventure play. Bar, food and live family entertainment. Only 4m from Ayr's beaches. David Bellamy Gold Conservation Award. M74, J12 to A70. Open: 23 March - 6 November. ★★★★★ BH&HPA NCC

### Girvan

(8m). Bennane Shore Holiday Park, Lendalfoot, Girvan, Ayrshire KA26 0JG. *01465 891233*. www.bennaneshore.com. A quiet, family park with beach frontage enjoying panoramic views across the Firth of Clyde to Ailsa Craig and Kintyre Peninsula. Laundry. Boating facilities with private slipway. Sea fishing. Cliff walks. 8m S of Girvan on A77 Stranraer to Ayr trunk road. Open: 1 March - 31 January. ★★★★

(10m). Queensland Holiday Park, Barrhill, Girvan, Ayrshire KA26 0PZ. *01465 821364*. www.queenslandholidaypark.co.uk. Peaceful woodland park. Excellent local fishing and golf. Ideal location for walking in Southern Upland Mountains. From Girvan take A714 heading SE, park on R 1m before Barrhill. Open: 1 March - 31 January. ★★★★

(3.5m). Turnberry Holiday Park, Girvan, Ayrshire KA26 9JW. *01655 331288*. www.turnberryholidaypark.co.uk. Surrounded by rolling hills, sandy beaches and golf courses, with an unspoilt view of Ailsa Craig and the Firth of Clyde. Open March 1-October 31. On A77 Turnberry to Girvan Road. 400 yards off main road. Open: 1 March - 31 October.

### Isle of Arran

(1m). Lochranza Campsite, Lochranza, Isle of Arran, Ayrshire KA27 8HL. *01770 830273*. www.arran-campsite.com. Ideal site for golfers, birdwatchers and walkers. Climbing, hill walking, canoeing etc close by. Level, grass site. Best hot showers, very clean facilities. Entrance opposite the distillery. In the village at N end of island, beside our own superb golf course. Open: 1 March - 31 October.

### Lamlash

Middletons Caravan & Camping Park, Lamlash, Ayrshire KA27 8NN. *01770 600255*. www.middletonscamping.com. Flat, grassy site. 5mins from beach. Night lighting. 0.25m from centre of Lamlash. Open: 15 March - 30 September. ★★★

### Largs

(2.25m). South Whittlieburn Farm, Brisbane Glen Road, Largs, Ayrshire KA30 8SN. *01475 675881*. www.SmoothHound.co.uk/hotels/whittlie.html. Fishing, hill walking, golf course, sailing, fishing, horse walking, diving. Ferries to Islands, shops, restaurants, doctor etc 2.5m. Swimming pool, theatre, putting green within easy reach. 4 star AA + STB. 'B&B' in Farmhouse. Owner supplied copy. Working sheep farm is situated NE of Largs - only 5mins from town centre. Travel about 0.5m along A78 shore road from town centre/pier, heading for Greenock, turn R at large signpost for Brisbane Glen Road. Drive 2.25m - it is the second farm on left hand side, but the only one on roadside. Open: All year. ★★★★

### Maybole

(3m). Culzean Castle Camping & Caravanning Club Site, Culzean, Maybole, Ayrshire KA19 8JX. *01655 760627*. www.campingandcaravanningclub.co.uk. The area has extensive views and spectacular sunsets. Non members welcome. All units accepted. The site is adjacent to the historic castle and country park. (There are 17m of country walks within easy access. Local attractions include sandy beaches, a deer park and an aviary). Special deals available for families and backpackers. From S on A77 turn L on to A719. Site 4m on L. From N on A77 turn R on to B7023 in Maybole. After 100yd turn L, site 4m. Open: 1 April - 31 October. ★★★★ NCC

(1.5m). The Ranch Caravan Club Site (CC Affiliated), Culzean Road, Maybole, Ayrshire KA19 8DU. *01655 882446*. www.theranchscotland.com. AFFILIATED CARAVAN CLUB SITE - MEMBERS ONLY. This award-winning pretty little site with its colourful rose beds and flowering shrubs is an excellent base for exploring this lovely part of South West Scotland. Toilet blocks, laundry facilities and MV service point. Play area, swimming pool and dog walk on site. Fishing, golf and NCN route nearby. Facilities for disabled. Ideal for families. Owner supplied copy. A77 to Ayr and Maybole. In Maybole turn R on B7023. Open: All year. NCC

Visit www.caravanclub.co.uk

# SCOTLAND

**(4m). The Walled Garden Caravan & Camping Park,** Kilkerran Estate, Crosshill, Maybole, Ayrshire KA19 7SG. *01655 740323.* www.walledgardencp.co.uk. Fishing in season on River Girvan on estate. Golf courses 3m & 5m. Nearest supermarket (Co-op) is 3m. Doctors 3 & 4m. PO 2m. Petrol station 5m. Open all year except February, Xmas/Boxing Day. From A77 (4m S of Ayr) pass through Minishant 200yd turn L at Hoggs Corner and follow brown and white tourist signs. From roundabout N of Girvan follow signs. Open: 16 March - 21 December. ★★★★ 🏠🐕🎵🦺🏊⛳🎣🚿♿ 10🚐 60🚗 Å

## Prestwick

**(1m). Prestwick Holiday Park,** Prestwick, Ayrshire KA9 1UH. *01292 479261.* Beach. Lounge bar. Games room. Laundry. Quiet, family run site, set between golf courses. 1m N of Prestwick site SP off A79. Open: 1 March - 31 October. ★★★ BH&HPA NCC ♀🏠🐕🎵📶🍴🍺🚿♿ 24🚐 36🚗 Å 155⛺

## Saltcoats

**(1.5m). Sandylands Holiday Park,** James Miller Crescent, Auchenharvie Park, Saltcoats, Ayrshire KA21 5JN. *01294 469411.* www.park-resortstouring.com. Indoor pool, water resorts programme, FREE kids club, amusements, shops, laundrette, takeaway, FREE family evening entertainment. Darts. Pool table. Ayr racecourse. David Bellamy Silver Conservation Award. From Glasgow take M77 to Prestwick airport/Kilmarnock. Follow signs then to Irvine, then Ardrossan. Follow A78 to Stevenson. Open: 20 March - 31 October. ★★★ BH&HPA NCC ♀🏠🍴♿🎵🎶🍺🏊🚿❌🍴 🔌♿🚐🚗 Å 530⛺

## Troon

**(0.25m). St Meddans Caravan Site,** Low St Meddans, Troon, Ayrshire KA10 6NS. *01292 312957.* Town centre, beaches, golf course - all within 5mins walk. Owner supplied copy. On A759. Off No 2 Dundonald Road, in town centre. Open: 1 March - 31 October. BH&HPA 🏠🐕🎵 ♿🚿🍴 2🚐 23🚗 Å

## CLACKMANNANSHIRE
### Alloa

**(2m). The Woods Caravan Club Site (CC Affiliated),** Diverswell Farm, Fishcross, Alloa, Clackmannanshire FK10 3AN. *01259 762802.* CARAVAN CLUB AFFILIATED SITE. Non members welcome. Ideal for families. Quiet and tranquil site with almost a 180 degree panorama to the Ochill Hills. Toilet blocks with privacy cubicles and laundrette. MV service point, vegetable preparation area and gas/gaz. Good area for walking, dog walk on site. Fishing, golf and NCN route nearby. Facilities for disabled. Owner supplied copy. 4m from Stirling. Open: All year. NCC 🏠🐕🎵♿ 🌳🚿🍴♿🚐 105🚗 Å

## Dollar

**(0.5m). Riverside Caravan Park (Dollar),** Dollarfield, Dollar, Clackmannanshire FK14 7LX. *01259 742896.* www.riverside-caravanpark.co.uk. Ideal base for exploring central Scotland and excellent base for hill walking, bird watching, fishing and golf. Close to many places of interest and Knockhill Racing Circuit. Owner supplied copy. On B913 Dollar to Dunfermline. Open: 1 March - 31 January. BH&HPA 🏠🐕🎵♿🚿🍴 30🚐 Å 38⛺

## DUMFRIES & GALLOWAY
### Annan

**(0.5m). Galabank Caravan Site,** North Street, Annan, Dumfries & Galloway DG12 7DQ. *01461 203539.* Nearby facilities include: shops, PO, doctor, golf and fishing. Owner supplied copy. At traffic lights in Annan centre, turn onto B722, to athletics club and site is on L. Open: 1 May - 30 September. ★★ 🏠🐕🎵🦺 🍴♿ 30🚐 30🚗 Å

**(4m). Queensberry Bay Caravan Park,** Powfoot, Annan, Dumfries & Galloway DG12 5PN. *01461 700205.* www.queensberrybay.co.uk. Family run park on the coast overlooking the Solway. Adult only touring areas. Many facilities including walking, cycling & bird watching. From Annan B724, 3m unclassified to Powfoot 1m. Open: 28 January - 25 November. ★★★★ BH&HPA 🏠🐕🎵♿🎶 🚿🍴♿ 10🚐 80🚗 Å 90⛺

## Castle Douglas

**Auchenlarie Holiday Park,** Gatehouse-of-Fleet, Castle Douglas, Dumfries & Galloway DG7 2EX. *01556 506200.* www.auchenlarie.co.uk. Friendly park overlooking Wigtown Bay with several golf courses nearby and both sea and coarse fishing. Excellent facilities. Entertainment, laundrette, 3 bars with meals, games room, amusement centre, crazy golf and three play areas. AA 4 pennants. Indoor swimming pool & leisure suite including gym, sauna, solarium, sports hall. On A 75. 5m W of Gatehouse-of-Fleet on S coast of Galloway with small sandy cove. Open: 1 March - 31 October. ★★★★ 4 BH&HPA 🏠🐕🎵♿🎶❌🍴🚿 ♿🚿 75🚐 Å 240⛺

**(5m). Barlochan Caravan Park,** Palnackie, Castle Douglas, Dumfries & Galloway DG7 1PF. *01557 870267.* www.gillespie-leisure.co.uk. Friendly park overlooking Urr estuary with nearby coarse fishing loch (free). Exceptional facilities. Laundrette and dishwashing. Games and TV rooms, mini-golf and play area. Pub nearby. On A711, 2.5m SW of Dalbeattie. Open: 4 April - 31 October. ★★★★ BH&HPA NCC ♀🏠🐕🎵 ♿🎶🍺🚿♿🍴 30🚐 Å 6⛺

**(3m). Cardoness Holiday Park,** Cardoness, Gatehouse-of-Fleet, Castle Douglas, Dumfries & Galloway DG7 2EP. *01557 840288.* Situated within 100-acres of an estate. 3m of sandy beaches and rocky coves. Nature trails, fishing, walks, tennis court, games room. David Bellamy Gold Conservation Award. Owner supplied copy. Off A75 Stranraer to Dumfries, on seaward side. Open: 1 April - 31 October. BH&HPA 🏠🐕🎵♿🚿🍴♿ 6🚐 190⛺

**(7m). Loch Ken Holiday Park,** Parton, Castle Douglas, Dumfries & Galloway DG7 3NE. *01644 470282.* www.lochkenholidaypark.co.uk. On the shores of the loch with sandy beach. Lovely natural park. Excellent fishing. Cycle hire. Canoeing, boating & sailing on site. Waterskiing, sailing and golf 7m. Charge for dogs. David Bellamy Gold Conservation Award. A713 Castle Douglas to Ayr road. Open: 1 March - 10 November. ★★★★ BH&HPA 🏠🐕🎵♿🎶🍺🚿 ♿🍴 10🚐 55🚗 Å 40⛺

**(0.25m). Lochside Caravan & Camping Site,** Lochside Park, Castle Douglas, Dumfries & Galloway DG7 1EZ. *01556 502949.* www.dumgal.gov.uk. Dogs on lead. Nearby facilities include: Doctor, PO, shops, tennis, swimming pool, golf, fishing, sailing, play area and park, boating, putting, Threave Gardens. Castle Douglas has been designated as the region's 'food town'. 3 pennants AA rating. Just off A75 at Castle Douglas. Site is located by Carlingwark Loch, Castle Douglas. Open: 4 April - 24 October. ★★★★ 3 🏠🐕 🎵♿❌🚿🍴♿ 108🚐 108🚗 Å

**(15m). Mossyard Caravan Park,** Gatehouse-of-Fleet, Castle Douglas, Dumfries & Galloway DG7 2ET. *01557 840226.* www.mossyard.co.uk. Family run park on the shores of the Fleet estuary. Ideal location for swimming, boating. Coarse fishing, swimming pool within 0.25m - nearest village, golf, tennis 5m away. On A75 Dumfries to Stranraer 4m beyond Gatehouse-of-Fleet. SP. Open: 30 March - 4 November. ★★★★ BH&HPA 🏠🐕🎵♿🚿🍴♿ 27🚐 37🚗 Å 22⛺

# SCOTLAND

**(5m). Sandgreen Caravan Park, Sandgreen, Gatehouse-of-Fleet, Castle Douglas, Dumfries & Galloway DG7 2DU.** 01557 814351. www.sandgreencaravanpark.co.uk. A stunning west coast location for your holiday home or lodge. Private beach and boat launch. Ideal holidays for all the family. Quiet secluded friendly park. David Bellamy Gold Conservation Award. Owner supplied copy. Off A75 Gatehouse-of-Fleet by-pass. Open: 1 March - 31 October. BH&HPA ⌂ ⚡ ⊘ ⏏ 220 ⛺ ⛱

## Dalbeattie

**(1m). Glenearly Caravan Park, Dalbeattie, Dumfries & Galloway DG5 4NE.** 01556 611393. www.glenearlycaravanpark.co.uk. Walking distance to shops in Dalbeattie. 6m to nearest beach. Golf courses within 10mins drive. Pony trekking, mountain biking, fishing, tennis, forest walks all available nearby. Owner supplied copy. From Dumfries take the A711 to Dalbeattie. See park entrance on R just before you enter Dalbeattie. Open: 1 March - 31 October. ★★★★ BH&HPA ⌂ ⚡ ⚘ ⌖ ⏏ ⏏ 40 ⛺ ⛱ 60 ⛱

**Islecroft Caravan & Camping Site, Colliston Park, Mill Street, Dalbeattie, Dumfries & Galloway DG5 4HE.** 01556 612236. www.islecroft.co.uk. Easy access to town. Dogs on lead. Nearby facilities include: Shops, PO, doctor, tennis, golf, beaches, play area and park, paddle boats, putting. Walking, cycle tracks. Site is in Dalbeattie. From A711 on to B793 in town. Take first left at The Cross into Islecroft Park. Open: 1 March - 31 October. ★★★★ ⌂ ⚡ ⌖ ⏏ ⏏ 30 ⛺ 30 ⛱ ⛱

**(3m). Kippford Holiday Park, Kippford, Dalbeattie, Dumfries & Galloway DG5 4LF.** 01556 620636. www.kippfordholidaypark.co.uk. Nominated top 100 park. Touring and tenting pitches are set in small groups attractively terraced and level with hardstand, individually screened, on sloping ground. Thistle award holiday caravan hire. 15mins stroll to the beautiful seaside village of Kippford, with two excellent pubs, and spectacular seaside walk to the beach and bay. Shop, cycle hire, golf & fishing adjacent. Long stay, group and family discounts. David Bellamy Gold Conservation Award. Open all year (winter booking required). 3m S of Dalbeattie on A710 towards Kippford (beautiful seaside village). Open: All year. ★★★★ BH&HPA NCC ⌂ ⚡ ⚘ ⏏ ⌖ ⏏ ⏏ ⏏ ⏏ 24 ⛺ 24 ⛱ 13 ⚐ 21 ⛱ 13 ⛱

**(6m). Sandyhills Bay Leisure Park, Sandyhills, Dalbeattie, Dumfries &** Galloway DG5 4NY. 01557 870267. www.gillespie-leisure.co.uk. Award winning park only a few yards from the finest beach in the area. Spectacular coastal walks. Smugglers cave. Excellent facilities. Showers, laundrette, dishwashing and takeaways. 18 hole golf course adjacent. Fishing, riding and eating out within walking distance. Advance bookings: 015578 70267. Exceptional facilities at Brighouse Bay are available. On A710 Dumfries to Dalbeattie. Open: 4 April - 31 October. ★★★★ BH&HPA NCC ⌂ ⚡ ⚘ ⌖ ⏏ ⏏ ⏏ ⏏ 25 ⛺ 31 ⛱

## Dumfries

**Anwoth Holiday Park, Garden Street, Gatehouse of Fleet, Dumfries, Dumfries & Galloway DG7 2JU.** 01557 814333. www.auchenlarie.co.uk. Managed by a friendly warden. Peaceful and tranquil yet with all the facilities of Galloway and Gatehouse-of-Fleet. Area of natural beauty and an excellent touring base. Within walking distance to shops and restaurants. In the centre of Gatehouse-of-Fleet. Open: 1 March - 31 October. ★★★★★ BH&HPA ⌂ ⚡ ⚘ ⌖ ⏏ ⏏ ⏏ 5 ⛺ 28 ⛱ 46 ⛱

**(8m). Beeswing Caravan Park, Kirkgunzeon, Dumfries, Dumfries & Galloway DG2 8JL.** 01387 760242. Site is rural, inland, quiet and an ideal touring base. Haven for wildlife. Excellent facilities. On right-hand side, 0.75m south of Beeswing on A711. Open: 1 March - 31 October. ★★★ BH&HPA ⌂ ⚡ ⚘ ⏏ ⏏ ⏏ 25 ⛱ 2 ⛱

**(3m). Halleaths Caravan Park, Lochmaben, Lockerbie, Dumfries, Dumfries & Galloway DG11 1NA.** 01387 810630. www.halleaths.co.uk. Kitchen area with microwave. Winter storage available. Well sheltered site surrounded by trees. Game and coarse fishing within 1m. 5 golf courses within 9m. From Lockerbie (M74) take A709 Lockerbie to Dumfries road. Site 0.5m on R after crossing river Annan. Open: 15 March - 15 November. ★★★★ BH&HPA ⌂ ⚡ ⚘ ⌖ ⏏ ⏏ ⏏ ⏏ 7 ⛺ 81 ⛱

**(8m). Mossband Caravan Park, Kirkgunzeon, Dumfries, Dumfries & Galloway DG2 8JP.** 01387 760505. Tennis court. Play area. Off A711. Open: 1 March - 31 October. ★★★ ⌂ ⚡ ⏏ ⏏ ⏏ 15 ⛺ 11 ⛱

**Newfield Caravan Park, Annan Road, Dumfries, Dumfries & Galloway DG1 3SE.** 01387 750228. newfieldcaravanpark.com. On A75 Carlisle to Dumfries next to Little Chef. Open: Contact site direct. ⌂ ⚡ ⏏ 20 ⛱

**(9m). The Park Of Brandedleys, Crocketford, Dumfries, Dumfries & Galloway DG2 8RG.** 0845 4561760. www.holgates.com. Indoor swimming pool, sauna, tennis and badminton courts, games room, recreational areas, bar and restaurant. Golfers will love no fewer than 25 challenging courses within a 20m radius of the park. Fishing - opportunity for sea fishing, trout and salmon as well as coarse fishing, within 20m radius. David Bellamy Gold Conservation Award. Off A75. At W end of Crocketford. Open: All year. ★★★★ BH&HPA ⌂ ⚡ ⚘ ⌖ ⏏ ⏏ ⏏ ⏏ ⏏ 40 ⛺ 65 ⛱ 65 ⛱

## Gretna

**(0.5m). Braids Caravan Park, Annan Road, Gretna, Dumfries & Galloway DG16 5DQ.** 01461 337409. www.thebraidscaravanpark.co.uk. Fishing information. Golf course nearby. PO, shops, doctor all within 0.75m. Bus service to Carlisle, Annan and Dumfries. 100mtrs from Stranraer Ferry Terminal. Calor Gas agency. B721 Gretna to Annan Road. Open: All year. ★★★★ 4 ⌂ ⚡ ⚘ ⌖ ⏏ ⏏ ⏏ 20 ⛺ 74 ⛱

**(3m). King Robert the Bruce's Cave Caravan & Camping Site, Kirkpatrick Fleming, Gretna, Dumfries & Galloway DG11 3AT.** 01461 800285. www.brucescave.co.uk. Wooded and secluded in grounds of 80-acre estate with coarse fishing on site in pond (small charge). Holiday suites available. Restricted facilities from October 31-March 1. Shop only available in summer. Quad riding, clay pigeon shooting, paintball nearby. BMX bikes on site. Turn off A74 at sign Kirkpatrick Fleming, then follow all signs to Bruce's Cave. Wooded and secluded in grounds of 80-acre estate with coarse fishing on site in pond (small charge). Holiday suites available. Restricted facilities from October 31-March 1. Shop only available in summer. Quad riding, clay pigeon shooting, paintball nearby. BMX bikes on site. Open: 22 April - 31 October. ★★★★ NCC ⌂ ⚡ ⚘ ⌖ ⏏ ⏏ ⏏ ⏏ 15 ⛺ 25 ⛱ 20 ⛱

## Kirkcudbright

**(6m). Brighouse Bay Holiday Park (Premier Park), Borgue Peninsula, Kirkcudbright, Dumfries & Galloway DG6 4TS.** 01557 870267. www.gilloopicleisure.co.uk. Hidden away within 1200 acres next to beach and bluebell woods. Exceptional amenities. Golf and leisure club with indoor pool, toddlers pool, steam room, Jacuzzi, bowling green. Also family lounge, function room, bar, bistro, games room with 10 pin easy bowl. 18-hole par

# SCOTLAND

73, 9 hole par 3 golf course, practice area and covered driving range. Slipway, mini golf, pond canoes, nature trails, bike hire. Pony trekking. Quad bikes. Luxury caravans and lodges for sale and hire. David Bellamy Gold Conservation Award. Off B727 Kirkcudbright to Borgue or take A755 (Kirkcudbright) off A75 2m W of Twynholm. Clear SP for 8m. Open: All year. ★★★★ BH&HPA NCC 120 120 A 35

(2.5m). **Seaward Caravan Park, Dhoon Bay, Kirkcudbright, Dumfries & Galloway DG6 4TJ.** *01557 870267. www.gillespie-leisure.co.uk*. Beautifully situated with exceptional panoramic views over bay. Award-winning park. Excellent facilities include heated outdoor pool, dishwashing, laundrette and showers. Sea angling, Beach picnic area nearby. Advance bookings 01557 870267. Games and TV room, 9 hole pitch & putt. Exceptional facilities at nearby Brighouse Bay available for use. From Kirkcudbright take A755 W, then B727 to Borgue. Open: 18 April - 31 October. ★★★★ BH&HPA NCC 10 20 A 56

(0.5m). **Silvercraigs Caravan and Camping Site, Silvercraigs Road, Kirkcudbright, Dumfries & Galloway DG6 4BT.** *01557 330123. www.dumgal.gov.uk*. No advance booking. Fees on application. Dogs on lead. Nearby facilities include: Shops, PO, doctor, tennis, swimming pool, golf, museum, wildlife park, fishing, sailing, beaches, play area and park. This elevated site overlooks the historical town of Kirkcudbright, providing panoramic views of the Solway coast - 3 pennants AA rating. Owner supplied copy. In Kirkcudbright off Silvercraigs road overlooking the town. Open: 4 April - 24 October. ★★★★ 3 50 50 A

### Lochmaben

(0.25m). **Kirk Loch Caravan Site, Kirkloch Brae, Lochmaben, Lochmaben, Dumfries & Galloway DG11 1PZ.** *01556 503806. www.dumgal.gov.uk/kirklochcs*. Nearby facilities include: shops, PO, doctor, golf, fishing, play area. This site is situated on the picturesque Kirkloch in the small historical town of Lochmaben - 2 pennants AA rating. Owner supplied copy. B709 at Lochmaben, near Lockerbie, Dumfriesshire. Enter site by Kirkloch Brae. Open: 4 April - 24 October. ★★★ 30 30 A

### Lockerbie

(5m). **Cressfield Caravan Park, Townfoot, Ecclefechan, Lockerbie, Dumfries & Galloway DG11 3DR.** *01576 300702. www.cressfieldcaravanpark.co.uk*. Peaceful country park with superb facilities. Sports field. Play area. Dog walk. Village amenities 0.25m. Good touring base or night halt. Golf, fishing 2m. Supermarket, cinema 5m. Holiday homes for sale. Leave A74 (M) at Ecclefechan J19. Follow B7076 for 0.5m to south side of village, SP. Open: All year. ★★★★ BH&HPA 20 20 A

**Hoddom Castle Caravan Park, Hoddom, Lockerbie, Dumfries & Galloway DG11 1AS.** *01576 300251. www.hoddomcastle.co.uk*. Peaceful site part of 10,000 acre estate. Bar, restaurant, golf, tennis, fishing, nature trails on site. AA 5 pennants, 5 stars Scottish Tourist Board. Cinema, shopping centre, 2x18 hole golf course within 5m. Exit A74 M, J19, follow signs. Open: 1 April - 31 October. ★★★★★ 200 A 54

### Moffat

(2m). **Craigielands Country Park, Beattock, Moffat, Dumfries & Galloway DG10 9RE.** *01683 300591. www.craigielands-countrypark.co.uk*. Mob: 07912 309464. Set in lovely country estate of over 56 acres with own loch and woodland walks. Pony-trekking. Public house and restaurant on site. Owner supplied copy. J15 off new M74, follow signs for Beattock, follow through village, we're at the end under the bridge. Open: All year. ★★★ 20 40 150 A

(0.25m). **Moffat Camping & Caravanning Club Site, Hammerlands, Moffat, Dumfries & Galloway DG10 9QL.** *01683 220436. www.campingandcaravanningclub.co.uk*. Perfect base for touring the picturesque border country. All units accepted. Non-members welcome. Local attractions include superb golf and fishing. A visit to the 300-year-old Drumlanrig Castle is a must. Local village of Moffat has won awards for the 'Best Kept Village in Scotland'. Special deals available for families and backpackers. From Moffat take A708 towards Selkirk, turn R at Int. sign. Turn L at Nursery. Follow club signs to site. Open: All year. ★★★★ NCC 180 180 A

### Newton Stewart

(22m). **Burrowhead Holiday Village, Tonderghie Road, Isle of Whithorn, Newton Stewart, Dumfries & Galloway DG8 8JB.** *01988 500252. www.burrowheadholidayvillage.co.uk*. Beautiful views of the Isle of Man. Indoor leisure complex with fun slide, sauna and Jacuzzi. Play area, club house and entertainment. Soft ball play area. A714 and A746 S from Newton Stewart to Isle of Whithorn. Open: 1 March - 5 January. BH&HPA NCC 25 60 A 120

(2m). **Castlewigg Holiday Park, Castlewigg, Whithorn, Newton Stewart, Dumfries & Galloway DG8 8DL.** *01988 500616. www.castlewiggcaravanpark.co.uk*. Fantastic location. Beaches only 5mins drive away. Beautifully maintained quiet park. Shops, PO, doctors and other shops only 2m away. Dogs must be kept on leads. Open for static owners 1 March - 7 January. N of Whithorn on A746. Open: 1 March - 31 October. ★★★ BH&HPA 5 6 A 14

(0.25m). **Creebridge Caravan Park, Newton Stewart, Dumfries & Galloway DG8 6AJ.** *01671 402324. www.creebridgecaravanpark.com*. Quiet, secluded site next to town. 0.5m into Newton Stewart, shops, PO etc. Golf course across road. Restaurants, cinema, theatre nearby. Owner supplied copy. Off A75, 1m E of Newton Stewart, head for Minnigaff. Site is 200yd before bridge over river. If in Newton Stewart go over old bridge to Minnigaff, site is 200yd on R. Open: 1 March - 1 December. ★★★ BH&HPA 25 55 A

(6m). **Creetown Caravan Park, Silver Street, Creetown, Newton Stewart, Dumfries & Galloway DG8 7HU.** *01671 820377. www.creetown-caravans.co.uk*. Reasonable rates, excellent toilet block. Outdoor heated swimming and paddling pool, games room and play area. Convenient for village amenities. Ideal centre for exploring SW Scotland. On A75 in village of Creetown. Open: 1 March - 31 October. ★★★★ NCC 10 22 A 55

(12m). **Drumroamin Farm Touring Site, 1 South Balfern, Kirkinner, Newton Stewart, Dumfries & Galloway DG8 9DB.** *01988 840613. www.drumroamin.co.uk*. Rural location but village shop and PO are 1.5m away. Golf course in Wigtown, book capital of Scotland. Doctors, butchers and Co-op all in Wigtown. Sea and river fishing all close by. Site also has shed for bike storage, as there are plenty of cycle routes about. 13m from Kirroughtree and mountain biking facilities. Owner supplied copy. A75 towards Newton Stewart, turn on to A714 towards Wigtown. Turn L on B7005 head through Bladnock, A746 through Kirkinner. Take B7004 Garlieston, turn 2nd L, campsite at end of lane. Open: All year. ★★★★

# SCOTLAND

**Garlieston Caravan Club Site, Garlieston, Newton Stewart, Dumfries & Galloway DG8 8BS.** *01988 600636.* www.caravanclub.co.uk. Ideal location for an undemanding, relaxing holiday on the Machars Peninsular. Toilet blocks, laundry facilities and MV service point. Good area for walking, and cycling nearby. Facilities for disabled. Quiet and peaceful off-peak. Site within 1min of the beach. Members only. No tents. See website for standard directions to site. Open: 23 March - 5 November. NCC

**(15m). Glenluce Caravan Park, Glenluce, Newton Stewart, Dumfries & Galloway DG8 0QR.** *01581 300412.* www.glenlucecaravan.co.uk. Secluded suntrap park close to village, sea, bowling, fishing, pony trekking, golf and superb walks all within 1m. Luxury caravans. Thistle Award. Owner supplied copy. Take A75 Dumfries to Stranraer, leave A75 at Glenluce SP, 10m E of Stranraer. Concealed entrance in centre of village opposite Brambles restaurant. Open: All year. ★★★★ BH&HPA

**(9m). Glentrool Holiday Park, Bargrennan, Newton Stewart, Dumfries & Galloway DG8 6RN.** *01671 840280.* www.glentroolholidaypark.co.uk. A pleasant, peaceful park in an ideal situation for touring and exploring the Galloway forest and hills. Super scenery. Static caravans available for hire. Cafe/restaurant, bird watching and fishing nearby, plus off road cycle routes. Cinema, swimming pool, golf, shops, cycle hire 9m. Off A714. N of Newton Stewart. Open: 1 March - 31 October. ★★★★ BH&HPA

**(0.3m). Kings Green Caravan Park, South Street, Port William, Newton Stewart, Dumfries & Galloway DG8 9SH.** *01988 700489.* www.portwilliam.com/kingsgreencaravansite. Toilet block with access for the disabled. Seaside location within walking distance of Port William with shops. Pubs and harbour. Many interesting places to visit, 4 golf courses within easy reach, fishing in abundance, or you may just want to enjoy the peace, tranquility and the view across Luce Bay. On A747. Open: 15 March - 31 October.

**(18m). Knock School Caravan Park, Monreith, Newton Stewart, Newton Stewart, Dumfries & Galloway DG8 8NJ.** *01988 700414.* www.knockschool.co.uk. Very small, peaceful touring park. Bird watching, archaeology and gardens locally. Golf, beaches and fishing all within 5mins. Hardstanding pitches available. Owner supplied copy. On A747. 3m S of Port William. Entrance by golf course and beaches. Open: 22 April - 30 September.

**(18m). West Barr Farm Caravan Site, Port William, Newton Stewart, Dumfries & Galloway DG8 9QS.** *01988 700367.* www.westbarrholidaypark.co.uk. Small, privately owned site on Luce Bay, close to sea and 1m from Port William. Owner supplied copy. On A747 2m N of Port William. Open: 1 March - 31 January.

**Whitecairn Holiday Park, Glenluce, Newton Stewart, Dumfries & Galloway DG8 0NZ.** *01581 300267.* www.whitecairncaravans.co.uk. Small, family run park within easy reach of many local attractions. Fully serviced pitches for touring caravans and campers. Caravans for sale or hire. 1.5m N of Glenluce village and 2m from A75. 12m from Stranraer. SP from village, main street. Open: All year. ★★★★ NCC

## Shawhead

**(6m). Barnsoul Farm Caravan Park, Shawhead, Dumfries & Galloway DG2 9SQ.** *01387 730249.* www.barnsoulfarm.co.uk. Unspoilt site with ponds and woodlands set in well-known wildlife area. Fishing close by. Mountain bikes, Mabie Forest, AE Forest all within 8m. AA 3 pennants. 8 wigwam bothies to hire - timber one roomed bothies with electricity, sleep 4/6, based on Scandinavian mountain huts. David Bellamy Gold Conservation Award. From Dumfries take A75 (Stranraer) for 6m turn R for Shawhead. At T-junction turn R then bear L (Dunscore). Farm is 1m on L. Open: 1 March - 31 October. ★★★ 3 BH&HPA

## Southerness

**Lighthouse Leisure, Southerness, Dumfries & Galloway DG2 8AZ.** *01387 880277.* www.lighthouseleisure.co.uk. Level, lawned family owned park. Leisure complex with Mermaid Bar, restaurant, heated pool, sauna, gym, ten pin bowling, amusements. Toytown. All facilities. Close to sweeping sandy beaches and championship golf course. From Dumfries follow A710 for 20minc turn off to Southerness on L - 5mins to site. Open: 1 March - 31 October. ★★★ BH&HPA

**(17m). Southerness Holiday Park, Off Sandy Lane, Southerness, Dumfries & Galloway DG2 8AZ.** *01387 880256.* www.parkdeanholidays.co.uk. A modern holiday village with separate touring park catering mainly for families. Licensed club, bar meals and indoor cafe with takeaway service, heated indoor swimming pool, family entertainment, amusement centre, adventure play park. Colour brochure on request. Championship golf, Pay and Play golf. Local attractions. David Bellamy Gold Conservation Award. Off A710. Follow Solway Coast signs from Dumfries. Open: 23 March - 30 October. ★★★★ BH&HPA NCC

## Stranraer

**(1m). Aird Donald Caravan Park, London Road, Stranraer, Dumfries & Galloway DG9 8RN.** *01776 702025.* www.aird-donald.co.uk. Small, sheltered site, level grass. Children's play park 500 yds. Excellently situated for ferries to Ireland. Tarmac hardstandings for wet weather. Excellent facilities. Shops, PO, doctor etc in Stranraer town 1m. Golf, river fishing 2m, sea fishing 1m. On A75 Newton Stewart to Stranraer. Open: All year. ★★★★ BH&HPA

**(6m). Cairnryan Caravan Park, Cairnryan, Stranraer, Dumfries & Galloway DG9 8QX.** *01581 200231.* www.cairnryancaravanpark.co.uk. Shop 500yd. On A77, opposite P&O ferry terminal, Cairnryan. Open: 25 February - 4 January. ★★★★ BH&HPA

**(0.75m). Castle Bay Holiday & Residential Park, Portpatrick, Stranraer, Dumfries & Galloway DG9 9AA.** *01776 810462.* www.castlebayholidaypark.co.uk. 22 acres of rolling countryside overlooking the Irish Sea and Dunskey Castle. 0.5m coastal walk to village of Portpatrick. Open all year for statics. From N take A77 S from Glasgow, from S take A75 W from Dumfries onto A77 to Portpatrick, follow caravan park sign. Open: 2 March - 29 October. ★★★ BH&HPA

**(17m). Clashwhannon Holiday Park, Drummore, Stranraer, Dumfries & Galloway DG9 9QE.** *01776 840632.* www.clashwhannon.co.uk. Bar. Restaurant. Games room. Golf course, riding school, shopping centre, leisure centre, charter boat hire all available nearby. Pets welcome but must be kept on leads whilst on park. On A716. From Strandaer to Mull of Galloway road, 1st exit on L as enter to Drummore village. Open: 1 March - 31 December. ★★ BH&HPA

# SCOTLAND

(7m). **Galloway Point Holiday Park, Portpatrick, Stranraer, Dumfries & Galloway DG9 9AA.** 01776 810561. gallowaypoint-holidaypark.co.uk. Excellent family park with stunning sea views. 5mins away from shops, pubs, restaurants in small fishing village of Portpatrick. Brand new state of the art shower/laundry block. David Bellamy Silver Conservation Award. Off A75, A77 S from Glasgow, A75 W from Dumfries. 1st L after 30mph on R, office at house/pub on L. Open: 12 March - 31 October. BH&HPA ★★★★ ♦ 10🚐 40🚐

(14m). **New England Bay Caravan Club Site, Port Logan, Stranraer, Dumfries & Galloway DG9 9NX.** 01776 860275. www.caravanclub.co.uk. This site is on the edge of Luce Bay and is carefully landscaped into seven intimate pitching areas with sea views. Non-members welcome. No tents. Advance booking essential BH and July-August. Toilet blocks with privacy cubicles and laundry facilities. Veg prep area, gas, dog walk nearby. MV service point. Games room. Play equipment. Ideal for families. Steel awning pegs required. Storage pitches, water sports and beach nearby. Quiet and peaceful off peak. See website for standard directions to site. Open: 23 March - 5 November. ★★★★★ NCC 158🚐 158🚐 A

(1m). **Ryan Bay Caravan Park, Innermessan, Stranraer, Dumfries & Galloway DG9 8QP.** 01776 889458. www.hagansleisure.co.uk. A truly beautiful caravan park, with its own clubhouse, on the sea shore of Ryan Bay. Off A77 between Innermessan and Stranraer. Open: 1 March - 31 October. ★★ BH&HPA NCC 16🚐 16🚐 A 55🚐

**Sands of Luce Holiday Park, Sandhead, Stranraer, Dumfries & Galloway DG9 9JN.** 01776 830456. www.sandsofluceholidaypark.co.uk. Located directly on the beautiful Luce Bay, Sands of Luce Holiday Park is a multi award winning family run park. At junction of B7084 and A716, S of Stranraer. Open: 1 May - 15 November. ★★★★★

(7m). **Sunnymeade Caravan Park (Stranraer), Portpatrick, Stranraer, Dumfries & Galloway DG9 8LN.** 01776 810293. www.sunny-meade.co.uk. Near beach and golf. Owner supplied copy. A75 to Portpatrick, turn L on entering Portpatrick. Site 0.5m on L. Open: 1 April - 30 September. BH&HPA 4🚐 15🚐 A 90🚐

(4m). **Wig Bay Holiday Park, Loch Ryan, Stranraer, Dumfries & Galloway DG9** 

OPS. 01776 853233. www.wigbayholidaypark.com. Heated indoor swimming pool. Play area. Bar. Telephone. On entering take A718 Kirkcolm road, right at roundabout, past garden centre. Park is on L. Open: 1 March - 31 October. ★★★★ BH&HPA NCC 24🚐 90🚐

### Thornhill

(2m). **Penpont Floors Caravan Park, Penpont, Thornhill, Dumfries & Galloway DG3 4BH.** 01848 330470. www.penpontleisure.com. Quiet, riverside park in beautiful country. 5mins walk to shop, local pub and PO. Golf course 3m. River and loch fishing, mountain bike trails available locally. Good cycling area. Owner supplied copy. At north end of Thornhill take the A702 to Penpont 2m. Park is on the L just before Penpont village. Open: 6 April - 31 October. BH&HPA 5🚐 10🚐 A 20🚐

### Wigtown

(6m). **Castle Cary Holiday Park, Creetown, Newton Stewart, Wigtown, Dumfries & Galloway DG8 7DQ.** 01671 820264. www.castlecary-caravans.com. Large heated outdoor swimming and paddling pool. Olde world country inn with bar meals and takeaway food. Sun patio. Playground. Public phone. Well-stocked coarse fishing lake. Super indoor pool. Adult snooker room. Woodland walks. Donkey park. Crazy golf. Village 0.25m distance to PO/butcher/craft shops/hotels/cafe/garage, etc. New timber lodge development around Loch Murray. Environmental colour holiday home caravans also for sale. AA 5 pennants. David Bellamy Bronze Conservation Award. Off A75. Main euro route UK-Northern Ireland. Open: All year. 5 BH&HPA 50🚐 50🚐 A 2🚐

(11m). **Three Lochs Holiday Park, Balminnoch, Newton Stewart, Wigtown, Dumfries & Galloway DG8 0EP.** 01671 830304. www.3lochs.co.uk. Bottled gas. Indoor heated pool. Fishing, sailing and wind-surfing. Full size snooker room. Golf courses, leisure centre, pony trekking all nearby. Off B7027 and A75. Follow A75 approximately 8m W of Newton Stewart and turn R at Dirnow crossroads and follow signs. Open: 1 March - 31 October. ★★★ BH&HPA NCC 45🚐 45🚐 A 10🚐

### DUNBARTONSHIRE

### Balloch

(0.25m). **Lomond Woods Holiday Park, Loch Lomond, Balloch,** 

Dunbartonshire G83 8QP. 01389 755000. www.holiday-parks.co.uk. Play area, games room, TV lounge, laundrette. Pine lodges and caravan holiday homes also for hire. Short walk to Loch Lomond and Balloch village for restaurants, bars, and shops. Huge variety of activities locally including water sports, golf and fishing. At gateway to Loch Lomond National Park and next to Loch Lomond Shores visitor experience. David Bellamy Gold Conservation Award. Turn R off A82, 17m N of Glasgow at roundabout SP Balloch. At next roundabout take a L following signs. A811 for Lomond Woods. Open: All year. ★★★★★ BH&HPA 120🚐 48🚐

## EAST LOTHIAN
### Dirleton

(2.5m). **Yellowcraig Caravan Club Site, North Berwick, Dirleton, East Lothian EH39 5DS.** 01620 850217. www.caravanclub.co.uk. This is an attractive site with grass covered sandy dunes, shrubs and dog roses creating private pitching areas. Non-members welcome. No tents. Advance booking essential BH and mid-July to mid-August. Some hardstandings. Toilet blocks with privacy cubicles and laundry facilities. Baby/toddler washroom. MV service point. Play area. Golf nearby. Ideal for families. Veg prep area, gas, dog walk nearby. Quiet and peaceful off-peak. Beach within 5m. See website for standard directions to site. Open: 23 March - 5 November. ★★★★★ NCC 116🚐 116🚐

### Dunbar

(0.5m). **Belhaven Bay Caravan & Camping Park, Dunbar, East Lothian EH42 1TU.** 01368 865956. www.meadowhead.co.uk. Peaceful setting located in the John Muir Country Park. Laundry, internet access available on the park. Children's play area. Sandy beaches only a short walk away. Thistle Award. Facilities within 15mins walking distance. David Bellamy Gold Conservation Award. From A1 N or S exit at roundabout W of Dunbar. Park about 0.5m down A1087 on left side of road. (From S, do not take first exit to Dunbar.) Open: 12 March - 31 October. ★★★★ BH&HPA NCC 27🚐 A 7🚐

**Dunbar Camping & Caravanning Club Site, Oxwellmains, Dunbar, East Lothian EH42 1WG.** 01368 866881. www.campingandcaravanningclub.co.uk. The site is located on Scotland's sunshine coast, with a long sandy surfing beach nearby. The town of Dunbar is less than 3m from site and Edinburgh a car ride away. Take

# SCOTLAND

A1087 off the A1. Open: 1 April - 31 October. ★★★★★ NCC 90 90

**(6m). Thorntonloch Caravan Park, Innerwick, Dunbar, East Lothian EH42 1QS.** *01368 840236.* thorntonlochcaravanpark.vpweb.co.uk. Shop on site open at weekends. Sea fishing, right on beach. Owner supplied copy. On A1. Open: 3 March - 31 October. 10 10 10 57

**(4m). Thurston Manor Holiday Home Park, Innerwick, Dunbar, East Lothian EH42 1SA.** *01368 840643.* www.thurstonmanor.co.uk. Close to sea and sandy beaches. Licensed club with entertainment. Family room. Heated indoor pool, fitness centre with sauna, steam room, solarium, spa and gymnasium. Bar meals and takeaway. Private trout lake. Sea fishing and golf within 4m. S of Dunbar, SP from A1. C Open: 1 March - 31 October. ★★★★★★ 100 595

## Edinburgh

**Edinburgh Caravan Club Site, 35-37 Marine Drive, Edinburgh, East Lothian EH4 5EN.** *01313 126874.* www.caravanclub.co.uk. This site is in an ideal location for a caravanning holiday. Situated to the N of the city on the Firth of Fourth, the site provides easy access to Edinburgh. Hardstandings; toilet block; laundry facilities and veg prep; play area; dog walk. Non-members and tent campers welcome. MV service point. Golf and water sports nearby. Serviced pitches, gas and gaz, ideal for families, beach within 5m. Significant interest nearby (zoo, holy road, etc). NCN cycle route within 5m. See website for standard directions to site. Open: All year. ★★★★★ NCC 197 197

**(4m). Mortonhall Caravan Park, 38 Mortonhall Gate, Frogston Road East, Edinburgh, East Lothian EH16 6TJ.** *01316 641533.* www.meadowhead.co.uk. Specimen Tree Arboretum on the park. Internet access/bar/restaurant, children's play areas. Golf, supermarket, dry ski slope all within 2m. Cinema/theatre 2.5m. Excellent access to Edinburgh City centre. David Bellamy Gold Conservation Award. From city by-pass A720 leave at Lothianburn Junction on (A702) or Straiton Junction on (A701) and follow signs for Mortonhall. Open: 15 March - 4 January. ★★★★ DII&IIPA 250 40

## Longniddry

**Aberlady Caravan Park, Aberlady, Longniddry, East Lothian EH32 0PZ.** *01875 870666.* www.aberladycaravanpark.co.uk. Quiet site. Ideal for touring, close enough to 20 golf courses, Edinburgh, Musselburgh Races or the Museum of Flight - home to Concorde. Gosford House. Aberlady village is a small coastal village 0.5m from the site with 2 hotels, a PO and a shop. 5m from Haddington on B6137, 3m from Longnddry on A198. Open: 1 March - 31 October. 5 15 2

**Seton Sands Holiday Village (Haven), Prestonpans, Longniddry, East Lothian EH32 0QF.** *0871 2310867.* www.caravancamping.co.uk. Heated indoor swimming pool. Club. Family entertainment. Direct beach access. Mini market. Free kids' clubs. Amusements, pool tables. Play area. Thistle Award. David Bellamy Silver Conservation Award. Take A1 to A198 slip road. Turn on to B6371 for Cockenzie then R on to B1348. Park is 1m along on the right hand side, SP from A1 N and S. Open: 18 March - 31 October. ★★★★ BH&HPA NCC 38 38 706

## Musselburgh

**(1.5m). Drum Mohr Caravan Park, Levenhall, Musselburgh, Musselburgh, East Lothian EH21 8JS.** *01316 656867.* www.drummohr.org. 108 mixed pitches. East Lothian's premier touring park secluded and well landscaped on edge of beautiful countryside yet only 20mins from Edinburgh to which there is an excellent bus service. 1.5m E of Musselburgh between B1348 and B1361. Open: All year. ★★★★ BH&HPA NCC 110 12

## North Berwick

**(1m). Gilsland Caravan Park, Grange Road, North Berwick, East Lothian EH39 5JA.** *01620 892205.* www.gilslandcaravanpark.co.uk. 0.5m from swimming pool and sports centre. Golf, sailing, shopping all within 1m. Between B1347 and A198. Along Grange Road. Open: 1 April - 31 October. ★★★ BH&HPA 114

**(0.5m). Tantallon Caravan & Camping Park, Dunbar Road, North Berwick, East Lothian EH39 5NJ.** *01620 893348.* www.meadowhoad.co.uk. Play area, 0 hole putting green. Internet access available on the park. 4 wigwams available for hire. Adjacent to Glen Golf Course. Cafe/restaurant and takeaway meals available nearby. Holiday homes for the disabled. Close to bus stop. Thistle Award. On the A198 immediately E of North Berwick. Open: 13 March - 31 October. ★★★★ BH&HPA 180 70

## FIFE

### Anstruther

**(0.25m). St Monans Caravan Park, The Common, St. Monans, Anstruther, Fife KY10 2DN.** *01333 730778.* www.abbeyfordscotland.com. Small quiet park beside park, village and seaside. David Bellamy Silver Conservation Award. Adjoining A917 E of St Monans. Open: 21 March - 31 October. ★★★ BH&HPA 18 18 112

### Burntisland

**(1m). Pettycur Bay Caravan Park, Kinghorn, Burntisland, Fife KY3 9YE.** *01592 892200* . www.pettycur.co.uk. Spectacular sea views and golden sands. Prime tourist area close to Edinburgh (35mins by road). Dogs allowed but not in hire vans. GS. Park next to one golf course, 2m from another. Sea and loch fishing within 2m. Local shopping in Kinghorn, Burntisland 1m & 2m on main bus route with stop at park. Rail station at Kinghorn and Burntisland. On A921. Open: 1 March - 31 October. BH&HPA 10 50 636

### Crail

**Sauchope Links Park, Crail, Fife KY10 3XJ.** *01333 450460.* www.caravanleisure-park.co.uk. On the seashore with heated outdoor swimming pool, games room, play area. Wash basins, shaver points. GS. David Bellamy Gold Conservation Award. On A917. Open: 21 March - 31 October. ★★★★ BH&HPA 50 84

### Glenrothes

**(2.25m). Balbirnie Park Caravan Club Site, Markinich, Glenrothes, Fife KY7 6NR.** *01592 759130.* www.caravanclub.co.uk. An attractive site set within 400 acres of parkland. Veg preparation area. Motorcaravan waste point. Toilet block. Non-members welcome. Tent camping very limited. Part hardstandings, part sloping. Steel awning pegs required. Gas, information room, dog walk nearby. Ideal for families, quiet and peaceful off peak. Water sports nearby. NCN cycle route within 5m. Advance booking advised all BH and July-August. See website for standard directions to site. 0.5m from Markinch. Open: 23 March

# SCOTLAND

- 5 November. ★★★★ NCC 76

## Leven

**(1m). Leven Beach Holiday Park, Promenade, Leven, Fife KY8 4HY.** 01592 892200. www.pettycur.co.uk/levenbeach.asp. Direct access to sandy beach and adjoining golf course. Bar, laundry, games room. Prime tourist area. Dogs not allowed in hire caravans. 3 local golf championship golf courses, local leisure centre and pool, shopping centre. A915 to Leven on to the A955 South. At promenade turn E along to Road End. Open: 1 March - 31 October. BH&HPA 40 20

**(2m). Shell Bay Caravan Park, Elie, Leven, Fife KY9 1HB.** 01333 330283. www.abbeyfordscotland.com. Lounge bar. Meals served. Laundry facilities. Private beach. Play park. Free showers and hot water. Fishing and water sports. Golf courses and leisure pool nearby. David Bellamy Gold Conservation Award. Off A917. Lounge bar. Meals served. Laundry facilities. Private beach. Play park. Free showers and hot water. Fishing and water sports. Golf courses and leisure pool nearby. David Bellamy Gold Conservation Award Open: 21 March - 31 October. ★★★ NCC 120 292

**(1m). Woodland Gardens Caravan Site (Leven), Blindwell Road, Lundin Links, Leven, Fife KY8 5QG.** 01333 360319. www.woodland-gardens.co.uk. Ideal centre for St Andrews and East Neuk of Fife. Small quiet family run site. ADULTS ONLY. Peace and tranquillity in a beautiful rural setting overlooking the river Forth to Edinburgh. Golf course 1m. Turn N off A915 at east end of Lundin Links. SP on A915 by international camping and caravanning signs. Open: 1 April - 31 October. ★★★★ 20 20 2

## St Andrews

**(1m). Cairnsmill Caravan Park, Largo Road, St Andrews, Fife KY16 8NN.** 01334 473604. Ideal touring base, in close proximity to a choice of golf courses and the east Fife coast. Indoor heated swimming pool. Coffee bar. GS. Fly fishing, bunkhouse. David Bellamy Gold Conservation Award. On A915 Leven to St Andrews, SW of town centre. Open: 1 April - 31 October. ★★★★ BH&HPA 10 80 5

**(1.5m). Craigtoun Meadows Holiday Park, Mount Melville, St Andrews, Fife KY16 8PQ.** 01334 475959. www.craigtounmeadows.co.uk. Licensed restaurant. AA 5 pennant. Indoor/outdoor games room, shop, telephone, tennis court. 1.5m to golf, cinema, shops, restaurants, hotels and pubs. David Bellamy Gold Conservation Award. Off A91, at Guardbridge turn R for Strathkiness, follow signs for Craigtoun. Open: 15 March - 31 October. ★★★★★ BH&HPA NCC 56 21

**(1m). Kinkell Braes Holiday Park, St Andrews, Fife KY16 8PX.** 01334 474583. www.abbeyfordscotland.com. Free showers & hot water. Unit for disabled. 15 min walk to town centre, beach and leisure centre 5min walk, golf courses (7) about 1.5m. Bar and restaurant servings meals, laundry, shop, play area and games room. Off A918 St Andrews to Crail. Open: 1 March - 31 October. ★★★ BH&HPA NCC 100 397

## Tayport

**(0.3m). Tayport Links Caravan Park, East Common, Tayport, Fife DD6 9ES.** 01382 552334. www.tayportlinkscaravanpark.co.uk. Dogs on lead welcome. Fishing, golf courses, forest walks extensive beaches all within 5m radius. 15mins to St Andrews, 10mins Dundee. All shops within walking distance surrounded by extensive council owned and maintained playing fields with children's play parks. Enter Tayport on B945 and follow park signs, on shore. Open: 1 March - 13 January. ★★★★ BH&HPA 94

## GLASGOW
### Glasgow

**(1.5m). Milarrochy Bay Camping & Caravanning Club Site, Balmaha, Drymen, Glasgow, Glasgow G63 0AL.** 01360 870236. www.campingandcaravanningclub.co.uk. On East bank of Loch Lomond in the heart of Rob Roy country adjacent to the West Highland way. You can hire a boat to take out onto the Loch yourself or enjoy a pleasure cruise. All units accepted. Non-members welcome. The Queen Elizabeth Forest Park with its 75,000 acres of forest is nearby. The site has a peaceful and quiet atmosphere. Special deals available for families and backpackers. AA's Best Campsite in Scotland award. Visit Scotland Thistle Award finalist. A811 Balloch to Stirling road take Drymen turning in Drymen take B837 to Balmaha after 5m road turns sharply R up Steep Hill. Site 1.5m further on. Open: 1 April - 31 October. ★★★★ NCC 150 150

## HIGHLAND
### Achnasheen

**(36m). Inverewe Gardens Camping & Caravanning Club Site, Poolewe, Achnasheen, Highland IV22 2LF.** 01445 781249. www.campingandcaravanningclub.co.uk. All units accepted. Non-members welcome. The site nestles in spectacular mountain scenery. The National Trust for Scotland organise some excellent walks led by a ranger. There is good sea and fly fishing close to the site. Wildlife includes seals, otters, and golden eagles. Special deals available for families and backpackers. On A832, just N of Poolewe, close to Inverewe Gardens and on shores of Loch Ewe. Open: 1 April - 31 October. ★★★★ NCC 55 55

**(8m). Kinlochewe Caravan Club Site, Kinlochewe, Achnasheen, Highland IV22 2PA.** 01445 760239. www.caravanclub.co.uk. A small and intimate site in a peaceful position at the foot of the rugged slopes of Ben Eighe. Non-members welcome. No tents. Advance booking essential BH and June-August. Toilet blocks. Laundry facilities. MV service point. Good area for walking. All hardstandings, steel awning pegs required, dog walk, quiet and peaceful off peak. See website for standard directions to site. Open: 5 April - 1 October. ★★★★★ NCC 56 56

### Arisaig

**(4m). Camusdarach, Arisaig, Highland PH39 4NT.** 01687 450221. www.camusdarach.com. Traigh golf club. 6m from Mallaig, restaurants, shops and ferries to the islands. Mobile shop calls. On B8008, 4m N of Arisaig on seaward side of road near to fine sandy beaches. Open: 1 March - 31 October. ★★★★ 20

**(1.5m). Invercaimbe Caravan Site, Invercaimbe, Arisaig, Highland PH39 4NT.** 01687 450375. www.invercaimbecaravansite.co.uk. On the beach. Golf nearby. Fishing & boat trips locally. Off A830. Open: 20 March - 31 October. 4 10 2

**(2m). Portnadoran Caravan Site, Portnadoran, Arisaig, Highland PH39 4NT.** 01687 450267. www.arisaigcampsite.co.uk. Beside sea and white sands. We have a small golf course nearby, distance to shops 2m. An ideal site for children with

# SCOTLAND

lots to do and see. Owner supplied copy. About 2m N of Arisaig Village on old road. Open: 22 April - 15 October.

## Aviemore

**(3m). Dalraddy Holiday Park, Aviemore, Highland PH22 1QB.** *01479 810330*. www.alvie-estate.co.uk. Laundrette. Static vans open for winter skiing. Play area. Licensed shop. Heated facilities block. Fishing, pony trekking and water sports. Quad bikes and 4x4 all within 2 miles. Owner supplied copy. On B9152 (old A9). Open: All year. ★★★★ BH&HPA NCC

**(7m). Glenmore Forest Holidays, Glenmore, Aviemore, Highland PH22 1QU.** *01479 861271*. www.forestholidays.co.uk. In the heart of the Cairngorms. An Area of Outstanding Natural Beauty, close to sandy beaches of Loch Morlich and Scotland's largest ski area. Bookings and brochure requests on 0845 1308221. David Bellamy Gold Conservation Award. From A9 turn on to B9152 S of Aviemore. At Aviemore, turn R on to B970, keeping R at Coylumbridge. Open: All year. **BH&HPA**

**(1.5m). Rothiemurchus Caravan Park, Coylumbridge, Aviemore, Highland PH22 1QH.** *01479 812800*. www.rothiemurchus.net. Touring pitches (hardstand) do vary in size as they are worked in around the trees. All have 16 amp and TV hook-ups. From Aviemore take ski road B970, park is situated on R in 1.5m. Open: 1 December - 31 October. **BH&HPA**

## Beauly

**(26m). Cannich Caravan & Camping Park, Cannich, Beauly, Highland IV4 7LN.** *01456 415364*. www.highland-camping.co.uk. Friendly site situated 0.5m from village centre where there is a shop, pub. Close to Glen Affric Nature Reserve. Highland and Lowland trails for walkers and mountain bikers. Site has 24 hour public telephone, laundry, play area, TV/rec room, indoor washing up facilities. Out of Inverness on A82 at Drumnadrochit take A831 to Cannich. 16m from Beauly. Open: All year. ★★★★ BH&HPA

## Boat of Garten

**Boat of Garten Caravan Park, Deshar Road, Boat of Garten, Highland PH24 3BN.** *01479 831652*. www.boatofgarten-holidaypark.com. Thistle Award Park. PO 300yd, fishing 500yd, golf and tennis 300yd, Railway 250yd. Beautiful forest walks all around. Osprey Hide 2m. Off A95 Grantown to Aviemore. From A9 take A95 SP Grantown on Spey then follow signs for boat of Garten. Situated in the centre of the village, 1st Carrbridge cut off both ways A9. Open: All year. ★★★★ BH&HPA NCC

**(1m). Loch Garten Lodges & Caravan Park, Loch Garten Road, Boat of Garten, Highland PH24 3BY.** *01479 831769*. www.lochgarten.co.uk. 3 golf courses, fishing within 1m. Bird watching at Osprey Centre 0.5m. Woodland walks in RSPB Nature Reserve next to site. Shopping 7m. Owner supplied copy. Leave A9 immediately N of Aviemore follow Boat of Garten signs, through village and cross river Spey, turn L on B970, first R to Tulloch, park on L overlooking river and Spey Valley. Aviemore 7m. Open: All year. ★★★★ BH&HPA

**(2m). Osprey Caravan Park, Boat of Garten, Highland PH24 3BY.** *01479 831380*. ospreycaravanparkandlpgaservices.com. Small, quiet site. Excellent base for touring, attractions to suit all tastes. Owner supplied copy. Off A9, on to B970 between Boat of Garten and Nethy Bridge. Near to RSPB site of Loch Garten (Ospreys) also on the side of River Spey (fishing). Open: 1 December - 31 October.

## Brora

**(1.5m). Dalchalm Caravan Club Site, Brora, Highland KW9 6LP.** *01408 621479*. www.caravanclub.co.uk. A site on the east coast of Sutherland just 300yd from a safe, sandy beach. Tent campers admitted. Non-members welcome. Advance booking advised June-August. Toilet blocks. Privacy cubicles. Laundry facilities. Veg prep. MV service point. Golf, fishing nearby. Good area for walking. Ideal for families. Some hardstandings, gas and gaz. Dog walk nearby, quiet and peaceful off peak. See website for standard directions to site. Open: 5 April - 1 October. ★★★★ NCC

## Caithness

**(0.25m). Inver Caravan Park, Houstry Road, Dunbeath, Caithness, Highland KW6 6EH.** *01593 731441*. www.inver-caravan-park.co.uk. 15 pitches in total. Smooth grassy site; 8 hardstandings, dump station. Free showers, beautiful views over Dunbeath Bay. Friendly welcome. Comfortable 6-berth holiday caravan for hire. Near shop and pub/restaurant. Convenient for exploring far north or for Orkney crossings. Owner supplied copy. Adjacent A9 just N of Dunbeath, 21m SW of Wick. Park entrance 40yd up road SP 'Houstry 3'. Open: All year. ★★★ 

## Dingwall

**(5m). Black Rock Caravan Park, Evanton, Dingwall, Highland IV16 9UN.** *01349 830917*. www.blackrockscotland.co.uk. Set in wooded glen on the banks of river Glass. Level, grassy and sheltered park within easy reach of west and east coasts. Free showers. Play area. Telephone. Laundry. Disabled facilities. Hard standing pitches. No single sex groups. Thistle Award. Off A9, 15m N from Inverness, turn L for Evanton B817, proceed for 0.75m. Open: 1 April - 31 October. ★★★★ BH&HPA

**(0.5m). Dingwall Camping & Caravanning Club Site, Jubilee Park Road, Dingwall, Highland IV15 9QZ.** *01349 862236*. www.campingandcaravanningclub.co.uk. Ideal base for exploring the Western Highlands. All units accepted. Non-members welcome. Site set in 6.5 acres. Nature lovers will enjoy the Millbuie Forest in the nearby Black Isle. There are also train excursions from Dingwall to the Kyle of Lochalsh available. Special deals available for families and backpackers. In Dingwall coming from S, take bypass and follow signs, first R down Hill Street, R at junction, L over railway bridge, then first L, SP. Open: 1 April - 31 October. ★★★★ NCC

## Dornoch

**(2.5m). Grannie's Heilan Hame Holiday Park, Embo, Dornoch, Highland IV25 3QD.** *0870 4580943*. www.parkdean-holidays.co.uk. Direct beach access. Free indoor pool and spa bath, solarium, sauna, bar, clubhouse, entertainment/meals, tennis court, playground, games room, mini bowling and pool. Caravan sales. David Bellamy Silver Conservation Award. Take A9 from Inverness northwards to Dornoch and Embo. Follow the road for Embo. Park is at the end of this road. Open: 23 March - 2 November. ★★★★ BH&HPA NCC

**(1.25m). Seaview Farm Caravan Park (Dornoch), Hilton, Dornoch, Highland IV25 3PW.** *01862 810294*. Caravanning &

# SCOTLAND

Camping Club member. Dogs allowed on leads. Flat site. Golf course nearby. Shops, PO, doctor in village. From Dornoch turn L at square. After 1.25m turn R at road junction by telephone box. Open: 1 April - 31 October. ★★★ 🏠🐕✏🏊🚐 16🚐 ⛺

## Dundonnell

(8m). **Badrallach Airstream D, Bothy, Little Loch Broom, Badrallach, Dundonnell, Highland IV23 2QP.** 01854 633281. www.badrallach.com. Tranquil lochshore site in a remote highland setting. Boats, bikes, kayaks, biokarts, kites to hire. Walk, see otters, deer, golden eagles, porpoise or just relax with a dram. 7m along the winding single track road off the A832. 1m E of the Dundonnell Hotel. Open: All year. ★★★★ 🏠🐕 ⛺🏊✏🔥🚗♿🚽 3🚐 3⛳ 17⛺ 1🏠 1🏕

## Fort William

 (2.5m). **Glen Nevis Caravan & Camping Park, Glen Nevis, Fort William, Highland PH33 6SX.** 01397 702191. www.glen-nevis.co.uk. Restaurant near site at foot of Ben Nevis. David Bellamy Gold Conservation Award. Off A82 at sp Glen Nevis on northern outskirts of Fort William. Site is about 2m from A82. Open: 13 March - 9 November. ★★★★★ BH&HPA ♀🏠🐕 ✏🏊🔥🚗♿🚽 250🚐 ⛺ 🏊

(5m). **Linnhe Lochside Holidays, Corpach, Fort William, Highland PH33 7NL.** 01397 772376. www.linnhe-lochside-holidays.co.uk. One of the best and most beautiful lochside parks in Scotland. Pets welcome. Free fishing. 18 hole golf, cinema 5m. PO, shops 0.5m. Brochure on request. On A830, 1m W of Corpach. 5m from Fort William. Open: 15 December - 31 October. ★★★★★ BH&HPA ♿ 🏠🐕✏🏊🔥🚗🚽 67🚐 ⛺ 285⛳

(2.5m). **Lochy Holiday Park, Camagheal, Fort William, Highland PH33 7NF.** 01397 703446. www.lochy-holiday-park.co.uk. Laundry shop, play area, showers, toilets. Golf 0.5m. Fishing 1m. Town centre 2m. On A830, off A82. Park is situated on the same road as the Medical centre/ High School in the District of Camaghael. Open: 15 March - 31 October. ★★★★ BH&HPA 🏠🐕✏🏊🔥🚗♿🚽 40🚐 40⛳ ⛺ 19🏕

## Fortrose

(0.5m). **Rosemarkie Camping & Caravanning Club Site, Ness Road East, Rosemarkie, Fortrose, Highland IV10 8SE.** 01381 621117. www.campingandcaravanningclub.co.uk. On the shore of the Black Isle in the small seaside village of Rosemarkie. Non-members welcome. All units accepted. Disabled facilities. The spectacular coastline is famous for its bottlenose dolphins. The area is a paradise for bird watchers, with many local nature reserves. Inverness with all its attractions is only a few miles away. Special deals available for families and backpackers. Loo Of The Year (4 stars). Take A832. A9 at Tore roundabout. Through Avoch, Fortrose then turn R at Police house Down Ness Road, first L, small turning sign Golf and Caravan Site. Open: 1 April - 31 October. ★★★★ NCC 🏠🐕✏🚐 🏊🔥🚗♿🚽 60🚐 60⛳ ⛺

## Gairloch

**Gairloch Caravan and Camping Park, Strath, Gairloch, Highland IV21 2BX.** 01445 712373. www.gairlochcaravanpark.com. Shower block, laundrette. Close to shops, pubs & restaurants. Wi-Fi Internet coverage to all pitches. Chemical toilet disposal point if required. 4 bed bunkhouse. AA 3 pennant rated. 70m from Inverness. From the A842 take the B8021 sign posted Melvaig, heading for the village of Strath. Approx 0.5 miles on right, just past Millcroft Hotel turn right. Immediately after hotel turn right again. Open: 26 March - 1 November. ★★★★ BH&HPA 🏠🐕 ✏🏊 🔥🚗♿🚽 34🚐 40⛳ 40⛺ 7🏕

(3m). **Sands Caravan & Camping, Gairloch, Highland IV21 2DL.** 01445 712152. www.sandscaravanandcamping.co.uk. Play area. Public phone. Slipway for boats. Beach adjoining. Full facilities May 2 to mid-September. Underfloor heated toilet and shower rooms. Free Loch fishing to residents. Owner supplied copy. Following A833 to Gairloch then take B8021 4m along this road will bring you to Sands Caravan & Camping. Open: 26 March - 24 October. ★★★ BH&HPA 🏠🐕✏🏊🔥🚗♿🚽 50⛳ 160⛺ 20🏕

## Glencoe

(0.25m). **Invercoe Caravan & Camping Park, Invercoe, Glencoe, Highland PH49 4HP.** 01855 811210. www.invercoe.co.uk. Holiday touring centre. Advance bookings for electric hook-ups. Thistle commendation. On B863, beside loch. Open: All year. ★★★★★ BH&HPA NCC 🏠🐕✏🚐 🏊🔥🚗♿🚽 55⛳ 4🏕

## Invergarry

(1m). **Faichemard Farm Touring Caravan & Camping Site, Invergarry, Highland PH35 4HG.** 01809 501314. www.faichemard-caravancamping.co.uk. Exclusively for adults. All pitches have own picnic tables. Laundry on site. Some individual pitches, hardstanding and hook ups available. To find us follow the signs with green writing off the A87 at Invergarry. Leave A87 1m W from junction with A82. Turn R and go past Ardgarry Farm, then turn R at sign A & D Grant. Open: 10 April - 20 October. ★★★★ 🏠🐕✏🚐 🏊♿ 12🚐 12⛳ 23⛺

## Invermoriston

(30m). **Loch Ness Holiday Park, Easter Port Clair, Invermoriston, Highland IV63 7YE.** 01320 351207. www.lochnessholidaypark.co.uk. The only park on Loch Ness. All vans have magnificent views. Fishing allowed, permits for salmon fishing with charge. Play area and lounge bar/family room with hot meals available. Laundry. New addition to park are the Hobbits, the new way to camp. Mobile shop. Adjacent to Great Glen walk. 5mins to Fort Augustus with 2 supermarkets. 1m to village, PO, shop and hotel. Golf course 5mins, indoor pool 9m. On A82 1.5m S of Invermoriston. Open: 1 February - 31 October. ★★★★★ BH&HPA ♀🏠 🏕🐕✏🔥🚗🚽♿🚽 54⛳ 6🏕

## Inverness

(10m). **Auchnahillin Caravan & Camping Park, Daviot East, Inverness, Highland IV2 5XQ.** 01463 772286. www.auchnahillin.co.uk. Friendly informal family owned park 10 acres in rural location only 8m from Inverness, ideal base for touring the Highlands, many attractions within easy drive, all amenities available in Inverness. 8m SE of Inverness off the A9 on B9154 (Moy/Daviot East). Friendly informal family owned park 10 acres in rural location only 8m from Inverness, ideal base for touring the Highlands, many attractions within easy drive, all amenities available in Inverness. Open: 15 April - 16 October. ★★★★ BH&HPA 🏠🐕✏ ✏🚐🏊🔥🚗♿🚽 45🚐 45⛳ 30⛺ 10🏕

(0.5m). **Bught Caravan Park, Bught Lane, Inverness, Highland IV3 5SR.** 01463 236920. www.invernesscaravanpark.com. A privately family run park situated in the City of Inverness, a 15mins walk from the Castle and 20mins walk from centre. Located in tourist area. Well equipped site. Tents welcome. Includes an internet cafe and small shop. Many sports facilities nearby. On A82, situated in the middle of Inverness, next to the Tomnahurich Canal Bridge and the

# SCOTLAND

Inverness Aqua Dome. Open: 23 March - 1 October. ★★★ 日日 ⚡ ♿ ♪ ⛱ 🐕 🚗 🚫 🍴 日日 ⚡ ♿ 60🔌 60⚡ 80⛺

**Culloden Moor Caravan Club Site, Newlands, Culloden Moor, Inverness, Highland IV2 5EF.** 01463 790625. www.caravanclub.co.uk. A gently sloping site facing a glorious view over the Nairn Valley. Vegetable preparation area. Motorhome waste point. Playframe. Toilet block with privacy cubicles. Advance booking advised June-August essential July and BH. Information room. Fishing. Good area for walking. Ideal for families. Significant area of interest nearby including Loch Ness. Hardstandings, part sloping, laundry, gas and gaz, dog walk nearby, quiet and peaceful off peak, beach within 5m. NCN cycle route within 5m. Non-members & tent campers welcome. See website for standard directions to site. Open: 30 March - 31 October. ★★★★★ NCC 🛁 ♿ ♪ 🚗 🐕 日 ⚡ 🍴 🛒 97🔌 97⚡

(16m). **Highland Riding Centre (Borlum Farm), Borlum Farm, Drumnadrochit, Inverness, Highland IV63 6XN.** 01456 450220. www.borlum.co.uk. Overlooking Loch Ness. BHS approved riding establishment on site. Working farm. On A82 Fort Augustus to Inverness. 1m S of Drumnadrochit. Open: All year. ★★★ BH&HPA 日 ♿ ♪ ❄ 🚗 🐕 🍴 12🔌 12⚡ ⛺

(1m). **Torvean Caravan Park, Glenurquhart Road, Inverness, Highland IV3 8JL.** 01463 220582. www.torveancaravanpark.co.uk. Peaceful park, 1m from town centre, overlooking golf course and canal. Laundrette. One small pet per outfit. Mobile shop. Thistle Commended holiday caravans for hire. On A82 on right after crossing canal bridge. Open: 26 March - 30 September. ★★★★★ BH&HPA NCC 日 ♿ ♪ 🚗 🐕 ♿ 50🔌 10⚡

## Isle of Benbecula

**Shell Bay Holiday Park, Liniclate, Isle of Benbecula, Highland HS7 5PJ.** 01870 602447. Near beaches and community school. Shop and restaurant available nearby. Site 23m from Lochboisdale on A865/B892. 21m from Lochmaddy. Open: 1 April - 31 October. ★★ 日 ⚡ ♪ 🛒 🍴 ♿ ⛺ ⚡ ⛺

## Isle of Lewis

**Eilean Fraoich Camping Site, North Shawbost, Isle of Lewis, Highland HS2 9BQ.** 01851 710504. www.eileanfraoich.co.uk. Small, friendly, family run site in Shawbost on the scenic west coast of Lewis. 19m from Stornoway. Take the A857 to Barabhas (Barvas). Turn left along the A858 to Siabost (Shawbost). Follow the main road through village, turn left after school building. Open: 1 May - 31 October. ★★★ 日日 ♪ 🚗 🔥 🍴 🛒 ⚡ ♿ 10⚡ ⛺

**Laxdale Holiday Park, 6 Laxdale Lane, Stornaway, Isle of Lewis, Highland HS2 0DR.** 01851 703234. www.laxdaleholidaypark.com. Quiet, family run park in peaceful tree lined surroundings. Owner supplied copy. From Stornaway ferry terminal take A857 for 1.5m, turn L just before Laxdale river, park is 100yd on L hand side. Open: 1 March - 31 October. ★★★★ 日 ⚡ ♪ 🚗 🐕 🛒 🍴 ♿ 6🔌 6⚡ ⛺ 11⛺

## John O'Groats

**John O'Groats Caravan Site, John O'Groats, Highland KW1 4YR.** 01955 611329. www.johnogroatscampsite.co.uk. 90 pitches in total. Magnificent cliff scenery 1.5m. Seal colony 4m. Harbour Hotel & snack bar within 200yd. Phone 100yd. PO, grocery store 600yd. Day trips by passenger ferry to Orkney. Owner supplied copy. At end of A99 on sea front overlooking Orkney Islands. Open: 1 April - 30 September. ★★★ 日 ♿ 🚗 🍴 ♿ 🐕 ⚡ 90⚡ ⛺

(2m). **Stroma View Camping Park, Stroma View, Huna, John O'Groats, Highland KW1 4YL.** 01955 611313. www.stromaview.co.uk. Free electrically heated showers. Craft shop. H&C water. Razor points. Play area. Owner supplied copy. On A836 John O'Groats to Thurso. Open: 1 March - 31 October. 日 ⚡ ♪ 🚗 🛒 🐕 ♿ 15🔌 15⚡ ⛺ 2⛺

## Kinlochleven

(3m). **Caolasnacon Caravan And Camping Park, Kinlochleven, Highland PH50 4RJ.** 01855 831279. www.kinlochlevencaravans.com. Lochside location - free sea loch fishing; golf course 4m. Shops, PO, doctor 3m. Off A82. On to B863 at Glencoe. Open: 1 April - 27 October. ★★★ BH&HPA 日 ⚡ 🐕 ♪ 🚗 ♿ 🛒 🍴 50🔌 50⚡ 50⛺ 18⛺

## Kyle of Lochalsh

(8m). **Ardelve Caravan Site, Ardelve, Dornie, Kyle of Lochalsh, Highland IV40 8DY.** 01599 555231. www.ardelvecaravanandcampingpark.co.uk. A short walk from the famous Eilean Donan Castle and the village of Domie where you will find a shop, PO, hotel and PH. Ideal location for touring: Skye Lochalsh, Outer Hebrides and Wester Ross. On A87. Invergarry to Kyle of Lochalsh. 1m beyond Eilean Donau Castle. Open: 22 April - 31 October. 日 ⚡ 🐕 ♪ ♿ 10⚡ 10⚡ ⛺ 2⛺

(3.5m). **Reraig Caravan Site, Balmacara, Kyle of Lochalsh, Highland IV40 8DH.** 01599 566215. www.reraig.com. No bookings. En route to Isle of Skye, bridge 4m. Not suitable for motorcaravans longer than 7.5m/25ft. Owner supplied copy. On A87, 1.75m W of junction with A890, by Balmacara Hotel. Open: 1 May - 1 October. ★★★★ 日 🐕 ♪ ⚡ 🍴 ♿ 40⚡

(16m). **Shielbridge Campsite, Shiel Bridge, Glenshiel, Kyle of Lochalsh, Highland IV40 8HW.** 01599 511221. www.shielbridgecaravanpark.co.uk. Cafe and PO on site. (PO open 8 hours week only). Fishing: sea and sea lochs, rivers and inland lochs - subject to permit. Open all year for tents. Owner supplied copy. On A87. Open: 17 March - 10 October. 日 ⚡ 🐕 ♪ 🚗 🍴 ♿ 🛒 ♿ 15⚡ ⛺

## Laide

**Gruinard Bay Caravan Park, Laide, Laide, Highland IV22 2ND.** 01445 731225. www.gruinard.scotshost.co.uk. Unspoilt, beachside park on beautiful bay with magnificent views to mountains and islands. Inverness to Ullapool road A835, at Braemore Junction, take A832 to Laide (29m). Gairloch 12m. Unspoilt, beachside park on beautiful bay with magnificent views to mountains and islands. Open: 1 April - 31 October. ★★★ BH&HPA 日 ⚡ 🐕 ♪ 🚗 ♿ 🛒 🍴 ♿ 18⚡ 17⛺ 15⛺

## Lairg

**Dunroamin Caravan Park, Main Street, Lairg, Highland IV27 4AR.** 01549 402447. www.lairgcaravanpark.co.uk. Perfect centre for exploring Highlands, fishing, hill walking and water sports. Licensed restaurant and laundry on site. Pay phone. PO, banks, shops and pubs 200yds. South side of A839 in village of Lairg, 300yd from Loch Shin. Open: 1 April - 31 October. ★★★★ BH&HPA 日 ⚡ 🐕 ♪ 🚗 ♿ 🍴 🛒 ♿ 10⚡ 10⚡ ⛺ 9⛺

(25m). **Grummore Caravan Club Site, Altnaharra, Lairg, Highland IV27 4UE.** 01549411226. www.caravanclub.co.uk. This site is perfect for those wanting to get away from it all, the nearest shops are 20m away! Own sanitation required. Fishing, water sports and NCN route nearby. Good area for walking. Quiet and peaceful off-peak. Members only. No tents. See website for standard directions to site. 2.75m from Altnaharra. Open: 5 April - 1 October. NCC 日 ⚡ 🐕 ♪ 🛒 ⚡ 24🔌 24⚡

CARAVAN & HOLIDAY PARKS 2012 165

# SCOTLAND

**(5m). Woodend Caravan & Camping Site**, Woodend, Achnairn, Lairg, Highland IV27 4DN. 01549 402248. AA 3 pennants. Laundrette. Calor Gas. Campers kitchen. Gold award for quality and service from International Caravanning & Camping Guide. Shops, PO, doctor within 5m. Golf course 14m. Owner supplied copy. A836 from Lairg on to A838 SP. Open: 22 April - 31 October. 3 ★ ★ ★ ★ ★ 53 ★ ★

### Lochinver

**(7m). Clachtoll Beach Campsite**, Clachtoll, Lochinver, Highland IV27 4JD. 01571 855377. www.clachtollbeachcampsite.co.uk. Breathtaking scenery. Owner supplied copy. Off A837 0.5m before Lochinver on to B869 site about 6m. 100yd from beautiful sandy beach. Open: 1 April - 29 September. ★ ★ ★ ★ 50 ★ ★

### Melvich

**(16m). Halladale Inn Caravan Site**, Halladale Inn, Melvich, Highland KW14 7YJ. 01641 531216. www.halladaleinn.co.uk. Small quiet site, next door to Halladale Inn. Beautiful scenery and sandy beach. Ideal for surfers, walking, bird watching. PO and shop about 1m. Golf course 6m. 16m W of Thurso along A836. Open: 1 April - 31 October. ★★★★ BH&HPA ★ ★ ★ ★ ★ ★ 6 ★ ★

### Nairn

**Nairn Camping & Caravanning Club Site**, Delnies Wood, Nairn, Highland IV12 5NX. 01667 455281 . www.campingandcaravanningclub.co.uk. Situated in wooded setting, 2m from the beach and close to the town of Nairn. 75 pitches set in 14 acres. Non-members welcome. Caravans, motorcaravans and tents accepted. Fort George, Loch Ness and Cawdor are all worth a visit. Dolphins often seen in waters of Firth. Special deals available for families and backpackers. Off the main A96 Inverness to Aberdeen road, 2m W of the town of Nairn. Look out for 'Delnies Wood' SP. 13m from Inverness. Open: 1 April - 31 October. ★★★★ NCC ★ ★ ★ ★ ★ ★ ★ 75 ★ 75 ★ ★ 6 ★

**(0.5m). Nairn Lochloy Holiday Park**, East Beach, Nairn, Highland IV12 5DE. 01667 453764. www.parkdeanholidays.co.uk. Set between a pretty marina and the dunes of Nairn East beach. Indoor heated pool, adventure play and amusements. Kids' club and crazy golf. Restaurant, bar and live family entertainment. David Bellamy Silver Conservation Award. A1 to Edinburgh, then A9 to Inverness, A96 to Nairn. Open: 23 March - 6 November. ★★★★ BH&HPA NCC ★ ★ ★ ★ ★ ★ ★ ★ ★ ★ ★ ★ ★ 10 ★ 10 ★ ★ 337 ★

### Newtonmore

**Spey Bridge Caravan Site**, Perth Road, Newtonmore, Highland PH20 1BB. 01540 673275. Family run site on the River Spey, S of Newtonmore, a thriving little Highland town. Level with 30 pitches. Take A9 north from Perth turn on to B9150 Newtonmore Road and continue for 0.5m, site on the right after crossing Spey Bridge. Open: 27 March - 31 October. ★ ★ ★ ★ ★ ★ ★ ★ 30 ★ ★

### Onich

**(8m). Bunree Caravan Club Site**, Onich, Highland PH33 6SE. 01855 821283. www.caravanclub.co.uk. On safe, sandy beach. Quiet and peaceful off peak. Laundry room, drying room. Play area and play frame. Toilet block with privacy cubicles. Baby and toddler washroom. Motorhome waste point. Non-members welcome. Advance booking advised BH and June-August. Recreation room. Information room. Boat launch site. Fishing from site, PH/restaurant within walking distance. Good for walking. Ideal for families. No tents. See website for standard directions to site. Open: 23 March - 7 January. ★★★★★ NCC ★ ★ ★ ★ ★ ★ ★ ★ ★ ★ 99 ★ 99 ★

### Shiel Bridge

**(13m). Morvich Caravan Club Site**, Inverinate, Shiel Bridge, Highland IV40 8HQ. 01599 511354. www.caravanclub.co.uk. Morvich is an ideal family holiday base. Tent campers and non-members welcome. Advance booking essential BH and June-August. Toilet blocks. Privacy cubicles. Laundry facilities. Baby washroom. Veg prep. MV service point. Games room. Info room. Public transport available. Good area for walking. Part hardstandings, steel awning pegs required, dog walk nearby. Quiet and peaceful off peak. Beach within 5m. See website for standard directions to site. 3m Shielbridge. Open: 23 March - 5 November. ★★★★★ NCC ★ ★ ★ ★ ★ ★ ★ ★ 106 ★ 106 ★

### Spean Bridge

**(2m). Gairlochy Holiday Park**, Old Station, Gairlochy Road, Spean Bridge, Highland PH34 4EQ. 01397 712711. www.theghp.co.uk. Play area. Public telephone. Laundrette. Great Glen walk 0.25m away at Caledonian Canal. Free fishing on Loch Lochy. Owner supplied copy. Off A82 on to B8004, at Commando Memorial, 1m N of Spean Bridge, site 1m on L and SP. Open: 23 April - 31 October. ★★★★ BH&HPA ★ ★ ★ ★ ★ ★ ★ 25 ★ ★ 10 ★

### Strathcarron

**Applecross Campsite**, Applecross, Strathcarron, Highland IV54 8ND. 01520 744268. www.applecross.uk.com. The local shop and PO is 1m, the local hotel is a 5mins walk. The Walled Garden restaurant is about 1m away. Also 5mins walk from the sea and centred in the middle of Applecross. 8m N of Lochcarron on A896, turn L onto Applecross Road. (Bealoch-na-Ba). Applecross 11m, road not suitable for caravans. Caravans proceed on A896 for 7m, turn L, SP Applecross, 24m. Open: 1 March - 30 November. ★★★ BH&HPA ★ ★ ★ ★ ★ ★ ★ ★ ★ ★ 60 ★ ★ 8 ★

### Strathpeffer

**(2m). Riverside Chalets Caravan Park (Contin)**, Contin, Strathpeffer, Highland IV14 9ES. 07765 633482. www.riverside-contin.co.uk. Tranquil, unspoilt riverside site with mini market. Garage, golf, fishing, forest walks all available locally within 2m. Close to Dingwall, Inverness and well situated for touring the West Coast. On A835 junction of Ullapool to Strathpeffer to Maryburgh in Contin village. Open: 1 March - 31 October. ★★ BH&HPA ★ ★ ★ ★ ★ ★ 15 ★ 15 ★ ★ 8 ★

### Sutherland

**(0.5m). Dornoch Caravan and Camping Park**, The Links, Dornoch, Sutherland, Highland IV25 3LX. 01862 810423. www.dornochcaravans.co.uk. Adjacent to beach & world famous golf course. Town centre 5mins walk. A9, 6m N of Tain. Turn R on to A949 E for 2m, entry via River Street. Open: 1 April - 24 October. ★★★★ BH&HPA ★ ★ ★ ★ ★ ★ ★ ★ ★ 125 ★ ★ 22 ★

**Sango Sands Oasis**, Durness, Sutherland, Highland IV27 4PZ. 01971 511262. www.sangosands.com. Cafe and restaurant, lounge bar. Gift shop. No advance bookings except for electric hook-ups. Golf course 1m. Shops, PO, doctor within 400yds. Overlooking safe, sandy beach. Adjacent A838 overlooking Sango Bay. Open: 1 April - 31 October. ★ ★ ★ ★ ★ ★ ★ ★ ★ ★ ★ 82 ★ ★ 3 ★

**Scourie Caravan and Camping Park**, Scourie, Lairg, Sutherland, Highland

# SCOTLAND

IV27 4TE. *01971 502060*. Holiday site. Hill walking. Handa Island bird watching. No bookings taken. Fees on application SAE. Near Scourie village. Overlooking Scourie Bay. At junction of Harbour Road and A894. 20m S of Cape Wrath. Open: 10 April - 30 September. ★★★ ♀ 🖼 🖼 🏕 ⚓ ⚙ ⛺ 🍴 ✕ 🏪 ⚓ ⛽ 30🚐 🏕

### Tain

(2m). **Dornoch Firth Caravan & Camping Park, Meikle Ferry South, Tain, Highland IV19 1JX.** *01862 892292*. www.dornochfirth.co.uk. Beautiful scenic location, ideal for touring Highlands. Bar/restaurant adjacent to park. New caravan holiday homes for sale. Owner supplied copy. A9 N from Inverness, past Tain to Meikle Ferry roundabout, A836: Dornoch Firth scenic route, 1st R Meikle Ferry South. Open: All year. ★★★★ BH&HPA 🖼 🏕 🐕 ⚙ 🔥 ✳ ⛽ 🍴 🏪 ⚓ 20🚐 20🔌 🏕 36🏕

### Thurso

(30m). **Craigdhu Caravan Site, Dunveaden House, Bettyhill, Thurso, Highland KW14 7SP.** *01641 521273*. Shop, restaurant, hotel and laundry nearby. Picturesque scenery with golden beaches, popular with botanists and geologists also bird watching. Near new swimming pool. Fishing, PO and fuel pumps available nearby. Owner supplied copy. On A836 Tongue to Thurso. Open: 1 April - 30 September. 🖼 🏕 🐕 ⚙ 🔥 ✳ ⛽ 30🚐 30🔌 🏕 30🏕

**Dunnet Bay Caravan Club Site, Dunnet, Thurso, Highland KW14 8XD.** *01847 821319*. www.caravanclub.co.uk. A good site for those who like to be solitary; you can look out to Dunnet Head, the northernmost point of mainland Britain. Toilet block, laundry facilities and motorhome service point. Fishing and water sports within 5m, ideal for families. Non-members and tent campers welcome. See website for standard directions to site. Open: 5 April - 1 October. ★★★★★ NCC 🖼 🏕 🐕 ⚙ 🔥 ✳ ⛽ 🍴 ⚓ 57🚐 57🔌 🏕

(0.5m). **Thurso Caravan and Camping Site, Smith Terrace, Scrabster Road, Thurso, Highland KW14 7JY.** *01847 894631*. Overlooking Thurso Bay to Orkney Islands from the 4.5 acre grassed park with many facilities including, cafeteria. Area renowned for surfing and sea angling etc. Owner supplied copy. On A882 Thurso to Scrabster road, within the town boundary. Open: 1 May - 30 September. ★★★ 🖼 🏕 🐕 ⚙ 🔥 ✕ 🏪 ⚓ ⛽ 105🚐 105🔌 🏕 10🏕

### Ullapool

(3m). **Ardmair Point Caravan Site, Ardmair, Ullapool, Highland IV26 2TN.** *01854 612054*. www.ardmair.com. Small site situated in beautiful location with panoramic views over the sea. Boat centre on site. Off A835, 3m N of Ullapool. Open: 1 May - 1 October. ★★★★ BH&HPA 🖼 🏕 🐕 ⚙ 🔥 ✳ ⛽ 🏪 ⚓ 45🚐 45🔌 🏕 1🏕 ⛺

**Broomfield Holiday Park, Shore Street, Ullapool, Highland IV26 2UT.** *01854 612020*. www.broomfieldhp.com. Supermarket 5mins. Restaurants, bars, cafes, museum, leisure centre, etc. all within 5mins walk from site. Turn 1st R after harbour then 1st L. Open: 6 April - 30 September. ★★★ 3 BH&HPA 🖼 🏕 🐕 ⚙ 🔥 ✳ ⛽ 🏪 ⚓ 140🚐 🏕

### Wick

(0.5m). **The Wick Caravan & Camping Site, Riverside Drive, Janetstown, Wick, Highland KW1 5SP.** *01955 605420*. www.wickcaravansite.co.uk. Tent campers welcome. Veg prep. Motorhome service point. Information room. Golf, fishing and water sports nearby. Laundry facilities, gas, dog walk nearby. Quiet and peaceful off peak, beach within 3m, good area for walking. Owner supplied copy. Off A882 into Riverside Drive in 0.5m. River Wick running beside site. Open: 22 April - 15 October. ★★★★ 🖼 🏕 🐕 ⚙ 🔥 ✳ ⛽ 🏪 ⚓ 15🚐 50🔌 25🏕

## INVERNESS-SHIRE
### Beauly

(1m). **Lovat Bridge Caravan and Camping Site, Lovat Bridge, Dunballoch Farm, Beauly, Inverness-shire IV4 7AY.** *01463 782374*. Set in the old Caledonian Forest next to the river Beauly. Woodland site. Park is undergoing major redevelopment to include new facilities and the addition of park homes for retired/semi retired living. Owner supplied copy. On A832 Inverness to Beauly. Open: 15 March - 15 October. 🖼 🏕 🐕 ⚙ ✕ 🏪 ⚓ 40🚐 40🔌 🏕

### Inverness

(3m). **Bunchrew Caravan Park, Bunchrew, Inverness, Inverness-shire IV3 8TD.** *01463 237802*. www.bunchrew-caravanpark.co.uk. Bunchrew Caravan Park is in a beautiful, quiet setting on the southern shore of the Beauly Firth. Situated in 20 acres of parkland. 14 thistle award caravans for hire (all sleep 6), licensed shop, children's play area, 125 grassy pitches and 50 electric hook-ups. Dogs welcome but not all breeds allowed. Internet access. 3m from Inverness on A862 Beauly road. Open: 15 March - 30 November. ★★★ 🖼 🏕 🐕 ⚙ 🔥 ✳ ⛽ 🏪 ⚓ 125🚐 🏕 14🏕

### Newtonmore

(3m). **Invernahavon Caravan Site, Glentruim, Newtonmore, Inverness-shire PH20 1BE.** *01540 673534*. CARAVAN CLUB AFFILIATED SITE. Level site close to river Truim. Surrounded by woods and mountains. Non members and tent campers welcome. Ideal family site. Good area for walking. 2 golf courses within 8m, pets welcome. Fishing permits for sale from site office. Mountain bike track 8m. Owner supplied copy. Off A9, S of Newtonmore 10m N of Dalwhinnie. Open: 20 March - 31 October. ★★★★ 🖼 🏕 🐕 ⚙ 🔥 ✳ ⛽ 🏪 ⚓ 25🚐 50🔌 🏕

### Roy Bridge

(0.3m). **Bunroy Park, Roy Bridge, Inverness-shire PH31 4AG.** *01397 712332*. www.bunroycamping.co.uk. Peaceful site surrounded by woodland on the banks of the River Spean. Two hotels/restaurants, shop and PO within a few minutes walk. Ideally positioned for touring, walking and outdoor activities. A82 from Fort William, on A86 Spean Bridge then 3m to Roy Bridge. At Stronlossit Hotel, turn R past school, follow signs for 350yd to end of road. 12m from Fort William. Open: 1 April - 31 October. ★★★ BH&HPA 🖼 🏕 🐕 ⚙ 🔥 ✳ ⛽ 🏪 ⚓ 19🚐 35🏕

## ISLE OF SKYE
### Glenbrittle

**Glenbrittle Camp Site, Glenbrittle, Isle of Skye IV47 8TA.** *01478 640404*. www.dunvegancastle.com. Safe swimming from sandy beach. Ideal for the outdoor activity lover and fans of wilderness camping. The centre for the Cuillins. Leave A850 at Sligachan and take A863 W for 5m. B8009 2.5m to Merkadale. Turn S on to road for 8m to site. Open: 1 April - 30 September. 🖼 🏕 🐕 ⚙ 🏪 ⚓ 8🚐 8🔌 🏕

### Portree

**Skye Camping & Caravanning Club Site, Loch Greshornish, Borve, Arnisort, Edinbane, Portree, Isle of Skye IV51 9PS.** *01470 582230*. www.campingandcaravanningclub.co.uk. Set on the shore of Loch Greshornish. Two camping pods are available. Book direct with site. Fresh fish available on site once a week. From A87 on to A850 Edinbane. Head to Flashader, signposted, site on L. Open: 1 April - 31 October. ★★★★ NCC 🖼 🏕 🐕 ⚙ 🔥 ✳ ⛽ 🏪 ⚓ 105🚐 105🔌 🏕

# SCOTLAND

Staffin Caravan Site, Staffin, Portree, Isle of Skye IV51 9JX. 01470 562213. www.staffincampsite.co.uk. Excellent fishing and hill walking available locally. Quiet location overlooking Western Isles. Restaurant and shops in village 0.25m from site. Owner supplied copy. Off A855 Portree to Staffin on south side of village. 16m from Portree. Open: 6 April - 30 September. ★★★ 🏠🏕🐕🚗🚿♿ 20🚐 🏕 🏠

(1m). Torvaig Caravan & Camping Site, Portree, Isle of Skye IV51 9HU. 01478 611849. www.portreecampsite.co.uk. Ideal for touring all parts of the island. Owner supplied copy. On A855 Staffin road on outskirts of village of Portree. Open: 2 April - 22 October. ★★★ 🏠 🍴🐕🏠🚿♿ 30🚐 30🚐 🏕

### Uig

(16m). Uig Bay Caravan & Camping Site, 10 Idrigill, Uig, Isle of Skye IV51 9XU. 01470 542714. www.uig-camping-skye.co.uk. Fishing from bottom of campsite, pub 100yds away. Fuel station, PO, doctors all close by. Walks. Beautiful place to mull away the time. Owner supplied copy. From Portree follow A87 to Uig, past PO on L, carry on for 1m passing Caledonian MacBrayne on the R. Campsite is 200yd away. Open: All year. ★★★ 🏠🏕🐕 🍴🏠🚿♿ 20🚐 20🚐 🏕

## LANARKSHIRE
### Abington

■ (0.25m). Mount View Caravan Park, Abington, Lanarkshire ML12 6RW. 01864 502808. www.mountviewcaravanpark.co.uk. Quiet site set in beautiful scenery. Ideal central location for visiting Glasgow, Edinburgh, Carlisle, Peebles, Ayr, Moffat. Good for overnight stops, weekends or holidays. Village shop, hotel and petrol station. Fishing and golf nearby. M74, J13 and take A702 S into Abington Village. Follow signs down Station Road. Park is on R. Open: 15 March - 31 October. ★★★★ BH&HPA 🏠🏕🐕🍴🏠🚗🚿 ♿ 50🚐 50🚐 5🏕 3🚐

### Glasgow

(0.5m). Craigendmuir Park, Lomond Place, Craigendmuir Park, Stepps, Glasgow, Lanarkshire G33 6AP. 0141 7794159. www.craigendmuir.co.uk. Ideally located for those wanting to explore the length and breadth of Scotland. Golf course 1.5m. Cinema, shopping centre 3m. From J11 M8 to Glasgow and from A80 follow signs for Stepps. From R at Cardowan Road, 2nd R to Clayhouse Road to roundabout, turn L, park on roundabout. Situated on the outskirts of Glasgow (6m). Only 10mins from one of Glasgow's newest shopping centres - the Fort. Open: All year. ★★★ BH&HPA NCC 🏠🏕🐕🍴🏠❄🚗🚿♿ 🏠♿ 30🚐 🏕 21🚐

### Lanark

(1m). Clyde Valley Caravan Park, Kirkfield Bank Bridge, Lanark, Lanarkshire ML11 9JW. 01555 663951. Off A73. Open: 1 April - 31 October. 🏠🍴 🐕🏠🚿 50🚐 🏕 50🚐

## MORAY
### Aberlour

 (1m). Aberlour Gardens Caravan Park, Aberlour-on-Spey, Aberlour, Moray AB38 9LD. 01340 871586. www.aberlourgardens.co.uk. Quiet sheltered site close to River Spey and Speyside Way on the Malt Whisky Trail. Shop, laundry and dishwashing facilities. Disabled/family room comprising shower, toilet, sink, baby changing table. Pets welcome. Small children's play area. Seasonal pitches available. David Bellamy Gold Conservation Award. Midway between Aberlour and Craigellachie off A95. Vehicles over 10'6" high use A941. Open: 1 March - 28 December. ★★★★★ BH&HPA 🏠🏕🐕🍴🏠🚗🚿♿ ♿ 35🚐 🏕 31🚐

(5m). Speyside Camping & Caravanning Club Site, Archiestown, Aberlour, Moray AB38 9SL. 01340 810414. www.campingandcaravanningclub.co.uk. Walk along the Speyside Way or visit one of the many seaside villages. Salmon and whiskey are the specialities of this area. All units accepted. Non-members welcome. Situated in 7 acres. The surrounding area has historic castles, National Trust properties and gardens to visit. Special deals available for families and backpackers. On A941 from Elgin towards Craigellachie, turn R on to B9102 for about 3m to site. Open: 1 April - 31 October. ★★★★ NCC 🏠🏕🐕🍴🏠🚗🚿♿ 75🚐 75🚐 🏕

### Buckie

Findochty Caravan Park, Jubilee Terrace, Findochty, Buckie, Moray AB56 4QA. 01542 835303. www.findochtycaravanpark.co.uk. Village pub/restaurant by entrance to park. Shops 200yd. Lawn bowling/golf/harbour/beaches adjacent to park. Owner supplied copy. From Buckie 3m E on A942 on west edge of the village by the harbour. Open: 1 March - 31 October. 🏠🏕🐕🍴 🏠♿ 25🚐 🏕 19🚐

(1.5m). Strathlene Caravan Park, Strathlene, Portessie, Buckie, Moray AB56 1SR. 01224 696679. Private caravan site situated by sea on Eastern outskirts of Buckie. Owner supplied copy. E of town centre on A942. Open: 1 April - 31 October. 🏠🏕🐕🍴🏠🚗🚿 26🚐 🏕 🚐

### Burghead

(0.25m). Burghead Beach Caravan Park, Station Road, Burghead, Moray IV30 5RP. 01343 830084. www.lossiemouthcaravans.co.uk/burghead.asp. Adjacent to beautiful sandy beach and close to local facilities and shops. North west of Elgin on the B9012. Open: 15 February - 15 January. BH&HPA 🏠🐕🏕 🍴🏠🚗🚿♿ 26🚐 🏕

### Cullen

(0.25m). Cullen Bay Holiday Park, Logie Drive, Cullen, Moray AB56 4TW. 01542 840766. www.cullenbayholidaypark.co.uk. Located on the NE coastal trail, overlooking Cullen Bay and the beautiful Moray coastline, this family run park with good amenities is just a 10mins walk to town. From the south, follow the motorway network to Perth. Then choose between the Deeside Tourist Route (A93) or the dual carriageway trunk route (A90). Open: 18 April - 31 October. ★★★★ BH&HPA 🏠🏕🐕🍴🏠🚗🚿♿ 11🚐 11🚐 3🚐

### Elgin

(5m). North Alves Caravan Park, Alves, Elgin, Moray IV30 8XD. 01343 850223. North Alves is a very well kept park with acres of grassland, 1m from beach. Several golf courses nearby. Off A96. Turn N to site at Alves village by the school. Forres 6m, Elgin 6m. Open: 1 April - 31 October. 🏠🏕🐕🍴🏠❄🚗🚿♿ 🏠♿ 40🚐 40🚐 🏕 20🚐

(0.5m). Riverside Caravan Park (Elgin), West Road, Elgin, Moray IV30 8UN. 01343 542813. www.riverside-caravan-park.co.uk. Statics plus 39 touring pitches with hook-up available. Hardstandings or river pitches. Ideal for visiting Elgin and surrounding area. On A96 Aberdeen to Inverness road on western outskirts of Elgin. Open: 1 April - 31 October. ★★★★ 🏠🏕🐕🍴🏠🚗🚿♿ ♿ 38🚐 🏕 31🚐

(7m). Station Caravan Park, West Beach, Hopeman, Elgin, Moray IV30 5RU. 01343 830880. www.stationcaravanpark.co.uk. Laundrette and pay phone. 5 golf courses within 10 mins driving distance. Shops & doctor's surgery in village, sea and river fishing nearby. Castle & whisky trails close by. Glorious views over Moray Firth. Pubs and takeaway food in

# SCOTLAND

village. On NE coast 7m from Elgin, 10m from Forres follow coast road from Elgin. Open: 1 April - 31 October. ★★★★ BH&HPA 占卜♿♨🍴🛒🏪♿ 35🅿 35⛺ 20🏕 83🛏

### Fochabers

(0.5m). Burnside Caravan Park (Fochabers), Keith Road, Fochabers, Moray IV32 7ET. *01343 820511.* 500yds from town. Swimming pool, sauna and spa on site. Ideal touring centre for north east Scotland. On A96. Open: 1 March - 31 October. BH&HPA 占卜♿♨🍴♿ 🏊🎣🍴🛒🛍🏪♿ 36🅿 36⛺ 15🏕 7🛏 2♿

### Forres

(5m). Findhorn Bay Holiday Park, Findhorn, Forres, Moray IV36 3TY. *01309 690203.* www.findhornbayholidaypark.com. Shop, pubs, restaurants, PO 150yd. 3m to golf and doctor. Off A96 at Forres roundabout to Kinloss and north at Findhorn SP at Kinloss junction, turn R at second caravan site sign leading to beach touring site. Open: 22 April - 31 October. ★★★★★ 占卜♿♨🍴♿ 🏊🎣🛍🏪♿ 5⛺ 45🏕

(3.5m). Old Mill Caravan Park (Brodie), Brodie, Forres, Moray IV36 2TD. *01309 641244.* www.theoldmillbrodie.com. Quiet, country site on Grampian/Highland border near the coast. Country Inn adjacent & fishing, golf & historical places nearby. On A96 Forres to Nairn. Open: 1 March - 31 October. ★★★★ 占卜♿♨🍴♿ 🏊🎣🛍🏪 27⛺ 65🏕

### Grantown-on-Spey

(0.5m). Grantown-on-Spey Caravan Park, Grantown-on-Spey, Moray PH26 3JQ. *01479 872474.* www.caravanscotland.com. CARAVAN CLUB AFFILIATED SITE. Set in the heart of the Highlands, quiet and peaceful off peak. Laundry, dishwashing and games room. Three chemical toilet disposal points. Motor car-

avan service point. Fully serviced pitches with Sky TV & Internet. From town centre turn N at Bank of Scotland. Park 0.5m straight forward. Open: 4 January - 21 December. ★★★★★ BH&HPA NCC 占卜♿♨🍴♿ 🏊🎣🛍🏪♿ 60🅿 110⛺ 60🏕

### Lossiemouth

(0.5m). Lossiemouth Bay Caravan Park, East Beach, Lossiemouth, Moray IV31 6NW. *01343 813980.* www.lossiemouth-caravans.co.uk. Adjacent to sandy beach and close to shops and facilities at sunny Lossiemouth. 2 golf courses 1m. Reached from A941. Open: 28 March - 31 October. 占♿♨🍴🛒🏪♿

(1m). Silver Sands Leisure Park, Covesea West Beach, Lossiemouth, Moray IV31 6SP. *01343 813262.* www.silver-sands.co.uk. On the Moray Firth with miles of unspoilt beaches. Ideal location to explore whisky distillers, castle and golf course. Excellent facilities for all the family. On B9040. Lossiemouth to Hopeman road, Elgin 6m. Open: 15 February - 15 January. ★★★★ 占卜♿♨🎵♿🍴🏊🎣🛍🏪♿ 140⛺ 200🏕

## ORKNEY ISLANDS

### Kirkwall

(0.25m). The Pickaquoy Caravan & Camping Park, Muddisdale Road, Kirkwall, Orkney Islands KW15 1LR. *01856 879900.* www.pickaquoy.co.uk. Largest campsite on Orkney, located in leisure complex with cinema. Near town centre. Has 80 pitches (28 electric) and modern shower block. Turn R off A965 when approaching Kirkwall and follow signs. Situated on the Pickaquoy Centre Campus. Open: 1 April - 31 October. ★★★★ 占卜♿♨🍴🛒🏪♿ 50⛺ 30🏕

### Stromness

Point of Ness Camping & Caravan Site, Point of Ness, Stromness, Orkney Islands KW16 3DL. *01856 873535.* Grass site adjacent to shore. Owner supplied copy. Follow signs on leaving ferry. Open: 30 April - 30 September. ★★★ 占♿ 🍴🛒🏪♿ 30⛺ 30🏕

## PERTH & KINROSS

### Auchterarder

(1m). Auchterarder Caravan Park, Nether Coul, Auchterarder, Perth & Kinross PH3 1ET. *01764 663119.* www.prestonpark.co.uk/caravan.htm. Ideal for couples and the active retired in the heart of Perthshire's golfing country. Lots of wildlife observation opportunities and good off-site dog walking facilities. Only 1m from the village of Auchterarder. Self catering chalet available for hire in adjacent, secluded area. Take B8062 (to Dunning). From A824 (between Auchterarder and Aberuthven) 1.5m from A9-Stirling/Perth. Open: All year. 占卜♿♨🍴♿ 🏊🎣🛍🏪♿ 23⛺ 23🏕

### Blairgowrie

(1m). Blairgowrie Holiday Park, Blairgowrie, Perth & Kinross PH10 7AL. *01250 876666.* www.holiday-parks.co.uk. Follow international signs. Friendly, family-run park. Excellent heated facilities. Laundrette. Adventure playground. Pine lodges and caravans for hire and for sale for holidays all year round. Fishing, swimming pool locally. Shops and restaurants within 1m. 6 golf courses within 5m. David Bellamy Gold Conservation Award. Off A93. 1m N of Blairgowrie town centre. Open: All year. ★★★★★ BH&HPA 占卜♿♨🍴♿🏊🎣🛍🏪♿ 5⛺ 20🏕 6🛏

(5m). Corriefodly Holiday Park, Bridge of Cally, Blairgowrie, Perth & Kinross PH10 7JG. *01250 886236.* www.holiday-parks.co.uk. Rural riverside park set in picturesque valley. Bar, function room and games room. Fishing. Caravan holiday homes for hire and for sale. Riverside and

**Mount View Caravan Park, Abington, Biggar, South Lanarkshire ML12 6RW**
Quiet site set in beautiful scenery. Ideal central location for visiting Glasgow, Edinburgh, Carlisle, Peebles, Ayr, Moffat. Good for overnight stops, weekends or holidays. Holiday homes for sale and hire. Tourers, motor homes and tents welcome.
Easy access being just 5 minutes from J13 off M54.
Tel: 01864 502808    www.mountviewcaravanpark.co.uk    info@mountviewcaravanpark.co.uk

# SCOTLAND

hill walking. Cycling, golf and horse riding nearby. 20m from Perth & Dundee. David Bellamy Gold Conservation Award. Follow A93, 6m N of Blairgowrie to Bridge of Cally. Turn L to Pitlochry road, at bridge and PO. Corriefodly is about 150yd on L. Open: 1 March - 31 October. ★★★★★ BH&HPA ♀ ⛺ ⚑ ∥ ⊘ ♨ ⚐ ✕ ⛔ ⛞ ⁂ ⛩ & 10⛺ 20⛺ 3⛺

**(0.8m). Five Roads Caravan Park, By Alyth, Blairgowrie, Perth & Kinross PH11 8NB.** 01828 632255. www.fiveroads-caravan-park.co.uk. Park is a small, friendly family run site, just lying on the outskirts of Alyth. Wi-Fi available. There is an inn adjacent to the park and the local shops are 0.5m away. 3 golf courses, 2 driving ranges within 1m. Local walks, fishing, pony trekking, bird watching and winter sports at Glenshee. PO, doctor, etc all within 0.5m from park. From Blairgowrie take A926. After 4.5m turn L into site at Blackbird Inn. Site lies just outside Alyth, an attractive little country town. Open: All year. ★★★★ BH&HPA ⛺ ⚑ ∥ ⊘ ♨ ⚐ ⛩ ⛞ & ⁂ 6⛺ 20⛺ A 2⛺

**(12m). Nether Craig Caravan Park, Alyth, Blairgowrie, Perth & Kinross PH11 8HN.** 01575 560204. www.nethercraigholidaypark.co.uk. Peaceful, family-run touring park suitable for all country pursuits and near much of historic interest. David Bellamy Gold Conservation Award. At the roundabout S of Alyth, join B954 SP Glenisla, follow caravan signs for 4m. Open: 15 February - 15 January. ★★★★★ BH&HPA ⛺ ⚑ ⊘ ♨ ⚐ ⛩ ⛞ ⁂ 40⛺ A

## Comrie

**(7m). Twenty Shilling Wood Caravan Park, Comrie, Perth & Kinross PH6 2JY.** 01764 670411. 10 mixed pitches in total. Located in a national scenic area. Family run park with spotless facilities all season. Peaceful and secluded. Security gates. Booking essential. Shops, PO, doctor, golf, fishing all within 1m. Calor 'Environmental Award' finalist. David Bellamy Gold Conservation Award. On A85, 0.50m W of Comrie. Open: 18 March - 22 October. BH&HPA ⛺ ⚑ ∥ ⊘ ♨ ⚐ ⛩ ⛞ S & 10⛺ 10⛺

**(1m). West Lodge Caravan Park, Comrie, Perth & Kinross PH6 2LS.** 01764 670354. www.westlodgecaravanpark.co.uk. Quiet, sheltered, family run park with free showers, electricity and good facilities. 10 mins walk from village. Good touring centre. Calor Gas and Camping Gaz for sale. Public telephone. Pre book high season. Static vans for hire. Tents, motorhomes and tourers welcome. Winter storage available. Good area for fishing, golf, walking, bowls. Water sports at Loch Earn. On A85 Crieff to Comrie. 4m W of Crieff, 1m East of Comrie. Open: 1 April - 31 October. ★★★★ BH&HPA ⛺ ⚑ ∥ ⊘ ♨ ⚐ ⛩ ⛞ & 5⛺ 10⛺ A 6⛺

## Crieff

**Braidhaugh Caravan Park, South Bridgend, Crieff, Perth & Kinross PH7 4DH.** 01764 652951. www.braidhaugh.co.uk. ★★★★ ⛺ ⚑ ⊘ ♨ ⚐ ⛩ ⛞ ✿ ⛔ ⛞ ⁂ ⛩ ⛞ ⛺

**(12m). Loch Earn Leisure Park, South Shore Road, St Fillans, Comrie, Crieff, Perth & Kinross PH6 2NL.** 01764 685270. www.loch-earn.com. Bar and restaurant. Marina and water sports. 0.5m to golf course. Long Shoreline to Loch Earn. Owner supplied copy. Turn L before entering St Fillans village (A85) after leaving Comrie. SP South Shore road. Open: 30 March - 29 October. BH&HPA NCC ⛺ ⚑ ∥ ⊘ ♨ ⚐ ⛩ ⛔ ✕ ⛞ ⁂ & 24⛺ 24⛺ 240⛺ 6⛺

## Dunkeld

**(1m). Inver Mill Farm Caravan Park, Inver, Dunkeld, Perth & Kinross PH8 0JR.** 01350 727477. www.visitdunkeld.com/perthshire-caravan-park.htm. Fishing available on site. Golf course 2m away. Shops, PO, doctor, bar, restaurants in Dunkeld 1m away. Owner supplied copy. Turn off A9 on to A822 then immediately R to Inver, follow road for 1m past the static site on the L, cross bridge and take first L to park. Open: 23 March - 28 October. ★★★★ ⛺ ⚑ ⊘ ♨ ⚐ ⛩ ⛞ ⁂ 65⛺ A

**(1m). The Erigmore Estate, Birnam, Dunkeld, Perth & Kinross PH8 0BJ.** 01350 727236. www.erigmore.co.uk. Indoor pool, spa bath, sauna, solarium, games room, restaurant, takeaway, laundrette, lounge bar with family entertainment, and adventure playground. Tennis courts. Golf course 1m. Cinema, shopping centre 12m. Local shop 2mins away. David Bellamy Gold Conservation Award. Owner supplied copy. 12m N of Perth on A9. Open: 1 March - 6 January. ★★★★ BH&HPA NCC ⛺ ⚑ ⛔ ⚐ ⛩ ⛞ ✕ ⛞ & ⁂ 117⛺ ⛺

## Killin

**(1m). Clachan Caravan Club Site, Aberfeldy Road, Killin, Perth & Kinross FK21 8TN.** 01567 820245. www.caravanclub.co.uk. This site is a find, with its several open pitching areas tucked quietly away in woodland ablaze with wild flowers, and with an amazing range of bird life. Own sanitation required. MV service point. Fishing, golf and NCN route nearby. Dog walk on site. Good area for walking. Quiet and peaceful off-peak. Members only. No tents. See website for standard directions to site. Open: 5 April - 29 October. NCC ⛞ ⛺ ∥ ⊘ ♨ ⚐ 45⛺ 45⛺

**(4m). Cruachan Caravan & Camping Park, North Loch, Tay Side, Killin, Perth & Kinross FK21 8TY.** 01567 820302. www.cruachanfarm.co.uk. Quiet, family run park adjacent to farm. Highland cattle. Hill and woodland walks, riding, golf, salmon and trout fishing on Loch Tay. Coffee shop, play area, gas and payphone. Licensed restaurant. Ideal touring centre. Owner supplied copy. On A827 Killin to Aberfeldy. Open: 15 March - 4 November. ★★★★ ⛺ ⚑ ∥ ⊘ ♨ ⚐ ⛩ ✕ ⛞ & 15⛺ 15⛺ A 37⛺

**Glen Dochart Caravan Park, Luib, Crianlarich, Killin, Perth & Kinross FK20 8QT.** 01567 820637. www.glendochart-caravanpark.co.uk. Calor Gas stockist. Tennis, golf and bowling available in nearby Killin (6m). On main A85 between Killin and Crianlarich. Open: 1 March - 30 November. ★★★★ BH&HPA ⛺ ⚑ ∥ ⊘ ♨ ⚐ ⛩ ⛞ ⁂ 45⛺ A 6⛺

**(2.5m). High Creagan Caravan Site, Killin, Perth & Kinross FK21 8TX.** 01567 820449. Ideal for fishing, bird watching or to relax. Small family run site, peaceful, elevated with panoramic view of Loch Tay and surrounding countryside. Within easy reach of the village of Killin and the famous Dochart Falls. Owner supplied copy. On the A827 Aberfeldy to Killin road. Well signposted. Open: 1 March - 31 October. ⛺ ⚑ ∥ ⊘ ♨ ⚐ ⛩ ⛞ 15⛺ 15⛺ A

**(0.25m). Maragowan Caravan Club Site, Aberfeldy Road, Killin, Perth & Kinross FK21 8TN.** 01567 820245. www.caravanclub.co.uk. The site is an ideal family holiday base, set on one bank of the river Lochay, and within walking distance of the shops and restaurants of Killin. Hardstandings. MV waste. Toilet block and laundry. Gas. Veg prep. Playframe. Salmon and trout fishing. Non-members welcome. No tents. Advance booking essential BH and June-August and advised for September. Ideal for families. Privacy cubicles. Dog walk nearby. Quiet and peaceful off peak. Good area for walking, golf and NCN cycle route within 5m, water sports nearby. See website for standard directions to site. Open: 23 March - 5 November. ★★★★ BH&HPA ⛺ ⚑ ∥ ⊘ ♨ ⚐ ⛩ ⛞ & 100⛺ 100⛺

# SCOTLAND

### Kinloch Rannoch

(3.75m). **Kilvrecht Campsite, Loch Rannoch, Kinloch Rannoch, Perth & Kinross PH17 2QU.** *01350 727284.* www.forestry.gov.uk. Woodland setting. Fishing nearby. Woodland walks. Food shop, gas, bar/pub, restaurant 3m. Owner supplied copy. Off B846 3.5m W of Kinloch Rannoch on south bank of Loch Rannoch. Open: 2 April - 21 October. 60

### Lochearnhead

(12m). **Balquhidder Braes Caravan & Camping Park, Balquhidder Station, Lochearnhead, Perth & Kinross FK19 8NX.** *01567 830293.* www.balquhidderbraes.co.uk. Beautiful scenery. Excellent restaurant beside site. Families welcome. Within first National Park in Scotland. Ideal base. Adjacent to route 7 cycleway and Rob Roy Way. Fishing & water sports 1m David Bellamy Silver Conservation Award. Owner-occupied caravans. 1.5 from Lochearnhead take A84 Stirling road, on left-hand side from Strathyre towards Lochearnhead 2m. Open: 1 March - 31 October. ★★★★ 10 35 17

### Perth

(10m). **Beech Hedge Caravan Park, Cargill, Perth, Perth & Kinross PH2 6DU.** *01250 883249.* www.beech-hedge-caravan-park.co.uk. Small, quiet site with wonderful views. Owner supplied copy. On A93 Perth to Blairgowrie. 10m N of Perth. Open: 1 January - 30 November. 26

**Scone Palace Camping & Caravanning Club Site, Scone Palace Caravan Park, Perth, Perth & Kinross PH2 6BB.** *01738 552323* . www.campingandcaravanningclub.co.uk. Ideally situated for touring Perthshire and central Scotland. All units accepted. Non-members welcome. Trout and salmon fishing is available from the nearby river Tay. There is beautiful countryside surrounding the site. Special deals available for families and backpackers. David Bellamy Gold Conservation Award. Follow signs for Scone Palace. Once through Perth continue for 2m and follow signs for racecourse. Site is at R of racecourse car park. Open: 1 March - 5 January. ★★★★ NCC 150 150 19

### Pitlochry

**Blair Castle Caravan Park, Blair Atholl, Pitlochry, Perth & Kinross PH18 5SR.** *01796 481263.* www.blaircastlecaravanpark.co.uk. Experience the freedom of 9 acres of green open space and a relaxed family-friendly atmosphere situated adjacent to the grounds of Blair Castle and surrounded by the spectacular mountain scenery of Highland Perthshire. Within 2hrs drive of Edinburgh, Glasgow, Aberdeen or Inverness, via A9. Open: 28 February - 28 November. ★★★★★ BH&HPA 27 248 20

(2m). **Faskally Caravan Park, Faskally Home Farm, Pitlochry, Perth & Kinross PH16 5LD.** *01796 472007.* www.faskally.co.uk. Bar and restaurant. Indoor heated leisure pool. Sauna, steam room and spa bath. On A9 (B8019 Killiecrankie) Perth to Inverness. Open: 15 March - 31 October. ★★★★ BH&HPA 215 40

(0.5m). **Milton of Fonab Caravan Site, Pitlochry, Perth & Kinross PH16 5NA.** *01796 472882.* www.fonab.co.uk. Fees on application. 5mins walk to Pitlochry festival theatre. 1m to 18 holes golf course. Fantastic scenery and fishing on doorstep. Off A9 0.5m S of Pitlochry, on the banks of river Tummel. Open: 29 March - 17 October. ★★★★ BH&HPA 20 200 36

**The River Tilt Park, Golf Course Road, Blair Atholl, Pitlochry, Perth & Kinross PH18 5TE.** *01796 481457.* www.river-tiltpark.co.uk. Take B8079 off A9, SP to Blair Atholl. On banks of river Tilt, next to golf course and 100yds from town and Blair Castle. Re-furbished heated shower block. Free showers. Calor Gas and Camping Gaz. Calor Best Park Scotland. New indoor heated pool. Sauna. Solarium. Steam room, gym and spa pool. Restaurant. GS. Open: 28 March - 9 November. ★★★★★ BH&HPA 31 35 65 42

(13m). **Tummel Valley Holiday Park, Tummel Bridge, Pitlochry, Perth & Kinross PH16 5SA.** *01882 634221.* www.parkdeanholidays.co.uk. Indoor pool and toddlers' splash pool, solarium and sauna. Kids' clubs and adventure play area, multi-sports court and amusements. Bar, food, and live family entertainment. David Bellamy Gold Conservation Award. A9 to Pitlochry B8019 to Tummel Bridge. Open: 23 March - 2 November. ★★★★ BH&HPA NCC 40 64

## RENFREWSHIRE
### Gourock

(2.5m). **Cloch Caravans Holiday Park, Cloch Road, Gourock, Renfrewshire PA19 1BA.** *01475 632675.* www.clochcaravans.com. On A770 Largs to Gourock. Entrance on L. Ferry 0.5m. Station 2m. Doctor, PO 2.5m. Fishing, golf, swimming pool nearby. Bus service at park entrance. Laundry facilities available. Licensed restaurant, bar, children's play park. Luxury caravans for hire and sale. Golf, shops, swimming pool 2m. Cinema 6m. Beautiful views, plentiful wildlife. David Bellamy Silver Conservation Award. Owner supplied copy. On A770 Largs to Gourock. Entrance on L. Open: 1 April - 30 November. BH&HPA NCC 185

### Wemyss Bay

(6m). **Wemyss Bay Holiday Home Park, Wemyss Bay, Renfrewshire PA18 6BA.** *01475 522589.* www.parkdean.com. Heated indoor pool, kids clubs and family entertainment. Mini market. Laundrette. Only 7m from the pretty seaside town of Largs. David Bellamy Gold Conservation Award. Owner supplied copy. From Glasgow follow M8 to Greenock. Take A78 to Wemyss Bay. Open: 19 March - 31 October. ★★★★ BH&HPA NCC 700

## SCOTTISH BORDERS
### Cockburnspath

(1m). **Chesterfield Country Retreat, The Neuk, Cockburnspath, Scottish Borders TD13 5YH.** *01368 830433.* www.chesterfieldcountryretreat.co.uk. Peaceful park set in breathtaking countryside of the Lammermuir hills. Historical towns of Cockburnspath & Dunbar just short walk away. From bypass follow the signs to Abbey St Bathans. Park approximately 0.5m on left from junction. Open: 1 March - 31 January. ★★★★ BH&HPA 10 33 70

(2m). **Pease Bay Leisure Park, Cockburnspath, Scottish Borders TD13 5YP.** *01368 830206.* www.peasebay.co.uk. Surfing, fishing, shops and doctors 10mins, PO 5mins. 3 top golf courses within a 15m radius. We are in the Clean Beach guide one of the cleanest beaches in Scotland. 5mins away from the A1 Scotland's major route on the East coast of England. Scottish wildlife reserve adjacent of caravan park. Owner supplied copy. 1.5m off A1 at Cockburnspath roundabout. 22m from Berwick on Tweed and 35m S of Edinburgh. 20mins to Berwick. 10mins to Dunbar. Open: 5 March - 22 January. ★★★★ BH&HPA 320

### Duns

(6m). Greenlaw (Blackadder) Caravan

# SCOTLAND

Park, Bank Street, Blackadder Touring Park, Greenlaw, Duns, Scottish Borders TD10 6XX. *01361 884075*. www.greenlawcaravanpark.co.uk. Riverside park with free fishing. Licensed bowling club. Shops nearby. Laundrette on site. New children's play area with swings. Owner supplied copy. 10m N of Coldstream and 37m S of Edinburgh on A697. SP in Greenlaw village at junction of A697 and A6105. Open: 22 April - 30 September. ★★★★ BH&HPA 150

### Eyemouth

(0.5m). Eyemouth Holiday Park, Fort Road, Eyemouth, Scottish Borders TD14 5BE. *01890 751050*. www.park-resorts-touring.com. New all weather sports court in 2008. Family bar, lounge, laundrette, amusements, outdoor play area. 18 hole golf course 1m, trout fishing 2.5m. David Bellamy Gold Conservation Award. From A1, follow signs to Eyemouth on A1107. On entering town, turn R after the petrol station and L at the bottom of the hill into Font Road. Open: 21 March - 31 October. ★★★★ BH&HPA NCC 22

(2m). Scoutscroft Holiday Centre, St Abbs Road, Coldingham, Eyemouth, Scottish Borders TD14 5NB. *01890 771338*. www.scoutscroft.co.uk. Holiday home rentals & sales. Few minutes walk from the beach, close to the fishing village of St Abbs. Bar, restaurant & games room. Turn off A1 on to A1107 head for St Abbs, site SP. Open: 1 March - 7 November. ★★★★ BH&HPA 2 70 132

### Hawick

(2m). Riverside Caravan Park (Hawick), Hornshole Bridge, Hawick, Scottish Borders TD9 8SY. *01450 373785*. www.riversidehawick.co.uk. Set on the banks of the river Teviot with free fishing. 8 acres including woods, quiet, family run site. Half price golf on our own nearby golf course (9 hole). Owner supplied copy. From A696 from Newcastle to Scottish Borders, A6088 to Hawick, from Carlisle A7 N to Hawick. Open: Contact site direct. ★★★★ BH&HPA 40 57

### Jedburgh

(1m). Jedburgh Camping & Caravanning Club Site, Elliot Park, Jedburgh, Scottish Borders TD8 6EF. *01835 863393*. www.campingandcaravanningclub.co.uk. Close to outskirts of Jedburgh historic town on direct route to Scotland. All units accepted. Some all-weather pitches available. Non-members welcome. There is a picturesque walk by the riverside to the town of Jedburgh 1m away. There is a good leisure centre in the town, as well as golf and fly fishing. Special deals available for families and backpackers. Off the A68 N of the town; SP. Directly opposite the Edinburgh and Jedburgh Woollen Mills. Open: 1 April - 31 October. ★★★★ NCC 60 60

(5m). Lilliardsedge Holiday Park, Jedburgh, Scottish Borders TD8 6TZ. *01835 830271*. www.lilliardsedgepark.co.uk. 9 hole golf course. Bar/food and entertainment. Redeveloped new super pitches in 2010 for tourers/motorhomes. New holiday home pitches. All amenities available in Jedburgh (5m). On A68, between Ancrum and St Boswells. Open: 1 March - 31 October. ★★★ BH&HPA 40 40 218

### Kelso

(1m). Springwood Caravan Park, Springwood Estate, Kelso, Scottish Borders TD5 8LS. *01573 224596*. www.springwood.biz. On site: play area, table tennis. Nearby: golf, swimming, pony trekking, tennis. Ideal for walking. David Bellamy Gold Conservation Award. On A699. Open: 27 March - 12 October. ★★★★ BH&HPA 10 20 200

### Lauder

(4m). Lauder Camping & Caravanning Club Site, Carfraemill, Oxton, Lauder, Scottish Borders TD2 6RA. *01578 750697*. www.campingandcaravanningclub.co.uk. 24m S of Edinburgh, close to Thirlestane Castle and a good fishing area. 4 self-catering timber chalets available to let. Non-members welcome. All units accepted. The site is set in a valley in the heart of the Scottish Borders complete with its own river. Special deals available for families and backpackers. From the town of Lauder, turn R at roundabout on to A697 then L at Lodge Hotel. Site on R behind Carfraemill Hotel. Open: 1 April - 31 October. ★★★★ NCC 60 60

(1m). Thirlestane Castle Caravan and Camping Park, Lauder, Scottish Borders TD2 6RU. *07976 231032*. www.thirlestanecastlepark.co.uk. Secluded site with glorious views across wooded countryside and near the river. Adjacent to the touring park, holiday homes (statics) area is being developed. SP just off A68 and A697 28m S of Edinburgh. Just outside Royal Burgh of Lauder which has excellent shops and pubs. 30m S of Edinburgh. Open: 1 April - 3 October. ★★★★ BH&HPA NCC 60 20

### Melrose

(1m). Gibson Park Caravan Club Site, High Street, Melrose, Scottish Borders TD6 9RY. *01896 822969*. www.caravanclub.co.uk. This is a level and peaceful site in the edge of Melrose, overlooked by the three hills. Non-members welcome. Shops adjacent. MV service pt. Toilet block with laundry facilities. Tent campers welcome. Fishing and golf within 5m. Good area for walking, some hardstanding, gas, dog walk, ideal for families, quiet and peaceful off peak. NCN cycle path within 5m. See website for standard directions to site. Open: All year. ★★★★★ NCC 60 60

### Newcastleton

Lidalia Caravan Park (Affiliated Caravan Club Site), Old Station Road, Moss Road, Newcastleton, Scottish Borders TD9 0RU. *01387 375819*. www.lidalia.co.uk. CARAVAN CLUB AFFILIATED CLUB - MEMBERS ONLY. This small site is very attractively landscaped in an interesting village within easy reach of the shops. Toilet blocks and laundry facilities. Dog walk nearby. Fishing and golf nearby. Good area for walking. Facilities for disabled. Quiet and peaceful off-peak. See website for standard directions to site. Open: All year. NCC 30

### Peebles

(0.5m). Crossburn Caravan Park, Edinburgh Road, Peebles, Scottish Borders EH45 8ED. *01721 720501*. www.crossburncaravans.co.uk. This site has 50 pitches (8 fully-serviced), a children's play area, a shop & new shower block - 45 minute drive from Edinburgh. On A703. Laundry. Full on-site facilities. Games room. Play area. Open: 1 April - 26 October. ★★★★ BH&HPA NCC 40 40 5

Rosetta Caravan & Camping Park, Rosetta Road, Peebles, Scottish Borders EH45 8PG. *01721 720770*. www.rosetta-caravanpark.co.uk. Set in picturesque town of Peebles. 47 acres of grounds surrounding a Georgian mansion. Plenty to do in the area & many walks. Well SP from Peebles. Open: 19 March - 31 October.

# SCOTLAND

## SELKIRKSHIRE
### Ettrick Valley

(19m). Angecroft Park, Ettrick Valley, Selkirkshire TD7 5HY. 01750 62355. www.angecroftpark.com. High class holiday park which offers peace & tranquillity. Excellent facilities and touring pitches. On B709 4m S of Tushielaw Inn, 26m E from M6 or A74. Leave dual carriageway at Lockerbie. Open: 26 February - 31 October. ★★★ BH&HPA NCC 40

## SHETLAND ISLANDS
### Lerwick

(1.5m). Clickimin Caravan & Camp Site, Clickimin Leisure Complex, Lochside, Lerwick, Shetland Islands ZE1 0PJ. 01595 741000. www.srt.org.uk. Recently refurbished site on outskirts of Lerwick. Excellent location for touring islands. Site is situated next to modern leisure complex with swimming pool, leisure waters, main hall, bowls hall and squash courts. Dogs must be kept on leads at all times on site. Owner supplied copy. From ferry terminal follow signs to Lerwick town centre, then at first roundabout follow signs to Clickimin Leisure complex. Open: 1 May - 30 September. ★★★★★ 5 20 20

## STIRLINGSHIRE
### Aberfoyle

 (3m). Trossachs Holiday Park, Aberfoyle, Stirlingshire FK8 3SA. 01877 382614. www.trossachsholiday.co.uk. 40 acre landscaped park with glorious oak and bluebell wood. Shop, games/TV lounge, play area, enclosed dog walk, all caravan pitches on hard standing, serviced and fully serviced available. Static Holiday Homes for hire. Nearby fishing 1m, golf 1m. David Bellamy Gold Conservation Award. S of Aberfoyle on A81. Open: 1 March - 31 October. ★★★★★ BH&HPA 40 45 10

### Blair Drummond

Blair Drummond Caravan Club Site, Cuthill Brae, Blair Drummond, Stirlingshire FK9 4UP. 01786 841208. www.blairdrummondcaravanpark.co.uk. CARAVAN CLUB AFFILIATED SITE - MEMBERS ONLY. A delightful and very attractive site, set in and around a walled garden, sheltered with mature trees and bright flowering shrubs. Laundry, vegetable preparation area. Playframe. Toilet block with privacy cubicles. Motorhome waste. Gas and Gaz. Dog walk nearby. Ideal for families. Quiet and peaceful off peak. NCN cycle route within 5m. Advance booking advisable at all times. Part hardstandings. Steel awning pegs required. Local attractions include Blair Drummond Safari park and Trossachs. Off A84, follow international caravan signs. 5m from Stirling. Open: 19 March - 3 January. ★★★★ NCC 88

### Callander

(1m). Gart Caravan Park, Stirling Road, Callander, Stirlingshire FK17 8LE. 01877 330002. www.callander-holiday-park.co.uk. Spacious park with level grass pitches. Outstanding shower & toilet facilities. Free fishing & children's play area. Touring caravans & private holiday homes. Golf course, swimming pool, pony trekking, sailing all nearby. Situated off the A84 on the left hand side, 1m from Callander. Open: 1 April - 15 October. ★★★★★ BH&HPA 128

(1m). Keltie Bridge Caravan Park, Callander, Stirlingshire FK17 8LQ. 01877 330606. 50 mixed pitches in total. Quiet riverside location, close to Callander in the scenic Trossachs area. Top quality shower block. Golf, sports centre 1m. On A84 between Doune and Callander. Open: 1 April - 31 October. ★★★★ BH&HPA 50 50 50

### Gartmore

(1.5m). Cobleland Forest Holidays, Station Road, Gartmore, Stirlingshire FK8 3RR. 01877 382392. www.forestholidays.co.uk. Set on the banks of the River Forth amidst majestic old trees, Cobleland sits in the heart of the Trossachs. Bookings and brochures: 0834 1308224. David Bellamy Gold Conservation Award. Off A81 Glasgow to Aberfoyle. Open: 1 April - 31 October. BH&HPA 126

### Rowardennan

(3m). Cashel Forest Holidays Site, Rowardennan, Stirlingshire G63 0AW. 01360 870234. www.forestholidays.co.uk. On the shores of Loch Lomond, Cashel is ideal for boating and walking. The West Highland Way passes the site entrance. No generators on site. Bookings and brochure requests on 0845 1308224. Off B837 Drymen-Rowardennan road 3m N of Balmaha. Open: 1 March - 31 October. ★★★★ BH&HPA 168

### Stirling

(3m). Witches Craig Caravan And Camping Park, Blairlogie, Stirling, Stirlingshire FK9 5PX. 01786 474947. www.witchescraig.co.uk. Graded excellent, Best Park in Scotland finalist. National Loo of the Year awards. Peacefully situated below picturesque Ochil Hills, ideal place to unwind but also a great base for travelling. Superb modern facilities. Also children's play park. Milk, newspapers and rolls sold daily. David Bellamy Gold Conservation Award. On A91, 3m E of Stirling. Open: 1 April - 31 October. ★★★★★ BH&HPA 60 60

### Strathyre

Immervoulin Caravan & Camping Park, Strathyre, Stirlingshire FK18 8NJ. 01877 384285. www.immervoulin-caravan-camping-park.co.uk. Situated in area of picturesque beauty alongside the river Balvaig. Within 300yd to village, PO and 3 pubs. Cycle hire on site. Fishing in river and Loch Lubnaig. Water sports centre in Lochearnhead. 9m N of Callander with easy and clearly marked access from the A84. Open: 1 March - 31 October. ★★★ 56

### Thornhill

(0.25m). Mains Farm Wigwams, Kippen Road, Thornhill, Stirlingshire FK8 3QR. 01786 850735. www.mainsfarmwigwams.com. Five acres with scenic views, ideal touring centre for Stirling, Loch Lomond and Trossachs. Children's play area. Shops, PO, doctor within 0.25m. Golf, tennis, swimming pool, cinema, shopping centre, all within 5-7m. 12 heated wooden wigwams for hire, avail-

# SCOTLAND / WALES

able all year. From M9 J10 take A84 for 6m. Then A873 for 3m. In Thornhill village L on to B822, site on R. Open: 1 April - 31 October. 🚐🐕🏇🚶🎣⛵🚿🚻♿ ⛽2⛺🏠

## WEST LOTHIAN
### East Calder

**(3m). Linwater Caravan Park,** West Clifton, East Calder, West Lothian EH53 0HT. 01313 333326. www.linwater.co.uk. A quiet country park - Ideal for Highland Showground, Edinburgh or call in on your journey N or S. David Bellamy Gold Conservation Award. 10m W of Edinburgh. Take B7030 from Newbridge J1 of M9 - and follow signs. Open: 16 March - 5 November. ★★★★ BH&HPA 🚐🏇 🚶🎣⛵🚿🚻♿🚗 60⛺ 60⛺ △

### Linlithgow

**(3m). Beecraigs Caravan & Camping Site,** Beecraigs Country Park, The Park Centre, Linlithgow, West Lothian EH49 6PL. 01506 844516. www.beecraigs. com. Set within Beecraigs Country Park, with miles of woodland walks, outdoor pursuit activities, fly-fishing, restaurant and visitor centre. Local shops available in Linlithgow. Excellent base for exploring Central Scotland. M9, J3 or J4, follow tourist signs for Beecraigs Country Park from Linlithgow. Open: All year. ★★★★ NCC 🚐🐕🏇🚶🎣⛵🚿❋✕🚗 🚻♿ 18⛺ 18⛺ △

**(1m). Loch House Farm Caravan Park,** Loch House Farm, Linlithgow, West Lothian EH49 7RG. 01506 842144. www.lochhousefarmcaravanpark.co.uk. Shops, doctor, restaurants within 1m or 10mins walk to High Street and train station. Regular service to Glasgow and Edinburgh. Owner supplied copy. From Linlithgow take A706 towards Bo'ness, take first left after motorway bridge. Open: All year. 🚐🐕🏇🚶🎣⛵🚿🚻🚗♿ 16⛺ 16⛺ △

## ANGLESEY
### Amlwch

**(1.5m). Point Lynas Caravan Park,** Llaneilian, Amlwch, Anglesey LL68 9LT. 01407 831130. www.pointlynas. com. Quiet park overlooking the sea by Point Lynas, access to coastal path, fishing, walking, swimming. Modern facilities block with launderette, showers etc. Shops, PO, bank, doctor 1.5m. Golf course 3m. From Anglesey Mowers on A5025, 1.5m in seaward direction, 200yd from Porth Eilian cove. Open: 30 April - 30 September. BH&HPA 🏇🚶🎣⛵ 🚗🚻♿ 12⛺ △ 51⛺

**(1m). Waen Farm Caravan Park,** Llanfechell, Anglesey, Amlwch, Anglesey LL68 0RG. 01407 711561. www.waenfarm.co.uk. Quiet farmland family run site with the picturesque seaside village of Cemaes Bay nearby. Fully equipped caravans for hire including bed linen. 8m down A5025 from Valley crossroads. 2m to Cemaes Bay. Open: 1 March - 31 October. ★★★★ BH&HPA 🚐🐕 🏇🚗⛺ 14⛺

### Beaumaris

**(1.5m). Kingsbridge Caravan and Camping Park,** Llanfaes, Beaumaris, Anglesey LL58 8LR. 01248 490636. www.kingsbridgecaravanpark.co.uk. A quiet, family, 4 star park in a rural location, close to beaches, golf, fishing, walking. 2 underfloor heated shower blocks. 1.5m from picturesque town of Beaumaris. David Bellamy Gold Conservation Award. Drive through Beaumaris, past castle, turn third L after 1.5m at first crossroads. Open: 1 March - 31 October. ★★★★ BH&HPA 🚐🐕🏇🚶🎣⛵🚗🚻♿ 4⛺ 48⛺ △ 29⛺

### Benllech

**(1.5m). Ad Astra Caravan Park,** Brynteg, Benllech, Anglesey LL78 7JH. 01248 853183. www.adastracaravanpark.co.uk. Small, quiet, rural park in open countryside. First class facilities. 10mins walk to pub/restaurant. 0.5m to golf course. 1.5m to shops and all services. Sea and coarse fishing 1.5m. Benllech 1.5m, from Benllech take B5108 to California Hotel, turn L park 0.25m on R. Open: 1 March - 31 October. ★★★★★ BH&HPA 🚐🐕🏇🚶🎣⛵🚿♿ 🚗🚻♿ 12⛺ 23⛺ 20△ 1⛺

**(0.5m). Bodafon Caravan Park,** Benllech, Anglesey LL74 8RU. 01248 852417. www.bodafonpark.co.uk. Within 0.5m of the village, 1m from the beach, convenient for the local area. Part of a group comprising of three parks. Through the village of Benllech on A5025 0.5m on L. Big yellow house. Open: 1 March - 31 October. ★★★ BH&HPA 🚐🐕🏇🚶🎣 🚗🚻♿ 4⛺ 10⛺ 16△ 2⛺

**Golden Sunset Camping and Touring Bay,** Golden Sunset Holidays, Benllech, Anglesey LL74 8SW. 01248 852345. www.goldensunsetholidays.com. Centre of village for shops, PO, doctors, tennis courts, bowls, golf. Elevated cliff side, well drained site with superb views over the bay and mountains beyond. Site entrance at Benllech Bay off A5025 from Bangor towards Amlwch. At the crossroads in Benllech. Turn R and the park is immediately on the L. Open: 1 April - 30 September. 🚐🐕🏇🚶🎣⛵🚿✕🚗 🚻♿ 50⛺ 40⛺ △ 7⛺

**Nant Newydd Caravan Park,** Brynteg, Benllech, Anglesey LL78 7JH. 01248 852842. www.nantnewydd.co.uk. Hardstanding with hook-up point, mains water and waste disposal. Quiet countryside 3m from coast. Dogs allowed. Fees on application. 3m SW. B5108 off A5025 at crossroads. At crossroads after 2m turn L. Site is 1m on R. Open: 1 April - 31 October. ★★★★ 🚐🐕🏇🚶🎣⛵ 🚿🚗✕🚻♿🚗⛽△

**(2m). Penparc Caravan Site,** Lon Las, Brynteg, Benllech, Anglesey LL78 7JG. 01248 852500. www.penparc.com. Fishing and golf course nearby. Owner supplied copy. On junction B5110 and B5108, Isle of Anglesey. Open: All year. ★🏇🎣❋🚿🚻🚗 26⛺ △ 22⛺

**(2m). Penrhos Caravan Club Site,** Brynteg, Benllech, Anglesey LL78 7JH. 01248 852617. www.caravanclub. co.uk. 5mins drive to safe, sandy beach. Close to a farm trail, bird sanctuary and sea zoo. Non-members welcome. No tents. Golf course within 5m. Play area & play equipment. Some hardstandings, part sloping. Baby and toddler washroom. MV service point, veg prep area. Dog walk nearby. Water sports, good walking, NCN cycle route all nearby. Ideal for families. Quiet and peaceful off peak. See website for standard directions to site. Open: 30 March - 8 October. ★★★★★ NCC 🚐🐕🏇 🚶🎣⛵🚿🚻♿ 90⛺ 90⛺

**(0.5m). Plas Uchaf Caravan & Camping Park,** Benllech, Anglesey LL74 8NU. 01407 763012. Well sheltered and level park within 1m of beach. Disabled friendly. Hot showers, hairdryers, and dishwashing facilities. Freezers. Play area. Patio seating and tables. Dog walk. Tarmacadam roads with street lights. Tradesmen call. Top 100 Award Park. Situated off A5025 SP on B5108. 0.5m from Benllech, SP by fire station. Open: 1 March - 31 October. 🚐🐕🏇 🚶🎣⛵🚿🚗🚻♿ 80⛺ 80⛺ △ 75⛺

### Brynsiencyn

**(0.5m). Fron Caravan and Camping Park,** Brynsiencyn, Anglesey LL61 6TX. 01248 430310. www.froncaravanpark. co.uk. Laundry room. Public telephone. Gas. Hot showers. Heated outdoor swimming pool with dome cover. Adventure playground. On A4080. 6.5m SW of Menai Bridge. Cross Britannia Bridge then first slip road marked Llanfairpwllgwyn, then L on to A4080 to Brynsiencyn. Site is 0.5m beyond village on right hand side. Open: 1 April - 30 September. ★★★★★ 🚐🐕🏇 🚶🎣⛵🚿🚻♿ 10⛺ 39⛺ △

# WALES

## Dulas

**(1m). Capel Elen Caravan Park, Lligwy Bay, Dulas, Anglesey LL70 9PQ.** *01248 410670.* www.capelelen.com. Fishing, coastal path, golf courses nearby. Shops, etc within 3m. On A5025 to village of Brynrefail, turn off opposite craft shop, park is 300yd on L. 2m from Moelfre. Open: 1 March - 31 October. BH&HPA

**(4m). Melin Rhos Caravan and Camping Park, Dulas, Anglesey LL70 9HQ.** *01248 852417.* www.bodafonpark.gbr.cc/. Close to lovely beach and good walks. 2m from nearest village. Golf course 5m. Medium size town 13m. David Bellamy Bronze Conservation Award. Off A5025 Bangor to Amlwch. Turn L at Moelfre roundabout, down hill, first R. Site is at bottom of hill, before bridge. 5m from Benllech. 2m from Moelfre. Open: 1 March - 31 October. ★★ BH&HPA

**(6m). Minffordd, Penrhoslligwy, Lligwy, Dulas, Anglesey LL70 9HJ.** *01248 410555.* www.minffordd-holidays.com. Beautiful garden park near the safe, sandy beach of Lligwy with parking alongside each caravan. Local facilities include golf, sailing, fishing, riding and sports centres. Dogs on leads by arrangement. Modern recent caravans and some caravans equipped for physically disabled guests. Winner 'Wales in Bloom' 2002-2007. Separate field for tourers. 9 hole golf course 3m, 18 hole golf course 7m. 14m to Bangor. Owner supplied copy. Off A5025 Benllech Bay to Amlwch. Lligwy 1m. Moelfre 2m. 5m from Amlwch. Open: All year. ★★★★★ BH&HPA 15

**(5m). Tyddyn Isaf Caravan and Camping Park, Lligwy Bay, Dulas, Anglesey LL70 9PQ.** *01248 410203.* www.tyddynisaf.co.uk. Private path to beach. 'Loo of the Year' winner for superb facilities. Voted Top 100 parks in Britain by Practical Caravan 2010 (16th position). David Bellamy Gold Conservation Award. Off A5025 through Benllech up to Brynrefail village, turn R at phone box towards Lligwy beach. Open: 1 April - 26 September. ★★★★★ BH&HPA NCC 40

## Gaerwen

**(0.25m). Mornest Caravan Park, Pentre Berw, Gaerwen, Anglesey LL60 6HU.** *01248 421725.* www.mornestcaravanpark.co.uk. Dairy produce delivered daily. Local shops within 500yd. Winter storage arranged on site. Pub and restaurant on site. Laundry facilities. J7 off A55, follow signs for caravan park, 1m through village of Gaerwen. Open: 1 March - 31 October. ★★★ BH&HPA 5 45 15

## Holyhead

**(6m). Bodowyr Caravan Park, Bodedern, Holyhead, Anglesey LL65 3SS.** *01407 741171.* www.bodowyrcaravanpark.co.uk. Family run touring site in rural countryside. Well located for beaches and ferries to Ireland. Excellent facilities and new licensed restaurant with home cooking. Advance booking advisable. Take the A55 towards Holyhead, turn off J4 direction Bodedern. Follow international camping signs, park on L after 0.5m. Open: 1 March - 31 October. ★★★ 30 30

**Gwyn Fair Caravan Park, Ravenspoint Road, Holyhead, Anglesey LL65 2AX.** *01407 860289.*

**(3m). The Lee Caravan Park, Trearddur Bay, Ravenspoint, Holyhead, Anglesey LL65 2AX.** *01407 860485.* www.theleecaravanpark.com . Slipway. Owner supplied copy. Off A5. Open: 1 March - 31 October. 165

**Tyn Rhos Camping Site, Ravenspoint Road, Trearddur Bay, Holyhead, Anglesey LL65 2BQ.** *01407 860369.* 200 mixed pitches in total. Family run rural site with modern facilities, within minutes of beautiful seaside resort. Coastal walks, bird watching and climbing. Water sports, from fishing to diving, local golf course and horse riding. Ferries to Ireland 3m. Much local history and attractions for all tastes. A55 to J2. Follow signs for Trearddur Bay B4545; about 1.5m onto Ravenspoint Road. (First R after Spar), about 1m to shared entrance, take L branch. Open: 1 March - 31 October. ★★★ 200

**(1m). Valley of the Rocks Caravan & Camping Park, Porthdafarch Road, Trearddur Bay, Holyhead, Anglesey LL65 2LL.** *01407 765787.* Touring/camping site is wild and natural, surrounded by lochs, trees. 1.5m to shops, doctors, PO. Licensed club next door. 10 mins walk/2 mins by car to the beach. Fishing, golf and water sports nearby. Follow A55 across Anglesey to where the road terminates at the roundabout. Take first L at roundabout then take immediate first R between two public houses (The Foresters and The Angel). Follow road for about 1m until you see the signpost for Valley of the Rocks caravan park. Turn L into site then fork R. Reception is on the L at site shop. Open: 1 March - 31 October. 14 11 48

## Llanbedrgoch

**(1m). Ty Newydd Caravan Park, Llanbedrgoch, Anglesey LL76 8TZ.** *01248 450677.* www.tynewydd.com. Club. Swimming pool. Restaurant. Golf course 0.5m. Fishing 1m. Off A5025 Isle of Anglesey. Pass through Pentraeth Village turn L after first lay by, park 1m on R. Open: 1 March - 31 October. ★★★★ BH&HPA 45 4

## Llanfwrog

**(9m). Penrhyn Bay Caravan Park, Llanfwrog, Anglesey LL65 4YG.** *01407 730496 .* www.penrhynbay.com. Coastal park near a sandy beach. Electricity, water and grey waste. Indoor heated swimming pool. Tennis court. Showers. Laundrette. Play area. PO 3m, golf 8m. A55 to Anglesey, Exit 3. A5025 through Llanfachraeth then 1st L, SP Penrhyn. Through farm to caravan park. Open: 13 March - 31 October. ★★★★ BH&HPA 10 100 80

## Lligwy

**(2m). Ty'n Rhos Caravan Park, Lligwy, Anglesey LL72 8NL.** *01248 852417.* www.bodafonpark.co.uk. Within 0.5m of sandy beach. Washing machine and dryer available. Good walks nearby. AA 3 pennants. Park conveniently located for visiting attractions all over Anglesey and travelling to Ireland. A5025 to Moelfre roundabout. R towards Moelfre. L at first T junction with bus stop. Proceed for 2m, site is on R. 50yd after lane leading to Lligwy Beach. Open: 1 March - 31 October. BH&HPA 4 42 70

## Marianglas

**Cae Mawr Caravan Club Site, Llangefni Road, Marianglas, Anglesey LL73 8NY.** *01248 853737.* www.caravanclub.co.uk. Sea fishing and boating. Safe, sandy beaches. Non-members welcome. No tents. Golf course within 5m. Chemical toilet disposal point. No toilet block. MV waste point, gas, dog walk. See website for standard directions to site. 2m from Benllech. Open: 30 March - 1 October. ★★★★ NCC 76 76

**(2m). Home Farm Touring & Holiday Park, Marianglas, Anglesey LL73 8PH.** *01248 410614.* www.homefarm-anglesey.co.uk. Has 107 pitches (67 hardstandings) on 5-star rated site. Two toilet blocks, tennis courts, indoor & outdoor children's play areas. From M6 take M56

# WALES

for North Wales, then A55 to Britannia Bridge. Take A5025 SP 'Benllech'. Approx 2m beyond Benllech keep L at roundabout. Entrance on L, 300yds beyond church. Open: 25 March - 31 October. ★★★★★ BH&HPA ... 54 102 22A 13

### Newborough

(0.5m). **Awelfryn Caravan Park, Newborough, Anglesey LL61 6SG.** 01248 440230. www.awelfryn.co.uk. Near Llanddwyn Isle and Newborough Warren (noted beauty spots). Fees on application. SAE. On A4080 about 10m SW of Menai Bridge and 20m from Holyhead. Open: 1 March - 31 October. ... 12 A

### Pentraeth

(2m). **Clai Mawr Caravan Park, Park Lodge, Pentraeth, Anglesey LL75 8DX.** 01248 450467. www.claimawr-holidays-anglesey.co.uk. Golf course, nearby and beaches. Pub, good food 10mins walk. Shops, garage, PO 2m. Doctor 3m. Owner supplied copy. Off A5025 Bangor to Amlwch, Isle of Anglesey. Go through Pentraeth to the start of 40mph sign. Clai Mawr on the right hand side after the sign. Open: 1 March - 31 October. ★★★ NCC ... 14 32

(0.75m). **Rhos Caravan Park, Rhos Farm, Pentraeth, Anglesey LL75 8DZ.** 01248 450214. Children's play area. Flat sheltered fields (grass & hedges). 10mins walk to Red Wharf Bay. Golf course nearby 2.5m. AA 3 pennants. Owner supplied copy. On A5025 on the L after Bull Hotel. N of Pentraeth. Open: 1 March - 31 October. 3 BH&HPA ... 10 50 A 68

### Red Wharf Bay

(1.5m). **St David's Park, Benllech, Red Wharf Bay, Anglesey LL75 8RL.** 01248 852341. www.stdavidspark.com. Private beach, boat park and slipway, children's play area. Gastropub 'The Tavern 1924'. Follow A55, after crossing the Britannia Bridge on to the island take the B5025 and follow for 8m follow signs for St David's Park and Red Wharf Bay on your R about 1m after passing through the town of Pentraeth. Open: 12 March - 1 October. ★★★★ BH&HPA NCC ... 95 A 140

### Rhosneigr

(0.5m). **Bodfan Farm, Bodfan, Rhosneigr, Anglesey LL64 5XA.** 01407 810706. www.bodfanfarm.co.uk. Quiet, family site near lake and sea. Electrical hook-ups must be prebooked. Showers, shaving points and dryers. Shops, PO, pub within 0.5m. Golf course, horse riding, tennis court, bowling green, water sports in village. A55 to A4080, next to primary school in Rhosneigr. Open: 6 April - 30 September. ... 25 40 60 A

(0.25m). **Shoreside Camping and Caravan Park, Station Road, Rhosneigr, Anglesey LL64 5QX.** 01407 810279. www.shoresidecamping.co.uk. Children welcome. Local amenities include bowling, tennis, plane spotters RAF valley. Restaurants/bars, shop, takeaway meals & laundry facilities all available nearby. Park established in 1925. Boat launch from park. Caravans available for season hire March/Sept. Ring for details. Storage for caravans and boats. Seasonal pitches touring vans. L off A55 J5 onto the A4080 Rhosneigr road, opposite Anglesey golf club. Open: 15 March - 31 October. ... 20 70 A 64

(0.5m). **Ty Hen, Station Road, Rhosneigr, Anglesey LL64 5QZ.** 01407 810331. www.tyhen.com. Heated swimming pool, coarse fishing, play park, wt/gym, sauna on park. Walks, wildlife, fresh air. Seaside Beach award. Sports, sea and coarse fishing, surfing, sub-aqua, tennis, golf and bowls all local. David Bellamy Gold Conservation Award. Owner supplied copy. A55 across Anglesey. At exit 5 take A4080 to Rhosneigr. Entrance adjacent to railway station, nr low bridge (on A4080). Open: 26 March - 29 October. ★★★ BH&HPA ... 38 A 42

(2m). **Bagnol Caravan Park, Ravenspoint Road, Trearddur Bay, Anglesey LL65 2AX.** 01407 860023. www.caravan-park-anglesey.co.uk. Site personally supervised. Offers 113 hardstanding pitches with modern Alpine-style toilet block. Has food hall with vending machines. Handy for Holyhead ferry. Off A5, B45 to Trearddur Bay, turn L into Ravenspoint Road, park 100yd on L. Open: 1 March - 31 October. BH&HPA ... 30 13 A

### Trearddur Bay

## BRIDGEND
### Porthcawl

(2m). **Trecco Bay Holiday Park, Bay View Road, Porthcawl, Bridgend CF36 5NG.** 0844 3353450. www.parkdean.com. Fun indoor heated pool. Sports and leisure centre. Licensed bars. Family entertainment centre. Bowling. Jungle Jims. Children's clubs, 2mins walk to beach. Dodgems. Adventure golf. Diner. Restaurant. Owner supplied copy. J37 off M4 Bridgend to Port Talbot. 0.5m from Porthcawl. Open: 19 March - 31 October. ★★★★ BH&HPA NCC ... 2441

## CAERPHILLY
### Bargoed

(4m). **Parc Cwm Darran, Deri, Bargoed, Caerphilly CF81 9NR.** 01443 875557. www.caerphilly.gov.uk. Visitor centre, coffee shop. Circular walks, coarse fishing lake. 5m cycle track. Events throughout the year. Shop, PO 1m. H&C water, showers (free), toilets. Owner supplied copy. Between Deri and Fochriw on unclassified road between A469 and A465. Situated in Parc Cwm Darran Country Park. Open: 1 April - 30 September. ... 30

## CARDIFF, SWANSEA & THE VALLEYS
### Cardiff

(0.5m). **Cardiff Caravan Park, Poncanna Fields, Sophia Close, Cardiff, Cardiff, Swansea & The Valleys CF11 9LB.** 02920 398362. www.cardiff.gov.uk. Local shops, PO, doctors, garages all within 200yd. Dogs allowed on leads. 10mins walk to city centre and Millennium Stadium. Approaching from A48 (T) take a turning into Cathedral Road and turn L in to Sophia Close. Passing National Sports Centre continue for 200yd to site. Open: All year. ★★★ ... 70 A

### Glyntawe

(15m). **Dan Yr Ogof Show Caves Campsite, Abercraf, Glyntawe, Cardiff, Swansea & The Valleys SA9 1GJ.** 01639 730284. www.showcaves.co.uk. Bordered by mountain river in Brecon Beacons National Park. Ski slope. Ideal walking area. Warden: A C Price. Dogs on leads at all times. Midway between Brecon and Swansea on the A4067 and within the Brecon Beacons National Park. Open: 1 April - 31 October. ... 40 40 40 A

### Merthyr Tydfil

(4m). **Grawen Caravan and Camping Park, Cwm Taf, Merthyr Tydfil, Cardiff, Swansea & The Valleys CF48 2HS.** 01685 723770. www.walescaravanandcamping.com. Picturesque forest, mountain and reservoir walks close to site in clean fresh air with easy access. Also

# WALES

a wealth of history in the town and valleys. On A470. Brecon Beacons road 2m from A465. Open: 1 March - 31 October. ★★★ BH&HPA NCC 🐕 ⛔ ✗ 🌳 ⛔ 🏪 🚐 ⛺ 🚿 ♿ 10🚐 20🚐 ⛺

### Oxwich

**Greenways Leisure Park**, Oxwich, Cardiff, Swansea & The Valleys SA3 1LY. 01792 390220. www.greenwaysleisure.co.uk. Showers. Laundry. Swimming pool. Bars. Children's adventure playground. Owner supplied copy. On A4118. About 15m from Swansea. Open: 1 April - 30 September. BH&HPA 🐕 ⛔ ⛺ 🚐 ⛺ 🏪 🚿 ♿ 🚐 200⛺ 125🚐 5🏊

**Oxwich Camping Park**, Oxwich, Cardiff, Swansea & The Valleys SA3 1LS. 07926 166096. A quiet, secluded, family park in the heart of the Gower Peninsula, 8m from Killay. Heated swimming pool, hot showers. Village amenities, shop, restaurant, beach in Oxwich village. Owner supplied copy. Take A4118 from Swansea, turn L at Oxwich SP, after 1m turn R, park 0.25m on the R. Open: 22 April - 6 September. ★★★ 🐕 ⛔ 🌳 ✗ 🏪 🚿 ♿ ⛺

### Port Eynon

(14m). **Newpark Holiday Park**, Port Eynon, Cardiff, Swansea & The Valleys SA3 1NP. 01792 390192. www.newparkholidaypark.co.uk. Uninterrupted views over bay. Play area & games room. On A4118. Open: 1 April - 31 October. ★★ BH&HPA 🐕 ⛔ ✗ 🌳 ⛔ 🏪 🚿 ♿ 40🚐 112⛺ ⛺ 14🏊

### Swansea

(15m). **Bank Farm Leisure Park**, Horton, Swansea, Cardiff, Swansea & The Valleys SA3 1LL. 01792 390418. www.bankfarmleisure.co.uk. Superb views overlooking Port Eynon Bay. Showers. Swimming pool. Shop, licensed bar and coffee bar, play area, Calor Gas. Also available 8 bungalows for hire. A4118 for Port Eynon, L turn for Horton 1m after Scurlage, site entrance on R. Open: 1 March - 13 November. ★★★ NCC 🐕 ⛔ ✗ 🌳 ⛔ 🏪 🚿 ♿ 🚐 180🚐 ⛺ 110🏊

**Gowerton Caravan Club Site**, Pont-y-Cob Road, Gowerton, Swansea, Cardiff, Swansea & The Valleys SA4 3QP. 01792 873150. www.caravanclub.co.uk. Easy driving distance of a whole range of superb beaches on the Gower Peninsula. Non-members welcome. No tents. Hardstandings. Toilet blocks. Privacy cubicles. Laundry facilities. Very Prep. MV Service point. Gas. Playframe. Information room. Dog walk. Storage, ideal for families, quiet and peaceful off peak. Good area for walking, NCN cycle route within 5m. See website for standard directions to site. Open: 23 March - 12 November. ★★★★ NCC 🐕 ⛔ ✗ 🌳 ⛔ 🏪 🚿 ♿ 135🚐 135⛺

(0.75m). **Hillend Camping & Caravan Park**, Hillend, Llangennith, Swansea, Cardiff, Swansea & The Valleys SA3 1JD. 01792 386204. www.hillendcamping.com. 🐕 ⛔ ⛺ 🌳 ⛔ ✗ 🏪 🚿 ♿ ⛺ ⛺

(1m). **Pitton Cross Caravan Park**, Rhossili, Swansea, Cardiff, Swansea & The Valleys SA3 1PH. 01792 390593. www.pittoncross.co.uk. Level site 1m from coast. Walking, sea fishing, surfing, bird-watching all nearby. Over 50? from £80 p/w off peak season inc. 4 for 3 offer - Sunday to Thursday, not Bank Holidays. Gower Kite centre and surf hire available. From Swansea - A4118 to Scurlage 16m, turn R, SP Rhossili, we are 2m on L. Open: All year. ★★★ 🐕 ⛔ ⛺ 🌳 ⛔ 🏪 🚿 ♿ ⛺ 🚐 50🚐 50🚐 50⛺

(4m). **Riverside Caravan Park** (Swansea), Ynysforgan Farm, Morriston, Swansea, Cardiff, Swansea & The Valleys SA6 6QL. 01792 775587. www.riverideswansea.com. Showers. Chemical toilet disposal point. Laundry room. Gas supplies. Picnic and barbecue area. Licensed club. Indoor swimming pool on site. Children welcome. Dogs allowed by arrangement (no breeds of dangerous dogs). J45 of M4, direct access to caravan park from roundabout under motorway. Open: All year. ★★★ ♿ ⛺ 🐕 ⛔ 🎵 ⛺ 🌳 ⛔ 🏪 🚿 ♿ 🚐 10🚐 120⛺ ⛺

**Three Cliffs Bay Caravan & Camping Site**, North Hills Farm, Penmaen, Swansea, Cardiff, Swansea & The Valleys SA3 2HB. 01792 371218. www.threecliffsbay.com. Fishing, shop on site (basics), PO 1m, golf course 3m, doctor 5m. A4118 from Swansea (8m). Site SP in village of Penmaen. Open: 1 April - 30 September. ★★★★ 🐕 ⛔ ✗ 🌳 ⛔ 🏪 🚿 ♿ 20⛺ ⛺

## CARMARTHENSHIRE

### Burry Port

(0.5m). **Shoreline Caravan & Chalet Park**, Heol Vaughan, Burry Port, Carmarthenshire SA16 OHD. 01554 832657. www.shorelinecaravanpark.co.uk. Bar. Laundrette. Showers. Playground. Family room. Regular entertainment. Cafe. Beach. Caravans & chalets for sale. Owner supplied copy. Leave A484 for B4311, follow signs to harbour and caravan park. Open: 1 March - 30 November. 🐕 ⛔ ✗ 🚐 15🚐 200⛺

### Carmarthen

(3m). **Afon Lodge Caravan Park**, St Clears, Carmarthen, Carmarthenshire SA33 4LG. 01994 230647. Beautiful, quiet, secluded park in wooded valley with countryside views. Ideal touring centre for West Wales. David Bellamy Gold Conservation Award. From traffic lights in St Clears take road to Llanboidy in 100yd fork R. 1.75m, 1st R, 0.75m 1st R continue for 0.25m. Open: 1 March - 9 January. ★★★ BH&HPA 🐕 ⛔ ✗ 🌳 ⛔ 🏪 🚿 ♿ 25🚐 25⛺ ⛺ 42🏊

(2m). **Antshill Caravan Park**, Laugharne, Carmarthen, Carmarthenshire SA33 4QN. 01994 427293. www.antshill.co.uk. 4-6 berth caravans for hire. Ideal for inland and coastal touring. Historic home town of Dylan Thomas and near the famous sands of Pendine. Clubhouse. Laundry facilities. Outdoor heated swimming pool. Play room & play area. AA 3 pennants. RAC appointed. On A4066 St Clears to Laugharne. Open: 1 March - 31 October. ★★★ 3 BH&HPA 🐕 ⛔ ⛺ 🌳 ✗ 🏪 🚿 ♿ 5🚐 60🚐 ⛺ 60🏊

(10m). **Pendine Sands Holiday Park**, Pendine, Carmarthen, Carmarthenshire SA33 4NZ. 0844 3353450. www.parkdean.com. Heated indoor swimming pool. Daytime and evening entertainment for whole family. Mini market. Bakery. Direct beach access. Kids clubs. Varied food choice available. Pembroke Castle, Caldey Island and a chocolate factory are all close to the park. Tenby is just 20mins drive away. Awarded Holiday Park Fair Trader Award by NCC. David Bellamy Gold Conservation Award. Take A40 Trunk Road from Carmarthen to St Clears. SP Pendine/Pentywyn along the A4066, 8m from A40 junction. Pass through Laugharne and the park reception is 5m further on the right hand side. Open: 1 March - 1 November. ★★★★ BH&HPA NCC 🐕 ⛔ ✗ 🌳 ⛔ 🏪 🚿 ♿ 600🚐

### Clunderwen

(0.5m). **Grondre Vale Holiday Park**, Clunderwen, Carmarthenshire SA66 7HD. 01437 563111. www.valeholidayparks.com. Park facilities: pub, pool, shop, showers, laundrette, games room. Local attractions: Oakwood Theme Park, Tenby, Saundersfoot, Folly Farm. 2m from Narberth. On A478 Cardigan road, just off A40. Open: 1 March - 31 October. DH&HPA 🐕 ⛔ ✗ 🌳 🎵 ⛺ 🏪 🚿 ♿ ✗ 🏪 🚿 ♿ 30🚐 30⛺ ⛺ 4🏊

### Kidwelly

**Carmarthen Bay Holiday Park**, Port Way, Kidwelly, Carmarthenshire SA17

CARAVAN & HOLIDAY PARKS 2012 177

# WALES

5HQ. *0871 6649722.* www.park-resorts.com. Indoor pool, restaurant, takeaway, children's clubs, sports & leisure facilities, crazy golf. Spa bath. Soft play area. Adventure playground. Family entertainment. David Bellamy Gold Conservation Award. M4 leave at J48. Take A4138 to Llanelli and then A484 or B4308 to Kidwelly. Park is SP once you pass Kidwelly. Open: 1 April - 31 October. ★★★ BH&HPA 480

**Tanylan Farm Holidays, Tanylan Farm, Kidwelly, Carmarthenshire SA17 5HJ.** *01267 267306.* www.tanylanfarmholidays.co.uk. Level site, 200yds from beach. Membership to park resorts available. Free hot water in showers. Owner supplied copy. M4-exit 48 to Kidwelly via Llanelli left at Spar supermarket, coast road to Ferryside 2m. Open: 15 March - 30 September. ★★★ 100

## Llandovery

(0.5m). **Erwlon Caravan & Camping Park, Brecon Road, Llandovery, Carmarthenshire SA20 0RD.** *01550 721021* . www.erwlon.co.uk. Set in the beautiful Towy Valley in mid-Wales. An ideal base for touring the beautiful hills and vales of Wales. Luxury amenity block and super pitches. Good access. Within 0.5m of Llandovery at the foothills of the Brecon Beacons. On A40 Brecon to Llandovery. Open: All year. ★★★★ BH&HPA 40 40 40A

(0.5m). **Erwlon Caravan & Camping Park (Premier Park), Brecon Road, Llandovery, Carmarthenshire SA20 0RD.** *01550 721021.* www.erwlon.co.uk. Set in the beautiful Towy Valley in mid-Wales. An ideal base for touring the beautiful hills and vales of Wales. Luxury amenity block and super pitches. Good access. Within 0.5m of Llandovery at the foothills of the Brecon Beacons. On A40 Brecon to Llandovery. Open: All year. ★★★★ 40 40 40A

(7m). **Rhandirmwyn Camping & Caravanning Club Site, Llandovery, Carmarthenshire SA20 0NT.** *01550 760257.* www.campingandcaravanningclub.co.uk. There is some spectacular countryside within easy reach of the site. The red kite, one of Britain's rarest birds, can often be seen flying above the site. There are lots of walks within easy reach of site. Non-members welcome. All units accepted. Special deals available for families and backpackers. From A483 in Llandovery take road SP Rhandirmwyn for 7m, turn L at PO, site is on the L before the river. From Llandovery take A483 at level crossing, turn L in 300yd by fire station signed Rhandirmwyn and continue 7m to village. Turn L at pub/PO, continue down steep hill past church for 0.5m to site on L before river bridge. The site is set in the beautiful Welsh countryside. Open: 1 April - 31 October. ★★★★ NCC 90 90

## Llanelli

**Black Lion Caravan and Camping Park, 78 Black Lion Road, Gorslas, Llanelli, Carmarthenshire SA14 6RU.** *01269 845365.* www.caravansite.com. Close to National Botanic Garden of Wales. Family owned park, peaceful, well maintained and friendly. Some hardstandings. Children's play area. Caravan storage. Shops 0.5m. Camping & Caravanning Club certificated. David Bellamy Gold Conservation Award. Just off A48. Follow brown touring signs from Cross Hands (1m). 4m from Ammanford. Open: 1 April - 30 September. ★★★★ BH&HPA 7 40 A

(6m). **Pembrey Country Park Caravan Club Site, Pembrey, Llanelli, Carmarthenshire SA16 0EJ.** *01554 834369.* www.caravanclub.co.uk. Set in a large country park with adventure playground and miles of sandy beaches. Non-members welcome. No Tents. Advance booking essential bank holidays and school holidays. Motorhome service point. Golf and water sports nearby. Ideal for walking and for families. Some hardstandings, steel awning pegs required. Baby and toddler washroom. Veg prep area. Play equipment, storage pitches, quiet and peaceful off peak, good walking area. NCN cycle route within 5m. See website for standard directions to site. Open: 23 March - 7 January. ★★★★★ NCC 130 130

## Llangadog

(1.5m). **Abermarlais Caravan Park, Llangadog, Carmarthenshire SA19 9NG.** *01550 777868.* www.abermarlaiscaravanpark.co.uk. Offering 88 grassed pitches set near Llandovery, bordered by tall trees and a stream. Shop & children's play area. On northern side of A40, near Llangadog and halfway between Llandovery and Llandeilo. If travelling through Llandovery, ignore sign for Llangadog and take sign for Llandeilo - far easier route. Open: 16 March - 16 November. ★★★★ BH&HPA 60 60

(6m). **Black Mountain Caravan & Camping Park, Llanddeusant, Llangadog, Carmarthenshire SA19 9YG.** *01550 740217.* www.blackmountainholidays.co.uk. Fishing & pony-trekking close by. Part of Brecon Beacons National Park, with unique wildlife. Excellent walking country. Good base for touring mid and south Wales. Cycle hire can be arranged locally. Red kite feeding station close to site (50yd), pub with good food adjacent to site. A40 from Brecon, follow SP Llandovery. At Trecastle turn L directly before pub Castle Coaching Inn (brown tourist sign) follow road for about 9m, turn R before pub Red Pig. Open: All year. ★★ BH&HPA 10 10 A 8

## Llangunnor

(1m). **Pant Farm Touring Caravan & Camping Park, Llangunnor Road, Llangunnor, Carmarthenshire SA31 2HY.** *01267 235665.* Convenient, flat, sheltered location. Tents welcome. Walking distance to station and town. Near Botanical Garden of Wales. Shops, PO, doctor, golf course, fishing all within 1m. Off M4 on B4300 at Carmarthen. Open: All year. 30

## Llanwrda

(10m). **Maesbach Caravan Park, Ffarmers, Llanwrda, Carmarthenshire SA19 8EX.** *01558 650650.* A tranquil family run peaceful retreat in 5 acres with magnificent countryside views. Quiet lanes for walking, cycling, horse riding, bird watching and sightings of Red Kite. Explore West Wales beaches, visit local attractions. Nearby everyday store/garage with Lampeter's shops, supermarkets, leisure facilities 7m away. Tourist information available from the park. 7m from Lampeter. Off A40 at Llanwrda take A482 Lampeter Road after passing Pumsaint, turn R after 1.5m for Ffarmers, follow signs. Open: 1 March - 31 October. 3 16 10

**Springwater Lakes, Harford, Llanwrda, Carmarthenshire SA19 8DT.** *01558 650788.* www.springwaterlakes.com. Quiet, peaceful, very well maintained, garage with convenience shop 500yds. Main shops 4m. No children's play facilities. 4 lakes to fish on site: 1x3acre mixed coarse, 1x3 acre specimen carp, 1 fly only (rainbow & browns), 1 small coarse pool. Fishing tackle shop. 4.5m E of Lampeter on A482. Open: 1 March - 31 October. ★★★★ BH&HPA 30 10A

## Newcastle Emlyn

(2m). **Afon Teifi Caravan & Camping**

# WALES

Park, Pentrecagal, Newcastle Emlyn, Carmarthenshire SA38 9HT. *01559 370532*. www.afonteifi.co.uk. Quiet, riverside site, an ideal touring base for Cardigan Bay. Family run site with playground and games room. Shop, pub and restaurant nearby. 25 hardstandings. All the usual facilities, well-lit and maintained to a high standard. Off A484. Open: 1 April - 31 October. ★★★ 15🚐 90⛺ A

**(3m). Cenarth Falls Holiday Centre, Cenarth, Newcastle Emlyn, Carmarthenshire SA38 9JS.** *01239 710345*. www.cenarth-holipark.co.uk. Luxurious heated indoor pool and health club, bars and restaurant area. Unheated outdoor pool open beginning June till end of August. Excellent caravan holiday homes, 5 cottages for hire and touring facilities. Family run award winning park. Superb beaches. Lovely walks. Golf. Fishing. Shop 1m. On the A484 Newcastle Emlyn to Cardigan road. Open: 1 March - 15 November. ★★★★★ BH&HPA 30🚐 30⛺ A 2

**(1.8m). Dolbryn Camping & Caravanning, Capel Iwan Road, Newcastle Emlyn, Carmarthenshire SA38 9LP.** *01239 710683*. www.dolbryn.co.uk. Peaceful site in sheltered valley. Half hour drive to sea. Licensed bar. Conservation and play area. Fishing on site. Rallies welcome. Shops, pubs, takeaway, leisure centre, restaurant all within 2m. Turn off on A484 in Newcastle Emlyn SP Leisure Centre follow camping signs, first R after garage. Open: 1 March - 27 October. ★★★ 60⛺ A

## CEREDIGION
### Aberaeron

**Aeron Coast Caravan Park, North Road, Aberaeron, Ceredigion SA46 0JF.** *01545 570349*. www.aeroncoast.co.uk. 22-acres of flat, coastal parkland. Club, recreational rooms, heated swimming pool and tennis court. Families only. 500yd from shops and picturesque harbour. Quiet out of high season - good facilities for children in school holidays, including free evening entertainment. On A487 Cardigan to Aberystwyth. Filling station at entrance. Brown SP, northern edge of town. Open: 1 March - 31 October. ★★★★ BH&HPA 100 A 200

**(5.5m). Ffos-Helyg Caravan Park, Cilcennin, Lampeter, Aberaeron, Ceredigion SA48 8RL.** *01570 471124*. www.ffoshelyg.vze.com. Off A482. Open: 1 April - 31 October. BH&HPA 45

**(0.75m). Wide Horizons Caravan & Chalet Park, Aberaeron, Ceredigion SA46 0ET.** *0845 0508176*. www.barker-sleisure.com. 0.25m from sea with panoramic sea views. Club house with lounge bar and family room. Entertainment peak periods. Access to sea. Gas sales. Adjacent to coastal path walks. Owner supplied copy. On A487 S of Aberaeron. 20mins from Aberystwyth. Open: 1 March - 9 January. BH&HPA 95

**(11m). Woodlands Holiday Park R (Aberaeron), Llanon, Aberaeron, Ceredigion SY23 5LX.** *01974 202342*. Level, secluded, tree-lined site with made-up roads. 200yd from sea. GS. David Bellamy Gold Conservation Award. From N A487 through Llanon, R at international caravan sign. Open: 1 March - 31 October. ★★★★ BH&HPA 40🚐 40⛺ A 41

### Aberystwyth

**(0.25m). Aberystwyth Holiday Village, Penparcau Road, Aberystwyth, Ceredigion SY23 1TH.** *01970 624211*. www.aberystwythholidays.co.uk. Near town and beach. Indoor swimming pool. 10 pin bowling centre. Shop, cafe, 2 bars, entertainment. Play area. Fishing, fitness centre. On A487. 0.25m S of town. Open: 1 March - 31 October. 50🚐 200⛺ A 230

**(10m). Aeron View Caravan Park, Blaenpennal, Aberystwyth, Ceredigion SY23 4TW.** *01974 251488*. www.aeron-view.com. Quiet, inland site with panoramic views yet only 15mins from the sea. Ideal for fishing, bird watching and relaxing. 1m off A485 Aberystwyth to Tregaron road, 4m from Tregaron. Open: 1 March - 31 October. 3🚐 3⛺ A 6

**(1.25m). Bryncarnedd Caravan Park, Clarach Road, Aberystwyth, Ceredigion SY23 3DG.** *01970 612444*. www.bryncottages.co.uk. Overnight stops. Dogs on lead only. Theatre nearby. Motorbikes welcome. Holiday cottages and lodges with Jacuzzi also available. NE of Aberystwyth via A487 for 1m then L on to B4572. Site 0.5m. Open: 22 April - 31 October.

**(5m). Brynowen Holiday Park, Brynowen Lane, Borth, Aberystwyth, Ceredigion SY24 5LS.** *01970 871366*. www.park-resorts.com. Heated indoor pool. Licensed entertainment complex. Amusement arcade. Free kids club. Free daytime & evening entertainment for all the family. Diner & takeaway. Playground. AA Holiday Centre. Investor in People. David Bellamy Gold Conservation Award. Take the B4353 off A487 (about 5m N of Aberystwyth and 12m S of Machynlleth). The entrance to Brynowen is 100yd from the southern end of Borth seafront. Open: 21 March - 31 October. ★★★ BH&HPA NCC 16🚐 85

**(4m). Clarach Bay Holiday Village, Clarach Bay, Aberystwyth, Ceredigion SY23 3DT.** *0845 0509716*. www.clarach-bay.com. Club. Full family entertainment. Outdoor heated swimming pool. Restaurant. Fish & chip takeaway. Mini-fairground. Laundrette. Supermarket. Fishing. Tennis. Owner supplied copy. On A487. Open: 1 April - 31 October. BH&HPA NCC 10🚐 10⛺ 255

**(12m). Erwbarfe Farm Caravan Park, Devil's Bridge, Aberystwyth, Ceredigion SY23 3JR.** *01970 890358*. www.erwbarfe.co.uk. Ideal base from which to tour mid-Wales area with walking, fishing, bird-watching etc. Close to Nantyr Arian mountain bike centre (2m). Owner supplied copy. On A4120 Ponterwyd to Devil's Bridge. Open: 1 March - 31 October. 10🚐 20⛺ A 50

**(2m). Glan Y Mor Leisure Park, Clarach, Aberystwyth, Ceredigion SY23 3DT.** *01970 828900*. www.sunbourne.com. Restaurant and takeaway. Supermarket. Amusements. Bowl and leisure centre. Licensed club. Laundrette. Free showers. Fitness gym. Sauna. Steam room. Whirlpool spa. Sunbeds. Entertainment. Dogs not allowed during Bank Holidays and school holidays. Off A487 Machynlleth to Aberystwyth. Open: 1 March - 1 November. ★★★★ BH&HPA 4🚐 42⛺ 100 A 40

**(1.5m). Midfield Holiday and Residential Park R, Southgate, Aberystwyth, Ceredigion SY23 4DX.** *01970 612542*. www.midfieldcaravanpark.co.uk. Mainly level hilltop site with panoramic views. Public phone. Free Wi-Fi broadband Internet access. Privately owned park. Touring, holiday & residential sites overlooking Aberystwyth and Cardigan Bay. Dogs must be on leads. Owner-occupied caravans, from 11/4/09 to 31/10/09. Owner supplied copy. On A4120 Aberystwyth to Devil's Bridge Road, 200yd from junction with A487, Aberystwyth end. Open: 1 April - 31 October. BH&HPA 75⛺ A 35

**(5m). Morfa Bychan Holiday Park, Llanfarian, Aberystwyth, Ceredigion SY23 4QQ.** *01970 617254*. www.hill-andale.co.uk. Set in over 110 acres of

# WALES

pastureland overlooking Cardigan Bay. Superb location from which to explore the area. Heated swimming pool. Cinema and town 3m. Golf 4m. David Bellamy Silver Conservation Award. Owner supplied copy. Off A487 southbound from Aberystwyth, first turning off A487, road unsuitable for caravans, proceed a further 2m to turning alongside radio masts. Open: All year. ★★★★ BH&HPA 50⊖ ▲ 218⊆

**(2m). Ocean View Caravan Park, Clarach Bay, Aberystwyth, Ceredigion SY23 3DL.** 01970 828425. www.oceanviewholidays.com. Peaceful, family run park near beach and with good sea views. Lovely area for touring and beach holidays. Excellent facilities a short walk. Free showers. Separate field as dog walk. Owner supplied copy. Off A487 N of Aberystwyth, turn for Clarach Bay. Follow road to beach, Ocean View is on R. Open: 15 March - 31 October. ★★★★ BH&HPA 5⊖ 24⊖ 50⊆

**(9m). Pengarreg Caravan Park, Llanrhystud, Aberystwyth, Ceredigion SY23 5DH.** 01974 202247. www.utowcaravans.co.uk. Fishing on site, golf 1m, PO 0.75m. Doctor 6m. Shop on site, laundry, office, licensed club, meals, children's room, 2 play areas. Hill walks. Boating ramp. Owner supplied copy. On A487 S of Aberystwyth, entrance opposite garage. Site situated on beach. Aberaeron 6m. Open: 1 March - 1 January. BH&HPA 8⊖ 50⊖ ▲ 155⊆

**(12m). Woodlands Caravan Park aka Devils Bridge, Devils Bridge, Aberystwyth, Ceredigion SY23 3JW.** 01970 890233. www.woodlandsdevilsbridge.co.uk. A peaceful country site adjoining farm. Ideal for walking, bird watching, touring, fishing and mountain biking. Beautiful scenery. Wales Tourist Board member. On A4120, 12m E of Aberystwyth or 3m S of A44 at Ponterwyd. Open: 6 April - 31 October. ★★★ 20⊖ 20⊖ 30▲

### Borth

**(0.5m). Glanlerry Caravan Park, Borth, Ceredigion SY24 5LU.** 01970 871413. www.glanlerrycaravanpark.co.uk. Laundry. Bathroom. Showers. Adventure playground, goal post. Wi-Fi available. Owner supplied copy. On B4353 between Bow St and Borth. Open: 1 March - 31 October. BH&HPA 90⊖ ▲ 100⊆

**(0.5m). Penygraig Farm Caravan Park, Borth, Ceredigion SY24 5NR.** 01970 871717. BH&HPA 85⊆

**(1m). The Mill House Caravan Park, Dol-y-bont, Borth, Ceredigion SY24 5LX.** 01970 871481. Quiet site, close mown grass. Fishing on site, shop, doctor, PO 1m. Golf 2m. Owner supplied copy. On A487 turn W at Rhydypenau Garage Corner (between Talybont and Bow Street) on to B4353 through Llandre. Proceed 1mile. Stop under railway bridge, by white railings, then fork R into Dolybont village, first R before hump-back bridge. Open: 1 March - 31 October. BH&HPA 5⊖ 10⊖ ▲ 15⊆

**(3m). Ty Mawr Holiday Home and Touring Park, Borth, Ceredigion SY24 5LB.** 01970 871327. www.tymawrcaravanpark.co.uk. Very quiet, sheltered, level site with panoramic views of hills, nature reserve and Dovey estuary. Fishing, golf course, shops, PO, doctor all very near. David Bellamy Gold Conservation Award. N of Borth on B4353 off A487. Open: 1 March - 31 October. BH&HPA 12⊖ 25⊖ ▲ 50⊆

### Cardigan

**(2.5m). Brongwyn Caravan & Touring Park, Brongwyn Mawr, Penparc, Cardigan, Ceredigion SA43 1SA.** 01239 613644. www.tentsandtourers.co.uk. A small, peaceful park with level pitches. Indoor pool and leisure facilities available (at extra charge), laundry etc. 5mins from the market town of Cardigan and beautiful sandy beaches at Mwnt and Aberporth. Golf course, cinema, theatre, shopping centre all 3m. Ideal location for walking, fishing and golf. On A487 Cardigan-Aberystwyth road, 2.5m N of Cardigan, turn L at crossroads in Penparc signposted Ferwig, carry on over next cross-roads, after 0.5m turn R into lane, opposite brown sign. Open: 18 May - 1 September. ★★★★ 5⊖ 10⊖ ▲ 7⊆

**(6m). Caerfelin Caravan Park, Aberporth, Cardigan, Ceredigion SA43 2BZ.** 01239 810540. NO TENTS. We have 5 touring pitches in total for either touring caravan or camper vans. Well-sheltered about 5mins walk to sandy beaches and village. Family park. Golf, cinema 6m. Owner supplied copy. Off A487 to B4333 at Blaenanerch R at St Cynwyls church to park 200yd on the L. Open: 19 March - 31 October. BH&HPA 5⊖ 100⊆

**Camping Blaenwaun, Mwnt, Cardigan, Ceredigion SA43 1QF.** 01239 613456. www.blaenwaunfarm.com. 0.5m from sea. Private coarse fishing lake. 4m NW of Cardigan. Take A487 for 0.25m W of Cardigan. Turn N on to B4548 towards Mwnt. After 0.5m turn right at SP to Mwnt. Follow signs to Mwnt. Site is 300yd from Mwnt beach camp sign. Open: 22 April - 31 October.

### Lampeter

**(6m). Hafod Brynog Caravan Park, Ystrad Aeron, Felinfach, Lampeter, Ceredigion SA48 8AE.** 01570 470084. Exceptionally well maintained park with plenty of space between caravans and modern shower block. Peaceful with lovely views. Ideal for coastal and inland touring or just relaxing. Walking distance to village with shops, garage, pubs. Laundrette on site. Golf course 6m. Fishing 3m. Owner supplied copy. On main A482 Lampeter to Aberaeron road in quiet village of Ystrad Aeron, entrance next to Brynog Arms pub. Open: 1 April - 30 September. 2⊖ 30⊖ 5▲ 40⊆

**(5m). Moorlands Caravan Park, Llangybi, Lampeter, Ceredigion SA48 8NN.** 01570 493543. www.moorlands-caravan-park.co.uk. Club. Swimming pool. Play area. Golf club within walking distance. Fishing and pony-trekking nearby. Close to many places of interest including Devil's Bridge and Llyn Brianne Dam. Mountain scenery. Cardigan Bay. David Bellamy Gold Conservation Award. Owner supplied copy. Off A485 Tregaron to Lampeter. Open: 1 March - 31 October. BH&HPA 62⊆

### Llanarth

**Shawsmead Caravan Club Site, Oakford, Llanarth, Ceredigion SA47 0RN.** 01545 580423. www.caravan-club.co.uk. 4m from the coast, dotted with lovely bays and beaches ideal for families. Non-members welcome. Some hardstandings. PO in village, garage/shop 1.5m, golf courses nearby. MV service point, veg prep area, water sports nearby. Quiet and peaceful off peak, good area for walking, beach and NCN cycle route within 5m. See website for standard directions to site. Open: 30 March - 8 October. NCC 50⊖ 50⊆

### Llandysul

**Brynawelon Touring and Camping Park, Sarnau, Llandysul, Ceredigion SA44 6RE.** 01239 654584. www.brynawelon cp.co.uk. A select tranquil park on the West coast of Wales. This unspoilt area has a lot to offer the family holiday maker who

# WALES

wants a quiet and relaxing holiday amidst beautiful scenery. N on A487, then turn R at Sarnau Chapel crossroads. 2m from coast. Site 0.25m on L down lane SP. 9m from Cardigan. Open: 1 March - 31 October. ★★★★ BH&HPA 🏠 📶 ✂ 🐾 🚿 🚻 ♿ 🚐 40🚗 ⚡

(3m). **Cardigan Bay Camping & Caravanning Club Site, LLwynhelyg, Cross Inn, Llandysul, Ceredigion SA44 6LW.** 01545 560029 . www.campingandcaravanningclub.co.uk. Well located site within easy reach of New Quay and Cardigan. Good coastal walks nearby. Close to golden beaches. Dolphins and porpoises have been spotted off the coast at New Quay Head. Non-members welcome. All units accepted. Special deals available for families and backpackers. On A486, 1m from New Quay. L at Penrhiwgaled Arms, turn R, about 0.75m. Site on R after 250yd. 10m from Cardigan. Open: 26 April - 27 September. ★★★★ NCC 🏠 📶 ♿ ✂ 🐾 🚿 🚻 🚐 ♿ 90🚗 90⚡ ⚡

**Dyffryn Bern Caravan Park, Penbryn Beach, Sarnau, Llandysul, Ceredigion SA44 6RD.** 01239 810900. www.dyffrynbern.co.uk. Fishing lake. Conservatory. Open Easter-October 31 for Hire. Owner supplied copy. Off A487. 7m from Cardigan. Open: 1 March - 31 December. BH&HPA 🏠 📶 ♿ 55⚡

(12m). **Maes Glas Caravan Park, Penbryn, Sarnau, Llandysul, Ceredigion SA44 6QE.** 01239 654268. www.maesglascaravanpark.co.uk. Peace and quiet. Dry ski slope 3m, golf course 4m, shops 9m. David Bellamy Gold Conservation Award. Owner supplied copy. Off A487 at Sarnau follow road down towards Penbryn Beach. 10m from Cardigan. Open: 22 April - 31 October. BH&HPA 🏠 📶 ✂ 🐾 ♿ 🚻 🚿 ⚡ 5🚗 5⚡ ♿ 45⚡

**Manorafon Park, Sarnau, Penbryn, Llandysul, Ceredigion SA44 6QH.** 01239 623633. www.coldatnight.co.uk. Nomad tents for hire and use of shared facilities. Luxury Geodesic dome tents for hire with their own decking and all mod cons. B&B basis for tents and farmhouse accommodation. Sauna on sites. Two pets allowed (£4 each). Local shop. On Ceredigion Coastal Path, ideal site for outdoor pursuits. Penbryn beach is a short walk away and is almost a private beach. Owner supplied copy. 0.75m from Penbryn beach in wooded valley. From A487 at Sarnau take Penbryn beach signs. Open: 1 April - 31 October. 🏠 📶 ♿ 🚐 ⚡

**Pilbach Holiday Park, Betws Ifan, Rhydlewis, Llandysul, Ceredigion SA44 5RT.** 0845 0508176. www.barkersleisure.com. Set in nearly 14 acres of land, this award-winning holiday park is surrounded by stunning countryside and close to Newquay with its picturesque harbour. Modern, refurbished club with live entertainment. Freshly prepared bar food. Owner supplied copy. From Midlands head for Shrewsbury, take A44 to Aberystwyth. From South Wales head for Carmarthen, take the A484 towards Newcastle Emlyn. Take A487 towards Cardigan. Turn off to Newcastle Emlyn on the B4333. Follow signs. Pilbach is on R. Open: 1 March - 9 January. ★★★★ BH&HPA NCC 🏠 📶 ✂ 🐾 🚿 🚻 ♿ 🚐 ⚡ 60🚗 60⚡ ♿ 96⚡

(8m). **Talywerydd Touring Caravan Park, Penbryn Sands, Sarnau, Llandysul, Ceredigion SA44 6QY.** 01239 810322. www.westwalescaravanandcamping.co.uk. Family run park with sea views. 2m from Penbryn National Trust beach and Ceredigion coastal path. Centrally located for touring mid-Wales. 600yds from farm shop, recommended booking for hardstanding pitches. Dog friendly. Owner supplied copy. From N or S off A487 take second Penbryn turn, site 600yd on L. Open: 7 March - 31 October. 🏠 📶 ✂ 🐾 🚿 🚻 ♿ 🚐 5⚡ 30⚡ ⚡

### Llanon

(2.5m). **Brynarian Caravan Park, Cross Inn, Llanon, Ceredigion SY23 5NA.** 0844 5617257. www.brynariancaravanpark.com. Quiet secluded family run park, set amongst mature beech trees. Large touring field, no overcrowding. Play area. H&C showers. Telephone for brochure. Golf, fishing nearby. Shop, restaurant, PO, garage 500yd from site. Off B4337, turn towards Llanon at Cross Inn second turning on L. 6m from Aberaeron. Open: 1 March - 31 October. BH&HPA 🏠 📶 ✂ 🐾 ♿ 🚿 🚻 ⚡ 🚐 20⚡ ♿ 45⚡

### Llanrhystud

(1m). **Morfa Farm Caravan Park, Llanrhystud, Ceredigion SY23 5BU.** 01974 202253. www.morfa.net. Laundry room. Tennis court. Slipway. Telephone. Calor Gas stockist. Snooker room. Golf course 1.5m. 9m to railway station. Dogs on lead. Owner supplied copy. On A487 Aberaeron to Aberystwyth. Open: 1 April - 31 October. 🏠 📶 ✂ 🐾 ♿ 🚿 🚻 ⚡ ♿ 10⚡ 20⚡ ♿ 152⚡

### New Quay

**Cei Bach Country Club, Parc-y-Brwcs, Cei Bach, New Quay, Ceredigion SA45 9SL.** 01545 580237. www.cei-bach.co.uk. Coastal walks. Overlooks Cei Bach beach, views along coastline, coastal walks to Aberaeron. All modern facilities. Children's play park and ball park. Heated shower block. Bookings essential in peak weeks. New Quay 1.5m by road, 1m along beach. Off A487. Take B4342 New Quay Road for 1.5m At Cambrian Hotel turn R. Follow signs for Cei Bach 1m. Open: 4 March - 30 October. 🏠 📶 ✂ 🐾 ♿ 🚿 🚻 ⚡ 40⚡ 40⚡ ⚡

(0.25m). **Neuadd Caravan Park, Neuadd Farm, New Quay, Ceredigion SA45 9TY.** 01545 560709. www.neuaddcaravanpark.com. 🏠 ✂ 🐾 60⚡ ♿ 85⚡

(2m). **Pencnwc Holiday Park, Cross Inn, New Quay, Ceredigion SA44 6NL.** 01545 560479. www.pencnwc.co.uk. Family owned park. 2m from New Quay. Clubhouse. Plenty of facilities. SP outskirts of village Cross Inn within 2m of New Quay on A486. Open: 1 March - 31 October. ★★★★ BH&HPA 🏠 📶 ✂ 🐾 ♿ 🚿 🚻 ⚡ ♿ 50⚡ 100⚡ ♿ 231⚡

(2.5m). **Penlon Caravan Park, Cross Inn, New Quay, Ceredigion SA44 6JY.** 0844 8000818. www.valeholidayparks.com. Showers, laundry, chemical toilet disposal point. Games room. Play area. Owner supplied copy. On A486 (SP Newquay) off A487 Aberystwyth to Cardigan main road. Open: 1 March - 3 January. BH&HPA 🏠 📶 ✂ 🐾 ♿ 🚿 🚻 ♿ 7⚡ ♿ 60⚡

(0.5m). **Quay West Holiday Park (Haven), Quay West, New Quay, Ceredigion SA45 9SE.** 0871 4680496. www.haven.com. Brilliant family holidays and short breaks at Cardigan Bay where the dolphins play. Heated fun and kids' pool and Kids' Club. Fantastic daily entertainment. 3 beautiful sandy beaches. Superb standard caravans and park. Welcome Host Award, Investor in People, Blue Flag Award. David Bellamy Gold Conservation Award. Take A487 coastal trunk road from Aberystwyth or A484 then A486 from Carmarthen. Join B4342 and the park is situated on the northern side of New Quay. Open: 18 March - 31 October. ★★★★ BH&HPA NCC 🏠 📶 ✂ 🐾 🚿 🚻 ♿ 🚐 ⚡ 782⚡

(2m). **Wern Mill Camping Site, Bressay, Gilfachreda, New Quay, Ceredigion SA45 9SP.** 01545 580699. Very sheltered level site near two sandy beaches. Ideal centre for touring Mid-Wales. Idyllic walks. Family site. Owner supplied copy. A487 Aberystwyth to Cardigan road, turn off at Llanarth to Newquay road B4342. Gilfachreda is 1.5m from Llanarth on the B4342. Open: 1 April - 30 September. 🏠 📶 ✂ 🐾 ♿ 🚿 🚻 ⚡ 10⚡ 30⚡ ⚡

## CONWY
### Abergele

(8m). **Abbeyford Holiday Camp, Bryn Road, Towyn, Abergele, Conwy LL22**

# WALES

9HN. *01745 334590*. www.abbeyford.com. Club with regular live entertainment. Close to beach and all amenities. Owner supplied copy. Off A548, Coast Road, or A55 take Abergele turn off and follow signs for Pensarn and Rhyl. Open: 21 March - 31 October. NCC ⚏ ⚑ ⚐ 120⚑

(3m). **Gaingc View, Gaingc Road, Towyn, Abergele, Conwy LL22 9HP.** *01745 342957*. www.gaingcview.co.uk. Owners' dogs allowed only. Owner supplied copy. Park is in the heart of Towyn, off Sandbank road. Open: 15 March - 31 October. ★★★★★ BH&HPA ⚑ 80⚑

(2.5m). **Henllys Farm, Towyn, Abergele, Conwy LL22 9HF.** *01745 351208*. www.henllys.com. Level, sheltered site overlooking open farmland. Close to all the amenities and entertainment in Towyn. Owner supplied copy. On S side of A548 at Towyn. Open: 21 April - 31 October. ★★★★ ⚑ 281⚑

(3.5m). **Hunters Hamlet Caravan Park, Sirior Goch Farm, Betws-yn-Rhos, Abergele, Conwy LL22 8PL.** *01745 832337*. www.huntershamlet.co.uk. Laundry room. Family bathroom. AA 4 pennants award-winning park. Superpitches. Free Wifi. Two 9 hole golf courses nearby + 18 hole golf course in Abergele 3.5m. Shop 0.5m, PO 1.5m. Off A55 J24 for Abergele then at 2nd set traffic lights L for A548 Llanwrst Road for 2.75m, turn R at crossroads, Hunters Hamlet is 0.5m on L. Open: 21 March - 31 October. BH&HPA ⚑ 23⚑ 23⚑

(2.5m). **Owens Caravan Park, (Gainc Bach), Towyn Road, Towyn, Abergele, Conwy LL22 9ES.** *01745 353639*. www.owenscp.co.uk. Family run quiet site. Excellent central location; only 5mins walk away from the amenities, entertainment, beach and cycle track, just opposite general store and PO. Owner supplied copy. Rhyl to Abergele coast road. 2m from Rhyl, 1st park just large church on R in Towyn. Open: 22 April - 30 September. BH&HPA ⚑ 12⚑ 300⚑

(1m). **Plas Farm Caravan Park, Betws yn Rhos, Abergele, Conwy LL22 8AU.** *01492 680254*. plasfarmcaravanpark.co.uk. Sian and John would like to welcome you to Plas Farm Touring Caravan Park. It's situated in the grounds of a stunning 16th century Grade II listed farmhouse, in a breathtaking location with a superb range of high quality facilities. The award-winning park is located within acres of unspoilt countryside with a woodland walk and outdoor play area, making it perfect for families and couples. It is only a short stroll away from the village shop and Country Inn and 3 miles to several beaches and stunning coastal walks. It is in easy reach of the A55 North Wales coast road and an ideal base for exploring a wealth of top attractions; from Anglesey to Chester and inland to beautiful Snowdonia. The park has won a David Bellamy Gold Conservation Award and has 4 AA pennants. Recommended route from junction 24. Leave the A55 at junction 24, drive through Abergele town centre on the A547, turn left and drive through Rhyd Y Foel. Our turning is left before the village Betws Yn Rhos. Open: 1 March - 31 October. ★★★★ 4 ⚑ ⚑ ⚑ 20⚑ 20⚑

(2m). **Seldon's Golden Gate Holiday Centre, Coast Road, Towyn, Abergele, Conwy LL22 9HU.** *01745 833048*. www.seldonsgoldengate.co.uk. Club. Open March-November. (10.5 months also offered). Owner supplied copy. On A548 Abergele to Prestatyn. Open: 1 March - 5 November. ⚑ 558⚑

(2m). **The Beach Caravan & Chalet Park, Llanddulas, Abergele, Conwy LL22 8HA.** *01492 515345*. www.thornleyleisure.co.uk. Club. Off A55. Open: 1 March - 30 November. ★★★★ BH&HPA NCC ⚑ 280⚑

(2m). **Ty Mawr Holiday Park, Towyn Road, Towyn, Abergele, Conwy LL22 9HG.** *01745 832079*. www.park-resorts-touring.com. Indoor pool. Adventure playground. All weather multi sports court. Free kids club. Free family entertainment day and night. Bar meals. Amusements. Darts. Pool table. Club room. David Bellamy Gold Conservation Award. Off A584 Rhyl to Abergele, W of Towyn. Open: 20 March - 31 October. ★★★★ BH&HPA NCC ⚑ 300⚑ 80⚑

▮ **Ty Gwyn Caravan Park, Towyn Road, Towyn, Abergele, Conwy LL22 9HA.** *01745 832275*. www.tygwynpark.co.uk. Located on the beautiful North Wales coast. A quiet, friendly park with direct access to the beach and coastal path for walking and cycling The park is conveniently situated for the local towns of Rhyl, Colwyn Bay and Llandudno. Snowdonia National Park and Anglesey are also easily accessible. The site has an area for touring caravans and also bases for static caravan homes. There are also 3-star graded chalets available for rent and pitches for seasonal tourers. On the A548 coastal road. 5 minutes from the A55, 3 miles from Rhyl. Open: 7 March - 17 October. ⚑

## Betws-y-Coed

(1m). **Cwmlanerch Caravan Park, Betws-y-Coed, Conwy LL24 0BG.** *01492 642770*. www.snowdonia-cwmlanerch.co.uk. Payphone. Play area. Deep freeze available on site. On B5106. Open: 1 March - 31 October. ★★★★ ⚑ 16⚑ 33⚑

(1m). **Hendre Farm Camping and Caravan Site, Holyhead Road, Betws-y-Coed, Conwy LL24 0BN.** *07879 437778*. www.snowdonia-campsite.co.uk. Showers, shaving point, washbasins and deep sink for clothes washing. Public telephone. Owner supplied copy. On A5 Betws-y-Coed to Capel Curig. Open: 16 April - 4 September. ⚑ 10⚑ 23⚑

**Riverside Caravan Park (Conwy), Old Church Road, Betws-y-Coed, Conwy LL24 0AL.** *01690 710310*. www.morris-leisure.co.uk. 8 acre site nestling in the Snowdonia National Park. Adjacent to golf course and river Conwy for fishing. 2mins walk from shops, restaurants, etc. Caravan Club affiliated site. Set close to centre of the town, just off the A5. Please follow signs. Open: 1 March - 31 December. BH&HPA ⚑ 60⚑ 60⚑ 29⚑ 68⚑

**Rynys Farm Camping Site, Betws-y-Coed, Conwy LL26 0RU.** *01690 710218*. www.rynys-camping.co.uk. Peaceful, scenic site in the hill of North Wales, close to Snowdonia peaks. Excellent clean facilities. Central for touring North Wales. Open all year for tents, Easter-October for caravans. Owner supplied copy. 2m S of Betws-Y-Coed on A5, opposite Conwy Falls. Open: 22 April - 31 October. ⚑

(8m). **Tyn Rhos Caravan Park (CL), Tyn Rhos Farm, Pentrefoelas, Betws-y-Coed, Conwy LL24 0LN.** *01690 770655*. www.tynrhoscaravanpark.co.uk. CARAVAN AND MOTORHOMES ONLY. Flat site within easy reach of Snowdonia and North Wales. Restaurant and pub 5mins walk. Go Karting 4m, Shop, PO, doctor's, fishing 6m, golf course 7m. Owner supplied copy. 5m N of Cerrigydrudion via A5. Turn S to Geeler Arms. Keep L after bridge to site. 7m SE of Betws-y-Coed. Open: 1 March - 31 October. ⚑ 20⚑ 20⚑

## Colwyn Bay

(3m). **Bron-Y-Wendon Touring Caravan Park, Wern Road, Llanddulas, Colwyn Bay, Conwy LL22 8HG.** *01492 512903*. www.northwales-holidays.co.uk. Award winning park with excellent modern facilities. All pitches have sea views and the beach is just a short walk away. Wi-Fi on the park. Ideal base for a seaside or touring holiday - Snowdonia, Llandudno and Chester are within easy reach. Colour bro-

# WALES

chure available. AA 4 pennants. Leave A55 at the Llanddulas (A547) interchange J23 and follow the tourist information signs to the park. Open: All year. ★★★★★ 5 🏕🏕🏕🏕 20🏕 110🏕

(0.5m). **Dinarth Hall, Rhos-on-Sea, Colwyn Bay, Conwy LL28 4PX.** *01492 548203.* members.fortunecity.com/dinarthhall. Touring centre. Fees on application. Golf course across the road. PO, Dr surgery within 15mins walk. Owner supplied copy. 2m NW of Colwyn Bay on B5115 to Dinarth Hall Road (opposite college). Open: 22 April - 31 October. ★★ 🏕🏕🏕🏕 20🏕 20🏕 🏕

### Conwy

(1.5m). **Conwy Touring Park, Trefriw Road, Bwlch Mawr, Conwy, Conwy LL32 8UX.** *01492 592856.* www.conwytouringpark.com. Sheltered, wooded site with splendid views. Close to beaches & Snowdonia. Special offers available. Storage facilities. 1.25m S of Conwy on B5106. Large slate-roofed sign on L. Open: 1 April - 26 September. ★★★ 🏕🏕🏕🏕 25🏕 320🏕 🏕

(5m). **Tyn Terfyn Touring Site, Talybont, Conwy, Conwy LL32 8YX.** *01492 660525.* www.tynterfyn.co.uk. Clean, quiet site on level ground. Hardstandings available. Excellent location for touring N Wales, castle, mountains, beaches, lakes, fishing etc. Butcher, PO, pubs, restaurants, papers, milk, groceries etc within 1.5m. Owner supplied copy. From Conwy Castle take B5106 for about 5m, first house on L after road sign 'Talybont'. Open: 14 March - 31 October. 🏕🏕🏕🏕 15🏕 15🏕 🏕

### Llandudno

(2m). **Maes Dolau Farm, Bryn Lupus Road, Llanrhos, Llandudno, Conwy LL30 1SR.** *01492 583461.* www.maesdolaucaravanpark.co.uk. Main services to all pitches. Booking only. Owner supplied copy. Off A546. Open: 21 March - 31 October. BH&HPA 🏕🏕 10🏕 100🏕

(3m). **Tan-y-Bryn Caravan Park (Llandudno), Bryn Pydew, Llandudno, Conwy LL31 9JZ.** *01492 546257.* www.northwalesstaticcaravanpark.com. 5min to all amenities. Small rural tranquil site. Car hardstanding for parking one vehicle by each static van. 4 golf courses, cinema and shopping centre all within 10mins. Owner supplied copy. Off A55. Detailed directions on request. Open: 1 March - 15 January. BH&HPA 🏕🏕 24🏕

### Llanrwst

(0.25m). **Bodnant Caravan Park, Nebo Road, Llanrwst, Conwy LL26 0SD.** *01492 640248.* www.bodnant-caravanpark.co.uk. 38 pitches (14 hardstandings) & 14 tent pitches on a working farm site. 26 years winner Wales in Bloom. Central for mountains & coast. A470 from Llanrwst town centre. Take B5427. Open: 1 March - 31 October. ★★★★ BH&HPA 🏕🏕🏕🏕 54🏕 38🏕 14🏕 2🏕

(0.5m). **Bron Derw Touring Caravan Park, Bron Derw, Llanrwst, Conwy LL26 0YT.** *01492 640494.* www.bronderw-wales.co.uk. A family run site in a quiet, secluded setting on the outskirts of the ancient market town of Llanrwst, with its variety of shops, cafes, restaurants, swimming pool and leisure centre. This location is ideal for exploring the Snowdonia mountain range and the North Wales coast. AA 5 pennant award and 5 star Visit Wales. Caravan storage compound. CaSSOA member - gold award. Additional adults only park open with 23 multi-service pitches. Follow A55 on to A470 For Betws-y-Coed and Llanrwst. On entering Llanrwst turn L into Parry Road (SP Llanddoged), at the T junction turn L. Then take first farm entrance, on the R signed 'Bron Derw' and continue up the drive until you reach the site. Open: 1 March - 31 October. ★★★★★ 5 BH&HPA 🏕🏕 🏕🏕🏕🏕 10🏕 33🏕

(2m). **Glyn Farm Caravans, Trefriw, Llanrwst, Conwy LL27 0RZ.** *01492 640442.* Dogs allowed only with tourers. Small family run site, very central for Snowdonia and coastal resorts. Lovely walking country, within picturesque village - homely and friendly atmosphere. Off B5106. Turn into car park opposite Trefriw Woollen Mills. Site situated approx 100yds on L. Open: 1 March - 31 October. ★★★★ 🏕🏕🏕 28🏕 2🏕

(2m). **Maenan Abbey Caravan Park, Maenan, Llanrwst, Conwy LL26 0UL.** *01492 660630.* www.thornleyleisure.co.uk. No tourers. Chalets for rent. On A470, 3m N of Llanrwst. Open: 1 March - 30 November. ★★★★★ BH&HPA NCC 🏕🏕🏕 80🏕

### Penmaenmawr

(1m). **Craiglwyd Hall Caravan Park, Craiglwyd Road, Penmaenmawr, Conwy LL34 6ER.** *01492 623355.* www.thornleyleisure.co.uk. Club. Golf. David Bellamy Silver Conservation Award. Off A55 into Penmaenmawr, turn L after pelican crossing, take second L uphill and turn L. Open: 1 March - 30 November. ★★★★ BH&HPA 🏕🏕🏕🏕 160🏕

# DENBIGHSHIRE

### Corwen

(2.5m). **Gaer Hyfryd Corwen Caravan Club (AS) Site, Plas Isaf, Corwen, Denbighshire LL21 0SN.** *01490 412189.* www.caravanclub.co.uk. CARAVAN CLUB AFFILIATED CLUB - MEMBERS ONLY. A simple rural site of charm and intimacy in the most breathtaking countryside. Toilet block and laundry facilities. Play area on site and dog walk nearby. Fishing nearby, good area for walkers. Quiet and peaceful off-peak. From Corwen on A5, follow signs for Betws-y-Coed. In 1.5m turn L after organic farm shop. Open: 25 March - 3 October. NCC 🏕🏕🏕🏕 35🏕

(8m). **Glan-Ceirw Caravan Park, Ty Nant, Corwen, Denbighshire LL21 0RF.** *01490 420346.* www.hiraethog.org.uk. Picturesque site with trout fishing. AA 3 pennants. David Bellamy Gold Conservation Award. Situated between Corwen and Betws y Coed on the A5 bordering Snowdonia National Park. Open: 1 March - 31 October. ★★★★ 3 BH&HPA 🏕🏕🏕🏕 6🏕 9🏕 29🏕

(4m). **Hendwr Caravan Park, Tyddyn Hendwr, Llandrillo, Corwen, Denbighshire LL21 0SN.** *01490 440210.* 40 pitches in total. Dishwashing room. Limited service during winter. Fishing nearby. Good walking area. 1m to pub restaurant. Very central location for touring North & Mid Wales. Open all year for owner occupied. Take B4401 from Corwen (A5) for 4m site on R. The site is SP from A5 at Corwen. Open: 18 April - 31 October. ★★★★ BH&HPA 🏕🏕🏕🏕 40🏕 🏕

(3.5m). **Llawrbetws Farm Caravan Park, Glan-yr-afon, Corwen, Denbighshire LL21 0HD.** *01490 460224.* Brochure by request. Gas supplies. Very quiet and peaceful, open country. Beautiful walks. Fly fishing available. On A494 off A5. Corwen to Bala road, 2nd R after Thomas Motor Mart. Open: 17 April - 31 October. ★★★★ BH&HPA 🏕🏕🏕🏕 10🏕 35🏕 68🏕

### Denbigh

(4m). **Station House Caravan Park, Bodfari, Denbigh, Denbighshire LL16 4DA.** *01745 710372.* stationhousecaravanpark.co.uk. Declared area of great natural beauty with walking on Offa's Dyke. Close to village shops and inn. Owner supplied copy. Off A541 Denbigh to Mold road, SP Tremeirchion with our directional

# WALES

signs B5429, 1st house on immediate L. Open: 10 March - 15 October. ★★★

### Llanferres

**(4m). Bryn Bowlio Caravan Park, Tafarn-Y-Gelyn, Llanferres, Denbighshire CH7 5SQ.** 01352 810484. www.brynbowlio-caravanpark.co.uk. Located on the edge of some of the country's most scenic walks and outdoor activities, in an Area of Outstanding Natural Beauty. 2 holiday cottages also available for hire. No cats, dogs on lead. Owner-occupied caravans. Take A494 from Mold to Ruthin, pass Loggerheads, go R at the sign for Moel Famau/Tafarn-Y-Gelyn. Pass the cottages on the L, entrance directly ahead. Open: 1 March - 14 January. ★★★ BH&HPA 10 12

**(5m). Ffynnon Park, Llanarmon Road, Llanferres, Denbighshire CH7 5TA.** 01824 780298. www.ffynnonpark.co.uk. New refurbished park set in beautiful scenery in an Area of Outstanding Natural Beauty. Plenty of walks, and places of interest to visit. Park is a small friendly quiet place to visit. Owner supplied copy. Take A494 from Mold to historic town of Ruthin, passing through Loggerheads and Llanferres. Continue for 1.5m and park is found on the L, SP. Open: 1 March - 31 October. 4 8 14

### Llangollen

**(1m). Ty Ucha Caravan Park, Maesmawr Road, Llangollen, Denbighshire LL20 7PP.** 01978 860677. 4 acre quiet AA 3-pennant site. Golf course 0.5m. Off A5, SP. Open: 1 April - 31 October. ★★ 3 10 30

**(0.5m). Wern Isaf Farm, Wern Isaf Farm, Llangollen, Denbighshire LL20 8DU.** 01978 860632. www.wernisaf.co.uk. Welcome Host Gold Award. Good touring centre for coast and Snowdonia. Quiet scenic site with views of the Dee Valley and Welsh mountains. Fishing, golf course, horse riding, white water rafting and many more sporting activities 0.75m from town centre. Owner supplied copy. Turn uphill behind Bridge End Hotel then R into Wern Road. Site 0.5m NE Llangollen at foot of Castell Dinas Bran (Crow Castle). Open: 6 April - 31 October. BH&HPA 6 20 3

### Prestatyn

**(0.5m). Nant Mill Touring Caravan and Tenting Park, Gronant Road, Prestatyn, Denbighshire LL19 9LY.** 01745 852360. www.nantmilltouring.co.uk. 150 mixed pitches in total. Dogs welcome but restrictions apply. 0.5m beach and town. Fishing, golf course, swimming, boating and horse riding all nearby. Ideal for sightseeing North Wales. On A548 Prestatyn coast road. Open: 25 March - 16 October. ★★★★ 150

**(3m). Presthaven Sands Holiday Park (Haven), Gronant, Prestatyn, Denbighshire LL19 9TT.** 0871 2310888. www.caravancamping.co.uk. 2 licensed club rooms and 1 family pub. Playground. Restaurant and takeaway. Go-karts. Mini ten pin bowling. All weather multi sports court. Heated indoor and outdoor pools. Entertainment for the whole family. Direct beach access from park. 2 golf courses within 5-10mins. Shopping town centre 10mins. Rhyl cinema 15mins from park. David Bellamy Gold Conservation Award. A55 then A5151 to Prestatyn. Follow A548 out of Prestatyn towards Gronant. Park SP L at the next set of traffic lights. Open: 18 March - 31 October. ★★★ BH&HPA NCC 220 220 1481

**(1m). Tan-y-Don Caravan Park, 263 Victoria Road, Prestatyn, Denbighshire LL19 7UT.** 01745 852563. www.bancroftleisure.co.uk. On A548 between Rhyl and Prestatyn. Select, family-run park near Ffrith Beach. Play area. Laundrette. Families welcome. Discounts for OAPs. Short breaks available during off peak. Caravans available for sale or hire. David Bellamy Silver Conservation Award. Open March 1-November 30. On A548 between Rhyl and Prestatyn. Open: 1 March - 30 November. ★★★★★ BH&HPA NCC 67

### Rhyl

**(3m). Golden Sands Holiday Park (Rhyl), Voryd, Kinmel Bay, Rhyl, Denbighshire LL18 5NA.** 01745 343606. www.goldensandsrhyl.co.uk. Perfectly located on the beautiful North Wales coast, Golden Sands is the ideal place to go on holiday or own a caravan. There is something for everyone, the park is literally a stones throw from the beach and close to the fun filled seaside town of Rhyl. The park boasts fantastic facilities such as an indoor pool, family club, indoor play area and a multi sports court to name a few! David Bellamy Silver Conservation Award. Owner supplied copy. From A55 leave at St Asaph and follow signs for Rhyl. Then A547 (Abergele) to first roundabout for Kimmel Bay. Follow to junction of A548 coast road and turn L. Park entrance 300yd on R at foot of stone bridge. Follow lane up side of bridge wall. Open: All year. ★★★★ BH&HPA 375 5

**(0.5m). Oakfield Caravan Park Ltd, Mofra Avenue, Kinmel Bay, Rhyl, Denbighshire LL18 5LH.** 01745 342455. www.oakfieldcaravanpark.co.uk. Close to all amenities including ASDA supermarket, PO and doctor. Local sea fishing, golf course within 2-3m. Nearest beach 10mins walk. Owner supplied copy. On A548 Abergele to Rhyl. Open: 9 April - 1 October. ★★★★ BH&HPA 245

**(1m). Palins Holiday Park, Morfa Avenue, Kinmel Bay, Rhyl, Denbighshire LL18 5LE.** 01745 342672. www.palinsholidaypark.co.uk. Indoor fun pool, family club with live nightly entertainment. Alamo Fort playground. Fish and chip bar. Amusement arcade. Football area. Pub/restaurant. Dragon Award. Owner supplied copy. On A548 Abergele to Rhyl. Open: 2 April - 29 October. 257

**(3m). Pleasant View Park, Abbey Road, Rhuddlan, Rhyl, Denbighshire LL18 5RL.** 01745 590282. www.pleasantviewholidaypark.com. Set in the beautiful Vale of Clwyd, adjacent to the river Clwyd and Rhuddlan Castle. Family run park offers the ideal location for visiting the many tourist attractions along the north Wales coast and Snowdonia. Owner supplied copy. ★ BH&HPA 5 5 100

### Ruthin

**(3m). Three Pigeons Inn, Graigfechan, Ruthin, Denbighshire LL15 2EU.** 01824 703178. www.threepigeonsinn.co.uk. 10 pitches for tourers and/or motorcaravans. Family room. Country inn, bar snacks and meals. PO, supermarkets, cafes, tourist attractions in nearby Ruthin, 3m. Owner supplied copy. From Wrexham A525 then on B5429. From Mold A494 then B5429. Open: 1 March - 31 October. 10

### St Asaph

**(2m). Penisa'r Mynydd Caravan Park, Caerwys Road, Rhuallt, St Asaph, Denbighshire LL17 0TY.** 01745 582227. www.penisarmynydd.co.uk. Quiet family site. Good access, hardstandings. Situated in open countryside with pleasant walks, including Offa's Dyke. Close to Rhyl, Prestatyn, Colwyn Bay and Llandudno. Fishing and golf courses close by. Shaver points. Laundrette. Seasonal pitches available. 0.5m off A55 express way, J29. Open: 1 March - 15 January. ★★★★★ BH&HPA 75

# WALES

## FLINTSHIRE
### Holywell

(3m). Silver Birch Caravan Park, Chester Road, Tyn-Y-Morfa, Gwespyr, Holywell, Flintshire CH8 9JN. 01745 852563. www.bancroftleisure.co.uk. Select, family-run, landscaped park, close to beaches and ideal for touring North Wales. Laundrette. Play area. Shop, pub, restaurant 100yd. David Bellamy Silver Conservation Award. On A548, between Talacre and Gronant. 2m from Prestatyn. Open: 1 March - 10 January. ★★★★★ BH&HPA NCC 108

### Mold

Barlow's Caravan Park, Pen-y-Cefn Road, Caerwys, Mold, Flintshire CH7 5BA. 01352 720273. www.caerwyslocal.co.uk/barlows_caravan_park.html. Take B5122. Off A55 and A541 and follow signs. Open: 25 March - 31 October. NCC 300

(4m). Fron Farm Caravan Park, Rhes-y-cae Road, Hendre, Mold, Flintshire CH7 5QW. 01352 741482. www.fronfarmcaravanpark.co.uk. Mob: 07710 596463. Working farm with animals and horses. Large playground. Fantastic views and walking. 4m to large market town. Take A541 towards Denbigh for about 5m, take right-hand turn for Rhes-y-Cae. Follow signposts all the way. Open: 1 March - 31 October. ★★ 75

### Prestatyn

(2m). Greenacres Caravan Park (Prestatyn), Shore Road, Gronant, Prestatyn, Flintshire LL19 9SS. 01745 854061. www.greenacrescaravanpark.co.uk. Pub, restaurant, indoor swimming pool and children's play are on site. No dogs, cats in tourer area or hire vans. Golf course 2m. Off A548. Open: 1 March - 31 October. BH&HPA 40 7

## GWENT
### Abergavenny

(5.25m). Pandy Caravan Club Site, Pandy, Abergavenny, Gwent NP7 8DR. 01873 890370. www.caravanclub.co.uk. Level site with views of the Black Mountains. Non-members welcome. No tents. Advance booking essential, some cubicles. Laundry facilities. Veg prep. Motorhome service point. Golf. Good area for walking. Dog walk. Quiet and peaceful off peak. NCN cycle route within 5m. Offa's Dyke path runs along the border of England and Wales. See website for standard directions to site. Open: 23 March - 5 November. ★★★★ NCC 53 53

(7m). Pont Kemys Caravan & Camping Park, Chainbridge, Abergavenny, Gwent NP7 9DS. 01873 880688. www.pontkemys.com. Pub 300yd, golf course 400yd. Usk Valley walk 300yd. Dogs charged for. Dog walk area. Mother and baby room. Booking advisable. Some hardstandings. 'Which Motorcaravan' site of the year 2010. 4m from Usk. On B4598 to Abergavenny. (M4, J24 N on A449, or from M5/M50/A40, S on A449 to Usk). Open: 2 March - 29 October. ★★★★ 20 45 10

(2m). Pyscodlyn Farm Caravan & Camping site, Abergavenny, Gwent NP7 7ER. 01873 853271. www.pyscodlyncaravanpark.com. 60 mixed pitches in total. Ideal area for exploring the Black Mountains and Brecon Beacons National Park. Fishing tickets available for river Usk. Golf and pony trekking nearby. W of Abergavenny on the A40 to Brecon. Open: 1 April - 31 October. ★★★ BH&HPA 60

(5m). Rising Sun, Old Hereford Road, Pandy, Abergavenny, Gwent NP7 8DL. 01873 890254. www.therisingsunpandy.com. Very popular bar restaurant. Bar food. Hot & cold showers. Children's play area. Owner supplied copy. 5m N of Abergavenny on A465 to Hereford at Pandy. Open: 1 March - 31 October. 15

### Newport

(2m). Cwmcarn Forest Drive Campsite, Cwmcarn, Crosskeys, Newport, Gwent NP11 7FA. 01495 272001. www.caerphilly.gov.uk/cwmcarnforest. Shower block. Telephone on site. Laundry facilities. Fishing nearby. Visitor centre with coffee shop and gift shop. Mountain bike trail and bike wash. New downhill track open. Events programme for 2008 including guided walks, children's events and Christmas fayre. J28 M4-A467 to Crosskeys and follow signs for site. Sited at entrance to Cwmcarn Forest Drive Tourist attraction. Open: All year. ★★★ 27 27

Tredegar House Country Park Caravan Club Site, Tredegar House, Coedkernew, Newport, Gwent NP10 0TW. 01633 815600. www.caravanclub.co.uk. This seven acre site is ideally located within 1m of the M4 and is only 7m from Cardiff. Adventure playground adjacent. Privacy cubicles. Veg prep. MV service point. Golf nearby. Non-members and tent campers welcome. Some hardstandings, gas, dog walk nearby. See website for standard directions to site. Open: All year. ★★★★ NCC 79 79

### Tredegar

(1.5m). Parc Bryn Bach, Countryside Centre, Merthyr Road, Tredegar, Gwent NP22 3AY. 01495 711816. www.parc-brynbach.co.uk. Caravan and campsite nestling alongside the lake and 100 metres away from the visitor centre with licensed bar and restaurant, gift shop, tourist info. 400 acre countryside park with 9 hole golf course, driving range, BMX track, bike hire, fishing, playground, adventure activities and much more! Owner supplied copy. A465 Tredegar, following signs to Parc Bryn Bach. Open: All year. ★★★ 30

## GWYNEDD
### Aberdaron

Mur Melyn Camping & Caravanning Site, Aberdaron, Gwynedd LL53 8LW. 01758 760522. murmelyncamping.co.uk. Quiet holiday site near end of Lleyn Peninsula. Grassy level and sheltered. Ideal for ramblers. Just over 1m from several beautiful sandy beaches and the village of Aberdaron. Booking advisable for caravans. Owner supplied copy. 17m SW of Pwllheli and 2m N of Aberdaron. W on B4413, fork R, SP 'Whistling Sands' and turn L at Pen-y-Bont House to site 0.5m. Open: 1 April - 31 October. 5

### Abersoch

(1m). Deucoch Touring and Camping Park, Sarn Bach, Abersoch, Gwynedd LL53 7LD. 01758 713293. www.deucoch.com. Flat, well-drained site, 15mins from beaches, closest campsite to Abersoch. Some serviced pitches. Sea view. Families only, children's playground. Dogs on leads. Cafe/restaurant nearby. Rail station 10m away. 1m S of Abersoch via the Sarn Bach road. TR at crossroads, school on L, campsite on R. Open: 1 March - 31 October. ★★★★ BH&HPA 10 70

(1m). Green Pastures Caravan Park, Sarn Bach, Abersoch, Gwynedd LL53 7LD. 01766 810519. www.thornleyleisure.co.uk. Near the village of Abersoch, with excellent sailing & water sports. Children's play area. Sandy beaches nearby & plenty of activities. Exclusive to holiday home owners. On A499 through town to Sarn Bach, turn R and follow road round for about 0.25m, turn R. Open: 1 March - 30 November. BH&HPA 62

# WALES

**(2.5m). Nant-y-Big Caravan Site, Cilan, Abersoch, Gwynedd LL53 7DB.** *01758 712686.* www.nantybig.co.uk. Shop 1m, golf course 18 hole 1.5m. Fishing on site, beach 150yd. Doctor 2.5m. All water sports at Abersoch. Pony trekking 1m. Coastal walks. Bird, dolphin watching. Railway station 9m. Pant-y-Branner is strictly a static holiday caravan and chalet site with all modern facilities. No pets in hire caravans. Only 6 persons per caravan. Owner supplied copy. S of Abersoch, through the village of Sarn Bach. Head for Cilan and Porth Ceiriad beach. Open: 1 March - 10 January. BH&HPA ★ ★ 10⚡ 44⚡ ▲ 13⚡

**Sarn Farm, Sarn Bach, Abersoch, Gwynedd LL53 5BG.** *01758 713583.* 40 mixed pitches in total. Hot water. Fridge & freezer. Dishwashing facilities. Golf course, beaches 20mins walk. Shops 1m. Bus stop. Owner supplied copy. Site is near Abersoch, in the village of Sarn Bach on the Abersoch to Cilan road. Open: 22 April - 31 October. ★★★★ ★ ★ 40⚡

**(1m). Trem-y-Mor, Sarn Bach, Abersoch, Gwynedd LL53 7ET.** *07967 050170.* www.tggroup.co.uk. Holiday site. AA approved. Family site. Short walk down quiet lane to beach. Through Abersoch to Sarn Bach, then sharp L, site 200yd on R. Open: 1 March - 30 September. ★★★★ BH&HPA ★ ★ 80⚡ 80⚡ ▲

**(0.5m). Tyn-y-Mur Camping & Touring Park, Lon Garmon, Abersoch, Gwynedd LL53 7UL.** *01758 712328.* www.tyn-y-mur.co.uk. It has level ground and panoramic views of Abersoch Bay to the south and Hells Mouth. One dog allowed per unit. New children's play area. Full size football pitch. David Bellamy Gold Conservation Award. Owner supplied copy. Turn sharp R at the Land & Sea Garage on the approach to Abersoch. Park 0.5m on left-hand side. Open: 22 April - 31 October. ★★★★ BH&HPA NCC ★ ★ 10⚡ 40⚡ ▲

## Bala

**(3m). Bala Camping & Caravanning Club Site, Crynierth Caravan Park, Cefn Ddwysarn, Bala, Gwynedd LL23 7LN.** *01678 530324.* www.campingandcaravanningclub.co.uk. Ideal for water sports. 4m from Bala Lake in Snowdonia National Park. All units accepted. Non-members welcome. Loo Of the Year - champions league, standard of Excellence Award. Barmouth and Welshpool are within easy reach of the site. Enjoy a ride on one of the many narrow gauge railways around Bala. Special deals available for families and backpackers. A5 on to A494 to Bala. Through Bethel and Sarnau villages. Pass Cefn-Ddwysarn sign. R up lane before red phone box. Site is 400yd on L. Open: 1 April - 31 October. ★★★★ NCC ★ ★ 50⚡ 50⚡ ▲

**(3m). Glanllyn Lakeside Caravan And Camping Park, Bala, Gwynedd LL23 7SS.** *01678 540227.* www.glanllyn.com. Plenty of outdoor activities available locally. Launching facilities. Lake side location. Level parkland with extensive views of the Aran, Arenig and Berwyn mountains. Central for touring north and mid Wales. SW of Bala on A494 - halfway between Bala and LLanuwchllyn. Open: 25 March - 9 October. BH&HPA ★ ★ 50⚡ 84⚡ ▲ 30⚡

**(0.5m). Pen y Bont Touring & Camping Park, Llangynog Road, Bala, Gwynedd LL23 7PH.** *01678 520549.* www.peny-bont-bala.co.uk. Closest park to Bala Town (10mins walk) and the sailing club. Modern shower block to include disabled facility and laundry room. Calor gas available on site. On B4391. Open: 23 March - 27 October. ★★★★ BH&HPA ★ ★ 31⚡ 31⚡ 36▲

**(2.5m). Ty Isaf Caravan Site, Llangynog Road, Bala, Gwynedd LL23 7PP.** *01678 520574.* www.tyisafbala.co.uk. Quiet, family site with level grass. Camp fires allowed. Gas sales. Free showers. Games area. Fishing on site; golf course, shops, PO, doctor all within 2.5m. Owner supplied copy. Off B4391 near telephone kiosk and post box. Open: 1 April - 31 October. ★ ★ 5⚡ 30⚡ ▲

**(4m). Tyn Cornel Camping & Caravan Park, Frongoch, Bala, Gwynedd LL23 7NU.** *01678 520759.* www.tyncornel.co.uk. We pride ourselves on running a clean and quiet campsite, just 4m outside the peaceful market town of Bala where you will find a swimming pool, cinema and golf course. Owner supplied copy. Take A4212 from Bala. Drive through Frongoch village, 1m beyond on L. Sharp turn over river bridge. Open: 2 April - 19 October. ★★★★ BH&HPA ★ ★ 12⚡ 25⚡ 25▲

## Bangor

**(3m). Dinas Farm Camping and Touring Site, Halfway Bridge, Bangor, Gwynedd LL57 4NB.** *01248 364227.* www.dinas-farmtouringpark.co.uk. Site is situated on the banks of the river Ogwen and enjoys an entirely sheltered setting amongst woodland. Fishing on site - by permit only. J11 on to A5 towards Bethesda, L off A55. For 1m then R towards Tregarth for 0.5m then Dinas Farm site on L. Open: 1 March - 31 October. ★ ★ 5⚡ 15⚡ ▲

**(5m) Ogwen Bank Caravan Park & Country Club, Ogwen Bank, Bethesda, Bangor, Gwynedd LL57 3LQ.** *01248 600486.* www.ogwenbank.co.uk. Set amidst 12-acres of glorious woodland. Members' club with entertainment and bar snacks in main season. Children welcome. Laundrette. Hill walking. On A5. Open: 1 March - 5 November. ★★★★ BH&HPA ★ ★ 130⚡

## Barmouth

**(4m). Bellaport Caravan Park (Adults only), Talybont, Barmouth, Gwynedd LL43 2BX.** *01341 247338.* ADULTS ONLY. No dogs in static van. Fishing, golf course nearby. Off A496, turn R at 40mph limit sign leaving Talybont village travelling N to top of lane. Barmouth 4m. 0.5m from village. Open: 1 March - 30 September. ★★★ ★ ★ 5⚡ 20⚡

**(5m). Benar Beach, Talybont, Barmouth, Gwynedd LL43 2AR.** *01341 247001.* Well-equipped family site 100yd from safe, sandy beach with miles of golden sand dunes. Satellite & TV hook-ups. Ideal touring base for Snowdonia & mid-Wales. Tents welcome. 5m N of Barmouth. On the seaward side of A496, mid-way Barmouth to Harlech. Open: 1 March - 31 October. ★ ★ 20⚡ 45⚡ ▲

**(2.5m). Caerddaniel Holiday Home Park, Llanaber, Barmouth, Gwynedd LL42 1RR.** *01341 280611.* www.barmouthholidays.co.uk. Site adjoins beautiful sandy beach, fabulous views and sunsets. Wayside Inn nearby. Perfect for walkers, golfers and those seeking the quiet life. 8m from Royal St Davids golf course. 2.5m from shops in Barmouth. New modern caravans. Owner supplied copy. Heading N along the A496, on the beach side of the main road on L. Open: 1 March - 5 January. ★★★★ ★ ★ 350⚡

**Dalar Farm, Tal-y-Bont, Barmouth, Gwynedd LL43 2BJ.** *01341 247221.* Flat, well-drained site near beaches. Fees on application. Shop, cafe/restaurant within few minutes. Owner supplied copy. 5m N of Barmouth. Leave A496 at Tal-y-Bont on to beach road. Turn R through green gate near station, follow track to farm. Open: 1 March - 31 October. ★ ★ 15⚡ ▲

**(1.5m). Hendre Coed Isaf Caravan Park, Llanaber, Barmouth, Gwynedd LL49 9RB.** *01341 280597.* www.hendrecoed-isaf.co.uk. Terraced caravan pitches with superb views over Cardigan Bay. Pet and pet-free caravans. Club, bar, restaurant. Swimming pool (July & August only). Games room. Caravan lets and

# WALES

sales. Sea, mountains, golf courses, fishing, walks and attractions all nearby. On main coastal road A496, Barmouth to Harlech. Approx 1.5m N of Barmouth. Open: 1 March - 10 January. ★★★★
🏠🚪🐕🛒🔌🚿♿🚻📶 113⚡️

**PREMIER PARKS 2011** (0.5m). **Hendre Mynach Touring Caravan & Camping Park, Barmouth, Gwynedd LL42 1YR.** *01341 280262.* www.hendremynach.co.uk. Ideally based for touring mid and north Wales. Heated toilet and shower blocks. Disabled facilities. Launderette. Shop/cafe with takeaway. Children's playground. Mother and baby room. 100 meters from a safe, sandy beach. 20mins safe and pleasant walk into Barmouth along the promenade. Pets welcome, dog walk nearby. Site near to public transport. 0.5m N of Barmouth on the A496 Harlech road. Open: 1 March - 9 January. ★★★★★ 🏠🚪🐕🛒🔌🚿♿🚻📶 🍴🛁🏊☕🎮 60⚡️ 🚗

(3.5m). **Islawrffordd Caravan & Camping Site, Tal-y-Bont, Barmouth, Gwynedd LL43 2AQ.** *01341 247269.* www.islawrffordd.co.uk. Family owned park for tourers & static holiday homes. Heated indoor swimming pool/sauna/Jacuzzi & tanning. Stunning coastline nearby. 4m N of Barmouth via A496. Turn L to beach at Tal-y-Bont. Site is second L. Open: All year. ★★★★★ BH&HPA 🏠🚪🐕🛒🔌🚿♿🚻📶 25⚡️ 25⚡️ 🚗

(5m). **Parc Caerelwan, Tal-y-bont, Barmouth, Gwynedd LL43 2AX.** *01341 247236.* www.parccaerelwan.co.uk. No tourers. Facilities for partially disabled. (1 unit). Indoor heated swimming pool. Launderette. Sauna, steam room, solarium, fitness room. Tot's fun room. Table tennis, pool tables, golf and pony trekking close by. Pets welcome. Shop opens from March 1-end of October. Beach, Golf course, cinema, shopping centre within 5m. Owner supplied copy. Off A496 Harlech to Barmouth. Turn L at 30mph sign when entering Talybont village. First caravan park on the R after the railway bridge. Open: 5 March - 26 November. ★★★★ BH&HPA NCC 🏠🚪🐕🛒 🔌🚿♿ 180⚡️

(5m). **Parc Isaf Farm, Dyffryn Ardudwy, Barmouth, Gwynedd LL44 2RJ.** *01341 247447.* www.parcisaf.co.uk. A lovely spot with a view of Cardigan Bay. Shops, PO, sandy beach, garage within 1m. Golf, fishing, historic castle, caverns within 5m. Woodland walk, lakes and mountain nearby. Owner supplied copy. Travel from Barmouth on the A496 through the village of Talybont, then about 0.25m there is a church on the L, few yards on there is a right hand turning through a pillar

gateway and we are the second farm on R. Open: 1 March - 31 October. 🏠🐕🛒🔌🚿♿ 20⚡️ 🚗

(4m). **Rowen Caravan Park, Talybont, Barmouth, Gwynedd LL43 2AD.** *01341 242626.* www.rowenpark.com. Small, quiet, family-run park for families. Footpath to beach, offering static caravans, lodges and chalets for hire. Owner supplied copy. Off A496, 4m N of Barmouth on the L. Open: 2 April - 29 October. ★★★★★ BH&HPA 🏠🚪🐕🛒 50⚡️

(4m). **Sarnfaen Holiday Park, Talybont, Barmouth, Gwynedd LL43 2AQ.** *01341 247241.* www.sarnfaen.com. Level landscaped site, 5mins walk to sandy beach. Brand new leisure club, heated indoor swimming pool. Coffee shop, games room, laundry. The site also has a dog walk and a new adventure play area for the children. Owner supplied copy. On main A496 coast road from Barmouth L turn on entering Talybont village, over railway halt and third entrance on R. Open: 1 March - 7 January. ★★★★ BH&HPA 🏠🚪🐕🛒🔌🚿♿ 140⚡️

(4m). **Sunnysands, Talybont, Barmouth, Gwynedd LL43 2LQ.** *01341 247301.* www.sunnysands.co.uk. Indoor pool complex. Slipway to beach. Licensed family club. Family amusement centre. Coffee shop. Leisure Centre 4m. Golf course, cinema & theatre 6m. On A496 Harlech to Barmouth. Open: 1 April - 31 October. 🏠🚪🐕🛒🔌🚿♿ 25⚡️ 25⚡️ 610⚡️

(2m). **Trawsdir Touring Caravans and Camping Park, Llanaber, Barmouth, Gwynedd LL42 1RR.** *01341 280999.* www.barmouthholidays.co.uk. Touring centre and overnight stop. Separate field for caravans. Advance bookings essential (main weeks). Fees on application. Seasonal pitches available. On A496 200yd N from Wayside Inn. Coastal site N of Barmouth. Open: 1 March - 6 January. 🏠🚪🐕🛒🔌🚿♿ 70⚡️ 70⚡️ 30 🚗

(2m). **Trawsdir Touring Caravans and Camping Park (Premier Park), Llanaber, Barmouth, Gwynedd LL42 1RR.** *01341 280999.* www.trawsdir.co.uk. Touring centre and overnight stop. Separate field for caravans. Advance bookings essential (main weeks). Fees on application. Seasonal pitches available. On A496 200yd N from Wayside Inn. Coastal site N of Barmouth. Open: 1 March - 6 January. 🏠🚪🐕🛒🔌🚿♿ 70⚡️ 70⚡️ 30 🚗

## Beddgelert

(0.75m). **Beddgelert Forest Holidays**

Site, Beddgelert, Gwynedd LL55 4UU. *01766 890288.* www.forestholidays.co.uk. In the heart of Snowdonia, within walking distance of Mount Snowdon. Three National Parks and five Areas of Outstanding Natural Beauty within driving distance. Bookings and brochure requests on 0845 1308224. 1m NW of Beddgelert on A4085. Open: All year. BH&HPA 🏠🚪🐕🛒🔌🚿♿🚻📶 195⚡️ 🚗

### Blaenau Ffestiniog

(2m). **Coed-Y-Llwyn Caravan Club Site, Gellilydan, Blaenau Ffestiniog, Gwynedd LL41 4EN.** *01766 590254.* www.caravanclub.co.uk. Landscaped within the Snowdonia National Park. Toilet blocks. Privacy cubicles. Laundry facilities. Veg prep. MV service point. Play equipment. Fishing and golf nearby. Significant places of interest nearby. Ideal for families. Members only. No tents. See website for standard directions to site. Open: 30 March - 29 October. NCC 🏠🚪🐕🛒🔌🚿♿🚻📶 96⚡️ 96⚡️

(4m). **Llechrwd Riverside Camping, Maentwrog, Blaenau Ffestiniog, Gwynedd LL41 4HF.** *01766 590240.* www.llechrwd.co.uk. Quiet, family run riverside site situated in Snowdonia National Park. Excellent centre for walking, mountain biking, slate mines, Ffestiniog Railway and climbing. Portmeirion Italianate village 4m. Safe beach 7m. Porthmadog 9m and Harlech 8m. Owner supplied copy. On A496 between Blaenau Ffestiniog (4m) and Maentwrog (1m). On left hand side travelling towards Blaenau Ffestiniog. Open: 1 April - 31 October. 🏠🚪🐕🛒🔌🚿♿ 8⚡️ 8⚡️ 🚗

### Caernarfon

(5m). **Bryn Gloch Caravan and Camping Park, Betws Garmon, Caernarfon, Gwynedd LL54 7YY.** *01286 650216.* www.northwalescamping.co.uk. All facilities available. Free hot showers. 2m from Mount Snowdon. Award-winning site. AA 4 pennants. Golf 5m, pony trekking 3m. On A4085 Beddgelert Caernarfon. On the bank of river Gwyrfai in the Vale of Betws. Open: 1 March - 31 October. ★★★★ 🏠🚪🐕🛒🔌🚿♿🚻📶 48⚡️ 148⚡️ 15 🚗

(6m). **Caernarfon Bay Caravan Park, Dinas Dinlle, Caernarfon, Gwynedd LL54 5LW.** *01286 830492.* www.caernarfonbaycaravanpark.com. Small park 50yd from beach and close to all amenities. Pets welcome. Off A499. Open: 1 March - 31 October. ★★★★ 🏠🚪🐕🛒🔌🚿♿ 20⚡️ 🚗

# WALES

**Coed Helen Caravan Club Site, Coed Helen Road, Caernarfon, Gwynedd LL54 5RS.** 01286 676770. www.caravanclub.co.uk. 45 pitches set around a two acre grassed site. The key appeal is its stunning location. 10 minute walk from the famous town of Caernarfon. See website for standard directions to site. Open: 25 March - 31 October.

(0.5m). **Cwm Cadnant Valley Caravan Park, Llanberis Road, Caernarfon, Gwynedd LL55 2DF.** 01286 673196. www.cwmcadnantvalley.co.uk. Well maintained site, set in a small peaceful valley. 0.5m walk to town castle. Easy distance Snowdon and Anglesey. Take A4086 from Caernarfon - Llanberis Road. Campsite next to fire station. Open: 14 March - 1 November.

(7m). **Dinlle Caravan Park, Dinas Dinlle, Caernarfon, Gwynedd LL54 5TW.** 01286 830324. www.thornleyleisure.co.uk. Laundrette. Licensed club. Heated swimming pool. Takeaway. Beach 300yd. SW of Caernarfon. Take A487-A499 from Caernarfon and Pwllheli. After 5.5m Dinas Dinlle is SP W past AA phone box. Dinlle Park is SP on beach road. Open: 1 March - 30 November.

(0.5m). **Is-Helen Farm, Caernarfon, Gwynedd LL54 5RN.** 01286 678497. www.ishelenfarm.co.uk. Within walking distance of a golf course and historic castle town of Caernarfon. Fishing, sailing & water sports facilities very close. 5mins walk to Menai Straits. 20mins away from the foot of Snowdon. Children can watch milking and feeding calves. Dogs must be kept on lead. Owner supplied copy. Off A499 to/from Caernarfon. Open: All year.

(7m) **Morfa Lodge Caravan Site, Dinas Dille, Caernarfon, Gwynedd LL54 5TP.** 01286 830205. www.morfalodge.co.uk. Family run and orientated holiday park within the perfect beach and nature reserve location. Offering high quality holiday home and lodge sales. Take A487 from Caernarfon followed by A499 Pwllheli. 7m from Caernarfon turn R for Dinas Dinlle and follow signs. Open: 1 March - 31 October.

(3m). **Plas Gwyn Caravan Park, Llanberis Road, Llanrug, Caernarfon, Gwynedd LL55 2AQ.** 01286 672619. www.plasgwyn.co.uk. Gas exchange service. Shop and laundry. Caravans for hire. Bed and breakfast on request. Horse riding, fishing nearby. Golf course 0.5m, shopping centre 3m, cinema 20m. Entrance off the A4086 on R 3m from Caernarfon, about half way to Llanberis. Open: 1 March - 31 October.

(1.5m). **Rhyd y Galen Caravan and Camping Park, Bethel, Caernarfon, Gwynedd LL55 1UL.** 01286 650216. www.wales-camping.co.uk. Quiet and truly beautiful park, 15mins from the Snowdon footpath, mountains, lakes and coast are on your doorstep. Perfect for family holidays. B4366 Caernarfon to Bethel Road. Open: 1 March - 31 October.

(2m). **Riverside Camping (Caernarfon), Seiont Nurseries, Pontrug, Caernarfon, Gwynedd LL55 2BB.** 01286 678781. www.riversidecamping.co.uk. Small, sheltered site bordered by river. Ideally situated in Snowdonia within easy reach of both sea and mountains. Modern toilets and separate disabled facilities. Children's playground. On site: cafe/restaurant in old mill, laundrette, fishing on association water - permits available. General provision shop and chip shop 1m. Indian restaurant within 8th mile. Golf 3m. PO and doctors 2m. 2m from Caernarfon on the right hand side of the A4086 (Caernarfon-Llanberis road). Entrance also signed Seiont Nurseries. Open: 22 April - 31 October.

**Snowdonia Park, Waunfawr, Caernarfon, Gwynedd LL55 4AQ.** 01286 650409. www.snowdonia-park.co.uk. Small site adjacent to a steam railway. Convenient for walkers wanting to climb Mount Snowdon, or visit Caernarfon. Food & real ale nearby. Off A4085. Open: All year.

(12m). **Talymignedd Caravan Site, Nantle, Caernarfon, Gwynedd LL54 6BT.** 01286 880374. Walking, climbing and fishing on 1300 acres. Quiet and peaceful site. 12m from Porthmadog railway station. Nearest village is Penygroes, good selection of shops, newsagents, PO, banks, chemist, doctor's surgery. Major tourist attraction The Welsh Highland Railway. Due West of Snowdon on the B4418 from Rhyd-ddu to Penygroes. About 2m from Rhyd-ddu. Walking, climbing and fishing on 1300 acres. Quiet and peaceful site. 12m from Porthmadog railway station. Nearest village is Penygroes, good selection of shops, newsagents, PO, banks, chemist, doctor surgery. Major tourist attraction The Welsh Highland Railway. Open: 1 March - 31 October.

(3m). **Tyn Rhos Farm Caravan Park, Saron, Llanwnda, Caernarfon, Gwynedd LL54 5UH.** 01286 830362. www.tynrhosfarm.co.uk. All pitches hardstandings. Golf 2.5m. Shop, PO, doctor, garage, leisure centre within 3m. Narrow gauge steam railway 1m. Cycle track. Beach 3m. Owner supplied copy. Turn R off A487 Caernarfon to Porthmadog road immediately after crossing Seiont Bridge into Pant Road (SP Saron). Site 3m on L. Open: 1 March - 31 October.

(6m). **West Point Beach Resort, The Beach, Pontllyfni, Caernarfon, Gwynedd LL54 5EH.** 01286 660400. Your own beach, all water sports. TV and Video. Full central heating and electric blankets. Villas for sale. Boat park and launch service. Also fishing: sea & river. Golf courses, shopping centre within half hour's drive. A487 on to A499 Caernarfon to Pwllheli Road. Open: 1 March - 1 November.

(3m). **White Tower Caravan Park, Llandwrog, Caernarfon, Gwynedd LL54 5UH.** 01286 830649. www.whitetowerpark.co.uk. Central heated shower block for tourers. Laundrette. Club. Games room. TV room. Calor Gas sales. Heated pool, entertainment, & children's play area. Seasonal touring pitches also available. Golf course 1.5m. From Caernarfon follow A487 Porthmadog road for about 0.25m go past McDonalds, straight ahead at roundabout take first R, park 3m on R. Open: 1 March - 10 January.

## Criccieth

(1m). **Eisteddfa Caravan & Camping Park, Eisteddfa Lodge, Pentrefelin, Criccieth, Gwynedd LL52 0PT.** 01766 522696. www.eisteddfapark.co.uk. Golf course and PO 1m away. Fishing lake next door. Cinema, swimming pool 3.5m. All amenities available in Criccieth. AA 4 pennants. Owner supplied copy. Come to Porthmadog and at roundabout follow the A497 towards Criccieth. Follow road for 3.5m through Pentrefelin take first R after Plasgwyn Eisteddfa. Open: 1 March - 31 October.

(3m). **Llanystumdwy Camping & Caravanning Club Site, Tyddyn Sianel, Llanystumdwy, Criccieth, Gwynedd LL52 0LS.** 01766 522855. www.campingandcaravanningclub.co.uk. There are

**300 yards from long sandy beach**

# ENJOY THE BEST OF BOTH WORLDS, BETWEEN SEA AND MOUNTAINS

## LUXURY HOLIDAY HOMES FOR SALE AND HIRE

- Licensed Club House
- Pets Welcome
- Heated Swimming Pool
- Games Room
- Super Pitches available
- Two Shower Blocks
- Two Children's Play Areas
- Touring & Camping on level grassland
- Washing-up and Laundry facilities
- Electrical Hook-ups available

To request a brochure please contact:
**Dinlle Caravan Park, Dinas Dinlle, Caernarfon LL54 5TW**
Tel: 01286 830324
www.thornleyleisure.co.uk

# WALES

scenic coastal views and sandy beaches close to the site. Close to Snowdonia National Park. Pleasant walks just below the village of Llanystumdwy. All units accepted. Non-members welcome. Special deals available for families and backpackers. From Criccieth take A497 W, 2nd R to Llanystumdwy, site on R. 1.5m from the attractive seaside resort of Criccieth. Open: 1 April - 31 October. ★★★ NCC ⌂▣⥋🐾♿⛱🚗🅿 ⛺♿ 70⚡ 70🔌 ⛺

(1m). **Llwyn Bugeilydd Farm, Criccieth, Gwynedd LL52 0PN.** 01766 522235. llwynbugeilydd.co.uk. Owner's mobile number: 07854 063192. 1m walk to beach and shops. Snowdon view from caravan site. One step to toilets/showers. Shaver and hairdryer points. Deep sinks for laundry and washing-up with free hot water. Senior citizens reduced rate low season. Criccieth golf course 18 hole, and also lake fishing is only 1.5m from the site. Regular bus service from site main entrance. Level site with sea and mountain views, situated away from traffic noise. Dog walking field. AA 2 pennants. From A55 take A487 through Caernarfon, then just past Bryncir, turn R on to the B4411, site on L 3.5m. From Porthmadog, take A497 then turn R in Criccieth town centre on to B4411, site on R in 1m. Open: 1 April - 31 October. ★★★★ 2⌂▣🐾 ⥋⛱🅿⛺♿ 5⚡ 30🔌 ⛺

(1m). **Mynydd-Du Caravan Park, Porthmadog Road, Criccieth, Gwynedd LL52 0PS.** 07810 386927. www.mynydddu.co.uk. New toilet blocks. Garages, fishing and golf courses in the area. Shops, PO and doctors within 1.5m. Owner-occupied caravans, from 1/3/11 to 15/1/12. Owner supplied copy. On A497. 3m W of Porthmadog, 1m E of Criccieth on the Criccieth side of Pentrefelin. Open: 1 March - 31 October. BH&HPA ⌂▣🐾 ⥋⛱🅿♿ 5⚡ 50🔌 ⛺ 12⛺ 🏠

(1.25m). **Tyddyn Morthwyl Campsite, Rhoslan, Criccieth, Gwynedd LL52 0NF.** 01766 522115. Sheltered site with good views and convenient for sea and mountains. Dogs on lead welcome. All amenities in the seaside town of Criccieth. Horse riding, local attractions nearby. On B4411 Criccieth to Caernarfon road. Open: 22 April - 31 October. ⌂🐾⥋⛱♿ 10🔌 10⚡ ⛺ 22🏠

## Dolgellau

(3m). **Dolgamedd Holiday Park, Bontnewydd, Brithdir, Dolgellau, Gwynedd LL40 2DG.** 01341 422624. 11 acre family run park, level and sheltered, set beside a river where camp fires are allowed. Street lights and picnic tables. Well appointed, spacious pitches available

to locate your own chosen holiday home. 3 separate fields available for tourers and campers. Swimming and fishing on site. Bird watchers paradise, excellent base for mountain biking. Top class facilities. Take A494 from Dolgellau, travel 3m towards Bala. Take B4416 for Brithdir, Dolgamedd on L after bridge, beside river Wnion. Open: 1 April - 31 October. ★★★ ⌂▣🐾⥋⛱🚗♿⛺ 5⚡ 38🔌 ⛺🏠

(4m). **Llwyn-yr-Helm Farm, Brithdir, Dolgellau, Gwynedd LL40 2SA.** 01341 450254. www.llwynyrhelmcaravanpark.co.uk. Small working farm park in scenic countryside. 2 toilets, shower block, disabled/family room. Laundry. Eggs available. Ideal for walkers, country lovers and the more enthusiastic mountain biker, also for relaxing and enjoying the views. Coast 10m. Owner supplied copy. Situated on minor road 0.5m off B4416 which is a loop road from A470 to A494. Open: 22 April - 31 October. ★★★ BH&HPA ⌂🐾⥋⛱♿ 10🔌 15⚡ ⛺

(6m). **Pant-y-Cae, Arthog, Dolgellau, Gwynedd LL39 1LJ.** 01341 250892. www.pantycae.co.uk. We are an organic farm in the foothills of Cadair Idris in the picturesque countryside for bird watching, walking, cycling, fishing only 4m from a sandy beach, shops. Owner supplied copy. Off A493 Towyn to Dolgellau on road to Cregennan lakes, SP after Arthog village. Open: All year. NCC ⌂▣🐾⥋ ⛱♿ 56🔌 54⚡ ⛺ 5🏠

(0.5m). **Tanyfron Camping And Caravan Site, Arran Road, Dolgellau, Gwynedd LL40 2AA.** 01341 422638. www.tanyfron.co.uk. Small family run quiet park, centrally located for touring. Less than 10mins/0.5m into Dolgellau where there are shops, cafes, restaurants etc. Tent prices include showers. No dogs on touring pitches. Take A470 from Welshpool, turn L Dolgellau. 0.5m on L by 30mph sign. Open: All year. ★★★★★ BH&HPA ⌂▣🐾⥋⛱🚗♿ ⛺ 13🔌 ⛺ 22🏠

## Dyffryn Ardudwy

(5m). **Dyffryn Seaside Estate, Dyffryn Ardudwy, Gwynedd LL44 2HD.** 01341 247220. www.dyffryn-seaside-estate.co.uk. Club. Dragon Award Park. On A496. Open: 1 March - 31 October. BH&HPA ⌂▣🐾⥋⛱🚗♿ 3⚡ 3🔌 ⛺ 40🏠

**Murmur-yr-Afon Touring Caravan & Camping Park, Dyffryn Ardudwy, Gwynedd LL44 2BE.** 01341 247353. www.murmuryrafon1@btinternet.com. Set in sheltered surroundings 1m from

the beach. Shop, Gas & Camping Gaz available in village which has off licence and hotel. Take A496 coast road from Barmouth to Harlech. Site entrance is 100yd from Bentley's garage in Dyffryn on right hand side. Open: 1 March - 31 October. ★★★★ ⌂▣🐾⥋🚗 ⛱⛺♿ 30⚡ 30🔌 37⛺

## Fairbourne

(1m). **Bwlch Gwyn Farm Caravan Park, Fairbourne, Gwynedd LL39 1BX.** 01341 250107. www.bwlchgwynfarm.co.uk. Small, quiet, farm park overlooking Mawddach Estuary and sea. 2.5m to sandy beach. Close to shops. Pony trekking. From Dolgellau follow A493 towards Fairbourne, park on left hand side. Open: 1 March - 31 October. BH&HPA ⌂🐾 ⥋▣⛱♿ 10🔌 ⛺ 20🏠

## Harlech

(4m). **Barcdy Touring Caravan & Camping Site, Talsarnau, Harlech, Gwynedd LL47 6YG.** 01766 770736. www.barcdy.co.uk. Ideal situation for touring Snowdonia. In quiet, picturesque surroundings. Wi-Fi available on all pitches. Garage, golf course 4m. Fishing nearby (10mins walk from park). Shops 1m, supermarkets 5m at Porthmadog. On A496 Blaenau Ffestiniog to Harlech. Open: 1 April - 30 September. ★★★★ BH&HPA ⌂▣🐾⥋⛱🚗♿ 8⚡ 32🔌 ⛺ 1🏠

(1m). **Min-Y-Don Caravan Park, Beach Road, Harlech, Gwynedd LL46 2UG.** 01766 780286. www.minydonholidayhomepark.co.uk. Central for Snowdonia. Below Harlech Castle. 5mins walk to railway station and bus stop. Near sandy beach and St Davids golf course. Doctor 5mins walk. Laundry facilities on site. Easily accessible off A596 coast road. Turn into Beach Road opposite Queens Hotel. Open: 1 March - 31 October. ⌂ 🐾⥋▣⛱🚗♿ 5⚡ 20🔌

## Llanrug

(3m). **Challoner Caravan Park, Erw Hywel Farm, Llanberis Road, Llanrug, Gwynedd LL55 2AJ.** 01286 672985. Small friendly camp site, surrounded by mountains and greenery, energetic or relaxing holidays, catered for, by a wealth of activities in the area, from deep water diving to golf. Mid week deals. Please ring for information. Wildlife meadow, bird hide: no dogs or unaccompanied children in this area. A4086 4m W of Llanberis and 3m E of Caernarfon. Open: 1 March - 10 January. ⌂▣🐾⥋⛱♿ 10🔌 10⚡ ⛺

# WALES

### Llwyngwril

(1m). **Sunbeach Holiday Park, Llwyngwril, Gwynedd LL37 2QN.** *01341 250263.* www.allencaravans.com. Own beach frontage. Club with restaurant. Fishing, golfing and horse riding nearby. Bus and train service. David Bellamy Silver Conservation Award. Owner supplied copy. On A493,1m S of Llwyngwril on R. 6m from Tywyn. Open: 7 March - 6 January. BH&HPA NCC 380

### Penmaenmawr

(1m). **Tyddyn Du Touring Park, Conwy Old Road, Penmaenmawr, Gwynedd LL34 6RE.** *01492 622300.* www.tyddyndutouringpark.co.uk. 100 pitches in total. Adults (over 18) only site with superb views across Conwy Bay. Ideal base for enjoying attractions of Snowdonia. Golf (0.5m), riding, walking, fishing (1m), local shops 10 mins walk & pubs nearby. David Bellamy Silver Conservation Award. Take A55 W of Conwy. Follow Tourist Info signs, 1st L at roundabout at junction 16 immediate L again towards Dwygyfylchi, site entrance 200yd on R after Gladstone Inn. Open: 22 March - 31 October. ★★★★ BH&HPA 100

### Porthmadog

(3m). **Black Rock Sands Touring & Camping Park, Black Rock Sands, Morfa Bychan, Porthmadog, Gwynedd LL49 9YH.** *01766 513919.* www.blackrocksands.webs.com. Shop & PO 1m, leisure centre 3m. David Bellamy Gold Conservation Award. After coming over toll gate into Porthmadog, turn sharp L by Factory Shop. Continue on through Morfa Bychan to the end, the park is opposite Black Rock cafe. Adjacent to 7m beach. Open: 1 March - 31 October. ★★★ BH&HPA 10 40

(1m). **Blaen Cefn, Penrhyndeudraeth, Porthmadog, Gwynedd LL48 6NA.** *07788 822003.* www.blaencefn.co.uk. 1m to shops and pubs. Fishing on site, horse riding 4m. Off A487 Porthmadog road, 1m E of Porthmadog. Open: 1 March - 31 October. 50 25

(2m). **Garreg Goch Caravan Park, Black Rock Sands, Morfa Bychan, Porthmadog, Gwynedd LL49 9YD.** *01766 512210.* www.garreggochpark.co.uk. Mainly caravan park but space for tents. Easy reach of beach. David Bellamy Gold Conservation Award. 2m W of Porthmadog. Turning for Morfa Bychan. Follow this road - pass BP filling station then turn L into Park. Open: 1 March - 10 January. ★★★★ BH&HPA 74 8

(2m). **Greenacres Holiday Park (Haven), Black Rock Sands, Morfa Bychan, Porthmadog, Gwynedd LL49 9YF.** *0871 2310886.* www.caravancamping.co.uk. Welcome Host Award, Investor In People. Heated indoor swimming pool. Mini market. Bakery. Pitch & putt. Kids' clubs. Access onto Black Rock Sands. Day and evening family entertainment. David Bellamy Gold Conservation Award. From Porthmadog High Street, turn between Woolworth's and the PO towards Black Rock Sands. Carry on for about 2m. The park entrance is just the other side of Morfa Bychan on the left hand side. Open: 18 March - 31 October. ★★★★ BH&HPA 48 48 1212

(0.5m). **Tyddyn Llwyn Farm Caravan & Camping Park, Morfa Bychan Road, Porthmadog, Gwynedd LL49 9UR.** *01766 512205.* www.tyddynllwyn.com. Tranquil location with level and elevated pitches. Razor points. Laundrette. Gas bottle for sale. Bar on site. All weather pitches available. Off A487. Turn at Woolworth's on Porthmadog High Street. Park on R side at bottom of hill. Open: 1 March - 31 October. ★★★★ BH&HPA 120 53

### Pwllheli

**Aberafon Holiday Park, Nefyn, Pwllheli, Gwynedd LL53 6LL.** *01758 720520.* www.haulfryn.co.uk. Wi-Fi internet access. Nefyn Golf Club. Maritime Museum. Cliff top walks, fishing, sailing. Owner supplied copy. From Pwllheli take A499 to Abersoch, about 1m. Turn R on to A497 to Nefyn. Through Nefyn taking Llithfaen Road, about 1m. on L. Open: 1 March - 10 January. 75

(1.5m). **Abererch Sands Holiday Centre, Abererch, Pwllheli, Gwynedd LL53 6PJ.** *01758 612327.* www.abererch-sands.co.uk. Heated indoor swimming pool. Fitness room. Play area for children. On A497 Criccieth to Pwllheli. Open: 1 March - 31 October. BH&HPA 70 85

(5m). **Bodwrog Camping & Caravanning Site, Llanbedrog, Pwllheli, Gwynedd LL53 7RE.** *01758 740341.* www.bodwrog.co.uk. Quiet family site. Close to beaches. Superb sea views. Disabled toilet. Electric hook-ups. Storage facilities. On Lof B4413, 1m from its junction with A499. Open: 1 March - 31 October. 30

**Bolmynydd Touring & Camping Park, Refail, Llanbedrog, Pwllheli, Gwynedd LL53 7UP.** *07882 850820.* www.bolmynydd.co.uk. Secluded park on Llanbedrog headland with glorious views. Within 10mins walk of two beautiful sandy beaches, pub and shop. Essential for tourers and motorhomes to book in advance. A499 from Pwllheli to Llanbedrog. Carry on towards Abersoch for 0.5m. Take first L lane after riding centre. Park 0.5m on L. Open: 1 April - 31 October. ★★★★★

(10m). **Cefn Hedog Caravan and Camping Site, Rhoshirwaun, Pwllheli, Gwynedd LL53 8HL.** *01758 760551.* www.cefnhedog.co.uk. Beautiful sea views, peaceful, coastal walks. 2m to shop, PO, beach. 4m to doctor. 3 golf courses within 10m. Hub cycle route, sea fishing 2m. Owner supplied copy. A499 W from Pwllheli. At Llanbedrog bear R on to B4413 for 5m then R on to Whistling Sands Road. Site 100yd on R. Open: 1 April - 31 October. NCC 15

(3m). **Hafan y Môr Holiday Park (Haven), Pwllheli, Pwllheli, Gwynedd LL53 6HJ.** *0871 2310887.* www.haven.com. Heated indoor swimming pool with flumes and slides. Daytime and evening family entertainment. Convenience store. Bakery. Direct beach access. Views of Snowdonia. Kid's clubs. All weather multi-sports court. New adventure golf. David Bellamy Gold Conservation Award. M54 to Telford, A5 past Oswestry and Llangollen. Take A494 to Bala, at traffic lights turn R following signs for Porthmadog, then SP for Criccieth and Pwllheli. Park is 3m on your L. Open: 18 March - 31 October. ★★★★ BH&HPA NCC 73 73 820

**Maes Carafanau Pen y Berth Caravan Park, Penrhos, Pwllheli, Gwynedd LL53 7HG.** *01758 612581.* www.pen-y-berth.co.uk.

(18m). **Tir Glyn Caravan Park, Tir Glyn, Aberdaron, Pwllheli, Gwynedd LL53 8DA.** *01758 760248.* www.tirglyn.com. Tir Glyn is a dairy farm situated at the tip of the Llyn Peninsula surrounded by National Trust Land. Dogs on lead. Local authority licence. All pitches located around the outside of the field. Washing machines, tumble dryers, freezer, washing up facilities. Shops and post 1m, doctor about 8m. Owner supplied copy. 0.5m from shops. Aberdaron, Uwchmynydd Road, (B4413) first L turn, site 0.25m. Above Fisherman's Cove. T Open: 1 April - 31 October. 30

# WALES

**(3m). Tyddyn Heilyn Caravan Park, Tyddyn Heilyn Farm, Chwilog, Pwllheli, Gwynedd LL53 6SW.** *01766 810441.* Beautiful scenic 10m walks passing through this farmland - overlooking Cardigan Bay/Snowdonia scenery. Ideal bird watching - coastal and country birds. Easy reach to shops, good eating out places and pubs. Near 2 fishing rivers and lakes, riding school, ample good golf, 20m safe cycle track nearby, also cycle routes here. Site very level and shaded. All amenities within 2.5m. Dogs must be kept on lead. Owner supplied copy. From A497 to B4354 and at village of Chwilog, before pub turn R in between houses opposite Povey butchers. 1.5m along, second site. Site marked. Open: 15 April - 31 October. BH&HPA

**(0.5m). Wern Newydd Tourer Park, Llanbedrog, Pwllheli, Gwynedd LL53 7PG.** *01758 740220.* www.wern-newydd.co.uk. Peaceful site. 15 mins walk to the beach, 5 mins to village. Good eating places, shops, PO, chemist, pubs, sailing, water sports facilities, golf, riding, fishing etc nearby. Doctor's surgery 4m. Turn R off A499 (Pwllheli-Abersoch) in Llanbedrog on to B4413 (Sp Aberdaron) continue through village, past the chemist on the R, then take first turning R on to unclassified road, called Lon Pin. Site entrance on the R in 700yd. Open: 1 March - 31 October. ★★★ BH&HPA NCC

**(4m). Wernol Caravan Park, Chwilog Fawr, Chwilog, Pwllheli, Gwynedd LL53 6SW.** *01766 810506.* www.wernol.co.uk. Free coarse fishing lake. Lovely country walks. 5 golf courses within 12m radius. 1m to village shop and country pub. 4m marina at Pwllheli. Cycle route. Panoramic views. From Porthmadog (A497), turn R on to B4354 - 1m to Chwilog. Turn R in Chwilog opposite butcher shop (blind turning). Park 1m on R. Open: 1 March - 15 January. ★★★★ BH&HPA

## Tyn-y-Gongl

**(1m). Bwlch Holiday Park, Bwlch, Tyn-y-Gongl, Gwynedd LL74 8RF.** *01248 852914.* www.bwlchholidaypark.co.uk/information.htm. All mains services. Fishing/golf about 0.5m away. Quiet park with all privately owned caravans. On A5025 then B5108 for 1.5m. Open: 1 March - 31 December. BH&HPA

**(0.5m). Pant Y Saer Caravan Park, Benllech, Tyn-y-Gongl, Gwynedd LL74 8SD.** *01248 852423.* 0.5m from village. Superb views. Beach 0.5m. Golf, shopping centre, doctors, PO within 0.5m. Wonderful coastal walks, quiet family run park, walking distance from Benllech village. From Benllech x roads on A5025. Off Llangefni road turn L down lane under Scots pine trees. Follow sign for Pant Y Saer farm. Open: All year. BH&HPA

## Tywyn

**Cwmrhwyddfor Camp Site, Talyllyn, Tal Y Llyn, Tywyn, Gwynedd LL36 9AJ.** *01654 761286.* Very clean park with hot showers, razor points, flush toilets. Disposal point. Electric Hook-ups. Tents also accepted. Tarmac road from main road to end of site. Touring caravan pitches available for summer and full season. Within easy reach of the sea. Excellent access. Ideal for walking. Fishing in stream. Craft shops. Pony trekking, golf course, shop nearby. Hotel and cafe less than 5mins walk away. Open all year for tents. On A487 6m from Dolgellau at bottom of Talyllyn Pass. White house on R at foot of Cader Idris mountain. Open: 1 March - 31 October.

**(5.5m). Glanywern Farm Caravan Site, Dysefin Farm, Llanegryn, Tywyn, Gwynedd LL36 9TH.** *01654 782247.* Fishing, golf course nearby. Shops 6m. Owner supplied copy. 3m E of the village of Llanegryn by Bird Rock. Open: 1 April - 31 October.

**Neptune Hall and Caravan Park, The Promenade, Tywyn, Gwynedd LL36 ODL.** *01654 710432.* Dogs allowed in owner-occupied if kept under control. Club on site. Owner supplied copy. Off A493. Open: 18 April - 31 October.

**(0.25m). Pall Mall Farm Caravan Park, Bryncrug Road, Tywyn, Gwynedd LL36 9RU.** *01654 710384.* Play area on site. Leisure centre, cinema, fishing, golf very near. Excellent beach and lots of lovely walks. Open Easter-end October (tourers), March 1-January 6 (statics). Owner supplied copy. Site is 1st farm on L 400yd W of Tywyn on A493. Open: 6 April - 31 October. BH&HPA

**(3m). Tynllwyn Caravan & Camping Park, Bryncrug, Tywyn, Gwynedd LL36 9RD.** *01654 710370.* www.tynllwyncaravanpark.co.uk. Small, friendly, family run site with excellent facilities. Telephone, laundry, play area. Talyllyn narrow gauge steam train runs past site. Off A493. Open: 1 March - 31 October. ★★★ BH&HPA NCC

**(4m). Waenfach Caravan Site, Llanegryn, Tywyn, Gwynedd LL36 9SB.** *01654 711052.* 10 pitches for tourers or motorcaravans. Beautiful views on working farm. Spacious amenities block with laundry facilities. Public telephone. Deep freeze. Dogs under control. Shops 2m; doctor, hospital, PO in Tywyn. Sea and river fishing, golf course 5m. Owner supplied copy. Off A493. Open: 1 March - 31 October.

**(1m). Ynysymaengwyn Holiday Park, Tywyn, Gwynedd LL36 9RY.** *01654 710684.* www.ynysy.co.uk. Relaxing, peaceful site. Tranquil woodland walks, lots of history. Fishing available. Tywyn town is short distance away with amenities. 1m out of Tywyn on the A493 towards Barmouth. Open: 1 April - 31 October. ★★★★ 3 NCC

# MONMOUTHSHIRE
## Monmouth

**(3m). Bridge Caravan Park & Camping Site, Dingestow, Monmouth, Monmouthshire NP25 4DY.** *01600 740241.* www.bridgecaravanpark.co.uk. In the heart of the Vale of Usk and Wye Valley next to the river Trothy. Fishing available to all visitors. A background of woodland completes the lovely setting of this select park. SP from Abergavenny junction of A449 trunk road. Open: 10 April - 31 October. ★★★★

**(2m). Glen Trothy Caravan & Camping Site, Mitchel Troy, Monmouth, Monmouthshire NP25 4BD.** *01600 712295.* www.glentrothy.co.uk. 1.5m from historic town of Monmouth in the Wye Valley and on the edge of the forest of Dean. Good range of facilities. Children's play area. Phone for free brochure. SW of Monmouth off new A40. Open: 1 March - 31 October. ★★★ BH&HPA NCC

**(0.5m). Monmouth Caravan Park, Southfield, Rockfield Road, Monmouth, Monmouthshire NP25 5BA.** *01600 714745.* Family run touring and camping park within easy walking distance of town. New facilities block and club house. Fishing available. 0.25m on B4233 Rockfield Road, just past fire and ambulance station. A40 to Monmouth. Leave to take the B4293 which then joins the B4233 to Abergavenny. Open: 1 March - 31 October. ★★★★ BH&HPA

**Monnow Bridge Caravan Site, Drybridge Street, Monmouth, Monmouthshire NP25 3AD.** *01600 714004.* Caravans for

# WALES

## PEMBROKESHIRE

### Amroth

**(1.25m). Amroth Bay Holidays, Amroth, Pembrokeshire SA67 8PR.** 01834 831259. www.amrothbay.co.uk. Heated pool, play area and laundrette. Well behaved dogs welcome. Dragon Award. Pub/restaurant 10mins walk. Situated in the National Park, just minutes from Amroth's Golden Sands. SC discounts, couples 30%, fortnight discounts. Off A477. At Llanteg in the direction of Tenby turn left at Murco garage. Park is about 1m on the R 1.25m from Amroth beach. Open: 1 March - 4 November. ★★★★★ BH&HPA 40

**(6m). Meadow House Holiday Park, Summerhill, Narberth, Amroth, Pembrokeshire SA67 8NS.** 01834 812438. www.celticholidayparks.co.uk. Indoor swimming pool. No dogs July 19-August 31. Direct access to Pembrokeshire National Park coastal footpath. David Bellamy Gold Conservation Award. 6m NE of Tenby. From Tenby take A478. After 3.5m turn R on to A477, turn R again at sign Amroth and Wisemans Bridge. From St Clears on A477 for 10m, after 'Stage Coach Inn' turn L at sign. 1m from beach. Indoor swimming pool. No dogs July 19-August 31. Direct access to Pembrokeshire National Park coastal footpath. David Bellamy Gold Conservation Award. Open: 1 March - 31 December. BH&HPA NCC 55

### Clynderwen

**(3.5m). Trefach Caravan Park, Mynachlog-ddu, Clynderwen, Pembrokeshire SA66 7RU.** 01994 419225. www.manorparks.com. Well-drained site in good walking area within Preseli National Park. 18-acre country site. Central to all Pembrokeshire, ideal for exploring by foot, car or horseback. Heated swimming pool. Play room. Restaurant. Bar. Fishing nearby. Owner supplied copy. 4m E of Maenclochog, 9m N of Narberth via A478 to 1m N of Efailwen, turn L by Cross Inn to site, 1m on R. Open: 1 March - 6 January. ★★★ BH&HPA 54

### Fishguard

**(3m). Fishguard Bay Caravan & Camping Park, Garn Gelli, Fishguard, Pembrokeshire SA65 9ET.** 01348 811415. www.fishguardbay.com. Well SP. Games/pool room, children's play area. TV common room. Laundrette. Cinema, town and swimming pool 3m. Golf course 5m. Take A487 Fishguard to Cardigan road. Turning on your L. Open: 1 March - 9 January. ★★★★ BH&HPA 20 30 11

**(0.25m). Fishguard Holiday Park, Greenacres, Fishguard, Pembrokeshire SA65 9JH.** 01348 872462. www.howellsleisure.co.uk. Club. Nightly entertainment. Swimming pool. Short breaks and weekly stays. Just a few minutes walk into town. Facilities for the disabled in accord with the disability access. Off A40 Haverfordwest to Fishguard Road. Open: 11 March - 29 October. ★★★★ BH&HPA 74

**(1.5m). Gwaun Vale Holiday Touring Park, Llanychaer, Fishguard, Pembrokeshire SA65 9TA.** 01348 874698. www.gwaunvale.co.uk. Local pub 0.5m. Laundrette. Telephone. Play area. Dog walk. Gas. Fishing, boating, swimming, coast and mountain walks and Irish ferry within 2m. Clean, unspoilt beaches. From Fishguard take B4313 SP Llanychaer and Gwaun Valley. Park 1.5m on R. Open: 1 April - 31 October. ★★★ BH&HPA 4 22

### Haverfordwest

**(8m). Brandy Brook Camping and Caravan Site, Rhodaston, Haycastle, Haverfordwest, Pembrokeshire SA62 5PR.** 01348 840563. www.brandybrookcampsite.co.uk. Secluded and quiet in a remote natural valley. A487 from Haverfordwest to Roch Motel. SP at the right-hand turn. Open: 22 April - 31 October. BH&HPA 33

**(5m). Creampots Touring Caravan and Camping Park, Broadway, Broad Haven, Haverfordwest, Pembrokeshire SA62 3TU.** 01437 781776. www.creampots.co.uk. Quiet and level with excellent heated facilities including free hot showers. Convenient for touring, beaches, coast path, water sports and bird sanctuaries. Excellent site for couples and young families. 1.5m to Broadhaven beach. From Haverfordwest take B4341 Broad Haven Road. At Broadway turn L, follow brown signs for Creampots. Open: 1 March - 31 October. ★★★★★ BH&HPA 10 60

**(7m). Hasguard Cross Caravan Park, Little Haven, Haverfordwest, Pembrokeshire SA62 3SL.** 01437 781443. www.hasguardcross.co.uk. Children allowed. Owner supplied copy. B4327 out of Haverfordwest. After 7m, turn R to Little Haven. Entrance 200yd on right-hand side. Open: All year. ★★★★ BH&HPA 25 42

**(2m). Hendre Eynon, St David's, Haverfordwest, Pembrokeshire SA62 6DB.** 01437 720474. www.hendreeynon.co.uk. Simple style on a working farm with superb facilities. Two perimeter pitching fields with sheltering trees. A haven for walkers, birdwatchers and botanists. Owner supplied copy. 2m NE of St David's on u/c road to Llanrhian. Open: 22 April - 30 September. ★★★★ BH&HPA 10 50

**Howelston Holiday Park, Howelston, Little Haven, Haverfordwest, Pembrokeshire SA62 3UU.** 01437 781818. www.sunnyvaleholidaypark.com. 200yd from coastal path. Owner supplied copy. Minor road on coast off B4327 and B4341. From Haverfordwest. Overlooking St Brides Bay and 1m from seaside village of Little Haven. Open: 1 March - 6 November.

**(9m). Mabws Bridge Caravan Park, Mathry, Haverfordwest, Pembrokeshire SA62 5JB.** 01348 831466. www.mabwsbridgecaravanpark.co.uk. Small, family owned and managed park in a tranquil, rural setting offering a secure and peaceful environment to all home owners. Disabled facilities, showers - hardstanding surfaces - and heated swimming pool. Children & pets allowed. Rallies welcome. GS. Golf (2m), horse riding, coast walking, quad biking, leisure parks, bird watching, water sports, Irish Ferry, fishing (3m). Open March 1-January 10 for holiday homes. St David's (9m) to Fishguard Road (4m) A487. Open: 1 March - 30 November. ★★★★ 40 40 30

**(7m). Newgale Camping Site, Wood Farm, Newgale, Haverfordwest, Pembrokeshire SA62 6AR.** 01437 710253. www.newgalecampingsite.co.uk. Next to beach popular for watersports. Pub and surf shop next door. Off A487. From Newgale take coast road to Nolton Haven, park 0.5m second turning on L. Open: 1 April - 30 September. BH&HPA NCC 120 120

**(12m). Nine Wells Caravan & Camping Site, Nine Wells, Solva, Haverfordwest, Pembrokeshire SA62 6UH.** 01437 721809. www.ninewellscamping.com. Fishing, sailing, boating and beaches nearby. PO, village shops, pubs and restaurants in Solva. 5mins walk down

# WALES

National Trust Valley to Pembrokeshire Coastal Footpath, the cove and sea. From Haverfordwest take A487 SP St Davids, go through Solva. After 0.5m at Nine Wells turn L at site sign. Open: 5 April - 21 October.

**(6m). Nolton Cross Caravan Site, Nolton, Haverfordwest, Pembrokeshire SA62 3NP.** *01437 710701.* www.noltoncrossholidays.co.uk. Coarse fishing lake on site. Mini market 3m. Central location for all of Pembrokeshire. Off A487 St David's to Haverfordwest, 1.5m from coast overlooking St Brides Bay. Open: 1 March - 15 December. ★★★ BH&HPA

**(17m). Prendergast Caravan Site, Trefin, Haverfordwest, Pembrokeshire SA62 5AU.** *01348 831368.* www.prendergastcaravanpark.co.uk. Fees on application No pets. No single sex groups. Owner supplied copy. 8m NE of St Davids. Via A487 to Trefin, SP. N for 1m to site. 0.25m from beach. Open: 2 April - 1 October. ★★★

**(15m). Rhosson Ganol, St David's, Haverfordwest, Pembrokeshire SA62 6PY.** *01437 720361.* On A487, 1m from St David's. Open: 22 April - 31 October. BH&HPA

**(12m). Solva (Llanungar Fach) Caravan Site, Solva, Haverfordwest, Pembrokeshire SA62 6UA.** *01437 721202.* On A487 Haverfordwest to St David's. Open: Contact site direct.

**(5m). South Cockett Touring Caravan & Camping Park, Broadway, Broad Haven, Haverfordwest, Pembrokeshire SA62 3TU.** *01437 781296.* www.southcockett.co.uk. 73 pitches for tourers and/or motorcaravans. Shop 1m. Hot water to basins. Freezer pack service. Calor Gas and Camping Gaz stocked. Clean site with excellent facilities. Category 3 disabled facilities (check with site). Visit Wales 3 stars, AA 3 pennants. Owner supplied copy. Take B4341 from Haverfordwest, turn L at official caravan & camping sign. Site 300yd on R. Open: 1 April - 31 October. 3

**St David's Camping & Caravanning Club Site, Dwr Cwmwdig Berea, St David's, Haverfordwest, Pembrokeshire SA62 6DW.** *01348 831276.* www.campingandcaravanningclub.co.uk. Site is set in 4 acres with 40 pitches accepting all units. Very convenient for the coast, being 0.5m by footpath from Abereiddy. The site is located in the beautiful Pembrokeshire countryside, just 1m from the heritage coast and close to Britain's smallest Cathedral City. Non-members welcome. Fishing 1m from the site. Special deals available for families and backpackers. From Fishguard on A487 after Croesgoch, fork R. Follow 'Abereiddy' signs. Site is 300yd W of crossroads. 5m from St David's. Open: 14 April - 26 September. ★★★ NCC

## Kilgetty

**(5m). Croft Holiday Park, Reynalton, Kilgetty, Pembrokeshire SA68 0PE.** *01834 860315.* www.celticholidayparks.co.uk. Dragon award. Licensed clubhouse. Playground. Fishing, horse riding 3m. Shops 4m. Golf 5m. Cinema 8m. Only 8m from Saundersfoot. David Bellamy Gold Conservation Award. Off A40. On A478 follow brown signs for 'Croft Park' from Templeton. Open: 1 March - 31 October. ★★★★ BH&HPA NCC

**(4.5m). Cross Park Holiday Centre, Broadmoor, Kilgetty, Pembrokeshire SA68 0RS.** *01834 811244.* www.valeholidayparks.com. Picturesque family park with excellent facilities, showbar with nightly entertainment, kids club, heated indoor swimming pool, shop, games room. etc, etc. Continue on A477 1m W of Kilgetty. Turn R at Cross Inn pub, park 250yd on L. Open: 1 March - 31 October. ★★★★ BH&HPA

**(0.75m). Stone Pitt Caravan Park, Begelly, Kilgetty, Pembrokeshire SA68 0XE.** *01834 811086.* www.stonepitt.co.uk. Quiet location but within easy reach of all the attractions Pembrokeshire has to offer. David Bellamy Gold Conservation Award. Owner supplied copy. From M4: take A48 to Carmarthen. A40 to St Clears. Branch L at roundabout on A477 towards Tenby. At roundabout go R on A478 towards Narberth. Straight on at next roundabout. Stone Pitt is 0.5m on L. Open: All year. ★★★ BH&HPA

## Little Haven

**(1.5m). Redlands Touring Caravan & Camping Park, Hasguard Cross, Little Haven, Pembrokeshire SA62 3SJ.** *01437 781300.* www.redlandstouring.co.uk. 5 acres of open grassland. Level, spacious pitches. Hardstandings. Immaculately kept facilities. Pets welcome. Convenient base for Pembrokeshire holidays. Close to beaches and famous coastal path. Highly recommended. On B4327 SW of Haverfordwest, do not approach via Broad Haven. Open: 1 March - 16 December. ★★★★ BH&HPA

## Milford Haven

**(4m). Sandy Haven Caravan & Camp Site, Herbrandston, Milford Haven, Pembrokeshire SA73 3ST.** *01646 698844.* www.sandyhavencampingpark.co.uk. Close to all Pembrokeshire attractions; Skomer Marine Reserve, castles etc. Ideal for families, coastal walkers. In Pembrokeshire Coast National Park. Waterside location. Fishing, boating, skiing, golf, riding - all close by. Sandy beaches and estuary. Wonderful for bird life. Owner supplied copy. Turn L at Taberna Inn in village, follow road down to beach. Open: 22 April - 5 September. ★★★★

## Narberth

**(5m). Little Kings Park, Amroth Road, Ludchurch, Narberth, Pembrokeshire SA67 8PG.** *01834 831330.* www.littlekings.co.uk. Quiet family park in country setting with easy access to explore Pembrokeshire. Residents bar and restaurant. Indoor pool, shop, 2 amenity blocks. 2 play areas. Dog walk. Beach 1.5m. No pets in holiday homes, maximum 2 dogs in bungalow. No booking from all male/all female parties of young people. Owner-occupied caravans, from 1/3/10 to 30/10/11. Open for hire caravans, from 1/4/11 to 30/9/11. From A477 turn L to Amroth and Wiseman's Bridge, take first turn R, SP Ludchurch, park 0.25m on L. Open: 1 March - 31 October. ★★★★★ BH&HPA

**(0.5m). Noble Court Holiday Park, Redstone Road, Narberth, Pembrokeshire SA67 7ES.** *01834 861908.* www.celticholidayparks.com. Club. Heated swimming pool, coarse fishing. Shops 0.5m. Walking distance from Narberth. Off A40 on B4313 road, 0.5m N of Narberth and 0.5m S of A40. Open: 1 March - 31 October. ★★★★ BH&HPA NCC

**(5m). Oakland Caravan Park (Narberth), Summerhill, Amroth, Narberth, Pembrokeshire SA67 8NS.** *01834 811051.* Small, quiet family park. 1m from beaches. Upgraded to high standard. One luxurious caravan, double glazed and central heated, set in a secluded corner for hire at reasonable rates. Caravans/vacant pitches occasionally available. Farm shop 0.5m. Sandy beach, food shop, pubs, restaurants, take away foods all 1m. Indoor

# WALES

heated pool and golf course 6m. Website: www.caravancampingsites.co.uk/pembrokeshire/oakland.htm. Owner supplied copy. 1.5m off A477 towards Wiseman's Bridge. (1m from Amroth, 2.5m from Saundersfoot). Kilgetty 3m. Open: 1 March - 9 January. 22

**(1.5m). Pinewood Caravan Park, Wisemans Bridge, Narberth, Pembrokeshire SA67 8NU.** 01834 811082. www.pinewoodholidaypark.co.uk. Small, peaceful, family run park adjacent to Pembrokeshire coastal path. 8 Dragon Award caravans for hire. No tourers, no tents. Owner supplied copy. 1.5m from Saundersfoot. 350yd to beach. Open: 10 March - 3 November. ★★★★★ BH&HPA 8

**(10m). Rosebush Caravan Park (Adults only), Rhoslwyn, Rosebush, Narberth, Pembrokeshire SA66 7QT.** 01437 532206. Boating. Coarse fishing. ADULTS ONLY. David Bellamy Gold Conservation Award. Owner supplied copy. On B4313. B4329 1m away. Open: 1 March - 31 October. BH&HPA 5 4 15

**(6m). Starre Gorse Caravan Site, Stepaside, Pleasant Valley, Narberth, Pembrokeshire SA67 8LR.** 01834 812428. starregorseholidaypark.co.uk. Heated swimming pool. Owner supplied copy. Off A477. Open: 14 March - 31 October. 100

**(2m). Wood Office Caravan Park, Cold Blow, Narberth, Pembrokeshire SA67 8RR.** 01834 860565. Central for touring. Flat site, well drained. Oakwood Park, Folly Farm and Heron's Brook all nearby. Restrictions apply on dog breeds (Pit bull, Rottweiler). On A40, B4315. Close to Oakwood Park A478, Folly Farm and Heron's Brook golf. Open: 22 April - 1 November. 45 45

## Newport

**Morawelon, Parrog, Newport, Pembrokeshire SA42 0RW.** 01239 820565. Close to sandy beach, safe bathing, good sailing, slipway for boat launching ideal for wind surfers. Sheltered site with beautiful sea views. 1m from local shopping area, doctor & PO. Golf course 4m. Park situated on the Pembrokeshire coastal path for wonderful walks. Owner supplied copy. On A487 in Newport turn N on road to Parrog. Site on sea front. Open: 1 March - 31 October. 5 5

**Tycanol Farm Camp Site, Newport, Pembrokeshire SA42 0ST.** 01239 820264. www.tycanolfarm.co.uk. Level, sheltered pitches, overlooking Newport Bay. By the coastal path with easy access to beaches and town. Free hot showers. Bicycle hire nearby. Nature walk for wildlife. BBQ free nightly. Owner supplied copy. On A487 near Newport. Sign to Tycanol on milk stand. Open: All year. ★★ 10 10

## Pembroke

**(10m). Castle Farm Camping Site, Angle, Pembroke, Pembrokeshire SA71 5AR.** 01646 641220. Limited number of touring vans. Situated directly behind village church. Site overlooking East Angle Bay. Very good shops in the village - PO twice a week, 2 pubs with food. Beach cafe, safe sandy beach. Enter opposite Glode Hotel in Angle or follow directions to Lifeboat station: Castle Farm is directly in front of you. Holiday site near entrance of Milford Haven, in National Park (Pembrokeshire). Open: 22 April - 31 October. 25 10

**(2.5m). Freshwater East Caravan Club Site, Trewent Hill, Freshwater East, Pembroke, Pembrokeshire SA71 5LJ.** 01646 672341. www.caravanclub.co.uk. Within the Pembrokeshire Coast National Park. Part sloping, information room, dog walk nearby. 2 toilet blocks. Privacy cubicles. Laundry facilities. Veg prep. MV waste point. Hardstandings (50%). Gas and gaz. Play area. Non-members and tent campers welcome. Do not tow to the beach. Fishing and water sports. Good area for walking. Ideal for families, quiet and peaceful off peak, within 5m of NCN cycle route. See website for standard directions to site. Open: 30 March - 8 October. ★★★★ NCC 130 130

**(3m). Upper Portclew Farm (CS), Freshwater East, Pembroke, Pembrokeshire SA71 5LA.** 01646 672112. Small, friendly site. Freshwater East beach can be seen from the site. Dog friendly pub within walking distance. Basic facilities. Off A4139, Tenby to Pembroke road. Open: 1 May - 30 September.

**(1m). Windmill Hill Caravan Park, Windmill Hill Farm, Pembroke, Pembrokeshire SA71 5BT.** 01646 682392. www.windmillhillcaravanpark.co.uk. Family run site. Close to the Pembrokeshire National Park with its beautiful beaches and 5mins from the ferry terminal to Ireland. Modern toilets and showers on the park. Situated 1m S of Pembroke town on the B4319. Open: 1 March - 5 January. ★★★★ 30

## Saundersfoot

**(5m). Beachdean Leisure Park, Reynalton, Kilgetty, Saundersfoot, Pembrokeshire SA68 0PE.** 01834 891643. www.beachdeanholidays.co.uk. Static Caravans only. Immaculately maintained and winner of Wales In Bloom Award. Central location for all Pembrokeshire's splendour. Holiday Homes for sale and rent. Safe secure quiet park. A477 to Kilgetty, A478 towards Narberth turn sharp L at Boar's Head, Templeton for Reynalton. Open: 1 March - 31 October. ★★★★★ BH&HPA 50

**(0.75m). Bonville's Court Caravan Park, Weighbridge Office, The Ridgeway, Saundersfoot, Pembrokeshire SA69 9NA.** 01834 812673. www.bonvillescourtholidaypark.co.uk. Fishing, golf, cycling and walking all nearby. We are a quiet park in mature grounds 10mins walk from Saundersfoot beach and harbour. There is a PO in the village, plenty of shops and lovely pubs and restaurants. We also have a detached 3 bed superb cottage for rent with stunning meadow views and a large garden, in quiet location 10mins walk from Saundersfoot. David Bellamy Silver Conservation Award. Owner supplied copy. A40 from Carmarthen to St Clears then A477 to Kilgetty roundabout, take Tenby to Saundersfoot road for 0.75m, Saundersfoot sign B4316 via Ridgeway Road, park is 0.5m on R. Open: 9 April - 30 November. BH&HPA 10 55

**(1.5m). Moreton Farm Leisure Park, Moreton, Saundersfoot, Pembrokeshire SA69 9EA.** 01834 812016. www.moretonfarm.co.uk. Set in peaceful surroundings. Modern facilities. Pine lodges and cottages. Bed linen provided. Play area. On A478 Kilgetty to Tenby 3.5m. Saundersfoot 1.5m. Open: 1 March - 31 October. ★★★★ BH&HPA 20

**(1m). Moysland Farm, Tenby Road, Saundersfoot, Saundersfoot, Pembrokeshire SA69 9DS.** 01834 812455. 14 motor caravans/tents pitches in total. 4 acres, level. Low level nighttime lighting. On cycle route Saundersfoot to Tenby. Free hot water and showers, dogs welcome under control. Booking advisable July-September. Public transport, fishing within 1m. Owner supplied copy. On A478 2.5m S of Begelly roundabout, 1m CW of Saundersfoot. Open: 22 April - 30 September. 3

**(1m). Sunnyvale Holiday Park (Saundersfoot), Valley Road, Saundersfoot, Pembrokeshire SA69

# WALES

9BT. 01834 814404. www.sunnyvaleholidaypark.com. Club. Nightly entertainment. Heated indoor swimming pool. Shop, kiddies play park. Owner supplied copy. Take A478 towards Tenby. 3m from Tenby. Enter Pentlepoir. Pass Murco petrol station on R, take next left into Valley Road. Park 150yd down on left hand side. Open: 11 February - 2 January. ★★★★
BH&HPA ⌂ ⚙ ✈ ⚘ ⌘ ⚒ ⚔ ⛏
⚡ ⚓ 3⛺ 47⚐ ⛺ 106⛵

(1m). **White Gate Caravan Park, Pleasant Valley, Stepaside, Saundersfoot, Pembrokeshire SA67 8NY.** 01834 811543. www.whitegate-caravanpark.co.uk. LETTING ONLY. Close to Saundersfoot and coastal path. Small, select park in peaceful wooded valley yet only 400yd from beach. Regret no pets. Green Dragon Environmental Award level 2. Folly Farm, Oakwood Heatherton etc, all within 15mins drive. Shopping in Kilgetty 2m away. Owner supplied copy. Off A477, at L turn for Wiseman's Bridge. Follow road through Stepaside and take lower road into Pleasant Valley. Open: 24 March - 29 September. ★★★★★
BH&HPA ⌂ ⚙ ⚐ ⛺ 8⛵

(75m). **Windy Hill Holiday Park, Sardis, Saundersfoot, Pembrokeshire SA67 8JX.** 01834 812766. www.windyhillholidaypark.com. Windy Hill is set on high level overlooking some 60sq miles of countryside, some of which is in the Pembrokeshire Coast National Park. Shopping is only 0.75m at Kilgetty with approximately 12 shops and a Co-op supermarket, garage and Post Office. Doctor at Saundersfoot only 1.25m away. Within 5m golf courses, fishing, theme parks, wild life parks, etc. Beaches 1m. Launderette & Children's play area on site. Owner supplied copy. Turn R off the A477. SP Kilgetty, then take first L (150yd), Sardis Road. We are then about 0.75m on R. Open: 17 March - 29 October.
⌂ ✈ ⚘ ⚒ 15⚐ 30⛺ 2⛵

## St Davids

(1m). **Caerfai Bay Caravan Park, St Davids, Pembrokeshire SA62 6QT.** 01437 720274. www.caerfaibay.co.uk. Panoramic sea views. Seaside Award. Bathing beach 200yd, adjacent to Pembrokeshire coastal path and numerous local outdoor pursuits. Takeaway. Cafe/restaurant nearby. Shops 0.75m, golf 2m. No season site pitches available. Pets restrictions in high season. A487 to St Davids, turn at visitor centre, Caerfai SP, park at end of road on R. Open: 1 March - 11 November. ★★★★
BH&HPA ⌂ ⚙ ⚐ ✈ ⚘ ⌘ ⚒ ⚔ ⛏
15⚐ 28⛺ 9⛵

**Lleithyr Farm Caravan Park, Lleithyr Farm, Whitesands, St Davids,** Pembrokeshire SA62 6PR. 01437 720245. www.whitesands-stdavids.co.uk. 0.5m from one of the UK's finest beaches, Whitesands. Off A487. Haverfordwest 17m, St David's 1.5m. Follow signs for Whitesands. We are SP 1m from Whitesands. Open: 1 March - 5 January.
★★★★ BH&HPA ⌂ ⚙ ⚐ ✈ ⚘ ⌘ ⚒
⚔ ⛏ ⚡ ⚓ 15⚐ 30⛺ ⛺ 46⛵

(1.5m). **Lleithyr Meadow Caravan Club Site, Whitesands, St Davids, Pembrokeshire SA62 6PR.** 01437 720401. www.caravanclub.co.uk. A marvellous holiday site nestled by three headlands of the Pembrokeshire coast. Toilet block. Privacy cubicles. Laundry facilities. Veg prep. Information room. Shop adjacent. Gas. Motorhome waste. Play equipment. Non-members welcome. No tents. Fishing, golf and water sports nearby. Good area for walking. Dog walk nearby, beach and NCN cycle route within 5m. See website for standard directions to site. Open: 30 March - 8 October.
★★★★ NCC ⌂ ⚙ ⚐ ✈ ⚘ ⌘ ⚒
⚔ ⚡ ⚓ 120⛺ 120⚐ ⛺

(1m). **Porthclais Farm Campsite, St Davids, Pembrokeshire SA62 6RR.** 07970 439310. www.porthclais-farm-campsite.co.uk. Family run with most beautiful sea views. 24 acres are available for tents and one field of 5 acres is licensed for 12 touring caravans and motorcaravans. Owner supplied copy. SW of St David's. From Haverfordwest on A487. Keep L at St David's and join Porthclais road. Site is L after 0.5m farm site which adjoins Porthclais Harbour. Open: 28 May - 1 September. BH&HPA ⌂ ⚙ ⚐ ✈ ⚘
⌘ ⚒ 12⛺ 12⚐ ⛺ 24⛵

(14m). **Tretio Caravan and Camping Park, Caravan & Camping Park, St Davids, Pembrokeshire SA62 6DE.** 01437 781600. www.tretio.com. 4.5 acre 9 hole pitch and putt course. PO, doctors, shops available in St David's, 3m. 1.5m to nearest beach. Off B3283. St David's 3m. On leaving St David's keep L at St David's R.F.C and continue straight for 3m until sign pointing R. Park 300yd. Park situated in Pembrokeshire National Park. 0.25m off coast road and 0.5m to coastal path, panoramic views. Open: 1 March - 31 October. ★★★ ⌂ ⚙ ⚐ ✈ ⚘ ⌘ ⚒
⚔ ⛏ 10⚐ ⛺ 3⛵

## Tenby

(5m). **Buttyland (Arreton) Touring Caravan and Tent Park, Station Road, Manorbier, Tenby, Pembrokeshire SA70 7SN.** 01834 871278. www.arreton.net. Cafe nearby. Fees on application. On A4139 Pembroke to Tenby. Pass through Penally and Lydstep. After Lydstep straight over crossroads and after 1m turn R at sign to Manorbier Station. Site is 150yd on R. Open: 22 April - 31 October. ⌂ ⚙ ✈ ⚘
⚒ ⚔ ⛏ ⚡ ⚓ 15⚐ 35⛺ ⛵

(2.5m). **Crackwell Holiday Park, Penally, Tenby, Pembrokeshire SA70 7RX.** 01834 842688. www.crackwell-holidaypark.co.uk. Level pitches. Friendly local staff. Laundrette. Small convenience shop. Play area. Coastal path, beaches and all leisurely pursuits nearby. Luxury holiday homes available for hire and also for sale. Most of Hire Fleet is 'no pets allowed'. Families only. Owner-occupied caravans, from 01/03 to 07/01. Owner supplied copy. A40 from Carmarthen, follow A4139 from Tenby 2.5m on right hand side. Open: 21 March - 31 October.
BH&HPA ⌂ ⚙ ✈ ⚘ ⌘ ⚒ ⚔ 25⚐
75⛺ ⛺ 70⛵

(5m). **Hazelbrook Caravan Park, Sageston, Milton, Tenby, Pembrokeshire SA70 8SY.** 01646 651351. www.hazelbrookcaravanpark.co.uk. Quiet, family site. Hard or grass standing. Free showers. Shop. Gas. Laundry and ironing facilities. Games room. Good for coast and country holidays. Shops, doctor in Tenby and Pembroke Dock 5m. Fishing, golf course 1.5m. PO 1.25m. Pub/restaurant 0.25m. Dogs on leads, walk off park. No single sex groups. Owner-occupied caravans, from 1/3/11 to 9/1/12. Open for Hire caravans, from 22/4/11 to 31/10/11. Owner supplied copy. Off A477 on to B4318 at Sageston roundabout, 20yd on the R. Open: 14 March - 9 January.
NCC ⌂ ⚙ ✈ ⚘ ⌘ ⚒ ⚔ ⛏ 10⛺ 70⚐
⛺ 58⛵

(1m). **Kiln Park Holiday Centre (Haven), Marsh Road, Tenby, Pembrokeshire SA70 7RB.** 0871 2310889. www.caravancamping.co.uk. 2 show bars. Heated indoor fun pool. Outdoor pool. Arcade. Cafe and takeaway food. Mini market. Petrol station. Direct beach access. Family entertainment. Pitch n putt, tennis courts, mini bowling, bouncy castle, play area. 2 golf courses within 5mins drive. Oakwood Theme Park 15mins. Cinema in Tenby. Blue Flag Award, Welcome Host Award, AA Award. David Bellamy Gold Conservation Award. Follow A477/A478 to Tenby for about 6m. Follow the caravan/camping signs to Penally. Kiln Park is 0.5m on your L. Open: 18 March - 31 October. ★★★★ BH&HPA NCC ⚐ ⌂ ⚙
⚔ ✈ ⚘ ♫ ⌘ ⚒ ⚓ ⛏ ⚡ ⛏ ⛵
⚒ ⚔ ⛏ 15⚐ 240⛺ ⛺ 794⛵

(10m). **Lawrenny Quay Caravan Site, Lawrenny Quay, Lawrenny, Kilgetty, Tenby, Pembrokeshire SA68 0PR.** 01646 651212. www.lawrennyyachtstation.co.uk. Waters edge hotel accommodation, yachtsman's and fisherman's bars. Showers. Petrol, diesel station, moorings

# WALES

swinging and pontoons. Chandlery. Owner supplied copy. Off A4075. Open: 1 March - 31 December.

**(1.5m). Lodge Farm Holiday Park, New Hedges, Tenby, Pembrokeshire SA70 8TN.** 01834 842468. 65 A 40

**(2m). Lydstep Beach Village (Haven), Lydstep Beach, Tenby, Pembrokeshire SA70 7SB.** 0871 4680496. www.haven.com. Blue Flag Award, Welcome Host Award. Owners lounge, bar, snooker room, spa bath, gym, sun beds, steam room, family entertainment, private bay with boat launch, sea views, shops and restaurants. Fishing, golf all nearby. David Bellamy Gold Conservation Award. A40 then A478 to Tenby. Take A4139 SP Penally. Passing Kiln Park on your L follow the main road for nearly 3m and the park entrance is on the L. Open: 18 March - 31 October. ★★★★ BH&HPA NCC 474

**(1.5m). Manorbier Country Park, Station Road, Manorbier, Tenby, Pembrokeshire SA70 7SN.** 01834 871952. www.countrypark.co.uk. Heated indoor pool. Rail station nearby. Swimming pool. Laundry. Facilities block. Selection of sporting activities nearby. 4.5m to Tenby, nearest golf course 4.5m. No pets. No group bookings, no single sex parties. From Tenby follow A4139 towards Pembroke. Road widens with chapel on R, take right hand turn for Manorbier-Newton Station, park 300yd on L. Open: 1 March - 30 November. ★★★★★ NCC 35 A 131

**(4m). Masterland Farm, Broadmoor, Kilgetty, Tenby, Pembrokeshire SA68 0RH.** 01834 813298. Ideal for beaches and touring, all modern facilities. Baby bathroom. Bar and restaurant. TV room. Booking advisable at peak times. A477 to Broadmoor, turn R at Croos Inn pub, after 300yd turn R for park. Open: 1 February - 9 January. ★★★ BH&HPA 38

**(4m). Milton Bridge Caravan Park, Milton, Tenby, Pembrokeshire SA70 8PH.** 01646 651204. www.miltonbridgecaravanpark.co.uk. Small, peaceful, family run park set in the National Park on river estuary. Convenient for visiting Pembroke's numerous attractions. Shop over road. Pub and restaurant at entrance to park. Owner supplied copy. Directly off the A477 at Milton, SP Cosheston. Open: 1 March - 31 October. BH&HPA 15 24

**Northcliff Caravan Park, North Cliff, Tenby, Pembrokeshire SA70 8AU.** 01834 843526. www.btinternet.com/~m.

calver/northcliff.html. Nearest site to beach and town. Phone (winter) 01782 303527. Owner supplied copy. Take L fork after passing 'Welcome to Tenby' sign on A478 into Narberth Road, at bottom of road turn L into The Croft, park at top of road. Open: 22 April - 30 September. 15

**(2m). Rowston Holiday Park, New Hedges, Tenby, Pembrokeshire SA70 8TL.** 01834 842178. www.rowston-holiday-park.co.uk. Flat to sloping park with sea views. Owner supplied copy. Follow signs for New Hedges through village mini-market on R, park is second turning on L. Open: 2 April - 29 October. BH&HPA 110 A 133

**(3m). Trevayne Farm Caravan Park, Saundersfoot, Tenby, Pembrokeshire SA69 9DL.** 01834 813402. www.camping-pembrokeshire.co.uk. We have a newly built block of showers, toilets and washing facilities. Access to Monkstone Bay, one of Pembrokeshire's finest beaches and beautiful scenic walks. Owner supplied copy. Off A478 Narberth to Tenby. 15mins walk from New Hedges village. Open: 1 April - 31 October. BH&HPA 35 97 A 80

**(6m). Tudor Glen Caravan Park, Jameston, Manorbier, Tenby, Pembrokeshire SA70 7SS.** 01834 871417. www.tudorglencaravanpark.com. Family site, no groups. 1m from Manorbier Beach and Pembrokeshire coastal path. Golf at Tenby with its superb beaches 5m away. Oakwood 10m. David Bellamy Gold Conservation Award. On A4139 .Tenby to Pembroke. Open: 1 March - 31 October. ★★★★ BH&HPA 30 A 20

**(1m). Well Park, New Hedges, Tenby, Pembrokeshire SA70 8TL.** 01834 842179. www.wellparkcaravans.co.uk. Excellent facilities - free showers. Holiday caravans and cottages for hire. Family run park convenient for all beaches and touring Pembrokeshire coast. Licensed bar. Wales in Bloom Award. Golf course nearby. 4 mins walk to shops, PO. Doctors 1m. 15 mins walk to Waterwynch beach. AA 4 pennants. On right-hand side of main A478 Tenby road. 1m before reaching Tenby. Open: 12 March - 31 October. ★★★★★ 4 BH&HPA 10 40 A 48

**(3m). Whitewell Holiday Park, Lydstep Beach, Penally, Tenby, Pembrokeshire SA70 7RY.** 01834 871569. www.whitewellholidaypark.com. Campers' bar. Club. Footpath to Lydstep beach. Theme and adventure park, golf course nearby. Off A4139 Tenby to Manorbier. Open: 1

March - 30 November. ★★ 20 20 A

**(1.5m). Wood Park Caravans, New Hedges, Tenby, Pembrokeshire SA70 8TL.** 01834 843414. www.woodpark.co.uk. Friendly, family park with games room, laundrette, excellent facilities block. No groups please. Small dogs only allowed, except Easter week, Spring bank holiday week and school holidays. No dogs allowed in hire caravans at any time. Owner supplied copy. At roundabout 2m N of Tenby take A478 then second R and R again. Open: 6 April - 30 September. ★★★★ BH&HPA 40 A 106

## Whitland

**(4m). Old Vicarage Caravan Park, Red Roses, Whitland, Pembrokeshire SA34 0PE.** 01834 831637. www.valeholidayparks.com. Close to beaches and central for touring S W Wales. Licensed club, bar meals, heated outdoor swimming pool, play area, facilities block and laundry. Separate field for ball games. On A477 in Red Roses. Open: 1 April - 31 October. BH&HPA 17 A 23

**(3m). Pantglas Farm Caravan Park, Tavernspite, Whitland, Pembrokeshire SA34 0NS.** 01834 831618. www.pantglasfarm.co.uk. Quiet, family run, rural park. Play area. New disabled wet room. Near Amroth, Saundersfoot and Tenby. Caravan storage. Shops, doctor, dentist, vets in Whitland 3m away. Golf 4m, fishing 1m. PO 3m. Bar on site open Friday/Saturday and weekdays during main school holidays. Games room open daily. On A477 to Tenby to Pembroke. Turn R Red Roses to Tavernspite. Take the middle road at village pump, Pantglas 600metres on L. Open: 23 March - 21 October. ★★★★ BH&HPA 22 83 24

# POWYS

## Brecon

**(4.5m). Aberbran Caravan Club Site, Aberbran, Brecon, Powys LD3 9NH.** 01874 622424. www.caravanclub.co.uk. On edge of Brecon Beacons National Park. Chemical toilet disposal point. Advance booking essential. Shipping length of outfit required due to size limitation of some pitches. No toilet block. Hardstandings. Gas. Dog walk. Fishing and golf nearby. Good area for walking. Members only. No tents. See website for standard directions to site. Open: 23 March - 29 October. ★★ NCC 24 24

# WALES

**(8m). Anchorage Caravan Park, Bronllys, Brecon, Powys LD3 0LD.** 01874 711246. www.anchoragecp.co.uk. SAE for brochure. High standard park with panoramic views. Children's play area, PO, hairdresser's, laundrette, TV room. Golf course, cinema 8m. Midway between Brecon and Hay-on-Wye in centre of Bronllys village. Nr Brecon Beacons. Open: All year. ★★★★ BH&HPA ⚏ ⛌ ⛾ ⚲ ⦿ ⚙ ❉ ⚐ ⛌ ♿ WC 10⛺ 60⛺ ⛺ 77⛺

**(1m). Bishops Meadow Caravan & Camping Park, Hay Road, Brecon, Powys LD3 9SW.** 01874 610000. www.bishops-meadow.co.uk. With spectacular views of the Brecon Beacons the park was opened in 1993 and its restaurant is open all day. Friendly lounge bar. Heated outdoor swimming pool. Play area. Dog exercise area. Situated on the B4602 about 1m from the town centre. Open: 1 March - 31 October. ★★★★★ ⚏ ⛌ ⛾ ⚲ ⦿ ⚙ ❉ ⚐ ⛌ ⛱ ⛌ ♿ WC ♿ ⛺ 80⛺ ⛺

**(1.5m). Brynich Caravan Club Site, Brynich, Brecon, Powys LD3 7SH.** 01874 623325. www.caravanclub.co.uk. Award winning family run park with panoramic views of the Brecon Beacons. Two immaculately clean, fully equipped amenity blocks including baby and disabled rooms. Play area, adventure playground and recreation field. Relaxing brookside walks and dog exercise field. Easy access, large level pitches with short grass. Well stocked shop (inc Off Licence). Restaurant adjoining site (Listed in Good Food Guide). Children's soft indoor play facility next door. On A470 200yd from A40-A470 roundabout. Open: 23 March - 29 October. ★★★★ BH&HPA ⚏ ⛌ ⛾ ⚲ ⦿ ⚙ ❉ ⚐ ⛌ ⛱ ⛌ ♿ WC 144⛺ 144⛺ ⛺

**(6m). Lakeside Caravan Park (Brecon), Llangorse Lake, Brecon, Powys LD3 7TR.** 01874 658226. www.llangorselake.co.uk. AA 3-pennants site. Excellent club house. Cafe, activity centre and local pubs nearby. Riding, climbing centres 1m. Indoor swimming pool, golf course, cinema, gliding, shop/market town all within 6m. David Bellamy Gold Conservation Award. Off A40 at Bwlch, then B4560 to Llangorse. SP to Llangorse lake and common. Open: 19 March - 5 November. ★★★ 3 BH&HPA ⚏ ⛌ ⛾ ⚲ ⦿ ⚙ ❉ ⛌ ♿ ⚞ ⛺ 10⛺ 20⛺ ⛺ 90⛺

**(6m). Llynfi Holiday Park, Llangorse, Brecon, Powys LD3 7TR.** 01874 658283. www.llynfi.com. LLangorse lake a short walk. Heated pool, licensed bar and all facilities. Off B4560. Park is on flat, secluded and grassy in the Brecon Beacons National Park. Open: 21 March - 8 November. BH&HPA ⚏ ⛌ ⛾ ⚲ ⦿ ⚙ ❉ 15⛺ 30⛺ ⛺

**(3m). Pencelli Castle, Pencelli, Brecon, Powys LD3 7LX.** 01874 665451. www.pencelli-castle.com. Peaceful, countryside park in the heart of Brecon Beacons National Park. Within walking distance of highest peaks. Adjoining Brecon Canal. Village pub 150yd. Bike hire. On bus route. Wi-Fi. Wales in Bloom Winner 2011, Loo of the Year Winner 2011. David Bellamy Gold Conservation Award. On B4558 off A40. 3m SE of Brecon. Open: 1 February - 30 November. ★★★★★ BH&HPA ⚏ ⛌ ⛾ ⚲ ⦿ ⚙ ❉ ⛌ ♿ WC 40⛺ 40⛺ ⛺

**(0.5m). Riverside International (Brecon), Bronllys, Brecon, Powys LD3 0HL.** 01874 712850. www.riversideinternational.co.uk. Licensed restaurant. Heated indoor swimming pool. Leisure complex, gym, sauna, Jacuzzi. Laundrette. Bathroom. Public phone. Takeaway service available. Fishing on site. Ideal site for cycling and walking. AA 3 pennants. Calor Gas Award. David Bellamy Bronze Conservation Award. W of Talgarth on A479 opposite Bronllys Castle. Open: 1 February - 31 December. ★★★★ BH&HPA ⚏ ⛌ ⛾ ⚲ ⦿ ⚙ ❉ ⛌ ⛱ ⛌ ♿ ⛺ 25⛺ 35⛺

## Builth Wells

**(4m). Fforest Fields Caravan & Camping Site, Hundred House, Builth Wells, Powys LD1 5RT.** 01982 570406. www.fforestfields.co.uk. Peaceful, level mown site straddling a mountain stream. Hardstandings. Clean, modern facilities with free showers. Laundry. Dogs welcome. Lovely forest and moorland walks direct from site, excellent for bird watching. Pub 1m. 101 Best Site 2007, Area Winner Wales. David Bellamy Gold Conservation Award. Easy access off A481, 0.5m from Hundred House village. Open: 6 April - 31 October. ★★★★ BH&HPA ⚏ ⛌ ⛾ ⚲ ⦿ ⚙ ❉ ⛌ ♿ WC 20⛺ 40⛺ ⛺

**(6m). Irfon River Caravan Park, Upper Chapel Road, Garth, Builth Wells, Powys LD4 4BH.** 01591 620310. Nestling between the Epynt and Cambrian mountains. A quiet, family run, quality park, on the banks of the river Irfon with trout fishing. Ideal for touring mid Wales. New and used holiday vans for sale. Seasonal pitches for Touring Caravans, with hardstandings. Cafe/restaurant 1m. 500yd S of Garth on B4519, W of Builth Wells. Open: 1 April - 31 October. ★★★★ BH&HPA ⚏ ⛌ ⛾ ⚲ ⦿ ⚙ ❉ ⛌ ♿ 12⛺ 12⛺ 47⛺

**(8m). Riverside Caravan Park (Builth Wells), Llangammarch Wells, Builth Wells, Powys LD4 4BY.** 01591 620465. www.riversidecaravans.com. Peaceful park with surrounding mountain views, many places of interest locally. Modern facilities. Shop nearby. Laundry room, BBQ area with large gazebo. Hard stand, lawned and riverside pitches, all year storage. Large safe play area. Fishing. Owner supplied copy. From Builth Wells take A483 and second L turn in Garth SP Llangammarch Wells 2m. Open: 1 April - 31 October. BH&HPA ⚏ ⛌ ⛾ ⚲ ⦿ ⚙ ❉ ⛌ ♿ WC 16⛺ 15⛺ ⛺ 12⛺

## Church Stoke

**Daisy Bank Caravan Park, Snead, Church Stoke, Powys SY15 6EB.** 01588 620471. www.daisy-bank.co.uk. Adults-only site featuring 55 fully-serviced pitches set in a laid back part of Wales. On-site are award winning loos & laundry room. Off A489 Lydham to Church Stoke road. Open: All year. ★★★★★ ⚏ ⛌ ⛾ ⚲ ⦿ ⚙ ❉ 50⛺ 50⛺ 10⛺

**(1.5m). Mellington Hall Holiday Home Park, Mellington, Church Stoke, Powys SY15 6HX.** 01588 620011. www.mellingtonhallcaravanpark.co.uk. 30 hardstanding pitches with open grassed areas overlooking lush parkland. Fishing & access to all the hotel's facilities. Many walks. Leave A489, W of Churchstoke, on to B4385 to Mellington. Open: All year. BH&HPA ⚏ ⛌ ⛾ ⚲ ⦿ ⚙ ❉ ⛌ ♿ 30⛺ 30⛺ ⛺ 95⛺

## Crickhowell

**(4m). Cwmdu Caravan & Camping Site, Cwmdu, Crickhowell, Powys NP8 1RU.** 01874 730441. www.campingbreconbeacons.com. Ideal base for exploring national park. Quiet location. Walking on Black Mountains from site. Refer to website for further details. On A479, turn off at Farmers Arms pub, Cwmdu and site is 300 metres distant. Open: 18 April - 31 October. ⚏ ⛌ ⛾ ⚲ ⦿ ⚙ ❉ ⛌ ♿ 10⛺ 50⛺ ⛺

**(0.25m). Riverside Caravan & Camping Park (Crickhowell), New Road, Crickhowell, Powys NP8 1AY.** 01873 810397. www.riversidecaravanscrickhowell.co.uk. Adults only. Level, grassy site. Canal nearby. Town 5 mins walk. Mountain walks. Restaurant 200yds. No single sex groups, hang or paragliders. Between A40 and B4558. Open: 1 March - 31 October. BH&HPA ⚏ ⛌ ⛾ ⚲ ⦿ ⚙ ❉ ⛌ ♿ 10⛺ 25⛺ ⛺ 20⛺

## Hay-on-Wye

**(1.5m). Borders Hideaway Holiday Home Park, Painscastle Road, Clyro,**

# WALES

**Hay-on-Wye, Powys HR2 5SG.** *01497 820156.* www.bhhhp.co.uk. Peace & tranquillity. Beautiful Herefordshire border countryside - historic town of Hay-on-Wye, second-hand book capital of the world! David Bellamy Silver Conservation Award. Owner supplied copy. From Leominster on A44, A4112, A438. Enter village of Clyro. Turn R SP Painscastle, 0.5m on R. Open: 15 March - 15 October. ★★★★ BH&HPA 🐕 ♿ ⚡ 🚿 18⚡ 18👤

## Llanbrynmair

**(1m). Cringoed Holiday Park, The Birches, Llanbrynmair, Powys SY19 7DR.** *01650 521237.* www.cringoed.co.uk. New facilities block and laundry room. Ideal base for touring mid Wales with its many attractions including castles, slate mines and the Alternative Technology Centre. Machynlleth 5m - golf course, shopping. Idyllic location for escaping the pressures of life. Nestling beside the river Twymyn with breathtaking scenery. David Bellamy Gold Conservation Award. Turn off A470 at Llanbrynmair on the B4518 for 1m. By river Twymyn. Open: 1 March - 31 October. ★★★★ BH&HPA NCC 🐕 ♿ ⚡ 🚿 6⚡ 35⚡ 👤 35👤

**Gwern-Y-Bwlch Caravan Club Site, Llanbrynmair, Powys SY19 7EB.** *01650 521351.* www.caravanclub.co.uk. A gem of a site in a lovely setting, lost in Mid Wales between Snowdonia and Montgomeryshire with splendid mountain views. Chemical toilet disposal point. Gas and Gaz. Shop 1.5m. Non-members welcome. No tents. No toilet block. Some hardstandings. Good area for walking. Dog walk. See website for standard directions to site. Open: 30 March - 1 October. ★★★★ NCC 🐕 ♿ ⚡ 🚿 37⚡ 37⚡

## Llandrindod Wells

**(3m). Disserth Caravan & Camping Park, Howey, Llandrindod Wells, Powys LD1 6NL.** *01597 860277.* www.disserth.com. Very good park with level, sheltered pitches in a peaceful riverside setting. Ideal touring centre. Licensed bar, free hot showers and dishwashing. Fishing on site. Shops, golf 3m. Cinema 6m. AA 3 pennants. 1m off A483 Llandrindod Wells to Builth Wells, by Disserth Church between Howey and Newbridge-on-Wye Brown signed. Open: 1 March - 31 October. ★ BH&HPA 🐕 ♿ ⚡ 🚿 25⚡ 25⚡ 👤

**(7m). The Pines Caravan Park, Pine Lodge, Doldowlod, Llandrindod Wells, Powys LD1 6NN.** *01597 810068.* www.pinescaravanpark.co.uk. Shop. Gas. Pub and restaurant adjacent. Wheelchair accessible caravan available for hire. Near Elan Valley reservoirs and Red Kite Centre. Excellent bird watching and walking. Swimming pool 4m. Golf course 8m. Cinema 9m. David Bellamy Gold Conservation Award. Owner supplied copy. 3.5m S of Rhayader on A470 to Builth Wells. Open: 1 March - 31 October. BH&HPA 🐕 ♿ ⚡ 🚿 34⚡

## Llangynog

**Glendower Caravan Park, Llangynog, Powys SY10 0EX.** *01691 860304.* www.glendowerpark.co.uk. Library/book exchange. Washing/drying facilities. 3 site BBQ's per year. Bird seed/nuts available for feeders. Crown green bowling in village. Walking distance to 2 good pubs. Shop/PO in next village. On B4391 from Oswestry to Bala. Open: 1 February - 30 December. ★★★★ BH&HPA 🐕 ♿ ⚡ 🚿 47⚡

**(0.5m). Henstent Park, Llangynog, Powys SY10 0EP.** *01691 860479.* www.henstent.co.uk. Stunning views. Peaceful country park near lakes Vyrnwy and Bala. Popular with bird watchers and walkers. Seasonal pitches, tourers/tents welcome all year. Two pubs nearby serving meals. Wi-Fi available. Owner supplied copy. Off B4391. From A5 follow signs for Bala, park on R, just before you reach Llangynog. Open: All year. BH&HPA 🐕 ♿ ⚡ 🚿 25⚡ 25⚡ 👤 40👤

## Llanidloes

**(0.5m). Clywedog Riverside Holiday Home Park, Van, Llanidloes, Powys SY18 6NE.** *01686 412682.* www.clywedogpark.co.uk. Laundry. Golf, sailing, fishing, sports centre and Clywedog Dam all nearby. Satellite TV. Within walking distance of Llanidloes town centre (15mins). From Llanidloes take the On B4518, SP Llynclywedog. We are 0.75m on the left hand side. Open: All year. 🐕 ♿ ⚡ 🚿

**(0.8m). Dol-Ilys Caravan Park, Dol-Ilys Farm, Llanidloes, Powys SY18 6JA.** *01686 412694.* Campers kitchen for walkers. Fishing in river Severn. Play area. Golf course, PO, doctor and sports centre all within 1m. Railway station 6m. From roundabout on A470 in Llanidloes take R4569. Past hospital, Fork R and site is 1st R. Open: 1 April - 31 October. ★★★ 🐕 ♿ ⚡ 🚿 20⚡ 👤

## Llansantffraed-ym-Mechain

**Bryn Vyrnwy Caravan Park, Bryn Vyrnwy, Llansantffraed-ym-Mechain,** **Powys SY22 6AY.** *01691 828252.* www.brynvyrnwyholidaypark.co.uk. Quiet park overlooking river Vyrnwy. Convenient for all mid-Wales beauty spots and NT locations. 0.5m to village shops, PO, doctor, fishing on site, golf course nearby. Main A495 at Llynclys, off main A483 Oswestry to Welshpool road, on left-hand side just outside of village. Open: 1 April - 1 November. 🐕 ♿ ⚡ 🚿

## Llanwddyn

**(1m). Fronheulog Caravan Park (Adults only), Lake Vyrnwy, LLanwddyn, Powys SY10 0NN.** *01691 870362.* www.fronheulog-caravan-park.co.uk. Quiet site with breathtaking views. Sorry we do not cater for children, but pets are welcome. Electric hook-ups available on our Caravan Club members site. Static caravans new and used usually for sale. 0.5m local shop, RSPB reserves, tea rooms and gift shops. Walkers and bird watchers paradise. Owner supplied copy. On B4393. 2m on right hand side before Lake Vyrnwy. Open: 1 April - 31 October. 🐕 ♿ ⚡ 5⚡ 5⚡ 35⚡

## Machynlleth

**(12m). Celyn Brithion Caravan & Camping Park, Dinas Mawddwy, Machynlleth, Powys SY20 9LP.** *01650 531344.* www.celynbrithion.co.uk. 4 hotels with bar and restaurant facilities. All within a short walking distance of the site. Garage and village shop with adjoining cafe. Mill shop and cafe close by. On A458 Shrewsbury to Barmouth. Situated on the A470 between Dolgellau and Machynlleth. Open: 1 March - 31 October. 🐕 ♿ ⚡ 🚿 13⚡ 👤 14👤

**(0.5m). Garth Holiday Park, Garth Road, Machynlleth, Powys SY20 8HQ.** *01654 702194.* www.garthholidaypark.co.uk. Fishing river. Hotel on site. Plus 15 log cabins sold and 1 new for sale. Shops, sports centre, swimming pool, golf, horse riding all nearby. David Bellamy Gold Conservation Award. Open all year for log cabins. Owner supplied copy. Off A489. In Machynlleth turn R between hospital and chip shop, R again behind hospital and follow Garth Road. Open: 1 March - 15 January. BH&HPA 🐕 ♿ ⚡ 🚿 100⚡

**(3m). Morben Isaf, Derwenlas, Machynlleth, Powys SY20 8SR.** *01654 781473.* Ideal for walking, fishing, bird watching, golfing etc. 10mins for beautiful sandy beach. Adjacent to Cors Dyfi Nature reserve with easy access. David Bellamy Silver Conservation Award. S

# WALES

of Machynlleth on A487 Aberystwyth Road. Open: 15 March - 31 October.
★★★★★ BH&HPA NCC 🏠 🏕 ⛱ 🚗 ✈ 📶 ♿ 🚻 12🚐 12⛺ 15▲

**(10m). Tynypwll Camping & Caravan Park, Dinas Mawddwy, Machynlleth, Powys SY20 9JF.** 01650 531286. Fishing. PO, shops within 0.5m. Lovely scenery and walks. Takeaway meals, shop, cafe/restaurant available nearby. Take A470 at Mallwyd for 1m, turn R by second garage for Dinas Mawddwy. Turn R by 'Red Lion' on the corner, site 200yd on L. Open: 31 March - 31 October. 🐕 🏕 ✈ 📶 ⛱ ♿ 🚻 ♿ 🚐 10⛺ ▲ 60⛺

## Montgomery

**(6m). Argae Hall Caravan Park, Garthmyl, Montgomery, Powys SY15 6RU.** 01686 640216. On the banks of the river Severn with free fishing. Hot showers. Laundrette. Chemical toilet disposal point. Playground. 9 hole golf course adjacent. Pub and club, food, entertainment. Most Improved Park in Wales. Calor Award. Owner supplied copy. A483 from Welshpool to Newtown then the B4385 to Montgomery. Open: 1 April - 31 October. 🐕 🏕 ✈ 📶 ⛱ ✖ ♿ 30🚐 30⛺ 101⛺

**(4m). Smithy Caravan Park (Montgomery), Abermule, Montgomery, Powys SY15 6ND.** 01584 711280. www.bestparks.co.uk. Very well run and very pretty garden like park all pitches are fully services and hardstanding. On banks of river Severn with 0.5m fishing, new toilet and shower block. Local shop within 300yd. Special rates for mid week and longer stays. Leave A483 and enter village of Abemule. Turn down lane opposite village shop and PO. Open: 1 March - 31 October. BH&HPA 🏠 🏕 ⛱ ✈ 📶 ⛱ ♿ 🚗 ♿ 🚻 ♿ 30🚐 30⛺ 55⛺

## New Radnor

**(0.25m). The Old Station Caravan Park, Smatcher Lane, New Radnor, Powys LD8 2SS.** 01544 350543. www.oldstationcaravanpark.co.uk. 12 mixed pitches in total. Situated on old railway buildings. New toilet block and showers - all disabled friendly. Pub, village shop, 500yd. Golf course 6m. Also nearby canoeing, walking, bird watching, biking and horse riding. Owner supplied copy. A44 from Kington (Herefordshire) to Rhayader. L turn before the village of New Radnor on R. Open: All year. BH&HPA 🏠 🏕 ✈ 📶 ⛱ ♿ 🚻 ♿ 12🚐 ▲ 13⛺

## Newtown

**(7m). Sunny View Holiday Home Park, Bwlch Y Ffridd, Newtown, Powys SY16 3JF.** 01686 688580. leylandsholidayhomeparks.co.uk. Quiet site, scenic walks over the hills. Pony trekking, fishing, golf nearest village Caersws 3m. Owner supplied copy. Follow A489 to Caersws, then turn R on the B4569 SP Aberhafesp. At first crossroads straight over the B4568 ignoring sign for Aberhafesp, at second crossroads turn L SP Bwlch Y Garreg. Farm and site 1m on R. Open: 1 February - 31 October. 🐕 🏕 ✈ 📶 ⛱ ♿ 🚻 34⛺

## Presteigne

**(1m). Rockbridge Park R, Presteigne, Powys LD8 2NF.** 01547 560300. www.rockbridgepark.co.uk. Small, tranquil park in wonderful scenery. Near Offa's Dyke. Sports centre, hotels, takeaway food, restaurants, bowling all available within 1m. On B4356 W of Presteigne. Small, tranquil park in wonderful scenery. Near Offa's Dyke. Open: 1 April - 31 October. 3 BH&HPA 🏠 🏕 ✈ 📶 ⛱ ✖ ♿ 🚻 10🚐 21⛺

**(5m). Walton Court Caravan & Camp Site, Walton, Presteigne, Powys LD8 2PY.** 01544 350259. www.waltoncourtcaravanandcampingsite.co.uk. In beautiful unspoilt countryside. Cottage available. Close to Offa's Dyke footpath, pub close by. Golf course, swimming pool & leisure centre 3m. Hay on Wye, town of books 16m. on A44. 3m North Kington. Open: 6 April - 31 October. 🏠 🏕 ✈ 📶 ⛱ ♿ 🚻 5🚐 10⛺ ▲ 20⛺

## Rhayader

**(0.5m). Gigrin Farm Caravan Site, South Street, Rhayader, Powys LD6 5BL.** 01597 810357. www.gigrin.co.uk. Shops, PO, doctor, takeaway meals etc within 0.5m. Bryafon Country House - meals 100yd. Fishing 3m, bus service 0.75m. Excellent TV/reception. Red Kite centre and nature trail open all year. Feeding Red Kites at 2 o'clock GMT, daily. Dogs on leads. Owner supplied copy. 0.5m S of Rhayader. Just off A470. Open: 3 January - 23 December. 🐕 🏕 ✈ 📶 ♿ 15⛺

**(0.25m). Wyeside Caravan & Camping Park, Llangurig Road, Rhayader, Powys LD6 5LB.** 01597 810183. www.wyesidecamping.co.uk. On the banks of the river Wye. Excellent facilities on site and in town. 3m Elan Valley. Colour brochure available. On the outskirts of Rhayader on the A470. Open: 1 March - 31 October. ★★★★ BH&HPA 🏠 🏕 ✈ 📶 ⛱ ♿ 🚻 20🚐 20⛺ ▲

## Welshpool

**(5m). Bank Farm Caravan Park, Middletown, Welshpool, Powys SY21 8EJ.** 01938 570526. www.bankfarmcaravans.co.uk. Family run park with beautiful views, part flat, part sloping. On A458 Shrewsbury to Welshpool, 12M W of Shrewsbury, 5m E of Welshpool. Open: 1 March - 31 October. ★★★★ BH&HPA 🏠 🏕 ✈ 📶 ⛱ ♿ 🚻 5🚐 20⛺ ▲ 35⛺

**(15m). Carmel Caravan Park, Cefn Coch, Welshpool, Powys SY21 0AJ.** 01938 810542. www.carmelcaravanpark.com. Fishing on site, golf course 6m. Shops, PO and doctor within 5m. Take A458 from Welshpool to Llanfair Caereinion. Turn L over bridge into town centre. Follow signs to Cefn Coch turn L before Inn, follow park signs for 2m. Open: 1 March - 1 November. ★★★ BH&HPA 🏠 🏕 ✈ 📶 ⛱ ♿ 🚻 8🚐 40⛺ ▲ 150⛺

**(6m). Henllan Caravan Park, Llangyniew, Welshpool, Powys SY21 9EJ.** 01938 810554. www.henllancaravanpark.co.uk. Pitch and putt course. Club. Bottled gas available. Fishing. Club/restaurant on park, play area. Owner supplied copy. Off A458 Welshpool to Dolgellau. Situated on meadowland adjoining river Banwy. Open: 1 March - 31 December. BH&HPA NCC 🏠 🏕 ✈ 📶 ⛱ ✖ ♿ 🚻 10🚐 6⛺ ▲ 66⛺

**River Meadow Holiday Centre, Minffordd, Llangadfan, Welshpool, Powys SY21 0PL.** 01938 820277. www.rivermeadow.co.uk. NCC 🏠 🏕 20🚐 50⛺

**(17m). Riverbend Caravan Park, Llangadfan, Llanfair Caereinion, Welshpool, Powys SY21 0PP.** 01938 820356. www.hillandale.co.uk. Level riverside touring field with extensive private fishing. Tranquil and unspoilt region of Wales. Shop 200m, pub 100m, golf, pony trekking nearby. Only short drive to the coast. On A458 Welshpool to Dolgellau, turn L in village of Llangadfan immediately before Cann Office Hotel. Open: All year. BH&HPA 🏠 🏕 ✈ 📶 ⛱ ♿ 🚻 50🚐 90⛺

**(1.5m). Severn Caravan and Camping Park, Cilcewydd Farm, Forden, Welshpool, Powys SY21 8RT.** 01938 580238. www.severnbunkhouse.co.uk. Hot showers, play area. Fishing on site. Golf course 3m, Powys Castle 1.5m. Small railway station 2m. Owner supplied copy. Off A490. Open: 1 April - 31 October. 🏠 🏕 ✈ 📶 ⛱ ♿ 🚻 20🚐 20⛺ ▲ 86⛺

# RHONDDA CYNON TAFF

## Aberdare

**(0.75m). Dare Valley Country Park, Aberdare, Rhondda Cynon Taff CF44 7RG.** 01685 874872. www.darevalley-

# WALES / IRELAND

countrypark.co.uk. Small site set in 500 acres of parkland. Two lakes, riding centre, miles of waymarked footpaths and cafeteria on site. Ideal base for visiting the Gower coast, Brecon Beacons etc. Owner supplied copy. Follow signs from town centre. Open: 4 January - 31 December. BH&HPA 25 A

## VALE OF GLAMORGAN
### Barry

(2m). Vale Touring Caravan Park, Port Road (West), Barry, Vale of Glamorgan CF62 3BT. 01446 719211. We cater for touring and motor caravans. H&C showers. Razor points. 100yd from Hotel. Good entrance to park 6yd wide off the A4050 road. Owner supplied copy. On R of A4226 Barry to Rhoose. From M4 J33 follow signs for Cardiff Airport. Open: 1 March - 1 December. 30

### Cowbridge

(3m). Llandow Caravan Park, Llandow, Cowbridge, Vale of Glamorgan CF71 7PB. 01446 794527. www.llandowcaravanpark.com. Sheltered, secluded park set in the Vale of Glamorgan. Seasonal pitches. Caravan storage. Exit M4 at junction 33 to Cardiff Airport. Take A48 to Cowbridge-Bridgend, bypass Cowbridge, first left to B4268 (Llantwit Major), keep on this road until brown signs. Open: 1 February - 30 November. ★★★★ BH&HPA 5 70 25 A

### Llantwit Major

(0.5m). Acorn Camping & Caravanning, Ham Lane South, Llantwit Major, Vale of Glamorgan CF61 1RP. 01446 794024. www.acorncamping.co.uk. About 1m from the beach in the Glamorgan Heritage coast. Hardstandings and serviced pitches available. M4 to J33 follow signs to Cardiff Airport then to Llantwit Major on B4265. Follow signs to site from Llantwit Major. Open: 3 February - 8 December.

★★★★ BH&HPA 10 40 45 A 24

## WREXHAM
### Eyton

★★★★★ PREMIER PARKS 2011 (0.5m). Plassey Leisure Park (Best of British), The Plassey, Eyton, Wrexham LL13 0SP. 01978 780277. www.plassey.com. Multi award winning park with many amenities including: 9 hole golf course, swimming pool, badminton courts, table tennis, sauna, restaurant, coffee shop, retail shops, craft workshops, adventure playground, garden centre, hairdresser, beauty salon and craft centre. David Bellamy Gold Conservation Award. Take Bangor-on-Dee exit (B5426) off A483 Chester-Oswestry bypass. 2.5m on L. Open: 10 February - 4 November. ★★★★ BH&HPA 20 60 A 15

### Ruabon

(5m). James' Caravan Park, Ruabon, Ruabon, Wrexham LL14 6DW. 01978 820148. Leisure centre nearby. Fees on application. Golf course, shops, PO, doctor etc 1m. 0.5m W of the A483/A539 junction to Llangollen. Open: All year. ★★★ 40 40

### Wrexham

(0.5m). Lady Margaret's Park Caravan Club Site, Chirk, Wrexham, Wrexham LL14 5AA. 01691 777200. www.caravanclub.co.uk. A beautiful wooded parkland site adjacent to Chirk Castle with many other castles and historic sites close by. Some hardstandings. Steel awning pegs required. Toilet blocks. Privacy cubicles. Laundry facilities. Baby and toddler washroom. Veg prep. MV Service point. Gas & gaz. Play equipment. Good area for walking. Ideally

suited for families. Members only. No tents. See website for standard directions to site. Open: All year. NCC 106 106

Trench Farm Fisheries and Touring Caravan Park, Red Hall Lane, Penley, Wrexham, Wrexham LL13 0NA. 01978 710098. www.trenchfarmfisheries.co.uk. Indoor dish wash area with microwave, fridge, washing machine, kettle. Ellesmere 3m. Accessed from A539 & A528. Open: 1 March - 31 October. 50 50 A

## NORTHERN IRELAND
## CO ANTRIM
### Antrim

(1m). Six Mile Water Caravan Park, Lough Road, Antrim, Co Antrim BT41 4DG. 02894 464963. www.antrim.gov.uk/caravanpark. Situated close to the shores of Lough Neagh - an area steeped in history and natural beauty with many attractions and activities for the holidaymaker to enjoy. Facilities include modern toilet and shower block, fully equipped laundry and electric hook-up for 20 pitches. The park is an ideal base for touring Northern Ireland and has a TV lounge and a games room. Follow SP for Antrim Forum/Lough Shore Park and turn off Dublin Road (A26) on to Lough Road. Open: 1 March - 31 October. ★★★★★ NCC 20 20 24 A

### Ballycastle

Silvercliffs Holiday Village, Clare Road, Causeway Coast, Ballycastle, Co Antrim BT54 6DB. 02820 762550. www.hagansleisure.co.uk. Situated on an elevated site, Silvercliffs Holiday Village commands a breathtaking view over Ballycastle Bay. Just a 20 mins drive from the world famous Giant's Causeway, it's the perfect base from which to explore Northern Ireland's magical Causeways Coast & Glens. Facilities include

### Six Mile Water Caravan Park & Camping Park
Lough Road, Antrim, BT41 4DG

The Six Mile Water Caravan & Camping Park, situated on the beautiful shores of Lough Neagh, is an ideal base for touring Northern Ireland. On-site facilities include: TV lounge, games room, modern toilet and shower block, payphone, fully equipped laundry room, electronic hook up for 37 pitches and 8 camping sites.

Maximum stay 7 night. Advance booking advisable. Open February—November.

For bookings or further information:
Tel: 028 9446 4963
Email: sixmilewater@antrim.gov.uk
www.antrim.gov.uk/caravanpark

# IRELAND

indoor heated pool, play area and a traditional bar with live entertainment. From A26, take A44 to Ballycastle. Go straight through Ballycastle and turn L at Marine Court Hotel roundabout, taking you to North Street and on to Clare Road. Park is 0.5m on R. Open: 1 March - 30 September.
★★ NCC ♀️🐕⚓〰️🚲⛱️🎮🍴 🚗✖️🛒🏪📶 80⚡ 80🔌 👤 347⛺

### Ballymena

**(1.8m). Cushendall Caravan Park, 62 Coast Road, Cushendall, Ballymena, Co Antrim BT44 0QW.** *02821 771699*. www.moyle-council.org. On A2. 25 miles from Larne ferry heading north, enjoying the picturesque Glens of Antrim on your journey. Open: 1 April - 31 October. ♿ 👤 4⚡ 25🔌 👤 64⛺

### Ballymoney

**(4m). Drumaheglis Marina & Caravan Park (Caravan Club Affiliated Site), 36 Glenstall Road, Ballymoney, Co Antrim BT53 7QN.** *02827 666466* . www.ballymoney.gov.uk. CARAVAN CLUB AFFILIATED SITE. Non-members and tent campers welcome. This award winning park is one of the few, and most attractive access points to the lower river Bann. Toilet blocks, laundry facilities and MV service point. Playground and play area on site. Ideal for families. Fishing, golf and water sports nearby. Facilities for the disabled. Well SP from the A26 Ballymoney to Coleraine Road. Open: 17 March - 31 October. ★★★★★ 🏪🐕⚓🚲♿ 🚗⛵🛒🏪📶 55⚡ 10🔌

### Bushmills

**Portballintrae Holiday Home Park, Ballaghmore Avenue, Bushmills, Co Antrim BT57 8RX.** *02820 731478*. Quiet family touring and static site. Reservations required for July and August. B17 to Bushmills, B145 to Portballintrae. Also SP A2-B145 junction in Portballintrae. Open: Contact site direct. 🏪〰️⚓🎮✖️🏪 ♿ 🏕️🔌 👤

### Cushendun

**Cushendun Caravan Park, 14 Glendun Road, Cushendun, Co Antrim BT44 0PX.** *02821 761254*. www.moyle-council.org. Refurbished park offering water & electricity connections to all sites. Set in woodland, 5 minutes walk from village centre & beach. From A2 take B92. Open: 22 April - 30 September. 🏪 ♿〰️⚓🎮 🛒📶 👤 ⛺

### Larne

**(3.5m). Carnfunnock Caravan Park & Campsite, Coast Road, Drains Bay, Larne, Co Antrim BT40 2QG.** *02828 270541* . Situated on the beautiful Antrim Coast within 191 hectares of parkland. Unique attractions include: walled garden, maze in shape of N Ireland, activity centre (with children's adventure playground, trampolines, 'mini-Silverstone' racetrack, face painting/glitter tattoos, putting and 9 hole golf course), Family Fun Zone (with miniature railway, 18 hole mini golf, laser clay pigeon shooting, bungee run, bouncy castle and remote control boats & lorries), woodland walks, golf driving range and academy, orienteering, picnic/BBQ areas and modern visitor centre with gift and coffee shop. On A2 Coast Road, 3.5m N of Larne between Drains Bay and Ballygally. Open: 12 March - 7 November. ★★★★★ 🏪🐕⚓〰️🚲🎮🚗✖️ 🛒📶♿ 🏕️ 31⚡ 👤

**Curran Court Caravan Park, 131 Curran Road, Larne, Co Antrim BT40 1BD.** *02828 273797*. Near leisure centre, hotel, bowling green and putting green. Hotel beside site (no music) town centre 400yd away, 2m to Cairndwu 18 hole golf course, 8m to Larne's 9 hole golf course. Sea fishing 0.5m. River fishing 1m. From town centre SP for leisure centre. 0.5m from ferry terminal and amenities. Open: 17 March - 31 October. ★★★ 🏪🐕 〰️⚓🏪🛒📶♿ 10⚡ 30🔌 👤

### Portrush

**(0.5m). Blairs Caravan Park, 29 Dhu Varren, Portrush, Co Antrim BT56 8EW.** *02870 823537*. 200yd from beach and nine hole pars golf course 2km. Royal Portrush championship links 1m, Giant's Causeway 7m. Caravan accessory shop. Owner supplied copy. Situated on coast road between Portrush and Portstewart. Open: 1 April - 31 October. NCC ♿ 🏕️ 25⚡ 115🔌

**Hilltop Holiday Park, 60 Loguestown Road, Portrush, Co Antrim BT56 8PD.** *02870 823537*. www.blairscaravans.com. Play area. Hardstandings. Owner supplied copy. On A29 Coleraine to Portrush. Open: 1 April - 31 October. NCC 🏪🐕〰️⚓🎮🛒🏪📶 20⚡ 50🔌 👤 421⛺

**(1m). Skerries Holiday Park, 126 Dunluce Road, Portrush, Co Antrim BT56 8NB.** *02870 822531*. skerriesholidaypark.co.uk. Family park. Play area. Tennis courts. Championship golf course within walking distance of park, sea views. Football pitch 15mins walk to town centre. Owner supplied copy. On A2 Bushmills to Portrush coast road. Open: 19 March - 11 October. 🏪🐕〰️🎮 ♿ 🛒🏪📶 20⚡ 70🔌 👤 780⛺

## CO ARMAGH
### Lurgan

**(2m). Kinnego Marina Caravan Park, Kinnego Marina, Oxford Island, Lurgan, Co Armagh BT66 6NJ.** *02838 327573*. Situated on Lough Neagh within Oxford Island National Nature Reserve, with striking views over Lough Neagh & Kinnego Marina. Off roundabout, 10 M1 Lurgan down embankment road to Oxford Island 0.25m. Based on the shore of Lough and nature reserve. Open: 1 April - 31 October. ★★ 🏪🐕〰️⚓🚲🛒✖️🏪📶♿ 10⚡ 10🔌

### Markethill

**(1m). Gosford Forest Park, 7 Gosford Demesne, Markethill, Co Armagh BT60 1GD.** *02837 551277*. www.gosford.co.uk. Hardstanding electrical hook-up sites. Picnic & barbecue areas. Function hall with basic kitchen heating, chairs and tables. Horse riding routes. Way-marked trails. Guided tours (bookable), orienteering routes, special events (arranged by permit). Heritage, poultry & rare breeds collection. Take A28 from Armagh 6m. A28 from Newry 11m. Open: 9 April - 30 September. ★★★ 🏪🐕〰️⚓🚲🎮 🚗✖️🛒🏪♿ 5⚡ 40🔌 50👤

## CO DOWN
### Castlewellan

**(0.3m). Castlewellan Forest Park, The Grange, Castlewellan, Co Down BT31 9BU.** *02843 778664*. www.nidirect.gov.uk/forests. 61 pitches for tourers and motorcaravans. Game fishing on site. Families only. 30m S of Belfast SP off the Belfast-Newcastle route. Open: 17 March - 31 October. 🏪🐕〰️⚓🎮✖️🏪📶 ♿ 🏕️ 61🔌 👤

### Downpatrick

**(6m). Edgewater Holiday Park, 50 Minerstown Road, Downpatrick, Co Down BT30 8LR.** *02844 851527*. www.edgewaterholidaypark.co.uk. 3m to shop & PO. 1m to golf course. Private beach. Owner supplied copy. NCC ♿ 🐕〰️🏪📶 🏕️🔌 162👤

### Kilkeel

**(4m). Chestnutt Holiday Park, 3 Grange Road, Cranfield West, Kilkeel, Co Down BT34 4LW.** *02841 762653*. www.chestnuttholidayparks.com. Excellent base to explore area. Beside Blue Flag beach. 16m from Newry and Newcastle. 4m from Kilkeel. Laundry and modern touring facilities. Owner supplied copy. Off A2. Follow signs for Cranfield West. Adjacent to award-winning Cranfield beach. Open:

# IRELAND

6 April - 15 September. ★★★★★
BH&HPA

(3m). **Sandilands Holiday Park**, 30 Cranfield Road, Cranfield East, Kilkeel, Co Down BT34 4LJ. *02841 763634*. www.chestnuttholidayparks.com. Multi hook-up for tourers. Private beach. Pitch & putt, golf course. Dogs must be kept on lead. Owner supplied copy. From Kilkeel, follow Greencastle road for about 3m, Park on L. Open: 19 March - 30 September. ★★★★★ BH&HPA

## Killyleagh

(1m). **Delamont Country Park Camping & Caravanning Club Site**, Downpatrick Road, Killyleagh, Co Down BT30 9TZ. *02844 821833*. www.campingandcaravanningclub.co.uk. Delamont Country Park is located in an area of outstanding natural beauty and has features to attract all kinds of visitors - plenty of walks, picnic areas, bird watching, Victorian walled garden and children's playground. Anglers will want to try sea fishing off Ardglass or opportunities for coarse and game fishing. Other local activities include walking, cycling, golf, horse riding. Non-members welcome. All units accepted. Some super pitches available. Special deals available for families and backpackers. Loo Of The Year (5 stars). David Bellamy Silver Conservation Award. Off A22 1m S of Killyleagh and 4m N of Down Patrick. The site is about 1hr from Belfast ferry and 1.30hrs from the port of Larne. Open: 15 March - 7 November. ★★★★★ NCC

## Newcastle

**Bonny's Newcastle Trailer Park**, 82 Tullybrannigan Road, Newcastle, Co Down BT33 0PD. *02843 722351*. www.bonnys.net. Entrances to hundreds of acres of forest walks 1m. Owner supplied copy. Proceed down Newcastle main street, turn R at Donard Park. Open: All year. NCC

(0.5m). **Bonny's Sunnyholme**, 33 Castlewellan Road, Newcastle, Co Down BT33 0JY. *02843 722739*. www.bonnys.net. New barbecue and children's play area. Owner supplied copy. On main Castlewellan to Newcastle road, Beside Burrendale Hotel. Open: 1 March - 1 November. BH&HPA

(1.5m). **Murlough Cottage Caravan Site**, 180-182 Dundrum Road, Lower Newcastle, Newcastle, Co Down BT33 0LN. *02843 723184*. www.murloughcottage.com. This family run park is set in an Area of Outstanding Natural Beauty which makes it an ideal central point to explore many of the local attractions. No dangerous dogs. On main Belfast road. Open: 1 March - 31 October. ★★★★★ BH&HPA NCC

(1m). **Windsor Caravan Park**, 138 Dundrum Road, Newcastle, Co Down BT33 0LN. *02843 723367*. A tranquil park situated within walking distance of the popular holiday resort of Newcastle, with its sandy beaches and championship golf course. On A24. Open: 1 March - 30 September. ★★ NCC

## Newry

**Annalong Caravan Park**, 38 Kilkeel Road, Annalong, Newry, Co Down BT34 4TJ. *02843 768248*. www.chestnuttholidayparks.com. Shops within 20yd from front gate. Park gently slopes to sea with touring pitches on seafront. Golf 6m. Shopping centre, cinema 20m. Owner supplied copy. On A2. In the centre of village. Open: 17 March - 31 October. ★★★★★ BH&HPA

(2.5m). **Leestone Caravan Park**, 60 Leestone Road, Maghereagh Kilkeel, Newry, Co Down BT34 4NW. *01693 762567*. www.leestonecaravanpark.co.uk. Off A2. North of Kilkeel on Kilkeel/Newcastle road. Open: 1 April - 31 October.

## Newtownards

(7m). **Ballywhiskin Caravan & Camping Park**, 216 Ballywalter Road, Millisle, Newtownards, Co Down BT21 2LY. *02891 862262*. www.ballywhiskincaravanandcamping.com. Open weekends during winter. Hard stands and laundry facilities. Situated close to beach. Small animal farm on site. Playing field and play park. Children welcome. Within easy reach of many places of interest. Golf, horse riding, tennis, swimming pool, shopping centre, cinema all available within 7m. From Newtownards take B172 E to Millisle, turn R on A2 towards Ballywalter, site on the R. Open: 17 March - 31 October. ★★★ BH&HPA

## Rostrevor

**Kilbroney Caravan Park**, Shore Road, Rostrevor, Co Down BT34 3DQ. *02841 738134*. Large areas of open space, riverside walks and arboretum. Owner supplied copy. About 0.5m from Rostrevor on main A2 road to Kilkeel. Open: 6 April - 31 October.

## CO FERMANAGH

### Enniskillen

(8m). **Blaney Caravan Park**, Blaney, Enniskillen, Co Fermanagh BT93 7ER. *02868 641634*. www.blaneycaravanpark.com. Hardstanding and waste hook-ups for touring caravans. 4 star park has a host of amenities with rural activities on its doorstep. On A46 from Enniskillen to Belleek. Open: 17 March - 23 October. ★★★★

### Irvinestown

(5m). **Castle Archdale Caravan Park**, Lisnarick, Irvinestown, Co Fermanagh BT94 1PP. *02868 621333*. www.castlearchdale.com. Restaurant, takeaway, play park, pony-trekking, cycle hire and ferry to White Island. 10m from Enniskillen off B82 Enniskillen to Kesh Road. On the shore of Lower Lough Erne. Situated in Castle Archdale Country Park. Open: 1 April - 31 October. NCC

### Lisnaskea

(3m). **Share Holiday Village**, Smith's Strand, Lisnaskea, Co Fermanagh BT92 0EQ. *02867 722122*. www.sharevillage.org. Share Holiday Village is a residential outdoor activity centre, all facilities have been purpose built for use by people with disabilities and able bodied people. Canoeing, sailing, archery, climbing wall and arts activities. Indoor swimming pool with ramped access. Coffee shop and takeaway. Shops, PO, doctor 3m from site. From A4 main Belfast to Enniskillen road turn off. Open: 6 April - 30 September.

## CO LONDONDERRY

### Coleraine

(6m). **Castlerock Caravan Club CL**, 91 Bishops Road, Castlerock, Coleraine, Co Londonderry BT51 4SE. *02870 848589*. www.thecaravanclub.ie. Park is located in the prime holiday resort of Castlerock on Northern Ireland's famous Causeway Coast. Enclosed play park. Golf and beaches nearby. Take A2 from Coleraine. Open: 1 April - 31 October.

(1m). **Tullans Farm Caravan Park**, Tullans Farm, 46 Newmills Road, Coleraine, Co Londonderry BT52 2JB. *02870 342309*. www.tullansfarm.co.uk. Cinema and swimming pool within 2m. Large children's play area. Snooker, pool,

# IRELAND

table tennis (indoors), TV room. Country ambience yet just 1m from Coleraine. 'Try the Tullans experience where people matter'. Off A26. Open: 17 March - 31 October.

### Limavady

(12m). **Benone Tourist Complex, 53 Benone Avenue, Magilligan, Limavady, Co Londonderry BT49 OLQ.** 02877 750555. www.limavady.gov.uk. Complex includes 9-hole, par 3 golf course, golf practice range. Outdoor heated splash pool. 4 tennis courts. Bowling green. Modern activity play area. Events programme and cafe opened during July/ August. Seasonal shop available. Situated on coast road about 10m from Coleraine. Open: 1 April - 30 September. ★★★★

(9m). **Golden Sands Caravan Park, 26 Benone Avenue, Magilligan, Limavady, Co Londonderry BT49 OLQ.** 02877 750324. www.goldensandsbenone.com. Dogs permitted only at discretion of manager. Owner supplied copy. N of Limavady on coast road to Coleraine. Beside extensive sandy beach on north coast. Open: 1 March - 31 October. **BH&HPA**

### Portstewart

(2m). **Ballyleese Town and Country Caravan Park, 34 Agherton Road, Portstewart, Co Londonderry BT55 7PJ.** 02870 833308. www.bonalstoncaravans.com. Close to beaches, golf courses and Portstewart promenade. Nearby towns easily accessible. Owner supplied copy. A2 from Coleraine, approach Portstewart and take L at Agherton road, opposite Tesco, park is 0.5m on left hand side. Open: 17 March - 31 October. ★★★★★ **NCC**

(1m). **Burnside Caravan Park (NI), 30A Burnside Road, Portstewart, Co Londonderry BT55 7SW.** 02870 833308. www.bonalstoncaravans.com. Close to beaches, golf courses and Portstewart Promenade. Nearby towns easily accessible. Owner supplied copy. Take A2 from Coleraine, on approach to Portstewart, turn L at first roundabout into Burnside Road, park 500yd on left hand side. Open: 17 March - 31 October. **NCC**

## CO TYRONE

### Clogher

**Clogher Valley Country Caravan Park, 9 Fardross Forest, Clogher, Co Tyrone BT76 OHG.** 02885 548932. www.caravanparknorthernireland.co.uk. Forest walks. Bird watching. Bicycles for hire. Owner supplied copy. SP off main A4 between Clogher and Fivemiletown. Open: All year.

### Dungannon

(1m). **Dungannon Park, Moy Road, Dungannon, Co Tyrone BT71 6DY.** 02887 728690. www.dungannon.gov.uk/index.cfm/area/page/pagekey/549. Catering for a wide range of visitor and recreational needs. Dungannon town centre (0.75m) has a broad range of supermarkets, restaurants, local markets and bus depot. PO, doctors 0.25m; golf course 1m. SP off the A29. A 70 acre parkland in the heartland of Ulster. Open: 1 March - 31 October. ★★★★

### Fivemiletown

(0.5m). **Round Lake Caravan Park, 20 Murley Road, Fivemiletown, Co Tyrone BT75 0QS.** 02889 521949. A tranquil destination amidst the lush Clogher Valley. Short walk to busy Fivemiletown adds to its rural attraction. SP from Fivemiletown on the Fintona Road. Open: 1 March - 30 September. ★★

# SOUTHERN IRELAND
## CO CAVAN

### Virginia

**Lough Ramor Caravan & Camping Park, Ryefield, Virginia, Co Cavan.** 00 353 87 2825976. www.camping-ireland.ie. Popular for angling and boating. Nearby are the historical sites of Newgrange, Loughcrew and Hill of Tara. Facilities include: toilets, washing area and boat hire. Restaurants, pubs and shops nearby. Site is located off N3 route, 3m S of Virginia on the scenic shores of Lough Ramor. Open: 1 July - 1 September.

## CO CLARE

### Corofin

**Corofin Hostel and Camping Park, Main Street, Corofin, Co Clare.** 00 353 65 6837683. www.corofincamping.com. Well sheltered site with games room and laundrette. Ideal for walking and cycling. Fishing lakes nearby. Cliffs of Moher 30mins. Nearest park to Burren National Park. From Ennis follow N85 and R476. From Galway City follow the N18 towards Gort, then R460 via Kilmacduagh to Corofin. Open: 1 April - 30 September. ★★★

### Doolin

(0.5m). **Nagle's Doolin Camping & Caravan Park, Doolin, Co Clare.** 00 353 65 7074458. www.doolincamping.com. Our site is a touring site only with 15 hardstands. Can accommodate touring vans and camper vans on the grass also and have electric points for all visitors. Overlooked by the Cliffs of Moher and just a short walk from three of Ireland's most famous pubs, with traditional music nightly. Excellent restaurants, Lahinch Seaworld and heated swimming pool nearby. Shop open from June 1st - August 31st. Pitch & putt only 200yd from site. From Lisdoonvarna go towards Cliff of Moher, turn R for Doolin and follow signs to Doolin Pier. Located beside Doolin Pier. Open: 16 March - 14 October. **NCC**

**Riverside Caravan & Camping Park (Doolin), Doolin, Co Clare.** 00 353 65 7074314. www.oconnorsdoolin.com/riverside_camping.htm. Situated in the centre of Doolin within 5 mins walk from pubs, shops & restaurants. Attractions in area include trips to Aran Islands, coastal walks, pot holing, Ailwee Caves, pony trekking, river and sea fishing, pitch & putt, bicycle hire. From Lisdoonvarna go towards Cliffs of Moher (N67) turn R for Doolin. Go straight at main crossroads in centre of Doolin. Park is situated over Aille River Bridge on left hand side of road, behind O'Connors B/B. Open: 15 March - 15 October. ★★★ **NCC**

### Mountshannon

(1.3m). **Lakeside Holiday Park (Mountshannon), Mountshannon, Co Clare.** 00 353 61 927225. www.lakesideireland.com. This natural lakeside watersport park is located on the shores of Lough Derg. Dogs allowed except during July-August. On site amenities include: tennis, boat hire, soccer pitch, table tennis, swimming and fishing. Pitch & Putt, cafe/bistro, bicycle hire, pony riding for children, golf course, pubs and shops available within 2m. Straight through Mountshannon, on Portumna Road (R352). First turn R, SP. Open: 1 May - 1 October.

## CO CORK

### Bantry

(3m). **Dunbeacon Camping Site, Durrus, Bantry, Co Cork.** 00 353 27 62851. Family run, beautifully landscaped secluded site with views overlooking Dunmanus Bay, ideally situated for touring West Cork. Pubs, restaurants, fishing, waters-

# IRELAND

ports, walking and archaeological sites all nearby. ICCC member. From Bantry take R591 to Durrus. After Durrus, continue on this road for a further 3m and you will see us on the left hand side. Open: 1 June - 30 September. ★ 🛏 🚿 👤 ✎ 🍽 🛒 🚐 🛒 🛎 8🚐 12👤

**(4m). Eagle Point Camping, Ballylickey, Bantry, Co Cork .** 00 353 27 50630. www.eaglepointcamping.com. CARAVAN CLUB AFFILIATED SITE. Top standard amenities and a relaxing base for touring the West Cork/South Kerry region. The park, situated on a peninsula, has a safe and sheltered coastline with pebbled beaches suitable for water sports. Activities include boating, windsurfing, sailing, swimming and fishing. Slipway allows for easy boat launch. Food store and petrol station at the park entrance. N71 Cork to Blandon, R586 Bandon to Bantry. N71 Bantry to Glengarriff. Entrance opposite EMO Petrol station. Open: 1 April - 30 September. NCC 🛏 🚿 👤 ✎ 🍽 🛒 🚐 125🚐 👤

## Beara

**Hungry Hill Camping Site, Adrigole Harbour, Beara, Co Cork .** 00 353 27 60228. www.hungryhilllodge.com. Idyllic rural setting at Adrigole - the jewel of Beara Peninsula. Pub on site, shop next door. Midway between Glengarriff and Castletownbere on R572. Open: 1 March - 31 October. ★★★ 🛏 🚿 👤 ✎ 🍽 🛒 10🚐 10🚐 👤

## Blarney

**(1.5m). Blarney Caravan And Camping Park, Stone View, Blarney, Co Cork .** 00 353 21 4516519. www.blarneycaravanpark.com. Set in countryside, spacious, well sheltered and well landscaped site, personally supervised giving a high standard of cleanliness and security. 18 hole pitch & putt course on site. Shops, restaurants, pubs within Blarney, coarse/game fishing nearby. N25 take N8 towards Cork City. From N8 take sign for north Ring Road/Limerick, N20 then Blarney R617. SP from Blarney filling station. Open: 1 April - 25 October. 🚿 👤 ✎ 🍽 🛒 🚐 40🚐 40👤

## Carrigtwohill

**(1m). Jasmine Villa Caravan Park, Carrigtwohill, Co Cork .** 00 353 21 4883234. www.camping-ireland.ie/caravan-parks/camping.php?id=51. Golf course, swimming pools, pitch and putt, beaches, fishing, laundry, disco, Jameson Heritage Centre, shopping, pubs, restaurants all available nearby. N25 Cork/Rosslare, 6m from Midleton, 9m from Cork City. Open: All year. NCC 🛏 🚿 👤 ✎ 🍽 🛒 🚐 17🚐 👤

## Clonakilty

**(0.6m). Desert House Caravan & Camping Park, Coast Road, Clonakilty, Co Cork .** 00 353 23 33331. www.camping-ireland.ie. Family run park. Small touring park situated on a dairy farm overlooking Clonakilty Bay. Nearby model village, water sports, tennis, golf, fishing, bird watching, sandy beaches & traditional pubs. From Cork N71 to Bandon and Clonakilty. Park is SP at roundabout in Clonakilty. Open: 1 May - 30 September. ★★ 🛏 🚿 👤 ✎ 🍽 🛒 🚐 14🚐 👤

**Sexton's Caravan & Camping Park, Timoleague-Clonakilty Road, Clonakilty, Co Cork .** 00 353 23 46347. www.sextonscamping.com. Games room, large play field, small play area. Sandy beaches, fishing, golfing, horse riding within 3m. Restaurants, music pubs, historical/archaeological sites within 2m. From Cork - coastal route - R600 Kinsale-Timoleague. Sexton's on the main route to Clonakilty. From Cork - Bandon - Clonakilty N71, turn L before town back on R600. Open: 1 May - 30 September. 🛏 🚿 👤 ✎ 🍽 🛒 🚐 70🚐

## Fermoy

**Blackwater Valley Caravan & Camping Park, Fermoy, Co Cork .** 00 353 25 32147. Family run top standard caravan park, situated on the banks of River Blackwater. Fishing on site. Within easy reach golf course, pitch & putt, pony trekking, cinema and youth centre. 200yd from shops, restaurants and singing pubs. Adjacent to Fermoy town park which has swimming pool, leisure centre and playground for children. Member of Irish Caravan Council- Bord Failte approved 3 stars. Static caravans for hire on site fully serviced. We are on N72 from Rosslare to Killarney. 200yd from Fermoy town on Malloy Road and exit 14 from M8 and R639. Open: 15 March - 31 October. ★★★ 🛏 🚿 👤 ✎ 🍽 🛒 🚐 15🚐 10🚐 👤 5

## Glandore

**(1m). The Meadow Camping Park, Glandore, Co Cork .** 00 353 28 33280. Family run park in a garden setting and the recipient of three environmental awards. It is best suited to people who prefer peace and tranquillity. The site is well sheltered surrounded by trees, shrubs and flowers. Off N71 at Rosscarbery or Leap take R597 to Glandore. Open: 5 April - 15 September. ★★ 🛏 🚿 👤 ✎ 🍽 🛒 6🚐 14🚐 👤

## Kinsale

**(6m). Garrettstown House Holiday Park, Kinsale, Co Cork .** 00 353 21 4778156. www.garrettstownhouse.com. Set in the grounds of an 18th century estate, the park provides numerous top class facilities for families in high season. Blue Flag beach 0.5m. The park is an ideal base for touring Cork, Kinsale, Clonakilty. AA 4 pennants award. Owner supplied copy. R600. Through Ballinspittle village, past school and football pitch on main road to beach. Open: 1 May - 18 September. 4 🛏 🚿 👤 ✎ 🍽 🛒 🚐 20🚐 👤

## Skibbereen

**(0.6m). The Hideaway Camping & Caravan Park, Skibbereen, Co Cork .** 00 353 28 22254. Family run park with excellent facilities in an ideal location for touring the southwest. Rural setting only 10 mins walk to Skibbereen town. VW, Honda and Hyundai garages in Skibbereen. Bird watching, golf course nearby. Ferries to islands of Cape Clear and Sherkin available from Baltimore. Lidl and Super Valu supermarkets in Skibbereen. On R596 to Castletownsend. Open: 5 April - 15 September. ★★★★ 🛏 🚿 👤 ✎ 🍽 🛒 25🚐 35🚐 👤

# CO DONEGAL

## Ballyshannon

**(0.5m). Lakeside Caravan & Camping, Belleek Road, Ballyshannon, Co Donegal .** 00 353 71 9852822. www.donegalbay.com. Tents welcome. Overlooking the waters of Assaroe Lake, well serviced and fully supervised modern site. Pubs & restaurants now on site. Shops, takeaways, leisure and entertainment facilities available in Ballyshannon. Facilities for rallies or groups, meetings; function room available for hire. Watersport centre (canoeing, kayaking, sailing, windsurfind) now open on site. From Ballyshannon take N3 for Belleek. Site is on the left hand side about 0.5m. Open: 14 March - 12 October. ★★★ 🛏 🚿 👤 ✎ 🍽 🛒 60🚐 60🚐 👤

## Portsalon

**Knockalla Caravan & Camping Park, Magherawarden, Portsalon, Co Donegal .** 00 353 74 59108. www.knockallacaravanpark.com. Miles of safe golden beach and awarded the 2nd most beautiful beach in the world. Local amenities: golf, pitch & putt, angling, mountain climbing, walks. Owner supplied copy. Situated near Portsalon on the Knockalla Coast Road, overlooking Ballymastocker Bay. Open: 23 April - 18 September. 🛏 🚿 👤 ✎ 🍽 🛒 🚐 90🚐 👤

# IRELAND

## CO GALWAY

### Clifden

**(1m). Shanaheever Camping & Caravan Park, Shanaheever, Westport Road, Clifden, Co Galway** . *00 353 95 22150*. www.clifdencamping.com. Sheltered in a valley at the foot of the Twelve Bens but within a few minutes drive of the sea, Shanaheever is ideally situated for the perfect holiday. 15mins walk to Clifden, the capital of Connemara and offers on hand information on the area with O.S. maps on loan. A covered dining area, clean washrooms and showers. Board games to loan out are available on site. Owner supplied copy. From Galway follow the N59 towards Westport. We are the 1st R (1m) after a lake on the R. From Westport, turn off L 1m before Clifden. Open: 6 April - 30 September. ★★♿

### Connemara

**(6m). Acton's Beachside Caravanning & Camping Eco Park, Streamstown Point, Claddaghduff, Clifden, Connemara, Co Galway** . *00 353 87 1267687*. www.actonsbeachsidecamping.com. Park is located on a small peninsula on a sandy private beach. Uncommercialised in an area of scientific interest. EU Machair habitat site, 10 plots privately spaced apart. From Clifden take N59 road (Westport Road) after about 3km turn L, for Claddaghduff for 6km. Open: All year.

### Renvyle

**Connemara Caravan & Camping Park, Lettergesh, Renvyle, Co Galway** . *00 353 95 43406*. www.connemaracaravans.com. Within 3m: salmon/sea trouts/sea angling, mountain climbing, windsurfing, canoeing, diving, golf, horse riding. Restaurants, pubs, shop, PO, laundrette, mobile bank, Irish traditional music. Dolphins often seen from site. Sandy beaches. Diving centre close by. Owner supplied copy. 5m S of Leenane, turn R off the main Westport/Clifden road (5m to site). Open: 1 May - 30 September.

**Renvyle Beach Caravan & Camping Park, Tullybeg, Renvyle, Co Galway** . *00 353 95 43162*. www.renvylebeach-caravanpark.com. The Park has direct access to the one of the most beautiful beaches to be found on the West Coast. High standard of cleanliness and hygiene. Dogs must be kept on a lead. 15mins walk to shops, pubs and restaurants. Mobile homes for hire. Nearest town Clifden. Turn L at Letterfrack. SP in Tullycross. Sign at entrance to site. Open: 1 April - 30 September. ★★

### Salthill

**(0.5m). Salthill Caravan & Camping Park, Salthill, Co Galway** . *00 353 91 523972*. www.salthillcaravanpark.com. Beautifully positioned site. 0.5m from sandy beach. Well-equipped family site. Boat trips from Galway and many holiday attractions at Salthill. Perfect location for touring Connemara, if hiking and you arrive into Galway, get the No 2 bus and it will bring you to the campsite. Owner supplied copy. 3m W of Galway on Salthill road. 0.5m outside Salthill. 2nd park on left hand side 50yd after the Top station which is on your right hand side. GPS:N53 degree.15.413/W9 degree.06.283. Open: 1 April - 29 September.

## CO KERRY

### Ardfert

**(6m). Sir Roger's Caravan Park, Banna, Ardfert, Co Kerry** . *00 353 66 7134730*. www.sirrogerscaravanpark.com. Family run park opened since 1999, modern and purpose designed newly extended with a new state of the art children's playground, also toilet facilities, laundrette etc. It is a safe, secure and pleasant for families. Banna Beach is just 200yd from park. Out the R551, about 0.5m from Ardfert on the main Ballyheigue Road. Open: 1 March - 1 November.

### Caherdaniel

**(1.2m). Glenbeg Caravan & Camping Park, Caherdaniel, Co Kerry** . *00 353 66 9475182*. Adjacent to a fine sandy beach. The park fronted by a sheltered cove in the Kenmare bay is an ideal location for water sports enthusiasts. Ideal base for hill walkers, horse riding, visiting historic sites. Restaurants, pubs and a hotel located within walking distance. Located on the Ring of Kerry Road, about 31m from Kenmare, 18m from Caherciveen. Open: 15 April - 1 October.

**(1m). Wave Crest Caravan And Camping Park, Caherdaniel, Co Kerry** . *00 353 66 9475188*. www.wavecrestcamping.com. Park overlooks Kenmare Bay. Safe sandy beaches and water sports available. Within 3m surfing, boat trips to nearby islands, deep sea fishing trips, swimming and diving. Located on the main Ring of Kerry Road, 30m from Kenmare and 20m from Cahirciveen. Open: 15 March - 15 October.

### Cahirciveen

**(0.5m). Mannix Point Camping & Caravan Park, Ring of Kerry Coast, Cahirciveen, Co Kerry** . *00 353 66 9472806*. www.campinginkerry.com. Site open out of season by prior arrangement. Site is surrounded on three side by mountains and faces the Atlantic islands of Valentia and Beginish on the south west. Nearby: water sports, diving, climbing, high and low levels walks, horse riding, sea, river and sea fishing, bird watching, golf, pitch & putt. Art galleries, potteries, pubs and restaurants. Supermarket 500yd. Traditional music and dancing. Failte Ireland/ICC 2003 The Award of Excellence - The Best Park in Ireland (2004, 2005), Overall winner plus Personal Choice Award. Owner voted 'The Greatest Ambassador for the Caravan and Camping industry'. Located on the coast, 300yd off N70 Ring of Kerry Road, 0.5m W of town centre. Open: 15 March - 15 October.

### Castlegregory

**Anchor Caravan Park, Castlegregory, Co Kerry** . *00 353 66 7139157*. Well run, sheltered park with a high standard in cleanliness and hygiene. Direct access to a beautiful sandy beach and safe bathing. Games room, TV room, playgrounds, laundry facilities, hot showers available on site. Nearby: golf, fishing, watersports, restaurants, bars, supermarkets, hotel and take-away. 12m from Tralee, on Tralee-Dingle coast road. Park SP from Camp junction. Open: 5 April - 30 September.

### Glenbeigh

**(0.5m). Glenross Caravan & Camping Site (Caravan Club Affiliated Site), Glenbeigh, Co Kerry** . *00 353 66 9768451* . www.campingkerry.com. CARAVAN CLUB AFFILIATED SITE. Fine view of Rossbeigh Beach. Ideal touring base for Dingle and Killarney. Popular venue for water sports, fishing, horse-riding, walking, mountain climbing. Bicycle hire. Motorcaravan service point. Brand new campers dining area and pot wash. Children's playground on Rossbeigh Beach (5 mins away). From Killarney/Killorglin take the N70 towards Glenbeigh. Park is on the R just before entering village. 10m from Killorglin. Open: 22 April - 25 September. ★★★★

### Killarney

**(3m). Beech Grove Caravan & Camping Park, Fossa, Killarney, Killarney, Co Kerry**

# IRELAND

. 00 353 64 31727. www.beechgrovecamping.net. A family run site with panoramic views overlooking Killarney's lower lake. Set in a wooded background. Registered with Bord Failte in excess of 25 years. From Killarney, Cork, Mallow and Limerick follow signs for the N72 Ring of Kerry/Killorglin Road. Beechgrove is W of Killarney and situated on the R after Golden Nugget Pub. Open: 28 March - 28 October.

(1m). **Fleming's White Bridge (Affiliated Caravan Club Site), OFF N22 Cork Road, Ballycasheen Road, Killarney, Co Kerry** . 00 353 64 6631590. www.killarneycamping.com. CARAVAN CLUB AFFILIATED SITE. GPS: N52:03.37 W09:28.45. 3 modern sanitation blocks, shop open daily (01/06 - 01/09), tourist information, 2 laundries, games room, TV lounge, sports field, fishing on site, bicycle hire and dog walks. Golf, cinema, shopping centre within 1m; 3m. 300yd off N22 Cork Road. E of Killarney. Open: 12 March - 5 October.

(3m). **Fossa Caravan & Camping Site, Fossa, Killarney, Co Kerry** . 00 353 64 6631497. www.camping-holidaysireland.com. Family run park set in wooded area, in the village of Fossa, overlooking the MacGillycuddy Reeks and just 5mins walk from Lough Leane. 4 stars under the Failte Ireland scheme. From Cork & Mallow Junction (N22/N72) - continue towards Killarney Town. At the top of the hill take second exit off the first roundabout, follow road till second roundabout - take third exit - (all the time following road signs for the N72 Ring of Kerry/Killorglin/Cahirciveen/Dingle road). Continue for about 3.5m. Fossa Caravan & Camping park is the second park on the R. Open: 1 April - 30 September.

**Killarney Flesk Caravan & Camping Park, Flesk Caravan and Camping, Muckross Road, Killarney, Co Kerry** . 00 353 64 31704. www.killarneyfleskcamping.com. Gateway to National Park and Lakes. At the start of the Kerry walk/cycle path from caravan park into National Park and Lakes. While being the nearest located caravan park to Killarney town centre.On site facilities: supermarket, cafe, takeaway, restaurant, bar/entertainment (high season), campers kitchen, laundry, TV lounge, bike rental, taxi service, wet weather shelter. 1m from Killarney town centre on the N71 road to Kenmare. Follow signs for the National Park and Lakes. Next door to the Gleneagle and Victoria House hotel. Open: 30 April - 30 September.

## Killorglin

(1m). **West's Caravan Park and Static Caravan Hire & Sales, Killarney Road, Ring of Kerry, Killorglin, Co Kerry** . 00 353 66 9761240. Great location for touring Ring of Kerry, Killarney, Dingle, mountains, Skelligs Rock, beaches, golf and peninsulas. Overlooking Ireland's highest mountain, on banks of river. Tennis, game fishing, play area, laundry etc on park. Pubs and food nearby. 8 golf courses within 8m, sea fishing 15m. ADAC, MCCI. Static caravans for sale on park from 7000 euros. David Bellamy Bronze Conservation Award. From Killorglin take the main Killarney Road and after 1m West's Caravan Park will be on your right hand side. Open: 2 April - 31 October. BH&HPA

## Lauragh

**Creveen Lodge Caravan Park, Healy Pass Road, Lauragh, Co Kerry** . 00 353 64 83131. www.creveenlodge.com. Creveen Lodge is a small park in the beautiful Ring of Beara. Personally supervised, fully serviced, well sheltered and boasting excellent amenities. The perfect place for a quiet holiday. Walk or cycle to Caha Mountains, rivers, lakes or Dereen Garden. Healy Pass sea angling (1m), pub and local shops (0.5m). Turn R at Sound BRidge R571, Castletownbere road on to Lauragh 15.5m, turn R to Healy Pass road R574 and watch out for signs. Open: 6 April - 31 October.

## Tralee

(0.5m). **Woodlands Caravan & Camping Park (Tralee), Dan Spring Road, Tralee, Co Kerry** . 00 353 66 7121235. www.kingdomcamping.com. Located on a 16 acre parkland setting just a 10 mins walk from the centre of Tralee town, connected by bridge to the Aqua Dome. Golf, bowling, sea angling, diving, horse riding, sailing, windsurfing all available locally. Irish Park of the Year 2005, Loo of the Year 2006, Alan Rogers Motorhome Award 2007. From N69, turn L at railway and follow signs N86. Open: 16 March - 30 September.

# CO KILDARE

## Athy

**Forest Farm Caravan & Camping Park, Dublin Road, Athy, Co Kildare** . 00 353 59 8631231. www.accommodationathy.com. Family run park on 140 acre working farm. Surrounded by mature trees, beech and evergreen. Recently opened and finished to a high standard. Fishing on river Barrow and Grand Canal in Athy. Bicycles for hire. Owner supplied copy. 3m from Athy Heritage town on Dublin road (N78) 38m from Dublin. Open: All year.

# CO KILKENNY

## Bennettsbridge

(2m). **Nore Valley Park, Bennettsbridge, Co Kilkenny** . 00 353 56 7727229. www.norevalleypark.com. Situated on an open farm. Patrons have free access to the farm and children are encouraged to assist in animal feeding. River walk through farm and woodland. Crazy golf, poolroom, children's play area, pedal go-karts and trailer rides. Indoor two storey maze. Swimming, fishing, canoeing, golf, horse riding all available within 10m. From Kilkenny take R700 to Bennettsbridge, just before bridge turn R at sign. Open: 1 March - 31 October.

## Kilkenny

(1m). **Tree Grove Caravan & Camping Park, Danville Park, Kilkenny, Co Kilkenny** . 00 353 56 7770302. www.treegrovecamping.com. Park is ideally located for touring Medieval Kilkenny and the south-east. Horse riding, fishing, golf and other outdoor pursuits are all within easy access of the park. Golf clubs, bikes available for hire. Free and unlimited hot showers, sheltered eating area. 1m from Kilkenny City Centre after roundabout on R700 in the direction of New Ross, or just ring. Open: 1 March - 15 November.

# CO LEITRIM

## Carrick-on-Shannon

(5m). **Battlebridge Caravan & Camping Park, Leitrim Village, Carrick-on-Shannon, Co Leitrim** . 00 353 71 9650824. battlebridgecaravanandcamping.ie. Cast a fishing line from your pitch, enjoy our private marina, on site traditional Irish pub, miles of forest, canal walks and nearby Carrick-on-Shannon. Local activities: boating, golfing, fishing, horse-riding, biking, scenic walks, bird-watching, traditional Irish music, swimming, dining in our fine restaurants and sight-seeing. On site facilities: children's playground, slipway for boating, beer garden with BBQ, indoor dining facilities. Owner supplied copy. From Carrick-on-Shannon take the R280 to Leitrim. Turn L towards Keadue (R284) 0.5m to Beirnes of Battlebridge (pub). Open: All year.

# IRELAND

## CO LIMERICK

### Adare

**(2.5m). Adare Camping & Caravan Park,** Adare, Co Limerick . 00 353 61 395376. www.adarecamping.com. Relaxing atmosphere, sheltered boundaries. Play area for children separate from parking area. Local amenities include old abbeys, churches, fishing (1m), golf (2.5m), pitch & putt, horse riding, bicycle hire, restaurants etc. Hot spa on site and campers kitchen. From Limerick N20/N21 for Tralee. Stay on N21 through Adare. Take L for R519 for Ballingarry and follow camp signs. Open: 1 April - 30 September. ★★★

### Kilcornan

**Curragh Chase Caravan & Camping Park,** Coillte Forest Park, Kilcornan, Co Limerick . 00 353 61 396349. www.coillte.ie. Fishing 10kms. From Limerick City take N69 coast road for 25km SW towards Foynes. The park is located in a 242 hectare Coillte Forest Park of exceptional beauty. Open: 6 April - 4 September. 40 40 40

## CO LOUTH

### Dundalk

**Gyles Quay Caravan Park,** Riverstown, Dundalk, Co Louth . 00 353 42 9376262. Within 1m: golf, fishing, mountain climbing, wind surfing, licensed pub on site. Live entertainment. Owner supplied copy. 10m from Dundalk. Travel 2m on the Dundalk/Newry Road. Turn R on to the coast road, travel 7m and turn R at signpost for Gyles Quay. Open: 1 May - 1 September. 139

## CO MAYO

### Achill Island

**Keel Sandybanks Caravan And Camping Park,** Keel, Achill Island, Co Mayo . 00 353 98 43211. www.achillcamping.com. Bridge-linked to mainland Mayo, Achill Island offers a variety of scenic beauty and a range of holiday opportunities unequalled anywhere. From Keel, explore the West of Ireland or enjoy boating, angling, sailboard lessons, surfing, mountain walking and golfing. Plenty of outdoor playing area for the children. ICC member. Rated 4 stars under Irish Failte scheme. From Castlebar (Co Mayo) travel to Achill Sound via Newport. Take the R319 to Keel (8km). Caravan Park is adjacent to Keel Beach, on L as you enter village. Open: 3 April - 8 September. ★★★★ 30 42 28

### Ballina

**(2m). Belleek Caravan & Camping,** Ballina, Co Mayo . 00 353 96 71533. www.belleekpark.com. Sheltered and tranquil location with excellent facilities and guaranteed high standards. Salmon fishing in River Moy. Nearby historical sites, blue flag beaches, 18 hole golf, deep sea angling and all leisure activities. All amenities in town of Ballina. 300yd off the Ballina to Killala Road, R3140. Open: 1 March - 1 November. ★★★★ NCC 25 25 25 10

### Castlebar

**Lough Lannagh Village,** Old Westport Road, Castlebar, Co Mayo . 00 353 94 9027111. www.loughlannagh.ie. Secluded lakeside setting and unique touring base. 10mins walk to Castlebar. 15mins drive to Westport. Boating, fishing, walking, swimming, golfing, bowling, cinema, shopping. Kids activities July and August only. N5 road around edge of Castlebar, straight through 2 roundabouts, second exit at the third roundabout, then immediately L. Refer to map on website. Open: 22 April - 30 September. 20

### Connemara

**(1m). Cong Caravan And Camping Park,** Lisloughhrey, Quay Road, Connemara, Co Mayo . 00 353 94 9546089. www.quietman-cong.com. 40 mixed pitches in total. A fisherman's paradise with rods and boats available and a plentiful supply of lakes, rivers and underground streams. Laundrette, children's playground, boat rental and shop on site. Bike rental. Mini golf themed on favourite fairy tale and nursery rhymes next door. 'The Quietman' film shown to residents in the mini cinema nightly. Pony trekking and falconry nearby. Forest walks, caving. Lake cruises. Holiday Hostel and B&B also available on site. From Cong, go out the Galway Road, past Ashford Castle entrance gates. Take the next turn R, the park is on your R after the cemetery/graveyard. Open: All year. ★★★★ 40

### Knock

**Knock Caravan & Camping Park,** Claremorris Road, Knock, Co Mayo . 00 353 94 9300100. www.knock-shrine.ie. CARAVAN CLUB AFFILIATED SITE. An excellent base for touring Mayo and the West of Ireland. Toilet blocks, laundry facilities and MV service point. TV rooms and play area. Dog walk nearby. Good area for walking. Fishing nearby. Quiet and peaceful off-peak. Owner supplied copy. Exit N17 for Knock, at roundabout take Claremorris Road for 1m, the park is located on the L, opposite filling station. Open: 1 March - 31 October. ★★★ NCC 58

## CO ROSCOMMON

### Ballaghaderreen

**(3.7m). Willowbrook Caravan & Camping Park,** Kiltybranks, Ballaghaderreen, Co Roscommon . 00 353 94 9861307. www.willowbrookpark.com. Warm and friendly, family run park set in the Lung Valley. Unspoiled and beautiful landscape ideal for a relaxing and leisurely holiday. Disabled toilet available. Tuck shop. On site activities include: archery, coarse fishing, adventure camp on 2nd two weeks in July (within 3kms). Tennis courts, 9 hole golf course nearby. Owner supplied copy. Take R293 from Ballaghaderreen towards Castlerea. Then R325 over the bridge and bear L for 1m, turn R at the sign post, park is 500yd. Open: 1 April - 30 September. ★★★ 10

### Boyle

**(2.5m). Lough Key Caravan & Camping Park,** Lough Key Forest and Activity Park, Boyle, Co Roscommon . 00 353 71 9662212. www.loughkey.ie. After major development the scenic and historic Lough Key now encompasses a landmark cluster of attractions unique to Ireland. The innovative Adventure House contains challenging activities and puzzles where only teamwork and trial and error allows you to progress. The outdoor Adventure play-zone provides entertaining activities for children of all ages. The estate also contains many trails through the woodlands and forest. Owner supplied copy. On the N4 National Primary Route, 2.5m E of Boyle. Open: 1 April - 4 September. 72

### Knockcroghery

**Gailey Bay Caravan & Camping Park,** Knockcroghery, Co Roscommon . 00 353 90 6661058. www.camping-ireland.ie. Friendly, family run, self-contained holiday park on the shores of Lough Rea where truly peaceful waters flow. Located in an area steeped in culture and heritage and suitable for sailing, fishing and water sports. From Athlone: N61 to Roscommon, turn R then immediately L before railway crossing (before Knockcroghery), continue 1m at Crossroad, turn R. Open: 15 April - 31 October. 27

# IRELAND

## CO SLIGO

### Enniscrone

**Atlantic Caravan Park, Enniscrone, Co Sligo .** 00 353 96 36132. www.atlantic-caravanpark.com. Long established family holiday resort. Adjacent to famous 3m golden beach. 18 hole Championship golf course, fishing, pony trekking all nearby. Off N11. Open: 27 March - 30 September. 50

### Riverstown

**Lough Arrow Touring Caravan Park (Adults only), Ballynarry, Riverstown, Co Sligo .** 00 353 71 9666018. www.lougharrowcaravanpark.com. Registered with Bord Failte and Irish Caravan Council. ADULT ONLY SITE. Fishing adjacent and within 5m (several lakes). 3 golf courses within 8m. Boat Hire on lake. Camp site on lake shore. On site facilities: boules pitch, golf practice nets. S on N4: L at Castlebaldwin. Follow signs to site. N on N4: first R past Boyle turning, follow signs to site. Open: 13 March - 31 October. 30 10

### Rosses Point

**Greenlands Caravan & Camping Park, Rosses Point, Co Sligo .** 00 353 71 9177113. www.sligocaravanandcamping.ie/greenlands_park.html. The ideal family site on a rise with direct access to two safe beaches. Golf beside the site. Sailing club at 100yd. Magnificent views, mountains and sea all around. All the attractions of the area are within a short drive. Hotel, restaurants, shop at 500yd. AA 4 pennants. 5m W of Sligo on R29 off N15. Open: 21 April - 15 September. 4 120

### Strandhill

**Strandhill Caravan & Camping Park, Strandhill, Co Sligo .** 00 353 71 9168111. www.camping-ireland.ie. The site is at Strandhill Beach, mecca for surfers from all around the world, while the flat sands of Culleenamore, more suitable for family fun, are just 1m away. Golf is 500yds, shops, pubs and restaurants within 100yds. Pitches on hardstandings. On N59 5m W of Sligo. Site is on airport road. Open: 4 April - 30 September. 65 65 75

## CO TIPPERARY

### Cahir

**(4m). The Apple Farm Caravan & Camping Park, Moorstown, Cahir, Co Tipperary .** 00 353 52 744 1459. www.theapplefarm.com. Our friendly site is located on an award winning fruit farm. You will be welcome to wander round the orchards, try some of the farm-pressed apple juice and help yourself to a few strawberries or raspberries when in season. On site facilities: free access to tennis courts and rackets, unlimited free hot water, spring water for drinking and large indoor area. Located about 300yd off the main Waterford/Limerick road (N24), between Clonmel and Cahir. Open: 1 May - 30 September. ★★★ 10 12 10

### Clogheen

**Parsons Green Holiday Park, Kilkenny Road, Clogheen, Co Tipperary .** 00 353 52 65290. www.clogheen.com. Small, family run park, centrally situated for touring the whole of the south of Ireland. Excellent on site facilities include: garden and river walks, pet field, farm museum, coffee shop, playground, pony, boat rides, picnic area, tennis and basketball court. Hot food takeaway. Golf, fishing, hill-walking nearby. Take R668 from Cahir and Lismore. Take R655 from Clonmel R655 from Mitchelstown. Open: All year. 40

### Glen of Aherlow

**Ballinacourty House, Ballinacourty, Glen of Aherlow, Co Tipperary .** 00 353 62 56559. www.camping.ie. Family run park offering facilities of high hygienic standards to those who enjoy holidays away from the crowds in a tranquil surrounding of unspoilt nature. Table tennis, tennis court, children's playground & mini golf on site. Horse riding, fishing, swimming pool all available locally. Graded 4 star Failte Ireland. At traffic lights in Tipperary Town turn L and follow signs for Glen Hotel. Take next R after Glen Hotel. Take next R (watch out for hairpin bends and steep incline). Open: 16 March - 14 October. 45

**Glen of Aherlow Caravan & Camping Park, Newtown, Glen of Aherlow, Co Tipperary .** 00 353 62 56555. www.tipperarycamping.com. CARAVAN CLUB AFFILIATED SITE. Spectacular scenery, top class amenities and a warm welcome await you at this site. Toilet blocks and laundry facilities. TV and games room. Dog walk on site. Good area for walking and golf nearby. Facilities for disabled. Quiet & peaceful off-peak. Off R663. Open: Contact site direct. NCC

### Roscrea

**(1.5m). Streamstown Caravan & Camping Park, Streamstown, Roscrea, Co Tipperary .** 00 353 50 521519. www.tipperarycaravanpark.com. Park is set on a dairy farm, in quiet surroundings. Beautifully landscaped. Good standard amenities and a relaxing atmosphere are guaranteed. 5 nights for the price of 4. Local activities include: horse riding, golf, historical sites, fishing, hill walking. Open Easter-October 1 and by appointment other times. Owner supplied copy. From Roscrea take R491 to Shinrone for 1.5m. Park is SP. Open: 6 April - 1 October. ★★★ 14 10

## CO WATERFORD

### Dungarvan

**(2m). Bayview Caravan & Camping Park, Gold Coast Golf Resort, Dungarvan, Co Waterford .** 00 353 58 45100. www.bayviewcaravancamping.com. Gold Coast Golf and Leisure Centre, restaurant, bar, swimming pool - all 200yd from park. Other amenities in area: angling, sailing, water-skiing, swimming, tennis, etc. Two 18 hole golf courses within 2m. From Dungarvan turn S off N25 on to Gold Coast Road and follow signs to park. Open: 1 April - 31 October. 26 26

**(3.5m). Casey's Caravan & Camping Park, Clonea, Dungarvan, Co Waterford .** 00 353 58 41919. www.camping-ireland.ie. Direct access to the beach. Top facilities available include playground, TV room, games room, crazy golf, telephone, shop adjacent to park. Top class angling, also sailing and sail boarding. Three golf courses in the area. Cards not accepted as method of payment. Follow SP off N25. From Dungarvan town take R675 coast road follow SP. GPS: N 52degree.05.683'; W 007degree.32.773'. Open: 21 April - 13 September. ★★★★ 81 81

### Tramore

**(2m). Newtown Cove Caravan Park, Newtown Road, Tramore, Co Waterford .** 00 353 51 381979. www.newtowncove.com. Family run park, in a peaceful setting, well sheltered. On site children's playground, TV & games rooms, shop, laundry. 400yd from sea swimming and fishing. 18 hole golf course. Open weekends only in April. From Tramore on R675 Coast Road to Dungarvan: 0.5m from town turn L at the top of the second hill, before roundabout. Open: 21 April - 25 September. ★★★★ 20 20 15

# IRELAND

## CO WESTMEATH
### Athlone

(3m). Hodson Bay Caravan Park, Hodson Bay, Kiltoom, Athlone, Co Westmeath . 00 353 90 6492448 . Quiet location beside lake, hotel, marina and golf course. On N61, from the western part of Athlone travel N for 3m turn R at sign for Hodson Bay. Open: 1 June - 31 August.

## CO WEXFORD
### Ballaghkeen

(2m). The Trading Post, Ballaghkeen, Co Wexford . 00 353 53 9127368. www.wexfordcamping.com. Designed and opened at the dawn of a new century for the free spirited who like the less beaten track. Facilities include: disabled facilities, TV room, laundrette, BBQ area, children's play area, service station deli and forecourt shop. Pub, golf courses, sandy beach all nearby. Out of season visitors can be catered for, contact owner. From Wexford take R741 for 14km. 'The Trading Post' service station and camper park is on your L. Open: 1 April - 30 September. ★★★★

### New Ross

Ocean Island Caravan & Camping Park, Fethard-on-Sea, New Ross, Co Wexford . 00 353 51 397148 . www.oceanislandmobilehomes.com. 1.25m to beach, horse riding, fishing, swimming, golf. Outdoor playground and shop. Indoor games room and laundry facilities. From Rosslare/Wexford take R733 to Duncannon road roundabout, turn L at roundabout, SP for Wellington Bridge, then follow signs for Fethard-on-Dea. From New Ross town take the Fethard-on-Sea road No. R734. Open: 6 April - 30 September.

### Rosslare Harbour

(1.5m). St Margaret's Beach, Carnsore Point, Lady's Island, Rosslare Harbour, Co Wexford . 00 353 53 9131169. www.campingstmargarets.ie. Located in an Area of Outstanding Natural Beauty, with an important nature preserve and bird sanctuary, St Margaret's is an attractive quiet place to spend a few days in - adjacent to Wexford coastal path and miles of safe sandy beach. Family run with the owners living on site. N25 to Tagoat, then follow signs to the L for Lady's Island/ Carne. Continue for 1.5m. After Butlers Bar turn L, continue for 1.5m, park is right hand side, SP. Open: 15 March - 31 October. ★★

### Wexford

Ferrybank Caravan & Camping Park, Ferrybank Leisure Centre, Wexford, Co Wexford . 00 353 53 9166926 . www.wexfordcorp.ie. Situated on seafront overlooking town and harbour. Heated indoor swimming pool and shop attached. Golf, fishing, surfing, sailing, Blue Flag beaches and tennis within easy reach. 5 mins walk across bridge on seafront on R741. Open: 29 April - 14 September.

## CO WICKLOW
### Donard

Moat Farm Caravan & Camping Park, Donard, Co Wicklow . 00 353 45 404727. www.camping-ireland.ie. Small, quiet, select family run park set in a tranquil rural setting, 1mins walk from the village. Modern, fully serviced park. Golf, fishing, pony trekking within easy reach. A walking paradise. Ideal base for touring. From Dun Laoghaire follow the signs for N4 and N7, then on to N81. 9m S of Blessington, turn L at the Old Toll House pub. See signs. Park is 1m from here. GPS - N53 01.289' W006 36.890'. Open: 15 March - 30 September.

### Rathdrum

Hidden Valley Holiday Park, Rathdrum, Co Wicklow . 00 353 86 7272872. www.irelandholidaypark.com. Quiet site on the banks of Avonmore river and on the edge of the Wicklow Mountains. 10mins walk away from village pubs, shops and restaurants. Trout fishing on site. From Dublin N11 to Rathnew, then R752. From Rosslare, N11 to Arklow, then R752. Open: 30 March - 23 September. ★★★★

### Redcross

River Valley Caravan And Camping Park (Caravan Club Affiliated Site), Redcross, Co Wicklow . 00 353 40 441647. www.rivervalleypark.com. CARAVAN CLUB AFFILIATED SITE. Situated in one of the most scenic areas of County Wicklow - an ideal base for exploring the many famous tourist attractions of the country. Golf, walking, trails, horse riding, water sports, shore and fresh water angling. Restaurant & bar. Dogs allowed in Secret Garden (area for couples only) during July and August. From Dublin N11 S, continue for 30m passing Beehive Pub on L, continue for another 2m to Lil Doyles Pub on R, turn for Redcross beside pub, site in village 3m. Open: 11 March - 30 October. ★★★★

### Roundwood

Roundwood Caravan Park, Roundwood Village, Roundwood, Co Wicklow . 00 353 12 818163. www.dublinwicklowcamping.com. A mature modern fully developed park in the heart of the Wicklow Mountains in the quaint village of Roundwood, overlooking Vartry Lakes and Forest. Shops, pubs, restaurants, markets and entertainment are all within a leisurely 5mins stroll. Walking is the most popular outdoor activity with endless mountain and forest walks. Golf, fishing, equestrian sports available nearby. Situated off N11. From Dublin and Dun Laoghaire turn R at Kilmacanogue from Rosslare, turn L at Ashford village. Open: 27 April - 2 September. ★★★★ NCC

## DUBLIN
### Rush

(1m). North Beach Caravan & Camping Park, North Beach, Rush, Dublin . 00 353 18 437131. www.northbeach.ie. Family owned, managed and operated. Picturesque peaceful secure location beside the Irish Sea. Rural surroundings. 200yd frontage and direct access to a sandy beach safe for swimming, water sports and fishing possible. Within walking distance to supermarket, shops, restaurant, PO. Owner supplied copy. From the South: N1, M1, M50. Leave N1 to R at the Esso filling station north of Swords, turn R at Lusk. Drive down. Rush main street, turn L at our sign post for North Beach, 50yd down the road. Turn R at next sign for North Beach. Open: 1 April - 30 September.

### Dublin

(5m). Camac Valley Caravan & Camping Park, Green Isle, Link Road, Naas Road, Dublin 22. 00 353 14 640644. www.camacvalley.com. Award winning park has now established itself as Dublin's premier Caravan & Camping Park with top class facilities. Groups and rallies well catered for in spacious park whilst the individual hardstands are both private and pleasant. The local village of Clondalkin has 2 large supermarkets, PO and bars & restaurants. There are numerous golf courses within easy reach and horse riding facilities are also nearby. M50 motorway, exit at no 9 and take N7 S, direction Cork for 2km ad follow international camping signs off the N7 to Green Isle Road. Open: All year. ★★★★

# Enjoy your UK holidays more with The Caravan Club

2012 EDITION £7.99

Troutbeck Head Caravan Club Site, one of The Club's eight sites in Cumbria

## Choose from 200 superb Club Sites in the finest locations

With the UK's increasing popularity as a holiday destination, there's no better way to discover Britain & Ireland's beauty and heritage than by staying at one of The Caravan Club's 200 quality Club Sites.

Caravan Club Sites are renowned for their excellence. With most of those graded achieving 4 or 5 stars from VisitBritain, you can be sure of consistently high standards.

And with over 40 Club Sites open all year, you can enjoy superb touring all year round.

You can be assured of excellent facilities and a friendly welcome from our Resident Wardens. Why not discover the best of Britain this year?

### Why choose a Caravan Club Site?

- Choice of superb locations throughout Britain & Ireland
- Sites are immaculately maintained
- Most Club Sites are in peaceful settings, ideal for a relaxing holiday
- Care for the local environment and wildlife is paramount

Clumber Park Caravan Club Site, Nottinghamshire

Trewethett Caravan Club Site, Cornwall

You don't have to be a member to stay on most Caravan Club Sites but members save £8 per night on pitch fees!

## For Caravan Club Site details and locations visit www.caravanclub.co.uk/parks

THE CARAVAN CLUB

QUATREM,
une équipe
de professionnels
au service
des hôteliers et
restaurateurs.

## QUATREM
Assurances Collectives

- ■ **Fidéliser le personnel.**
- ■ **Optimiser les charges salariales.**
- ■ **Gérer la mise en place des 35 heures.**

QUATREM vous propose les réponses adaptées à votre établissement.

QUATREM,
partenaire des Tables et
Auberges de France
www.quatrem.fr

Votre interlocuteur
**Daniel Barcelo**
Tél. 01 53 32 67 06
e-mail : daniel.barcelo@quatrem.fr

# Votre coup de coeur sélection dans le Guide 2001 TROPHEE

**Catégorie TABLE DE PRESTIGE**

**Table de Prestige**

Nom de l'établissement : ........................................
Code postal : ........................................
Ville : ........................................

*Vos appréciations et commentaires (entrée, plat et dessert) sont les bienvenus*
........................................
........................................
........................................

**Catégorie TABLE GASTRONOMIQUE**

**Table Gastronomique**

Nom de l'établissement : ........................................
Code postal : ........................................
Ville : ........................................

*Vos appréciations et commentaires (entrée, plat et dessert) sont les bienvenus*
........................................
........................................
........................................

**Catégorie TABLE DE TERROIR**

**Table de Terroir**

Nom de l'établissement : ........................................
Code postal : ........................................
Ville : ........................................

*Vos appréciations et commentaires (entrée, plat et dessert) sont les bienvenus*
........................................
........................................
........................................

**Votre adresse** - Your address - Su dirección - Ihre Adresse

**Nom Prénom** ........................................   **N°/Rue** ........................................
*Name Firstname - Apellido nombre - Name Vorname*    *Road - Calle - Straße/Nr*

**Ville** ........................................   **Code Postal** ........................................   **Pays** ........................................
*City - Ciudad - Stadt*    *Post Code - Código postal - Postleitzahl*    *Country - País - Land*

**Remerciements : Crédit photos** : le CDT Haute-Garonne, CRT Midi-Pyrénées, P Journou, D.Viet, J. Sierpinski CDTHG. **Traductions** : Mmes V. Theau, L. Darenes, S. Rasponi, Mme Garaud et Mme Van der Spek. Malgré les soins apportés à l'édition de ce guide et conformément à la Jurisprudence, la responsabilité de l'éditeur ne saurait être engagée en cas d'erreur ou d'omission involontaire ; tous les tarifs indiqués n'engagent en aucun cas la responsabilité de la Fédération des Tables & Auberges de France.

Guide National édité à l'initiative de la Fédération Nationale des Tables & Auberges de France 2, rue Lanternières BP 47 - 31012 Toulouse cedex 06
Directeur de la publication : Jean Lanau - Responsable de la rédaction : Michel Garnier
Conception, réalisation et fabrication : FNTAF - Métropole Médias - Toulouse - Tél. : 05 61 62 15 00
Dépôt légal : février 2001
TVA Intracommunautaire : FR51403118875830750672 - ISBN 2-95109055-2

# VOS COMMENTAIRES ET VOS APPRÉCIATIONS, LES PLUS OBJECTIFS, SONT LES BIENVENUS

*Your comments and appreciations, the most objective, are welcome - Sus comentarios y sus apreciaciones, los más objetivos, son bienvenidos Ihre Kommentare und Beurteilungen, so objektiv wie möglich, sind uns willkommen.*

 Table de prestige      Table gastronomique      Table de Terroir

| | Très satisfaisant<br>Excellent<br>Muy satisfactorio<br>Sehr Zufriedenstellend | Satisfaisant<br>Good<br>Satisfactorio<br>Zufriedenstellend | Peu satisfaisant<br>Unsatisfactory<br>Poco satisfactorio<br>wenig Zufriedenstellend | Pas du tout satisfaisant<br>Bad<br>No satisfactorio<br>ganz und gar nicht Zufriedenstellend |
|---|---|---|---|---|
| **Accueil**<br>Reception - Acogida - Empfang | ❏ | ❏ | ❏ | ❏ |
| **Service en salle**<br>Service Staff - Servicio en sala - Bedienung | ❏ | ❏ | ❏ | ❏ |
| **Cuisine: qualité de la Table**<br>Cooking/quality : - Cocina : calidad de la Comida : - Küche : Qualität der Tische : | ❏ | ❏ | ❏ | ❏ |
| **Qualité / Prix**<br>Quality/price - Calidad/Precio - Qualität/Preis | ❏ | ❏ | ❏ | ❏ |
| **Aménagements, cadre, Agrément et calme**<br>Fitting out, laying out, quietness - Instalaciones, ambiente, atracción y calma - Einrichtungen, Rahmen - Annehmlichkeiten, Ruhe | ❏ | ❏ | ❏ | ❏ |
| **Propreté générale**<br>Hygiene - Limpieza general - Sauberkeit | ❏ | ❏ | ❏ | ❏ |

Le classement national du restaurant Table de Terroir, Table Gastronomique ou Table de Prestige vous semble-t-il cohérent et correspondre aux prestations offertes ?    ❏ oui    ❏ non

**Nom de l'établissement -** .................................................
*Name of the establishment - Nombre del establecimiento - Name des Hauses :*

**Ville** ..................................................    **Code Postal** ..................................
*City - Ciudada - Stadt*    *Post Code - Código postal - Postleitzahl*

**Date de votre passage dans cet établissement** ..................................
*Date of the visit to the establishment - Fecha de su paso por este establecimiento - Datum Ihres Aufenthalts*

---

**Votre adresse** - *Your address - Su dirección - Ihre Adresse*

**Nom Prénom** ............................  **N°/Rue** ............................................
*Name Firstname - Apellido nombre - Name Vorname*    *Road - Calle - Straße/Nr*

**Ville** ......................  **Code Postal** ..................  **Pays** ....................
*City - Ciudad - Stadt*    *Post Code - Código postal - Postleitzahl*    *Country - País - Land*

**Fédération des Tables & Auberges de France - 2, rue Lanternières BP 47 - 31 012 Toulouse cédex 0**

*Tables & Auberges de France se réserve le droit d'exploiter les informations collectées conformément à la loi Informatique et Liberté du 6 01 1978. Droit d'accès, de retrait et de modifications garant*

www.tables-auberges.com • réservation gratuite (0% de commission)